# Violent *Femmes*

The female spy has long exerted a strong grip on the popular imagination. With reference to popular fiction, film and television *Violent Femmes* examines the figure of the female spy as a nexus of contradictory ideas about femininity, power, sexuality and national identity. Fictional representations of women as spies have recurrently traced the dynamic of women's changing roles in British and American culture. Employing the central trope of women who work as spies, Rosie White examines cultural shifts during the twentieth century regarding the role of women in the professional workplace. Beginning with an examination of the male spy in popular fiction, White's revealing book then moves on to examine female spies, comparing and contrasting numerous female spies in investigative case studies with the aim of answering the following questions:

- How have depictions of the female spy changed over the twentieth century?
- What can Modesty Blaise tell us about women in the 1960s and 1970s?
- Does *Alias* offer an ideal vision of the working woman in the twenty-first century?
- Are women in Western culture now seen as agents of their own futures?

In the twentieth century, a period when women's relationship with public life and state authority was changing radically, the female spy in all her forms offers a suggestive account of the effects of, and resistances to, such transformations. *Violent Femmes* examines the female spy as a figure in popular discourse which simultaneously conforms to cultural stereotypes *and* raises questions about women's roles in British and American culture, in terms of gender, sexuality and national identity.

Immensely useful for a wide range of courses such as Film and Television Studies, English, Cultural Studies, Women's Studies, Gender Studies, Media Studies, Communications, and History, this book will appeal to students from undergraduate level upwards.

**Rosie White** is Senior Lecturer in English and Programme Leader for the degree in English and Film Studies at Northumbria University.

# Transformations: Thinking through Feminism

Edited by:
Maureen McNeil, *Institute of Women's Studies, Lancaster University*
Lynne Pearce, *Department of English, Lancaster University*

Other books in the series include:

# Violent *Femmes*

Women as spies in popular culture

**Rosie White**

Routledge
Taylor & Francis Group

LONDON AND NEW YORK

First published 2007
by Routledge
2 Park Square, Milton Park, Abingdon, Oxon OX14 4RN

Simultaneously published in the USA and Canada
by Routledge
270 Madison Avenue, New York, NY 10016

*Routledge is an imprint of the Taylor & Francis Group, an informa business*

Typeset in Times by
Taylor & Francis Books
Printed and bound in Great Britain by
TJ International Ltd, Padstow, Cornwall

*British Library Cataloguing in Publication Data*
A catalogue record for this book is available from the British Library

*Library of Congress Cataloging in Publication Data*
White, Rosie, 1964–
    Violent femmes: women as spies in popular culture / Rosie White.
      p. cm.
    Includes bibliographical references and index.
    1. Women spies on television. 2. Women spies in motion pictures.
    3. Women spies in literature. 4. Spies in literature. I. Title.
PN1992.8.S67W45 2007
791.43′658–dc22

ISBN 978–0–415–37077–6 (hbk)
ISBN 978–0–415–37078–3 (pbk)
ISBN 978–0–203–03057–8 (ebk)

For my mother and father, Ann and Bill White

# Contents

# Illustrations

# Acknowledgements

The author and publisher would like to thank the *Evening Standard* for permission to reproduce Modesty Blaise strips, MPTV/London Features International Ltd for the image of Lindsay Wagner in *The Bionic Woman* and Pictorial Press for permission to reproduce all other film and television stills. Every effort has been made to obtain permissions; if any proper acknowledgement has not been made, we invite copyright holders to inform us of the oversight.

I would like to thank the series editors Lynne Pearce and Maureen McNeil, together with Ulrike Swientek and Gerhard Boomgaarden at Routledge for their help in producing this book. I would also like to acknowledge the help and support of friends and colleagues, in particular Richard Armstrong, Victoria Bazin, Lynn Edmonds, Hilary Fawcett, Kathy Hedley, Amanda Holmes, Peter Hutchings, Sarah Leahy, Kate McGuinness, Julie Scanlon and Mo White. I am indebted to the Division of English and the School of Arts and Social Sciences at Northumbria University for research leave which enabled me to complete this project.

# Introduction

The spy is a suggestive figure. While spies and espionage have existed at least since biblical times, popular accounts of the secret agent are wired to a distinctly twentieth-century anxiety regarding personal and national identity. The spy embodies fears that national identity is under threat and that in order to maintain the status quo, clandestine activities normally considered illegal or invasive must be endorsed – that special measures must be taken (Cawelti and Rosenberg 1987: 2). Spy fictions, often come to the fore at moments when social and political change is being felt; James Bond in 1950s fiction and 1960s film reflects upon a new era while also displaying a nostalgia for a disappearing world. This book is concerned with how the fictional female spy-protagonist reflects upon such modern and postmodern unease, particularly at those moments marked by changes in gender roles. My examination of women spies in a variety of media across the twentieth and into the twenty-first century thus maps the construction and reconstruction of femininity as a shifting, multiple discourse. Women as spies in popular culture are read as commentaries on specific temporal and cultural femininities, from Mata Hari to Sydney Bristow, aligning them with other indicators of cultural anxiety about femininity, such as the femme fatale and the New Woman.

Spying is an appropriate trope to employ when discussing gender, as femininity, like masculinity, is always undercover – a covert operation with powerful far-reaching effects. Women spies are violent *femmes* because they expose some of the contradictions embedded in those covert operations. In particular, women spies in fiction, film and television are licensed to be violent agents and, thus, confound the western binary understanding of gender that aligns femininity with objectified passivity. Unlike the femme fatale, however, the 'good' woman spy disturbs any easy recuperation of the violent or active woman, again doing violence to the symbolic map that has structured popular understandings of gender in the past two centuries. The woman spy also offers a version of the New Woman across the twentieth and into the twenty-first century; she is rarely depicted as maternal and more often situated within the professional workplace. The fictional spy may be aligned with doctors, teachers, managers, lawyers and architects and, thus, understood as an account of the cultural shift a growing number of women in the professions have effected and experienced. The female spy-protagonist is doubly contradictory by being a female protagonist in a male-dominated genre, just as female spies are out of place in a male-dominated profession. In short, this study reads espionage fictions as critical accounts of bureaucracies in which the woman spy is an inherently volatile signifier.

Although the fictional spy is most often characterised as male, the covert aspect of espionage links it to an attribute pejoratively ascribed to femininity – it is based on deception. Spying employs 'feminine' skills such as disguise and dissimulation, while spies are masculinised as observers and agents. The spy is, thus, a hermaphrodite figure within popular culture, destabilising unitary formulations of gender identity in favour of a more mobile subjectivity. In popular imagination, spies operate between legal and illegal spheres, between public and private spaces, between fact and fiction. The operations of secret agents and secret agencies are, by definition, clandestine, uncharted and unseen and, therefore, unverifiable. Spying in this way lends itself to fiction in its creation of cover stories, false identities and conspiracy theories. Intelligence agencies' refusal to release information has led to more, rather than less, fictional accounts of the work they do (Miller 2003: 38). Spies trade in information which is 'classified' but not always reliable, a discourse which is authoritative but also unofficial and, consequently, a source of knowledge which relies on trust. In fiction and in fact, espionage makes apparent the link between knowledge and power. Spy fictions in print, on film and television may thus be understood as a means of examining the operations of hegemonic discourse. This makes academic study itself a covert operation. In the wake of post-structuralism, the project of late twentieth-century cultural studies has been to decode popular texts. Arthur Asa Berger goes so far as to propose that the academic is also a spy:

> I am a self-employed secret agent who searches, relentlessly, for hidden meanings and latent functions. I like to think that, like all secret agents, I shake the very foundations of society. For if society maintains itself on the basis of the unrecognized functions people engage in, when I point out these latent functions I make them recognizable (manifest), and the equilibrium of society is disturbed.
>
> (Berger 1974: 70–1)

That is the ambition of this book: to examine women spies and spy fictions as complex and contradictory accounts of the modern and postmodern West. Women as spies in fiction, film and television map shifts in the politics of gender across the twentieth century and into the twenty-first, disturbing the equilibrium of popular culture.

Like most popular genres, spy fictions do not constitute a singular dynamic. Popular fictions reach into the labyrinthine imagination of their many readers to produce often contradictory and unstable renderings of power and resistance: 'Successful story patterns like the western persist ... not because they embody some particular ideology or psychological dynamic, but because they maximize a great many such dynamics' (Cawelti 1976: 30). It is thus not a case of 'one size fits all' in popular culture – the dismissive idea that genre fictions offer all readers all the same pleasures all the time – but of a formula that is sufficiently elastic to engage with a range of readers and readings. Spy fictions are particularly elastic; there are certain formulae, yes, but an infinite range of combinations and readings to be made of those formulae (see Atkins 1984, Denning 1987, Bloom 1990). In her examination of British genre film, Marcia Landy proposes that spy films are fictions of identity and power, with women often central to a nexus of public and sexual politics (Landy 1991: 124–6). This book takes that definition to heart by making women spy-protagonists its focus. Like their sisters in hardboiled detective fictions and film noir, women in spy narratives have often meant trouble, following the long shadow cast by the myth of Mata Hari (Miller 2003: 154–69). Yet, by the late twentieth century, female spies were emerging as protagonists and heroes, rather than the marginal love interest or villain. This intervention, however rare, is significant because espionage offers an overt account of power through representing both the power of the individual and the power of the state. Moreover, the spy thriller usually deals with threats to the state and to the status quo (Chapman 2002: 20). The *good* female spy thus offers a powerfully ambivalent account of the nation-state and the status quo because of the discrepancy between femininity and public forms of power in the history of Britain and the USA. Figures released on 5 January 2006 by the British Equal Opportunities Commission as part of its annual survey of women's representation in positions of power suggest equality between men and women will take twenty years in the top management of the Civil Service, forty years at the director level of FTSE 100 companies, forty years in the senior judiciary, and up to 200 years – another forty elections – in Parliament.

By her very existence, the female spy comments on her male counterpart in her role as femme fatale (Mata Hari), the desirable 'girl' (Bennett and Woollacott 1987), or the female professional (*Alias*). The first two figures are visible in most popular spy fictions, but the third became more prevalent as the twentieth century drew to a close. This refracts political and social change as more women entered the professions, but it does not represent an equality that has been achieved. Spies, doctors, actors, poets and artists are seen as predominantly male in the West; hence, the *woman* doctor and the *woman* poet. In this fashion, women remain spies within Western culture – still added on as a prefix to distinguish us from the 'real' doctors, the 'real' poets. British and American cultures still struggle to make room for women. Women are still forging roles for themselves within the public arena; the calls for universal childcare in the feminist movements of the 1970s have not been heard, and women entering a male-dominated profession often find themselves subject to abuse. If spies are agents, then the woman spy is doubly transgressive because she crosses the line that ordinarily designates woman as object rather than subject. Women spies in popular fiction, film and television represent an uneasy rapprochement between women spies as agents/subjects *and* as objects. Depictions of female spies thus reflect upon women's conundrum at the turn of the twenty-first century in the wake of alleged equal opportunities: the doubled emphasis on work *and* on the work of femininity – that women be beautiful, make a home, have children, care for them. Where John Berger once asserted that, 'men act and women appear' in his foundational account of art history, in the twenty-first century, privileged white women are often required to both act *and* appear (Berger 1972: 47). Women spy-protagonists in popular fictions map this dynamic. In many popular narratives, women spies cross the boundaries of femininity and are shepherded back to it by visual codes of beauty, whiteness and heterosexuality. They both break out and are contained, becoming an amphibious combination of radical and reactionary. In this way, the woman as spy in popular culture tests the bounds of gender and is encrypted both as a cipher of social change and of resistance to change.

Hence, this study examines women spies who are protagonists in popular fiction, film and television, rather than the more prevalent character who appears in the margin of spy narratives. In their exhaustive list of female spies from 1960s film and television, Tom Lisanti and Louis Paul categorise women as falling into four main character types: 'the helpful spy ... the innocent ... the bad-girl-turned-good ... the villainess/*femme fatale*/assassin' (Lisanti and Paul 2002: 14–16). Of the 107 women profiled, few play protagonists. Honor Blackman (Cathy Gale), Diana Rigg (Emma Peel) and Joanna Lumley (Purdey) share a central status in *The Avengers* and *The New Avengers*, and Stefanie Powers is an exception as the short-lived *Girl from U.N.C.L.E.* (Lisanti and Paul 2002). Yet, by the 1990s, one could cite a range of active female protagonists in film and television series: Ripley, Sarah Connor, Thelma and Louise, Lara Croft, Buffy, Xena. Feminist academics in Britain and America, such as Yvonne Tasker (1993, 1998) and Lynda Hart (1994), began mapping this phenomenon in the 1990s, while collections such as *Action Chicks* (Inness 2004) and *Reel Knockouts* (McCaughey and King 2001) contribute to a continuing debate about what such representations mean. *La Femme Nikita* and *Alias* are part of this contingent in representing a new kind of female spy, one who is objectified but also represents a version of the increasing numbers of women entering the professions. They are professional spies and the protagonists of popular adventure series but are still the exception rather than the rule.

During the twentieth century, spying became a business, with the British and American intelligence agencies developing their own systems of training and bureaucracy (Knightley 2003). As with many professions, twentieth-century espionage devoted itself to specialisation and produced experts in a range of fields (Miller 2003: 28). Unlike most professions, however, the intelligence service has an intimate history with fictions about itself. In Britain writers such as E. Phillips Oppenheim and William Le Queux fuelled popular concerns about enemy spies operating on British soil before and during the First World War (Murray 1988, Radaker 1988). Such fictions fed into the political will to establish a British secret service in 1909, as a means to combat the perceived enemy at the gate (Knightley 2003: 7–28). The twentieth century has subsequently established an elastic boundary between fact and fiction regarding popular conceptions of espionage that continues into the twenty-first century (Knightley 2003, Der Derian 1992: 40–70, Beer 2001, Wark 1990, Hiley 1990). It is, therefore, not surprising that spy fictions have consistently shadowed our understanding of modern society since the early twentieth century in their representation of white-collar work. British and American intelligence agencies, from their inception in the early twentieth century, were part of the move towards a bureaucracy of surveillance as a means of social control (Dandeker 1990: 110–49, Lyon 1994: 114–16). Consequently, fictional accounts of espionage both glamorise and critique modern bureaucracies, such as le Carré's arcane and inefficient Circus, or the hyperreal office space of *24*. This fascination with the mundane details and working practices of intelligence agencies is evident even in early cinema. In his account of Fritz Lang's *Spies* (1928), Geoffrey O'Brien writes:

> Spy stories are a century-long graphing of our psychic (spy-kick?) relation to an eluctable bureaucracy conceived alternately as protector and oppressor, invader and home team. Bureaucracy is everywhere and nowhere; like the Chinese poet trying to describe the mountain, we can hardly conceptualize it because we're inside it. ... In *Spies* Lang constructs a model kit of modernity ...
>
> (O'Brien 1995: 68)

If Lang produced a 'model kit of modernity' in 1928, the fictions that followed, in print as on film and television, have offered their own accounts of spying as an indicator of modernity and postmodernity. Unlike its close relations, the western, detective fiction and science fiction, the spy narrative thus offers a particular frisson regarding its relation to the real (Wark 1990). On the one hand, Dame Eliza Manningham-Buller, the current Director General of MI5, recently commented, 'I wish life were like [the BBC television series] *Spooks* where everything is (a) knowable and (b) soluble by six people', and a former MI6 agent asserted: 'A lot of the time you spend at the desk.' Yet MI5 was said to be delighted with *Spooks* and the rise in applications it produced, while the MI6 website both distances itself from the Bond myth and employs it as an aid to recruitment (Norton-Taylor 2006).

Although intelligence agencies may be pleased to employ fictional spies as aids to recruitment, they are not so sanguine where it comes to questions of authentication. Espionage deals in information, and intelligence agencies' status is dependent on their ability to provide the right information at the right time. This makes spying a particularly pertinent business in modern corporate culture, where information as a currency is privileged over hard industries and hard cash. It is logical, therefore, that the twentieth century should be the moment when espionage became subject to bureaucratic structures, as a means of certifying the accuracy of the information which it accrues and as a means of legitimating its existence as a profession. It has been said that, 'modern intelligence systems emerged not so much by the conscious will of the central government as by a process of creeping bureaucratic growth' (Christopher Andrew, cited in Knightley 2003: 264). Those twentieth-century spy fictions with claims to realism thus tend to describe professional bureaucracies. Norman Mailer, in his best-selling spy novel, *Harlot's Ghost*, examines the workings of the CIA, an allegory not just of the USA but also of the white-collar bureaucracies which have come to dominate late Western capitalism. The titular 'Harlot,' a CIA maven called Hugh Montague, describes his profession to an audience of trainees and upper-echelon officers:

> 'This, gentlemen,' said Harlot, 'is espionage – a middle-class activity that depends on stability, money, a keen eye for the architecture of anxiety, large doses of hypocrisy on both sides, insurance plans, grievances, underlying loyalty, constant inclinations towards treachery, and an immersion in white-collar work.'
>
> (Mailer 1991: 412)

Spying, from this account, is inherent to the functioning of bureaucratic capitalism and ineluctably masculine – 'gentlemen'. What Harlot does not countenance is the impact of the female spy within this masculine environment. Yet women have been at the centre of espionage bureaucracies from their establishment. Tammy Proctor, in her account of the founding of British intelligence during the First World War, cites the central role of women in MI5: 'As clerks, supervisors, report writers, translators, printers, searchers, messengers, and historians, women made it possible for a tiny spy-tracking office created in 1909 to become a massive information clearinghouse by the end of the war' (Proctor 2003: 53). More recently, Dame Stella Rimington became the first woman Director General of MI5, having worked her way through all areas of the secret service. This is not to say that espionage is an equal-opportunities profession. While most of MI5's staff is female, few women occupy senior positions (Bennett 2002: 207–9).

As spying became a bureaucratised profession and spy fictions followed suit, they imbued the commonplace with meaning – the everyday phrases employed as passwords or recognitions and the mundane locations used for exchanging information. The fictional spy is, thus, a fantasy of agency for the subject in an increasingly confused and confusing world. Spies offer a material sense of self and agency that appears to be increasingly unavailable in Western culture. Michael Denning argues that this is a central aspect of spy fictions' popularity:

> it serves as a way of narrating individual political agency in a world of institutions and states that seem to block all action and paralyze all opposition. In its two main traditions, the thriller redeems the worlds of white-collar work and consumerist leisure: in the thriller of work, the anxieties of the organization man take on a secret coherence, and bureaucratic routines are invested with political meaning; in the thriller of leisure, the sports and games that kill time become a killing time, a time of dangerous political contests.
>
> (Denning 1987: 151)

Women spy-protagonists offer women readers and viewers this fantasy of individual agency. There are not many such figures in fiction, film and television, but this book examines some of the most popular women spies. In the process of that examination, it becomes evident that rather than 'redeem[ing] the world of white-collar work', women spies do not sit easily within such bureaucratic power structures. If, as Denning argues, spy fictions invest bureaucracies with political meaning, women spies in such settings raise questions about the kinds of politics such fictions endorse. Female spies in these terms work against the grain of the genre and mirror the poststructuralist practices of feminist academics. Christine Bold, in her rereading of women in the James Bond novels, argues that 'Reversing dominant reading practices in this case may be a step towards rewriting women's agency within the closed world of fictive clandestinity, refeminising the secret sphere of influence, and changing the rules of the "great game" and the socio-political matrix it trails with it' (Bold 2003: 181). Women spy-protagonists in fiction, film and television begin that process of rereading by raising questions about 'the "great game" and the socio-political matrix' which are never fully resolved.

As I began researching this book, the materials around it expanded at an exponential rate so that the story of its writing is also one of attempting to manage a baggy monster of sources, contexts and media. My focus, therefore, became very selective, moving from mythologies about real women in the early twentieth century to the most hyperbolically fictional representations of the woman spy on twenty-first-century television. This movement from historical to cultural material mimics the shift from modern to postmodern, in an attempt to chart the archaeology of mythologies around women as spies since 1900. Chapters 1 to 4, therefore, present a historical overview of mythologies, fictional representations and critical work regarding women spies in popular culture, while Chapters 5 and 6 offer more detailed analyses of popular television representations of the woman spy since the 1980s. My research proposes that the fiction of the female spy is emblematic of the changes wrought in understandings of white middle-class femininity across the twentieth century and into the twenty-first. From Mata Hari to Sydney Bristow, fictional spies may be read as indicative of debates about professional women's role in Western culture.

My research has been informed by a number of cognate works. There are now several volumes examining the recent phenomenon of active or violent women in popular media. Yvonne Tasker's *Working Girls: Gender and Sexuality in Popular Cinema* (1998) focuses on 'new Hollywood' and takes the figure of the prostitute or 'working girl' as a central trope. Sherrie Inness's *Tough Girls: Women Warriors and Wonder Women in Popular Culture* (1999) takes a broader view, including contemporary television, film, women's magazines and comic books. Other writers have provided invaluable historical and cultural resources, including Julie Wheelwright's *The Fatal Lover: Mata Hari and the Myth of Women in Espionage* (1992) and James Chapman's *Saints and Avengers: British Adventure Series of the 1960s* (2002). A number of statutory texts on popular culture include material on the spy but tend not to deal in detail with female spies in popular fiction or on film and television. Toby Miller's *Spyscreen: Espionage on Film and TV from the 1930s to the 1960s* (2003) is one exception, as it includes a chapter on the woman spy: 'Women Making Trouble: *The Avengers*, *Honey West* and *Modesty Blaise*'. This study endeavours to expand that account by assaying a broader historical scope and including examinations of printed media. Nevertheless, there are gaps and elisions in any survey, and I am all too aware of the absences.

One of the areas of examination barely touched upon is the spy spoof. A notable cinematic example merges spy-action-comedy with teen movie (in the tradition of John Hughes and Amy Heckerling) to produce the lesbian spy film, *D.E.B.S.* (Angela Robinson, 2005). Set in a college for super-spies, the top trainee is captured by a master criminal, the famous Lucy Diamond (Jordana Brewster) and willingly held hostage, only to be rescued by her teammates. Sending up the conventions of the teen drama and the spy film, these young spies are, as the strapline says, 'crime-fighting hotties with killer bodies.' Seductively presented for the viewer as Britneyesque teens in tartan mini skirts, *D.E.B.S.* nonetheless demonstrates the cultural elasticity of the female spy in twenty-first-century media. Disney/Pixar animation feature *The Incredibles* (Brad Bird, 2004) literally presented an elastic female spy – a family of superhero spies with Elastigirl, the stretchably strong working mother, Helen Parr (voiced by Holly Hunter). *She Spies* (2002–3) was a one-season attempt to capitalise on the success of the *Charlie's Angels* films, with Natasha Henstridge, Kristen Miller and Natashia Williams playing convicted criminals recruited by a secret government organisation. These and other examples demonstrate how the woman as spy fits neatly into the multigenre, multimedia economy of twenty-first-century popular culture, yet also has the potential to expand and subvert its limited account of femininity.

The first chapter examines male spies in British popular fiction, with particular reference to the Scarlet Pimpernel, Richard Hannay, James Bond and Alec Leamas. The focus is entirely on British fiction, as this tradition established grounding assumptions that continue to resonate in popular understandings of espionage. Nevertheless, such masculine models are less monolithically secure than they at first appear. My reading of Orczy, Buchan, Fleming and le Carré consequently unravels the ambivalence within espionage as a masculine endeavour. This leads to a closer examination of the women who surround the male spy in popular fiction. While such women appear to shore up his masculinity, they also, by their very presence, indicate anxieties regarding 'innate' or 'natural' discourses of gender. Chapter 2 discusses representations of the female spy from the turn of the twentieth century to the 1950s. The mythologised and demonised Mata Hari inflects all subsequent accounts of women in espionage, while Edith Cavell offers an early incarnation of the woman spy as hero. These opposing figures, whose stories were mobilised as propaganda in the First World War, lay the foundations for debate about the woman as spy in popular culture. The chapter concludes with a selective survey of cinematic accounts of the (good) woman spy on film from the 1930s to the 1950s. Women spies in the early twentieth century chart anxieties about the New Woman – those white, middle-class professionals who were gaining the franchise and moving beyond the domestic arena.

Chapter 3 focuses on the 1960s, with male and female spies featuring in popular television series. Beginning with an overview of critical work to date on central figures such as Emma Peel, I then address less well documented women spies. Modesty Blaise and Emily Pollifax are eccentric in that they have few peers during the 1960s or since. While Modesty Blaise is often mentioned in critical works, she is rarely examined in detail. The comic strips and novels in which she appears offer unresolved and contradictory accounts of Modesty as an active and attractive woman spy. Emily Pollifax is less well known but has featured in a series of popular novels by Dorothy Gilman since the 1960s. As an elderly spy, and as an account of an ageing woman in active work, she has few peers. The 1970s marked a renegotiation of women's social roles in response to second-wave feminisms. While many of the aims of those 1970s movements have not been met, they shifted the terms of debates about gender. In Chapter 4, *The Bionic Woman* and *The New Avengers* are examined as popular responses to the second wave, as attempts to imagine women as heroes rather than heroines (Brunsdon 1997: 48). Jaime Sommers and Purdey were new women addressing a new audience – the so-called 'Cosmo Girl' – but they are often unconvincing in their efforts to represent 'liberation'. Jaime and Purdey are hermaphrodite heroes, combining hyper-feminine appearance with masculine activities, and the contradictions of their roles do not sit comfortably within the medium they inhabit. Purdey and Jaime's power and femininity are commented upon within both series and, particularly in *The New Avengers*, humour is employed as a way of dealing with the paradox – but this does not render such contradictions invisible and nor does it ultimately resolve them.

Chapter 5 moves on to the 1990s to study three versions of Nikita: Luc Besson's 1990 film, its American remake and the subsequent television series *La Femme Nikita*. The spy drama as an allegory of corporate culture comes to the fore in this examination of a postmodern female spy. In the Nikita narratives, modern bureaucracies are fictionalised as dramatic arenas in which world-changing events occur. Yet such spy dramas may also be read as indicative of the inadequacy of late Western capitalism's response to feminism in their depiction of professional women in the new economy. The final chapter focuses on the most hyperbolic representation of the woman spy to date: Sydney Bristow in *Alias*. *Alias* is one of many new quality television drama series designed to appeal to an affluent, urban demographic. In this sense, it is as incorporated as *La Femme Nikita* or earlier television spy series such as *The Avengers* or *The Bionic Woman*. Yet, in its multiple address across genres, media and demographics, *Alias* is open to a range of readings. This concluding account of the woman as spy in popular culture does not attempt to classify Sydney Bristow as a progressive or reactionary representation of a woman in the professions. Instead Sydney, like many of her earlier sisters, is a mobile and suggestive signifier.

Just as espionage itself tracks the shifts from modernity to postmodernity, so women spies in popular culture shadow the advances and compromises of feminist politics in Britain and the USA. Although women spies in fiction, film and television often appear to follow the most conformist agendas – mimicking their male counterparts in serving the nation – their activities as women lend them a queer inflection. Women have often been regarded as suited to spying because white middle-class women are seen as above or beyond suspicion. One of the reasons women have been successful as spies – in fiction and in fact – may be the talents engendered by a career in femininity. As a subordinate group, even within a privileged class or race, women are often forced to work undercover to gain some measure of power over their own lives. In this way, as this book argues, representations of women spies make explicit the continuing contradiction between femininity and agency in Western culture across the twentieth century and into the twenty-first.

# 1 Spies, lies and sexual outlaws

## Male spies in popular fiction

This chapter examines the male spy in twentieth-century British popular fiction. While this may appear to reinforce the cultural authority of masculinity, proposing the male spy as origin and the female spy as his pale imitation, that is not my intention. The purpose of this approach is, rather, to trace contradictions and absences within literary representations of masculinity, following the growing body of work which bears witness to its social and historical specificity (see Mangan and Walvin 1987, Roper and Tosh 1991, Rutherford 1997, Boyd 2003). To this end, the discussion centres on four influential fictional spies: the Scarlet Pimpernel, Richard Hannay, James Bond and Alec Leamas. These characters mark shifts in literary accounts of espionage, from the 'great game' to a more muddied world. They also map an eccentric history of modern England from 1900 to the 1960s. This was a foundational period for the mythology of the spy. British fictions established a template against which later spies in fact and fiction are measured; yet, these figures are shaky constructs, embodying fantasies of monolithic power and agency while barely suppressing the Others they allegedly oppose. This chapter thus examines four male spies in the light of so-called 'queer' theory, which argues that dominant social norms are predicated upon subordinated categories (see Butler 1990, Sedgewick 1991). Fragmentation, foreignness and femininity haunt these heroes, yet they also depend upon these opposing forces. Male spies in fiction consequently initiate debate about spies in the early twentieth century, while the femmes fatales and good women who inhabit the margins of their narratives call attention to the mutability of masculinity and to contemporary debates about the role of women in public life.

At the turn of the twentieth century, English masculinity was understood as white, middle-class and heterosexual (Rutherford 1997). The Victorian and Edwardian cult of 'manliness' may have been established in Britain through the public-school system, but was exported to the USA as part of a new fascination with physical and mental health (Park 1987). Contrary to such ideals of nobility, Christianity and honour, the male spy is required by his profession to acquire skills that are antithetical to his national and gender identities. In particular, the spy is required to develop criminal attributes, to deceive others and disguise himself to evade capture or to gain information. Such masquerades run counter to late nineteenth- and early twentieth-century accounts of white masculinity, as they employ character- istics more often projected onto a deviant other. Despite his role as a heroic protagonist, the male spy is thus shadowed by deviance; to spy is to be *devious*, after all. In effect, the male spy must acquire skills that are stereo- typically and pejoratively ascribed not only to criminality but also to femininity – he must be sneaky, double-faced and underhand. In early spy fictions, such as Buchan's Hannay novels, these skills are primarily evident in his foreign foes; hence, femininity and the foreign threat to England's nationhood are frequently elided (Hiley 1990: 73). This trope is depicted variously in the work of key authors who have helped shape popular understandings of espionage, from Buchan to Fleming and le Carré, as they refract the concerns and contexts of their particular moments.[1] As the twentieth century advances, fictions about the English spy present a gentle- man whose profession works against any gentlemanly mode of conduct.

## The aristocratic spy: Baroness Orczy's *The Scarlet Pimpernel*

In her essay on spies in nineteenth-century American popular fiction, Christine Bold notes how authors 'masculinized the "great game," allied espionage with the frontier myth to discover heroic characteristics for the spy, and used the figure to make sense of a social order undergoing rapid change' (Bold 1990: 18). Although the frontier spirit is specific to an American context, the difficulty of ascribing a properly heroic character to a spy protagonist is a problem common to all spy fiction. Many representa- tions of the spy compensate for this by emphasising the pleasure he takes in adventure, moral standpoint and appropriate resolution, yet such emphases also serve to highlight the contradictory nature of the spy's role. While spy protagonists may represent attempts to 'make sense of a social order undergoing rapid change' during the twentieth century, they also indicate absences and inconsistencies in the ideologies that shape such social orders. Male spies are thus hegemonic characters, as they serve the dominant order *and* question it. One such contradictory figure appears in an early twentieth- century popular novel which struggles even to achieve classification as spy fiction: the Scarlet Pimpernel. If William Le Queux wrote spy novels that veered into the genre of the 'love-romance', Baroness Orczy's most famous creation is lodged in the romantic genre and often only considered spy fic- tion on sufferance (McCormick 1977: 147, Panek 1981: 5–16). *The Scarlet Pimpernel* was initially rejected by at least a dozen publishers. Orczy and her husband, undaunted, made the manuscript into a play, which was per- formed to great success in Nottingham in 1903; the novel was subsequently published in 1905 (McCormick 1977: 147–8, Staples 1988: 232–3). The main character, Sir Percy Blakeney, survived for several more novels and inspi- red a number of film and television adaptations. The most successful film version, which is largely faithful to Orczy's novel, is Harold Young's *The Scarlet Pimpernel* (1934) starring Leslie Howard.

Set during the French Revolution, *The Scarlet Pimpernel* recounts the adventures of a French actress, Marguerite St Just, married to Sir Percy Blakeney and unaware of her husband's secret identity as the Scarlet Pimpernel, mysterious liberator of the French nobility. The narrative follows a romantic trajectory, as the estranged husband and wife are unwittingly united against Chauvelin, the devious republican spy, and ultimately restored to marital union. At the beginning of the novel, they have been married for a year but were separated twenty-four hours after their wedding by Marguerite's inadvertent betrayal of the Marquis de St Cyr and his subsequent execution. All the major characters are secret agents; Percy Blakeney as the leader of an amateur English spy ring, Chauvelin as professional spy for Revolutionary France and Marguerite who, with her history of betrayal, is forced by Chauvelin to betray the Pimpernel in order to save her brother, Armand. The distinction between the heroic Blakeney and the villainous Chauvelin is made clear throughout; their opposition endorses the innate dominance of the 'natural' aristocrat over the common man. Yet Blakeney constitutes a mercurial hero whose skills in disguise and dissimulation are preternatural.

Part of Blakeney's 'cover' is his role as a foppish nobleman. Sir Percy is a distinctive character in English high society, obsessed with the minutiae of fashion and leisure, yet able to disguise himself with ease on the other side of the Channel. He first appears in the novel as an old woman driving a cartload of concealed aristocrats through the gates of Paris; in the final adventure of the novel, he is back on French soil and disguised as a Jew. The Pimpernel thus cross-dresses in terms of gender, class and race, confirming his reputedly magical ability to evade capture. His performances also compromise his identity as an Englishman, however; if he is such a skilled actor, then the 'true' identity of Percy Blakeney may also be a disguise. This early example of the spy as romantic hero reveals the contradictions upon which British spy fiction rests. Blakeney's aristocratic birth, thirst for adventure and omniscient leadership make him a typical *fin-de-siècle* protagonist. Kelly Boyd argues that the function of such heroes in Victorian boys' magazines was to 'crystallise the link between masculinity and class status ... at a time when the category was undergoing refinement, especially for the middle classes' (Boyd 2003: 47). Blakeney fits this model but also problematises it through his theatrical use of disguise. While his exploits conform to those of a *Boys' Own* hero, the means by which he achieves his successes do not.

In *Cover Stories: Narrative and Ideology in the British Spy Thriller*, Michael Denning describes how the spy thriller is formally constructed in terms of a game, with its own rules and set players:

> Moreover, this concern for games is founded historically in the ethic of sportsmanship of the public schools of the late nineteenth and early twentieth century, an ethic that was disseminated and popularised by

the 'school stories' of popular boys' weeklies, by a variety of popular fiction forms including the thriller, and by youth organisations like the Boy Scouts. The myth of the Newbolt man with his mystical loyalty to school, nation and Empire, and his philistine muscular Christianity, set the tone for the early thrillers of Childers, Buchan and Sapper. It was an ethic that took the school cricket pitch, the celebrated playing fields of Eton, as a figure for social life, thus combining an institutional loyalty and reverence for hierarchical structures with a sense that social and political conflict was a game, to be played in a spirit of fairness, amateurism, and manliness.

(Denning 1987: 33)

The novel's account of Blakeney's fairness and amateurism is aligned with his social role as an English aristocrat, but his manliness is compromised both by his foppish masquerade in London society and by his disguises in France. The reader sees little of the 'real' Blakeney or his manliness, as that is his *secret* identity as the Scarlet Pimpernel. While *The Scarlet Pimpernel* is a historical novel, it is a fiction that engages with concerns regarding national identity and gender at the turn of the twentieth century. Blakeney's heroic deeds make him a *Boys' Own* hero, but the ease with which he becomes the dandy feminises him. The setting of the novel places Blakeney as a contemporary of Beau Brummel, the nineteenth-century dandy, but its publication in 1905 places the narrative in the wake of a *fin-de-siècle* decadence that gave the dandy a new significance. The aesthete's obsessive interest in clothing and decor aligned him with women's role as consumers in the new department stores and thus made him a rare and exotic creature; the 'feminized male' (Felski 1995: 91–7).

Blakeney's ambiguity is most evident in the competing generic demands of romantic fiction and the spy thriller, where the former requires the hero to be an object of desire and the latter requires him to be an active subject. The narrative point of view in *The Scarlet Pimpernel* is primarily that of Marguerite, who spends much time observing her husband and musing on the change he has undergone since they were first married. In this sense, he plays the role of the hero in romantic fiction who remains an enigma until the final denouement (Modleski 1984):

Marguerite looked at him tentatively once or twice; she could see his handsome profile, and one lazy eye, with its straight fine brow and drooping lid.

The face in the moonlight looked singularly earnest, and recalled to Marguerite's aching heart those happy days of courtship, before he had become the lazy nincompoop, the effete fop, whose life seemed spent in card- and supper-rooms.

But now, in the moonlight, she could not catch the expression of the lazy blue eyes; she could only see the outline of the firm chin, the corner of the strong mouth, the well-cut massive shape of the forehead; truly, nature had meant well by Sir Percy ...

(Orczy 1905: 141)

As with Joseph Conrad's *The Secret Agent* (1907), *The Scarlet Pimpernel* offers an external view of Englishness, told largely from the point of view of the French exile Marguerite rather than Blakeney. The effect of this is to make Blakeney strange, so that *he* becomes the mysterious 'other' rather than Marguerite, who is a point of identification for the reader. For Marguerite and for the reader, Blakeney is unknown and unknowable. Even as he masterfully drives his coach and four on long journeys through the night, he holds the reins 'in his slender feminine hands' (Orczy 1905: 78). His gender identity is fluid, and the implication throughout the novel is that Blakeney, while powerful, is mercurial in his ability to transform himself.

The second Scarlet Pimpernel novel attempts to fix Blakeney more securely as a heroic figure:

The full magnetism of the man was apparent now. ... The man of the world – the fastidious dandy – had shed his mask; there stood the leader, calm, serene in the very face of the most deadly danger that had encompassed any man, looking that danger fully in the face, not striving to belittle it or to exaggerate it, but weighing it in the balance with what there was to accomplish; the rescue of a martyred, innocent child from the hands of fiends who were destroying his very soul even more completely than his body.

(Orczy 1913: 71)

This description is much more aligned with the adventure heroes of the late nineteenth century, which promoted a Victorian manliness based on aristocratic birth, arrogance and omniscient leadership (Boyd 2003: 50–1). Yet Blakeney compromises even this already-outdated heroism by slipping back into the dandy persona: 'His usual *débonnair* [*sic*] manner was on him once again, his laziness, his careless *insouciance*. He was even at this moment deeply engaged in flicking off a grain of dust from the immaculate Mechlin cuff at his wrist' (Orczy 1913: 77). In *Eldorado* (1913), Blakeney is engaged in a plot to rescue the infant dauphin from the squalid Temple Prison; once again, the innate heroism of the nobility wins out against brutish Republican foes. Set amid such a rigidly delineated battle between the upper and lower classes, Blakeney cuts a strange figure, able to pass as a common stonemason and furniture remover, due to his 'abnormal physique and iron nerve' (Orczy 1913: 127). Blakeney's double identity as foppish English aristocrat and Scarlet Pimpernel, compounded with his many transformations, contradict any secure heroic persona.

This unstable hero is also an odd English gentleman, for while he is a nobleman with the ear of the Prince of Wales, his background is compromised by a mentally unstable mother, apparently driven mad by marriage: 'His father, the late Sir Algernon Blakeney, had had the terrible misfortune of seeing an idolised young wife become hopelessly insane after two years of happily married life' (Orczy 1905: 48). To avoid the scandal of insanity in the family, Algernon Blakeney takes his wife and child to an unspecified 'abroad', where Percy grows up, eventually settling in England with his French bride. Blakeney's fluency in French is thus explicable, but his background is consequently more European than English. This is another aspect of the novel where the genres of romantic and spy fiction clash: Blakeney's background and mysterious identity make him an effective romantic hero but, as a spy, his skills in deception and disguise ally him with the evil Other of the novel, the wicked Chauvelin. Blakeney's mutable identity also problematises his motivation for becoming the Scarlet Pimpernel in the first place; if Blakeney is faking it as an aristocratic English buffoon, Englishness is also part of his motivation. Blakeney is nothing if not a gentleman spy setting out with his followers to play the 'great game' on French soil. Why, with a childhood spent 'abroad', does Blakeney assay an English cause? Within the novel, such concerns are explained in terms of class loyalty; Blakeney sets out to save fellow aristocrats, although the narrative asserts the superiority of English aristocracy above all others.

*The Scarlet Pimpernel* thus offers an early example of the confusions and contradictions of spy fiction and the male spy. The plot transports the protagonists from France to England and back to France, ending as the happy couple set foot on English soil again with all misunderstandings resolved and Monsieur Chauvelin banished from London society. As a romantic adventure, Orczy's novel offers the pleasures of foreign travel without any of the inconveniences. The reader is transported from the cosy order of the Fisherman's Rest in Dover to the squalid chaos of the Chat Gris in Calais, without any doubt that these hostelries represent the opposing characteristics of England and France. In Harold Young's film, the adventures of the Pimpernel are irrevocably linked to a 'timeless' Englishness by Leslie Howard, as Percy Blakeney, reciting the 'this England' speech from *Richard II* in the closing scenes. Such romances seem to offer simple oppositions between masculinity and femininity, England and the enemy, but they also raise questions about such apparently simple categories.

## The gentleman spy: John Buchan's Richard Hannay

Like Percy Blakeney, John Buchan's Richard Hannay is also an amateur spy, although he arguably becomes more of a professional as the series of novels progress (Cawelti and Rosenberg 1987: 90, Bloom 1990: 5, Trotter 1990: 42). Buchan's hero embodies principles of amateur gamesmanship which are pitted against a narrow professionalism (Panek 1981: 56). Hannay first appears in *The Thirty-Nine Steps* (1915) and is inadvertently caught up in international espionage. He thus enters the world of the spy by chance rather than choice, and this, to a large extent, absolves him of the need to examine too closely the ethics of spying (Macintosh 1990). In this first novel, he adopts the disguises and deceptions of the spy out of necessity, as he is on the run from the fellowship of the Black Stone and also from the police. Hannay's motive for becoming involved is explained as a personal obligation and sense of duty: 'Somehow or other the sight of Scudder's dead face had made me a passionate believer in his scheme. He was gone, but he had taken me into his confidence, and I was pretty well bound to carry on his work' (Buchan 1915: 27).

'Schoolboy-honour' runs high in these novels (Atkins 1984: 140), and Hannay's subsequent comment – that the 'long knife would not be the end of Scudder if I could play the game in his place' (Buchan 1915: 27) – speaks of a social contract rooted in class, gender and nation. While such language recalls public-school Englishness, it is confounded by Hannay's initial impression of England. As a Scottish ex-pat recently returned from South Africa, Hannay confesses that he regarded England as an exotic destination – 'England was a sort of Arabian Nights to me' – and a huge disappointment: 'I had been three months in the Old Country, and was fed up with it. ... The weather made me liverish, the talk of the ordinary Englishman made me sick, I couldn't get enough exercise and the amusements of London seemed as flat as soda-water' (Buchan 1915: 13).

England is both strange and decadent to this returning colonial. The unhealthy Englishman Hannay describes is indicative of contemporary concerns regarding the physical and mental health of the nation; an anxiety also felt across the Atlantic (Park 1987, Richardson 2004). Baden-Powell's *Scouting for Boys* (1908) made a direct connection between the colonial experience and a manliness that many saw as lacking in native Englishmen (Warren 1987). The Hannay novels outline a debate about what constitutes Englishness – and what kind of England is being fought for. *The Thirty-Nine Steps* was published a year into the Great War but is set shortly before it begins. From the outset, Englishness appears vulnerable – in *The Thirty-Nine Steps* the threat is envisaged as an insidious foreign invasion of master spies on British soil, yet the solution to that threat also comes from beyond the national boundaries of England itself. Franklin P. Scudder, the agent whose death invokes Hannay's allegiance, is a journalist and linguist from Kentucky who brings news of an international conspiracy against England.

In this first novel, 'the ordinary Englishman' appears ill-equipped to fight such cunning foes; while Hannay admires the working men that he meets, he is scathing about the chattering middle classes (Panek 1981: 58). The old country is in danger of losing its ability to fight, having become fat and lazy on the profits of Empire. Hannay has little time for bureaucracy and middle-class suburbia, as the Englishness favoured here is that of an idealised working man who knows his place, together with a ruling class who know theirs. Scudder describes the conspiracy he is fighting in the following terms:

I gathered that most of the people in it were the sort of educated anarchists that make revolutions, but that beside them there were financiers who were playing for money. A clever man can make big profits on a falling market, and it suited the book of both classes to set Europe by the ears. ...

When I asked why, he said that the anarchist lot thought it would give them their chance. Everything would be in the melting-pot, and they looked to see a new world emerge. The capitalists would rake in the shekels, and make fortunes by buying up wreckage. Capital, he said, had no conscience and no fatherland. Besides, the Jew was behind it, and the Jew hated Russia worse than hell.

(Buchan 1915: 16–17)

This statement makes clear the ground of battle; this conflict is about national and racial identity. Scudder's story of an international conspiracy, later exposed as an overheated interpretation of events, is superseded by a less complex but equally terrifying plot to steal British naval secrets: 'By displacing one plot by another, one villain by another, Buchan is able to produce a more convincing if no less implausible plot and villain' (Denning 1987: 47). Nevertheless, the echo of Scudder's voice resounds throughout the Hannay novels, for there is no convincing explanation as to why foreign foes so regularly assault English territories. To provide one would involve a more critical scrutiny of the British imperial project.

As a colonial, Hannay appears eminently qualified to combat the pernicious forces that assail England, primarily because of his idealistic patriotism, keeping the flame of Englishness alive in the healthy environment of the colonies. He is also, as the text notes at several points, 'a white man', where whiteness indicates integrity and honour; the enemy organisation is predictably named the Black Stone. As with *The Scarlet Pimpernel*, Scudder's narrative is casually anti-Semitic – in both cases, the figure of the Jew is employed to represent contemporary discomfort with the cosmopolitan modernity of the early twentieth century (Rutherford 1997: 57). Despite their disparate settings, *The Scarlet Pimpernel* and *The Thirty-Nine Steps* each evoke a nostalgic account of homogenous Englishness; Blakeney, like Hannay, offers an idealised representation of the true Englishman who is a last line of defence against foreign invasion. In neither case should this be taken as a simple reflection of their author's political tendencies; nor should it be read as a straightforward reflection of contemporary attitudes (Butts 1990: 53, Donald 1990: 60–5). John G. Cawelti asserts that such simple oppositions tend to indicate a cynicism on the part of the author regarding his or her perceived readership, that formula fictions offer lazy archetypes as a matter of course to provide their readers with simple solutions to difficult issues (Cawelti 1976: 31–2). In Buchan's Hannay novels, however, there is increasing evidence that such simple solutions are insufficient even for the narratives themselves.

*The Thirty-Nine Steps* is set shortly before the First World War, and Hannay remains within the British Isles, travelling only from London to Scotland and back again. Scudder, however, offers a different kind of modern subject, as his evidence for the conspiracy has been gathered all over Europe:

> 'I got the first hint in an inn on the Achensee in Tyrol. That set me inquiring, and I collected my other clues in a fur-shop in the Galician quarter of Buda, in a Strangers' Club in Vienna, and in a little book-shop off the Rachnitz-strasse in Leipsic [*sic*]. I completed my evidence ten days ago in Paris.'
>
> (Buchan 1915: 19)

Scudder represents a spy more familiar to later readers in the form of Fleming's Bond and his imitators. He is a cipher of modernity, able to move across Europe at the speed of a sentence and not entirely approved of by the intelligence hierarchy. *The Thirty-Nine Steps* introduces Hannay's 'M', Sir Walter Bullivant of the Foreign Office, who says of Scudder, 'He was half crank, half genius, but he was wholly honest. The trouble about him was his partiality for playing a lone hand. That made him pretty well useless in any Secret Service – a pity, for he had uncommon gifts' (Buchan 1915: 93). Scudder also mirrors the Scarlet Pimpernel's ability to transform himself:

> 'I left Paris a dandified young French-American, and I sailed from Hamburg a Jew diamond merchant. In Norway I was an English student of Ibsen collecting material for lectures, but when I left Bergen I was a cinema-man with special ski films. And I came here from Leith with a lot of pulp-wood propositions in my pocket to put before the London newspapers.'
>
> (Buchan 1915: 19)

Scudder's disguises move him across race and class but also indicate the coming information technologies. The diamond merchant and student can also become a 'cinema man' or supplier of raw materials to the papers. Scudder works in the modern profession Richard Hannay tumbles into; the world of international espionage in which anyone can be anything. It is also a world already informed by popular fiction: as the literary innkeeper gasps, 'it is all pure Rider Haggard and Conan Doyle' (Buchan 1915: 41). For Hannay and his allies, however, this is not an egalitarian Europe but a dangerous world where traditional hierarchies are under threat and in need of protection. Scudder's disguises provide a dark warning about the ability of enemy agents to transform themselves; indeed, much of Hannay's work is to discern the enemy behind an English façade. The Hannay novels clearly perceive the emergence of a new world order, evoking conservative fears of what such change may bring and concomitant anxieties about national security and the demise of a mythic Englishness.

After a breathless chase across the Scottish Highlands, Hannay returns to England to identify his foe and is horrified to discern the lineaments of the Black Stone on a village tennis court in Kent. The enemy is truly at the gate and so well disguised as retired stockbrokers that Hannay continues to doubt his own instincts until the final showdown. The chief skill of enemy agents rests in their ability to become someone else: 'Those chaps didn't need to act, they just turned a handle and passed into another life, which came as naturally to them as the first' (Buchan 1915: 118). The Black Stone, and their leader, whom Hannay first encounters as 'the bald archaeologist', are not adept at disguise; their skill comes from a *lack* of identity. In this novel, as elsewhere, there is a horror of fluidity, of the abyss, of the unknown futures that modernity offers. The Black Stone are able to pass as Englishmen, as archaeologists, as a First Sea Lord of the new British Navy. They are able to do so because they are nebulous wraiths, diametrically opposed to the secured identity of the true Englishman, Richard Hannay: 'In this way, the enemy is that which the hero is not: *faceless*, soulless, amorphous automata who blindly obey unseen masters and whose autonomy and individuality is absolutely curtailed by obedience to absolutism itself' (Bloom 1990: 4).

Yet, Hannay also employs disguise in order to evade capture. In this first novel, he is a milkman, a road mender and a beggar called Ned Ainslie. The good spy is thus allied with the bad, and the narrative works hard to provide some distinction between the two. In *The Thirty-Nine Steps* it is a matter of ability. As the bald archaeologist says to Hannay, 'You are a clever actor, but not quite clever enough' (Buchan 1915: 74). Hannay is hampered in his abilities as a spy by too secure an identity – he is too much an Englishman to dissemble. His lack of 'cleverness' in this regard marks him as morally superior to the brotherhood of the Black Stone, who stand for slippery modernity. Disguise is thus an indicator of evil; where Hannay employs disguise, he only succeeds in fooling the enemy for a while. The distinction is also that of the professional and the amateur. Where the Black Stone are professional spies, trained in disguise and subterfuge, Richard Hannay is an amateur whose skills rely on his background as a soldier in the Boer War and his friendship with the Afrikaner scout, Peter Pienaar. Pienaar appears in later novels, but in *The Thirty-Nine Steps*, he is present only in Hannay's memory, proving invaluable as Hannay attempts to unmask the Black Stone. Modern professionalism is thus set against the traditions of amateur gamesmanship, and, in this first novel, the latter is clearly the victor. As the Hannay series progresses, however, the distinction between the modern and the traditional – England's future and its past – are less distinct, as the narratives address the question of what will become of England and Englishness after the Great War.

For Buchan's protagonist, this is a moral journey, and Peter Pienaar, together with the constant references to Bunyan's *Pilgrim's Progress*, represents Hannay's spiritual and ethical touchstone (Cawelti and Rosenberg

1987: 82). Leroy L. Panek notes the link between the spiritual and the physical in Buchan's novels, particularly apparent in Hannay's largely pointless trek across the Alps in *Mr Standfast*: 'The point is that Buchan *via* Bunyan saw climbing as a means of showing character and that one could not accept a final reward without having been pitted against the physical and psychological stress of climbing' (Panek 1981: 52). Hannay, at this point, as in the rigours of his flight across Scotland and England, exhibits an almost masochistic pleasure in the privations thrust upon him. The notion of duty, of having to strive to *deserve* the 'final reward', is embedded in the discourses of masculinity which prevail in the early twentieth century:

> The imaginary Englishman with his stiff upper lip and masterly control over world affairs was invented during another era of uncertainty, in the years between 1870 and the outbreak of the First World War. This period saw the appearance of hundreds of boys' adventure stories, eulogising Britain's empire builders. Life for the fictitious imperial hero was a series of opportunities to exercise his prowess and demonstrate supremacy over foreigners and the working classes.
>
> (Rutherford 1997: 12)

The 'stiff upper lipped' Englishman does not tell the whole story regarding masculinity at this time; Kelly Boyd and others have mapped the move away from the manly hero as an aristocratic individualist to a more community-oriented subject (Boyd 2003). Victorian and Edwardian middle-class masculinity was reformulating itself to deal with the new challenges of the twentieth century (Mangan and Walvin 1987). One aspect of this shift is apparent in *The Thirty-Nine Steps*, in Hannay's relation to middle-class England. The novel ends as it begins, with Hannay finding himself in an exoticised urban environment where he is ill at ease. Still doubting his own instincts, Hannay meets the brotherhood of the Black Stone in their suburban Kentish villa. The enemy spies are hiding in plain sight, pretending to be Englishmen. During this final confrontation, Hannay is thrust into the one arena where he is uncomfortable:

> A man of my sort, who has travelled the world in rough places, gets on perfectly well with two classes, what you may call the upper and the lower. He understands them and they understand him. I was at home with herds and tramps and roadmen, and I was sufficiently at my ease with people like Sir Walter and the men I had met the night before. I can't explain why, but it is a fact. What fellows like me don't understand is the great comfortable, satisfied middle-class world, the folk that live in villas and suburbs. He doesn't know how they look at things, he doesn't understand their conventions, and he is as shy of them as of a black mamba.
>
> (Buchan 1915: 119)

Hannay is finally able to discern the enemy who gives himself away by repeating a small gesture that Hannay recalls from his flight through Scotland. Sitting in an ordinary suburban house, surrounded by the police, the alien threat has truly come home to roost, and the location of this final sequence is heavily symbolic. The expanding suburbs and their inhabitants are thus depicted as ripe for infiltration by foreign enemies and alien ideas, such as socialism and feminism.

This mistrust of the middle classes is significant, for concurrent with Richard Hannay's development as a professional spy is the development of Hannay as domesticated Englishman rather than restless colonial. If the Hannay novels take the protagonist on a journey from amateur to professional, they also map his development from lonely bachelor to contented husband. Hannay's emotional journey in the novels represents a spiritual journey towards an understanding of England and Englishness (Panek 1981: 57). The quest is played out through Hannay's romance with Mary Lamington, whom he first encounters in a shell-shock hospital in the Cotswolds in the third novel of the series, *Mr Standfast*. Mary is burdened with symbolic weight, which may explain why she appears as little more than a cipher, and an ambiguous one at that: 'She smiled demurely as she arranged the tea-things, and I thought I had never seen eyes at once so merry and so grave. I stared after her as she walked across the lawn, and I remember noticing that she walked with the free grace of an athletic boy' (Buchan 1919: 17).

Mary is suggestively associated with the traditional English song 'Cherry Ripe' and, like England, she is the motivation and destination for Hannay in this novel. The dissatisfaction with England, which Hannay voiced at the beginning of *The Thirty-Nine Steps*, is resolved in *Mr Standfast*. At the beginning of the latter novel, Hannay notes his changing perspective, as he arrives at Fosse Manor and surveys the rolling countryside of the Home Counties:

> In that moment I had a kind of revelation. I had a vision of what I had been fighting for, what we were all fighting for. It was peace, deep and holy and ancient, peace older than the oldest wars, peace which would endure when all our swords were hammered into ploughshares. It was more; for in that hour England first took hold of me. Before my country had been South Africa, and when I thought of home it had been the wide sun-steeped spaces of the veld or some scented glen of the Berg. But now I realised that I had a new home. I understood what a precious thing this little England was, how old and kindly and comforting, how wholly worth striving for.
>
> (Buchan 1919: 21)

The characteristics of this 'little England' are difficult to pin down, and that difficulty may be perceived via the figure of Mary Lamington. Mary's ambiguity – her boyish femininity – together with her lack of characterisation in the novel represent the problem that Hannay wrestles with in *Mr Standfast*. Men of Hannay's generation faced a conflict between manliness and domesticity: 'The generation which grew up after 1860 displayed an insecurity in their masculine identities which manifested itself in a flight from domesticity, a growing disparagement of the "feminine," a readiness to go abroad and an increasing refusal amongst late Victorian men to marry' (Rutherford 1997: 19). *Mr Standfast*, thus, represents an attempt to reconcile the hero not only to domesticity, as home for Hannay becomes little England rather than the sweeping vistas of the veld, but also an attempt to imagine a future for the hero in peacetime. While the novel is set during the First World War – and the closing chapters take place on the Front Line in France – it was published in 1919 and offers a prescient account of the interest in new social movements that was to dominate political life in the inter-war period (Boyd 2003: 101).

Mary represents one aspect of this despite her flat characterisation; she is a version of the New Woman in her role as female operative and professional colleague (Felski 1995: 146). Towards the end of the novel, she allows herself to be used as a decoy, a 'honey-trap' for the enemy agent, Moxon Ivery. When Hannay primly objects to this degradation, she is the one to talk him round:

> 'Look at me, Dick, look at your someday-to-be espousèd saint. I'm nineteen years of age next August. Before the war I should have been the kind of shivering débutante who blushes when she's spoken to, and oh! I should have thought such silly, silly things about life. ... Well, in the last two years I've been close to it, and to death. I've nursed the dying. I've seen souls in agony and in triumph. England has allowed me to serve her as she allows her sons. Oh, I'm a robust young woman now, and indeed I think women were always robuster than men. ... Dick, dear Dick, we're lovers, but we're comrades too – always comrades, and comrades trust each other.'
>
> (Buchan 1919: 230)

This proto-feminist sentiment sits strangely in the deeply traditionalist Hannay novels. Buchan's own politics were not simple, however: 'although he was politically a Tory, Buchan supported many of the progressive issues of his times: he wrote in favour of women's suffrage, voted for the recognition of the Soviet Union, and appealed for the release of conscientious objectors after the First World War' (Panek 1981: 43). Whether Mary's speech is a reflection of Buchan's more liberal political leanings or not, this account of gender relations and the 'ideal' partnership of (relatively) equals echoes the socialist ideals of the radical suburban community which Hannay initially has to infiltrate. Hannay is forced to live in the environment he most despises – middle-class suburbia – amongst the people he most disapproves of – a community of cranky pacifists – and this, like his tramp across the Alps, is part of his pilgrim's progress towards a fuller understanding of England. He and Mary work together in the Garden City of Biggleswick, and their emotional bond, together with his friendship with the conscientious objector, Lawrence Wake, map a discussion of the value and political constituency of Englishness.

Hannay's relationship with Lawrence Wake moves from deep suspicion of his principles as a conscientious objector and a mistaken assumption that he is an enemy spy, to frank admiration for his courage in death at the Front Line: 'He was the Faithful among us pilgrims, who had finished his journey before the rest. Mary had foreseen it. "There is a price to be paid," she had said – "the best of us"' (Buchan 1919: 341–2). Naturally, at the end of the novel, thoughts of Mary lead to thoughts of England and peacetime:

> I had a vision of a green English landscape, with its far-flung scents of wood and meadow and garden. ... And that face of all my dreams, with the eyes so childlike and brave and honest, as if they, too, saw beyond the dark to a radiant country.
>
> (Buchan 1919: 342)

What emerges from Hannay's meditations on England is a liberal form of Tory politics based on Christian fortitude and morality. Hannay's time in Biggleswick is unusually stationary – he is forced to meditate on the shortcomings and the strengths of the cranky radicals who live there. His purpose in Biggleswick is to flush out the enemy spy, Moxon Ivery, another blank-faced foe who, according to Hannay's colleague Blenkiron, 'hasn't got any personality either – he's got fifty, and there's no one he could call his own' (Buchan 1919: 55). Yet Hannay's own identity is strangely difficult to pin down; if Moxon Ivery is the evil other, Richard Hannay is the good self – a self based on a set of assumptions about masculinity and Englishness that are being renegotiated as the novels progress.

The gender politics of Buchan's Hannay novels are less confused than those of Orczy's *The Scarlet Pimpernel*, but they rest on a model of difference which requires the reader to agree with a logic which is full of absences. This is most explicit in the novels' female characters. While Richard Hannay is the protagonist, and his male friends and colleagues mark a wider understanding of the world in which he operates, Mary Lamington and Englishness constitute a symbolic destination for the hero and little more. Hannay appears strangely sexless, commenting in *Greenmantle* on his monk-like existence at the age of forty and admitting that he has little knowledge of women (Buchan 1916: 256). Such distance from femininity tallies with Hannay's Edwardian manliness. To be a man is to serve the Empire, to do one's duty and avoid the emotional messiness represented by the world of women, whether domestic or sexual. Women in the novels are ciphers; whether coded as good or evil, they are equally blank. Hilda Von

Einem, the villain at the centre of *Greenmantle*, lacks background or motivation; she simply exists like some force of nature. She is described as a fanatic, an ancient god and as having a mask-like face; she first appears disguised as 'The Lady of the Mantilla'. Despite her role as villain, both Hannay and Sandy Arbuthnot have romantic and/or sexual feelings for her; at several points, Hannay admires Hilda as one would admire a splendid wild animal. *Greenmantle* ends with the death of Hilda Von Einem and Sandy's noble desire to give her a burial on the mountaintop: 'Dick, we must bury her here ... You see, she ... she liked me. I can make her no return but this' (Buchan 1916: 335). Hilda barely exists in the novel except as a trope loosely based on Mata Hari, her only purpose to demonstrate the nobility of a good man. The Hannay novels are largely concerned with homosocial relationships (Panek 1981: 45). Hannay's male friends are his personal and professional touchstone, but Mary represents an ideal that is essentially untouchable. In the opposition between Mary and Hilda Von Einem, Buchan establishes the trope of the good and bad female spy discussed in the next chapter. Mary is associated with nation and (in later novels) motherhood, while Hilda represents a decadent, oriental sexuality which Hannay and Arbuthnot find fascinating (Donald 1990: 69–70). Despite Sandy's laudatory – and fearful – description of Von Einem as a 'Superwoman', neither she nor Mary is made complex in this novel; their common difference *as* women is mobilised to confirm the masculinity of the hero.

## Bond's girls

Of all the spies examined in this book, James Bond is the most analysed and theorised. In addition to essays and chapters devoted to Bond in books that generally examine spy fiction and film, there are several academic studies of Fleming's hero. Of these, Tony Bennett and Janet Woollacott's ground-breaking *Bond and Beyond: The Political Career of a Popular Hero* (1987) remains an authoritative examination of the novels and films. It is supplemented by more recent studies such as James Chapman's *Licence to Thrill: A Cultural History of the James Bond Films* (1999), Jeremy Black's *The Politics of James Bond* (2001) and Christoph Lindner's *The James Bond Phenomenon: A Critical Reader* (2003). Bond has also caught the attention of high-profile theorists such as Umberto Eco (1981) and Roland Barthes (1982). James Bond, as these commentaries attest, is more than a fictional figure; he is a cultural phenomenon. Far more than the Scarlet Pimpernel or Richard Hannay – or later fictional spies translated for film and television such as Deighton's Harry Palmer or le Carré's George Smiley – Bond has a visual role in popular culture, albeit one which changes as the actors have changed. It may seem perverse, in the light of that dominant visual field, to focus on the novels which feature James Bond, yet it is in the novels that Bond's gender is most problematic: 'the films ... reconstruct Fleming's plots, add the gadgets absent in the novels, rewrite the dialogue and provide a stable image of the hero unavailable in the books' (Panek 1981: 201). In a doubly perverse move, the discussion will centre on the women in Fleming's texts as particular moments in the novels that question Bond's status while appearing to endorse it.

In *Bond and Beyond*, Tony Bennett and Janet Woollacott examine the structural function of the Bond girl in Fleming's fictions and conclude that she embodies two forms of narrative 'problem': the enigma of her gender, as a 'girl' who is not fully aligned with heteropatriarchy, and the question of whether Bond can or will act to 'fix' her into normative femininity, usually through sexual conquest or awakening. Through her encounter with Bond, the 'girl' is thus cured of her problematic sexual identity, whether she is frigid, a virgin or a lesbian. The Bond girl is thus put back into place within 'the regime of the phallus'; she embodies a 'free and independent sexuality' but only insofar as it conforms to hyperbolised heterosexuality (Bennett and Woollacott 1987: 118). This reading of Bond marks him as an exemplary figure of 'compulsory heterosexuality' (Rich 1981, Bold 2003: 173). While the 'girl' is put in her place by Bond's dubious sexual therapy, James Bond is also 'fixed' within 'the regime of the phallus' by his relations with her – an unequal relationship which is just as circumscribed by the sex/gender system (Rubin 1975, Butler 1990: 72–5). While the Bond girl's purpose in the novel is to service Bond, she also indicates how Bond's heteromasculinity is dys-functional. The repeated sexual conquests bespeak a narrative anxiety about Bond's gender identity, which is inseparable in these fictions from his sexual performance. Several critics, from Bennett and Woollacott on, have focused their attention on Bond's phallic persona, but few have acknowledged the extent to which it is a delicate construct, so vulnerable that it requires con-stant support (Bennett and Woollacott 1987: 114–27, Miller 2003: 122–53). Christine Bold cites Judith Butler in her argument that Bond needs his 'girls' in order to assert his gender and national identity (Bold 2003: 177). Bond's sexuality is hysterical in its repetition; his role as a hysterical subject is manifest in the repeated ordeals each job entails (Woolf 1990: 87). To be a spy, for James Bond, is to suffer torture at the hands of England's enemies and to encounter exotic women who serve to reiterate his sexual potency. In Bennett and Woollacott's analysis of the 'phallic code' of Fleming's fictions, the 'girl' and the 'enemy' are aligned:

> Ultimately, the threat of ideological disruption embodied in both the villain's conspiracy and 'the girl's out-of-placeness' is avoided because Bond – as delegated representative of M, the holding centre of England and the patriarchal order – proves 'man enough' for the task. It is also by the operation of the 'phallic code' that the two centres of narrative tension constituted in the relations between Bond and the villain and Bond and the girl are connected: figuratively speaking, their interconnection might be expressed by saying that Bond puts England

back on top at the same time as he places 'the girl' back in place beneath him.

(Bennett and Woollacott 1987: 140–1)

Bond and M also need the girl and the villain in order to certify their patriarchal roles. The villain allows M to be confirmed as good rather than evil, while the girl allows Bond to be confirmed as fully heterosexual.

While popular fiction in general, and spy fiction in particular, is based on the pleasures of repetition, Fleming's novels mimic the structures of pornographic literature in their mechanical reproduction of heterosexuality (Denning 1987: 102). As *Bond and Beyond* notes, James responds to the challenging enigma of 'the girl' by 'putting her back into place beneath him (both literally and metaphorically)' (Bennett and Woollacott 1987: 116); for Bond sex is always penetrative, he is always on top (literally and metaphorically), and it is always the missionary position. As in much pornography, in these novels, sex is always the same thing. It is also similarly commodified. Just as Bond fixes 'the girl' within the libidinal economy of heterosexuality, so the pleasure she represents is fixed within consumer culture by Bond's gaze. There is little explicit description of the sexual act in these novels, but much description of the visual pleasure of looking at 'the girl'. Her unusual and suggestive name – Pussy Galore, Honeychile Rider – merely marks her as a different brand in the stream of disposable consumer goods that pass through Bond's hands. 'The girl' is thus part of Bond's role as consumer and connoisseur, and his pleasure in looking invites the reader to join him in his voyeurism. The Bond girl is 'part of the "view"' (Denning 1987: 105), while Bond's role as spectator is part of his professional, phallic persona: 'For Bond's pornographic imagination is structured not so much around explicit depictions of sexual acts as around Bond as voyeur, Bond as spy' (Denning 1987: 110). In this sense, Bond is the ultimate male spy as he embodies and repeatedly demonstrates anxieties about heteromasculinity.

For the desiring subject, of course, one 'view' is never enough. Bond himself appears to acknowledge this problem at the end of *The Man with the Golden Gun*, where he muses on a happy convalescence with Mary Goodnight after his battle with Scaramanga: 'he knew, deep down, that love from Mary Goodnight, or from any other woman, was not enough for him. It would be like taking "a room with a view." For James Bond, the same view would always pall' (Fleming 1965: 191). This odd statement, while consistent with Bond's lifestyle, is indicative of the problem Bond constitutes as a heteromasculine figure. Bond refuses to contemplate homosexual desire – the narratives instead project homosexual characteristics and tendencies onto his opponents (Bold 2003: 175–6) – but he is unable to satisfy himself within heterosexual terms. Bond can never settle for domesticity in the form of a single lover and is thus condemned to endless repetition. Even novelty can pall because, for James Bond, 'the same view' is always the next Bond girl. The weary statement at the end of *The Man with the Golden Gun*

is a metaphor not only for the sexual cul-de-sac which Fleming's protagonist represents but also for the potential boredom of his readers. It is
appropriate that *The Man with the Golden* Gun first appeared as a serial in
*Playboy*, for it represents the jaded appetites to which many of that magazine's readers aspire (Panek 1981: 214). If Bond's many conquests ultimately represent 'the same view', then Bond himself is always the same and
unable to change. On the one hand, as many critics have affirmed, Bond
appears to be a constant in Fleming's novels. Confronted by marriage, impo-
tence, madness and the loss of his identity, Bond suffers momentarily but is
always ready for his next job (Bennett and Woollacott 1987: 125–6). He is
unable to cope with an ordinary life of routine, cast into 'dog-days' depression
by unwelcome inactivity. Even when, as at the beginning of *The Man with
the Golden Gun*, Bond is clearly unfit for his job, M appears to correctly
prescribe another assignment as a means of helping him recover from brain-
washing by the KGB.

When we are offered a different view of Bond, however, the gaps and
contradictions become apparent. *The Spy who Loved Me* is narrated by
Vivienne Michel, a French Canadian who stumbles on an insurance scam
and is rescued by Bond. When she first encounters Bond, she mistakes him
for one of the gangsters who are holding her hostage in a remote motel in
the Adirondacks:

> At first glance I inwardly groaned – God, it's another of them! He stood
> there so quiet and controlled and somehow with the same quality of
> deadliness as the others. And he wore that uniform that the films make
> one associate with gangsters – a dark-blue, belted raincoat and a soft
> black hat pulled rather far down. He was good-looking in a dark,
> rather cruel way and a scar showed whitely down his left cheek. I
> quickly put my hand up to hide my nakedness. Then he smiled and
> suddenly I thought I might be all right.
>
> (Fleming 1962: 108)

Vivienne ventriloquises the usual narrative voice of these fictions – a voice
which is confidently aligned with Bond's world view, including his obsessive
concern with clothing and accessories. Yet this odd novel is not a comfortable read. Divided into three sections, it addresses Vivienne's background
in 'Me', the threatening appearance of the gangsters in 'Them' and Bond's
heroic rescue in 'Him'. For the Bond series, this is something of an experimental, even modernist, work, allowing Fleming to replicate gangster slang
in an unusual American setting. Fleming admired the American hard-boiled
school of detective writing, particularly the work of Raymond Chandler
(Chapman 1999: 2), and Vivienne even gives Bond a classic hard-boiled
persona: 'No woman had ever held this man. None ever would. He was a
solitary, a man who walked alone and kept his heart to himself' (Fleming
1962: 130). This novel also contains one of Bond's attempts to think about

his role as a spy. Aligning himself with the tradition of spying as the 'great game', Bond describes his work as 'a complicated game', but then quickly agrees with Vivienne that his profession is outdated, implying that he is less than convinced by his own role (Fleming 1962: 120). Significantly, this conversation takes place when Bond is forced to sit quietly, having been captured by Sluggsy Morant and Sol Horowitz, and the intelligence work he indiscreetly outlines to a complete stranger is that of Cold War politics. The peculiar juxtaposition in this novel between Vivienne's narration, the hard-boiled gangster formula and Bond's Cold War persona make for uncomfortable bedfellows. *The Spy who Loved Me*, with its experimental format and comparatively realist plot and setting, can be read as a sustained example of the tension apparent throughout the Bond series between the spy fiction of sensation – of action, sex and excitement – and a more realist spy fiction of meditation, frustration and doubt (Chapman 1999: 32). In these terms, Bond straddles the early twentieth-century certainties of Buchan's Hannay and the Cold War uncertainties of later fictions by writers such as Deighton and le Carré (Chapman 1999: 26–7).

Other moments where this tension breaks through include the opening passage of *Goldfinger* where Bond thinks about life and death in existentialist terms: 'It was part of his profession to kill people. He had never liked doing it and when he had to kill he did it as well as he knew how and forgot about it. ... Regret was unprofessional – worse, it was death-watch beetle in the soul' (Fleming 1959: 7). It is also visible in *On Her Majesty's Secret Service*, where Bond, for once, appears to be about to have a life beyond his work. He marries Tracy (La Comtesse Teresa di Vicenzo) at the end of the novel, and she is almost instantly killed, thus fulfilling the traditional role of the good woman in thrillers – to provide a motive for the hero. While the conclusion of the novel puts Bond neatly back in his place in the patriarchal world of Fleming's fictions, *On Her Majesty's Secret Service* also reveals a surprising aspect of Bond's character:

> I'm fed up with all these untidy, casual affairs that leave me with a bad conscience. I wouldn't mind having children. I've got no social background into which she would or wouldn't fit. We're two of a pair, really. Why not make it for always?
>
> Bond found his voice saying those words he had never said in his life before, never expected to say.
>
> 'Tracy. I love you. Will you marry me?'
>
> (Fleming 1963: 183)

The notion of a conscience about his sexual relationships, the desire for children and for long-term female companionship via marriage is a surprise to any reader familiar with the Bond character. It is as if Bond himself has suddenly realised the limitations of his character and attempts momentarily to break out of the endless cycle of repetition. The sensational Bond, who thrives on constant action and sexual conquest, confronts the realist Bond, who admits to conscience and desires a future rather than a repetitively existential present.

It is no surprise when Tracy dies so soon after their marriage – a death almost invited by Bond's assertion that they have 'all the time in the world' (Fleming 1963: 258) – for Bond represents a fantasy of masculinity that does not allow for attachment to women. Even his impulsive decision to marry seems little more than a momentary desire to be ordinary. He barely knows Tracy, and their relationship is predicated on her submission to his orders; he tells her what to do and how much to drink. Bond's affection for her father, Marc-Ange, is far more palpable. As head of the Corsican Mafia, the Union Corse, Marc-Ange Draco should be one of Bond's enemies but is instantly recognised as a friend: 'The man had such a delightful face, so lit with humour and mischief and magnetism that, at least in the man's present role, Bond could no more have killed him than he could have killed, well, Tracy' (Fleming 1963: 37). The connection that Bond makes between Marc-Ange and Tracy is more than familial here. Marc-Ange is an unconventional father; his first action on meeting Bond is to bribe him to marry his daughter and rescue her from suicidal tendencies. This attempt to straighten his daughter out (in every sense) is highly symbolic, as it makes explicit the position of women in the Bond narratives – as gifts between men, rather than subjects in and of themselves. It also makes explicit the nature of Bond's relations with men. This is what Luce Irigaray terms homosexual relations, more commonly known as homosocial relations – an exchange which employs the body of a woman to express desire between men, sexual or otherwise (Irigaray 1981, Sedgwick 1991). As with Buchan's Hannay novels, the purpose of women in Fleming's fiction is to certify the hero's masculinity.

## Doubtful professionals: le Carré's Alec Leamas

The success of Fleming's hero produced imitations in fiction and on film and television (see Cawelti and Rosenberg 1987: 151–2), but Bond also spawned his antithesis. While Fleming's fictions were regarded as 'dirty' in some quarters because of their pornographic tendencies, Deighton and le Carré offer a differently dirty evocation of espionage – a far muddier account of the profession. Their worlds are not the glamorous jet-set lifestyle of James Bond, nor the upper-class society of Richard Hannay. Instead, their heroes are seedy little men, who are professionals but not gentlemen. The British secret service in these fictions is a bureaucracy in decline, liable to inter-agency rivalries, betrayal, infiltration by enemy operatives and the human emotions of greed and ambition. Several critics have noted that Deighton and le Carré's secret service is peopled by white-collar workers, where the old school tie is often a cover for something more sinister (Cawelti and Rosenberg 1987, Denning 1987, Bradbury 1990).

Michael Hayes cites Kingsley Amis's comment on *The Spy who Came in from the Cold* (1963) as 'a farewell' to the subject and genre, and this early novel certainly contradicts the heroic exploits of Orczy's, Buchan's and Fleming's spy heroes (Hayes 1990: 116).

*The Spy who Came in from the Cold* begins with the death of an agent and a failed mission in East Berlin. There are no clear distinctions between le Carré's Circus and the enemy. The novel's protagonist and anti-hero, Alec Leamas, offers a direct contrast to Bond:

> His eyes were brown and small; Irish, some said. It was hard to place Leamas. If he were to walk into a London club the porter would certainly not mistake him for a member; in a Berlin night club they usually gave him the best table. He looked like a man who could make trouble, a man who looked after his money, a man who was not quite a gentleman.
>
> (le Carré 1963: 15)

Leamas is distanced from the public-school tradition of espionage; indeed, the description above questions his national identity – is he English at all? Like le Carré's other anti-hero, George Smiley, Leamas has a personal code of honour, but he is unable to put it into practice and finds himself at odds with the British secret service, used as their patsy to ensure the position of a Soviet double agent. Leamas's world view is shaped by a post-war political landscape that questions the certainties Blakeney, Hannay and Bond take for granted, to the extent that any nostalgic belief in Englishness becomes untenable (Bradbury 1990: 134–5). Like many of le Carré's protagonists, Leamas is a burnt-out professional, the opposite of Buchan's breathless amateur (Cawelti and Rosenberg 1987: 159). Leroy L. Panek astutely states that le Carré, 'uses the spy organization to examine not necessarily spies, but the way in which men serve institutions and institutions serve men' (Panek 1981: 236), inadvertently marking the gendered focus of the novels. As with class and national identity, however, Leamas offers a different masculinity to that of Hannay and Bond.

This is apparent in his relations with women in the novel. While establishing his cover identity working in a library, Leamas becomes involved with Liz Gold. Liz is the only character to call Leamas by his first name, and their intimacy leaves him professionally vulnerable. At the end of the novel, after he has been interrogated by the East German secret service and his target, Mundt, stands accused of being a double agent (which, in fact, he is), Liz is called upon to give evidence that discredits Leamas as a witness. Ultimately, both Liz and Leamas are shot while trying to cross the wall into West Berlin. Liz is not the glamorous 'girl' who appears in the Bond novels but an ordinary woman and a member of the British Communist Party who, through her encounter with Alec, is caught up in a dangerous game. Nevertheless, she fulfils a stereotypical function in the narrative, as a romantic spinster who subsumes her own needs and desires to those of Leamas. This is a different representation of femininity and heterosexual relations from that in Fleming's work, but one which still places women within recognisable gender roles – in this case, woman as helpmeet and inadvertent trap.

Other female characters do not fare much better. In the process of being recruited as a KGB informer, Leamas is taken to a strip club in Soho where the scenario is, again, the antithesis of Bond's glamorous milieu:

> A girl performed a striptease, a young, drab girl with a dark bruise on her thigh. She had that pitiful, spindly nakedness which is embarrassing because it is not erotic; because it is artless and undesiring. She turned slowly, jerking sporadically with her arms and legs as if she only heard the music in snatches, and all the time she looked at them with the precocious interest of a child in adult company. The tempo of the music increased abruptly, and the girl responded like a dog to the whistle, scampering back and forth. Removing her brassière on the last note, she held it above her head, displaying her meagre body with its three tawdry patches of tinsel hanging from it like old Christmas decorations. They watched in silence, Leamas and Kiever.
>
> (le Carré 1963: 60)

Le Carré offers the reader a different view of espionage than that presented by Fleming, but the women in these narratives perform a structural function similar to that of Bond's girls: they are on the periphery of the action and, if not part of the scenery, then an obstacle to the hero's success. Just as Bond's desiring gaze fixes the girls he meets in the masculine economy – insuring his position as vendor/consumer rather than object of exchange – so Leamas and Kiever's dispassionate gaze reasserts that economy, albeit in a more self-conscious manner. There is a different mood here, but the power structures are the same. The lush description of Honeychile Rider's first appearance on the beach in *Dr No* is in sharp contrast to this strangely disembodied account of a young stripper, but it is still men who look and women who are the objects of their attention. The difference resides in a lack of confidence in the view; these fictions foreground the seedy desperation of both the viewers and the object of their gaze. Le Carré's fiction is premised on a postmodern society where hope is a nostalgic emotion.

If there is a difference between the masculinities of Fleming's and le Carré's male protagonists, it is that of emotional focus. Bond is largely emotionless, whereas le Carré's heroes are emotionally complex, often damaged and damaging to those around them. The dramas in these later spy fictions are also more clearly played out against a corporate background. The organisation of espionage is as much the subject of these narratives as the spy protagonist. Where Fleming's fiction offered 'comforting fantasies' about intelligence agencies as benign bureaucracies that license secret desires for violence and sex (Cawelti and Rosenberg 1987: 136), le Carré's narratives are played out against a background of private and professional betrayal. Liz Gold's arrival in the East German courtroom makes this evident, as she is forced to betray Leamas and he is made to betray his affection for her (le Carré 1963: 162–98). For Leamas and Smiley, espionage entails a binding of their personal and professional lives, where their profession is not about combat and action but the slow accumulation of information (Denning 1987: 136–7). These later twentieth-century spy fictions map a society where agents' motives are always suspect and hopelessness is all pervasive. *The Looking-Glass War* marks out a new world of pointless operations in its account of misguided and mismanaged expeditions into Soviet territory:

> Avery was already familiar, during his short association with the Department, with the phenomenon of organic motivation; with operations which had no discernible genesis and no conclusion, which formed part of an unending pattern of activity until they ceased to have any further identity; with that progress of fruitless courtships which, in the aggregate, passed for an active love life.
>
> (le Carré 1965: 128)

This mindless bureaucracy, symbolically aligned in this passage with sexuality, represents a late-twentieth-century response to the successful agents of Buchan and Fleming. The Deighton and le Carré school of espionage is populated by failed operations and betrayed agents. Where Buchan and Fleming describe fantasies of individual agency, Deighton and le Carré indicate a lack of agency, describing anti-heroic little men locked within bureaucratic machines. The female spy protagonists discussed in the following chapters offer different views on twentieth-century society. It is notable, however, that as the twentieth century draws to a close and second-wave feminism begins to take effect, representations of female spies follow their male compatriots in their focus on the profession as a public and private arena of betrayal.

# 2 Femmes fatales and British grit

## Women spies in the First and Second World Wars

This chapter examines representations of women spies from 1900 to the 1950s. This was an era of dramatic change in women's public life, particularly for the white middle classes of Europe and the USA. Suffrage campaigns on both sides of the Atlantic, together with the prospect of higher education and a professional career for some privileged women, were accompanied by shifting discourses of gender and modernity. My discussion begins with Mata Hari, the infamous spy executed by the French during the First World War, whose name shadows all subsequent accounts of women spies. Since Mata Hari, the female spy has most often been understood as a femme fatale. Her real story is a morality tale of a different kind, as it maps the changing roles of women in modern Europe. In this sense, she may be a feminist forerunner, but her myth is dependent on derogated accounts of gender, race and class. Above all, Mata Hari's mythology feeds into the stereotype of the villainess. William Le Queux's novel *The Temptress* (1919) depicts a French femme fatale who brings disaster with her fiendish plans to seduce and murder any who get in her way. Like Buchan's Hilda Von Einem, she exhibits no motivation other than desire for wealth and lack of inhibition. Finally unmasked, she commits suicide with an overdose of morphine, and the remaining characters are married off. Lord Hugh Trethowen, the central protagonist and victim closes the novel: 'I feel assured we shall now be happy and contented. Let us look only to a bright and prosperous future, and let us forget forever the grim shadow that fell upon us, the shadow of THE TEMPTRESS' (Le Queux 1919: 250).

Le Queux's novel was published two years after Mata Hari's execution and employs that 'shadow' of continental femininity to naturalise Trethowen's aristocracy, wealth and honour, just as Mata Hari's prosecutors mobilised gender and racial stereotypes to represent her as the source of France's troubles. Mata Hari fed into projections, fears and anxieties regarding women and modernity that emerged in the late nineteenth century (Huyssen 1986: 52). This archetypal spy, like other femmes fatales, is thus 'not the subject of feminism, but a symptom of male fears about feminism' (Doane 1991: 2–3). Mata Hari is complemented by the emergent figure of the good woman spy. The propaganda surrounding Edith Cavell, a British agent executed during the German occupation of Belgium, together with later films such as *Nurse Edith Cavell* (Herbert Wilcox, 1939), depict women spies who are pure, white and feminine. In the early twentieth century, the female spy thus represents a modern femininity which is either eroticised and demonised as exotic or fetishised as the epitome of pure British womanhood. As the century proceeds, however, these binaries disintegrate, and a more complex account of the woman spy begins to appear on film.

## Mata Hari (1876–1917): female spy as femme fatale

The femme fatale, like her sister the New Woman, shadows nineteenth-century *fin-de-siècle* shifts in gender roles. The suffrage movements in Britain and America, together with legislative changes in marital property law and the development of university education for some privileged women, produced the distinctly middle-class phenomenon of the New Woman (Richardson 2004: 242–3). The femme fatale was less distinct in her class identity, often moving up the social scale through her immoral activities. Like the cities she inhabited, the modern femme fatale presented a fluid identity which combined new technologies and 'primitive' cultures:

> If, as Christine Buci-Glucksmann points out, the archaeology of modernity is 'haunted by the feminine,' the femme fatale is one of its most persistent incarnations. She is associated with the styles of Decadence, Symbolism, and Art Nouveau as well as with the attention to decoration and excessive detail linked to a persistent and popular Orientalism (in the constant return, for instance, to the figures of Salome and Cleopatra). Her appearance marks the confluence of modernity, urbanization, Freudian psychoanalysis and new technologies of production and reproduction (photography, the cinema), born of the Industrial Revolution.
>
> (Doane 1991: 1)

Although the focus in this chapter is femininity, the assertions made in the preceding chapter regarding masculinity continue to resonate; if the femme fatale represents a projection of fears around masculinity, then she, with the New Woman, is the opposite number of the Newbolt man. Rebecca Stott, in her examination of the late Victorian femme fatale, maps anxieties apparent in late-nineteenth-century British imperialism, as opposed to the more confident colonialism of the early Victorians. This produced fictions about external threats to the nation, as evident in Orczy's *The Scarlet Pimpernel*, Buchan's Hannay series and boys' magazine stories (Stott 1992: 10–11). Yet, where such fear of the Other focused on a woman, it became doubly virulent in its condemnation of sexualised femininity and exoticism.

Born in 1876 into a middle-class Dutch family, Margaretha Geertruida Zelle, or Mata Hari, is emblematic of the opportunities and dangers that *fin-de-siècle* Europe offered women. Margaretha arrived in Paris in 1904, following a disastrous marriage to Rudolph MacLeod, a Dutch colonial army captain twenty-one years her senior whom she met through a newspaper advertisement. Their son had been murdered by his Malay nurse in Sumatra, in revenge for disciplinary action MacLeod carried out against one of his own soldiers, and Rudolph had taken their daughter, leaving Margaretha penniless. By the time she began her dancing career, Margaretha was already a femme fatale, as a woman whose sexuality was not confined to marriage and as a divorcée who did not fulfil the maternal ideal. Whereas the fictional femme fatale is rarely given a history, one does not have to read too deeply into accounts of Margaretha's early life to imagine its effect. Her mother died when she was fourteen, following a nine-month separation from her father, leaving Margaretha in the care of her godfather (Wheelwright 1992: 8–30). Margaretha was, thus, already modern in her experience of trauma, familial separation and migration.

Margaretha's response to Rudolf's advertisement, despite its unhappy outcome, indicates her desire for activity rather than the passivity assigned to respectable middle-class women in this period (Dijkstra 1986: 26). This active role marks her out as not 'proper', not 'feminine'; in her wifely behaviour as in her subsequent career, she exceeded the bounds of her gender, class and race. Rita Felski notes the different models of modernity offered by Marshall Berman and Gail Finney, the former arguing for a masculine modernity, focusing on the importance of Faust, Marx and Baudelaire, and the latter arguing for the 'imaginative centrality of female psychology and sexuality to representations of modernity in the European *fin de siècle*,' citing Hedda Gabler, Salomé and Lulu (Felski 1995: 2–3). Margaretha as Mata Hari does not fit either model. Like the 'hysterics' who fascinated Charcot and Freud, Mata Hari performed femininity for a range of spectators (Showalter 1985: 145–64). Her final audience, the prosecution at her trial in Paris in July 1917, imagined her as the threat of unconfined femininity – worse, a woman who allegedly engaged in the masculine sphere of international intelligence. In these terms, Mata Hari offers a transgender account of modernity, slipping between masculine and feminine, public and private, self and other, Occident and Orient.[1]

During their marriage, the MacLeods had lived in Sumatra and Java. This brief encounter with the East was later mined for Mata Hari's public persona. After her marriage, Margaretha headed for Paris, initially existing on the margins of respectable society. The Paris of 1904 was the modern metropolis par excellence (Wilson 1991: 47–64). A first attempt to be an artist's model sent her back to Holland, but she returned and, with the help of a French diplomat whom she had met at The Hague, launched herself in 1905 as a dancer in the Parisian salons (Wheelwright 1992: 13). Mata Hari placed herself beyond respectable middle-class femininity by entering a profession allied to that of the courtesan. Rita Felski notes the mythic position of the middle-class woman as angel of the house: 'woman became a symbol of nonalienated, and hence nonmodern, identity' (1995: 18). In real terms, this bore little relation to an urban environment where many women were moving into modern forms of industrial labour (Wilson 1991: 49). The streetwalker epitomised such contradictions, combining commodification, sexuality and contamination (Felski 1995: 19). Such women exemplified the dangers and desires of the modern cities, and Mata Hari, like the prostitute, was a 'figure of public pleasure', her artificiality visible in her use of veils, exotic make-up and props (Baudelaire, cited in Felski 1995: 19).

Mata Hari's persona fed into contemporary fascination with the Orient as a feminised and decadent territory where 'nature' in all its savagery still reigned (Wheelwright 1992: 14). This rich terrain was mined by other dancers of the period, such as Maud Allan, in her performances as Salomé (Showalter 1990: 144–68, Bentley 2002). The perceived threat of the new dancers – whose number included Isadora Duncan – was rooted in their implicit and provocative questioning of the absolute separation between public and private life, as many of them performed both in theatres and in private salons. They also raised difficult questions about what their performances meant to different viewers:

> Male viewers might appreciate their form and applaud the rebellion of their naked limbs and fluid movements, but the men were disturbed when their wives or daughters imitated these steps. The dancer's threat to the 'sanctity of the fireside' offered upper-class ladies the fantasy of release from stifling social constraints.
>
> (Wheelwright 1992: 23)

For many women, Oriental performances, literature and fashions were emblematic of an escape from modern constraints into a world of premodern pleasures and unconfined eroticism (Felski 1995: 115–41, Fawcett 2004). Yet, this fantasy of an elsewhere beyond the modern worked to consolidate the 'hegemonic centrality of the European perspective that it simultaneously seeks to escape' (Felski 1995: 141). It also played to dominant understandings of race and gender. Male members of Mata Hari's audiences could view her performances as evidence of Woman's innate atavism: 'turn-of-the-century men adored the stage spectacle of a woman who lapsed into self-induced fits of orgiastic transport – and all in the name of art. What could be more intriguing than to watch a woman, safely isolated from the audience, revert publicly to the "savage" source of her being?' (Dijkstra 1986: 246).

*Fin-de-siècle* discourses of gender, sexuality and race, thus, gestured towards liberation but also served to reinforce a colonial politics that aligned women and non-Europeans as regressive and aberrant. Women were seen as more closely related to the mysterious East, particularly when that Orientalised version of the Other was perceived as harbouring some ancient thrilling secret (Stott 1992: 34). The fascination of *fin-de-siècle* scientists and sexologists with the mystery of women's sexuality is thus aligned with the fascination of imperial powers with their colonial spoils (Stott 1992: 35–6). Mata Hari embodied such Orientalist fantasies in her fictitious Eastern character and performances, which were loosely based on Margaretha's memories of life in the Dutch East Indies.

After early successes, Margaretha became fully absorbed in her new identity, outdoing rivals in her determination to continue the illusion beyond the stage door (Wheelwright 1992: 17–18; 27–8, Proctor 2003: 127). In interviews, she created stories about her background, the sources of her inspiration and the character of the Oriental woman, fascinating audiences in Paris, Berlin and Monte Carlo. Once the novelty had worn thin and Margaretha began to get older, however, her performances as Mata Hari became increasingly problematic, but that persona was difficult to replace. Despite forays into Spanish dance and other forms, Margaretha was unable to find an equally profitable act. Her role as a courtesan was a logical sideline. As a woman working in an unstable profession, Margaretha was practical about the financial realities of her situation, often attracting older men who could become her patrons. This was another aspect of her life that would play into the hands of her accusers; the seductive spy-courtesan was a potent myth – and one that Margaretha herself perhaps believed (Wheelwright 1992: 28–39, Proctor 2003: 124–5). By 1913, Mata Hari was already past her peak and worried by the resurgence of interest in rivals such as Isadora Duncan. While the 'divine Isadora' played the grand theatres, Mata Hari was consigned to a 'café-*chantant*-cinema' in Palermo, where she performed in front of a rolling film on a bill that included a performing dog (Wheelwright 1992: 38).

Mata Hari was, literally and metaphorically, out of place as the war began, stuck in Berlin, waiting for her show at the Metropol to commence. Struggling to get back to Paris, already accused of being a spy, she must have also been struggling to come to terms with the speed at which her fortunes had changed (Wheelwright 1992: 39–41). In a Europe already anxious about the New Woman and changing gender roles, the First World War brought scrutiny of any individual or group perceived as threatening the status quo (Ledger 1997). The woman as temptress, as carrier of sexual diseases and as a mother of fatherless children was a particular concern. New acts were introduced in Britain and France to regulate women's movements and sexual conduct; few voices raised the issue of men's role in sexual activity (Grayzel 1999: 121–56). Even before the war, anti-feminist sentiments were circulating in popular literature and high culture. Michelle Perrot cites writers such as François Mauriac and André Breton: 'These men denounced the social and domestic power of women (as did Georges Deherme in *Le pouvoir social des femmes*, 1912) – perceived as an occult, diffuse and secret power for which men are mere playthings' (Perrot 1987: 59). In the popular imagination, female spies embodied such feminine power, crossing the line between domestic and public spheres. Like the prostitute, the woman spy laboured in public and private arenas, making her doubly effective but also doubly dangerous (Proctor 2003: 124). The war made Mata Hari's exotic image a liability, and it was only a matter of time before she was charged.[2] Remaining quietly in Holland for a year, she missed her Parisian life. Attempts to revive her career on the Dutch stage faltered, and Mata Hari returned to Paris in 1915, travelling via England and Spain in order to gain access. In returning to France, she was placing herself in extreme danger. As a woman and as a public figure, Mata Hari presented a disturbingly mobile femininity. Her trial became an attempt to fix that mobility within the regime of French sexual and imperial relations. It was not important what Mata Hari had actually done but, rather, what she represented; the profitable image that Margaretha had created became her worst enemy and, ultimately, the cause of her death (Wheelwright 1992: 60). Mata Hari is, consequently, not only a femme fatale, fixed within the terms of the period's sexual politics but also an archetypal woman spy, existing in the half-light of fact and fiction.

Arrested in her hotel room on 13 February 1917, Mata Hari was prose-cuted by Captain Pierre Bouchardon, acting on information provided by Georges Ladoux, whom she knew as her contact in the *Deuxième Bureau*, French military intelligence. Ladoux had recruited Mata Hari as an agent at their first meeting in August 1916. Mata Hari sought Ladoux's help in get-ting a travel pass to visit her lover, and, in the course of the meeting, he suggested that she could work for French interests, despite his alleged sus-picion that she was already a German agent (Wheelwright 1992: 51–2). The assignments Mata Hari conducted between this meeting and her arrest were neither discreet nor successful; she had little idea of how to go about being a spy, beyond the dramatic images rendered in popular fiction and theatre of the time (Wheelwright 1992: 50–64). Wheelwright argues that Ladoux used the Mata Hari case to consolidate his position as the wartime head of French counter-intelligence, and Bouchardon was a willing aide in this, regarding Mata Hari as a 'savage' and a 'negress'. In her abject state as an exposed traitor and imprisoned woman, Bouchardon appears to have pro-jected onto Mata Hari 'the underside of the racist "Oriental" fantasy' (Wheelwright 1992: 77). As Tammy Proctor observes, Mata Hari fitted the stereotype of the female spy and filled a convenient role as scapegoat: 'Mata Hari died not for her great success as a master spy but because she was a symbol of the contagion of decadence and treason that seemed to be undermining France, especially in 1917, when widespread mutinies infected the French armies at the front' (Proctor 2003: 126).

In addition to representing all that was rotten within French culture, Mata Hari also served as a symbolic Other to French European identity. She was implicitly condemned for being a woman whose nationality was not easily defined and as a woman whose sexuality had run beyond the bounds of bourgeois respectability:

'Neither the type, nor the character, nor her culture, nor her coloured skin, nor her mentality – nothing of her belongs to our latitudes,' commented Inspector Alfred Morain, the Metropolitan Police Commissioner of Paris. 'She had something of the primitive savage about her and at the same time something refined – sacerdotal.'

(Wheelwright 1992: 84–5)

Morain, like Bouchardon, was aware that Mata Hari's Oriental persona was an invention, yet her abject role as prisoner and traitor appeared to entail identification with racist forms of Otherness. This was aided, for such commentators, by their recognition that Mata Hari was no longer young. Bouchardon was disgusted by the deterioration in her appearance, as the grey began to show through her dyed black hair. He equated this appearance with her alleged racial difference and inferiority, as did the prison doctor, Dr Bizard. In the latter's description of her ambivalent appearance, he alleges that she is 'not at all feminine' (Wheelwright 1992: 85). Such accounts clearly made it easier for her prosecutors to convince themselves that Mata Hari was not only guilty but also something less than human. Her sentence to death by firing squad on 15 October 1917 continues to be contested. Most biographical accounts now acknowledge that the French had little or no evidence on which to convict her and that some evidence was probably invented to support the prosecution's case.

## Mata Hari in Hollywood

The fictions perpetuated first by Mata Hari and then by her prosecution have proved resilient through her many mythic rebirths across Western culture.[3] It is no coincidence that the rise of the femme fatale mirrors that of new technologies of mass communication – in particular, the prevalence of photography and cinema (Doane 1991: 1). Mata Hari employed tinted photographic postcards as part of her publicity material, and the images of Mata Hari as an Oriental beauty in jewelled headdress and breastplates have informed subsequent fashion and films. Oriental stylings are to the fore in cinematic accounts of Mata Hari, but they are invariably inflected by contemporary concerns. The most well known Hollywood version is Greta Garbo's *Mata Hari* (George Fitzmaurice, 1931). The film was one of Garbo's early talking roles. *Anna Christie* (Clarence Brown, 1930) was the first, with a German-language version made in the same year, directed by Jacques Feyder and completely recast apart from Garbo. When the talkies arrived, the Hollywood studios were keen to capitalise on foreign stars' ability to perform in English and foreign-language versions of the same film (Berry 2000: 117). Garbo's multilingual skill suited the star persona fostered by MGM; she was one of a number of non-domestic stars marketed as an exotic product:

The European stars Greta Garbo, Marlene Dietrich and Lil Dagover were ... 'Orientalized' in many films and described as embodying a 'pale exoticism.' The casting of Euramerican actors in 'ethnic' roles was commonplace in Hollywood, and the process of transforming them via elaborate character-makeup techniques was often discussed and illustrated in magazines.

(Berry 2000: 111)

Such trans-racial performances were often cited as evidence of actors' versatility, but the cross-dressing was only one way; 'ethnic' actors rarely played 'white' roles (Berry 2000: 111). Hollywood studios thus engaged in a raced doublespeak in which ethnicity was free-floating *and* carefully policed.

Garbo's star persona tapped into similar discourses to those that had surrounded Mata Hari as a New Woman and through her identification with the aesthetic of art deco. Garbo's roles on screen and in her Hollywood publicity depicted her as an avatar of unconventional and independent femininity; one commentator even described her as 'an outgrowth of modernity' (Biery, cited in Fischer 2002). Garbo's version of the modern woman lent itself to the art-deco style of the studio era. The deco style was an international aesthetic in furnishings, fashion and jewellery popular between 1910 and 1935. Its name came from an abbreviation of the Paris International Exposition of Decorative and Industrial Modern Arts of 1925, and it epitomised modernity in its fascination with advanced mass-production techniques and synthetic materials, together with 'ancient' styles and exotic motifs (Fischer 2002). Art deco had a significant influence on Hollywood, particularly art directors such as Cedric Gibbons and costume designers such as Adrian; both worked at MGM with Garbo. Several of Garbo's films explicitly reference deco style and relate her independent, sensual persona to that of the New Woman, none more so than *Mata Hari* (Fischer 2002).

From the 'Oriental' music that accompanies the title sequence to the sumptuous costumes and sets, Mata Hari is fetishised as an exotic woman. The star persona of Garbo, like the deco style, exemplifies the interchangeability of ethnic identities, as this Mata Hari expands the boundaries of the Orient to Eastern Europe, several of the costumes evoking a Russian or Cossack style. Orientalism is, thus, mobilised to offer a potent fantasy of liberation from modern constraints, just as it had earlier been deployed to market consumer goods (Berry 2000: 133, Fawcett 2004). Garbo, performing as Mata Hari in costumes designed by Adrian, was part of an Orientalist fashion during the 1930s which 'also signified stylistic modernity' (Berry 2000: 136). Three years later, Garbo starred in *The Painted Veil* (Richard Boleslawski, 1934), in which Chinese-style costumes indicate her modern sophistication (Berry 2000: 137). Discursive shifts regarding the Orient, femininity and modernity are, thus, made evident in these popular products. Mata Hari's famous dancing is barely visible in the Hollywood film – the critic Mary Cass Canfield wrote in her 'Letter to Garbo' in

*Theatre Arts Monthly* that she, 'walked through it like some superior and unperturbed mannequin' (Bainbridge 1955: 161). Just as the role was rife with contradictions regarding ethnicity – a Swede playing a Dutch woman pretending to be a Javanese dancer – so the role contradicted Garbo's star persona. Mata Hari's dance of Eastern passion became what *Variety* called 'a polite cooch', in a brief scene where Garbo moves slowly round a huge statue of Shiva (Paris 1995: 213). This desultory performance did nothing to dent the film's success – 'Its windfall $879,000 profit for MGM was larger than that of all but one of the films she ever made' (Paris 1995: 213) – and endorsed the idea that Garbo was more potent as a static rather than a moving image, inviting the 'to-be-looked-at-ness' of the Hollywood goddess (Mulvey 1989: 19).

Mata Hari's East Indian Orientalism is commuted to Eastern European Orientalism in the Garbo film to fit with the persona of the star and avoid the taint of miscegenation, just as the complexities surrounding Mata Hari's conviction were elided and made secure.[4] Yet, as with any stereotype, contradictory aspects of Garbo-as-Mata-Hari cannot be fully contained. With the advent of talking pictures, Hollywood found itself serving at least three different audiences: the home market, which enjoyed the 'spice' of exoticism; the newly immigrant Americans (mainly Jewish, Italian and Eastern European

*Figure 2.1*   Greta Garbo and Ramon Navarro in *Mata Hari* (dir. George Fitzmaurice, 1931).

migrants); and the global audience outside the States (Berry 2000: 117). In such a polyphonic context, images, narratives and characters are liable to elicit a variety of responses despite the studios' attempts to control their product by producing films geared to particular markets, such as the German-language version of *Anna Christie*. Barry Paris notes that the German Anna is 'more relaxed, less declamatory – and a heavier smoker' (Paris 1995: 194). The studios' desire to promote their films across a range of markets also made some of their product inadvertently more liberal than the race politics of 1930s America in which they were produced (Berry 2000: 117). It allowed for a complex intersection of discourses regarding race and gender to appear on screen in films such as *Mata Hari*.

The contradictory discourses surrounding Mata Hari continue to reso-nate in later representations of her, albeit transformed to fit new contexts. Just as Mata Hari constituted an Orientalism which fed into the desires and fears of her audiences (and later her interrogators), so Garbo's Mata Hari fed into the desires and fears of audiences in the 1930s. Mata Hari con-tinues to represent an ambivalent encounter between white and non-white; West and East; modern and ancient. Mata Hari as a spy is similarly equi-vocal: professional and amateur, masculine and feminine, active and passive. Garbo's Mata Hari is unequivocally guilty; as the foreword to the action asserts, 'In 1917, war-ridden France dealt summarily with traitors and spies.' She is an archetypal femme fatale who appears to betray France for little reason other than pure evil; there is a symbolic sequence where, in the process of seduction, Mata Hari insists that a lamp on a house shrine to the Madonna is extinguished.[5] Yet, the film also represents her as a sympathetic figure, a woman caught because of her love for the heroic Alexei (Ramon Navarro). *Mata Hari* was a vehicle for the two stars, the narrative played for melodrama. There is no doubt in this film that Mata Hari is anything but a bad woman redeemed by the love of a good man. The contradictions and complexities of the historical Mata Hari are subsumed in her image so that the questions she raised are answered by the drama of her appearance. Just as the face of Garbo was enshrined on celluloid as a blank page which offers everything and nothing to its reader, so Mata Hari has become a stereotype onto whose surface an audience can project their fears and desires.[6] The resilience of this image indicates Western culture's continuing fascination with the exotic and, through Mata Hari's mythic heritage, a nostalgic past in which the East, the Other and femininity remain myster-ious territories.[7]

## The good spy: Edith Cavell (1865–1915)

While Mata Hari has come to represent the female spy as femme fatale, she is historically complemented by Edith Cavell. Cavell established the role of the good female spy, primarily because she worked for the right side but also because she was understood as a secular saint and martyr through her role as a nurse rather than as a spy. Despite their distinct differences within the popular imagination, both Mata Hari and Edith Cavell were necessarily engaged in contradictory discourses surrounding women and war work during the First World War. Sharon Oudit describes the Voluntary Aid Detachment as providing a place in which middle-class English women could take an active role in war work; work which was understood as a natural extension of the feminine predilection for nurture: 'This form of public recognition was dependent on a feminine piety that implied deference to masculinity, militarism and the patriarchal nation state' (Oudit 1994: 7). Women who took on caring roles during the war were thus understood in terms of a conventional bourgeois femininity. Women who stepped outside such roles were regarded with some horror. The Women's Army Auxiliary Corps of the British Army, for example, was greeted upon establishment in 1917, by letters to the papers decrying the unnaturally militaristic tendencies of its officers. Such evident discomfort was riddled with overt or implicit concerns about the connections between any change in women's roles and the issue of the franchise – a debate that had effectively been halted at the outbreak of war – and by the not unconnected question of deviant sexuality. The pre-war association of feminism with lesbianism continued to effect discussion of women's roles:

> Women who displayed 'symptoms' of lesbianism (an inclination to dress up in masculine clothes, to drill, and to shoot) were considered not only distasteful but abnormal and in need of medical help. Any attacks on them were thus fully justified. Women in military organisations were a target for those who held such views, and it was not uncommon during the First World War for women who joined the military services to be regarded as peculiar at least, if not downright immoral.
>
> (Gould 1987: 121)

Yet women had been active in intelligence long before the war began, and became key during the First World War – indeed, their diligent and poorly paid work kept the British intelligence services going (Proctor 2003: 27). In roles ranging from the Girl Guides employed as messengers in MI5 to the employment of more than 3,500 women by MI9, the Postal Censorship Branch, women were central to the daily functioning of British intelligence services (Proctor 2003: 53–73). Even here, however, there was ambivalence about women's work. While women offered a plentiful, cheap and obedient workforce, the organisations that employed them began to develop a gendered understanding of agents in the field as opposed to intelligence-gathering: 'Espionage was generally referred to as domestic, hidden, and sneaky – in other words, it was feminine. Intelligence, on the other hand, was professional, bureaucratic, and officially secret – or masculine in its endeavours' (Proctor 2003: 30). This was also an attempt to draw a moral distinction between the imagined enemy agents who threatened Britain from within before and during the First World War and the developing secret services established by the British Government. The artificial distinction between feminine and masculine roles bears no relation to the numbers of women employed within the bureaucracy of intelligence gathering.[8]

The imaginary distinction between the bad, feminine spy and the good, masculine intelligence officer is visible in the opposing figures of Mata Hari and Edith Cavell. Like Mata Hari, Edith Cavell's public image owed much to popular mythology. In their examination of women spies in fiction of the First World War, Craig and Cadogan note that, like Mata Hari, Edith Cavell, 'seems to be as much the end result of late Victorian and Edwardian fictional projections as an influence on the espionage stories that came after her' (Craig and Cadogan 1981: 54). Both women are, thus, framed by discourses that preceded and succeeded them. During the First World War, women played key roles not only in British intelligence but also in the intelligence networks in occupied countries. The *La Dame Blanche* network in Belgium was a militarised espionage group for both men and women – albeit dropping the term 'spy' in favour of 'agent' or 'soldier' (Proctor 2003: 78–9). *La Dame Blanche* was remarkably egalitarian, basing its rankings on service to the organisation rather than an individual's age, class or gender and often including whole families within its ranks (Proctor 2003: 91–2). After the war, however, the women of *La Dame Blanche* were largely forgotten, in part because of fluctuating definitions of wartime activities, 'soldiers' and the home front. Proctor asserts that for the women of *La Dame Blanche*, their homes were in occupied territory so that the distinction between the battlefield and the domestic arena was not absolute: 'The women of *La Dame Blanche* had no concept of a home front because their own homes became fronts when their nations were occupied' (Proctor 2003: 98). Once the war was over, such women were rapidly erased from public memory in favour of more sensational images of female spies – namely, Mata Hari and Edith Cavell. In this manner, the contradictions evident in wartime femininity were effaced, just as distinctions between the battlefield and the domestic arena were re-established after the war.

Cavell was a middle-class Englishwoman who grew up in East Anglia and trained as a nurse. In 1907, she moved to Brussels to establish a nursing school, having already worked as an instructor in Britain. She was forty-eight when war broke out in August 1914 – ten years older than Mata Hari and far more successful as an agent of the Allied resistance in occupied Belgium. She was not really a spy as such; Cavell's resistance work consisted not of gathering information or passing on secrets but of organising an escape network for Allied soldiers (Proctor 2003: 100–1). The humanitarian aspect of her work fitted well with public perceptions of the nursing profession, so that when she was caught, arrested and imprisoned in August 1915, she was a martyr-in-waiting. Unlike Mata Hari, Edith Cavell freely admitted her role in hiding and transporting Allied soldiers out of Belgium. She was tried with thirty-five other prisoners, found guilty and executed on

12 October 1915. Philippe Baucq, a Belgian architect who helped to plan and organise the escape routes, was executed with her. Comtesse Jean de Belle-ville, Louise Thuliez and Louis Severin had their death sentences commuted following appeals on their behalf (Proctor 2003: 102).

The story of Cavell's life and death was immediately employed in a pro-paganda war between Germany and the Allies. While the Germans sought to use Cavell's fate as a warning to other activists in occupied territories, the public outcry in several countries, particularly the USA and Canada, quickly produced a backlash from the Allies that began the reconstruction of Cavell as passive victim rather than active agent (Proctor 2003: 102–3). Cavell's death inspired a range of patriotic images on postcards distributed as pro-paganda by the Allies; they present a marked contrast to the publicity postcards promoting Mata Hari's exotic image. Cavell is almost exclusively depicted clothed in white and either nursing soldiers or lying supine as a monstrous German shoots her. A series of six cards published in 1915 depicts her 'story' from 'Miss Cavell as a nurse' through to the memorial in Brussels, while the Italian artist Tito Corbella designed an allegorical series which pits Cavell against 'Kultur' and the 'Kaiser'.[9] Cavell is described as a 'martyr' or 'victim' in the captions for such images, reiterating the visual depiction. Cavell was represented as madonna in opposition to Mata Hari's archetypal whore and femme fatale. This binary understanding of the two women is endorsed by one of Cavell's colleagues. Louise Thuliez, who escaped execu-tion for life imprisonment, commented in her 1934 autobiography:

> In trying to defend themselves the Germans have pushed their insolence so far as to compare Edith Cavell to Mata Hari. Edith Cavell had worked for her country, consecrating to this noble task all her career of faith and sacrifice. Mata Hari, thinking only of her personal charms, had sold herself to the highest bidder. While Edith Cavell, at the bed-side of the wounded men she was tending, wept over the sufferings of her fellow-countrymen, Mata Hari in the luxury of palaces betrayed indiscriminately all who approached her. Which of these two women deserves to be called a 'spy'?
>
> (Thuliez, cited in Wheelwright 1992: 120)

If nothing else, this statement, written nearly two decades after the deaths of Cavell and Mata Hari, denotes the extent to which both women have entered the realm of mythology. They have exceeded the limits of memory and been rewritten as types instead of individuals. While Mata Hari is the villainous traitor, femme fatale and spy, Cavell is the innocent, virginal patriot. Whereas her prosecutors saw Mata Hari as 'primitive' and 'savage', Cavell has become whiter than white – representing a femininity symbolic of Great Britain's 'civilisation'. The discourses surrounding both women are written across stereotypes of gender and of race, making them complicit with debates about racial purity and difference during the first half of the twentieth century (see Bergman 2004, Richardson 2004). Rather than examining the work of women in intelligence, post-war accounts of espionage on the Allied front tended to ignore women's activities as spies or to forget them altogether: 'Descriptions of spy-martyrs usually emphasized the moral character, generosity, patriotism, and naïve spirit of the women who died for their nations. Why are these women celebrated more than the female agents who survived the war without declaration or capture?' (Proctor 2003: 100). Cavell's white garb in images contemporary with her death continued to resonate as she was recreated on celluloid.

## Cavell on film

Such a simplified understanding of Cavell is evident in *Nurse Edith Cavell* (Herbert Wilcox, 1939). Wilcox had already produced a silent version of the Cavell story, *Dawn* (1928), starring Sybil Thorndike, which was censored by Austen Chamberlain, then Foreign Minister of the Conservative Government, as likely to damage British relations with Germany but nevertheless exhibited with the approval of the London County Council (Wilcox 1967: 73–4, 79–83). The talking version of Cavell's story was no less controversial. Released as the Second World War began, the patriotic iconography of Cavell's life was replayed for British and American audiences in this film – a reminder to the former of what was being fought for, and to the latter of what was at stake in the battle. The director/producer Herbert Wilcox claimed in his autobiography that it was 'the first British-Hollywood co-production' but also stated that the film led to accusations of propaganda: 'There was a broadside of criticism alleging breach of the Neutrality Code; but *Nurse Cavell* weathered the storm and was accepted as a film of first-class entertainment' (Wilcox 1967: 124). Indeed, its star and Wilcox's later wife Anna Neagle was nominated for a Best Actress Oscar for her performance. While Wilcox and Neagle were not official propagandists, it is hard to miss the ideological thrust of their work. Herbert Wilcox directed Neagle in thirty-two films, often in historical roles with national resonance, such as Queen Victoria, Florence Nightingale and Amy Johnson (Dolan 2000: 26). Contemporary critics saw Neagle as 'as much a part of Britain as Dover's white cliffs' (Street 1997: 124), and that appeal was to the fore in *Nurse Edith Cavell*:

> Her screen roles ... celebrated individual stoicism in the face of adversity as a means of communicating the overall liberal-conservative political ideology of the Wilcox-Neagle films. Neagle epitomised middle-class values of thrift, hard work, stoicism and feminine modesty. Just as the White Cliffs of Dover are associated with Britain's self-consciousness as an island, vulnerable to foreign invasion, Neagle also represented a resolutely British, non-European and white identity.
>
> (Street 1997: 126)

Questions of class and conflict are repressed in these films in favour of a mythologised English stoicism. This elision is evident in *Nurse Edith Cavell* where Cavell mixes happily with the soldiers she rescues, most notably a chirpy cockney, and reminisces with one of the men she is treating about cricket and Norwich. There are no apparent divisions between this middle-class woman and the men she tends and commands.

In this biopic, Neagle as Cavell takes on a saintly aura, inspired to set up the escape route while reading the Bible in her bed. Even captured, imprisoned and informed of her fate, Cavell is a model of otherworldly calm, saying, 'I thank God for these few quiet weeks ... This time of rest has been a great mercy.' At times, Cavell's stoicism appears trance-like as she floats through her scenes, dressed throughout in her nurse's uniform. Anna Neagle's performance in *Nurse Edith Cavell* reiterates her cinematic persona through costume, physical posture and acting style. Marcia Landy describes her performance in *Victoria the Great* (Herbert Wilcox, 1937):

> The actress looks and behaves according to preconceptions and myths of 1930s female gentility. Her demeanor, not unlike that of the other British female stars of the era, such as Deborah Kerr and Phyllis Calvert, is restrained. Her status is defined by rather stiff body movements, a walk that is measured, giving her the impression of gliding, and gestures and looks that are imperious. Her expensive costumes are fashionable but decorous, unlike the sexually provocative costumes of the 1940s Gainsborough melodramas. Her image is matronly. ... The men in the film are dwarfed by her presence. As actress and as character, she monopolises the screen.
>
> (Landy 1991: 69)

While Edith Cavell is a different role to Queen Victoria, Neagle's performance draws upon a similar range of reference. Both films, released in 1937 and 1939, are examples of the roles that made Neagle a transatlantic star during the 1930s, 1940s and 1950s. The film foregrounds her professional identity as a nurse, prefacing the narrative with a tribute to Cavell's fortitude and that of her profession:

> This is a tale, based on fact, of heroic life and a conflict of loyalties, told in reverence and without bitterness. ... Nursing is a dedication to mercy and healing. War is a dedication to brutal force. Neither admits distinction of race or person. Each is the uncompromising foe of the other.

Thus, even in the opening titles, Cavell's role as an active agent of resistance in occupied territory is obscured in favour of a more passive representation of saintly femininity. Cavell is made to represent the ultimate nurse-mother-virgin, inhuman in her heroic fortitude. While *Nurse Edith*

*Cavell* does show the escape route through Belgium as a group effort, the other women are merely supporting characters, often given comedic or pathetic roles. Their main function is to be displayed as victims of an oppressive German military and thus to remind audiences of the moral distinction between the Allies and the enemy. In this way, the film offers a depiction of strong women but curtails their radical potential by emphasising the individual hero rather than a collective enterprise. Richard Dyer writes how such whiter-than-white women were lit in photographs and films; the use of lighting effects and filters combine to make such figures appear saintly, often giving them a literal 'halo' of light: 'Idealised white women are bathed in and permeated by light. It streams through them and falls from above. In short, they glow' (Dyer 1997: 122). In the sequence following the announcement of her death sentence, Cavell is shown kneeling in her cell before a crucifix; a beam of light shines down on her face so brightly it erases her features. While Neagle's heroic performance often depicts Cavell as the 'glowing' white woman Dyer describes, this image takes that trope to its mythic limit in virtually erasing Cavell's face.

## English women spies on film, 1930s–1940s

Spy films between the two world wars were inevitably 'attuned to the possibility of another war' (Landy 1991: 123), and women playing spies were often depicted as ambiguous figures, drawing on the mythologies of Mata Hari and Edith Cavell. Marcia Landy writes of Vivien Leigh's role as a First World War double agent for the British in *Dark Journey* (Victor Saville, 1937): 'Characteristic of the espionage film, the female is treated as a mysterious, exotic object of desire whose motives are ambiguous. ... Before her identity is known, she is presented as a femme fatale, a mysterious Mata Hari' (Landy 1991: 124). Towards the end of the 1930s, there was a flurry of spy films (Aldgate and Richards 1986: 79; Landy 1991: 126; Chapman 1998: 93–4), several of which placed their female leads at the centre of a nexus of public and sexual politics regarding identity and power. Anna Neagle's role in *The Yellow Canary* (Herbert Wilcox, 1943) played upon public expectations and her star persona; trailers promoting the film implied that she was cast against type (Street 1997: 127). The film opens in London, September 1940. Air-raid wardens debating Shakespeare, Bacon and Samuel Johnson as bombs rain around them epitomise the spirit of the Blitz as Buckingham Palace comes under attack. A 'timeless' Englishness is thus evoked via literary history and royal heritage. In the middle of this, Sally Maitland, played by Neagle, is signalling enemy planes. In subsequent scenes, she is publicly humiliated by a nightclub comedian and endures an uncomfortable breakfast with her family because of her notorious reputation as a Nazi sympathiser. Sally is a double agent for the British, assigned to infiltrate the ranks of Nazis hiding in Canada. She succeeds, unmasking a spy ring in Halifax, Nova Scotia, which plots to destroy the harbour, the 'gateway to the battle of the Atlantic' and falling for Lieutenant Commander Garrick (Richard Greene) who is assigned to watch her during her mission. The film closes with Sally, already married and in uniform, restored to her family. Family, nation, heterosexuality and femininity are thus aligned and given closure in *The Yellow Canary*. Casting Neagle against type, however, sets an odd precedent in a film where many of the characters have double identities and even the staunch patriot, Miss Cholmondley (Margaret Rutherford), inadvertently consorts with the enemy. Wartime identities are shown to be deceptive and changeable.

Valerie Hobson played several leading roles as a spy. During her early career, she had been under contract to Universal, starring in Hollywood shockers such as James Whale's *The Bride of Frankenstein* (1935). In the late 1930s, Hobson returned to England and developed a successful career in roles that depicted her as the quintessential Englishwoman. She took the female lead in three spy dramas at the end of the 1930s: *Q Planes* (Tim Whelan, 1939), *The Spy in Black* (Michael Powell, 1939) and *Contraband* (Michael Powell, 1940). In *Q Planes*, Hobson plays Kay Lawrence – an investigative journalist who at one point is called 'a newspaper spy'. Lawrence/Hobson is working undercover in the cafeteria of a factory developing experimental aircraft which are being stolen by enemy forces who shoot them with a ray-gun over the sea and then 'rescue' the plane and its crew once they have crash-landed on water. The main protagonist is Kay Lawrence's brother, an intelligence officer called Major Hammond, played by Ralph Richardson, while Laurence Olivier has a romantic role as the test pilot Tony McVane. Major Hammond was an inspiration for Steed in 1960s spy series *The Avengers* (Rogers 1989: 18, Richards 1998: 247). Hobson's role appears influenced by the style of the Hollywood screwball comedies of the 1930s but is also a forerunner of Diana Rigg as Emma Peel: a woman who stands her ground as a professional. Indeed, Kay's spirited defence of journalism elicits a soliloquy from Major Hammond that aligns women with destructive modernity:

> That's the modern woman for you. ... Women, women, what should we do without them? I tell you, McVane, I love everything about them. Their touching loyalty. Their astonishing self-sacrifice. Their still more astonishing sacrifice of everybody else. Their modesty. Their conceit. Their preposterous dress. Their ridiculous hats. Their silly little hand-bags with the pathetic little bunch of things they carry around inside. Little purses, mirrors, sticky lipsticks, nonsensical compacts ...

In this ambivalent list of women's characteristics and consumer goods, Hammond light-heartedly voices discomfort with the new woman. *Q Planes'* odd mixture of witty romantic comedy, spy thriller and science fiction offers a foretaste of 1960s spy films and television series that dealt lightly with changes in gender relations while portraying a nostalgic Englishness.

Richardson's intelligence officer is an endearing eccentric who sniffs out the truth, while Hobson's 'newspaper spy' is confident and right-headed, despite early intimations that she might be an enemy agent. The film ends with Hobson marrying Laurence Olivier's test pilot, while Hammond is comically astonished that 'Daphne', whom he has repeatedly stood up throughout the film in a running-joke phone-call sequence, has married someone else. Threats to national borders and gender roles are, thus, neatly curtailed, and espionage is once again depicted as a great game.

In Michael Powell's *The Spy in Black*, also released in 1939, Hobson plays another ambivalent character; indeed, in her early scenes, it is not clear who she works for. The film is set during the First World War and begins with an innocent schoolmistress killed on her way to a job in the Orkneys by two female German spies. Hobson takes her place, working as a double agent for the British, and becomes a schoolmistress on the Old Man of Hoy, a strategic naval outpost. Conrad Veidt, as a German U-boat commander, is put ashore and hidden in Hobson's schoolhouse. The relationship between them is ambiguous throughout. While Veidt plays a naval captain, Hobson's undercover schoolmistress is in command. Gender roles are topsy-turvy, and this carries through into the dialogue, as they debate the ethics of war. This is followed by a scene in which Hobson is distressed that her actions have led to the death of the U-boat crews. The simple moralities of a propaganda war are questioned in *The Spy in Black*. Sue Harper notes an exchange between Hobson and Veidt at one point:

'You are English! I am German! We are enemies!'
'I like that better!'
'So do I! It simplifies everything!'

She reads this as evidence of a moment in Veidt's career when Britain mobilised for war: 'The balance between the good and bad Germans which had informed Veidt's earlier 1930s films was no longer welcome' (Harper 1998: 135). The exchange may also be read as a comment on the oversimplification of national identities during wartime. Veidt's U-boat captain becomes increasingly hysterical, Hobson's spy increasingly confused; the absolute binaries mobilised in wartime propaganda are challenged as the film draws to a close. In the final minutes, Veidt follows Hobson onto the steamer taking her back to the mainland, then takes over the boat by freeing the German prisoners of war on board. Hobson voices her feelings against the war shortly before the steamer, commanded by Veidt, is shelled by his own craft. The film ends with Veidt's U-boat sunk by a British destroyer while he remains on board the sinking steamer. Hobson weeps on a life-raft as she sees him go down with the boat. Hobson's ambivalent role in *The Spy in Black* is carried through into the narrative itself; nothing is secure in this film, and the conflict of war is exposed as traumatic and complex, rather than straightforwardly patriotic. By *Contraband* (1940), another Hobson and Veidt/Powell and Pressburger production, such ambiguities had been closed off: even Powell noted that Pressburger's script was 'all pure corn, but corn served up by professionals, and it works' (Harper 1998: 136).[10]

Nevertheless, such films reveal a potential for ambiguity. The English female spy is a figure ripe for multiple readings which may be made available by the script, the production or an actor's performance. Some of the films cited explore that ambiguity – *Q Planes, The Spy in Black* – while others attempt to contain it – *Contraband, The Yellow Canary* – or to shut it down completely in favour of a more straightforwardly patriotic narrative – *Nurse Edith Cavell*. All these films are more or less successful in their resistance to the unsaid other of white femininity, for they are shadowed by the figure of Mata Hari and her sisters. The slur of aberrant feminine sexuality tracks such narratives, and each film attempts, in its own way, to 'purify' its heroine; most obviously in *Nurse Edith Cavell* by creating a mythic figure who is almost inhuman in her stoical martyrdom. These dichotomous stereotypes even impinge on autobiographical accounts of the real women involved in secret-service work during the First and Second World Wars, as Deborah Van Seters observes in her examination of such writings:

> Consciously and unconsciously, these women indicate the extent to which, as individuals, they both conformed to, and departed from, contemporary stereotypes. Thus, not only do these accounts illustrate certain traits that have previously been noted as being common to female autobiographies in general, they also offer reflections specifically concerning the realm of the secret services that are more complex and less predictable than those characterising their fictional sisters.
>
> (Van Seters 1992: 412)

It is important to note, again, the distance between women's real experience of the secret services and representations of such women in popular fiction and film. Antonia Lant remarks how such representations attempted to close down or efface the contradictions inherent in wartime reformulations of femininity even as they bore witness to the anxieties such contradictions aroused. She cites Christine Gledhill's argument that stereotypes 'potentially open up a challenge to patriarchal assumptions, making visible a whole regime of practices, modes of feeling and thought which generally go unrecognised even by women themselves' (Lant 1991: 89). It would seem, from Van Seter's account, that even women who understood the gap between their real secret-service work and fictional versions of it were unable to ignore the cultural weight of Mata Hari/Edith Cavell – to the extent of measuring their experience in relation to such popular stereotypes. Despite, or perhaps because of, that binary heritage, the woman as spy, agent or resistance activist throws into question the West's investment in passive femininity.

## Women spies on film in the 1950s: *Odette* and *Carve Her Name with Pride*

If this was visible in films made before and during the Second World War, it was to become increasingly evident after the war, as cinematic styles changed and a new realism was possible. While Garbo's performance as *Mata Hari* in 1931 and Neagle's performance as Cavell in 1939 were informed, respectively, by Hollywood and the British theatre, the realism introduced during and after the Second World War in Hollywood and British cinema made a grittier representation of women spies possible. Such realism led to strange hybrids in American film, such as the bizarre marriage of expressionism and realism in film noir, while in Britain it marked a journey towards the British 'new wave' of the 1960s. Two popular post-war British films offer differing accounts of the female spy during the Second World War: *Odette* (Herbert Wilcox, 1950) and *Carve Her Name with Pride* (Lewis Gilbert, 1958). These films chart a parallel course: both are based on the real experience of women agents in the British Special Operations Executive (SOE) in occupied France. *Odette* is based on the autobiography of Odette Churchill, who was also technical adviser on the film (Wilcox 1967: 183–9), while *Carve Her Name with Pride* is based on the life of Violette Szabo. Both Odette and Violette were captured on active service in France, taken to the notorious Fresnes prison in Paris, interrogated and tortured at Gestapo Headquarters in the Avenue Foch and finally sent to Ravensbrück concentration camp. Violette was executed at Ravensbrück, but Odette survived and married her SOE colleague Peter Churchill. While on active service, she already had three children by her first marriage, and Violette also had a daughter by her French husband, Etienne Szabo, following a wartime marriage. All of these aspects are visible in the two films, but they are employed in different ways.

The Wilcox–Neagle production of *Odette* moves a little beyond their usual style; as Jeffrey Richards observes, it is a 'memorable account ... filmed in 1950 on the actual locations of the events themselves in a sober semi-documentary style' (Richards 1997: 132). Herbert Wilcox was keen to stress the documentary aspect of the film, writing in his autobiography how he and Anna Neagle took Odette and Peter Churchill, together with the writer Warren Chetham Strode, on a tour of Odette's wartime operations in France. However harrowing the experience may have been for the Churchills, Wilcox asserts that it produced the best performance of Neagle's career, albeit pushing her to the point of breakdown (Wilcox 1967: 183–9). The film also featured a cameo role by Odette's commanding officer, Colonel Maurice 'Buck' Buckmaster, playing himself, as head of the French office of the SOE. This is a shift from the virginal English heroism of Nurse Edith Cavell, as Odette is a Frenchwoman separated from her English husband. Neagle's performance is less stiff and glamorous than in *Nurse Edith Cavell* or *The Yellow Canary*. Her first appearance on screen is in her living room, listening to the Home Service on the radio, a scenario frequently employed in wartime British cinema to connote domestic order and national spirit (Lant 1991: 45). The settings and costumes throughout tend towards realism rather than glamour, an effect produced by location shooting and low-key dialogue, costumes and performances. Trevor Howard, as Peter Churchill, reproduces a form of irascible Englishness on screen, at first unsure of Odette's abilities but rapidly becoming convinced of her courage.

Despite the realist tendencies of *Odette*, however, the production perpetuates Wilcox and Neagle's conventional understanding of the individual heroine. Odette's struggle with her maternal instincts is depicted in harrowing phone calls to her daughters before and after her SOE work, while the romance between Odette and Peter Churchill provides a romantic frame to the narrative, ending with a kiss. Thus, the unconventionality of Odette's active service is mitigated by more conventional feminine traits. Most tellingly, the epilogue provided by Odette Churchill contradicts the narrative, as it states, 'I would like [the film] to be a window through which may be seen those very gallant women with which I had the honour to serve.' Yet the film only features Odette herself, surrounded by men in the SOE offices in London and on active service in France. The conflict within the film between Odette as an exceptional heroine and the attempt to depict the real experience of an SOE agent becomes most evident in the torture sequences. While the cinematography to this point largely follows the conventions of narrative realism in not disrupting spectatorial viewpoint with unusual or expressionist camera techniques, the scene in her cell in Fresnes with Henri (Marius Goring), the German intelligence officer, introduces off-kilter camerawork with low- and high-angle framing. The subsequent scene, where Odette is tortured at Gestapo headquarters becomes distinctly *noir*, with low-angle shots and shadows offering a distorted perspective and only a partial view of this graphic scenario.

On the one hand, such techniques from film noir offer a means of indicating the horror of such events without having to depict them explicitly, thus avoiding censorship. Yet they also indicate a tension within the film between Neagle's star persona and the character she is playing; if the part pushed its star to the point of breakdown, then the film itself breaks down in its struggle to represent a 'real' woman and an heroic figure. Odette after the torture sequences is very different; lighting and make-up contribute to her gaunt expression, while Neagle twists her body and shuffles on her heels to indicate the pain Odette was subjected to.[11] The distorted camera angles and expressionist lighting are complemented by Neagle's performance, which extends from her physical transformation to the hysterical repetition – 'I have nothing to say' – in response to her interrogators. Despite all these indications that the world is out of kilter, Odette continues to be the moral centre of the narrative, concerned to protect Peter Churchill from her own fate and berating those who deny their responsibility for her condition. At one point she wittily responds to the news that she has been condemned as 'a French woman and a British agent' with the retort: 'You must make your own choice. I can only die once.' The contradictions within Neagle's performance and the visual style of the film expose an unstable narrative which is uncertain how to treat a female protagonist who is not easily assimilable within binary understandings of femininity.

Eight years later, the parallel narrative of Violette Szabo's life story was rendered for the screen in *Carve Her Name with Pride*. While there are some similarities in style between the two films, I want to focus on their differences. Violette, played by Virginia McKenna, is framed in this narrative by her 'ordinariness': she is of a different class and generation to Odette Churchill in the Wilcox–Neagle film. The opening and closing sequences of the film are crane shots which zoom in on an 'ordinary' London street, with children playing. Violette is introduced within a family of respectable working-class Londoners, though her mother is French. Life during wartime is shown as disruptive of normative gender roles; Violette meets an old schoolfriend who is now a woman conductor on a London bus, and asserts, 'If I'd been a man, I'd like to have been a professional soldier.' Even before she is recruited by the SOE, she voices her desire for a more active role, and the film does not present this as a problem but rather as an indication of changing sensibilities. Violette's athleticism is commented upon within the film, and her father describes her as 'the toughest one in the family' following a play fight with her brother. McKenna's youth and energy represent a younger generation bringing with it a new modernity and the 'new woman' (Geraghty 2000: 21–37, 155–74).

Throughout the narrative, Violette is surrounded by female friends. When she first meets her husband-to-be, Etienne Szabo, an officer in the French Foreign Legion on leave in London, she is with her friend Winnie Watson (Billie Whitelaw). In the subsequent whirlwind romance, the visual vignettes offer a comic subtext as the camera repeatedly pans from the happy couple to Winnie, their chaperone and gooseberry. Even the relationship with Tony Frazer (Paul Scofield), which develops during her training for the SOE following Etienne's death at El Alamein, is initially secondary to her camaraderie with fellow female trainees. This is another way in which *Carve Her Name with Pride* differs from *Odette*. Whereas in *Odette* the female spy is represented as an exceptional individual and a lucky amateur, Violette is shown in several sequences training in hand-to-hand combat, with weaponry and as a parachutist. This later film offers a version of the female spy as a trained professional, whose femininity does not preclude success. Indeed, her friendship with Denise Bloch and Lilian Rolfe lasts throughout the narrative, ending when they are shot by a firing squad at Ravensbrück. Before they die, Violette's only comment is, 'We're all together.' While this can be related to a late-1950s nostalgia for the communal spirit of the Blitz, it can also be understood as a commentary on the film's representation of the life of a female spy.

Rather than a solitary and eccentric heroine, Violette Szabo, in *Carve Her Name with Pride*, is part of a community. While the officers at her training camp are all male, they are not offered the reverent portrayal of *Odette*. Following her chastisement by a judo instructor, Violette makes an aside to her friends, 'If only he'd break his bloody neck!' During their training, the 'girls' are constituted as a disobedient but proficient group; in a prank raid on command headquarters to steal whisky, Violette knocks out the commanding officer with one punch. As a more youthful, working-class woman, McKenna's performance as Violette Szabo indicates the possibilities of representing a professional female agent on screen, without the necessity of enshrining her as a national heroine, as in *Odette*. This version of the female spy may be understood as a forerunner of later representations, in its matter-of-fact account of a woman at work. The SOE in this later film, while dominated by male officers, also features 'Vera Atkins', a senior officer involved in Violette's recruitment and whom Violette entrusts with her will. Again, there is a sense here that women are supporting women. The film's conclusion indicates that, while Szabo's death marks the end of her espionage career, she is remembered as a public and as a private figure. The closing scenes offer a sentimental depiction of Szabo's young daughter going to Buckingham Palace to collect the George Cross for her mother. The final shot reverses the opening sequence, as her daughter joins other children playing in the street and the camera zooms out. Virginia McKenna, like Anna Neagle, was associated with a specifically English identity, but McKenna's 'English rose' star persona 'operated ... in ways that shed light on the difficulties that the new woman posed for fifties [British] cinema' (Geraghty 2000: 160). McKenna was one of the few women stars that British cinema produced in the 1950s. British popular films often featured accounts of femininity that were 'out of line with the contemporary views about mature femininity that found a ready outlet in other forms of popular culture such as women's magazines and fiction' (Geraghty 2000: 159). *Carve Her Name with Pride* offers one of the few attempts to represent a mature woman on screen and, despite its limitations, marks a distinct improvement on many earlier cinematic accounts of women spies.

This chapter has traced an optimistic trajectory in the historical development of representations of women as spies. From Mata Hari to Virginia McKenna as Violette Szabo, these figures mark particular moments in twentieth-century accounts of femininity and modernity. In many ways, this is a progressive narrative, conjuring a positivist history of women that moves from a myth to more complex and contradictory accounts of femininity. To some extent, this indicates the changes that have occurred for many middle-class women in Britain: better access to education, to work and to public life. But it is also a fictional account of representations rather than women's experience. Even for the privileged white middle classes, early twentieth-century histories are more complex than representations of those experiences can allow. I hope that some of the gaps between the real and the representation were evident in my accounts of Mata Hari and Edith Cavell. In the next chapter, however, my focus moves to entirely fictional and fantastic accounts of women as spies. If, as Mary Ann Doane argued, the *fin-de-siècle* femme fatale found a home in the 'new technologies of production and reproduction (photography, the cinema)' (Doane 1991: 1), post-war women spies were drawn to postmodern technologies. *Odette* and *To Carve Her Name with Pride* are cinematic attempts to deal with the new woman of the 1950s, but by the 1960s a newer and more malleable medium – television – was presenting even more challenging representations of women as spies, as professionals and as sexual beings.

# 3   Dolly birds

## Female spies in the 1960s

By the 1960s, spies were in fashion. Following the success of *Dr No* (Terence Young, 1962), spy fictions proliferated across a range of media in Britain and the USA. Numerically, there were more spy series on American networks in the 1950s, but the end of sponsors' direct control of programme content as post-McCarthyite blacklists loosened their grip and the Kennedy presidency began made the spy series a logical apogee for the newly affluent pop culture (Andrae 1996: 113–14, Worland 1994: 152–4). Conspicuous consumption, the 'white heat' of new technologies, an ambivalent fascination with new freedoms – 1960s modernity inhered in television series such as *The Man From U.N.C.L.E.*, *The Prisoner* and *The Avengers* (Sandbrook 2006: 44–56). Spy fictions on film, television and in print reflected on social shifts and, although such representations looked glossily modern, they were often infused with nostalgia for the old order. Many of the more successful British spy series on television, for example, present a fantasy England in which the establishment is challenged but ultimately triumphant. These are agents of the state, after all. This chapter examines women spies on television, in strip cartoons and popular fiction. Emma Peel, Modesty Blaise and Mrs Emily Pollifax offer an optimistic narrative of changing social mores, but they each represent different negotiations with the 1960s.

### Women spies on television: *The Avengers*

In her study of women and popular cinema, Janet Thumim notes the 1960s' central concern with personal liberation, together with 'an insistent privileging of the young and the new ... structures of class, nationality and power being interrogated to reveal their justifications in terms of the individual' (1992: 74). There are few mainstream 1960s films with women in key roles, and those which do have female protagonists often focus on debates about shifts in power, in particular, 'the question of power, its morality and its meanings' (Thumim 1992: 81).[1] A similar dynamic is visible on the small screen. In Britain, television was linked to national identity through institutions such as the British Broadcasting Corporation and events such as the screening of the Coronation in 1953. After the war, television sets began to sell in earnest, so that by 1963, 89 per cent of the British population had a television in their home: 'The television set was a signifier of modernity, and its ownership signified not just status among friends and relatives, but also the presence of the "modern home"' (Oswell 1999: 67; see also Sandbrook 2006: 376). Although the television set signified wealth and modernity, the spy series broadcast through the 1960s offered a more contradictory account of the modern West, as an expanding middle class and an increasingly affluent working class brought fresh concerns about social mobility and national identity. Television spies like John Steed, Catherine Gale, Emma Peel (*The Avengers*), Richard Barrett, Sharron Macready (*The Champions*) and John Drake (*Danger Man*) offered a newly exportable Englishness. Like the cinematic Bond, television spies negotiate a new modernity *and* myths of national identity embedded in discourses of class, tradition and empire (Buxton 1990: 86–7).

*The Avengers* spanned the 1960s, offering a vision of that era refracted through the lens of a rapidly developing British television industry. As part of the movement from film to videotape, from live recording to edited transmission and from black and white to colour, *The Avengers* also marked a shift from domestic product for a home audience to an exportable account of British culture for American viewers (Chapman 2000: 37–46, O'Regan 2000: 315–16, Chapman 2002: 7–9). James Chapman observes that the most successful series were those that offered a predominantly English cast and that such 'national fantasies in which the decline of British power never took place' were entirely out of step with reality. In particular, they contradicted the spy scandals of the 1950s and 1960s featuring Burgess, Maclean and Philby (Chapman 2002: 11–12). *The Avengers*' fantasy England was designed to appeal to American audiences. Brian Clemens, the series' producer, writer and story editor, commented, 'We became terribly British ... A car is a car is a car, and not an automobile. A lift is a lift is a lift, never an elevator. It is this Britishness that fits the fantasy world so appealing to the Americans' (Rogers 1989: 90). The postmodern reflexivity of *The Avengers* is visible in episodes such as 'Never, Never Say Die' (Series 5, Episode 10, 18 March 1967), which opens with Emma Peel watching 'The Cybernauts' (Series 4, Episode 7, 16 October 1965) on her black-and-white television, until the transmission is interrupted by Steed appearing on screen in colour to say 'Mrs Peel – we're needed.'

John Steed (Patrick McNee) was a constant throughout the series; a whimsical English gentleman with bowler hat and umbrella, which often doubled as his only weapons. By the time Cathy Gale (Honor Blackman) was replaced by Emma Peel (Diana Rigg) in the autumn of 1965, it was widely acknowledged that Steed represented English tradition, despite his modern tailored suits; as *The Avengers Annual* 1967 stated: 'Emma Peel plays mod to Steed's trad' (Chibnall 1985: 476). To complement Steed's benevolent account of the establishment, the producers invented Mrs Peel as a youthful model of the 'swinging London' which spy fictions were keen to emulate:

the England of 1965 *was* a radically different place from its predecessor of, say, 1960. There was a Labour government; unemployment was low, exports high, the touted 'white heat of technological change' cast a morale-boosting glow in which the newly empowered 'young meteors' (as Jonathan Aitken, then a journalist, apostrophised the yuppies of the time) could caper unconstrained. Even the BBC, under Hugh Carleton Greene, was casting aside its Reithian hauteur, and not merely joining, but often hosting the party. Not everyone was in favour of the new society, but the old guard were definitely in retreat.

(Green 1999: 71)

Like many of its peers, *The Avengers* was Janus-faced in its vision of England's mythic imperial past beside a youthful London-based culture. This combination of pastiche and nostalgia was part of the new medium's postmodern appeal (Jameson 1988: 15–20). The Bond films' stylised sets, costumes and gadgets were imitated in British and American spy series such as *Danger Man*, *The Prisoner*, *The Man From U.N.C.L.E.* and its female spin-off series, *The Girl From U.N.C.L.E.* These were dramas of surface appearance rather than realist 'depth': 'Characters in [television] series were no longer social archetypes representing various facets of "human nature" but designed to double as fashion models' (Buxton 1990: 74).

Yet, this playful concern with fashion and artifice also raised questions about gender, class and sexuality. Bond films marked the advent of targeting consumers across a range of markets, so that 'Masculinity [was] no longer the exclusive province of men, either as spectators, consumers or agents of power' (Miller 2003: 139), and television spies followed that route. The marketing of *The Avengers* via fashion, and fashion via *The Avengers*, is well documented (Rogers 1989: 89–90, Buxton 1990: 75). By 1965, 'The Avengers Collection' – modified versions of Diana Rigg's costumes – was available on high streets across Britain and overseas: 'the collection took as its theme the black and white of the television medium – the "lines" from which the TV screen is made up' (Rogers 1989: 89). Women and the new popular medium were thus united in a democratisation of style. Whether this offered liberation through consumption, however, is debatable. David Buxton proposes that 'the spy genre became the dominant fictional form of the pop ethic' because of the spy's characteristic 'cultural mobility' (Buxton 1990: 76), but Jonathan Green argues that, barring a few token figures, class divisions did not shift in the 1960s but were merely repackaged (Green 1999: 69, 72).

Series like *The Avengers* did, however, reveal a fascination with the *idea* of mobility. This is evident in episodes such as 'The £50,000 Breakfast' (Series 5, Episode 20, 14 October 1967), where the plot centres on Steed and Mrs Peel's investigation of the Litoff corporation, a multinational company they suspect is illegally trading in diamonds. The narrative gradually reveals that Alex Litoff, the Armenian industrialist who owns the company, is dead, and his assistant, Miss Pegram, is the mastermind behind a diamond-smuggling caper. During the investigation, Emma visits Litoff's niece, who works in a Carnaby Street-style tie shop decorated in op-art monochrome. The shop sells a variety of school ties, both genuine and fake, such as the 'Old Anonians' for those without a public-school background. 'The £50,000 Breakfast' overtly references social mobility through the tie shop and covertly indicates anxieties about women in senior management through the vilification of Miss Pegram. No one in this episode is what they seem: Litoff's presence is faked via impersonation and audiotape, while the woman in the tie shop is actually the niece of his butler, Glover. Glover himself is revealed as an avaricious underling who declares a passionate desire to be 'rude to a great number of women' once he has his £11 million cut. Litoff's doctor is complicit in the deception, also swayed by the financial imperative. These English gentlemen professionals are exposed as grasping criminals and foolish dupes of Miss Pegram; they appear unaware that she has murdered her boss. Class and gender are mobile in this episode, but they are also the focus of anxiety; the shifts in class order and gender distinction within the workplace are irrevocably linked to deviant practices. Miss Pegram, in particular, represents a counterpoint to Emma's jaunty heterofemininity, in her role as head of a financial and criminal organisation and as a masculinised woman; she describes herself as an 'ideas man'. Clearly, such ideas are dangerous in this context, but the status quo is inverted only temporarily with Steed and Mrs Peel on hand to restore order.

Despite such reassuring conclusions, 1960s spy series were offering new accounts of the modern man and woman. That such representations engaged with fantasies and anxieties regarding individual agency, sexual liberation and class mobility is entirely predictable. The new spies were also complex amalgamations of generic forms. James Chapman argues that *Danger Man* was related to the police/detective series of the late 1950s but was also the first of the new, stylish secret agent series (2002: 19). Like *The Avengers*, *Danger Man* went through different phases of production and broadcast, adding to its visual and generic diversity as its production team kept pace with a rapidly changing industry (Chapman 2002: 16). Series featuring female protagonists added further complexities. Toby Miller argues that women spies 'make trouble' by adding femininity and feminism to the mix (2003: 154–69). Where the woman is a protagonist rather than a marginal dalliance for the hero, she presents a structural problem *as* an agent in the very fact of her agency: 'there is a question of legitimacy hanging over the female agent – a fundamental untrustworthiness pervades her representation, and not only in terms of her honesty' (Miller 2003: 155).

Nevertheless, 1960s series appeared to accommodate female spies more easily than female private eyes. Charting the distinctions between British series featuring secret agents (*Danger Man*, *The Avengers*, *The Champions* and *Department S*) and those featuring crime fighters (*The Saint*, *Adam Adamant Lives!*, *Man in a Suitcase* and *The Persuaders!*), James Chapman inadvertently highlights a gender gap; three out of four of the former feature female protagonists but none of the latter do (Chapman 2002: 12–13). It is tempting to argue that hard-boiled detective fiction privileges masculine heroes, while espionage is open to more feminised figures. Whatever the case, detective stories and spy thrillers share a common focus on identity that highlights the contradictions inherent in bourgeois society (Mandel 1984: 65). In the 1960s, such contradictions were played out through an expanding consumer culture. Although the USA had enjoyed an affluent consumer culture since the early 1940s, a comparable economy was not visible in Europe until the late 1950s (Marwick 1998: 41–2). As in the America of the 1950s, British women in the 1960s were central to domestic consumption. Much like the television set itself, women were at the heart of the home and the consumer economy, but female spies on television mark disparities between women as consumers and as consumable images.

## Television spies and the new women professionals

In the 1960s, female spies on screen and in print in Britain and America traced changes in the workplace as consumer culture took precedence over heavy industry, and 'feminine' skills began to take priority over masculine inheritance. Thomas Andrae describes this 'crisis of masculinity' in Freudian terms: 'The paternal signifier was further undermined by the erosion of bourgeois entrepreneurship by the corporate state: the male's desire for autonomy and independence, ideals inherent in proprietorship, were displaced by the organisation man syndrome in which he became an alienated but conforming employee of a large corporate bureaucracy' (Andrae 1996: 119). If the new era threatened some middle-class men, the 1960s offered opportunities for women, ethnic minorities and the working classes which were largely unavailable to their parents' generation (Marwick 1998, 2000). In Britain, there were shifts in the education and class systems that had their roots in a move towards a more egalitarian social framework, even if the material effects of such shifts in ideology would not become visible until the 1970s. Male spies inadvertently embodied the disturbance these changes caused amongst those who had come to see themselves as inevitable inheritors of such benefits. *The Prisoner*, for example, offers itself as a subversive text, with a title sequence showing the male spy's rebellion against corporate bureaucracy, and the protagonist's resistant assertion, 'I am not a number: I am a free man!' Yet, the series tended to treat its female characters 'with a mixture of fear and suspicion'; the protagonist's struggle is with men and masculinity (Gregory 1997: 199–208):

> Like Leavisite literary criticism, to which the series is distantly related, this was a gratifying world view for an educated middle class, enabling at once resistance to a commodified, mass-mediatised society and a rejection of the mindless consumption habits of the 'masses.' The right

to have a 'name' and the cultured sensitivity that went with it, to exist as more than a cog in the machine, was finally founded on the value of rejection. It is only by resigning and positioning himself against the backdrop of the village – which, without work, is also without social classes – that Number Six can impress upon us the true singularity of his existence.

(Buxton 1990: 96)

The 1960s may have presented uncomfortable choices for men on television – to become a 'cog in the machine' or to break out of the new corporate prisons – but for women, the 1960s offered greater access to professional roles (Andrae 1996: 121). This was camouflaged by their performance as 'dolly birds' – women who are decorative and consumable.

In her famous 1929 essay on masquerade, Joan Riviere describes how 'women who wish for masculinity may put on a mask of womanliness to avert anxiety and the retribution feared from men', referring specifically to the woman intellectual (Riviere 1986: 35). The dolly-bird spies of the 1960s enacted a similar masquerade, disguising professional ability with a coating of acceptable femininity. The contradiction between what women television spies did and how they appeared may explain why there were few equivalent examples of Cathy Gale or Mrs Peel in American television series. Toby Miller follows Julie D'Acci in arguing that ABC's *Honey West* was a spy by proxy, as she 'referenced espionage in her visual style rather than her actantial [*sic*] position, which was as a private detective' (Miller 2003: 160). Agent or detective, *Honey West* only lasted one season, as did NBC's *The Girl from U.N.C.L.E.*, starring Stephanie Powers, in the following year: 'The networks found it more fiscally sound to channel their efforts involving the new single woman into cheaper, more formulaic, and more predictable situation comedies' (D'Acci 1997: 87). Like most successful American spy series, *The Man from U.N.C.L.E.* treated its intermittent female spies in much the same manner as the cinematic Bond; women provided scopophilic pleasure and shored up the heteromasculinity of the male leads. One of the few exceptions was the comedy spy series *Get Smart*, where bumbling Agent Smart (Don Adams) is repeatedly saved by efficient Agent 99 (Barbara Feldon). This was hardly an ideal pairing, however: 'Though he would take credit for her ideas, take advantage of her devotion and his seniority as a CONTROL agent, and make a snide comment or two (he once remarked, "You're too statuesque, 99!"), 99 endearingly followed him through adventure after adventure' (Lisanti and Paul 2002: 126). Agent 99 was often undercover in stereotypical roles – manicurist, harem girl, maid – and the series ended with her marrying Smart and having twins. Despite this, Barbara Feldon later claimed that 99 had inspired women: 'Because she was smart and she always had the right answer. And that was one of the first roles on television that showed women that way' (Lisanti and Paul 2002: 127). While the variety of viewers' responses cannot be underestimated, the predominance of stereotypical accounts of femininity cannot be denied. In one of the novels based on *The Man from U.N.C.L.E.*, an enemy spy constitutes little more than an extension of the setting:

> Napoleon Solo studied the long-legged brunette raising herself from a languorous position on the gilded love seat. Denise Fairmount was worth more than one look. Her amber eyes looked beautiful even in anger. Her silver lamé gown shimmered as she rose, emphasizing the almost feline beauty of her body. Solo reflected briefly that the Hotel Internationale's plush, brocaded Suite Four One One was a completely appropriate setting for her. She was like some regal holdover from another century of French beauty – with just enough Americanizing to make her doubly interesting.
>
> (Avallone 1965: 10)

Denise Fairmount is disembodied, her physique compared to that of an animal and aligned with the hotel furniture. The shimmering gown fits her into the 'brocaded' suite, and the final sentence positions her as a fascinating object within a neo-colonial museum of culture. Like Bond's girls, Denise Fairmount is 'put back in her place' by this description (Bennett and Woollacott 1987: 116).

April Dancer (Stephanie Powers), the girl from U.N.C.L.E., fared little better. The publisher's blurb on the back cover of her second published adventure is ambivalent:

> She moves with trained-to-kill reflexes, clicks with an IBM brain. She's cool, ingenious ... and sexy. She's a pro from the top of her beautiful head to the tip of her painted toenails. She's Mr. Waverly's right-hand girl and her heart belongs to U.N.C.L.E.
>
> Watch her infiltrate the ranks of THRUSH as she tries to reach kidnapped Mark Slate, an U.N.C.L.E. agent who's being held for ransom that's too high to pay. See her in action – 5ft. 5ins. ... 108lbs of dynamite ... U.N.C.L.E.'s newest weapon ... APRIL DANCER
>
> (Avallone 1966)

This passage speaks of a discomfort with the new women of the 1960s.[2] April Dancer is, first, a computer with 'an IBM brain' and, last, a 'weapon', 'dynamite.' She is an explosive combination of machine and sexuality – 'a pro' with 'painted toenails', which begs the question of whether the 'pro' is an abbreviation for professional or prostitute – and she is infantilised as 'Mr. Waverly's right-hand girl' whose 'heart belongs to U.N.C.L.E.' All this works against the main thrust of the narrative, that she saves her colleague Mark Slate from enemy agents. This short piece of copy outlines the contradictions the female spy embodies as a woman in a professional role. April Dancer, like the women who briefly appear in *The Man from U.N.C.L.E.*, is contained by a femininity that constantly works to 'put [her] back in her place' (Bennett and Woollacott 1987: 116). Such tension cannot be maintained if the female spy is to be anything but a clownish figure; April Dancer could not last.[3] This is not to say that women were not watching spy series in significant numbers. Women were one of the main audiences for *The Man from U.N.C.L.E.*, leading to sponsorship from Chanel and Maybelline. A *Newsweek* article claimed the series was an 'aphrodisiac', and much of the fan mail from women was directed to David McCallum, the British actor who played Illya Kuryakin. Nicknamed the 'blonde Beatle', McCallum's fan base was so strong that when he was shown kissing a woman in one episode the studio was besieged with threatening letters. A promotional appearance was cancelled when more than 15,000 fans began to riot in a New York branch of Macy's (Enns 2000: 130–1). It was these fans who were most vociferous in their opposition to *The Girl from U.N.C.L.E.*, as they feared that the spin-off series would lead to the demise of *The Man from U.N.C.L.E.* (Enns 2000: 131). Female fans, it appeared, were more powerful than April Dancer.

## Dolly-bird spies and the new England

Across the Atlantic, the British 'dolly bird' offered a different kind of femininity. This is not to say that she was an ideal – she represents a disturbingly pre-pubescent femininity (Green 1999: 76) – but this version of the 1960s 'dolly bird' was a more *mobile* figure. Twiggy and Jean Shrimpton were often photographed as if caught in motion, and the mini-skirt, although 'sexy', was also supposed to introduce a new freedom of movement for the women who wore it. Carnaby Street fashions broke away from the corseted female figure embodied by Dior's New Look silhouette of the 1940s and Hollywood icons in the 1950s (Green 1999: 79). These skinny, gawky British girls challenged the static 'to-be-looked-at-ness' of classical Hollywood (Mulvey 1989: 19). The 'dolly bird' was borne out of a mythic recreation of London as a 'happening' city, the focal point of everything youthful, modern and hip, which was largely the creation of features editors on either side of the Atlantic (Green 1999: 70–2). While they mythologised the new London, even these fictions offered a thinly disguised version of past mores. The 'shocking' new styles and behaviours catalogued by newspapers and magazines were dependent for their shock-value – and saleability – on the perceived entrenchment of the Establishment (Marwick 1998: 56). The central figure of 'swinging London' was the 'dolly bird':

> topless dresses, mini-skirts, hipster trousers, edible knickers, see through blouses, nudity onstage, streakers, the word 'fuck' first heard on British television – all the ephemeral images of Swinging London said that Britain had abandoned conventional morality and replaced it with the most frivolous forms of hedonism. The culture of fun cohered in the

single icon of the dolly-bird. She symbolised everything that was new, liberated, daring, sexually abandoned, independent and free.

(Linda Grant, cited in Green 1999: 76)

Female spies appearing on British television were inflected by this mythology of a new, youthful femininity. It was a symbolic shift when *The Avengers* replaced Honor Blackman as Cathy Gale – a figure still embedded in 1950s style – with the young Diana Rigg as Emma Peel (Chapman 2000: 53–4). Such women spies were not simply 'new' or completely removed from their forerunners. Rather, the swinging chick or dolly bird offered a modern take on the femme-fatale/angel-of-the-house dichotomy. The female spies of the 1960s, like the medium on which they were appearing, were as full of contradictions as ever. British television, with all its aspirations to modernity, was still looking to the future and chained to the past.

The high modernity of the 1960s gradually shifted into an ironic, self-reflexive postmodernity visible in *The Prisoner* and later seasons of *The Avengers*, both offering refractory accounts of debates about Englishness and modernity (Chapman 2000: 58–64). Figures such as Cathy Gale and Emma Peel represent contradictory versions of 1960s British femininity. Despite the different connotations of their roles, Blackman's and Rigg's professional backgrounds in theatre, together with their cinematic predecessors, connected both actors and their characters to a distinctly British tradition:

> Cathy Gale and Emma Peel belong to the same tradition of well-bred upper-middle-class girls portrayed in British films by the likes of Madeleine Carroll and Margaret Lockwood. They are sophisticated, fashionable, witty, and above all modern; they have careers of their own, they do not need men to look after them, and while they may resort to domesticity in the end this is the result of a conscious choice rather than patriarchal oppression.
>
> (Chapman 2000: 53; see also Chapman 2002: 76–7)

Gale and Peel offer a fantasy of the empowered white, middle-class woman professional as unthreatening. Sherrie Inness argues that such figures are contained by their lack of 'toughness' – that Emma Peel is 'semi-tough' because her active role is mitigated by her sexualised appearance and repeated use of disguise – yet these new women are also more directly engaged in the action than their predecessors on the cinema screen (Inness 1999: 33–7). Such characters rarely found depiction other than as femme-fatale figures, and even then their weapons of choice rarely included hand-to-hand combat. For the women of *The Avengers*, the 'sex war' found literal representation in their physical challenges to opponents of both sexes. Both these performances are more central and more physically active than Alexandra Bastedo's performance as Sharron Macready in *The Champions*, or

*Figure 3.1*   Diana Rigg as Emma Peel.

Rosemary Nicols' performance as Annabelle Hurst in *Department S*. Macready and Hurst were the only women in the team, often appearing token and stereotypical as they reacted emotionally in dangerous situations and rarely engaged in active combat.

   An indication of the industry's view of such female stars may be gleaned from promotional trailers for *The Champions*. Filmed towards the end of 1967 and aimed primarily at the American market, three trailers each featured a lead actor speaking to camera and introducing him/herself and the series as an exciting new addition to the schedules. A fourth featuring all three rounded up the campaign. The difference between the trailers for the two male leads and that for Alexandra Bastedo now appears comical. William Gaunt and Stuart Damon walk through a studio set in shirt-sleeves carrying their scripts, but Alexandra Bastedo is dressed in a shim-mering off-the-shoulder, short, blue evening gown carrying an evening bag. Her hair and make-up is immaculate, while Gaunt and Damon appear in casual clothes and adopt a businesslike manner, addressing the camera with information about the new show and ending the sequence by sitting with their backs to the viewer to study their scripts in canvas chairs featuring the actors' names. Having invited the viewer to 'make a date with me each week', Bastedo closes her sequence with, 'Keep that date, won't you. See you soon.' She also turns to sit with her back to the camera, but in this case she faces a studio make-up mirror which frames her in mid-shot and in which she combs her long blonde hair.[4] While the two male leads are depicted as serious professionals, concerned to study their lines, Alexandra Bastedo is eye candy. Rosemary Nichols, who played Annabelle Hurst in *Department S*, later said that she felt she 'was only there to add glamour to the show' (Lisanti and Paul 2002: 228).

*The Champions* and *Department S* offered cosmopolitan English spies for American audiences; both series were produced by Lew Grade's ITC for export to the USA and were not located in the quirky 'England' of *The Avengers*. Despite their limitations, female spies and spy series were at the cutting edge of the developing television industries in Britain and America. These shows offered a fantasy of modern consumer capitalism and began to break boundaries – not merely in terms of international travel and trade but also as a form of fictionalised proto-feminism. Before the second series of *The Avengers* began transmission in September 1962, Honor Blackman stated in a publicity interview: 'I'm a first for television. The first feminist to come into a television serial; the first woman to fight back' (Rogers 1989: 32). In contrast to film, where Bond girls were interchangeable and marginal, tele-vision in the 1960s could give women a more central role as modern pro-fessionals whose glamorous façades belie a steely determination. Spies like Emma Peel represent a 1960s femininity, which was physically active, intel-ligent and sexualised, and yet they were not demonised as femmes fatales.

## Women spies in print: Modesty Blaise

While there are many critical accounts of *The Avengers* (Buxton 1990, Andrae 1996, Inness 1999, Chapman 2000, 2002, O'Day 2001, Miller 2003), as well as useful fan literature and journalism (see, for example, Rogers 1989 and Chibnall 1985), other female spies from the 1960s have not garnered such detailed attention. Several of these accounts briefly mention Modesty Blaise (Buxton 1990, Chapman 2002, Miller 2003), but there is little substantial analysis of the novels or the daily newspaper comic strips in which she first appeared. Miller, in particular, focuses on the Joseph Losey film, *Modesty Blaise* (1966), which bears little relation to the original print versions by Peter O'Donnell (Miller 2003: 163–9). Most critics tend to write Modesty Blaise off as an ersatz female Bond. In *The Lady Investigates: Women Detectives and Spies in Fiction*, for example, Modesty Blaise only takes up a couple of pages, and she is dismissed as 'a sexual object' (Craig and Cadogan 1981: 220). It is for this very reason that I want to examine Modesty Blaise, in the comic strips and the novels, as an exemplary account of the 1960s spy in all her contradictory glory.

In the form of a comic strip in the London *Evening Standard*, a series of popular novels and a bizarre film adaptation (*Modesty Blaise*, Joseph Losey, 1966), Modesty Blaise takes a parallel course to Cathy Gale and Emma Peel. In 1962, Peter O'Donnell was commissioned by Beaverbrook Newspapers to create a new daily comic strip (O'Donnell 2004, Paterson 2004). The Modesty Blaise strip narratives first appeared in 1963, written by O'Donnell and drawn by Jim Holdaway (1963–70), Enrique Badia Romero (1970–9), John Burns and Pat Wright (1979–80) and, finally, Neville Colvin (1980–6) (O'Donnell and Holdaway 2004). The strips were initially published in the *Evening Standard* but were rapidly syndicated worldwide, giving rise to thirteen novels by O'Donnell (1963–96) and three film versions, of which Losey's is the most well known.[5] Fans and critics regard O'Donnell as the 'author' of Modesty Blaise, despite the crucial role of the artists who gave her visual form. O'Donnell's account of her creation offers two significant contexts in which she can be understood: as a character who moves across popular genres and as a character who represents particular ideals regarding human agency.

O'Donnell cites his career trajectory in the early 1960s, which saw him as a freelance writer providing copy for comic strips in national newspapers, most of which featured 'macho male heroes', and serial fiction for women's magazines which largely focused on romance (O'Donnell 2004). He describes the effect of these genres in the following terms:

> For some time before the call from [the Strip Cartoon Editor of the *Express* group of newspapers] Bill Aitken, I had been intrigued by the idea of bringing these two genres together by creating a woman who, though fully feminine, would be as good in combat and action as any male, if not better.
>
> (O'Donnell 2004)

This brief account situates Modesty Blaise as a product of consumer culture and an epitome of 'the pop ethic'. David Buxton argues that the strength of 'pop' culture is 'its ability to take form in several different media', citing *Modesty Blaise* as one of his examples (Buxton 1990: 76). Adding O'Donnell's account to Buxton's analysis makes evident the extent to which Modesty Blaise not only moves across media but also across genres. She appears in comic strips, novels, films and graphic novels while the narratives in all these media combine action and romance – the 'macho' genre of the comic strips and the women's magazine romance genre. Modesty Blaise has also become a cultural signifier, referenced in 1960s novels (Diment 1967: 47) and in contemporary film, such as the scene in *Pulp Fiction* (Quentin Tarantino, 1994) where Vincent Vega (John Travolta) sits on the toilet reading a Modesty Blaise novel. The 'brand' signifies subcultural knowledge; while not being so obscure that most of the readers or viewers will fail to recognise her, Modesty Blaise offers cultural capital. Although the trans-media aspect of 'pop' figures like Modesty contributed to their mass dissemination and consumption, the trans-genre aspect of Modesty Blaise was less successful. The clash between Modesty's femininity and her masculine role is evident in the comic strips and becomes a subject for comment in the novels.

There is a visual contradiction between Modesty's role and her appearance in the comic strips. For example, in *La Machine*, the first strip story published in the *Evening Standard* from May to September 1963, Modesty is drawn as a classic femme fatale, with full, dark lips and eyes and a voluptuous figure (O'Donnell and Holdaway 2004). This gives her fight scenes a curious twist; while her partner Willie Garvin is clearly designed for action, Modesty appears more at home in the frames where she assumes the poses of a porn star such as Betty Page. She is frequently depicted half-naked, in bed or changing her clothes (see Figure 3.2). *La Machine* is also notable for its gendered division of labour when it depicts violence. Willie is shown punching two women (for their own safety) and dealing with assassins who have been set up to kill him; Modesty, however, merely executes some basic self-defence in order to dispose of an over-eager date (see Figure 3.3). Most disturbingly, the frames where the women are knocked out are drawn in a cinematic style that invites voyeurism; Modesty lies below Willie in a seductively unconscious pose while Willie's girlfriend Pernod Mimi is pictured in the foreground, her ecstatic face dominating the frame and emitting an orgasmic 'uhh!' (see Figure 3.4). Neither woman is seriously hurt, and one could argue that they appear if not to enjoy the experience then at least to be *designed* to be struck in such a manner. There is also a gender division in terms of Modesty and Willie's responses to the aftermath of their adventure; Modesty weeps in Willie's arms, while Willie relies on his 'little address book' to unwind (see Figure 3.5). O'Donnell's account of the cross-genre inspiration for the Modesty stories does not include the pornographic reference of the comic-strip narratives.[6] In visual terms, Modesty, like other young women in the series, is fetishistically depicted, with an emphasis on her lips, eyes, jutting breasts and elegant legs. She is also frequently shown as a captive, tied up and reclining, in frames that suggest sadomasochistic scenarios. The cultural sophistication of the newspaper comic strips entails a 'liberated' heterosexuality, referencing the 'kinkiness' for which *The Avengers* was also famous. In effect, the beautiful artwork of the strip illustrators works to elide the contradictions at the centre of Modesty's characterisation; her hyperbolic appearance insists that we don't examine too closely the logic of her character but focus on the spectacular reproduction of her physical attributes.

O'Donnell and Holdaway appear conscious of these contradictions in their attempts to explain Modesty's exceptional status. O'Donnell has given several interviews about the inspiration for Modesty and has published an autobiographical account which provides the background to Modesty's

*Figure 3.2*   Modesty Blaise in 'La Machine', from *The Gabriel Set-Up*, by Peter O'Donnell and Jim Holdaway (Titan Books, 2004).

*Figure 3.3*   Modesty Blaise in 'La Machine', from *The Gabriel Set-Up*, by Peter O'Donnell and Jim Holdaway (Titan Books, 2004).

*Figure 3.4*   Willie Garvin in 'La Machine', from *The Gabriel Set-Up*, by Peter O'Donnell and Jim Holdaway (Titan Books, 2004).

*Figure 3.5*    Modesty Blaise in 'La Machine', from *The Gabriel Set-Up*, by Peter O'Donnell and Jim Holdaway (Titan Books, 2004).

creation. When stationed with a mobile radio detachment in Persia (now Iran) during the Second World War, O'Donnell encountered a young girl travelling across country on her own, one of the trickle of refugees fleeing the Balkans ahead of the German invasion:

> I was very curious about her because although her hair was black and she was deeply tanned, she didn't seem to be an Arab child. This was hard to define, but she was simply not quite like the many Arab children we had seen during our time in Persia and Iraq.
>
> I told Jock to heat another tin of McConnochie's [stew], and as the four of us talked, I found we all had the same feeling – that this child might well be one of the long term refugees from the Balkan country who had lost whatever group or family she had been with. If this was so, the loss was surely not recent, for the little girl was very much in charge of herself, clearly used to being alone, wary but not afraid, and with no expectation of help from anybody.
>
> (O'Donnell 2004)

The soldiers offer the girl stew and tea, which she warily takes, and then she walks away across country: 'To this day I can see in my mind's eye the smile she had given us and the sight of that upright little figure walking like a princess as she moved away from us on those brave skinny legs' (O'Donnell 2004). This episode forms the origins of Modesty Blaise, fleshed out in the 1966 strip narrative 'In The Beginning', which was designed to introduce the character to new readers whose papers were picking up the strip in the middle of its run (O'Donnell and Holdaway 2004). In the strip narrative, O'Donnell invents a more detailed background for the girl: she is a Hungarian orphan and refugee in the displaced-persons camps of the Second World War, who makes friends with a Jewish professor from Bucharest. They travel around the Middle East together, and he teaches her all he knows. The professor gives Modesty her first name, and she chooses her surname from the stories of King Arthur; Merlin's tutor was named Blaise. After the professor's death, the seventeen-year-old Modesty works for a gang in Tangier and takes over the operation when its leader is killed, eventually building it into a multinational criminal organisation called The Network.[7] This is Modesty's back story to the newspaper comic strips and the novels, a criminal past which is oddly honourable:

> She was, as far as she knew, only twenty – and the name of Modesty Blaise was already notorious. But nothing could ever be proved against her. ... The Network dealt in many crimes, but never drugs or vice. Modesty Blaise loathed human degradation and those who dealt in it. For this she would kill ...
>
> ('In The Beginning', O'Donnell and Holdaway 2004)

Indeed, according to Modesty's sidekick Willie Garvin, in one of the later novels:

> She didn't just run the smartest organization since crime began, she ran the cleanest. Sometimes it seemed we spent more time breaking up dirty mobs than bringing in loot. And I remember we passed up a fifty-grand job once, because we couldn't figure a way to do it without a couple of fuzz getting hurt. Certainly she's signed a few people off, but it's always been the kind of bastard whose going leaves the world smelling a lot sweeter.
>
> (O'Donnell 1972: 66)

Like Philip Marlowe, Modesty Blaise operates with an old-fashioned sense of honour in the dirty modern world. While money and perverse pleasures drive her opponents, Modesty and Willie, after their retirement from The Network, follow sybaritic lifestyles and egalitarian principle, motivated only by a need for excitement and a desire to uphold the law. In this, *Modesty Blaise* represents a particular formulation of post-war ennui; like the demobilised forces returning from the Second World War, Modesty and Willie find it hard to settle down in civilian life. As Willie's comment indicates, the background of The Network endorses a mythology of honour amongst thieves, while also casting Modesty Blaise simultaneously as criminal and judiciary.

The first novel opens after Modesty and Willie's retirement, when Sir Gerald Tarrant of the British Secret Service asks for their help, setting in motion their friendship and professional alliance. Like her contemporaries – Bond, the U.N.C.L.E. agents and the Avengers – Modesty is a model of urbane living. The novels are packed with detail of her apartments, her clothes and the meals she eats. Like other spies of the 1960s, Modesty and Willie are at ease with the burgeoning global consumer culture. On Tarrant's first visit to Modesty's Hyde Park penthouse, he observes furnishings drawn from a museum of international culture and colonial history: 'a scattering of ornaments – a porcelain-mounted lion clock after Caffieri, backed by a pair of Sèvres plates; a jade dragon bowl of the Chia Ch'ing period, and a silver vinaigrette; three superb ivories, a Clodion statuette, and an antique mahogany knife-urn' (O'Donnell 1965: 11).

The list indicates that Modesty has good taste, a characteristic narratively aligned with her role as moral arbiter. Unlike Bond and Mrs Peel, however, she does not have a class background, which makes her relation to such items that of the colonial inheritor. Modesty's origins as an orphaned refugee from Eastern Europe, together with the cockney heritage of Willie Garvin, give her a different position in relation to such cultural capital; in short, both she and Willie are self-educated and self-made. As Robbie Goh observes:

> In this period of transition [Britain's construction of its national image in the 1960s and 1970s], Fleming's works must be seen as a retrospective, inertial vision of an older, imperialistic Britain, while O'Donnell's novels develop a 'new liberal' image of Britain as a racially tolerant system governed by the motor forces of 'enterprise.'
>
> (Goh 1999: 29)

Where Cathy Gale and Emma Peel are eminently British, Modesty's origins are in the Eastern deserts, making her an 'ideal immigrant':

> Not only is she essentially law-abiding, moral and patriotic, she also brings into the nation the at that time fabulous fortune of half a million sterling, as well as the peculiar professional skills (surveillance, disguise, security, and occasionally execution) that suit her to serve the interests of the nation and its people.
>
> (Goh 1999: 33)

Modesty Blaise, with her companion Willie Garvin, represents a fantasy of the new England; C. P. Snow's vision of a national meritocracy (Sandbrook 2006: 48–9). Despite the egalitarian ethos of the novels, however, Western culture is always dominant. Like the objects in Modesty's apartment, the clothes she wears and the cuisine she favours, non-European culture in *Modesty Blaise* is to be consumed and assimilated. While Modesty herself is of Eastern origin, her allegiance is unquestionably to England and Englishness. Her surname, linking her to Arthurian legend, together with her platonic partnership with Garvin – he is described as being a courtier to her queen and fondly refers to Modesty throughout as 'princess' – attaches her to English mythologies of monarchy and heritage.

Despite this traditional frame, Modesty Blaise pushes the boundaries of nationality, legality and gender identity. She does go beyond the 'placed' identities of the Bond girls or of Cathy Gale and Emma Peel (Bennett and Woollacott 1987: 116). Her back story is one part of this, but her criminal past and incongruously moral agenda also entail a different relation to the state authorities she sometimes works for. While Sir Gerald Tarrant uses her services, she is not paid by him and is not an employee of the secret service he represents. In this sense, Modesty and Willie are not agents of the state, but independent operatives who have an ethical role. Modesty and Willie represent the triumph of good over evil, and this reassuring aesthetic fuels much of the pleasure in reading these popular fictions. Such narratives offered fantasies of freedom and agency in an era when the power of multinational capital was becoming increasingly evident. In these terms, Modesty and Willie represent modern ideals in a postmodern setting; like James Bond, they are able to assert their will over that of their enemies, many of whom are engaged in global enterprise.

Modesty's independence is evident in *The Long Lever* strip, originally published 23 September 1963–15 January 1964 in the *Evening Standard* (O'Donnell and Holdaway 2004). In this story, Modesty and Willie are called on by Sir Gerald to rescue a Hungarian scientist, Dr Kossuth, who has been kidnapped by Soviet agents. Modesty takes on the 'caper' because she recognises Kossuth as a fellow refugee; he spent time in a Greek internment camp after the Second World War, and Modesty recalls her experience of the same 'hell-hole' when she was six years old. When they find Kossuth, it emerges that he is returning to Hungary willingly, as his daughter is being held in a prison camp there, her mother having died during the birth. This again strikes a chord with Modesty's own childhood in the camps, and she sets Kossuth free to return to Hungary, knocking Willie out so that he doesn't have to take responsibility for her actions. In her report to Sir Gerald Modesty, she states, 'I don't give a damn about a scientist going one way or the other, Sir Gerald – it's nothing new, and it never seems to make much difference in the long run ... For me, what twisted the thumbscrews was choosing whether to fail *you* or fail the child' (O'Donnell and Holdaway 2004). It emerges that Kossuth has been killed by a Soviet agent in any case, but the child is now freed from hostage, and Sir Gerald's response is to forgive Modesty's insubordination, seeing the event as a 'non-recurring factor'. Modesty takes the moral high ground and provides an opportunity for Sir Gerald to implicitly endorse such moral fortitude, thereby shoring up the image of the state as an honourable entity rather than a body driven by economic imperatives.

In this narrative, Modesty's choice is driven by emotion; her memories of a childhood in the displaced-persons camps and her desire for parents who would return. This is a rare insight into Modesty's interior life; most of the strip and fiction narratives represent her as completely self-contained. The skills exhibited by Modesty and Willie in their various adventures are professionally honed, the result of many years' training. In addition to remarkable physical ability and skill with their chosen weapons, Modesty and Willie are able to suppress anxiety, pain and even to lose consciousness at will. In this sense, Modesty Blaise represents the perfect modern agent – the epitome of Enlightenment individualism, she is a fantasy of agency in a disorienting post-war environment – a subject who is able to effect change and take control of events. Above all, she is in control of her body, using it in several adventures to gain control of dangerous situations. In a later novel, *The Night of Morningstar*, Modesty employs muscular manipulation, based on a technique learned from an Indian holy man, to expel a drug injected into her thigh (O'Donnell 1982: 199, 234). Most notoriously, Modesty occasionally employs The Nailer, walking into a room of armed men naked to the waist in order to gain a few seconds' advantage (O'Donnell 1965: 26; O'Donnell 1966: 153–4). In this manner, Modesty is constructed as a masculine agent in a feminine body, able to compartmentalise her experience and employ her stunning physical attributes as weapons. Throughout the strip comics and the popular novels, Modesty's sexuality and gender are in the spotlight, ostensibly marking her as a product of the new freedoms of liberated sexuality and consumerism, but also indicating how *strange* this female agent is. There are many examples of the narratives themselves commenting upon Modesty's uniqueness, and it is notable that other women who feature in the novels are also often marked as 'different', albeit not as perfect as Modesty herself.[8]

Bond and the other male spies of 1960s fiction, film and television enact similar fantasies of affluence, ability and agency. Philip McAlpine (Diment 1967, 1968) and Napoleon Solo, like Bond, demonstrate such agency through their sexual prowess. Modesty, like the masculine models she emulates, is also depicted as sexually liberated, yet this is a problem for the narrative. Modesty's sexuality is a topic of debate, whereas for Bond et al., it is simply a given, providing evidence of their heteromasculinity. When Modesty is working for Tarrant in *Sabre-Tooth*, she encounters an old flame, Mike Delgado:

> It was five years or more since she had last felt the touch of his hand and the weight of his lean body upon her, but now it might have been yesterday. She had known other men through the years ... not many, not few. With them she had given, and been given, warmth and joy and the great leap to the summit and the glowing peace of fulfilment. But of them all, only three had carried her beyond the summit and into a blazing golden world of the eternal moment, when it seemed that the body's very essence was on the verge of being unmade.
>
> (O'Donnell 1966: 99)

This passage offers another rare insight into Modesty's psyche, but what a strangely purple turn of phrase she adopts, employing the euphemistic language of romantic fiction, with a 'great leap to the summit' rather than 'climax' and a 'blazing golden world of the eternal moment' rather than 'orgasm'. This sits strangely with the more graphic language of action sequences:

> Modesty took a long swerving stride. The bottle dropped from Emilio's hand and he snatched for his gun. Her leg swung with the whole impetus of her body behind it. Her toes were arched back and the ball

of her foot hit Emilio squarely on the solar plexus with the explosive energy of her hundred and thirty pounds behind it.

(O'Donnell 1966: 154)

The novels draw on incompatible styles of popular genre fiction. While popular fiction is notable for its ability to synthesise forms and produce new subgenres and combinations, in this case it offers a disjunctive style and narrative voice (Gelder 2004: 40–74). Modesty's transgenre representation is less than successful, but all the more interesting. The novels themselves appear to acknowledge such interest in their repeated return to Modesty's gender identity.

Steve Collier, Modesty's lover in *I, Lucifer*, describes her as 'a splendidly earthy creature' (O'Donnell 1967: 69), and this attempt at categorisation continues throughout the novels. By *A Taste for Death* (1969), Collier's appreciation of Modesty's sexuality is mitigated by an understanding of her professional abilities:

> Collier watched, not speaking. There was something in her face and in her manner that he did not like, a kind of animal ferocity, a controlled fury against her enemies which made her incapable of compromise. ...
> ... again he saw something flare deep in her eyes, like the momentary red glow of a dog's eyes picked out by headlights in the dark; or a wolf's eyes, Collier thought. He knew that it was the feral glow of her will, that this quality alone had kept her alive against all odds in early childhood, and that this alone might save his own life now, as it had done before.
> But still, in some strange way, it repelled and saddened him. She had been all things to him and he loved her, but this was a part of her with which he could make no contact. He knew that she had surprising depths of charity and compassion, of humour and warmth; that she was intelligent, with a serene but joyous zest for life; that she could give a man supreme happiness or give him rest; and that, despite her dangerous skills, she was wholly feminine. But this, now, was something else. She was on ground where he could never hope to walk with her, where perhaps Willie Garvin alone could walk with her.

(O'Donnell 1969: 210–11)

By the end of this novel, Stephen Collier has begun a relationship with Dinah Pilgrim, whom he later marries, so this passage marks the end of his sexual relationship with Modesty, yet it is not unique in its elaboration of her 'difference'. Here is Modesty herself, reflecting on her own femininity in conversation with Garvin:

> 'I grew up as a kind of hermaphrodite polecat, all sharp teeth and claws.' She gave a half laugh. 'It hardly dawned on me that I was a girl until I looked down one day and found I was growing knockers. But I

went on being just as mean and nasty and bloody-minded as before. So I'm sort of different.' She touched his hand as it lay on the balustrade. 'Not better. Worse if anything, but different.'

(O'Donnell 1977: 150)

These awkward passages set out to solve the ideological problem of Modesty's 'difference'; while 'wholly feminine' (whatever that means), she is capable of performing as well as, if not better than, the men around her.[9] Her predilection for combat is attributed to her childhood, yet this alone is clearly not enough; both passages are notable for their use of animal imagery to denote how far beyond ordinary humanity Modesty is. The novels thus admit to the central contradiction of Modesty's characterisation; she is, indeed, a 'hermaphrodite'. These passages describe how Modesty differs from normative femininity; but they also expose the artificial construction of gender difference per se. Modesty's own language – the peculiar use of the word 'knockers' to denote her breasts – indicate the extent to which she embodies heterofemininity; she cannot see herself as a woman because a woman could not do what she does. Therefore, she sees herself in masculine terms, through masculine eyes and in masculine language. Modesty may be self-made in the novels and the newspaper comic strips, but she is made in man's image. Like the fetishised femme fatale figure of classic film noir, Modesty is a woman who seduces and kills; unlike the femme fatale, she is depicted as the protagonist in these adventures and also given a voice. It is when she attempts to describe herself that the characterisation begins to unravel. At these moments, Modesty Blaise inadvertently exposes the contradictions of heterofemininity.

Continually marked as 'different' from other women, Modesty is a fantasy of 'liberated' (hetero)sexuality and super-human ability. When the narratives examine Modesty, however, the answers are not satisfactory. In *Sabre-Tooth*, Modesty and Willie adopt Lucille, who, like Modesty, is an orphan. Lucille is taken hostage and used by the villain, Karz to ensure Modesty and Willie's cooperation in a planned attack on Kuwait. Both Willie and Modesty admit that they do not feel much connection with Lucille but take on the challenge because of the more abstract threat to children in Kuwait. Once they have succeeded, Lucille is shipped off to a family in America, with Willie/Modesty and the child declared 'incompatible' by psychoanalysts (O'Donnell 1966: 278). In this 'caper', Modesty puts herself in a military bordello, where she is raped by Karz's mercenaries. This aspect of the job distresses Willie (and Tarrant) more than Modesty herself:

'My bit wasn't funny. ... ' A spark of wry humour touched her eyes.
    'But it wasn't a fate-worse-than-death, either!'
She pressed his hand a little tighter against her cheek.
'Listen, Willie. You know I never lie to you. I was a thousand miles away.

'It was nothing like when it happened to me long ago, when I was twelve. I was frightened then, until I passed out.

'And even that's gone now. I shut it out long ago. It happened to somebody else. So did this ... '

(O'Donnell 1966: 145)

On the one hand, these aspects of Modesty's character – her confessed lack of maternal feeling, her refusal to be defined by sexual assault – suggest a feminist sensibility, but this sits ill with the constant references to her *über*-femininity and sexual appeal. While many aspects of Modesty Blaise imply liberation and a new world order – her stateless origins, her passionate friendship with Garvin, her role as central mover in these narratives – ultimately, she is delimited by the insistence on her 'femininity' as something that demands comment, as expressed by her tears after a difficult job and her pointed heterosexual prowess. This makes Modesty a fascinating subject for analysis, just as the novels and strips make fascinating popular fiction.

### Women spies in print: Mrs Pollifax

Dorothy Gilman's Mrs Pollifax novels take the female spy a step further than Modesty Blaise. Emily Pollifax is a widow and grandmother from New Brunswick, New Jersey, who first appears in *The Unexpected Mrs Pollifax* in 1966. This is the only novel of the series published in the 1960s, however, and these fictions, as a serial narrative, are more in tune with the politics of 1970s left-wing liberalism than 1960s ideas about sexual liberation.[10] In the first novel, Emily Pollifax asserts her dissatisfaction with the usual round of volunteering and offers her services to the CIA, fulfilling a childhood ambition to be a spy. Despite their initial reluctance, she is employed as a courier by Carstairs who, with his assistant Bishop, becomes Mrs Pollifax's agency 'handler'. From the outset, Mrs Pollifax does not fit the stereotype of the spy, and, indeed, that's what gets her this first assignment:

'I've come to volunteer. I'm quite alone, you see, with no encumbrances or responsibilities. It's true that my only qualifications are those of character, but when you reach my age character is what you have the most of. I've raised two children and run a home. I drive a car and know first aid, I never shrink from the sight of blood and I'm very good in emergencies.'

Mr Mason looked oddly stricken.

(Gilman 1966: 9)

Naturally, Mrs Pollifax takes to spying extremely well, embarking on a series of adventures that take her to a variety of exotic destinations. Unlike Modesty Blaise, who is at home everywhere, Emily Pollifax is an American abroad (one of the novels is titled *Mrs Pollifax, Innocent Tourist*), yet these fictions do not espouse a neo-colonial ethic but rather seek to efface the realities of American foreign policy in the 1970s. Where the USA engaged in forays into South American politics, Mrs Pollifax, in this first novel, is kidnapped in Mexico by Chinese agents and transported to Albania where she befriends her fellow prisoner and captured agent, Farrell. In her encounter with the 'Red Chinese', Emily Pollifax's main weapons are her ability to improvise and to forge connections with those around her, including a Soviet agent and her Albanian guards. She represents the triumph of Western liberal ideals over the totalitarian regimes of communist states – the eccentric individual is lauded over the political masses.

As a depiction of the female spy, however, Mrs Pollifax is a radical departure; she is supremely conventional, and this ordinary quality, together with her age, brings her through the most dangerous escapades. The novels are told in the third person but largely from her point of view, so that we do get an insight into Mrs Pollifax's mind, unlike that of Modesty. These are clearly designed to be comic thrillers, gently satirising the conventions of 1960s spy fictions, yet also quietly examining the role of the professional spy. Farrell, a CIA operative she encounters in the first novel, reappears in several later novels, including *Mrs Pollifax on Safari* (1976), *Mrs Pollifax and the Second Thief* (1993) and *Mrs Pollifax Unveiled* (2000) as a disaffected retired agent who occasionally freelances for his former employers. In the second novel, *The Amazing Mrs Pollifax* (1970), Emily is dispatched to help another woman spy escape from Communist kidnappers in Istanbul. Their encounter is an interesting depiction of what Mrs Pollifax herself describes as 'an amateur confronted by her professional counterpart' (Gilman 1970: 2). Magda Ferenci-Sabo has been a spy since the First World War, becoming a member of the French resistance in the Second World War and then a Cold War agent in the 1950s. By the time in which the novel is set, this professional agent wants to retire, admitting, 'agents are not supposed to survive as long as I, they are supposed to die violently and early' (Gilman 1970: 82). Magda lists her reasons for wanting to retire from the 'double game':

> 'I am tired of violence, of uncertainty and betrayals, of remaining always detached lest someone I grow to like must be betrayed, or betray me. Most, I am tired of acting the double part ... '
>
> Mrs Pollifax looked at her and was curiously touched. She thought of the *Times* biography which could not know or possibly describe – no-one could – the complications or dangers which this woman must have met and mastered with intelligence and courage, and always alone. But she thought the story was written clearly in the lines of Magda's face: *Those are good lines*, she thought, *lines of humor and compassion and deep sadness. And I heard her laugh – how did she escape corruption from all this?* Her hand went out to touch Magda's hand and squeeze it.
>
> (Gilman 1970: 82–3)

In this encounter, Mrs Pollifax acknowledges the personal cost of professional espionage and respects her colleague's experience and fortitude. In this the Pollifax novels differ from the 1960s female spies on film, television and in popular fictions, as they indicate specific problems regarding espionage as a profession – the cost to the individual and the dubious intentions of state bodies. While the CIA remains largely unexamined, the Pollifax novels travel beyond the internal politics of the USA to investigate apartheid in South Africa (Gilman 1976: 92–3) and the politics of the Middle East (Gilman 1973: 175), as well as noting feminist and ecological issues.

Emily Pollifax, thus, offers a gently critical account of the violent fictional world she inhabits. Each novel begins with her being called to Carstairs' office for another assignment, and her domestic life in New Brunswick acts as an amusing counterpoint to the dangerous international locations she travels to. Mrs Pollifax breaks new ground as an older woman who reflects on the decline in her own body but refuses to be defined by the stereotype of aging femininity: ' "Wrinkled," she noted crossly as she glimpsed herself in the mirror, and sighed over her multiplying hobbies – environment, karate, Garden Club, Yoga, a little spying now and then – that left her so little time for grooming' (Gilman 1973: 8). Unfortunately, she has few peers in popular spy fiction and even fewer in depictions of women as spies in popular film and television. Her closest sister, as many reviewers have noted, is Agatha Christie's Jane Marple, but Emily Pollifax goes further than Christie's spinster detective; she encounters romance as well as danger in the Mrs Pollifax novels, eventually marrying the American lawyer Cyrus Reed, following their liaison in *Mrs Pollifax on Safari* (1976), and sharing a tender moment with the mysterious Tsanko in *The Elusive Mrs Pollifax* (Gilman 1971: 177–80). The examples of women spies in the chapters which follow map her development through the 1970s, 1980s, 1990s and 2000s, with reference to some of the most high-profile representations of the female spy on the large and small screen. They are, without exception, white, young, slim and heterosexual. Like Modesty Blaise, aspects of these representations disrupt the smooth surface of white heterofemininity, but none of them mark as critical a departure from the mainstream as Mrs Emily Pollifax of New Brunswick, New Jersey.

# 4 English roses and all-American girls

*The New Avengers* and *The Bionic Woman*

This chapter examines parallel representations of the female spy on British and American television during the 1970s: Purdey in *The New Avengers* (1976–7) and Jaime Sommers in *The Bionic Woman* (1976–8). In each series, the female protagonist is framed within a masculine economy; they are both employed by government agencies with a male commanding officer. Steed is Purdey's superior, just as Oscar Goldman is Jaime's 'manager', although there are ambiguities in these relationships. Unlike 1960s spy series such as *The Avengers*, however, *The Bionic Woman* and *The New Avengers* were produced and screened at a time when feminist politics were the subject of popular debate, elements of which are visible in television and film (Wood 1986: 202–5, Brunsdon 1997: 48). Second-wave feminisms were offering radical reassessments of gender relations, and traces of this are evident in *The Bionic Woman* and *The New Avengers* – in the performances of Lindsay Wagner and Joanna Lumley and in narrative references to the difficulties and possibilities such changes involved for women. Charlotte Brunsdon argues that female protagonists on screen from the 1970s to the 1990s renegotiated femininity in relation to three ideas: women's right to fulfilment beyond domesticity; women's financial independence; and women's sexuality outside marriage: 'In narrative terms, what was posed was the existence of female characters who were more like a hero than a heroine' (Brunsdon 1997: 48). Jaime and Purdey were such heroes. *The Bionic Woman* and *The New Avengers*, thus, represent attempts by the popular media to incorporate social change – attempts which, however modified and diluted, make feminism and femininity visible.

Although *The Bionic Woman* and *The New Avengers* sought to market the new middle-class professional woman as a consumable item, they also represented contradictions confronting such women in a society that had not substantially risen to the challenge of second-wave feminism. Indeed, the New Woman with her recently acquired disposable income was perceived as a market for consumer goods: 'The "new woman," as she is defined by aspects of the mass media, is indeed independent and self-assertive, but the implications of her new identity are not altogether what the women's movement had in mind' (Cagan 1978: 6). As representations of this 'New Woman', Jaime Sommers and Purdey are inevitably compromised in their delicate negotiation of popular feminism and consumer culture. Jaime and Purdey, like the public personae of the actors that played them, were thoroughly imbricated in 1970s discourses of femininity and consumer culture (Douglas 1994: 211; Inness 1999: 46–8). Both characters were a means of marketing their shows and the focus for various forms of merchandise, such as the Bionic Woman doll complete with 'the mission purse, faithful tote bag for hair brush, make-up, secret plans, and orders from O.S.I.'[1] Purdey's mushroom bob was widely imitated, much like Farrah Fawcett-Majors' 'flick' hairstyle in *Charlie's Angels*. Jaime and Purdey were active, intelligent and (largely) independent professional women, but all these qualities were contained in a glamorous and marketable package. These 1970s female spies are active women *and* consumable images, so that Jaime Sommers and Purdey, like Modesty Blaise, expose contradictions within hetero-femininity. Jaime's bionic powers enabled her not only to serve as an agent for the Office of Strategic Intelligence (OSI) but also to do her housework in double-quick time. Was this the brave new world women were being offered? Purdey defeated her (male) opponents in hand-to-hand combat wearing high heels and trailing chiffon scarves. Would other female professionals also have to overplay their femininity while taking on more 'masculine' roles?

## Production histories

*The Bionic Woman* and *The New Avengers* were popular prime-time dramas running concurrently on British and American television. The original broadcast dates of the series offer them as historical parallels, but they emerged from different national contexts of production and reception. *The Bionic Woman* was first broadcast on prime-time network television in the USA from January 1976 to May 1978, running for three seasons before it was dropped from the schedules. Like its close relation, *Charlie's Angels*, *The Bionic Woman* was produced by the American Broadcasting Company (ABC) under the reign of Fred Silverman, president of ABC's Entertainment division from 1975 to 1978. Throughout his career, Silverman was notorious for lowest-common-denominator programming (Gitlin 1994: 68). Master of the spin-off series, Silverman's success at ABC 'set the tone for American network television for the balance of the seventies' (Baughman 1997: 152). Under his direction, ABC broadcast a range of dramas and sitcoms with ambitions only to garner the largest viewing figures; sexual images and activity featured prominently in the drama series, while the sitcoms were designed to be as inoffensive as possible. Despite this limited remit, several series, such as *Roots* and *Charlie's Angels* tapped into contemporary concerns regarding race and gender. This is not to say that a liberal ethos was behind such programmes, rather that these were shows that people would watch in large numbers:

In 1976, [Silverman's] first full year at the network, ABC's earnings rose 186 percent. *Charlie's Angels* and *Roots* (some 130 million Americans, or 85 percent of all TV homes, watched all or part of the miniseries) had allowed ABC to overcome CBS for the overall ratings leadership for the 1976–77 season.

(Baughman 1997: 153)

Like *Charlie's Angels* and *Roots*, *The Bionic Woman* was successful in packaging a quasi-liberal politics within a deeply conservative medium.

The production history of its English equivalent is very different. The first season of *The New Avengers* was broadcast on British television from October 1976 to March 1977, but even before it was shown, the programme was dogged by disagreement. The ITV network could not agree a common slot for the show, so that it was shown at different times in different regions, none of them as high profile as the Saturday-night slot which *The Avengers* had occupied (Rogers 1989: 226). American networks bought the series two years later, but CBS once again buried *The New Avengers* in the schedules, broadcasting it at 11.30 p.m. due to its violent content (Rogers 1989: 227, Lumley 1989: 146). The production was dogged by dissent, and funding wavered. Dave Rogers argues that the show's demise was due to pressure from the French financiers to cater to their home market by making Purdey 'more sexy' and dressing her in French *haute couture* rather than British-designed outfits. The British cast and crew resisted these attempts to change the Avengers brand and secured backing from a Canadian company for the second series, which was aired in Britain from September to December 1977, but this was its last season (Rogers 1989: 226–7).[2] While *The Avengers* provided the initial impetus to produce *The New Avengers*, the latter was inevitably in its parent's shadow.

Like *The Bionic Woman*, *The New Avengers* was a spin-off series. *The New Avengers* was broadcast on British television seven years after the last episode of *The Avengers*; *The Bionic Woman* was an American network spin-off which ran concurrently with *The Six Million Dollar Man*, ending its run when the parent show was dropped. Although both programmes were spin-offs, they each had different relations to their originary series. *The New Avengers* was defined by *The Avengers*. Linda Thorson, who played Tara King in *The Avengers*, was very popular with French audiences, and this is widely cited as the reason the series was initially produced with French funding (Rogers 1989: 218). Crew who had worked with Diana Rigg on the earlier series called Joanna Lumley 'Diana' onset (Lumley 1989: 133). *The New Avengers* had little identity of its own; it was not so much a spin-off as an attempt to remake the 1960s series, and, in these terms, it was doomed to fail. Most popular and academic accounts mention *The New Avengers* only as an afterthought and compare it unfavourably with *The Avengers* (Chapman 2002: 94–7, Miller 2003: 97, Britton 2004: 74–7). *The Bionic Woman* had a more distinct identity. Although it was an attempt to capitalise on the popularity of *The Six Million Dollar Man*, it outdid its predecessor in the ratings and garnered its female star a more generous salary – Lindsay

Wagner earned $500,000 a season, while Lee Majors got $300,000 a season
for his role as Steve Austin in *The Six Million Dollar Man* (Inness 1999: 46).
*The Bionic Woman* was clearly a product of American network television in the
1970s, but *The New Avengers* had a more international background, funded by
French and Canadian money and devised and produced by a British team.

## Feminism and television in the 1970s

*The Bionic Woman* and *The New Avengers* were part of an array of mainstream films and television programmes in the 1970s which not only represented the 'New Woman' but were also addressed to a 'new' audience, the
liberated '*Cosmo* girl':

> White, youngish, heterosexual and an aspirant professional ... *Cosmo*
> girl aspires to the sexual satisfaction that was connotatively denied to
> the 'career girl' of the 1960s. Moving into the 1980s, *Cosmo* girl has
> options and makes choices. However her new subject position is
> potentially contradictory, retaining femininity, while moving into tradi-
> tionally masculine modes (alert, aggressive, ambitious). There is thus a
> constant tension in the way she must always already be desirable (fem-
> inine), as well as desiring.
>
> (Brunsdon 1997: 54–5)

Jaime and Purdey were not fully *Cosmo* girls; they displayed little desire
for sexual satisfaction and were primarily desirable rather than desiring.
Nonetheless, as active 1970s female protagonists, they predate the 1980s
*Cosmo* girl in their contradictory assumption of masculine and feminine roles.
The tension between their desirability and their actions is evident in each series;
there is an overt contradiction between how they look and what they do.

As new women, Jaime and Purdey were part of a shift in television roles
for women which was typified by Mary Richards, the lead character on *The
Mary Tyler Moore Show* (Dow 2005). Women had long been a target audience for commercial television in North America and Britain: 'Since
researchers first identified the quintessential consumer as female and between
the ages of 18 and 35, television has pandered to women, promoting a vision
of the good life in which they play a key part and feeding an obsession with
youth, affluence, beauty and glamor' (Cashmore 1994: 115). Yet, despite
their power as a desirable consumer group, women on television in the
1950s and 1960s tended to be placed within domestic settings and in subordinate roles (Downing 1974; Cashmore 1994: 115–16; Dow 2005: 379). As
Nancy S. Tedesco observed in her study of gender roles on prime-time
American television 1969–72:

> Males have adventures and get into violent situations. They are power-
> ful and smart, and their independence requires that they be relatively

unattached (not married) and thus able to take risks. Females, on the other hand, are presented as lacking independence. They are not usually found in adventure situations; they are younger, more likely to be married, and less likely to be employed.

The focus on different dramatic situations and other dissimilarities based on sex alone makes it difficult for men to view women as equals, for women to view themselves as equal to men, and for both sexes not to view the male role as necessarily the more active, powerful, and independent role.

(Tedesco 1974: 122–3)

In this fashion, series such as *The Bionic Woman* and *The New Avengers* did push the boundaries of traditional prime-time drama by placing Jaime and Purdey in 'masculine' roles which were relatively independent, central to the action and engaged in adventures which often led to violent situations.

Not only did Jaime and Purdey engage in 'masculine' roles, but they also played central roles in action-adventure series, a genre not known in the 1970s for its female protagonists or as a form of programming which delivered the desirable female demographic to advertisers. Sitcoms and soap operas were the locus for female protagonists and 'women's issues', offering 'a reformist or liberal feminism as "progressive" even while it simultaneously [worked] to disavow it' (Rabinovitz 1989: 3). Popular television thus works to contain disruptive images and ideas, rendering the new and the radical as safe and traditional in an attempt to attract viewers but not to disturb them. Nonetheless, in representing shifts in social structures, popular television retains a potential for divergent readings. Mary Ellen Brown argues that soap operas both construct women as a consumer group and offer pleasures that are not easily defined: 'I am suggesting that consumers can use the products of a consumer society, in this case television, in order to constitute acts of resistance while still remaining within the dominant economic order' (Brown 1990a: 210). A 1970s study of daytime soap operas not only acknowledges the low status of the genre but also alludes to the space it offers older, powerful female characters: 'The woman in primetime drama is under a greater compulsion to be young, insignificant, and subservient to the interests of the male characters' (Downing 1974: 134). *The Bionic Woman* often conforms to elements of soap-opera style in its attempts to render Jaime unthreatening, with its contemporary small-town setting and emphasis on the emotional aspect of the plot (Downing 1974: 131). Jaime also accedes to the demand for youthful glamour and is 'subservient to the interests' of Oscar Goldman, yet she often works alone and is invariably successful in her endeavours. She is hyper-feminine *and* heroic, a combination that makes her appear comical or 'camp' to contemporary viewers.[3] In these terms, figures like Jaime and Purdey offer contradictory accounts of popular feminism on television in the 1970s.

The ambiguities in Jaime's role are reflected by the production process itself. Ben Stein and James L. Baughman bear witness to the constant struggle between production companies and networks, together with the centrality of Hollywood as a location and cultural influence (via the film industry) for American television series (Stein 1980: 3, Baughman 1997: 143–74, Cantor and Cantor 1992: 66–7). These are not accounts of an industry which is

*Figure 4.1*   Lindsay Wagner in *The Bionic Woman*.

unified or politically motivated; rather, they make clear the extent to which television production in the 1970s was driven by economic imperatives above all, and if feminism was a selling point, then feminism was incorporated into the television series. Christine Gledhill cites this type of manoeuvre as an example of cultural hegemony: 'In this process, bourgeois society adapts to new pressures, while at the same time bringing them under control' (1998: 242). *The Bionic Woman*, like *Charlie's Angels*, was not enlightened broadcasting; initial intentions to make *Charlie's Angels* a feminist detective series were quickly brought into line so that the show was derided as 'jigglevision' (Baughman 1997: 153, Gitlin 1994: 71–3).

The success of series such as *Charlie's Angels* and *The Bionic Woman* is indicative of the popular media's ability to incorporate feminist issues and language for consumerist ends (Cagan 1978, Rabinovitz 1989, White 2006). Once feminism became a popular movement, advertisers were quick to respond to the shift in their target audience. Despite direct action by feminist groups such as the National Organization for Women (NOW), mainly responding to advertisements which insulted, exploited and stereotyped women, advertising agencies were able to employ the language of liberation to sell their products: 'By the early 1970s both the advertisements and the editorial copy of popular women's magazines had become fixed on redefining feminism as simply a new form of consumerism' (Craig 2003: 20). Most notoriously, the campaign to promote Virginia Slims cigarettes, launched in 1968, was one of several new brands specifically designed to draw on the cultural capital created by feminism. Marketed to women as a cigarette that promoted weight loss and offered the smoker both glamour and independence, the campaign slogan became a national catchphrase: 'You've come a long way, baby.' NOW condemned the campaign, and feminist graffiti appeared on the posters, reading ' … and don't call me baby', but the Virginia Slims campaign was a huge success, changing the terms of advertising campaigns aimed at women in the USA (Craig 2003: 18–19).

The first episode of *The Bionic Woman*, 'Welcome Home Jaime, Part 2', ('Welcome Home Jaime, Part 1' was initially broadcast as an episode of *The Six Million Dollar Man*), directly references the Virginia Slims campaign, as Jaime is shown in her classroom on Ventura Airforce Base engaged in discussion with her students about the Declaration of Independence. An African American girl asserts that while there were no women signatories on the Declaration, there would be a lot of women signing it now, to which a young white boy responds, 'You've come a long way, baby', and the class laughs. *The Bionic Woman* thus takes a phrase from popular feminism and employs it to establish the show's liberal agenda. The series presents a muted version of 1970s liberal politics, endorsing equal rights, civil liberties and social justice. These issues are frequently diluted beyond recognition and never examined in a manner that advocates disrupting the status quo. Yet, that these issues are referenced at all on a popular prime-time series indicates change in the USA's political geography. When Lyndon B. Johnson was elected in 1964, he introduced a raft of legislation combating racism and expanding welfare provision. Despite the Cold Warrior persona that took America into Vietnam and eventually lost Johnson the Presidency, the 1960s continued to represent an era of collective action and the radicalisation of subordinate populations: women, African Americans, Native Americans and Chicanos (Reeves 2000: 179–97). This is the perspective that *The Bionic Woman* offers, albeit in very curtailed form.

David Allen Case argues that 'American culture in the seventies ... can be defined as the extension of avant-garde sixties values to a suburban audience, the domestication of rebellion', citing *The Partridge Family* and *Bewitched* as examples (2000: 196). *The Bionic Woman* also domesticates rebellion, from Jaime's progressive classroom debates to the moral authority of her actions on OSI assignments. Jaime is always related to state authorities; even her work as a schoolteacher is located on the Ventura Airforce Base. This conveniently puts her on the spot for her work with OSI, but it also situates her as representative of a benevolent, humanitarian government that has the interests of all its people at heart. Jaime's domestic, amateur status makes her an advocate of the American way as both private individual and government agent. Just as her feminine exterior masks a complex technological interior, so Jaime's political and social positioning is often ambiguous. She is a double agent in terms of the ideologies she deploys, always undercover, with bionic powers that are harnessed to endorse US policy at home and abroad.

### *The Bionic Woman* as social commentary

Although *The Bionic Woman* may have cynically referenced feminism, this counters assertions that television drama did not acknowledge the women's movement at all. In her survey of prime-time American network television during 1973, Jean C. McNeil argues that:

> Television series programming does not acknowledge the existence of the feminist movement. ... this is a world without feminism, a world in which the truly independent woman is so rare as to have little meaning as representative of an alternate lifestyle. ... If feminism is, as one historian has said, 'the most radical social phenomenon in all history,' it is clear that the average viewer will not know of its significance from television.
>
> (McNeil 1975: 267, 269)

McNeil's evidence regarding television contradicts Steve Craig's discussion of 'post-feminist' advertising in the early 1970s – one could deduce that advertising campaigns aimed at specific markets were quicker to employ 'feminist' terms than prime-time series aimed at the widest potential audience. Nevertheless, it does indicate the extent to which programmes such as

*The Bionic Woman* were breaking new ground, albeit in a tentative manner. Jaime is an independent working woman. She is the title character of a prime-time action-adventure series. Her past as a professional tennis player, as well as her present roles as schoolteacher and bionic agent, takes her away from the usual domestic soap and sitcom roles for female characters. Yet, Jaime is situated within *The Bionic Woman* in a manner that limits her independence and 'alternate lifestyle'. Jaime lives in a converted barn on the Austins' ranch in Ojai; she is their surrogate daughter and potential daughter-in-law, frequently depicted in a family setting. While Steve Austin works in Washington, Jaime lives and works in provincial California, and their long-drawn-out romance is a constant reminder of Jaime's status in relation to him. Several of the plots centre on characters Jaime knows in Ojai, such as 'A Thing of the Past' (Series 1, Episode 3, 18 February 1976), where the school-bus driver is exposed as the witness to a mob killing in Chicago, or 'Claws' (Series 1, Episode 4, 25 February 1976), where Jaime helps a female animal trainer who buys a local ranch. In this way, Jaime remains local, while Steve is more often situated within the OSI head-quarters as an international agent. She is coded as domestic and provincial, an amateur part-time agent – a willing volunteer for Oscar – rather than a full-time professional.

The series' ambivalent account of feminism is carried through in other political issues *The Bionic Woman* addresses. In 'Canyon of Death' (Series 1, Episode 9, 14 April 1976), for example, Jaime has a new and troubled Native American student, John Littlebear, who has constructed a fictional identity for himself as a warrior brave, performing rituals for his dead grandfather on the Native American burial grounds at the edge of the Ventura base. John's aunt visits Jaime at school, and it emerges that his identity is based on a fallacious book about American Indians by a white author from Brooklyn. His aunt also corrects John's account of his grand-father as a great warrior: 'His name was Many Horses. The kids used to call him Many Bottles.' He was an alcoholic who died of exposure and was found by John. Jaime's response is to assert that John (who calls himself Paco) is struggling to find an identity. Following a parallel story in which the burial grounds are exposed as the hiding place of a mercenary gang who are trying to steal OSI's latest invention, Jaime identifies the burial platform John/Paco has built as inauthentic for the tribe he is from. She and the boy end the episode as friends, Jaime asserting that they will have to get him some books written by 'real Indians'. It is a white teacher who will restore him to his culture. Clearly, this narrative offers a paternalistic and patron-ising solution to a complex historical and social situation, but the episode does not entirely efface the issues it references. The complexity of John/Paco's identity is not dismissed or demonised; his grandfather's real life of alcoholism and early death, as opposed to the heroic life his grandson con-structs, indicate the social reality of many Native American people (Reeves 2000: 191). What the episode does not do, of course, is acknowledge the extent to which this was a situation created by an American government who, by the end of the nineteenth century, had settled Indian territories and destroyed their means of survival (Reeves 2000: 18). In this way, *The Bionic Woman* dips its toe into contemporary political debate but rapidly backs away as the water gets too hot.

Jaime's beauty – predicated on a dominant white, slim, middle-class model – is offered as the angelic solution to such problems; John/Paco, on witnessing her bionic abilities, symbolically decides she is a 'spirit'. Episodes like 'Canyon of Death' endorse the status quo; the governmental system is not questioned; rather, it is depicted as being led by just and moral figures (represented by Jaime Sommers and Oscar Goldman) who are not driven by monetary gain: 'The military men who send Jaime off on her missions are invariably good and well-intentioned people' (Stein 1980: 39). The threat in this episode, as in many others, comes from external forces – in this case a criminal gang who want to sell military secrets to the highest bidder. In several episodes, political issues are addressed in a superficial manner, often with the effect of simultaneously implying liberal and conservative agendas. In 'Angel of Mercy' (Series 1, Episode 2, 28 January 1976), Jaime goes undercover as a squeamish army nurse on a mission to save an American diplomat and his wife trapped in a military base in South America. Her gruff helicopter pilot, Jack Starkey, is not happy about taking this pretty young woman into a war zone and derides her 'sense of duty'. During their adventures en route to the base, she twice hides her abilities from Jack, despite his sexist remarks, pretending that it is his bravery and strength that saves them. They find the ambassador and his wife, acquiring a friendly Chicano boy on the way, and all take off for São Paolo. The boy, Julio, goes to a foster home, accompanied by Starkey, who has been converted from a sexist, uncaring old soldier to a rehabilitated new man. He tells Jaime, 'I think you're some special lady.' Jaime is the one who saves the day, not only with her bionic skills but also with her positive, can-do attitude. This liberal feminist agenda sits ill with the national politics of the storyline, as the South American country is clearly Cuba, and the guerrillas are depicted as crazed fighters. What they are fighting for is not made clear; but in case there should be any doubt as to the location, the leader of the guerrilla group is credited as a character simply called 'Castro Beard.' Contemporary politics – be it feminism, Native American rights or American foreign policy – are thus referenced in *The Bionic Woman*, but they are inevitably framed by a personal, rather than a political context. A similar dynamic was visible in 1970s cinema: 'In Hollywood films – even the most determinedly progressive – there is no "Women's Movement"; there are only individual women who feel personally constrained' (Wood 1986: 202). Rather than the 'personal is political', this is a liberal agenda where the political is personal; in *The Bionic Woman*, radical politics are disassociated from their social and historical context and defused by each episode's happy ending.

## 'Some special lady': Jaime Sommers' bionic powers

Although feminist politics were defused in *The Bionic Woman*, questions surrounding Jaime's femininity are rendered more contradictory by her exceptional qualities. Jaime Sommers differs from the other female spies discussed in this book because of her bionic abilities; she represents a link between the spy and the superhero. Superman, Spiderman and Wonder Woman are related to the spy in their 'undercover' roles as Clark Kent, Peter Parker and Diana Prince, as well as in their efforts to fight crime and uphold the American way. In the mid-1980s, several comic-book heroes were rewritten in a manner that reflected critically on the conservative politics of the original stories; most notably Batman in the Dark Knight series of graphic novels (Miller 1986, see also Moore and Gibbons 1987). Jaime Sommers precedes such radical rereadings, offering an overtly uncritical account of American politics: she is made by the state and endorses the US government as a benevolent power which is unremittingly masculine. Jaime's bionic transformation is entirely governed by male figures. In 'Welcome Home Jaime, Part 1', Steve Austin (the 6-million-dollar man) demands that his boss, Oscar Goldman, make Jaime bionic following a fatal skydiving accident. Oscar accedes to Steve's requests, and the government Office of Scientific Information provides facilities and finance for the medical work. Dr Rudy Wells oversees the initial operation, and Dr Michael Marcetti saves Jaime when her body rejects her bionic implants. There are no women here, and in these terms, Jaime is a classic 'cyborg' figure; like a car or a computer, she is something that men work upon, which has an unpredictable tendency to break down (Plant 1997: 503).

In the novel based on the 'Welcome Home Jaime' episodes that chart Jaime's reconstitution as a successful bionic experiment, she is referred to as 'the second bionic creature' and 'a most gratifying example of creative scientific progress' (Willis 1976: 27, 32), thus situating her as an example of quasi-biblical evolution. Only when Jaime returns to Ojai does she encounter another significant female character, Helen Austin, Steve's mother, who is a surrogate mother to Jaime and an occasional figure in her adventures. In this manner, *The Bionic Woman* conforms to traditional binaries regarding gender and professional life; the male characters are skilled professionals, scientists, doctors and managers, while the women are amateurs, primarily concerned with the domestic and emotional realm. Jaime is the character who bridges this gap. She is both feminine and masculine, domestic and professional. When on assignment, she is usually an autonomous agent, clearly able to think for herself in a crisis, so that in narrative terms she is both hero and heroine (Brunsdon 1997: 48). Jaime's secret bionic identity is at the centre of this transgender boundary-crossing.

Like the 6-million-dollar man, the bionic woman is an all-American weapon, built by the OSI and paternally 'owned' by them through the figure of Oscar Goldman. Contemporary reviewers saw her bionic powers as comical:

inevitably, with the perfect American woman came a whole new package of realized dreams: horror-stricken, I watched last night as the perfect housewife cleaned house bionically, scrubbing floors, polishing windows, killing all known germs dead, in less time than it takes to tell. Juggling three-piece suites as a wonderful prospective daughter-in-law, bringing order to classroom chaos as a bionic schoolmarm, plonking warm and wonderful kisses from her superlips on all and sundry, she filled one not with misery at the depths to which bionics had plummeted, but also with dread for the further depths yet to be plumbed.

(Coren 1976)

In the 1990s, critics have noted the compromised quality of Jaime's special powers, calling her a 'bionic bimbo' (Douglas 1994: 211) and arguing that her 'ladylike' qualities undermine her toughness (Inness 1999: 48). I want to take those accounts a step further to argue that the very elements that undermine Jaime Sommers' feminist credentials also open up a space within the series for a feminist critique of femininity. In many episodes, as Alan Coren notes above, Jaime's bionic abilities are used to domestic ends, often to comic effect. Although Jaime's bionic running and strength is depicted in slow motion (as is Steve Austin's bionic activity), her bionic cooking and cleaning activities are speeded up, adding to the comic effect. While this can be read as trivialising Jaime's 'unnatural' strength, it can also be read as an ironic comment on traditional femininity and how this was beginning to change.

Although Jaime's 'angelic' persona is offered as the solution for a variety of political and social problems, her bionic identity problematises any notion of natural or innate femininity. *Charlie's Angels* began its broadcast life in the same year as *The Bionic Woman* – 1976 – but, unlike Jaime Sommers, the Angels continued until 1981 and have recently been revived in a series of movie remakes.[4] One reason for this longer shelf life may be that the Angels offer a less problematic account of femininity. They are fully human, all-natural, all-American women, embodying ideologies regarding what it means to be human, natural and American through their performances. Sabrina (Kate Jackson), Jill (Farrah Fawcett-Majors), Kelly (Jaclyn Smith) and their successors on the small screen represented a surprisingly moral depiction of women as the ethical and legal arbiters in a variety of familial and criminal disputes. Referred to as 'Angels' by their employer, the eponymous Charlie, and Bosley, his comedic ambassador, they represent a 1970s account of the Angel in the House – the Angel in the City, perhaps. The Angels' labour is often tempered by an insight into their compassionate personae, such as in 'To Kill an Angel' (Series 1, Episode 7, 10 November 1976), where Kelly's friendship with an autistic boy highlights her maternal qualities. The Angels' physical beauty is matched by an inner sweetness. The Angels are never angry or unhappy. Unlike the demonic femme fatale, these beautiful women offer exactly what the viewer sees – goodness all the way through.

Despite their 'feminist' sorority and frequent references to 'chauvinism' in the shows, the series is careful to distance the Angels from anything that is not heterofeminine, as in the notorious 'Angels in Chains' episode (Series 1, Episode 4, 20 October 1976), where the imprisoned Angels are hosed down by a 'butch' female guard called Max, or in 'The Killing Kind' (Series 1, Episode 6, 3 November 1976), where the main villain is Inge, a murderous Swedish masseuse. 'Lesbian' figures are included to spice up the action, but they are inevitably villains defeated by the Angels' skill and their witty dialogue. Such characters guarantee the Angels' heterofeminine credentials, despite their lack of long-term boyfriends, fiancés or husbands. Once fiancés or husbands appear, they usually herald a character's departure (Dresner 2007: 67–8).

Jaime's inside, by contrast, does not match her heterofeminine appearance. While she is blonde and beautiful, she is also superhumanly strong and fast. In effect, she should be a femme fatale but is depicted as another angelic woman, resolving conflicts and setting the world to rights. She is a violent *femme*; a *femme* who does not prove fatal for her male colleagues and whose actions are driven by truth, justice and the American way, rather than selfish avarice. This contradiction is most overtly expressed in Jaime's use of her bionic power for domestic purposes. 'The Deadly Missiles' (Series 1, Episode 5, 3 March 1976) begins with Jaime in the kitchen using her bionic speed to make a pie, rolling out the pastry superfast and bionically pushing in a bolt that has come loose from her cooker; she is food processor and power drill in one short sequence. Jaime becomes a domestic appliance again in 'Mirror Image' (Series 1, Episode 12, 19 May 1976), where Steve's father takes Jaime to task on the state of her apartment as she leaves for a holiday in Nassau. There follows a sequence where Jaime bionically cleans up – dusting, doing her dishes, watering her plants, etc. – as Mr Austin looks on, smiling approvingly: 'All that in five minutes? Jaime you're incredible!' Jaime's professional, undercover role thus becomes an aspect of her domestic life, creating a ridiculous spectacle which contemporary commentators noted:

> What distinguishes [*Charlie's Angels*] – and a number of other TV excursions into feminine adventure, such as *Police Woman* and *Bionic Woman* – is a frank and total lack of pretence. They all seem to proceed from the belief that a television series should not aspire to any greater emotional or intellectual depth than a standard comic book. The dialogue is apparently borrowed from old *Batman* balloons.
>
> ('Charlie's Trio of Sexy Angels,' *Time*, 22 November 1976: 65)

The series itself acknowledges Jaime's incongruity with an early reference in the second episode of the first season, 'Angel of Mercy'. Oscar arrives to collect Jaime for an OSI assignment and, when an audiotape machine will not play the tape he has brought with him, Jaime uses her bionic hand to rewind it manually, at which point Oscar comments, 'Do you realize how much money we could make if I patented you as a household tool?' He then immediately voices his misgivings about sending Jaime on her own, specifically because of how she looks; he can think of her as a cyborg, but he sees her as a woman. In 'Welcome Home Jaime, Part 1', an episode originally broadcast as part of *The Six Million Dollar Man* (11 January 1976), Jaime responds to concerns about sending her out on assignment with the comment, 'You guys are afraid that I'm going to blow another fuse, aren't you?', overtly referencing her status as a man-made machine.

In this way, *The Bionic Woman* registers its own contradictions and, by extension, contemporary discomfort with the new women professionals. While working women had been a feature of company offices since the Second World War, the 'feminine mystique' had followed them from the suburban home:

> By 1971, the usual median weekly wage for full-time clerical workers in the United States was lower than that in every type of 'blue-collar' work. The only occupational category remaining below clerical work was service work, also predominantly female. Technological and structural changes in clerical work had facilitated women's entry into it; the preponderance of women clerical workers led, in turn, to further downgrading and deskilling of the work itself.
>
> (Gatlin 1987: 28)

Yet, by the early 1970s, new legislation was expanding the kinds of work women could apply for and was also beginning to offer protection rather than prejudice in the workplace (Gatlin 1987: 42; see also Tarr-Whelan 1978). By the late 1960s, there was a burgeoning women's movement visible in a range of women's groups, many of which engaged in direct action (Echols 1989). Television series such as *The Bionic Woman* were probably derided at the time by such activists, but even in this most conservative of media there is an acknowledgement that women's roles are shifting. In its unwieldy combination of technology and femininity, action and glamour, *The Bionic Woman* highlights political and social discomfort with newly independent white middle-class women – even if these women were not a majority but merely a potential.[5] As Shulamith Firestone wrote in her scathing critique of the modern media's role in disseminating the heteropatriarchal 'Culture of Romance', 'in its amplification of sex indoctrination, the media have unconsciously exposed the degradation of "femininity"' (Firestone 1979: 146).

## A 'no-nonsense head girl of a secret agent': Purdey as New Woman

If *The Bionic Woman* offered viewers an all-American spy, *The New Avengers* was emphatically British. Yet, the impetus and initial funding to produce the series came from a French producer, Rudolf Roffi, who employed

Linda Thorson and Patrick MacNee in a 1975 French television commercial for champagne. Thorson had played Steed's third female partner, Tara King, in the sixth and final season of *The Avengers* broadcast in 1969. She was very popular with French audiences and, following the commercial's broadcast, Roffi approached Brian Clemens to produce a new *Avengers* series, possibly assuming that Thorson would play the lead again (Lumley 1989: 133). Clemens rapidly formed an independent production company with two other members of the original *Avengers* team, Albert Fennell and Laurie Johnson. They auditioned new faces for the roles of Purdey and Gambit once Patrick MacNee had agreed to reprise his role as Steed. The original *Avengers* double-act was now a three-part piece, with Gareth Hunt as Gambit providing a rough-diamond substitute in action sequences for an ageing MacNee (Rogers 1989: 218–25). On 8 March 1976, the *Daily Mail's* Nigel Dempster announced that 'debby-voiced Miss Joanna Lumley, 29' had got the part of the new Avengers girl, and from the beginning the publicity campaign promoted her sexuality and sexual liberation as a means of selling the show: 'Prior to filming, Clemens told the media, "Purdey will be a stockings and suspenders girl – giving lots of glimpses of thigh. She will be tough, yet vulnerable, with a huge sense of humour. The *Avengers* girls will have gone full circle with Joanna. So much so that she won't have to burn her bra – she can put it back on"' (Rogers 1989: 221). Purdey was, thus, presented as a New Woman in terms of feminism and femininity, 'post-feminist' in her return to a more traditional femininity. In 'Dirtier by the Dozen' (Series 1, Episode 12, 13 March 1977), Purdey and Gambit are cornered, and she gives him her bra to use as a slingshot. Gambit asks her why she didn't burn it, and Purdey replies, 'I didn't need to. I knew I was liberated.' Purdey is 'liberated' only as a consumable image. As with *The Bionic Woman*, the feminism that *The New Avengers* occasionally referenced was a domesticated, consumer-friendly version of the second wave.

Joanna Lumley appears to have been aware of the contradictions of her role, recounting comic tales of ill-conceived Purdey merchandise and promotional appearances, as well as the rigours of low-budget filming (Lumley 1989: 125–44). Purdey was launched much like a 'Bond girl'. Lumley, unlike Honor Blackman and Diana Rigg, who went on from *The Avengers* to be 'Bond girls', had already appeared in a Bond film. She had one line in *On Her Majesty's Secret Service* (Peter R. Hunt, 1969), which starred Diana Rigg as the first and only Mrs Bond (Lumley 1989: 84–8). Purdey's stockings and suspenders were a short-lived publicity stunt, resisted by Lumley, who deliberately turned up to the press launch in tights (Lumley 1989: 127).

While she had little control over her costumes, Joanna Lumley did manage to negotiate a new hairstyle – the Purdey 'mushroom' cut designed by John Frieda – and suggested the name 'Purdey' when the original 'Charley' was rejected because it was also the name of a high-profile perfume (Lumley

*Figure 4.2*  Joanna Lumley as Purdey.

1989: 127, Rogers 1989: 221). Revlon's *Charlie*, launched in 1973 in the USA, was one of a range of products (like Virginia Slims) marketed to women via 'counter-stereotype' advertising: '*Charlie* advertisements featured what purported to be a no-nonsense single and independent working "girl" with a fashion model face and figure, usually pictured in a pantsuit. *Charlie* swept the market in less than a year, and other fragrance companies rushed to introduce their own "liberated" scents' (Craig 2003: 21). In Britain and

America, the perfume was promoted by a television advert featuring an androgynously beautiful model in a mannish three-piece suit who enters a gentleman's club in disguise, then sweeps off her hat to reveal tousled blonde hair. The commercial was produced in the USA and first broadcast in 1973 to launch the new perfume. The model was Shelley Hack who later played Tiffany Wells in the 1979 season of *Charlie's Angels. Charlie's* androgynous name, together with an image signifying independence, adventure and playful femininity, sold well, giving it a shelf life that extends into the twenty-first century.

Joanna Lumley as Purdey offered a similarly potent combination of glamorous 'New Woman' and nostalgia for a mythical English upper class: 'I had taken pains to present Purdey as a keen, no-nonsense head girl of a secret agent, with easy-to-keep hair and no real boyfriends. I wanted her to be tough and reliable, competent in scrapes but in bed alone by eleven' (Lumley 1989: 133). Purdey is a visibly classed model of English femininity redrawn to fit the New Woman refracted in media accounts of second-wave feminism. Lumley's 'debby' accent, together with Purdey's background – the daughter of a spy, whose stepfather is a bishop and whose early career includes a stint in the corps at the Royal Ballet – are signifiers of her upper-class persona. Lumley has employed this persona through much of her career, inflecting the 'posh' element of her roles with the humour that Purdey displays in *The New Avengers.*[6] Like the woman in the Charlie advertisement, Purdey represents tradition and modernity – a woman who doesn't need to 'burn her bra' because if she is playfully feminine, all doors are open to her. Purdey, like Jaime Sommers, is a double agent within 1970s discourses of feminism and femininity; she smuggles the latter under the guise of the former, and vice versa. Like Jaime, Purdey is a hyper-feminine woman capable of killing and authorised by the state to do so. These are not representations of female spies as femmes fatales but as skilled chameleons; in this sense, they may be understood as representing the contradictions that women in 1970s Britain and America frequently had to negotiate. If Jaime and Purdey offer acceptable accounts of women who are 'liberated' and 'feminine', they also represent overtly artificial versions of femininity. The delimited femininities they offer are grounds for feminist critique, but the overtly fictive, fantastic aspect of those representations are grounds for feminist analysis.

Neither show is realist in outlook. *The Bionic Woman* is clearly grounded in a science-fiction tradition, and the special effects that accompany Jaime's bionic actions signal their fantastic nature. While *The New Avengers* aimed for a more realist style than *The Avengers*, the dialogue frequently undermines any realism or makes reference to Purdey's unusual status. In 'The Midas Touch' (Series 1, Episode 4, 7 November 1976), Purdey and Gambit casually discuss who directed *The Treasure of the Sierra Madre* during a high-speed car chase, with Purdey peeling and eating an orange. *The Avengers* was famous for this ironic style, but it jars with *The New Avengers'* more realist approach. Purdey's femininity is often the subject of comment. In 'Obsession' (Series 2, Episode 5, 7 October 1977), Purdey is central to the narrative, as an old flame attempts to destroy the Government in revenge for his father's death. Purdey finds this encounter with her past traumatic, and the story is played as romantic melodrama, but she also disobeys Steed and Gambit to engineer a final confrontation with her former lover. The episode begins and ends with Steed and Gambit agreeing, 'She's Purdey. She's a woman.' This dictum appears both to comment on Purdey's universality as 'a woman' *and* on her exceptional status: 'She's Purdey.' The contradictions Purdey represents as a woman who is feminine *and* active are exposed in *The New Avengers* by the emphasis on her flawless appearance; like the bionic woman, Purdey is clearly a fantasy. In 'Trap' (Series 2, Episode 6, 14 October 1977), a visiting CIA agent (played by Stuart Damon, former star of 1960s spy series *The Champions*) asks Steed, 'She's not bionic is she? Purdey, I mean, she's just so perfect I thought maybe somebody had made her.' Lumley's brittle, witty performance as a 'no-nonsense head girl' elides the contradictions of her role by foregrounding Purdey's English upper-class persona, but this strategy also serves to highlight the character's artificiality.

Purdey's contradictory features are visible from the first episode, 'The Eagle's Nest' (17 October 1976), where she demonstrates an improbable fighting skill. Whereas Catherine Gale was a judo expert, and Emma Peel excelled at karate, Purdey has a more girlish talent. Trained at the Royal Ballet (a background later fleshed out in 'Obsession'), Purdey employs ballet moves in hand-to-hand combat (Lumley 1989: 128). In the final fight sequence in 'The Eagle's Nest', Purdey strips down to a low-cut green spandex leotard and red ankle boots, pirouetting towards her nonplussed adversaries before kicking them unconscious. The scene is played as light comedy, Purdey telling Steed that she was thrown out of the Royal Ballet for being too tall. In this, as in many other aspects of *The New Avengers*, Purdey does not fit. Other episodes employ similarly disjointed scenarios, often playing on Purdey's appearance. During 'Three Handed Game' (Series 1, Episode 11, 19 January 1977), Purdey is assigned to protect Masgard, an agent who has a 'memory man' act. While he is onstage, she waits in his dressing room and, apparently to pass the time, puts on full clown make-up, complete with wig. The subsequent sequences, which feature Masgard being captured by the enemy agents and Purdey searching for him backstage, have a surreal quality as her immaculate dress is topped by a clown face and fright wig. Surreal touches were typical of *The Avengers*, but *The New Avengers* careers between realist and surreal modes with Purdey often central to such dislocations.

Most notably, Purdey's outfits often involve an element of cross-dressing. One aspect of this is visible in terms of the gendering of her outfits. This is driven by the 1970s fashion for 'mannish' evening suits in 'To Catch a Rat' (Series 1, Episode 7, 28 November 1976), where Purdey has a dinner date with a double agent, Cromwell, and wears a dark velvet dinner suit, shirt and tie. The outfit recalls Yves Saint Laurent's reinterpretation of the tuxedo as evening wear for women in his *le smoking* outfit for the 1966 Rive Gauche *prêt-à-porter* collection, a ready-to-wear style that epitomised glamour, independence and chic (Arnold 2001: 104). When Cromwell expresses surprise at her evident skill in needlework, Purdey responds that she has 'all the virtues', listing a range of feminine attributes and concluding with the ability to 'break your back in three places.' Her cross-dressing clearly extends from fashion to behaviour. Elsewhere, as in 'Cat Amongst the Pigeons' (Series 1, Episode 5, 14 November 1976), Purdey's costume shifts from a formal black and white dress, then jeans, T-shirt and biker boots and, finally, a diaphanous green off-the-shoulder gown. At one point, Purdey rides her motorbike in the green dress; one of many scenes where her clothes are overtly impractical. As Joanna Lumley comments in her autobiography, the skills required for the role were varied: 'I learned how to skid a car with the handbrake, how to strip down and reassemble a Beretta and how to run over rocks in high heels' (Lumley 1989: 131). Lumley's costumes, while sometimes including trouser suits or leggings, are almost invariably paired with high-heeled boots, shoes and strappy sandals, so that it seems incredible that she can move at speed, let alone engage in hand-to-hand combat.

More specifically, Purdey's class background, endorsed by Lumley's performance and her public persona, is cross-dressed as she transgresses the early twentieth-century stereotype of the Lady, an arbiter of upper-class 'good taste' and modest behaviour. The Lady was allied to the Angel of the House in her passive dependence on her husband or father's wealth (Arnold 2001: 13). Purdey is a 1970s adaptation of the Lady, whose status relies on her class background but whose independence is visible in her professional expertise. Much of this expertise is made palatable in *The New Avengers* through Purdey's effortless femininity; her many costume changes and unruffled appearance following combat bespeak a gendering that is 'natural' and innate – that she can wear anything because underneath it all she is a Lady. Lumley's account of making the series undermines this smooth surface, as she describes the discomforts of filming and the labour involved in her earlier career as a model (Lumley 1989). Even within the two seasons of *The New Avengers*, such 'natural' femininity is parodied and placed in the foreground of the visual narrative.

In 'Sleeper' (Series 1, Episode 10, 19 December 1976), a gang steals a new sedative 'dust' and uses it to put central London to sleep. Steed, Purdey and Gambit are immune as they have been inoculated during a demonstration of this new weapon and spend the episode moving about a ghostly modern cityscape. Steed and Gambit work together, but Purdey is on her own and, chased by some of the mercenaries guarding the perimeter of the 'sleeping' area, takes refuge in a boutique, posing as a mannequin in the window. She fools her two pursuers for a moment, despite assuming different 'model' postures, as her silk pyjama pants keep falling down. This finally gives her away, and she kicks one opponent unconscious, then uses a rail of dresses to fend off the other, taking his belt once he is defeated. The sequence references Lumley's earlier career as a model and parodies Purdey's 'natural' style, for Purdey, like the mannequins she imitates, is fleshless, blonde and flawlessly made up. While she sucks in her cheeks and assumes the strange postures of a shop dummy, her appearance allows her to pass as something other than human.[7] A similarly parodic moment occurs in 'Emily' (Series 2, Episode 12, 25 November 1977), where the only lead on a double agent is his handprint on the roof of a vintage car. When the Avengers track the car down, it is about to go through a carwash, so Purdey throws herself across the roof and is shown going through the carwash, only to emerge as if from a beauty salon, with her wool sweater and skirt having shrunk. Such sequences play on Lumley's appearance and background and, while the intention may be to amuse and titillate the viewer, they also inadvertently throw Purdey's femininity into sharp relief. Her willowy, girlish character precludes any convincing performance as an action hero, so that the series becomes increasingly dependent on Lumley's 'head girl' persona and comic timing.

This led to a new career for Joanna Lumley once her roles in popular television action series had dwindled. She was a regular guest on Ruby Wax's comedy series *The Full Wax* in the early 1990s, where she sent up her star persona:

> [her performance] ... as a washed-up drugged-out actress ... initiated the revival of her career. This performance instantly transformed her from an idealised myth of feminine perfection, to reveal a more complex and humorous persona. Shortly after revealing her talent for comedy and self-parody, through a stroke of pertinent casting, Joanna Lumley became Patsy Stone, the ageing, neurotic 'Fash-Mag-Slag' for *Absolutely Fabulous* (1992–95). ... Lumley gives an immensely entertaining performance, but also, because of her on and off-screen persona, she creates in Patsy a hilarious and hideous satire around the expectations of glamour and refinement assigned to her.[8]

Yet, this satirical undertone is already evident in *The New Avengers* and is not merely an autonomous production by an individual actor but an indication that social and political debates about gender were visible in mainstream popular media. One of Lumley's appearances on *The Full Wax* featured Ruby Wax persuading her to relive the role of Purdey. She does indeed appear as 'a washed-up, drugged out actress' in a Purdey wig and leotard, struggling to reprise her former role. Barely fifteen years after *The New Avengers* was first broadcast, Purdey was an anachronism. Purdey, like Patsy Stone, was a woman out of step with the 1990s, but they are both characters whose independence and ruthless ability to survive are part of their appeal.

Joanna Lumley's performance of upper-class English femininity in *The New Avengers* may recall older and more restrictive national models of class and gender, but by the 1970s, the British class system was in flux. Purdey as a 'no-nonsense head girl of a secret agent' offered an upper-class femininity which was clearly a performance, not a natural or ahistorical phenomenon. Arguments over Purdey's costumes were not only national struggles between the French funders and British production team but also part of wider debates about fashion in the 1970s. Haute couture had lost its role as an arbiter of good taste in the 1960s with the advent of more youthful, disposable styles. Feminist debates about fashion in the 1970s and 1980s also challenged high fashion and high-street styles in questioning the role of fashion in women's subordination. As Elizabeth Wilson argues, however, feminist fashion – even when it represents itself as anti-fashion – is a style in itself, and one where the 'natural' look is as artificially constructed as anything on the catwalk (Wilson 2003: 228–47). In the mid-1980s, Wilson noted that 'an unresolved tension between "authenticity" and "modernism" haunts contemporary feminism' (2003: 231), and *The Bionic Woman* and *The New Avengers* can both be read in these terms. Jaime Sommers, with her 'natural' hair and make-up, casual jeans and knitwear, visually referenced the American 1960s liberation movements (Brunsdon 1997: 49). She represents a new 'authenticity', yet one which is clearly a construct of particular geographic, historical and political moments. Jaime's authenticity is, moreover, undermined by her bionic additions; she is nature and science combined. She is not entirely human, as contemporary critics and characters within the series noted, and thus offers an awkward compromise between competing discourses of feminism and femininity. Purdey, however, represents 'modernism' through the brittle wit of her repartee and her many (and inappropriate) costume changes, yet the series attempts to 'put her in her place' (Bennett and Woollacott 1987: 114–27) as both a Lady and as 'woman' – the eternal feminine. Neither of these characters are feminist figures, but they trace the dynamics around which late-twentieth-century representations of feminism and femininity vacillate.

While *The New Avengers* was produced and broadcast in the 1970s, 'Purdey was a girl of the 1980s' (Rogers 1989: 221). If Jaime Sommers looks back to 1960s egalitarian ideals – a domesticated version of liberal feminism – Purdey looks forward to the 1980s and what Susan Douglas terms 'narcissism as liberation' (Douglas 1994: 245–68). Noting the success of Christopher Lasch's *The Culture of Narcissism* in 1979, Douglas argues that such narcissistic individualism and insecurity were things that women were all too familiar with. In the 1980s, this reached its apogee in the figure of the 'New Woman' in advertisements featuring a white, middle-class woman cognisant of the cultural capital of masculinity yet still a lady: 'These women were huge successes at managing the impressions they gave to others, coming across as distinctive, nonconformist women who nonetheless conform perfectly to dominant standards of beauty' (Douglas 1994: 249). In

*The New Avengers*, this is summarised as 'She's a woman. She's Purdey', which could easily be the slogan promoting a new scent. At times, Purdey's beautiful façade slipped, as when she put on the clown make-up or imitated the mannequin, yet this façade did not conceal an 'authentic' inner core, but merely a more playful account of femininity as masquerade, as always-already in disguise. As Susan Douglas states above, the 'New Woman' of 1980s advertising was all about appearance, about 'managing the impressions they gave to others', and, while these appearances may be seen as part of a backlash against the feminism of the 1970s, they also offered an account of femininity that was compromised. When Purdey emerges from the car-wash with coiffed hair and a mini-skirt that was once maxi, it does not simply put her back in her place with the Bond girls of the 1960s; it also sends up the construction of appearance that constitutes feminine beauty.

# 5 *Nikita*

## From French cinema to American television

Luc Besson's 1990 hit *Nikita* spawned two Hong Kong versions in 1991 and 1992, a Hollywood remake in 1993, and an American television series in the late 1990s. The Hong Kong films *Black Cat* (dir. Stephen Shin, 1991) and *Black Cat II* (dir. Stephen Shin, 1992) take the narrative of *Nikita* as the basis for a series starring Jade Leung (see Grindstaff, 2001). For the purposes of my argument, however, the American remake *Point of No Return* (dir. John Badham, 1993), also known as *Assassin*, continues the transatlantic dynamic of earlier chapters and offers a rereading of the French original. It also introduces the Warner Brothers series *La Femme Nikita* (1997–2001), as the studio produced both Badham's film and the television series having bought the rights to Besson's *Nikita*. While *Nikita*, *Point of No Return* and *La Femme Nikita* may be understood as a series of adaptations across different national contexts, they offer a consistent focus on the corporate organisation of espionage as well as the corporal form of its central protagonist. This chapter reads the three Nikita narratives in relation to two main frameworks: French and American cinema and television in the 1990s and discourses of modernity and postmodernity after the 1980s. Although *Nikita*, *Point of No Return* and *La Femme Nikita* are inflected by different national and institutional backgrounds, all offer accounts of how film and television have attempted to address shifts in the professions; in particular, the growing dominance of bureaucracies and responses to the New Woman in Western culture.

These are very different accounts of the female spy than those examined in previous chapters. Whereas *The Avengers*, *The New Avengers* and *The Bionic Woman* offered little evidence of the organisations that employed their protagonists, all three Western versions of Nikita depict her in relation to an espionage bureaucracy. In the 1990s, it appeared, female spies were incorporated into late Western capitalism, offering more cynically postmodern representations of femininity, morality and state powers. In the French *polar* of the late 1980s, police and criminals were almost indistinguishable:

> This type of thriller suggests not just the increasing Americanization of
> French society as French cinema audiences began to be attracted more

to American films, but also a more general amorality prevalent throughout the western world during the materialistic 1980s. Typically, it was women characters who carried the burden for a changing society which no longer quite knew what its identity was in a postmodern and increasingly Americanized environment.

(Powrie 2003: 124)

The Nikita films and television series grew out of and spoke to this moment. In each case, the narrative recounts that she is a drug addict and criminal rehabilitated by an intelligence organisation to serve the state as an elite assassin. This story of capture, reform and incorporation alludes to cultural discomfort with the alleged rise of the female professional. Combining the fetishistic image of the femme fatale with an ongoing narrative about Nikita's emotional life – in particular, her relationship with her agency mentor – each version of Nikita offers an explosive combination of narrative genres and symbolic modes.

The films and television series also offer an exemplary account of current representations of active/violent women as targeting a range of spectators, epitomising shifts in the organisation of cinema and television industries in response to an alleged liberalisation of gender politics. While the New Hollywood appears to offer a more liberal and liberated account of female professionals, Nikita exemplifies the extent to which such representations are still dependent on historical types such as the femme fatale, employing them as a means of marketing films across a range of audiences in a global market. Thomas Austin's account of the marketing of *Basic Instinct* (dir. Paul Verhoeven, 1992) describes that film as a 'dispersible text':

The film's multiple address across genders and diverse sexualities was amplified, and its commercial and social reach extended, by a proliferation of secondary texts. Canonical references to film noir and Hitchcock were stressed in the press pack circulated to journalists, and were picked up in some magazine and broadsheet press reviews. The film's sex, violence and stars were pitched at a wider audience, flagged in television spots, cinema trailers, press advertising and poster art. Invited to approach the film in various ways, prospective spectators were promised these attractions and others, such as a 'whodunit' thriller plot, auteurist touches, glossy visuals, the topicality of Stone's character as a 'post-feminist' New Woman for the 90s, or the 'must-see' appeal of a controversial film which 'everyone' was talking about. The interpretations and uses made of *Basic Instinct* by its audiences often drew on these popular media readings and on criticisms of the film. But real spectators' reactions were far from being confined by such frameworks. The array of secondary texts worked to cue, inform or guide spectatorial interpretations and responses, but never simply determined them.

(Austin 1999: 148)

*Nikita, Point of No Return* and *La Femme Nikita* are borne of the same commercial moment and also tap into this range of address, albeit with differing emphases in each case. This chapter charts some of the hegemonic strategies evident in the films and television series, strategies which evince a late-twentieth-century sensibility regarding the moral authority of state powers, the role of the individual and the position of women in corporate settings. In these fictions, the motives of the secret service are questionable, and the demands and desires of the main protagonists are often in conflict with those of their employers. These narratives of individual rebellion do not, however, inevitably make Nikita a radical figure in any of her incarnations.

## *Nikita* (dir. Luc Besson, 1990)

As with Thomas Austin's account of the marketing of *Basic Instinct*, a number of contexts inform critical understandings of Besson's film and Badham's remake. The most prolifically documented is that of American film noir and Hollywood neo-*noir* cinema of the 1980s and 1990s. The American thrillers which were produced during and after the Second World War, and released en masse in France once the war was over, were recognised by French critics as offering a literal and metaphorical darkness. While films noirs addressed a variety of topics, they tended to represent a corrupt and dysfunctional society, often employing the family as an allegory of wider social ills (Harvey 1998). The most scandalous and charismatic figure in many classic American films noirs from the 1940s to the 1950s was the femme fatale. While the femme fatale had emerged in visual art and theatre of the nineteenth century (see Chapter 2), film noir offered a particularly deadly version of the femme fatale's combination of desire and fear (Doane 1991: 1). In Billy Wilder's *Double Indemnity* (1944), she was a vampiric figure, her face mask-like with pale skin and dark lips. Barbara Stanwyck's performance as Phyllis Dietrichson was one of the most extreme representations of the femme fatale as a manipulative serial killer, drawing the male protagonist into her net and shooting him when he threatened to betray her. The femme fatale of American *noir* in the 1940s was bad through and through – and enough of a stereotype that Rita Hayworth as Gilda in Vidor's 1946 film of that name was able to play against narrative expectations. As police inspector Obregon (Joseph Calleia) says to Johnny Farrell (Glenn Ford), 'Gilda didn't do any of those things you've been losing sleep over – not any of them. It was just an act, every bit of it.' The *noir* femme fatale thus carries a heavy symbolic load; she is a deathly figure who signifies the mutability of identity, her appearance concealing a lack of identity rather than a true self. Such authenticity was often assigned to the male protagonists she destroyed, and the lack of it placed the femme fatale at the centre of *noir* cinema's critique of Western society.

When *noir* stylings were reincarnated in the Hollywood neo-*noirs* of the 1980s and 1990s, the femme fatale was once more at the centre of the plot. Sharon Stone as Catherine Trammell in *Basic Instinct* (dir. Paul Verhoeven, 1992) was an icy blonde who visually referenced Hitchcock's women but had none of their sexual repression. The neo-*noir* femme fatale is all about sexuality, often representing 'deviant' desires and straddling the narrow margin between mainstream cinema and pornography (Stables 1998). Yet the neo-*noir* femme fatale also offers a commentary on the rise of women in the professions, most overtly in *Fatal Attraction* (Adrian Lyne, 1987), where Glenn Close as Alex depicts the female professional as an insecure, sexually frustrated hysteric who quickly turns into a psychotic killer. While some neo-*noirs* offered misogynistic accounts of the New Woman, others were more ambivalent: Kathryn Bigelow's *Blue Steel* (1990) put a female police officer at the centre of the cinematic narrative and presented an *homme fatal* in the psychotic stockbroker who stalks her. With a critical mass of theoretical work on both film noir and the femme fatale behind them, the films of the 1980s and 1990s were self-conscious, often overtly referencing the scenes and styles of classic *noirs* (Erickson 1996). Luc Besson is of this generation of film-makers: aware of the kudos *noir* stylings entail and of the symbolic heritage they offer as a means of social commentary (Tasker 1998: 117).

*Nikita* visually references *noir* from the opening shot of a wet Parisian street lit with neon. Nikita and her fellow junkies march towards the pharmacy to find their fix, but the visual reference to *noir* is quickly combined with other generic styles such as action cinema and the road movie. Critical accounts of the film have noted its range of reference, from the music video and comic strip in its fast-cut aesthetic, to French New Wave directors such as Godard in its radical use of colour (Austin 1996: 130, Hayward 1998: 16, 128). In the context of French cinema studies, Besson's films are classified as *cinéma du look*: 'characterised not by any collective ideology but rather by a technical mastery of the medium, a cinephile tendency to cite from other films and a spectacular visual style (*le look*)' (Austin 1996: 119). Besson is bracketed with other *cinéma du look* directors, such as Jean-Jacques Beineix (*Diva*, 1980) and Léos Carax (*Mauvais Sang*, 1986) but is also differentiated from them as the director 'who has received the most sustained ridicule from the critics while proving a consistent hit with the public' (Austin 1996: 126). Besson, like Beineix and Carax, was critiqued by *Cahiers du Cinéma* for his dependence on 'inferior' popular culture rather than the psychological realism of 'great' French cinema (Austin 1996: 119). Such combinations of high/low art forms and the alleged superficiality of the *cinéma du look* were taken as a sign that political cinema was finished in France; its 'postcard aesthetics' cynically postmodern (Vincendeau 1996: 50). Yet the transcultural referentiality of Besson's work may also be understood as the sign of a new politics, and one which does not merely endorse the superficiality of appearances in the *cinéma du look* but also critiques it. Despite the critical attacks cited above, Besson has also been seen as a 'new moralist of the 1980s and 1990s', particularly in regard to consumer culture (Hayward

1998: 17). In *Nikita*, Besson deploys American popular culture – including film noir – but does so with a critical European eye, often turning the table on transatlantic influences (Powrie 2003: 123).

The visual and narrative references in *Nikita* to both French and American cinema may be read through the use of colour – the opening sequence sets the blue light of the pharmacy against the red night-sights of the armed police called to quell the gang. The red and blue of the French and American flags are already visible, and the white light which presages Nikita's fake death and quasi-rebirth in the cell of the secret service rapidly completes the tricolour. Besson has asserted his desire to combine American and French cinematic styles, and *Nikita* apparently succeeded in this, garnering healthy audiences in France (3.7 million), the USA (3 million) and worldwide (nearly 4 million) (Hayward 1998: 40–1, 52). Yet Anne Parillaud's performance as Nikita does not sit easily with the neo-*noir* femmes fatales of American cinema. Parillaud herself regarded the role as a significant career move – 'it broke the entire baby-doll image I had been dragging behind me' – but if it destroyed this childlike image, it was only to reassert Parillaud's persona as a different kind of youth (Hayward 1998: 55). While she is 'dressed to kill' by her mentor Amande (Jeanne Moreau) in a fetishistic outfit for her first assignment, which references both classic and neo-*noir femmes*, she is not the overtly sexualised woman of the new Hollywood *noirs*.[1] Instead, she appears androgynously pre-pubescent, boyishly gamine in her little black dress, despite her ability to attract and desire both her mentor (Bob, played by Tchéky Karyo) and her boyfriend (Marco, played by Jean-Hughes Anglade). While Nikita is often in disguise, and the viewer gets little sense of her inner life, she is also coded as authentic rather than as a hollow façade. This compromises Nikita's construction as femme fatale as, in classic and neo-*noir* cinema, the male protagonist, however 'dumb', is the source of authenticity (Rich 1995). In Besson's film, however, Nikita's childlike responses are visually and narratively linked to a symbolically 'authentic' youth culture.

The gang with which Nikita is first seen represents a disenfranchised generation of French youth, the alienated *génération Mitterrand*, borne out of a period of economic recession and widespread unemployment during the Mitterrand presidency 1981–95 (Hayward 1998: 25). Nikita's rehabilitation and employment by the state as a government assassin may be read as an ironic allegory of youth training and redeployment which endorses the more cynical responses to Mitterrand's attempts to alleviate youth unemployment in the early 1980s (Hayward 1998: 23–4). Her punk background also gives a different slant to the film's take on the New Woman. If *The Bionic Woman* and *The New Avengers* had attempted to incorporate and adapt feminism in the 1970s, Hollywood continued this strategy through the 1980s and 1990s, specifically through its depiction of women as managers and professionals. French popular culture also pursued this issue, albeit layered within national debate about indigenous French culture and the prevalence of American popular forms:

*Figure 5.1*   Anne Parillaud in *Nikita* (dir. Luc Besson, 1990).

[French] popular culture both reflected and portrayed the maelstrom of sociocultural developments in the 1970s: the films of the period were either American imports or French analyses of the new complexities of – say – relations between men and women, or the difficulties of life in an increasingly post-industrial society.

(Dauncey 2003: 13)

During the 1980s, audiovisual media became a prime platform for and subject of French debates over popular culture and national identity. The freeing up of television and radio broadcasting in 1982 precipitated shifts in the economic organisation of production, with the emphasis on technology and commerce, which have informed Besson's work (Dauncey 2003: 13).

Central to such shifts in political economy and social debate in Europe and in America is the figure of the New Woman. Yvonne Tasker proposes the figure of the 'working girl' or prostitute as a literal and metaphorical allegory of how Hollywood has responded to the New Woman, arguing that sexuality is still central to the ways women are represented in mainstream cinema: 'Across a variety of popular genres, Hollywood representation is characterised by an insistent equation between working women, women's work and some form of sexual(ised) performance' (Tasker 1998: 3). Tasker argues that the New Hollywood has moved the sexually attractive woman of classical Hollywood from the home or social space (bars, dancehalls, etc.) to the workplace (Tasker 1998: 121). *Nikita*, however, is not merely a hyperbolic representation of a working woman but also a redeployment of the female professional in a critical examination of white-collar work. While films such as *Presumed Innocent* (dir. Alan J. Pakula, 1990), *Disclosure* (dir. Barry Levinson, 1994) and *The Last Seduction* (dir. John Dahl, 1993) offer 'a distinct inflection of the [femme fatale] archetype, literalising/embodying the threat of male redundancy whilst retaining the association between working women and sexuality' (Tasker 1998: 5), the Nikita narratives take that equation a step further. These narratives are not only about the rise of women in the professions – or rather male paranoia about that perceived shift in gender roles – they also raise questions about the professional environments which women are beginning to inhabit in more significant numbers. *Nikita* may be understood as a narrative not only of (resistance to) socialisation, as Hayward proposes in her psychoanalytic readings of *Nikita* (Hayward 1997, 1998: 127–68) but also as a narrative of disillusionment. In the films and the television series, the protagonist rejects her employment, her employers and, by extension, the principles on which they work. In each narrative, the organisation – more or less explicitly attached to the state – is shown to be morally questionable, employing Nikita to assassinate targets which are not evidently aggressive. By the time *Nikita* became reinscribed as John Badham's *Point of No Return*, the first Gulf war (1991) had taken place, and American foreign policy was once more under scrutiny. The Nikita narratives are, thus, debates about moral imperatives; most clearly about state violence but also about the (a)morality of bureaucracies. In these late-twentieth-century representations of the workplace – for spies are nothing if not agents of a secret *service* – corporate organisations are figured as complex, compromised and ultimately corrupt.

This is most visible in *Nikita*, as in the American remakes, in its representation of surveillance. Susan Hayward aligns surveillance in Besson's film with French discourses of youth in crisis – the *génération Mitterrand* and fears about social disorder which served to justify forms of social surveillance such as CCTV – and with psychoanalytic theories of the cinematic gaze (Hayward 1998: 80–99). It may also be understood as emblematic of modern bureaucracy. While forms of surveillance such as census have existed since the fifteenth century BC, modernity made it central to all institutions in a manner that pervades every aspect of social life: 'Systematic surveillance … came with the growth of military organization, industrial towns and cities, government administration, and the capitalistic business enterprise within European nation-states' (Lyon 1994: 24). In particular, modern surveillance is concerned with the management of workers within modern bureaucracies (Lyon 1994: 25; see also Dandeker 1990). Bob manages Nikita's training, and his surveillance of her in her room or in training becomes an extension of the camera's point of view. His gaze is enabled by a (post)modern grey workspace of glass and steel; this is a panoptical office without walls where all employees are visible all the time. Once she has graduated and is on assignment, the surveillance implicitly continues so that her employers are able to locate and activate her at any moment. This is the carceral society that Nikita can only escape by disappearing completely, enacting a symbolic death (Foucault 1977: 293–308).

Visible and invisible forms of surveillance have become central to spy fictions in the late twentieth and early twenty-first centuries. In *La Femme Nikita*, the open-plan command centre is overlooked by Operations' glass-panelled eyrie, a workspace replicated in *24* with a central raised glass-walled office within a larger open-plan space. Both *24* and *Alias* employ their glass-panelled offices to narrative effect with shots of the main characters watching each other and being watched. Such set designs reference the Benthamite panopticon and science-fiction cinema in a suitably post-modern combination of early and late modern styles. New communications technologies are also fetishised in spy fictions. In *24*, as in *Casino Royale* (dir. Martin Campbell, 2006), mobile phones become a part of the action, while in *La Femme Nikita*, as in *Alias*, ear-pieces are dispensed with to imply a high-tech communications system that is completely invisible. In the television movie *Jane Doe: Yes I Remember it Well* (dir. Armand Mastroianni, 2006), the central protagonist is a retired secret-service agent called back into the field. Thinking she is being followed by another car, 'Jane' (Lea Thompson) phones her commanding officer and asks if he can use the car's satellite navigation system to track her; he replies that they've already located her via her mobile phone. Contemporary spy fictions depict the technology of surveillance and, in doing so, dramatise a paranoid state which is all seeing.

Modern bureaucracy is, thus, aligned with capitalism, state power and surveillance: 'Like the capitalist enterprise, the modern state is a rational structure of domination and surveillance, in that it comprises a relationship between leaders and led that is mediated by a bureaucracy' (Dandeker 1990: 10). Postmodern spy fictions such as the Nikita narratives, *24* and *Alias* play out this relationship but do not necessarily endorse it. Weber argues that, 'The legitimacy of the modern state rests on the fact that its orders are established and exercised in a way that is recognised to be legal' (Dandeker 1990: 11). While Weber's definition does not entail substantive or ethical legalities such as freedom and democracy, the Nikita narratives are notable for their consistent representation of the secret service acting in an illegal manner. Legality, in Weber's model, recruits a minimal level of consent, which the modern state requires to sustain its bureaucratic system of control, yet, in *Nikita*, the central protagonist is recruited without her consent and in an illegal manner. In order to conscript Nikita, the state first 'kills' her and then gives her no option but to comply under threat of real annihilation. Thus, from the outset, all the Nikita narratives are predicated upon a state that is questionable. The secret service into which Nikita is conscripted is both mundane in its representation of a bureaucratic organisation and sinister in its account of what the organisation does and how it does it. By extension, the state itself is morally redundant, and the Nikita narratives thus (inadvertently) provide a critique of late Western capitalism.

In this light, the reason Nikita is offered for submitting to her new role may only be understood as ironic. When Nikita asks why she should submit to the 'education' Bob describes in the initial scenes in her cell, he responds that she will be educated 'To serve your country.' But serving her country in this case means doing 'wet work' – becoming an assassin for a state that also requires that Nikita does not question its motives: 'she is obliged to recycle her murdering skills within the legitimate arena of the State – more specifically within the arena of France's Secret Service, surely *the* institutional centre of the centre (within the social order, the law), *the* eye of the society of surveillance' (Hayward 1998: 87). Serving one's country is offered as an outmoded ideal in all the Nikita narratives, where countries are no longer ideologically unified or morally accountable. The interests of multinational corporations have inflected the nation-state, and the Nikita narratives offer a critique of this shift; the secret service is no longer driven by a government concerned with the welfare of its subjects but by a state engaged in global commerce. Nikita, in each version, is not recruited but conscripted; her very employment puts the state apparatus in question. How can one endorse a system that is so clearly undemocratic, so clearly dependent on violence? The figure of the spy – and, most pointedly, a female spy – is called into play in all three versions to offer a perspective on state organisations that are dehumanised and dehumanising. In *Nikita* and *Point of No Return*, Nikita and Maggie both assert that Bob is damaged by his work: in the Besson film, Nikita says, 'You're sick Bob … your job's a sewer for you' and accuses him of sadism. The emphasis on service, on work and training – on a promotional structure, as Nikita moves on to bigger tasks each time – widens the scope of this commentary to include corporate bureaucracies.

If serving one's country is outmoded, then so is the ideal of serving the company. In all the Nikita narratives, serving one's country has been absorbed into the interests of the corporation. Bob is a company man, whose only aberration appears to be his affection for Nikita. In Besson's film, Bob is initially a humourless, efficient government servant, but his encounters with Nikita break through that carapace to reveal a vulnerable masculinity. Witness, on the one hand, his evident delight at Nikita's unorthodox early responses to combat training, and on the other, his devastation at her assertion that she will never kiss him again. Nikita is a redemptive figure for Bob, but while she asserts that Bob is 'sick', she tells Marco that he is a 'beautiful person'. Marco is Bob's opposite: shy, vulnerable and completely loving. Whereas Bob is a cog in the corporate machine, Marco is an ineffective supermarket cashier, who gives up his job to become a boatbuilder. If Nikita is a version of the New Woman, Marco is an account of the much-derided New Man. He is the one who taught her to smile, Nikita says, not Amande. Amande's demand that Nikita perform femininity through a vacuous grin clearly requires that she fake it. In this way, *Nikita* sets authentic emotion – expressed by Nikita before *and* after her training – against the roles she is taught to perform. Corporate culture requires not only that Nikita look a certain way but also that she expresses only the right emotion at the right time. White-collar bureaucracy and bourgeois femininity are aligned here as something to be mastered and then rejected.

Despite this critical approach to bureaucracies, *Nikita, Point of No Return* and *La Femme Nikita* (and later *Alias*) offer pleasurable depictions of the working environment as one of clean efficiency and organisation – a rational world. Recent television series, such as *CSI: Crime Scene Investigation* and its franchises, offer similarly pleasurable depictions of rational, dedicated teams of individuals who subsume their personal lives into the world of work and science in search of a higher, purer truth. As the producers of *La Femme Nikita* comment in their DVD commentary on the first episode, both reviewers and fans rapidly understood the series as 'an extreme version of what it's like to go to the office every day' (see also Britton 2004: 260). Yet these spy narratives, which centre on female protagonists, also depict the rational bureaucratic world of work as oppressive systems to be negotiated and resisted. These hegemonic depictions of work offer viewers a perversely pleasurable account of white-collar labour in late Western capitalism, where information is the main currency. Besson's *Nikita* sets off this narrative stream, and the remakes take it in different directions by placing it within other national and media contexts. These accounts of transformation, incorporation and disillusionment offer a useful commentary, not only on white-collar bureaucracies but also on the female professional.

Women in the professions have had a chequered history on screen; as characters who combine femininity and authority, they are always already-ambiguous figures, contradicting the traditional formation of femininity as powerless and passive. Amelia Jones describes how such women are punished in mainstream Hollywood cinema: 'The intensity with which these films work to mutilate or reincorporate the characters who represent a new femininity suggests that the new woman is a highly threatening figure to a still extant, if floundering, fantasy of the nuclear family' (Jones 1991: 298). The Nikita narratives, however, offer a version of the New Woman who is not simply 'mutilated' nor fully 'reincorporated'. In each version, Nikita represents a challenge to the symbolic order – a deviant, androgynous female – who is apparently reincorporated through her grooming as an agent and as a fully feminised woman and then rejects the role she has been trained to play. In Besson's film, the targets she is assigned to kill are not anarchic or even apparently deviant, but simply foreign: 'The violent elements in society, tamed, are to be used not to repress violence, then, but difference' (Smith 2001: 31). In walking out of the frame, away from Bob and Marco, Nikita refuses to repress difference – either her own wild femininity or the targets chosen by the state. This is the radical, pleasurable element of the Nikita narratives, and while that element is not unmitigated, it still offers potential pleasures.

## *Point of No Return* (dir. John Badham, 1993)

> *Nikita* presents itself as a fantasy about 'justice', seen as the neutralisation of a danger to all the values of an ordered society, a danger constructed by the film in the first sequence. This fantasy, however, is not unequivocally endorsed by the film at any time and, indeed, is more and more clearly shown to contain within itself elements which negate it.
>
> (Smith 2001: 29)

'Justice' is a central thread running through all the Nikita narratives – as through all thrillers – and in the two American remakes that succeeded *Nikita* on film and television, justice appears increasingly equivocal. *Point of No Return* and *La Femme Nikita* both go beyond Besson's *Nikita* in questioning the state organisation by which the protagonist is conscripted. *Point of No Return* distinguishes itself from *Nikita* by placing the action at the heart of American national politics, with opening shots of Capitol Hill, and by recreating Nikita as Maggie (Bridget Fonda), an American protagonist who moves from East to West Coast. In its locations as in its protagonist, *Point of No Return* is fully Americanised, and this extends to a more emphatic connection between the agency which conscripts Maggie and the US government and judicial system. Unlike the Bob character in *Nikita*, Bob (Gabriel Byrne) in *Point of No Return* is visibly present in the courtroom as Maggie is sentenced and is also at the scene of her 'execution'. This does not, however, lend Badham's film an unequivocally radical edge as an indictment of American justice, for Maggie as an American protagonist is inevitably located within a cinematic history in which the renegade individual has an impressive genealogy. Maggie's idiosyncrasy resides only in the fact that she is female, rather than male; and even this has become a new variant on old stereotypes in 1990s Hollywood.

In addition to the cinematic contexts that informed *Nikita*, *Point of No Return* may also be understood in relation to a new type of Hollywood product which centres on violent female protagonists. By the late 1990s, feminist academics were responding to a new kind of fatal woman on screen – a woman who kills for all the 'right' reasons rather than the femme fatale who kills for all the wrong ones – with a range of studies (see, for example, Tasker 1998, Inness 1999 and 2004, Read 2000, McCaughey and King 2001). As Jacinda Read argues, in her succinct account of these discussions, the debate has often been tied to two binary axes: the alignment of masculinity-activity/femininity-passivity and an oppositional account of feminism and femininity (Read 2004: 205–10). Such binaries are difficult to sustain in the face of the New Hollywood, or what Thomas Schatz describes as 'the "new" New Hollywood' (2004: 7). Critical accounts of Hollywood cinema have come to acknowledge a shift in aesthetics in the late 1960s and early 1970s towards a more art-house style of film-making, in part as a consequence of the foreign films imported to American audiences in the 1950s and 1960s. Schatz cites Japanese, Italian and British cinemas as influential sources, but French New Wave directors also had an impact on emerging American film-makers such as Martin Scorsese. The Hollywood New Wave of the 1960s, like the French New Wave, was attuned to the emerging youth cultures and political movements of that era. Another shift is visible in the 1980s with the emergence of a 'new' New Hollywood, which Schatz characterises: 'with its commercially savvy producer-auteurs like Lucas and Spielberg, its obsession with big-budget blockbusters and multi-media franchises, its multiplexes and younger-skewed youth market, its increasingly stabilized ratings system, its ever-growing ancillary markets and a resurgent "studio system" geared to an era of global media consumption' (Shatz 2004: 7–8).

This is the context in which Badham's *Point of No Return* was released in 1993. As a faithful remake of Besson's film, it gestured towards the politics and aesthetics of the 1960s New Hollywood, while as commodity ripe for television adaptation it was very much part of the 'new' New Hollywood Schatz describes above. At this moment, in this form, 'Nikita' became a brand, with the willing cooperation of Besson, who approved the American remake (Hayward 1998: 54). Warner Brothers bought the rights to *Nikita* to make *Point of No Return* and went on to produce *La Femme Nikita*; footage from Badham's film (such as the explosion in the kitchen and Maggie's exit through the rubbish chute, copied from *Nikita*) were recycled in the opening episode of the television series.

The Nikita narratives thus represent an alliance of left aesthetics and cor-porate multinationals. As with the deployment of liberal politics in 1970s series such as *The Bionic Woman*, commercial film and television are more than happy to depict anti-establishment renegades if that is what sells. In this sense, these products are always already politically compromised; incorporated into the marketplace of late Western capitalism. The contra-dictions between what the narratives represent and the contexts of their production and distribution remain startling, however. They each raise a number of questions, not least because of the differences between the three versions. In Badham's film, one notable difference from Besson's *Nikita* is the stress on Maggie's feminine education. Unlike *Nikita*, where there are only two scenes regarding Nikita's transformation from androgynous punk to chic femininity – and these scenes only feature Nikita and Amande – *Point of No Return* offers a series of sequences regarding Maggie's accul-turation. While this begins with an individual consultation with Amanda (Anne Bancroft), it also extends to group lessons where Maggie is taught posture, elocution and how to behave at a dinner party. Amanda also pro-vides her with a phrase that Maggie eventually employs when confronted with the full horror of Victor's role as 'cleaner':

> AMANDA: What do you do when you're uncomfortable? When you're angry or scared?
> MAGGIE: I hit.

AMANDA: You might want to try smiling. Just smile a little smile and say
  something offhand. It doesn't have to fit the situation really. Say …
  say 'I never did mind about the little things.'
(MAGGIE is silent.)
AMANDA: *Say it!*
(MAGGIE tries to move away, but AMANDA, with a roar, grabs her arm.)
AMANDA: Please dear. The smile and the sentence.
MAGGIE: I never did mind … I never did mind about the little things.

Amanda literally puts words into Maggie's mouth, a phrase that is later
used in the most incongruous circumstances. This airy dictum represents
not only Maggie's rebirth as a properly smiling, 'feminine' woman but also
her reinvention as a middle-class professional. *Point of No Return* places
more emphasis than *Nikita* on Maggie's acquisition of feminine skills, and
these skills are evidently classed as well as gendered. In this sense, the masquerade which Maggie's transformation makes visible is, like Nikita in Besson's film, comparable to other Pygmalion fictions (Grindstaff 2001). Jeffrey
A. Brown contrasts *Point of No Return* with *Educating Rita* (dir. Lewis
Gilbert, 1983) and *Pretty Woman* (dir. Garry Marshall, 1990) on the
grounds that these films are more about class transformations than Badham's film (Brown 1996: 67). Yet, Maggie's transformation is about class as
it maps her movement from anarchic street person and drug addict into the
role of the professional. In the sequence where Maggie shows her 'finished'
self, she is not only visually transformed into acceptable white femininity (as
was Nikita), but also socially transformed, in her ability to speak gramma-
tically correct American English and fluent French. The acquisition of such
language skills gives Maggie the appearance of a refined education and an
aura of social sophistication – she gains cultural capital. As in Besson's film,
Maggie's transformation sequences make explicit the labour involved in
(re)producing white middle-class femininity. This transformation is given an
additional twist in Badham's film as Bridget Fonda, playing Maggie, comes
from a famous Hollywood dynasty.

The American remake of *Nikita* is interesting for these minor differences;
on release, it was recognised as a largely slavish reproduction of the original
(see, for example, Brown 1996: 63, Durham 1998: 175–7). Carolyn Durham
argues that the sexual relationship between Maggie and Bob is more highly
eroticised in *Point of No Return*, but its perversity is downplayed, as Bob's
parental role is not as evident as in *Nikita* (Durham 1998: 176). The eroti-
cisation of Maggie is along the lines of the neo-*noir* femme fatale, as her
sexuality – particularly in relation to Bob – is far cruder and more overt
than in Besson's film. It is signified through 'sexualized speech', a prime
characteristic of the new *fatale* for whom talking about sex is graphically
aligned with sexual acts (Stables 1998: 174–8). Maggie first cites her name
as 'Maggie Blowjob' and her translation of Nina Simone's 'Put a Little
Sugar in My Bowl' is, 'She's just saying, "Ooh baby, stick it in me twice a

day and I'll do anything for you. I'll lick the ground you walk on.'" Yet this does not appear to represent any authentic desire on Maggie's part. Both these exchanges are with male characters symbolic of state control: her police interrogator and Bob. Outside state institutions, however, Maggie is similarly unsexed. Her boyfriend, J.P. – the equivalent of the Marco character in Besson's film – says that living with her 'is like living with a ghost', and this comment offers a tacit summary of Fonda's performance. Maggie is, in every sense, a 'spook'. Where Anne Parillaud's Nikita is feral and lively, Fonda's Maggie always appears to be faking it. There is no *jouissance* in the American remake; rather, this is a disillusioned rebel who drifts through the film as an absence, an *aporia*. Maggie's final disappearance into the mist is emblematic of her role throughout the film; she is barely present. This makes *Point of No Return* more problematic than *Nikita*; whereas Parillaud's performance speaks of wildness in Nikita's raucous moments of glee, Fonda's Maggie is barely alive. Yet the ethereal quality of Fonda's performance also aligns femininity with artifice, femininity as masquerade. Maggie is always and only performing, thus offering a different critique of the cultural conditions from which she emerges to that in *Nikita*.

Both *Nikita* and *Point of No Return* may be termed postmodern films, but the former evokes a revolutionary postmodernity – the deconstruction of cultural hierarchies – while the latter suggests a more reactionary postmodernity of hopelessness and *ennui*. Where Nikita is shown in her spray-painted cell watching an old black-and-white costume drama, Maggie watches MTV. *Point of No Return*'s landscape is that of social and cultural pastiche, in Jameson's sense of the word (1988: 15–16). There is no common language here, no authentic traditions or gestures on which Maggie can call, only depthless imitation. *Point of No Return* problematises the linear trajectory of the remake (from original to copy) because it was based on a film that was already American in style: 'All creations involve re-creations, and all presentations re-presentations' (Grindstaff 2001: 151). The film's use of Nina Simone as a soundtrack gestures towards some vaguely historical authenticity, but even this device is evidently flawed, as a skinny white woman professes her liking for the work of a black singer with civil-rights credentials. Maggie likes Nina Simone because her mother would play the records, and this background, like the film's cinematic source, offer an artificial 'taste' of difference, of other cultures beyond white America. 'Nina' is also her codename for assignments, rather than the 'Josephine' of *Nikita* and *La Femme Nikita*, as a reference to the music Maggie describes as 'so passionate, so savage.' Black American music is thus reduced to yet another element of cultural capital, yet another element of the film's 'multiple address' (Austin 1999: 148). In this sense, critical responses which saw Badham's remake as a hollow copy arguably miss the point, because the point of *Point of No Return* is that there is no original, authentic source to call upon. This pessimistic reading echoes both films' account of professional bureaucracies as hollow and life-denying. Nikita/Maggie is literally an assassin, but the state agency for which she works is killing by more subtle means.

In all these versions, espionage is a simulation of corporate business; the office sets of the agency (symbolically located below ground in both films and the television series) replicate the open-plan offices, hierarchies and promotional structures of multinational corporations. Such fictions offer a fetishised account of white-collar labour as glamorous and important – the office worker as government agent, as part of a whole which is impacting on world politics, and all the while looking stylish and in control. The literal connections between office work and espionage here feed into fantasies of agency in situations where agency is often unavailable; the office worker as assassin, as spy, becomes someone more important than a cog in a paper machine. Yet, these narratives also present Nikita as a double agent within the secret organisation; she is not fully incorporated, does not fully believe in her assigned role. While the environment is postmodern, the Nikita narratives evince a modern desire for authenticity. In all her guises, Nikita is rehabilitated to become a good worker, a professional woman, learning to dress and pass as a white middle-class operative, but the organisation is questioned and questionable. In *Nikita*, she rejects her role as assassin of difference; in *Point of No Return*, Maggie also rejects the homogeneity of the organisation that recruits her. In these films, corporate life requires its workers to become grey and undifferentiated; Maggie is taught to be the same but rejects sameness. Her story fits with ideologies of American individualism; as the renegade, the rebel, she refuses to be incorporated. The irony is that, in an American context, Hollywood itself is bounded by corporate capital, and the renegade thus becomes a saleable item. The films and the television series all endorse the individual as source of authenticity and agency, a mythology embedded in Western culture; the only wrinkle here is that the individual is female, and a female protagonist has rarely had such cultural weight behind her.

## *La Femme Nikita* (1997–2001)

In her transition from film to television, Nikita traces shifts in the landscape of visual media. Just as *Point of No Return* may be understood in terms of 'new New Hollywood', so *La Femme Nikita* may be understood within the context of New Television. While the link between Hollywood cinema and television was not new, it entered a new phase in the 1990s: 'In contrast with the present moment, earlier stages of television might be usefully designated as Live Television, Filmed-series Television and "Quality" Television' (Moran 2005: 291). Because of changes in the technologies of transmission and reception, we are now in the era of New Television, characterised by 'the rapid multiplication of services of every kind' (Moran 2005: 292) and marking a distinct break from the histories of centralised broadcasting focused on British and American markets. The multiplication of channels, networks, forms of broadcast and distribution have opened the industry to new corporate interests, both within the industry and from related sectors, such as computing and newspapers. Concurrent developments in interactive media, such as computers and mobile phones, have further changed the ways in which television is consumed and have opened up greater potential to cater for specific interests (Moran 2005: 292–3).

Contemporary spy series overtly reference such shifts through their use of computer and communications technology. One has only to consider how *24*'s Jack Bauer employs his mobile phone. *La Femme Nikita*, also produced by *24*'s Joel Surnow, introduced this emphasis on new technologies with spectacular visuals such as the holographic screen employed during briefing sessions, as well as the more mundane image of characters frequently working at computer consoles. In the producers' DVD commentary on the opening episode, they describe the set design for Section One as 'five minutes into the future' with a 'no paper' aesthetic. While the intention may have been to make the series appear futuristic, it also represents a stylish version of contemporary office space. As the series progressed, computer-screen graphics often overlaid live-action shots, implying the scope of Section One's surveillance and the pervasiveness of information technology. In this way, like the films that preceded it, *La Femme Nikita* represents white-collar work as primarily engaged with new technologies; several episodes feature virtual-reality devices and even, in 'Getting Out of Reverse' (Series 4, Episode 1, 9 January 2000), a holographic Michael (the equivalent of the Bob character in the films). The use of information technology is a logical step for a programme about espionage, yet, like other American television series that represent the professions (such as *ER* and *CSI*), *La Femme Nikita* also fetishises the accoutrements of labour, so that the style of the series becomes paramount.

*La Femme Nikita* was rapidly noted for its stylish aesthetic, with an emphasis on the visual representation of the secret service that conscripts Nikita – here called Section One – and on the framing and costumes of its lead characters (Tung 2004: 97–8). The Australian Peta Wilson was cast as Nikita for her non-American accent, as was the French-Canadian actor Roy Dupuis, who played Michael, the series equivalent of the Bob character in the two films. Only one of the six central characters – Operations (Eugene Glazer) – was played by an American actor. *La Femme Nikita* was shot in Toronto, which, Surnow claims in his DVD commentary for 'Mercy' (Series 1, Episode 22, 5 October 1997), gave the outside broadcast sequences a fresh and European feel, as the city had rarely been used as a location for American television series. In these ways, the series is given an international quality designed to offer a taste of sophistication to home audiences and potentially making the programme more exportable as a product which is not easily classifiable *as* American. This transcultural chic is naturally linked to class as to race. The series looked European, looked 'classy' and offered a beguilingly hyperreal account of white-collar labour.

Symbolically, the producers decided not to have a literal communications system for agents on assignment but rather have the actors speak as if they can be heard, an 'invisible' earpiece that *really* isn't there. The style of *La Femme Nikita* thus offers a fetishistic account of white-collar work, replicating the glamour and social aspiration of the professions. The class aspirations of the narrative also extended to race aspirations, as in Peta Wilson, Nikita reaches her apogee as an Aryan figure: athletic, blonde and blue-eyed. In this series, as in the earlier films, white Europeans do white-collar work. While *Point of No Return* gave Maggie several African American colleagues, *La Femme Nikita* featured few non-European characters. Black actors rarely appear, and the few roles for Asian or Asian American actors (such as Michael's wife Simone in Episode 3 of the first season, members of terrorist groups or characters in the background of scenes in Section One) tend to conform to stereotypes of helplessness and inactivity (Tung 2004: 116). In its representation of Section One and Nikita as glamorous and efficient, as in the homogeneously Eurocentric focus of its casting, *La Femme Nikita* offers an account of professional lives that are unproblematically corporate and incorporated. Like the films, however, the television series also examines the cost of the work in which Section One and Nikita are engaged. From the first episode, where the back story of Nikita's recruitment is quickly glossed, she is placed at the moral centre of the series.

In contrast to the films, this Nikita is *falsely* accused of killing a police officer; each credit sequence shows her being discovered with a bloody knife, but as the opening episode makes clear, she has stumbled upon the crime scene and is thus not a killer at the outset. While this shift in Nikita's back story is driven by the constraints of network television – a prime-time protagonist who is a killer being perceived as problematic – it also lends weight to her moral dilemma. In the television series, Nikita is not so effective an assassin. In a number of episodes, such as 'Mercy', Nikita refuses to kill in cold blood and thereby puts Section One at risk, forcing Michael to cover for her. Consequently, the morals of Section One itself are consistently under scrutiny. In her essay on the series, Charlene Tung argues:

> While Nikita may continuously question the killing Section One engages in, the viewers do not. We are to see that Section One is the only thing between us (the West) and chaos. Taken from this perspective, the show is anything but transgressive, relying as it does on Western imperialist discourses.
>
> (Tung 2004: 107)

Yet, *La Femme Nikita* does not offer its viewers such a unitary position on the activities of Section One. From the outset, with Nikita being *mistakenly* recruited as an innocent rather than a natural-born killer, the television series presents Section One as fallible; it makes mistakes. Throughout its five seasons, the ethics of this secret service are questioned, in part through the emotional response and moral position of Nikita herself but also through revelations about the techniques Section One employs to gain information.

The character of Madeline (Alberta Watson) is central to this questioning. Madeline is *La Femme Nikita*'s version of Amande in Besson's film and Amanda in *Point of No Return*, an older woman employed by Section One to convert Nikita from street punk to glamorous young woman. In the first episode, the scene in front of the mirror from the films is replayed, with Madeline saying, 'There's no weapon as powerful as your femininity.' Yet even here, a conflict emerges: when Madeline asserts, 'They own you now', Nikita replies, 'I didn't know I was for sale.' The punk rebellion of Nikita against the totalitarian regime of Section One is rapidly established and becomes a central theme within the series. Nikita is constantly battling for freedom, to escape from Section One and its surveillance, while Operations and Madeline work to confound her efforts. That the series was partly inspired by cult 1960s series *The Prisoner* comes as no surprise.[2] There is a Freudian structure to the drama, with Madeline becoming increasingly significant; in the first episode, Michael tells Nikita before her first meeting with Madeline that he is taking her to meet her 'new mother', and Madeline tells Nikita, 'We're family now.' In the fourth season ('No One Lives Forever,' Series 4, Episode 8, 12 March 2000), Nikita is told that Operations is her father, a plot twist which is a logical extension of the familial structure of Section One. By Season 5, Nikita learns that her *real* father is 'Mr Jones' (Edward Woodward), the mysterious head of Center. While this mystery over Nikita's origins lends itself to a psychoanalytic reading of the series, it also emphasises the hegemonic power of masculinity. One father figure is easily replaced by another so that the system that entraps Nikita is all-pervasive and inescapable. The family is linked to the bureaucracy of Section One, which, in turn, is linked to state power. Nikita and Madeline are caught up in this power structure, and, while Nikita fights to escape and Madeline plots to entrap her, both are emblematic of the New Woman within late Western capitalism.

As the series progresses, Madeline becomes increasingly compromised. During the first season, it emerges that while her role involves psychologically monitoring the operatives in Section One, particularly Nikita, Madeline's job also involves the torture and interrogation of enemy agents. Although she does not do the dirty work herself, it is Madeline who appears at the beginning and end of interrogation scenes, often introducing a pair of besuited torturers, male and female, who carry metal cases and leave their subjects slumped and docile. These ordinary, sinister figures do something unspecified to their victims, leaving two small incisions under their eyes. Physical and psychological torture is implied but not shown, and Madeline is the commanding officer in this scenario. Throughout the series, Section One subjects enemy agents to torture, and innocent bystanders are caught in the crossfire during active operations. This inevitably distresses Nikita:

'Section let those people get slaughtered. Who are these butchers we're working for Michael?' ('Love', Series 1, Episode 6, 17 February 1997). By the fourth season, Nikita's lack of distress at such slaughter is seen as evidence of her successful 'reprogramming' at Madeline's hands. Right from the start, Madeline is the voice of Section One's (lack of) ethics: 'Shades of grey. There's no such thing as the enemy any more. As long as Bauer [a dealer in chemical weapons] is willing to play both sides of the fence, we'll continue to do business' ('Love', Series 1, Episode 6, 17 February 1997). From the outset, Section One's 'business' is compromised, shown to be ethically and morally unsound. Nikita's resistance to Section One's demands, and her on-off relationship with Michael, sets an Orwellian humanity against the needs of Big Brother. 'Gambit' (Series 1, Episode 14, 29 June 1997) opens with Madeline engaging in a homicidal scenario in virtual reality, effectively aligning the new technologies which saturate Section One's activities with its moral redundancy.[3] Madeline faces the cliché of psychological profilers in television drama when in this episode her opponent, Gregor Koestler, says they are the same. Yet unlike many detective series (such as *Millennium* or *Cracker*) where the moral distinction between detective and criminal is made clear, *La Femme Nikita* constantly reminds its audience of Section One's lack of ethics. Madeline and Operations often consider killing, or 'cancelling', their own agents, including, at various points, Nikita and Michael. In 'Treason' (Series 1, Episode 7, 24 February 1997), Nikita asks what happens to older agents, and Madeline's response – that it's 'highly classified' – implies that they are simply disposed of. This leads into a story regarding one of Nikita's colleagues, Roger, being blackmailed by an enemy organisation which has kidnapped his son. The child is returned to his adoptive parents and never discovers that Roger is his real father, but the episode closes with the revelation that Roger has been 'cancelled' because he betrayed Section One.

Section One's scant regard for the lives of its operatives, together with its disregard of their human rights, offers a scathing critique of both the espionage bureaucracy and the powers that support it. Section One's ethics – that the requirements of Section One are paramount and that any and all its operatives may be sacrificed for its survival – are those of a totalitarian state. Section One displays many of the characteristics of Orwell's Big Brother, yet this is an American agency with links to the CIA. In its cynical account of American intelligence agencies, *La Femme Nikita* is post-Watergate and pre-9/11. Arguably, the series' dark view of American politics derives from the perspective of its Canadian-based production team, offering an external commentary on a near-neighbour (Takacs 2005: 154). Yet, while the show is 'a veritable postmodern pastiche of intercultural referents' (Grindstaff 2001: 162), the profits go back to Warner Brothers, the kind of organisation that *La Femme Nikita* appears to critique. In this way, narrative agency is counterbalanced by economic determinism in a hegemonic strategy that deploys 'radical' politics in the service of containment. In the economic realpolitik of the television series, as in its internal storyline, the status quo remains. Internally, in its account of Section One and its use of information technologies, and externally, in its production and marketing, *La Femme Nikita* is, thus, an exemplary account of the new television and the new economy. It is also an account of women's position within that economy through its representation of Nikita as a woman constantly fighting to escape incorporation – and here, unlike the films, constantly failing – and in its representation of Madeline as a professional woman profoundly implicated in the darker dealings of the agency.

Stacy Takacs defines the 'New Economy' as a particularly American phenomenon, closely linked to new technologies:

> Technology, enthusiasts contend, has enabled corporations to decentralize their networks of production and distribution, institute 'flexible' labor relations, and specialize production and delivery, thereby distributing goods and services to consumers more efficiently. Unlike the older, more sluggish, mass-production economy, this New Economy would evade the crises of overproduction that stall economic growth and achieve virtually unlimited expansion.
>
> (Takacs 2005: 148)

Those who support this 'electronic capitalism' advocate its democratic ethos, its potential to transform the workplace and distribute its profits through the 'trickle-down' effect of laissez-faire economics. The social responsibility of the state for its citizens is replaced by multinational corporations competing within a global market (Takacs 2005: 148–50). While the New Economy is often sold (in the UK as in the USA) on the basis of individual rights, its effect on those at the bottom of the economy becomes ever more evident. Takacs argues that the original broadcasts of *La Femme Nikita* (1997–2001) coincide with the booming New Economy in the USA: 'Unlike New Economic discourse, however, the program emphasizes the desocializing effects of a networked society in which power is deterritorialized and dispersed but omnipresent' (2005: 152). In her incorporation into Section One – ultimately moving beyond it as head of Center – Nikita represents the ideal subject of electronic capitalism. She is self-surveilling, has no life other than Section One and is willing to 'cancel' any opposition: 'like the common labourer under electronic-capitalism ... her subjection reveals the negative impact of the New Economy on the lives of individual workers' (Takacs 2005: 165).

There is a deep irony in this account of a glossy television series read as a neo-Marxist account of labour relations, yet Takacs' argument is convincing. If anything, Nikita's haute-couture outfits and the stylish sets, together with statutory music-video action sequences, underline the extent to which the glossy surfaces of late Western capitalism disguise the poverty of groups beyond the white middle class. In these terms, *La Femme Nikita*'s 'whiteness' is completely appropriate, as is the protagonist's visual framing as a femme fatale:

> The femme fatale has typically responded to her reduction to an image-commodity by inhabiting the role and turning it to her advantage. An astute information processor, she becomes the ideal postindustrial laborer whose behavior, nonetheless, reveals some of the cracks in the monolith of the New Economy and its Empire of control.
>
> (Takacs 2005: 166)

*La Femme Nikita* coincides with, and comments upon, not only 'New Television' and the New Economy but also the New Feminism. I take this term from the title of Natasha Walter's book about a necessary shift in feminist thought away from the second-wave feminisms of the 1960s and 1970s rooted in Left politics and towards a more commercially viable 'new' feminism which is allegedly less constricting (Walter 1998). Walter is an English author, but her work echoes that of American writers such as Naomi Wolf, Katie Roiphe, Christina Hoff Sommers and Camille Paglia. All emerged in the early 1990s and rode a wave of publicity fuelled by the 'scandal' of feminism being attacked from within. While such accounts of the second wave were often unrecognisable, they brought debates about gender to the media table and also inspired a number of academic publications and conferences on the state of feminist praxis in the 1990s. Bonnie Dow summarises the New Feminism advocated by the American authors in the following terms:

> All see feminism strangling in the grip of an ideology that claims all women are passive victims of sexual violence, economic exploitation, beauty images, or sexual harassment (in particular, they share a profound distaste for antipornography feminists such as Catherine MacKinnon and Andrea Dworkin, to whom they attribute hegemonic power over feminist ideology). All reject difference feminism and claim for women the right to be as sexually aggressive and power seeking as men are presumed to be, and all have a tendency to cite the discourse of academic feminists as evidence of the feminist 'party line' they are critiquing. Finally, all of these authors are privileged, well-educated white women, and they clearly presume their target audience to be much like themselves.
>
> (Dow 1996: 203)

The Nikita narratives ironically reveal the consequences of such New Feminism in their accounts of femininity and incorporation. The two films and the television series indicate the lack of room for women in the new economy. Nikita, in all her incarnations, is required to perform white middle-class femininity (albeit while shooting people) while remaining under the surveillance and control of the agency that recruits her. Her only escape, in the films, is to disappear from sight, to go underground and escape the gaze of the screen, the social gaze of Bob and his superiors. New Feminism is anti-collective, pro-individualism, but the Nikita narratives reveal the consequences of such strategies: entrapment and coercion or a symbolic death. Bonnie Dow critiques the white middle-class heroines of prime-time television for being what the New Feminists would regard as ideal role models: 'As these critics describe it, feminism is being undermined by an emphasis on collective victimization, and the individualism that has always ruled television's representations is precisely what they claim the movement needs' (Dow 1996: 210–11). *La Femme Nikita* indicates the limits of such individualism and, as the series progresses, Madeline represents the destination of women who align themselves with corporate power; she is absorbed by it and becomes Nikita's greatest threat. By the final series, Madeline is dead, and Nikita has been conscripted to become head of Center. There is no feminist future here.

# 6 *Alias*

## Quality television and the working woman

At the beginning of the twenty-first century, spies in television series such as *Spooks* and *24* represent a hyperreal vision of corporate professionals within a homogenously affluent, postmodern milieu. This chapter finally focuses on a single television series; *Alias* (2001–6) is the most recent and most hyperbolic account of the woman spy. Sydney Bristow is a fantastic representation of the new New Woman in twenty-first-century economies of white-collar labour. She is fetishised as a femme fatale – an active woman who kills – yet also occupies the role of central protagonist and moral touchstone. In this, *Alias* continues the debate begun by *La Femme Nikita*, and the two series have much in common – not least the drama around Sydney and Nikita's parentage. As a far more successful series, however, *Alias* (re)negotiates its version of the spy as New Woman across discourses of American quality television, placing Sydney in debate with the new New Hollywood and the new femmes fatales. As a postmodern figure in a postmodern medium, Sydney takes the discussion regarding women spies as representations of New Women in the New Economy to its limit. *Alias*, like the Nikita narratives, may be read as feminist and reactionary at the same time. This chapter does not attempt to claim either position as a final destination for the series, even after its demise in 2006, but seeks to map the means by which it keeps a foot in every camp, satisfying no one but its producers in their hope of garnering the largest audience for their product.

Like *La Femme Nikita*, *Alias* offers an intricately plotted version of the female spy. Sydney is a college student recruited by SD6, a division of the CIA, as an intelligence agent engaged on international missions that require her to adopt a range of glamorous disguises. Her father also works for SD6, and during the first series, she discovers that SD6 is not the CIA but an enemy agency engaged in selling secrets to the highest bidder. Sydney approaches the CIA with this information and is recruited as a double agent – like her father. The production values of the series, together with its complex storylines, make *Alias* a typical example of American 'quality' programming within the new television economy (Moran 2005). Like other American 'quality' series featuring a female protagonist (such as *Ally McBeal* or *Buffy the Vampire Slayer*), *Alias* focuses on the conflicts of

Sydney's professional and emotional lives. As the series progresses, Sydney not only works with her father, Jack Bristow, but also with her mother, Irina Derevko, and her half-sister, Nadia, and is often engaged in conflict with her aunts, Yekaterina and Elena Derevko. In its representation of post-Cold War espionage and familial relationships, *Alias* straddles the drama series and soap serial, with long-term story arcs as well as short-term gratification in its episodic action sequences. While the series offers scopophilic pleasure in seeing Sydney in a range of fetishistic costumes and Hong Kong-style action sequences, the plot centres on her relationships with family, friends and CIA 'handler'. *Alias* attempts to rationalise and efface the contradictions of public and private demands on the female professional, consequently opening up gaps and elisions in the series' internal logic; not least in the juxtaposition of fast-paced action and soft-focus melodrama. The series is also an evocation of contradictions inherent in American white middle-class femininity, played out in the continuous procession of revelations about Sydney in which her family background is entwined with sinister machinations by intelligence agencies. In this way, *Alias* relates the personal to the political, the familial with the social and the private family dynamic to the public question of American state governance. *Alias* offers a range of (feminist) reading positions to its viewers: it can be read as a celebratory account of 'post-feminist' agency, as a fetishistic representation of the female professional, or as a contradictory narrative which makes explicit the mismatch between femininity and power. Like much quality television, the series' self-conscious multiplicity of address renders it available to a variety of interpretations.

## Spy series as quality television

Spy series in the twenty-first century have become a staple of prime-time television drama (Britton 2004: 252–5). In Britain, there is currently *Spooks* (BBC, 2002–), together with a range of historical dramas about spies and spying, such as *The Cambridge Spies* (BBC, 2003), which returned to the story of Blunt, Burgess and MacLean. Such dramas address mythologies of nation and identity; at once questioning such mythologies, in their narratives of treachery and betrayal, and shoring them up, through a nostalgic account of 'traditional' values. On British television, contemporary series stand in the shadow of BBC mini-series of the 1970s and 1980s, particularly those based on John le Carré's spy novels, such as *Tinker, Tailor, Soldier, Spy* (BBC, 1979), *Smiley's People* (BBC, 1982) and *The Perfect Spy* (BBC, 1987). These British series were rapidly imported by the American PBS network: 'Le Carré's world of shadow governments and suspicious double-dealings within intelligence organizations can also be seen as the precursor to many [American] shows with similar themes, such as *The Equalizer*, *The X-Files*, and *La Femme Nikita*' (Britton 2004: 213). *Spooks* continues that transatlantic drift: 'In July 2003, *Spooks* came to the American A&E cable network, retitled *MI-5* in the spirit of other acronym titles like *CSI*, *JAG*, and the new *NCIS*' (Britton 2004: 254). In this way, espionage series, like the forensic detection series which are their close cousins, constitute a strand of contemporary quality-television programming. The espionage series also shadows critical discussion about what constitutes quality television, not least because the spy as an indicator of national identity is implicated in long-standing debates regarding culture, class and entertainment on the small screen.

British television dramas addressing espionage, such as those cited above, frequently represent quality programming in very British terms; they turn upon a heritage version of Englishness, however skewed (Brunsdon 1997, Thomas 2002). Charlotte Brunsdon characterised a specifically British understanding of quality television in the late 1980s as 'Brideshead in the Crown,' following critical accounts of *Brideshead Revisited* (Granada, 1981) and *The Jewel in the Crown* (Granada, 1984). This British notion of quality is predicated on its literary source, 'name' actors, high production values and its potential as an exportable account of heritage culture (Brunsdon 1997: 142–3). While there have been shifts in this debate since the 1980s, the 'heritage' aspect of quality British television remains. Recent dramatisations of *Bleak House* (BBC, 2005) and *Jane Eyre* (BBC, 2006) maintain the British tradition in quality programming. Contemporary British spy dramas, however, borrow from their American counterparts in equal measure; the transatlantic exchange works both ways (see Rixon 2003). Spy thrillers such as *The Grid* (BBC, 2004) and *The State Within* (BBC, 2006) depict a global political arena, featuring American actors and an international plot. These series lean toward a Hollywood aesthetic in offering cinematic production values and a complex multilayered narrative style. This has also produced a shift within long-running series such as *Spooks*, whose fifth season featured fight sequences and camera work clearly influenced by American spy series such as *24*.[1]

American television offers a different account of quality, relying less on the guarantees of literary source and heritage than on the 'high-concept' production values of new New Hollywood (Smith 1998: 12–13). Aesthetically and economically, the Hollywood studios have had a hand in the North American networks since the early days of television; in the 1950s, movie executives were quick to recognise the competition television represented and also the outlet for cinematic product that it provided (Neale 1998). By 1955, MGM, Fox and Warners had followed Disney in producing filmed series for television and also selling their movie stockpile to the networks for screening on television: 'By 1960 virtually all prime time fictional series were produced on film in Hollywood, with the traditional studio powers dominating this trend' (Schatz 1993: 12). In the 1970s, this relationship between the New Hollywood and television was further cemented with the use of television as an advertising medium for cinematic product, the end of tri-network domination of commercial television with the development of pay TV and satellite services, and the development of home video systems with a subsequent demand for Hollywood blockbusters in the video market (Schatz 1993: 21–2). One consequence of this fiscal intimacy between the large and small screen was that since 1975 many mainstream films have been made with the knowledge that they are more likely to be viewed on television than in the cinema: 'cinematic technique is adjusted accordingly, conforming with the small screen's "most hypnotic images," its ads. Visual and spatial scale are downsized, action is repetitiously foregrounded and centered, pace and transitions are quicker, music and montage are more prevalent, and slick production values and special effects abound' (Schatz 1993: 32).

While Thomas Schatz is addressing New Hollywood, this is effectively a description of American networks' version of quality television and also an accurate description of the aesthetic that drives *Alias*. Like classical Hollywood, the television networks have had to confront the threat of new media – the multifunctionality of the television set (as games console and computer screen, for example) is matched by a 'multiplying non-exclusivity of content' (Moran 2005: 292–3). The relationship between film and television in the twenty-first century is more than intimate; it has become interchangeable as stars, directors, producers and narratives shift between media. The moving image is now available across a range of viewing technologies and can be redeployed across a range of media; as comics, computer games, novels, soundtracks and so on (Moran 2005: 294). In these terms, popular television dramas are brands rather than bounded narratives. *Alias* is currently available in game format – *Alias: The Game* (2003) – and as a series of novels, including a range of prequels that fill in the back story to the series.[2]

Such multimedia awareness is clear in the content and the style of *Alias* as a quality programme; as with *La Femme Nikita*, microtechnology is to the fore, with Marshall J. Flinkman the equivalent of 'Q' in the Bond films. While 'Q' is an elderly upper-class English gentleman, however, Marshall represents the stereotype of the Silicon Valley computer geek. He is young, gauche and engagingly eccentric, not only producing gadgets for Sydney's assignments but also collecting Pez dispensers and making paper pop-up books in his spare moments (Ruditis 2005: 43). Marshall offers a point of identification for fan cultures around *Alias*; like the Lone Gunmen in *The X-Files* and the Three in *Buffy the Vampire Slayer*, he is a representation of the fan-boy. *Alias*, thus, follows its predecessors in courting an active fan-base (Gwenllian Jones 2003: 166). While Sydney lives a fantasy urban professional lifestyle, Marshall's home life is clearly suburban and domestic; living with his mother in the first two series, by Season 3, Marshall has a wife and young son. In this way, the content of quality series like *Alias* combines high technology and the everyday to produce a glossy and often comic juxtaposition. Such programmes are aware of the world around television, self-consciously offering themselves as subjects for debate in magazine reviews, online discussions and academic studies. By the second season, the promotional material around *Alias* was 'self-reflexive, parodying the show itself and reflecting an understanding of its own audience' (Coon 2005: 8). Kevin Weisman, who plays Marshall, is the nominal editor of an 'unauthorised' collection of essays on the series: *Alias Assumed: Sex, Lies and SD-6* (2005). This is one aspect of television's postmodernity, evident in series like *Alias* that 'demonstrate an increasingly sophisticated knowledge of the conditions of their production, circulation, and eventual reception' (Collins 1992: 332). Such intimacy should not be taken as a sign of democratisation, however; while online fan sites and chat rooms are a rich source of information for journalists and programme-makers, the production companies are also concerned to police their copyright (Gwenllian Jones 2003).

*Alias*'s visual style is also tempered by a multimedia aesthetic; Sydney's action sequences are cut with the speed of a music video and invariably feature an appropriate soundtrack. This technique is brought to the fore in the title sequence for the fourth season, where a montage of Sydney's disguises is cut to the rhythm of the title music. This is the high-concept new New Hollywood aesthetic Schatz, Smith and Maltby describe, and Jennifer Garner has successfully used her role as Sydney Bristow as a calling card for film work. As Sydney Bristow, she has received four consecutive Emmy nominations, four Golden Globe nominations – winning one – and two Screen Actors Guild nominations, again winning one. Garner's role as Electra in *Daredevil* (dir. Mark Steven Johnson, 2003), and the subsequent *Electra* (dir. Rob Bowman, 2005), took the fantasy element of *Alias* to its logical limit by literally presenting her as a superhero. The multimedia aesthetic of *Alias*, together with its status as an award-winning show, lends itself to the quality aspects of Hollywood television.[3] Like other quality series (such as *CSI* and *ER*), *Alias* has featured a list of high-profile guest stars (such as Quentin Tarantino, Faye Dunaway, Ethan Hawke, Christian Slater and Ricky Gervais) and co-stars (such as Angela Bassett, Lena Olin and Isabella Rossellini), who add their film and television star personae to the 'high-concept' *Alias* aesthetic (Maltby 1998: 37–8). Such exchanges are characteristic of the twenty-first century mediascape that *Alias* both replicates and comments on, to the extent that the competing agencies in *Alias* appear to echo the multiple mergers and buy-outs of the new Hollywood (Maltby 1998, Balio 1998). When ABC (the network that bought *Alias*) was bought by Disney in 1995, it was a move that mirrored the vertically integrated production and distribution system of classical Hollywood. In 1999, the two corporations merged their production and programming to create the ABC Entertainment Television Group, one of several bodies to take advantage of the deregulation of American television in the mid-1990s (Holt 2003: 19–20). *Alias*'s burgeoning landscape of competing agencies offers a hyperbolic account of this corporate arena in which new competitors are constantly emerging. Unlike the media landscape from which it emerges, however, *Alias* delineates 'bad' and 'good' agencies: on the sinister side, the Alliance, Section Disparu (Cell 6) (SD6), K-Directorate, FTL and Prophet Five; and for the American government, the Central Intelligence Agency (CIA), Federal Bureau of Investigation (FBI), National Security Agency (NSA), Department of Special Research (DSR), National Security Council (NSC) and 'Authorized Personnel Only' (APO) (see Ruditis 2005: 50–7). In this way, despite the variable allegiances of individual characters (notably Arvin Sloane), *Alias* puts a moral gloss on its corporate environments.

## Quality and middle-class professionals

American quality drama in the early twenty-first century thus exhibits these characteristics: it is glossy, self-aware, visually informed by new New Hollywood and new media, recruits an active fan base and promotes itself as a quality product. Above all, it is a 'dispersible text' (Austin 1999: 148), addressing a range of audiences, with the potential to be franchised across a variety of media. *Alias* neatly fits this definition; indeed, popular discussion about the series makes clear the extent to which the discourse of quality is now employed by television companies as a means of marketing its product. In a November 2005 press release from ABC announcing the end of the series, Mark Pedowitz, President of Touchstone Television which produces *Alias*, said, '*Alias* has sustained its identity as a critical favorite because J. J. Abrams and everyone in this series set the bar for quality entertainment.'[4] This statement underlines the extent to which 'quality' has entered public discourse and also how it remains attached to notions of authorship, in naming Abrams as the show's 'creator'. Despite (or because of) the new-media emphasis in quality American television and its multiple address to a range of audiences, there is still a nostalgic desire for the Romantic ideal of the author as a source of originality and creativity.

Genre television drama, like the generic product of classical Hollywood, combats any denigration of its mass-produced consumer aesthetic with claims for the *auteur* status of the creative geniuses behind them (Feuer 1992: 142). Joss Whedon became the public face promoting *Buffy the Vampire Slayer* and, in the case of *Alias*, J. J. Abrams is promoted as much as the stars of the series. In American television, the producer of a programme is its 'author' rather than, as in British television, its writer (Shattuc 2005: 142–3). Just as Joel Surnow is cited as the creator of *La Femme Nikita*, and later *24* (2001–), so Abrams has become synonymous with the stylish visuals and complex story arcs of *Alias* and, more recently, *Lost* (2004–). Ironically, the similar style of these series indicates the limited originality of such products, contradicting the promotional and critical language that heralds their creators' innovations. Like Surnow, Abrams' style rewards viewers who follow the series religiously. They are, thus, part of a new shift in quality broadcasting toward 'must-see TV': 'These programmes have also been referred to as "date" or "appointment" television, and they are distinguished by the compulsive viewing practices of dedicated audiences who organize their schedules around these shows' (Jancovich and Lyons 2003: 2). This is a style of drama that offers little in the way of exegesis but demands that viewers have a thorough knowledge of the programme and take inexplicable plot twists on trust. It is also television that demands that the viewer watch attentively; another indicator of quality drama, as opposed to the 'lesser' quality of so-called wallpaper television such as soaps, life-style programmes or reality series.

These characteristics are driven (but not determined) by the economic requirements of the medium. The growing phenomenon of 'must-see TV' (a phrase originally used as a brand slogan for NBC) was one result of declining viewing figures for the networks following the spread of cable and satellite channels. American networks fought back by specifically targeting a 'quality' audience:

> In other words, the compulsiveness of 'must see' television is designed to appeal to affluent, highly educated consumers who value the literary qualities of these programmes, and they are used by the networks to hook this valuable cohort of viewers into their schedules. The other transition discernable here is the shift from networks as facilitators of a national public sphere to a situation in which these organisations are increasingly preoccupied with garnering international niche audiences. Interestingly, this transition has also been instrumental in television acquisition of greater cultural legitimacy. As Nicholas Garnham points out, the decline in the audience for a popular medium means that a taste for it becomes increasingly rare. The result is that the medium is then open to appropriation and legitimation by the middle classes.
>
> (Jancovich and Lyons 2003: 3)

The deregulation of broadcasting, and the subsequent pressure to access affluent 'international niche audiences', has put an industrial emphasis on producing middle-class product targeted at the middle classes (Mullan 1997: 76–7). Espionage and detection series are at the heart of this strategy, refracting the professional middle classes back to themselves at twice their original size: 'while many "must-see" shows have been praised for their quality, they have also been criticised for displaying an overwhelming pre-occupation with the white, affluent, urban middle classes' (Jancovich and Lyons 2003: 3). Such series are designed to attract this most lucrative audience by presenting drama that satisfies their newly defined cultural capital. Thus high-end detection and espionage series flatter their viewers with intricate story arcs and transcultural references, often acquiring 'cult' status. As Diane Werts of *Newsday* noted when *Alias* premiered in 2001, the series is an example of 'TV's longtime trend toward delayed drama gratification. Trying to reflect reality and deepen character, plots can stretch on for weeks' (Werts, cited in Britton 2004: 250). Whether the delayed gratification of these story arcs is an attempt at realism or rather a technique to keep those white, affluent middle classes watching is open to debate. Certainly, both *Alias* and *La Femme Nikita* have become recognisable as 'cult' series, thus tapping into the paradox of a niche market which is open to a range of viewers. *La Femme Nikita*'s status as a 'cult' show supported by an active fan base was clear: when the series was cancelled after four seasons by the USA Network cable channel, an internet campaign crashed the channel's e-mail system and inspired the screening of a further eight episodes in a curtailed 'final season' (Tung 2004: 108). Tim Cuprisin argues that this is not the full story:

> Neilsen Media Research data released by USA Network shows that nearly a quarter of the show's viewers live in households earning more than $75,000, 27% of the households tuning in are headed by college graduates and 60% of the audience comes from the 18–49 age group. That's the demographic group advertisers want most. The big lesson of the *Nikita* fan campaign is that you have greater chance of success saving a cable show than you would a network program. Cable shows can survive, even thrive, with audiences that would be considered microscopic by the network standards. But the key is just who makes up that tiny audience.
>
> (Cuprisin 2000)

In this way, the audience for such shows has a limited power to influence their production and distribution but only because they constitute a desirable market for advertising and only, in this case, because cable channels are more reliant on their profit margins. *Alias* fans have not been so fortunate; following ABC's press release, at least two websites were set up to coordinate online and postal campaigns to avert the show's demise, but this did not prevent the series ending with its fifth season (Blair 2005).

The corporate culture required to produce such television is apparent both in the working conditions of *Alias*' production team and in the work ethic of its characters; in this sense, art imitates life. Raymond Williams saw television as paradigmatic of late twentieth-century cultural production in its emphasis on market value: 'This dependency on the market presaged the final and current phase of artist in the marketplace – the corporate professional – the term Williams applies to television makers. Here, the writer or artist is wholly an employee of a corporation' (Shattuc 2005: 149). Jane M. Shattuc cites *Law and Order* as the most pronounced example of working practices in new television's deregulated media economy: '*Law and Order*'s makers are interchangeable – actors, writers, and directors have rotated in and out of the program for over a decade. They are the embodiment of classic corporate professionals' (2005: 150). *Alias* operates within a similar economy of labour. The series composer Michael Giacchino offers the following account of his experience of working on *Alias*:

The thing that always sticks in my mind is that I get about three days to do a show. That's regardless of how we're doing it. I get three days to do 20 to 25 minutes worth of music. Which is a lot. I end up working night and day doing it, but it never bothers me because I know the guys who have handed off the tape to me have been doing exactly the same thing. Everybody is working just as hard. You never feel, 'God, I can't believe I have to do this.' You feel like you have something to live up to, because the people behind you just handed you something that's great and you have to do something that's worthy of that product.

(Gross 2003: 52)

This brief statement offers one account of corporate labour within the new economy: tight deadlines, long hours and a great deal of pressure to 'live up to' an ideal, all framed within a market economy where 'product' must sell to exist at all. While television drama is not a simple reflection of social reality, it does have the capacity to refract social experience. In *Alias*, professional experience is refracted back to its (middle-class professional) audience through a lens that repackages 'life at the office' as a glamorous, jet-set lifestyle. The glossy surfaces and scopophilic pleasures of *Alias* – not least of which feature Jennifer Garner in a range of fetishistic outfits on assignment – would seem to predicate the series as a fantasy which bears little relation to most people's working lives. Yet, like the fast-forward schedule of its production crew, the content of *Alias* represents an articulation of contemporary corporate life.

## Sydney Bristow and the New Economy

*Alias* is, like *La Femme Nikita*, a representation of the new economy of 'electronic capitalism' (Takacs 2005), which has brought with it a new style of management. Several terms have been coined to describe this shift: 'New managerialism, which is also referred to as neoliberalism in the United Kingdom and Total Quality Management in the United States, is a system of the government of individuals invented during the Thatcher and Reagan years' (Davies et al. 2005: 360). In an article that examines the effects of this shift on women at work in academia, Bronwyn Davies and her colleagues describe the philosophy of this new managerial approach: 'Neoliberalism is characterized by the "death of society" and the rise of "individuals" who are in need of a new kind of management, surveillance and control' (Davies et al. 2005: 344). Sydney Bristow, like Nikita before her, embodies such control in her professional behaviour and her physical prowess. She is both surveilled and self-surveilling in her role as agent for SD6 and double agent for the CIA. As the perfect spy, and thus the perfect subject, Sydney has internalised the panoptical gaze of her employers and, while she may question the motives of individuals within the CIA, she does not question its moral right to use extreme force. In this way, Sydney represents a postmodern shift in working practices, which may be seen within education and other public services:

> The cold instrumentality of these new work practices is neatly encapsulated in the notion of 'performativity' ... Drawing on Wittgenstein's philosophy of 'language games,' Lyotard suggests that the knowledge sector of society has, in the postmodern era, undergone a shift of interest from concerns with human life, to pragmatic concerns interested only in the optimal performance of means; a move to performativity.
>
> (Whitehead 1999: 110)

Sydney does not simply represent a shift from the human to the performative, however, as the series is as much concerned with the contradictions between her private life and her professional performativity. Sydney is undoubtedly efficient – to an extreme that suggests both a superhuman ability to perform and a parodic account of the professional sphere – yet, she is also caught in a nexus of emotional issues: moral, familial and romantic. This provides melodrama, the series' soap heritage, which is a feature of other American quality dramas, such as *Buffy the Vampire Slayer*, *The Sopranos* and *The X-Files*. The contradictions between Sydney's professional and private lives were played out in early seasons through the destruction of her friends because of her work, and continued in later seasons through the on-off relationship with Vaughn and her tangled familial relations.

Sydney thus embodies the new 'New Woman' in the neo-liberal New Economy: she offers a hyperbolic account of the contradictions between professional and personal life. Most obviously, this is played out in the professional demands which make it impossible for her to have a social life outside the workplace (Nye 2005). This corresponds to the New Economy's stress on its professional workforce, that personal needs be subordinated to the needs of the corporation. In this twenty-first century working environment, the individual is placed under enormous pressure to perform a variety of roles, and failure to perform effectively entails the threat of demotion or dismissal:

> In neoliberal discourse primacy is given to the flexible individual who acts 'responsibly' in relation to the market and who is valued in market terms. Individuals must respond to the market and also anticipate it, and must always be ready to be rejected as relevant players if they are no longer of any (monetary) value.
>
> (Davies et al. 2005: 347)

Nikita in *La Femme Nikita*, like Sydney in the first two seasons of *Alias*, is under constant threat of 'cancellation' or assassination by the agency that employs her. While such extreme practice does not hold in 'real' life, few working in the public sector are unaware of the threat of redundancy. *Alias* thus comments on the New Economy through drawing parallels between Sydney's espionage adventures and her cover as a bank executive. Following an assignment where she is unable to prevent a CIA team being killed, Sydney catches up with best friend and housemate Francie, who believes she works for an international bank:

> FRANCIE: 'Hey, how was your trip?'
> SYDNEY: 'Oh ... not good ... I was working with these people who ... um ... they were terminated.'
> FRANCIE: 'Oh man. The economy *sucks.*'
>
> (*Alias*, 'Reckoning', Series 1, Episode 6, 18 November 2001)

This brief exchange makes explicit the linguistic and allegorical resonance between Sydney's missions and her day-to-day cover story as a banking executive and, thus, between Sydney and the New Economy. The resonance is echoed in 'Bob' (Series 5, Episode 8), where Sydney's new colleague, Rachel, is undercover as an IT executive at a convention. She describes her working life in terms that cover both her espionage work and her corporate cover story: 'Sometimes at these work events I feel that I'm in over my head. I just started in a new division. It's a lot more responsibility, more risks.' Despite the fact that recent studies have disputed the decline in long-term employment (see Perrons 2003: 71), working practices are increasingly predicated on a mobile economy and a flexible workforce. The information age, founded on communications and computer technologies, has allegedly introduced a much more fluid employment market. Some commentators see this as the way forward, offering potential benefits to those traditionally excluded from the labour market: 'The Internet is said to be free of gender (and race) bias because communication is impersonal and gender-neutral. Thus Internet-based trade and business (e-commerce) could be a fruitful source of new occupations for women on an equal basis with men' (Stanworth 2000: 21). The potential for flexible working hours in a range of locations (including the home) is often cited as beneficial to women, particularly those with children. However, this optimistic scenario is undermined by evidence that information technology, computers and telecommunications (ICT) work 'physically and contractually outside organisational boundaries is often isolated and exploitative, for women especially where skills are low, easily replaceable or undervalued' (Stanworth 2000: 21).

Yet Sydney and her colleagues emphatically do *not* represent such a dispossessed underclass of low paid, out-sourced workers; instead, they offer one of many accounts of a super-competent professionals on the small screen. Sydney, Nikita and their television sisters in quality drama perform the role of the privileged middle-class professional. They are separate from the masses, from the often unseen and undifferentiated 'ordinary' women who exist around them (Radner 1995: 5). Slim, (predominantly) white, immaculately presented and committed to their work, they embody professional efficiency. Vivian Johnson (Marianne Jean-Baptiste) in *Without a Trace* (2002–), Neela Rasgotra (Parminder Nagra) in *ER* (1994–), Alexx Woods (Khandi Alexander) in *CSI Miami* (2002–) and Cristina Yang (Sandra Oh) in *Grey's Anatomy* (2005–) are notable exceptions to the Eurocentric casting of professional women. Most prime-time dramas feature female professionals with a Hispanic or Italian-American background – such as Stella Bonasera (Melina Kanakaredes) in *CSI New York* (2004–) – but they tend to be assimilated as a different kind of glamour. Professional women on television are compromised by problems in their personal life, just as such characters are punished and demonised in mainstream Hollywood films, indicating the threat they still hold for masculine forms of power (Jones 1991, Brunsdon 1997: 90–4). In Sydney's case, the threat of her professional ability is also contained through hyperbole and fetishisation. Sydney's ability to perform on assignment is clearly superhuman; like her avatar in the *Alias* computer game, she is knocked down only to revive again, time after time. Her indestructibility is matched by her hyper-sexualisation on assignment. Sydney on the job is almost unfailingly dressed to kill in revealing outfits; Sydney in the office is a paragon of twenty-first-century officewear, in dark colours and body-concealing suits. Sydney's spy work is here aligned with that of the 'working girl', as in Yvonne Tasker's analysis of contemporary Hollywood product: 'Across a variety of popular genres, Hollywood representation is characterised by an insistent equation between working women, women's work and some form of sexual(ised) performance' (Tasker 1998: 3).

Sydney and Nikita are supremely professional *and* supremely feminine – and those two skills are combined in the many sequences where they perform their femininity as a professional alias, where they go undercover. In this, they overtly mimic the 'working girls' that shadow working women on screen; through their cross-dressed identities, Sydney and Nikita embody the 'head for business and a bod for sin' which Tess McGill (Melanie Griffiths) ascribes herself in *Working Girl* (Mike Nichols, 1988) (Tasker 1998: 39–43). Femininity and female sexuality thus become *work* for these female spies, an image to be performed and discarded. John Berger famously argued that 'men act and women appear' (Berger 1972: 47); in these new fictions on television, as on the cinema screen, that simple binary is disturbed by women who occupy both sides of the divide. Such women act and also appear – like their real counterparts, these fictional figures have double the workload: to play the man at work and also to accomplish the role of femininity. These figures do not represent a feminism that is achieved but, rather, a mutable account of femininity. Most notably, both Peta Wilson and Jennifer Garner, like many of their cinematic counterparts, are physically different from action women on screen in the 1960s and 1970s. Unlike Lindsay Wagner or Farrah Fawcett-Majors, these women are muscular and visibly strong. While they wear fetishistic outfits, there is little movement on their fleshless frames and, at the moments where they are hyper-sexually dressed, they often appear masculine – there is a mismatch between the hyper-feminine costume and the muscular female body. Such moments offer a discomforting vision of transgender identities. What Nikita and Sydney's aliases make evident is the transgender identity of the woman in the professions, that they are women out of place, in environments that clearly do not account for femininity but only work on masculine frames. While *La Femme Nikita* and *Alias* offer problematic accounts of living through the 'third wave' – echoing the gaps and elisions of many real women in the professions – they can gesture towards a third sex, a different performance of gender.

In this, they echo a shift in roles for women on the big screen. Hilary Radner notes the emergence of the 'psycho*femme*', or the neo-*noir* femme fatale, as a figure that 'rock[s] the boat of heterosexuality' upon which Hollywood predicates its profits (Radner 1998: 248). Radner elaborates with reference to Sarah Connor (Linda Hamilton) in *Terminator 2: Judgement Day* (James Cameron, 1991) and Marge Gunderson (Frances McDormand) in *Fargo* (Ethan Coen, 1996). Linda Hamilton's muscular physique represents a body which 'positions itself at the limits of erotic fascination, a gesture that reworks the status of that body as the limit between that which is human and that which is machine,' a theme which *Terminator 2* plays out repeatedly (Radner 1998: 251). Frances McDormand, on the other hand, was padded out to appear pregnant and ungainly throughout *Fargo*, representing a body which refuses to be eroticised, refuses the traditional scopophilic role of women within Hollywood cinema (Radner 1998: 253). These strategies are echoed in *Alias*, where Sydney initially plays out a version of Sarah Connor in *Terminator 2*, taking her professional (and personal) ethos to the limit, in a body that privileges muscularity over feminine softness. In Season 5, however, Sydney's body changes dramatically (as Jennifer Garner also became pregnant), offering an unprecedented representation of the pregnant woman spy. *Alias* is, thus, an instance of Hollywood-inflected American quality television offering its viewers something other than contained femininity. This is not to say that the series is 'feminist' or that it reflects any current social reality for women, simply that these diversions from the mainstream open up cracks in the façade of heteropatriarchy.

In many ways, the visual images presented by these models of the new young woman conform to contemporary critiques of the 'third wave' or 'new feminism.' Both Nikita and Sydney are fetishistically dressed for action in leather and rubber outfits. The producers' DVD commentaries on episodes from the first season of *Alias* make reverent reference to the electric blue rubber mini-dress that Sydney changed into from a maid's uniform on her assignment in 'So It Begins' (Series 1, Episode 2). In this sequence, Sydney simply changes from one fetishistic costume to another, in a paradigmatic example of the many outfits she dons during the series. These early aliases epitomise the working woman as 'working girl' (Tasker 1998), but the sequences that precede and succeed such costumes undermine any single reading of their significance; Sydney is also an obedient worker and a killer. The blue-rubber-dress image featured on an early poster promoting the series: 'Written across her left breast in small text are two phrases: "Not just a secret agent. She's a concealed weapon"' (Coon 2005: 7). These series are written across the small screens of contemporary television whose aesthetic increasingly appears to epitomise postmodernity: 'a world where notions of metaphysical truth, being and identity are deconstructed and replaced with an emphasis on flux, becoming and subjective perspectives' (DiTommaso 2003: 1). In postmodern adventure series such as *La Femme Nikita* and *Alias*, the lengthy story arcs, together with generic attributes that play with the boundaries of realism and fantasy, offer them as an ongoing debate over modernity/postmodernity. As these are spy fictions, this becomes a debate over the subject and agency; and because they are women at the turn of the twenty-first century, this debate entails feminist contexts.

Although these fictions are often claimed by those espousing a 'third wave' or 'new feminism' as the sign of cultural if not social change in gender relations, they may also be understood as revealing the political limitations of so-called post-feminism (Levy 2005: 75). Many advocates of the third wave offer distorted and homogenised accounts of 1970s second-wave feminist politics which, albeit inadvertently, support negative media stereotypes of feminists as shrill, unreasonable and outdated (Segal 1997: 6–7). While women's poverty on a global scale has increased in the past twenty years, some Western women have benefited from changes in legislation in the aftermath of the second wave (Segal 1997: 11). It is largely this privi-leged group that writes about, endorses or espouses a 'third wave', a politics complicit with the shift to the right in American politics which is echoed in other Western nations: 'neo-conservative politicians and corporate market-ing strategies have successfully normalized an astonishingly reactionary definition of feminism in the United States. Feminist success is now widely equated with any socio-economic gain that is achieved by any individual woman by any means necessary' (Smith 1997: 33).

Nikita, Sydney and their sisters on prime-time television appear to embody such a limited understanding of 'feminist success', yet they also give the lie to any unquestioning celebration of a third wave. The conflicts between these characters' private and professional lives are played out on the small screen as fantasy, but they also refract the realities of audiences which are tuning in; that desired, affluent middle-class international niche market. Television may be a hydra-headed media oligopoly – 'the Disney-ABC/Time Warner-Turner-CNN/General Electric-NBC/Westinghouse-CBS/Murdoch-Fox/Viacom-Paramount-MTV/Bertellsman swamp' – yet it also offers a terrain for debate, for instances of momentary questioning of the very corporations that dominate its production (Smith 1997: 33).

## The new New Woman as a 'free agent individual'

Nikita, as a conscripted agent for an agency which appears increasingly sinister, may be read as an overtly critical account of the New Economy, whereas Sydney is more fully incorporated and uncritical of the organisations that employ her. Once Sydney discovers SD6 is not the CIA, her allegiance is quickly switched to the CIA, and she remains within its hegemonic discourse of American patriarchy. Even when operating outside the remit of her agency, she still works within a patriarchal structure, often with her father or with Vaughn. In this way, Sydney Bristow represents the ideal (fantasy) subject of the New Economy. She is self-motivated, driven and highly efficient. Most importantly, she can deal with dramatic changes in structure – such as the revelation that SD6 is not the CIA or that she has been a brainwashed enemy assassin (working undercover for the CIA) for two years – without compromising her professional role. Sydney's professional life is totally geared towards the exigencies of the New Economy, making her a dream employee for neo-liberal employers. Most accounts of the New Economy in the information age note the increasing stress (both literal and rhetorical) on the individual:

> The theme of employment-by-self and the growth of 'enterprise' runs through both the European and the US information age literature. Technical work transforming information into knowledge, the archetypal work of the information age, is predicted to be carried out in 'virtual' organizations, described as dynamic coalitions of technical specialists linked by global computer networks. The diffusion of the 'virtual' organizational form is said to be driven both by the technological imperative and by the chaotic external environment. One form of virtuality is the sophisticated subcontracting chain, another is the lean hub of employed staff surrounded by a shifting army of own account self-employed workers. Negroponte (1995) and Barnatt (1997) foresee the predominance of 'free agent individuals' in future labour markets.
>
> (Stanworth 2000: 24)

While within the series both SD6 and the CIA have a visible 'hub of employed staff', they are supported by a network of independent agents and offices, linked by information technology. In 'So It Begins' (Series 1, Episode 2, 7 October 2001), Sydney tells her new CIA handler, Michael C. Vaughn, that she intends to help them destroy SD6 and then leave espionage behind her. He shows her the CIA's organisational map of SD6 – a huge grid covering most of the world – and tells her that her work is 'complicated, political and long term'. If the CIA in *Alias* is organised along the same lines – which it must be in order to combat a network like SD6 – then, like SD6, it must have a similarly 'virtual' structure. Both agencies are hierarchical, with a clear sense of management structure, yet, within the series,

Sydney appears to confound this with her startling insight and professional prowess. In 'Parity' (Series 1, Episode 3, 14 October 2001), when the CIA attempt to replace Vaughn with a more experienced officer, she bluntly rejects the replacement and gets Vaughn promoted in the process. It is notable that Vaughn's replacement, Seth Lambert, is characterised as not only older but as representing an 'older' sensibility, as he comments on Sydney's good looks and arranges a pointless meeting with her where he gets her murdered fiancé's name wrong. This is a rare instance of an inefficient operative in *Alias*, and he is quickly dispatched. Sydney, Vaughn and their colleagues (including enemy counterparts) are unfailingly efficient and dedicated to their work.

If *Alias* represents the CIA, SD6 and APO as 'virtual' organisations in the information-age economy Stanworth describes above, it is tempting to see Sydney Bristow as a model of the 'free agent individual'. This ideal employee is incorporated into predictions regarding the future of information technologies and the professional workplace: 'A scenario of atomized individuals bearing the risk of generating a sufficient income flow and operating in a global environment is predicted for the majority of the workforce' (Stanworth 2000: 24). In this sense, Sydney represents the future, but only a future for the white middle classes – a future that entails inordinate pressure to perform unfailingly in dangerous (economic) environments across the globe. In the face of a 'chaotic external environment', whether it be the threat of terrorism in *Alias* or the chaotic imperative of the new economy, the new professionals are expected to deal with it. While this is a fantasy, it may also appear to offer some form of agency in the person of these agents who individually (and regularly) save the world. Sydney Bristow and her sisters can be seen as allegories for 'the neoliberal/new managerialist demand for personal control of and responsibility for the self, which may seem liberating but is also dangerous in that the self is compelled never to rest. The controlled self must always be flexible, propelling itself into the ever-reinvented demands of the institution' (Davies et al. 2005: 351). Joanne Entwistle reads this new self within an explicitly Foucauldian frame, employing Foucault's 'technologies of the self' to propose that power-dressed career women in the 1990s constituted 'a technology of the (female, professional) self' (1997: 315):

> This 'technology of the self' can be seen to correlate with new work regimes developing from the 1970s onwards, a technology of the self commonly referred to as the 'enterprising self' because it is produced by a regime of work which emphasises internal self-management and relative autonomy on the part of the individual.
>
> (Entwistle 1997: 316)

Nikita (specifically in *La Femme Nikita*) and Sydney Bristow represent a fantasy of this self-managing self; a (female) self that goes to extreme measures to ensure that the job is done. The thin, muscular bodies of Peta Wilson and Jennifer Garner make evident the labour involved in maintaining such a self, while Nikita and Sydney's emotional crises indicate the cost and psychic discipline required to continue in their roles. It is no coincidence that these figures emerge on television and on film in parallel with the effects of second-wave feminism; Nikita and Sydney represent one outcome of that social shift: that women are present in the professional workplace, but that the demands made on professionals are increasingly inhuman. Such figures are fantastic representations of the New Woman which reflect upon the limitations of liberation.

Other significant female figures in the series – Sydney's mother, Irina Derevko, her aunts, Katya Derevko and Elena Derevko, and Vaughn's wife, Lauren Reed – are revealed as duplicitous figures working with enemy agencies. *Alias* plays upon the early twentieth-century opposition between evil, Oriental spies (feminine) and good, Occidental intelligence agents (masculine). In this sense, the series is a return to the old order of representation regarding women as spies, despite its postmodern credentials. *Alias* thus offers a 'double articulation' (Fiske 1987: 189), perpetuating the Mata Hari stereotype but also commenting upon it in early seasons by revealing that Irina is 'the Man', the mysterious leader of an enemy organisation dedicated to collecting the Rambaldi artefacts, and by offering Sydney as her opposite number. By the end of the series, however, Sydney and her mother are directly opposed as the good and the bad spy. Although Sydney is of mixed parentage, the child of an enemy Russian agent and a CIA father, she is subsumed within a masculine economy that is explicitly aligned with American interests. The Derevko women are increasingly revealed to be duplicitous, interested only in their own power. *Alias*, thus, takes a step back from addressing its own politics by presenting them as excess, and thus unresolved: 'Excess does not necessarily lead to subversive or interrogative readings: it allows for an overspill of meaning that escapes ideological control and that makes alternative readings possible' (Fiske 1987: 193). Any alternative reading in this case involves a critical account of Sydney Bristow, which the series itself gestures towards but never fully confronts. While many of the characters around her may switch their allegiances, if only temporarily, Sydney remains a touchstone of truth with a clear moral vision. It is left to the viewer to critique her monotonous success in the workplace and the crises in her private life.

By Season 4, Sydney's life beyond the new 'black ops' agency, APO, is almost indistinguishable from her life at work, as work also concerns her family relationships. Sydney no longer lives in a graduate-student house in a leafy suburb but a slick urban apartment which she invites her half-sister, Nadia, to share. In 'Détente' (Series 4, Episode 7, 16 February 2005), Arvin Sloane, the morally ambiguous leader of first SD6 and then APO visits his daughter Nadia at Sydney's apartment, and she is horrified to find him there; yet, this is only the most extreme example of how work enters Sydney

Bristow's personal life, and vice versa. This is true for most of the major protagonists in the series who have family within secret agencies and, in the case of Vaughn, Sydney and Nadia, are fascinated by a deceased parent. The internecine familial plots in *Alias* would appear to offer it for psychoanalytic interpretation, yet the extreme nature of the family relationships are, like the account of professional life, a hyperreal pastiche of familial dysfunction. Sydney's mother Irina Derevko is first thought to be dead, then is found to be alive but working as an enemy agent who takes out a contract on her daughter's life. Sydney's father, Jack Bristow, has Irina killed in order to save Sydney, but it later emerges that a genetic duplicate of Irina was killed in her place, so she is still alive but being kept prisoner and tortured by her sister, Elena Derevko. Towards the end of the fourth season, Nadia and Sydney rescue and release their mother, Irina, with Jack Bristow's help. The family narratives of *Alias* grow ever more bizarre as the series progresses, so that by the fourth season, Sydney's private and professional worlds have effectively combined.

## Mothers and daughters

*Alias* represents a masculine economy of emotion where 'male power … is associated with lack of emotion … the ability to keep one's vulnerabilities concealed' (Wright 2005: 203). It also privileges masculine forms of power, (self-)control and cultural capital. The emphasis on family drama, together with a romantic narrative, allies *La Femme Nikita* and *Alias* to soap opera, a form which has traditionally been seen as privileging feminine concerns (Modleski 1984: 85–109, Fiske 1987: 179–97). Yet, these series inevitably return to the father as a source of epistemological authority. In *La Femme Nikita*, this is played out by the revelation that Nikita is the daughter of the power behind Section One, a daddy's girl after all, despite her punkish rebellion. Sydney, likewise, is caught up in her relationship with her father, Jack Bristow, who is her prime source of truth and knowledge. Mothers are always untrustworthy, as older women in these series tend to occupy a sinister role – exemplified by Madeline in *La Femme Nikita* and Irina, Katya and Elena Derevko in *Alias*. Yet, all these characters offer accounts of women who are subsumed within a masculine economy: they are women whose role in the professional sphere has become their identity, but they have conformed to its demands rather than shifting the terms on which it operates. In this sense, Madeline and the Derevko sisters do not represent a post-feminist aesthetic but, rather, the politics of a pre-feminist work environment. With Sydney following their lead, it appears that little has changed, even in this apparently post-feminist and postmodern fantasy.

Madeline and the Derevko sisters represent a potential (and feared) future for Nikita and Sydney. Their roles as manipulators and traitors are contrasted with the moral and ethical figures of Nikita and Sydney. While they are desired (by Operations in *La Femme Nikita* and Jack Bristow – despite himself – in *Alias*), they are not authentically desiring as Nikita and Sydney are. The younger women have 'real' emotions, while the older women fake emotion in order to get what they want, and their aims are not ethical. Because such quality television privileges a masculine economy – and a 'New Economy', which is as damaging for men as it is for women in the workplace – older female characters like Madeline and Irina Derevko reveal the limited options open to professional women when they are no longer young. Whereas Nikita and Sydney might be proposed as representations of an 'empowered' new feminism, their older counterparts give the lie to any assumption that the workplace has changed. In the fifth and final season of *Alias*, maternal issues are foregrounded by Sydney's pregnancy and final revelations concerning her mother, Irina Derevko.

Irina is gradually revealed as the mastermind behind the machinations of APO's latest adversary, Prophet Five. In a grandstanding finale where Irina destroys both the twelve members of Prophet Five and APO's Los Angeles base, she is also revealed as an 'unnatural' mother who has relinquished any bond with her child in favour of her own power. This revelation begins in the appropriately titled episode 'Maternal Instinct' (Series 5, Episode 11). As Sydney gives birth to a daughter, Irina states that she had never wanted a child and that she had Sydney on KGB orders, to cement her relationship with Jack. Once she had a child, Irina decided that she couldn't be an agent and a mother, so she decided not to be a mother, and tells Sydney, 'You can't do both.' This bizarre commentary on working motherhood proceeds to the final episode where Irina tries to kill Sydney, calling her a 'complication in my life' before falling to her death through a glass skylight (a glass ceiling?) as she reaches for the precious Rambaldi artefact she dedicated her life to obtaining. The morality tale is fairly explicit: Irina relinquished her 'natural' role as a mother, and her desire for power ultimately destroys her. Sloane is left in a similar predicament. Haunted by Nadia, the daughter he killed, he is destroyed by a dying Jack Bristow, who heroically blows them both up so that Sloane, who has achieved life everlasting from the Rambaldi artefact, is entombed for eternity. There is an unambiguous natural justice for 'bad' mothers and fathers in this explosive finale.

Sydney's role as the moral arbiter of *Alias* is endorsed both by her battle with Irina and by the concluding frames of the series. In the final episode, Sydney is tasked by her father to eliminate her mother – 'You're the only one who can beat her … You have to stop your mother' ('All The Time In The World,' Series 5, Episode 17) – and, thus, becomes his avatar in their battle. Sydney's position in the masculine economy is underscored once again. As her mother says before their final confrontation, 'We're very different Sydney. You still cling to naïve ideals. I learned at a very young age the only currency worth anything in this world is power.' Sydney is positioned against this raw expression of unnatural desire, not only through her battles with enemy agencies and the Derevko women throughout the series but also through the different representation of maternity she offers in

Season 5. In early episodes, the heavily pregnant Sydney is shown in active service, still playing out a number of aliases and employing her pregnancy as part of her performance. In 'Mockingbird' (Series 5, Episode 4), Sydney is undercover at a casino in Monte Carlo, rolling dice on her belly and referring to herself as 'Momma.' The manager is disgusted when he discovers that the pregnant American has been cheating, to which Sydney responds, 'What can I say, sir. I'm not like other moms.' Indeed, despite Irina's claim that 'you can't do both', Sydney appears to be a successful working mother. In 'There's Only One Sydney Bristow' (Series 5, Episode 12), two besuited CIA babysitters arrive to provide security and childcare for her newly born daughter, Isabelle; as Sydney states, 'Momma's got to go to work.' Above all, Sydney is depicted as a good and 'natural' mother, nervous before the birth but overjoyed by her daughter and expressing fears in 'Reprisal' (Series 5, Episode 16) that Isabelle might have to grow up without her.

The different kind of mothering Sydney represents is crystallised by the final sequence of the series. Jack and Irina are dead, Sloane is buried alive and Marcus R. Dixon, Sydney's former partner, is Deputy Director of the CIA. Isabelle is now a young girl and living with Sydney and Vaughn in a beach house far removed from the dramas of espionage. 'Uncle Dixon' arrives and meets Sydney and Vaughn's new son, Jack, before asking Sydney to come back to work and assume another alias for a job that needs her special talents. Vaughn suggests they discuss it after dinner, and they all go out for a walk on the beach. Isabelle follows them, having completed a wooden puzzle which we saw the child Sydney complete in an earlier flashback; it is a CIA 'indicator' of exceptional skill in three-dimensional reasoning. The final frames are a slow motion long shot of Sydney, Vaughn, Dixon and the two young children, walking towards the surf. The beach is symbolic within the fifth season as an ideal fantasy or dream space for Sydney: in 'The Horizon' (Series 5, Episode 9) Sydney is drugged and interrogated by Prophet 5 and imagines herself on a beach talking to Vaughn. Are we then to understand this final sequence, with its saturated colours and slow motion, as a dream rather than a reality? Sydney appears to have been recuperated within the economies of heterosexuality and femininity: she is no longer in her work suit or the glamorous outfits of her aliases but in a simple cotton dress, the epitome of contented motherhood. She appears to have given up her professional role for the 'real' work of being a wife and mother. Is this the 'real' Sydney? Considering the twists and turns of the preceding five seasons, it is hard to take this final episode as a conclusive ending. Will Sydney return to active service? Will Isabelle, as the puzzle sequence implies, follow her mother into a career in espionage?

While this final sequence reproduces the hegemonic ideal of the nuclear family, neatly arrayed as mom/dad/daughter/son, the cosy advertisement-style scenario raises more questions than it answers. Any viewer who has watched the series and followed Sydney through the twists and turns of her familial, romantic and social relationships knows that anyone can betray her, and anyone (even Sydney herself) can be replicated and replaced. It is hard to see this final attempt to 'fix' Sydney as successful. The dreamlike quality of the beach scene, its heightened colours and temporal disjunction, all tend to undermine its status as a *final* scenario, as Sydney's destination. For, if nothing else, *Alias* has always been about movement, about Sydney strutting to pounding music in a tight dress and a different wig and the protagonists travelling between global locations with impossible speed. More than this, however, *Alias*'s central philosophy is that everyone has an alias, all the time. At work, at home, at play, the characters are always performing different identities, for better or worse reasons. In this, *Alias* epitomises the central trope of espionage as effecting change by employing deception; more, it reifies the woman spy as the embodiment of an unfixed signifier. Despite her worthy moral perspective, Sydney Bristow's world is a frightening melange of betrayal, conspiracies and false identities. Nothing is secure. Sydney, like her professional compatriots across the television-drama spectrum, is not a role model. Instead, the multiple address of *Alias* as a high-concept example of quality in North American new television's landscape opens it up to multiple audiences, for multiple identifications and interpretations. One result of this is that *Alias* as a whole, and Sydney in particular, makes available divergent accounts of dominant Western discourses regarding femininity and the family. Consequently, the attempt to close down that multiplicity of gazes, both within the series and in its external reach as it references other formats and other visual and aural texts, is marked only by its impossibility. Sydney at rest, at home and at peace appears as fictional as any of her other aliases.

*Alias* embodies the multiple subjectivities of contemporary television; its multi-audience and multimedia appeal epitomise quality American series. Yet, while *Alias* speaks to these postmodern indicators, one reading of the series is as a commentary on late Western capitalism. More than this, because of its multiplicity of address, its slippery social and political perspectives, *Alias* exemplifies the complexity and contradictions of femininity and feminism within contemporary British and American culture. Setting this most postmodern of spies against the mythologised modern figure of Mata Hari offers a vertiginous perspective on Western popular culture. It is tempting to argue for some progressive historical overview here, yet it is hard to see the playful and exploitative surfaces of *Alias* as an unequivocally positive replacement for the abject, othered figure of Mata Hari, the female spy as femme fatale.

# Notes

## 1 Spies, lies and sexual outlaws: male spies in popular fiction

1 It is interesting to note that all three authors were, at some point in their careers, involved in the British intelligence services. It would be dangerous to assume, however, that any of these fictional representations of espionage offer realist accounts of the profession. Clearly, such a professional background enabled these authors to draw upon experience, but their fictions are also riddled with the ideologies, prejudices and stereotypes of the worlds into which such novels were cast, as well as the worlds out of which such novels emerged. Under Lloyd George, Buchan became Director of Information and later Director of Intelligence; in 1939, Fleming became the Personal Assistant of Admiral John Godfrey, the Director of Naval Intelligence (McCormick 1977: 34, 72). Le Carré, aka David Cornwell, may have worked for the British secret services in the Second World War, but the 'disinformation' about his life, much like his fiction, makes it difficult to establish concrete facts – some commentators believe him to have been directly inspired by his own experiences of espionage (Britton 2005: 126).

## 2 Femmes fatales and British grit: women spies in the First and Second World Wars

1 My references to Orientalist fantasy are inevitably informed by the work of Edward Said (1978). For a succinct account of the absence of women in Said's work see Lewis 1996: 15–35.
2 Mata Hari's rival, Maud Allen, also became embroiled in a London libel case based on fears regarding national security. In the summer of 1918, Noel Pemberton Billing MP claimed to have a 'Black List' of high-ranking traitors and spies in Britain, many of whom were said to attend Allen's performances as *Salomé*:

> Maud Allen, accused of immorality and lesbian proclivities, became a central figure in this national spectacle as an outsider (Canadian), an exotic dancer (she was compared to Mata Hari, who had been executed less than a year before in Paris), and the lead actress in a play whose central themes were symbolic castration and sexual perversion.
>
> (Proctor 2003: 40)

3 Mata Hari's name has been used as a brand for such diverse products as on-line slot machines and absinthe. See http://www.igtonline.com/games/new_games/mata_hari.html and http://www.absinthe.at/productinfo_e.html. Both sites accessed 19 September 2003.

4 'Miscegenation was identified as "race suicide" and was included in the Motion Picture Producers and Distributors of America (MPPDA) list of representational prohibitions when Will Hays became president in 1922, removing the possibility that any Hollywood film narrative could include a non-tragic cross-racial romance' (Berry 2000: 116).

5 British censors objected to the use of a religious image in this scene, and a retake, in which a picture of her lover's mother is substituted for the Madonna, was edited into the version released in Britain (Paris 1995: 215).

6 This is a reference to the notorious episode during the filming of *Queen Christina* (Rouben Mamoulian, 1933), where Garbo asked for direction on how to play the final shot of Christina at the prow of a ship leaving Sweden, and Mamoulian replied, 'Darling, just make your face a blank' (Paris 1995: 305). For a seminal account of Garbo's mythology, see Roland Barthes (1972: 62–4).

7 Mata Hari remains a potent reference in glamour and fashion photography. One recent example of this may be seen in *Femme Fatale: The Timeless Style of Beautiful Women*, a collection of images celebrating the work of hairstylist Serge Normant which offers an imaginary history of the twentieth century decade by decade. The 1910–19 section features 'Elizabeth Hurley: The Temptress'. While Mata Hari is not mentioned by name, the metallic breastplates and kohl-eyed make-up clearly reference her Oriental image (Normant 2001).

8 Tammy Proctor notes that the Postal Censorship Branch (MI9) had 'more than thirty-five hundred women on its payroll in November 1918, compared to only thirteen hundred men' (2003: 55) and that 'MI5's Registry – a huge card file of suspects and information – was staffed entirely by women after November 1914' (2003: 57).

9 See http://www.ww1-propaganda-cards.com/miss_edith_cavell.html. The site also has a range of Mata Hari postcards: http://www.ww1-propaganda-cards.com/mata_hari.html. Both sites accessed 5 September 2005.

10 Harper also notes that the shift between the two Powell and Pressburger productions was driven by their contract, for *Contraband*, with British National: 'a less ambitious studio' (Harper 1998: 136).

11 In his autobiography, Herbert Wilcox recounts Odette Churchill's torture, together with her miraculous recovery from tuberculosis in her cell at Ravensbrück. He also writes about an accident on location, where Anna Neagle had a bad fall which injured her back, 'At the very same spot Odette had injured her spine.' Such injuries may have contributed to the verisimilitude of Neagle's performance (Wilcox 1967: 184–5).

## 3 Dolly birds: female spies in the 1960s

1 Thumim examines *Marnie* (Alfred Hitchcock, 1964) and *Mary Poppins* (Robert Stevenson, 1965) as popular examples which place a female character at the centre of the narrative. One could also cite more art-house productions, such as *Darling* (John Schlesinger, 1965) and *Girl on a Motorcycle* (Jack Cardiff, 1968), which offer representations of the 'dolly bird'.

2 And also, possibly, a discomfort with the depiction of a female spy battling THRUSH.

3 It is notable that April Dancer's male partner, Mark Slate, was very specifically located as not only English but part of the 'swinging' culture of the time:

The confirmed bachelor bought all his clothes on Carnaby Street and one of the closets was a veritable warehouse of tweeds and loud westkits [*sic*]. Another contained a guitar, and stacks of rock-and-roll records. In line with inverse snobbery, belied by his indolent manner of speech and languorous movement, a third closet secreted almost everything that an RAF veteran might find worth keeping. Ever since Slate had transferred from London Headquarters to New York, he had tried to keep England with him wherever he went. But his love of women, his passion for sports cars, his Cambridge attainments and his Olympic ski skills, marked him for the international man of the world that he was.

(Avallone 1966: 19)

4 See Disk 2 Extras, *The Champions: The Complete Series* (ITC Entertainment Group Ltd, 1968: Carlton Visual Entertainment Ltd, 2004). For a critical account of both *The Champions* and *Department S*, see Chapman (2002: 171–98).

5 Peter O'Donnell scripted a television film in 1982, the ABC pilot for a series which never went into production, and also gave his approval to the straight-to-video *My Name Is Modesty* (Scott Spiegel, 2003), marketed with Quentin Tarantino's name over the title, which tells Modesty's back story in Tangier. O'Donnell was not happy with Losey's version; it was very different from his vision of Modesty and was a commercial flop (Sandbrook 2006: 381–2).

6 For an account of female protagonists in 1960s comic strips, see Horn (1977: 188–221), where the *Modesty Blaise* strip is listed alongside *Barbarella*, *Jodelle* and *Blanche Epiphanie*. The pornographic reference of Modesty Blaise continues, with a contemporary burlesque artiste naming herself Immodesty Blaize.

7 This account of Modesty Blaise's background is reproduced, with minor variations on a number of websites; see, for example, the 'Introduction to Modesty Blaise' at http://www.cs.umu.se/~kenth/Modesty/mbintro.html and 'Interview with Peter O'Donnell' at http://www.cs.umu.se/~kenth/Modesty/podint.html (both accessed 11 June 2002). An interview with Peter O'Donnell in which he recounts his career and the inspiration for Modesty Blaise is an extra on the DVD of *My Name Is Modesty*.

8 Examples of other 'exceptional' women in the novels include Dinah Collier, née Pilgrim, who is blind but has extra sensory perception (O'Donnell 1969, 1972, 1977) and Lady Janet, who lost a leg in a car crash but manages a farm near Willie's pub, the Treadmill (O'Donnell 1972). In an online interview with Kent Hedlundh, Peter O'Donnell responds to questions from fans, the first of which is why he has introduced disabled characters like Dinah, Janet and Lucifer to the Modesty Blaise narratives. O'Donnell responds that there is no conscious reason for this and that he would rather not examine any 'subconscious reasons'. See http://www.cs.umu.se/~kenth/Modesty/podint2.html (accessed 11 June 2002).

9 An earlier discussion of this issue was published as 'Agents of the State? Violent Women in Popular Culture', in *Diegesis: Journal of the Association for Research in Popular Fictions*, 2 (summer 1998): 10–17.

10 There are two film versions of the Mrs Pollifax novels. *Mrs Pollifax-Spy* (Leslie Martinson, 1971) stars Rosalind Russell (who also allegedly wrote the screenplay) and is fairly faithful to the plot of the first novel in the series, *The Unexpected Mrs Pollifax* (1966). The television film, *The Unexpected Mrs Pollifax* (Anthony Pullen Shaw, 1999), starring Angela Lansbury, changes the initial location from Mexico to Morocco and mixes the plot of the first novel with that of the fourth, *A Palm for Mrs Pollifax* (1973).

## 4  English roses and all-American girls: *The New Avengers* and *The Bionic Woman*

1 See http://www.bugeyedmonster.com/toys/smdm/bionicwoman.shtml (accessed 31 October 2001).

2 See also Dave Matthews at http://www.personal.u-net.com/~carnfort/NewAvengers/ navg.htm, and http://theavengers.tv/forever/newave-prod2htm for similar accounts of the production problems.

3 Twenty-first-century students viewing episodes of *The Bionic Woman* as part of a third-year course on active female protagonists have invariably found Lindsay Wagner's performance amusing.

4 Whitney Womack offers an interesting assessment of the television series and the recent films in her article 'Reevaluating "Jiggle TV": *Charlie's Angels* at Twenty-Five', in Inness (2003: 151–71); see also Jacinda Read's essay ' "Once Upon a Time There Were Three Little Girls ... ": Girls, Violence, and *Charlie's Angels*' (Read 2004).

5 For example, a 1977 *Joint Economic Committee Report on Women and Full Employment* comments on the increase in women working as managers: 'In that area, women have moved from nine percent to 21 percent of the manager job titles in the period of 1960–1974, but during that same period, there was a growth in the occupation of 2,000 percent' (Tarr-Whelan 1978: 13).

6 Joanna Lumley's subsequent roles included Sapphire in *Sapphire and Steel* with David McCallum, the former man from U.N.C.L.E., as Steel; the louche Patsy Stone in *Absolutely Fabulous*; and a current advertising campaign for Privilege Insurance, in which Lumley again sends up her upper-class persona with the slogan, 'You don't have to be posh to be privileged.' For a reading of *Absolutely Fabulous* as a comedy about the impossibility of femininity, see Kirkham and Skeggs (1998).

7 Denys Fisher produced a Purdey doll, presented on a card which featured a drawing of Purdey in her leotard, although the doll itself was fully clothed. The back cover of the packaging endorsed her chameleon quality: 'Purdey leads such an exciting life, she needs an outfit for every occasion', urging the consumer to 'complete your collection of exclusive Purdey outfits.' Although Steed and Gambit figures were advertised, they were never issued. See Rogers (1989: 280) and http://deadduck.theavengers.tv/images/purdeydollfront.jpg (accessed 9 January 2007).

8 Nicola Foster's biography of Joanna Lumley is published online at http://www.museum.tv/archives/etv/L/htmlL/lumleyjoann/lumleyjoann.htm (accessed 10 July 2006).

## 5 *Nikita*: from French cinema to American television

1 Jeanne Moreau is a very symbolic choice for the role of Amande, as one of her most famous roles was the femme fatale Florence Carala in *Ascenseur pour l'échafaud/Lift to the Scaffold* (dir. Louis Malle, 1958).

2 Audio commentary by Joel Surnow, creative consultant Robert Cochran and director Jon Cassar on 'Nikita' (Series 1, Episode 1, 13 January 1997).

3 In 'A Girl who Wasn't There' (Series 5, Episode 2), the dead Madeline is resurrected as a holographic simulation, once again aligning her with new technologies.

## 6 *Alias*: quality television and the working woman

1 I'm indebted to Peter Hutchings for noting this shift.

2 Bantam Books, an imprint of Random House, produce the prequel series, including titles such as *Alias: Father Figure* by Laura Peyton Roberts (2003).

3 David Roger Coon's essay on the marketing of *Alias* argues that it is comparable to the promotion surrounding *Charlie's Angels* (McG, 2000) and that both campaigns play to a regressive account of gender regarding their female stars (Coon 2005).

4 See 'ABC set to begin countdown to *Alias* series finale' at http://www.abcmedianet.com/pressrel/dispDNR.html?id = 112305_01.

# Bibliography

Aldgate, A. and Richards, J. (1986) *Britain Can Take It: The British Cinema in the Second World War*, Oxford: Basil Blackwell.

Allen, R. C. (ed.) (1992) *Channels of Discourse, Reassembled: Television and Contemporary Criticism*, 2nd edn, London: Routledge.

Andrae, T. (1996) 'Television's First Feminist: *The Avengers* and Female Spectatorship', *Discourse*, 18 (3): 114–36.

Arnold, R. (2001) *Fashion, Desire and Anxiety: Image and Morality in the Twentieth Century*, London: I. B. Tauris.

Atkins, J. (1984) *The British Spy Novel*, London: John Calder.

Austin, G. (1996) *Contemporary French Cinema: An Introduction*, Manchester: Manchester University Press.

Austin, T. (1999) '"Desperate to See It": Straight Men Watching *Basic Instinct*', in M. Stokes and R. Maltby (eds) *Identifying Hollywood's Audiences: Cultural Identity and the Movies*, London: BFI.

Avallone, M. (1965) *The Man from UNCLE*, London: Souvenir Press.

——(1966) *The Girl from UNCLE No. 2: The Birds of a Feather Affair*, London: Souvenir Press.

Bainbridge, J. (1955) *Garbo*, New York: Doubleday and Company.

Balio, T (1998) '"A Major Presence in All of the World's Important Markets": The Globalization of Hollywood in the 1990s', in S. Neale and M. Smith (eds) *Contemporary Hollywood Cinema*, London: Routledge.

Barnatt, C. (1997) 'Virtual Organization in the Small Business Sector: The Case of Cavendish Management Resources', *International Small Business Journal*, 15 (4): 36–48.

Barnouw, E. (1975) *Tube of Plenty: The Evolution of American Television*, New York and Oxford: Oxford University Press.

Barthes, R. (1972) *Mythologies*, London: Paladin.

——(1982) *Image, Music, Text*, London: Flamingo.

Baughman, J. L. (1997) *The Republic of Mass Culture: Journalism, Filmmaking and Broadcasting in America since 1941*, 2nd edn, Baltimore, Md. and London: Johns Hopkins University Press.

Beer, S. (2001) 'The Third Man', *History Today*, May: 45–51.

Bennett, R. M. (2002) *Espionage: An Encyclopedia of Spies and Secrets*, London: Virgin Books.

Bennett, T. and Woollacott, J. (1987) *Bond and Beyond: The Political Career of a Popular Hero*, London: Macmillan Education.

Bentley, T. (2002) *Sisters of Salome*, London and New Haven, Conn.: Yale University Press.

Berger, A. A. (1974) 'Secret Agent', *Journal of Communication*, 24 (2): 70–4.

Berger, J. (1972) *Ways of Seeing*, London: BBC and Penguin Books.

Bergman, J. (2004) 'Whiteness and the American New Woman in the General Federation of Women's Clubs', in A. Heilmann and M. Beetham (eds), *New Woman Hybridities: Femininity, Feminism and International Consumer Culture, 1880–1930*, London: Routledge.

Berry, S. (2000) *Screen Style: Fashion and Femininity in 1930s Hollywood*, London and Minneapolis, Minn.: University of Minnesota Press.

Black, J. (2001) *The Politics of James Bond: From Fleming's Novels to the Big Screen*, London: Praeger.

Blair, A. S. (2005) '*Alias* Fans Rally to Save the Show', 6 December, available at: http://www.berubians.com/postboard/index.cgi?noframes;read=1280 (accessed 7 September 2006).

Bloom, C. (ed.) (1990) *Spy Thrillers: From Buchan to Le Carré*, London: Macmillan.

Bold, C. (1990) 'Secret Negotiations: the Spy Figure in Nineteenth-Century American Popular Fiction', *Intelligence and National Security*, Special Issue on Spy Fictions, Spy Films and Real Intelligence, 5 (4): 17–29.

——(2003) '"Under the Very Skirts of Britannia": Re-Reading Women in the James Bond Novels', in C. Lindner (ed.) *The James Bond Phenomenon: A Critical Reader*, Manchester: Manchester University Press.

Boyd, K. (2003) *Manliness and the Boys' Story Paper in Britain: A Cultural History, 1855–1940*, Basingstoke and New York: Palgrave Macmillan.

Bradbury, R. (1990) 'Reading John Le Carré', in C. Bloom (ed.) *Spy Thrillers: From Buchan to Le Carré*, London: Macmillan.

Britton, W. (2004) *Spy Television*, Westport, Conn.: Praeger.

——(2005) *Beyond Bond: Spies in Fiction and Film*, Westport, Conn.: Praeger.

Brown, J. A. (1996) 'Gender and the Action Heroine: Hardbodies and the *Point of No Return*', *Cinema Journal* 35 (3, spring): 52–71.

Brown, M. E. (1990a) 'Consumption and Resistance: The Problem of Pleasure', in M. E. Brown (ed.) *Television and Women's Culture: The Politics of the Popular*, London: Sage.

——(ed.) (1990b) *Television and Women's Culture: The Politics of the Popular*, London: Sage.

Brunsdon, C. (1997) *Screen Tastes: Soap Opera to Satellite Dishes*, London: Routledge.

Buchan, J. (1915) *The Thirty-Nine Steps*, London: Penguin.

——(1916) 'Greenmantle', in *The Complete Richard Hannay*, London: Penguin.

——(1919) *Mr Standfast*, London: Penguin.

Buscombe, E. (ed.) (2000) *British Television: A Reader*, Oxford: Oxford University Press.

Butler, J. (1990) *Gender Trouble: Feminism and the Subversion of Identity*, London and New York: Routledge.

Butts, D. (1990) 'The Hunter and the Hunted: The Suspense Novels of John Buchan', in C. Bloom (ed.) *Spy Thrillers: From Buchan to Le Carré*, London: Macmillan.

Buxton, D. (1990) *From The Avengers to Miami Vice: Form and Ideology in Television Series*, Manchester: Manchester University Press.

Cagan, E. (1978) 'The Selling of the Women's Movement', *Social Policy*, 8 (May/June): 4–12.

Cantor, M. G. and Cantor, J. M. (1992) *Prime-Time Television: Content and Control*, 2nd edn, London: Sage.

Case, D. A. (2000) 'Domesticating the Enemy: *Bewitched* and the Seventies Sitcom', in S. Waldrep (ed.), *The Seventies: The Age of Glitter in Popular Culture*, London: Routledge.

Cashmore, E. (1994) *... And There Was Television*, London: Routledge.

Cawelti, J. G. (1976) *Adventure, Mystery and Romance: Formula Stories as Art and Popular Culture*, Chicago, Ill. and London: University of Chicago Press.

Cawelti, J. G. and Rosenberg, B. A. (1987) *The Spy Story*, Chicago, Ill. and London: University of Chicago Press.

Chapman, J. (1998) 'Celluloid Shockers', in J. Richards (ed.) *The Unknown 1930s: An Alternative History of the British Cinema 1929–1939*, London: I. B. Tauris.

——(1999) *Licence to Thrill: A Cultural History of the James Bond Films*, London: I. B. Tauris.

——(2000) '*The Avengers*: Television and Popular Culture During the "High Sixties"', in A. Aldgate, J. Chapman and A. Marwick (eds) *Windows on the Sixties: Exploring Key Texts of Media and Culture*, London: I. B. Tauris.

——(2002) *Saints and Avengers: British Adventure Series of the 1960s*, London: I. B. Tauris.

Chibnall, S. (1985) 'Avenging the Past', *New Society*, 28 March, pp. 476–7.

Collins, J. (1992) 'Television and Postmodernism', in R. C. Allen (ed.), *Channels of Discourse, Reassembled: Television and Contemporary Criticism*, 2nd edn, London: Routledge.

Collins, J., Radner, H. and Preacher Collins, A. (eds) (1993) *Film Theory Goes to the Movies*, London: Routledge.

Conrad, J. (1907) *The Secret Agent*, Harmondsworth: Penguin.

Coon, D. R. (2005) 'Two Steps Forward, One Step Back: The Selling of *Charlie's Angels* and *Alias*', *Journal of Popular Film and Television*, 33 (1, spring): 2–11.

Coren, A. (1976) '*The Bionic Woman*', *The Times*, 2 July: 11.

Craig, P. and Cadogan, M. (1981) *The Lady Investigates: Women Detectives and Spies in Fiction*, London: Victor Gollancz.

Craig, S. (2003) 'Madison Avenue Versus *The Feminine Mystique*: The Advertising Industry's Response to the Women's Movement', in S. A. Inness (ed.), *Disco Divas: Women and Popular Culture in the 1970s*, Philadelphia, Pa.: University of Pennsylvania Press.

Cray, D. (2004) 'Rise of the Machines', *Time*, 163 (24): 73–4.

Cuprisin, T. (2000) 'Viewers Extend Life of USA's *Nikita*', *Milwaukee Journal Sentinel*, Tuesday December 19, available at http://www.findarticles.com/p/articles/mi_qn4196/is_20001219/ai_n10663576/print (accessed 3 May 2006).

Czerneda, J. E. (2005) 'Over Suds (In Which Experts Discuss the Relevance of Homely Details to the Appeal of a Certain Female Spy) (With Occasional Interruption by an Uncle)', in K. Weisman with G. Yeffeth (eds) *Alias Assumed: Sex, Lies and SD-6*, Dallas, Tex.: Benbella Books.

D'Acci, J. (1997) 'Nobody's Woman? *Honey West* and The New Sexuality', in L. Spigel and M. Curtin (eds) *The Revolution Wasn't Televised: Sixties Television and Social Conflict*, London: Routledge.

Dandeker, C (1990) *Surveillance, Power and Modernity: Bureaucracy and Discipline from 1700 to the Present Day*, Cambridge: Polity Press.

Dauncey, H. (ed.) (2003) *French Popular Culture: An Introduction*, London: Arnold.

Davies, B., Browne, J., Gannon, S., Honan, E., and Somerville, M. (2005) 'Embodied Women at Work in Neoliberal Times and Places', *Gender, Work and Organization*, 12 (4, July): 343–62.

Denning, M. (1987) *Cover Stories: Narrative and Ideology in the British Spy Thriller*, London: Routledge and Kegan Paul.

Der Derian, J. (1992) *Antidiplomacy: Spies, Terror, Speed and War*, Oxford: Blackwell.

Dijkstra, B. (1986) *Idols of Perversity: Fantasies of Feminine Evil in Fin-de-Siècle Culture*, Oxford: Oxford University Press.

Diment, A. (1967) *The Dolly Dolly Spy*, London: Pan Books.

——(1968) *The Great Spy Race*, London: Pan Books.

DiTommaso, T. (2003) 'The Aesthetics of Television', *Crossings*, 3 (1), available at http://crossings.tcd.ie/issues/3:1/DiTommaso. (Accessed 16 October 2006.)

Doane, M. A. (1991) *Femmes Fatales: Feminism, Film Theory, Psychoanalysis*, London: Routledge.

Dolan, J. (2000) '*They Flew Alone* and "The Angel of the Air": Crossings between Respectability, Nation and Empire', *Visual Culture in Britain*, 1 (2): 25–41.

Donald, M. (1990) 'John Buchan: The Reader's Trap', in C. Bloom (ed.), *Spy Thrillers: From Buchan to Le Carré*, London: Macmillan.

Douglas, S. J. (1994) *Where the Girls Are: Growing Up Female With the Mass Media*, London: Penguin.

Dow, B. J. (1996) *Prime-Time Feminism*, Philadelphia, Pa.: University of Pennsylvania Press.

——(2005) '"How Will You Make It on Your Own?": Television and Feminism Since 1970', in J. Wasko (ed.), *A Companion to Television*, Oxford: Blackwell.

Downing, M. (1974) 'Heroine of the Daytime Serial', *Journal of Communication*, 24 (2): 130–7.

Dresner, L. M. (2007) *The Female Investigator in Literature, Film and Popular Culture*, Jefferson, NC: McFarland.

Durham, C. A. (1998) *Double Takes: Culture and Gender in French Films and Their American Remakes*, Hanover, NH and London: University Press of New England.

Dyer, R. (1997) *White*, London, New York: Routledge.

Echols, A. (1989) *Daring to Be Bad: Radical Feminism in America 1967–1975*, London and Minneapolis, Minn.: University of Minnesota Press.

Eco, U. (1981) *The Role of the Reader: Explorations in the Semiotics of Texts*, London: Hutchinson.

Enns, A. (2000) 'The Fans from U.N.C.L.E.: The Marketing and Reception of the Swinging '60s Spy Phenomenon', *Journal of Popular Film and Television*, 28 (3): 124–32.

Entwistle, J. (1997) '"Power Dressing" and the Construction of the Career Woman', in M. Nava, A. Blake, I. MacRury and B. Richards (eds) *Buy This Book: Studies in Advertising and Consumption*, London: Routledge.

Erickson, T. (1996) 'Kill Me Again: Movement Becomes Genre', in A. Silver and J. Ursini (eds), *Film Noir Reader*, New York: Limelight Editions.

Fawcett, H. (2004) 'Romance, Glamour and the Exotic: Femininity and Fashion in Britain in the 1900s', in A. Heilmann and M. Beetham (eds), *New Woman Hybridities: Femininity, Feminism and International Consumer Culture, 1880–1930*, London and New York: Routledge.

Felski, R. (1995) *The Gender of Modernity*, Cambridge, Mass.: Harvard University Press.

Feuer, J. (1992) 'Genre Study', in R. C. Allen (ed.), *Channels of Discourse, Reassembled: Television and Contemporary Criticism*, 2nd edn, London: Routledge.

Firestone, S. (1979) *The Dialectic of Sex: The Case for a Feminist Revolution*, originally published 1970, London: The Women's Press.

Fischer, L. (2002) 'Greta Garbo and Silent Cinema: The Actress as Art Deco Icon', *Camera Obscura*, May, available at http://web5.infotrac.galegroup.com/itw/infomark/990/227/87669994w5/purl = rcl_SPO 24 May 06. (Accessed 24 May 2006.)

Fiske, J. (1987) *Television Culture*, London: Routledge.

Fleming, I. (1958) *Dr No*, London: Pan.

——(1959) *Goldfinger*, London: Pan.

——(1962) *The Spy Who Loved Me*, London: Pan.

——(1963) *On Her Majesty's Secret Service*, London: Penguin.

——(1965) *The Man with the Golden Gun*, London: Pan.

Foucault, M. (1977) *Discipline and Punish: The Birth of the Prison*, translated by Alan Sheridan (originally published in French by Éditions Gallimard 1975), London: Penguin.

Fratantuono, L. (2005) 'Classical Mythology, Prime-Time Television: Sydney Bristow and the Quest for Female Identity', in K. Weisman with G. Yeffeth (eds), *Alias Assumed: Sex, Lies and SD-6*, Dallas, Tex.: Benbella Books.

Garrett, S. M. (2005) 'You've Come a Long Way, Baby: A Forty-Year Leap for the Spygirl from the Swingin' Sixties to the Naughty Oughties', in K. Weisman with G. Yeffeth (eds), *Alias Assumed: Sex, Lies and SD-6*, Dallas, Tex.: Benbella Books.

Gatlin, R. (1987) *American Women Since 1945*, Jackson, Miss. and London: University Press of Mississippi.

Gelder, K. (2004) *Popular Fiction: The Logics and Practices of a Literary Field*, London: Routledge.

Geraghty, C. (2000) *British Cinema in the Fifties: Gender, Genre and the 'New Look'*, London: Routledge.

Gilman, D. (1966) *The Unexpected Mrs Pollifax*, New York: Fawcett Books.

——(1970) *The Amazing Mrs Pollifax*, New York: Fawcett Crest.

——(1971) *The Elusive Mrs Pollifax*, New York: Fawcett Crest.

——(1973) *A Palm for Mrs Pollifax*, New York: Fawcett Books.

——(1976) *Mrs Pollifax on Safari*, New York: Fawcett Books.

——(1993) *Mrs Pollifax and the Second Thief*, New York: Fawcett Books.

——(2000) *Mrs Pollifax Unveiled*, New York: Ballantine Books.

Gitlin, T. (1994) *Inside Prime Time*, 3rd edn, London: Routledge.

Gledhill, C. (1998) 'Pleasurable Negotiations', in J. Storey (ed.), *Cultural Theory and Popular Culture: A Reader*, London: Prentice.

Goh, R. B. H. (1999) 'Peter O'Donnell, Race Relations and National Identity: The Dynamics of Representation in 1960s and 1970s Britain', *Journal of Popular Culture*, 32 (4): 29–43.

Gould, J. (1987) 'Women's Military Services in First World War Britain', in M.R. Higonnet, J. Jenson, S. Michel and M.C. Weitz (eds) *Behind the Lines: Gender and the Two World Wars*, London and New Haven, Conn.: Yale University Press.

Grayzel, S.R. (1999) *Women's Identities at War: Gender, Motherhood and Politics in Britain and France During the First World War*, Chapel Hill, NC and London: University of North Carolina Press.

Green, J. (1999) *All Dressed Up: The Sixties and the Counterculture*, London: Pimlico.

Gregory, C. (1997) *Be Seeing You ... : Decoding The Prisoner*, Luton: University of Luton Press.

Grindstaff, L. (2001) 'A Pygmalion Tale Retold: Remaking *La Femme Nikita*', *Camera Obscura* 47, 16 (2): 133–75.

Gross, E. (2003) 'Hi, Hi Miss American Spy', *SFX Magazine*, 102 (March): 46–54.

Gwenllian Jones, S. (2003) 'Web Wars: Resistance, Online Fandom and Studio Censorship', in M. Jancovich and J. Lyons (eds), *Quality Popular Television*, London: BFI.

Harper, S. (1998) '"Thinking Forward and Up": The British Films of Conrad Veidt', in J. Richards (ed.) *The Unknown 1930s: An Alternative History of the British Cinema 1929–1939*, London: I. B. Tauris.

Hart, L. (1994) *Fatal Women: Lesbian Sexuality and the Mark of Aggression*, Princeton, NJ: Princeton University Press.

Harvey, S. (1998) 'Woman's Place: The Absent Family of Film Noir', in E. Ann Kaplan (ed.), *Women in Film Noir*, 2nd edn, London: BFI Publishing.

Hayes, M. J. (1990) 'Are You Telling Me Lies David? The Work of John le Carré', in C. Bloom (ed.), *Spy Thrillers: From Buchan to le Carré*, London: Macmillan.

Hayward, S. (1997) 'Sex-Violence-Surveillance: Questions of Containment and Displacement in Besson's Film *Nikita*', *Journal of the Institute of Romance Studies*, 5: 245–54.

——(1998) *Luc Besson*, Manchester: Manchester University Press.

Heilmann, A. and Beetham, M. (eds) (2004) *New Woman Hybridities: Femininity, Feminism and International Consumer Culture, 1880–1930*, London: Routledge.

Higonnet, M.R., Jenson, J., Michel S. and Weitz, M.C. (eds) (1987) *Behind the Lines: Gender and the Two World Wars*, London and New Haven, Conn.: Yale University Press.

Hiley, N. (1990) 'Decoding German Spies: British Spy Fiction 1908–1918', *Intelligence and National Security*, Special Issue on Spy Fictions, Spy Films and Real Intelligence, 5 (4): 55–79.

Hollows, J. (2000) *Feminism, Femininity and Popular Culture*, Manchester: Manchester University Press.

Holt, J. (2003) 'Vertical Vision: Deregulation, Industrial Economy and Prime-Time Design', in M. Jancovich and J. Lyons (eds), *Quality Popular Television*, London: BFI.

Horn, M. (1977) *Women in the Comics*, New York: Chelsea House Publishers.

Huyssen, A. (1986) *After the Great Divide: Modernism, Mass Culture, Postmodernism*, Bloomington, Ind.: Indiana University Press.

Inness, S. A. (1999) *Tough Girls: Women Warriors and Wonder Women in Popular Culture*, Philadelphia, Pa.: University of Pennsylvania Press.

——(ed.) (2003) *Disco Divas: Women and Popular Culture in the 1970s*, Philadelphia, Pa.: University of Pennsylvania Press.

——(ed.) (2004) *Action Chicks: New Images of Tough Women in Popular Culture*, New York: Palgrave Macmillan.

Irigaray, L. (1981) 'When the Goods Get Together', in E. Marks and I. de Courtivron (eds), *New French Feminisms: An Anthology*, Hemel Hempstead: Harvester.

Jameson, F. (1988) 'Postmodernism and Consumer Society', in E. A. Kaplan (ed.), *Postmodernism and Its Discontents: Theories, Practices*, London: Verso.

Jancovich, M. and Lyons, J. (eds) (2003) *Quality Popular Television*, London: BFI.

Jones, A. (1991) '"She Was Bad News": Male Paranoia and the Contemporary New Woman', *Camera Obscura*, 25–6 (January–May): 297–320.

Kaplan, E. A. (ed.) (1988) *Postmodernism and Its Discontents: Theories, Practices,* London: Verso.

——(1998) *Women in Film Noir,* 2nd edn, London: BFI Publishing.

Kemp, S. and Squires, J. (eds) (1997) *Feminisms,* Oxford and New York: Oxford University Press.

Kirkham, P. and Skeggs, B. (1998) *'Absolutely Fabulous*: Absolutely Feminist?', in C. Geraghty and D. Lusted (eds), *The Television Studies Book,* London: Arnold.

Knightley, P. (2003) *The Second Oldest Profession: Spies and Spying in the Twentieth Century,* London: Pimlico.

Landy, M. (1991) *British Genres: Cinema and Society, 1930–1960,* Princeton, NJ: Princeton University Press.

Lant, A. (1991) *Blackout: Reinventing Women for Wartime British Cinema,* Princeton, NJ: Princeton University Press.

le Carré, J. (1963) *The Spy who Came in from the Cold,* London: Coronet.

——(1965) *The Looking-Glass War,* London: Pan.

Ledger, S. (1997) *The New Woman: Fiction and Feminism at the Fin de Siècle,* Manchester: Manchester University Press.

Le Queux, W. (1919) *The Temptress,* London: Ward, Lock & Co.

Levy, A. (2005) *Female Chauvinist Pigs: Women and the Rise of Raunch Culture,* London: Pocket Books.

Lewis, R. (1996) *Gendering Orientalism: Race, Femininity and Representation,* London and New York: Routledge.

Lindner, C. (ed.) (2003) *The James Bond Phenomenon: A Critical Reader,* Manchester: Manchester University Press.

Lisanti, T. and Paul, L. (2002) *Film Fatales: Women in Espionage Films and Television, 1962–1973,* Jefferson, NC and London: McFarland.

Lumley, J. (1989) *Stare Back and Smile: Memoirs,* London: Penguin.

Lyon, D. (1994) *The Electronic Eye: The Rise of Surveillance Society,* Cambridge: Polity Press.

Macintosh, J.J. (1990) 'Ethics and Spy Fiction', *Intelligence and National Security,* Special Issue on Spy Fictions, Spy Films and Real Intelligence, 5 (4): 161–84.

Mailer, N. (1991) *Harlot's Ghost,* London: Abacus.

Maltby, R. (1998) '"Nobody Knows Everything": Post-Classical Historiographies and Consolidated Entertainment', in S. Neale and M. Smith (eds), *Contemporary Hollywood Cinema,* London: Routledge.

Mandel, E. (1984) *A Social History of the Crime Story,* London: Pluto Press.

Mangan, J. A. and Walvin, J. (eds) (1987) *Manliness and Morality: Middle-Class Masculinity in Britain and America, 1800–1940,* Manchester: Manchester University Press.

Marwick, A. (1998) *The Sixties: Cultural Revolution in Britain, France, Italy and the United States, c.1958–c.1974,* Oxford: Oxford University Press.

——(2000) 'Introduction: Locating Key Texts Amid the Distinctive Landscape of the Sixties', in A. Aldgate, J. Chapman and A. Marwick (eds), *Windows on the Sixties: Exploring Key Texts of Media and Culture,* London: I. B. Tauris.

Mazdon, L. (ed.) (2001) *France on Film: Reflections on Popular French Cinema,* London: Wallflower Press.

McCaughey, M. and King, N. (eds) (2001) *Reel Knockouts: Violent Women in the Movies,* Austin, Tex.: University of Texas Press.

McCormick, D. (1977) *Who's Who in Spy Fiction,* London: Elm Tree Books.

McNay, L. (2000) *Gender and Agency: Reconfiguring the Subject in Feminist and Social Theory*, Cambridge: Polity Press.

McNeil, J. C. (1975) 'Feminism, Femininity, and the Television Series: A Content Analysis', *Journal of Broadcasting*, 19 (3): 259–71.

Miller, F. (1986) *Batman: The Dark Knight Returns*, London: Titan Books.

Miller, T. (2003) *Spyscreen: Espionage on Film and TV From the 1930s to the 1960s*, Oxford: Oxford University Press.

Modleski, T. (1984) *Loving with a Vengeance: Mass-Produced Fantasies for Women*, London: Methuen.

Moore, A. and Gibbons, D. (1987) *Watchmen*, London: Titan Books.

Moran, A. (2005) 'Configurations of the New Television Landscape', in J. Wasko (ed.), *A Companion to Television*, Oxford: Blackwell.

Mullan, B. (1997) *Consuming Television: Television and Its Audience*, Oxford: Blackwell.

Mulvey, L. (1989) *Visual and Other Pleasures*, London and Basingstoke: Macmillan.

Murray, W. (1988) 'E. Phillips Oppenheim', in B. Benstock and T. F. Staley (eds) *Dictionary of Literary Biography Volume 70: British Mystery Writers 1860–1919*, Detroit, Mich. and London: Gale Research.

Nava, M., Blake, A., MacRury, I. and Richards, B. (eds) (1997) *Buy this Book: Studies in Advertising and Consumption*, London: Routledge.

Neale, S. (1998) 'Widescreen Composition in the Age of Television', in S. Neale and M. Smith (eds), *Contemporary Hollywood Cinema*, London: Routledge.

Negroponte, N. (1995) *Being Digital*, London: Hodder & Stoughton.

Normant, S. (2001) *Femme Fatale: The Timeless Style of Beautiful Women*, London: Thames & Hudson.

Norton-Taylor, R. (2006) 'Fact and Fiction: How Real-Life Spies See Bond', *The Guardian*, Saturday 11 November: 21.

Nye, J. L. (2005) 'Why Sydney Has No Social Life', in K. Weisman with G. Yeffeth (eds), *Alias Assumed: Sex, Lies and SD-6*, Dallas, Tex.: Benbella Books.

O'Brien, G. (1995) 'Fritz Lang's *Spies*: Now and Forever', *Film Comment*, 31 (4, July–August): 66–9.

O'Day, M. (2001) 'Of Leather Suits and Kinky Boots: *The Avengers*, Style and Popular Culture', in B. Osgerby and A. Gough-Yates (eds), *Action TV: Tough Guys, Smooth Operators and Foxy Chicks*, London: Routledge.

O'Donnell, P. (1965) *Modesty Blaise*, London: Pan Books.

——(1966) *Sabre-Tooth*, London: Pan Books.

——(1967) *I, Lucifer*, London: Pan Books.

——(1969) *A Taste for Death*, London: Souvenir Press.

——(1972) *Pieces of Modesty*, London: Pan Books.

——(1977) *Last Day in Limbo*, London: Pan Books.

——(1982) *The Night of Morningstar*, London: Souvenir Press.

——(2004) 'Girl Walking', in P. O'Donnell and J. Holdaway, *The Gabriel Set-Up*, London: Titan Books.

O'Donnell, P. and J. Holdaway (2004) *The Gabriel Set-Up*, London: Titan Books.

O'Regan, T. (2000) 'The International Circulation of British Television', in E. Buscombe (ed.), *British Television: A Reader*, Oxford: Oxford University Press.

Orczy, B. (1905) *The Scarlet Pimpernel*, London: Heron Books.

——(1913) *Eldorado*, London: Hodder & Stoughton.

Osgerby, B. and Gough-Yates, A. (eds) (2001) *Action TV: Tough Guys, Smooth Operators and Foxy Chicks*, London: Routledge.

Oswell, D. (1999) 'And What Might Our Children Become? Future Visions, Governance and the Child Television Audience in Postwar Britain', *Screen* 40 (1, spring): 66–87.

Ouditt, S. (1994) *Fighting Forces, Writing Women: Identity and Ideology in the First World War*, London: Routledge.

Panek, L. L. (1981) *The Special Branch: The British Spy Novel 1890–1980,* Bowling Green, Ohio: Bowling Green University Popular Press.

Paris, B. (1995) *Garbo: A Biography*, London: Sidgwick & Jackson.

Park, R. J. (1987) 'Biological Thought, Athletics and the Formation of a "Man of Character" 1830–1900', in J. A. Mangan and J. Walvin (eds), *Manliness and Morality: Middle-Class Masculinity in Britain and America, 1800–1940*, Manchester: Manchester University Press.

Paterson, M. (2004) 'Blaise of Glory: The Modesty Blaise Phenomenon', in P. O'Donnell and J. Holdaway (eds), *The Gabriel Set-up*, London: Titan Books.

Perrons, D. (2003) 'The New Economy and the Work-Life Balance: Conceptual Explorations and a Case Study of New Media', *Gender, Work and Organization*, 10 (1, January): 65–93.

Perrot, M. (1987) 'The New Eve and the Old Adam: Changes in French Women's Condition at the Turn of the Century', in M. R. Higonnet, J. Jenson, S. Michel and M. C. Weitz (eds), *Behind the Lines: Gender and the Two World Wars*, London and New Haven, Conn.: Yale University Press.

Peyton Roberts, L. (2003) *Alias: Father Figure*, New York: Bantam Books.

Plant, S. (1997) 'Beyond the Screens: Film, Cyberpunk and Cyberfeminism', in S. Kemp and J. Squires (eds) *Feminisms*, New York and Oxford: Oxford University Press.

Powrie, P. (2003) 'Cinema', in H. Dauncey (ed.), *French Popular Culture: An Introduction*, London: Arnold.

Proctor, T. M. (2003) *Female Intelligence: Women and Espionage in the First World War*, London and New York: New York University Press.

Rabinovitz, L. (1989) 'Sitcoms and Single Moms: Representations of Feminism on American TV', *Cinema Journal*, 29 (1, autumn): 3–19.

Radaker, K. (1988) 'William Le Queux', in B. Benstock and T. F. Staley (eds), *Dictionary of Literary Biography Volume 70: British Mystery Writers 1860–1919*, Detroit, Mich. and London: Gale Research.

Radner, H. (1995) *Shopping Around: Feminine Culture and the Pursuit of Pleasure*, London: Routledge.

——(1998) 'New Hollywood's New Women: Murder in Mind – Sarah and Margie', in S. Neale and M. Smith (eds), *Contemporary Hollywood Cinema*, London: Routledge.

Read, J. (2000) *The New Avengers: Feminism, Femininity and the Rape-Revenge Cycle*, Manchester: Manchester University Press.

——(2004) '"Once Upon a Time There Were Three Little Girls ... "': Girls, Violence, and *Charlie's Angels*' in S. J. Schneider (ed.) *New Hollywood Violence*, Manchester: Manchester University Press.

Reeves, T. C. (2000) *Twentieth-Century America: A Brief History*, New York and Oxford: Oxford University Press.

Rich, A. (1981) *Compulsory Heterosexuality and Lesbian Existence*, London: Onlywomen Press.

Rich, B. R. (1995) 'Dumb Lugs and *Femmes Fatales*', *Sight and Sound*, 5 (1, November): 6–10.

Richards, J. (1997) *Films and British National Identity: From Dickens to Dad's Army*, Manchester: Manchester University Press.

——(ed.) (1998) *The Unknown 1930s: An Alternative History of the British Cinema 1929–1939*, London: I. B. Tauris.

Richardson, A. (2004) 'The Birth of National Hygiene and Efficiency: Women and Eugenics in Britain and America 1865–1915', in A. Heilmann and M. Beetham (eds), *New Woman Hybridities: Femininity, Feminism and International Consumer Culture, 1880–1930*, London: Routledge.

Riviere, J. (1986) 'Womanliness as a Masquerade' (originally published in *The International Journal of Psychoanalysis*, Vol. 10, 1929), in V. Burgin, J. Donald and C. Kaplan (eds), *Formations of Fantasy*, London: Routledge.

Rixon, P. (2003) 'The Changing Face of American Television Programmes on British Screens', in M. Jancovich and J. Lyons (eds), *Quality Popular Television*, London: BFI.

Rogers, D. (1989) *The Complete Avengers*, New York: St Martin's Press.

Roper, M. and Tosh, J. (1991) *Manful Assertions: Masculinities in Britain since 1800*, London: Routledge.

Roseneil, S. and Seymour, J. (eds) (1999) *Practising Identities: Power and Resistance*, Basingstoke: Macmillan.

Rubin, G. (1975) 'The Traffic in Women: Notes on the Political Economy of Sex' in R. A. Reiter (ed.), *Toward an Anthropology of Women*, New York: Monthly Review Press.

Ruditis, P. (2005) *Alias: Authorized Personnel Only*, New York: Simon Spotlight Entertainment.

Rutherford, J. (1997) *Forever England: Reflections on Masculinity and Empire*, London: Lawrence & Wishart.

Said, E. W. (1978) *Orientalism*, Harmondsworth: Penguin.

Sandbrook, D. (2006) *White Heat: A History of Britain in the Swinging Sixties*, London: Little, Brown.

Schatz, T. (1993) 'The New Hollywood', in J. Collins, H. Radner and A. Preacher Collins (eds), *Film Theory Goes to the Movies*, London: Routledge.

——(2004) 'Introduction', in S. J. Schneider (ed.), *New Hollywood Violence*, Manchester: Manchester University Press.

Schneider, S. J. (ed.) (2004) *New Hollywood Violence*, Manchester: Manchester University Press.

Schrader, P. (1972) 'Notes on *Film Noir*', *Film Comment*, (spring): 8–13.

Sedgewick, E. K. (1991) *Epistemology of the Closet*, Hemel Hempstead: Harvester Wheatsheaf.

Segal, L. (1997) 'Generations of Feminism', *Radical Philosophy*, 83 (May/June): 6–16.

Shattuc, J. M. (2005) 'Television Production: Who Makes American TV?', in J. Wasko (ed.), *A Companion to Television*, Oxford: Blackwell.

Showalter, E. (1985) *The Female Malady: Women, Madness and English Culture 1830–1980*, London: Virago.

——(1990) *Sexual Anarchy: Gender and Culture at the Fin de Siècle*, London: Virago.

Silver, A. and Ursini, J. (eds) (1996) *Film Noir Reader*, New York: Limelight Editions.

Smith, A. (2001) '*Nikita* as Social Fantasy', in L. Mazdon (ed.), *France on Film: Reflections on Popular French Cinema*, London: Wallflower Press.

Smith, A.-M. (1997) 'Feminist Activism and Presidential Politics: Theorizing the Costs of the "Insider Strategy"', *Radical Philosophy*, 83 (May/June): 25–35.

Smith, M. (1998) 'Theses on the Philosophy of Hollywood History', in S. Neale and M. Smith (eds), *Contemporary Hollywood Cinema*, London: Routledge.

Spigel, L. and Curtin, M. (eds) (1997) *The Revolution Wasn't Televised: Sixties Television and Social Conflict*, London: Routledge.

Stables, K. (1998) 'The Postmodern Always Rings Twice: Constructing the *Femme Fatale* in 90s Cinema', in E. Ann Kaplan (ed.), *Women in Film Noir*, 2nd edn, London: BFI Publishing.

Stanworth, C. (2000) 'Women and Work in the Information Age', *Gender, Work and Organization*, 7 (1, January): 20–32.

Staples, K. (1988) 'Emma, Baroness Orczy', in B. Benstock and T. F. Staley (eds), *Dictionary of Literary Biography, Volume 70: British Mystery Writers 1860–1919*, Detroit, Mich. and London: Gale Research.

Stein, B. (1980) *The View from Sunset Boulevard: America as Brought to You by the People who Make Television*, New York: Anchor Books.

Stokes, M. and Maltby, R. (eds) (1999) *Identifying Hollywood's Audiences: Cultural Identity and the Movies*, London: British Film Institute.

Storey, J. (ed.) (1998) *Cultural Theory and Popular Culture: A Reader*, London: Prentice.

Stott, R. (1992) *The Fabrication of the Late-Victorian Femme Fatale: The Kiss of Death*, London: Macmillan.

Street, S. (1997) *British National Cinema*, London: Routledge.

Takacs, S. (2005) 'Speculations on a New Economy: *La Femme Nikita*, the Series', *Cultural Critique*, 61 (autumn): 148–85.

Tarr-Whelan, L. (1978) 'Women Workers and Organized Labor', *Social Policy*, 8 (May/June): 13–17.

Tasker, Y. (1993) *Spectacular Bodies: Gender, Genre and the Action Cinema*, London: Routledge.

——(1998) *Working Girls: Gender and Sexuality in Popular Cinema*, London: Routledge.

Tedesco, N. S. (1974) 'Patterns in Prime Time', *Journal of Communication*, 24 (2): 119–24.

Thomas, L. (2002) *Fans, Feminisms and 'Quality' Media*, London: Routledge.

Thumim, J. (1992) *Celluloid Sisters: Women and Popular Cinema*, London: Macmillan.

Trotter, D. (1990) 'The Politics of Adventure in the Early Spy Novel', *Intelligence and National Security*, Special Issue on Spy Fictions, Spy Films and Real Intelligence, 5 (4): 30–54.

Tung, C. (2004) 'Embodying an Image: Gender, Race and Sexuality in *La Femme Nikita*', in Sherrie A. Inness (ed.), *Action Chicks: New Images of Tough Women in Popular Culture*, New York: Palgrave Macmillan.

Van Seters, D. (1992) 'Hardly Hollywood's Ideal: Female Autobiographies of Secret Service Work, 1914–45', *Intelligence and National Security*, 7 (4): 403–24.

Vincendeau, G. (1996) *The Companion to French Cinema*, London: BFI.

Waldrep, S. (ed.) (2000) *The Seventies: The Age of Glitter in Popular Culture*, London: Routledge.

Walter, N. (1998) *The New Feminism*, London: Little, Brown.

Wark, W. K. (1990) 'Introduction: Fictions of History', *Intelligence and National Security*, 5 (4): 1–16.

Warren, A. (1987) 'Popular Manliness: Baden-Powell, Scouting, and the Development of Manly Character', in J. A. Mangan and J. Walvin (eds) *Manliness and Morality: Middle-Class Masculinity in Britain and America, 1800–1940*, Manchester: Manchester University Press.

Wasko, J. (ed.) (2005) *A Companion to Television*, Oxford: Blackwell.

Weisman, K. (ed.) (2005) *Alias Assumed: Sex, Lies and SD-6*, Dallas, Tex.: Benbella Books.

Wheelwright, J. (1992) *The Fatal Lover: Mata Hari and the Myth of Women in Espionage*, London: Collins & Brown.

White, R. (1998) 'Agents of the State? Violent Women in Popular Culture', *Diegesis: Journal of the Association for Research in Popular Fictions*, (2, summer): 10–17.

——(2006) 'Lipgloss Feminists: *Charlie's Angels* and *The Bionic Woman*', *Story-telling: A Critical Journal of Popular Narrative*, 5 (3): 171–83.

Whitehead, S. (1999) 'Contingent Masculinities: Disruptions to "Man"agerialist Identity', in S. Roseneil and J. Seymour (eds) *Practising Identities: Power and Resistance*, Basingstoke: Macmillan.

Wilcox, H. (1967) *Twenty-Five Thousand Sunsets: The Autobiography of Herbert Wilcox*, London: The Bodley Head.

Willis, M. (1976) *The Bionic Woman: Double Identity*, London: Wyndham Publications.

Wilson, E. (1991) *The Sphinx in the City: Urban Life, the Control of Disorder, and Women*, London: Virago.

——(2003) *Adorned in Dreams: Fashion and Modernity*, new edn, London: I. B. Tauris.

Wood, R. (1986) *Hollywood from Vietnam to Reagan*, New York: Columbia University Press.

Woolf, M. (1990) 'Ian Fleming's Enigmas and Variations', in C. Bloom (ed.) *Spy Thrillers: From Buchan to Le Carré*, London: Macmillan.

Worland, R. (1994) 'The Cold War Mannerists: *The Man From U.N.C.L.E.* and TV Espionage in the 1960s', *Journal of Popular Film and Television*, 21 (4, winter): 150–61.

Wright, L. A. (2005) 'Only Ourselves to Blame', in K. Weisman (ed.) *Alias Assumed: Sex, Lies and SD-6*, Dallas, Tex.: Benbella Books.

# Index

This book examines the early work of William Carlos Williams in relationship to a woman's tradition of American poetry, as represented by Mina Loy, Denise Levertov, and Kathleen Fraser – three generations of women poets working in or directly from a modernist tradition. Joining revisionary studies of literary history, Professor Kinnahan sees Williams's work as both developing from the poetics of women and as influencing subsequent generations of American women poets. Williams's poetry and prose of the 1910s and 1920s is read as a struggle with issues of gender authority in relationship to poetic tradition and voice. Linda A. Kinnahan traces notions of the feminine and the maternal that develop as Williams seeks to create a modern poetics. The impact of first-wave American feminism is examined through an extended analysis of Mina Loy's poetry as a source of a feminist modernism for Williams. Levertov and Fraser are discussed as poetic daughters of Williams who strive to define their voices as women and to reclaim an enabling poetic tradition. In the process, each woman's negotiations with poetic authority and tradition call into question the relationship of poetic father and daughter. Positioning Williams in relationship to these three generations of Anglo-American women writing within or descending from the modernist movement, the book pursues two questions: What can women poets, writing with an informed awareness of Williams, teach us about his modernist poetics of contact, and just as importantly, what can they teach us about the process, for women, of constructing a writing self within a male-dominated tradition?

CAMBRIDGE STUDIES IN AMERICAN LITERATURE AND CULTURE

**Poetics of the Feminine**

# CAMBRIDGE STUDIES IN AMERICAN LITERATURE AND CULTURE

*Books in the series*

Continued on pages following the Index

# Poetics of the Feminine
*Authority and Literary Tradition in William Carlos Williams, Mina Loy, Denise Levertov, and Kathleen Fraser*

LINDA A. KINNAHAN
*Duquesne University*

CAMBRIDGE
UNIVERSITY PRESS

Published by the Press Syndicate of the University of Cambridge
The Pitt Building, Trumpington Street, Cambridge CB2 1RP
40 West 20th Street, New York, NY 10011–4211, USA
10 Stamford Road, Oakleigh, Melbourne 3166, Australia

First published 1994

Printed in the United States of America

*Library of Congress Cataloging-in-Publication Data*
Kinnahan, Linda A.
Poetics of the feminine : authority and literary tradition in
William Carlos Williams, Mina Loy, Denise Levertov, and Kathleen
Fraser / Linda A. Kinnahan.
    p.    cm.
Includes bibliographical references and index.
ISBN 0–521–45127–2 (hc)
1. American poetry – Women authors – History and criticism.
2. Feminism and literature – United States – History – 20th century.
3. Women and literature – United States – History – 20th century.
4. Fraser, Kathleen, 1937–      – Criticism and interpretation.
5. Levertov, Denise, 1923–      – Criticism and interpretation.
6. American poetry—20th century – history and criticism.
7. Williams, William Carlos, 1883–1963 – Influence.   8. Loy, Mina –
Criticism and interpretation.   9. Influence (Literary, artistic,
etc.)   10. Authority in literature.   I. Title.
PS151.T38    1994
811′.5099287 – dc20                                              93–5483
                                                                    CIP

A catalog record for this book is available from the British Library.

ISBN 0–521–45127–2 hardback

*For Tom*

# Contents

# Acknowledgments

I am happy to finally be able to express my appreciation to those people and institutions who have helped make this book possible. The English Department of the University of Notre Dame granted me a fellowship at the beginning of this project that allowed me a concentrated year with pen, paper, and lots of books. Duquesne University has provided generous support through release time, for which I thank Dean John McDonald and Professor Joseph Keenan, English Department Chair. Through classes, conversations, colloquia, and other interchanges, my colleagues and the students at Duquesne have been a constant source of intellectual stimulation and encouragement. My particular thanks go to Dan Watkins, who has been an invaluable mentor, and to the graduate students at Duquesne, who continually energize me with their desire to learn and teach me through their own discoveries.

Early readers of this book include John Matthias and Jacqueline Brogan, whose interest in my ideas about poetry convinced me of their worth. I extend special thanks to Charlene Avallone for her extremely careful and sensitive reading of manuscript drafts, generosity of time in dialogue, and sharing of interests; and to Stephen Fredman, who kept me sane, provided incredible direction, and taught me much about many things. I would also like to thank Kathleen Fraser for engaging in long conversations with me and, on a larger scale, helping to develop connections among writers and critics interested in women experimental writers. For their quality editing work, I thank Sandy Graham and Melinda Mousouris.

I wrote my first draft with a fountain pen gifted to me by my very good friend Peter Campbell, and I continue to treasure both the pen and Pete. For inspiring me to listen to the language of poetry, I thank Susan Facknitz. For teaching me about art and books, and for their belief in me, I will always be grateful to my parents, Edith and Jim Arbaugh. For always reminding me that it's better to be pleasant than smart (influenced by Jimmy Stewart), for helping me laugh through many, many years, and through offering a constant refuge, I thank Kathy Corrigan and her family, Tony, Aaron, Lena, and Maggie. Most of all, I thank Tom Kinnahan for his humor, gentleness, sanity, and love. This book is for Tom and for all he makes possible.

Portions of Chapter 1 appeared in different form and under the name of Linda A. Taylor in "Lines of Contact: Mina Loy and William Carlos Williams," *William Carlos Williams Review* 16.2 (Fall 1990). Copyright © 1990 by Peter Schmidt, reprinted by permission of the *William Carlos Williams Review*.

Portions of Chapter 4 appeared in different form and under the name of Linda A. Taylor in " 'A Seizure of Voice': Language Innovation and a Feminist Poetics in the Works of Kathleen Fraser," *Contemporary Literature* 33.2 (Summer 1992), special editor Thomas Gardner. Copyright © 1992 by the Board of Regents of the University of Wisconsin System, reprinted by permission of the University of Wisconsin Press.

In addition, I acknowledge permission to cite excerpts from the following, reprinted by permission of New Directions Publishing Company:

William Carlos Williams, *Collected Poems 1909–1939* Volume I, copyright 1938 by New Directions Publishing Corporation;

William Carlos Williams, *Collected Poems 1939–1963* Volume II, copyright 1944, 1948, © 1962 by William Carlos Williams;

William Carlos Williams, *In the American Grain*, copyright 1933 by William Carlos Williams;

William Carlos Williams, *Paterson*, copyright 1946, 1948, © 1958 by William Carlos Williams;

William Carlos Williams, *Selected Essays*, copyright 1954 by William Carlos Williams;

Denise Levertov, *The Poet and the World*, copyright © 1973 by Denise Levertov Goodman;

Denise Levertov, *Collected Early Poems 1940–1960*, copyright © 1957, 1958, 1968 by Denise Levertov;

Denise Levertov, *Poems 1968–1972*, copyright © 1968, 1970, 1972 by Denise Levertov Goodman. Copyright © 1971, 1972, 1987 by Denise Levertov;

Denise Levertov, *The Freeing of the Dust*, copyright © 1975 by Denise Levertov;

Denise Levertov, *Life in the Forest*, copyright © 1978 by Denise Levertov;

Denise Levertov, *Candles in Babylon*, copyright © 1982 by Denise Levertov;

Denise Levertov, *Oblique Prayers*, copyright © 1982 by Denise Levertov;

Denise Levertov, *Breathing the Water*, copyright © 1987 by Denise Levertov.

Grateful acknowledgment is made for permission to cite excerpts from the following:

Kathleen Fraser, "Locations" and "The Flood" from *New Shoes*, copyright © 1978 by Kathleen Fraser, reprinted by permission of Harper-Collins Publishing Corporation;

Kathleen Fraser, *Each Next*, copyright © 1980 by Kathleen Fraser, reprinted by permission of Figures Press;

Kathleen Fraser, *Notes Preceding Trust*, copyright © 1987 by Kathleen Fraser, reprinted by permission of Lapis Press.

I also acknowledge permission to cite excerpts from the following poems from Mina Loy, *The Last Lunar Baedeker*, edited by Roger L. Conover (Highlands, North Carolina: The Jargon Society, 1982), reprinted here by permission of Roger L. Conover: "Parturition," "Love Songs to Joannes," "Giovanni Franchi," "The Black Virginity," "Joyce's *Ulysses*," "Lunar Baedeker," "Apology of Genius," "Anglo-Mongrels and the Rose," and "Gertrude Stein."

# Introduction

From the moment I began thinking about the shape of this book, I found I could never easily designate its center, and that as I wrote, the center kept altering, slipping, transforming. Just as simultaneity characterizes the modernist endeavor to reconsider reality, and a nonlinear layering of thought compels much postmodern poetics, this study takes shape as shifting, overlapping planes moving through a flattened space so that at any one moment we see numerous perspectives configured in changing relationship to each other. Is it a book about Williams, or modernism, or poetic daughters in a male tradition, or language innovation, or feminist poetics? William Carlos Williams is certainly the "big daddy" of the four poets examined here, a modernist giant looming with other male poets over Denise Levertov and Kathleen Fraser, and a modernist privileged in a literary history that has erased his radical contemporary, Mina Loy. Obviously, Williams remains the binding presence throughout the book, but I would encourage thinking about this presence as a translucent gauze that changes in tone, texture, shape, and even substance as various lights shine through it. To a significant degree, this shifting quality emerges when we recognize the impact of different gender-inflected strains of modernism upon Williams's writings. Operating at an intersection of a modernism practiced by men and a counterstrain practiced by women, Williams's work and his poetic theories traverse questions of subjectivity, tradition, and language, illuminating the gender dimensions of such questions and the process of poetic production.[1]

In exploring such concerns through the forms and subjects of his poetry and prose, Williams joins a line of woman modernists whose work, recently retrieved, is expanding our notion of the cultural moment of "modernism" and challenging the politics of its canonical formation. This recovery of women authors who practiced, edited, and influenced experimental writing early in the twentieth century revises and potentially repoliticizes our reading of modernism and of subsequent generations of writers. Positioning Williams in relationship to women writing within and descending from the modernist movement, this study looks at the shape Williams's modernism takes on when considered through the poetic efforts of Mina Loy, Denise Levertov, and Kathleen Fraser – three women belonging to three different generations of Anglo-American poets and writing within different historical contexts. By considering their encounters with a male-dominated tradition, this study asks a double question in regard to these women writers: What can women poets, writing with an informed awareness of Williams, teach us about him, and just as importantly, what can they teach us about the process, for women, of constructing a writing self within a male tradition?

Janet Wolff, discussing the gender dynamics of literary tradition, encourages attention to the "clear, if complex, relationship between woman as cultural producer and woman as 'sign' " that informs the experience of a woman artist within a male-dominated tradition (*Feminine Sentences* 113). The obvious centrality of "woman as 'sign' " within Williams's works has motivated numerous studies of images of women and ideas of the feminine in his poetry and prose;[2] particularly through the efforts of feminist criticism and theory, a groundwork has been laid for rethinking Williams's modernism as a site for gender struggle. By bringing Loy, Levertov, and Fraser, as cultural producers, into the equation, I am not interested in demonstrating a conventional line of influence; rather, this study investigates the negotiations of all four poets with the masculinist authority of tradition and resituates Williams through the reexplorations of modernism that these women, in different ways, exhibit in their work.

My study began with the observation of the frequency with which women poets, writing within varied strains of American poetry, have claimed Williams as an enabling predecessor. I first began to consider what such a claim meant for both the father and daughter figures and why Williams in particular kept cropping up as a poet who provided space for women writing explicitly woman-centered poetry. Denise Levertov, establishing early on a direct line to Williams, says he "cleared ground . . . gave us tools" to "discover the rhythms of our experience" (*PIW* 245). Diane Wakoski writes that Williams created a "set of possibilities" for the American poet; in her eyes, "there is no poet who has created more possibilities of roads to travel in my own American journey," and as a result, her poetry, her "own little song of self, exist[s] partially because of permission I receive from Dr. Williams to take these particulars of my life, as if they had a common grain" ("William Carlos Williams" 47). Alice Notley, penning an article entitled "Dr. Williams' Heiresses," emphatically stresses: "It's because of Williams that you can include every thing that's things – & maybe everything that's words – is that going too far? – if you are only up to noticing everything that your life does include. Which is hard. Too many people have always already been telling you for years what your life includes" (4). To which Rachel Blau DuPlessis responds "Including Williams," a terse rejoinder revealing the restrictiveness of influence at play in the same plane of empowerment. About her own poetic relationship with Williams, DuPlessis sees herself

> enabled by his enabling
> disenfranchised by my position in his enabling
> wobble wobble wobble
>
> (*Pink Guitar* 62)

Similarly, Susan Howe admits that "as a poet I feel closer to Williams's writing about writing . . . than I do to most critical studies . . . by professional scholars," even though the "ambiguous paths of kinship pull me in opposite ways at once" ("Introduction," *My Emily Dickinson* 7).

This sense of ambiguity, of a simultaneous enabling and disenfranchisement, compels one overarching set of questions that arise in reading Williams in conjunction with women poets, particularly through the ways they negotiate masculinized notions of poetic authority and creativity. Positioned as daughters within a predominately male tradition, many twentieth-century women poets have explored and challenged the gendered assumptions defining "the poet," and their work becomes a record of that challenge, whether leveled explicitly or suggested through subversive, implicit tactics. When we begin to consider those challenges, we begin – as many critics and poets are currently doing – to engage in important revisions of literary history. Given received (male) versions of literary history, we are accustomed to reading Williams back through a Ginsberg or an Olson or a Silliman or a Creeley; we think of Williams in conjunction with Pound or Eliot or Stevens, measuring his modernism against theirs. This study redirects such readings of Williams, considering him within a context of female poets. When we read him through the works of Loy, Levertov, and Fraser, he becomes a different kind of modernist, more closely akin, in deconstructing prevalant, gendered ideologies of poetic authority, to a group of women modernists that includes Stein, Loy, Moore, and H.D. More precisely, in the midst of his self-conscious formulation of a modern poetry, his absorption of the gender-inflected poetics of these modernist women helps shape a poetry bearing the marks of a tradition of innovative women writers. Often these marks are overwritten; at other times his debt to women, particularly Moore and Stein, is unequivocally voiced. Drawn to different modernisms at once, Williams stands as a bridge between a Poundian modernism and a female counterstrain, a position that is often conflicted and contradictory.

The first two chapters examine Williams's early poetry and prose, focusing particularly on journal publications in the 1910s (the *Egoist, Others,* and *The Masses*); the collections *Al Que Quiere!* (1917), *Sour Grapes* (1921), and *Spring and All* (1923); and the essays in *In the American Grain* (1925). Discussing these texts within the historically specific framework of first-wave American feminism, these chapters seek to redefine Williams's relationship to ideas of modernism centered on Ezra Pound, to feminist politics of the time, and to the works of women modernists. In the 1910s and 1920s, Williams is formulating a self-consciously modernist poetics, moving away from the Keatsian verse of his first book toward a modernism of language innovation. His struggle during these years with a new poetics – a restructuring of language that reconceives its relationship to experience – manifests itself forcefully in the 1923 *Spring and All,* his manifesto of the modernist imagination. The movement toward this volume and its collaged expression of a modernist poetics engaged Williams in reconsiderations of traditional ideas, forms, and institutions that ranged beyond the literary but, in his mind, were inseparably linked to literature and language.

To advocate the modern and the new, Williams, like his contemporaries, relentlessly questioned the old; yet, as numerous recent critics argue, this questioning on the part of most male modernists rarely extended to the grounds of gender. In fact, the masculinization of modernism reinforced with a vengeance the status quo of sexual ideology. Marianne DeKoven, warning against a conflation of avant-garde writing and *écriture féminine,* reminds us that "male supremacism and misogyny" coexisted comfortably within the modernist project for many writers ("Male Signature" 79). Equally blunt, Rachel Blau DuPlessis asserts that "Modernist agendas concealed highly conventional metaphors and narratives of gender" (*Pink Guitar* 44). Positing a striking example of such a narrative, Carolyn Burke demonstrates Pound's masculinization of creativity, a gesture excluding women as creators and situating them as material upon which the explicitly phallic potency of the male poet could force itself in shaping new forms from a feminized chaos ("Getting Spliced"). Andreas Huyssen, also arguing against a general characterization of modernism as feminine writing, identifies the "powerful masculinist and misogynist current within the trajectory of modernism" ("Mass Culture as Woman" 49). As Janet Wolff urges, reconstructing a history of modernism involves not just an expansion of the canon but a more complex "necessary task": "to dismantle a particular [masculine] ideology of modernism" (*Feminine Sentences* 56).[3]

Attentive to modernism's masculine gestures, this study of Williams's early modernist works identifies the struggle with issues of gender taking place within the writings most foundational to his efforts to create a modern poetics. While asserting a poetic voice, the early poems continually interrogate the claim to authority enabling such assertion; significantly, this concern with poetic authority takes on highly gendered configurations as the poems explore and often question the materiality of male authority, particularly as linked to poetic creativity and production. Thus, in these poems we can trace a concern with the movement from mundane, daily particulars (the local) to overarching systems and institutions of power, linked through structures of gender. Developing during Williams's formative poetic years, a consuming struggle with the traditional association of poetic voice and male creativity radiates into considerations of the relationship between these literary assumptions and the ideologies of gender regulating the cultural, economic, historical, religious, and social realms of American life.

As Williams works through the question of authority in his early poetry, its contingent relationship with structures and conventions of gender is repeatedly brought to the surface, questioned, challenged, exposed. Significantly, these texts foreground Williams's position as a male poet in relationship to these dynamics, and that position alternately oscillates between ambivalence, self-condemnation, vulnerability, and complicity with the status quo, while often ultimately undermining his own basis for poetic authority. Constantly linking poetic speech to gendered relations of power, he scrutinizes his own authority to speak when based upon a (masculinized) power structured through gendered hierarchy, through relations of dominance and submission. Williams, as a result, moves toward a different formulation of authority – an authority envisioned as a model of contact or contiguity that allows for difference rather than suppressing it through hierarchy.

Williams's struggle with poetic authority does not occur in a vacuum, and a central concern of this study is to contextualize these early works within first-wave feminism, particularly in its impact upon concurrent formulations of modernism. For decades a neglected force within narratives of history, American and British feminism of the early century is now being reconsidered as a powerful presence to which modernist writers, male and female, responded.[4] While at times displaying an anxiety over challenges to the sexual status quo, Williams also participates to an important and previously unconsidered degree in feminism's reconsiderations of patriarchal structures of power. A vigorous and plural movement, conspicuously public, the feminist movement in the 1910s defied conventional notions of womanhood, of family, and of masculine power; we see this defiance inflected within Williams's early poetry and in his resistance to Ezra Pound's more masculinized ideas of modernism.

Williams's admiration of Mina Loy's feminist modernism underscores this resistance. The impact of feminist thought upon Williams's poetry

of the late teens and early twenties coincides with his closest involvement
with the poetry and person of Mina Loy, a British woman whose radical
embrace of feminism clearly defines her poetry and her poetic reception
in America. Loy's interest in American feminism predated her arrival in
New York in 1917; by that date, New York circles of the avant-garde
would already be familiar with her poetry and its feminist slant through
publication in such journals as Alfred Stieglitz's *Camera Work*. Through
their association with the same artistic circles in New York, Williams
came to know Loy and her poetry, admiring both. Although Loy's name
would fade from New Critical narratives of literary modernism, she was
considered an important innovative poet in her time, cited by her contemporaries as a major player in the modernist movement. In reclaiming
Loy as a significant and influential modernist writer, as with reclamations
of other women writers, we begin to discern what Janet Wolff terms the
"new literary and visual forms and strategies [that] were invented and
deployed to capture and represent the changed situation of women in
the modern world, both in the private and public arenas" (61). Loy's
example demonstrates an important intersection of modernism and feminism involving a rejection of traditional definitions of gender as an
integral part of a claim to new forms of literature. This interaction between feminism and modernism, which characterizes the work of many
women modernists, provides the context in Chapter 1 for examining the
early poems of Williams in specific relationship to Loy's works, particularly in their critique of gender authority.

Loy's impact upon Williams is part of a broader pattern of interaction
between the male poet and female modernists. The final chapter and the
Conclusion return to this topic to discuss the implications of Williams's
adaptation of formal strategies practiced by women writers as modes of
cultural critique. Rather than looking only at Williams's contemporaries,
however, Chapter 4 draws upon a more recent generation of experimental
writers who have uncovered and incorporated a feminist formal heritage
from women modernists. The work of Kathleen Fraser is extensively
discussed to help establish a groundwork for understanding a tradition
attentive to the complex relationships between women's innovative writing and a resistance to patriarchal structures. Williams's *Spring and All*
is then read in relationship to this formal mode of resistance and the
directions taken by Fraser in working out of a tradition of women experimental writers. The Conclusion briefly discusses *Paterson* in light of
this tradition, reading the epic as a conflicted site of lineage – a poem
claiming a paternal line and a masculinist potency yet simultaneously
undermining the basis for such potency in its yearning toward a maternal
configuration of creativity and lineage. This late work remains painfully
unresolved in its sexual politics; underscoring this lack of resolution, the

concluding comments of this study aim to suggest ways of approaching the epic through the gender-inflected struggle with poetic authority linking his early writing with the works of modernist women.

Thus, Williams's historical orientation in relationship to first-wave feminism and women modernists, themselves influenced by the light cast by feminism upon modes of patriarchy, forms an essential framework for my reading of his concern with gender. Though Williams has alternately been taken to task for displaying sexist attitudes toward women and celebrated for valorizing them, these are two sides of the same reductionist coin. It has served to bring important considerations of gender into currency but now needs to be carried further. Williams speaks of women often; women populate his poems richly; "woman" is articulated in terms of a poetic principle at various points in his career. While I am centrally concerned with Williams's conception of the feminine, his representation of the female, and his appropriation of a feminine/maternal creativity, I want to argue against a narrowly quick and familiar accusation of essentialism, for despite the universalizing gesture motivating many of his articulations of "the female principle," this gesture is complicated by the deessentializing recognition of gender as a culturally constructed process, especially in the early work.

Williams's conception of the feminine has been discussed from various angles but is most typically regarded as his designation of the material upon and from which the poet works. Within this framework, the poet is male and the inert material female, replicating familiar dichotomies of gender. However, the dichotomy is neither so clear nor so stable. In an important essay defining his poetics, written in 1946, Williams refers to the need for the poet to engage in the "turmoil" of the present and refers to this material context as the "supplying female" ("Letter to an Australian Editor" 208). Commenting upon Williams's use of this phrase, Peter Schmidt perceptively urges us to resist accusing the poet of sexual essentialism. Rather than suggesting a natural and fixed nature for women, the phrase illuminates "Williams' emphasis on the cultural and historical contexts in which all art must be understood." Insisting upon the relationship of art to socioeconomic systems, Williams's designation of the "female" becomes "his metaphor (or personification, giving voice) to all that has been excluded by a dominant culture. Therefore, his definition of the 'supplying female', of what is excluded and silenced, may be seen as a cultural construction subject to contestation and revision" ("Introduction" 6).

This concept of the female long predates the 1946 essay. The revisionary historical essays written and compiled in the early 1920s for *In the American Grain* point to the "feminine" as the excluded and oppressed and silenced, yet simultaneously as the source of a disruptive resistance to masculinist containment. This disruptiveness is clearly linked to the quality of contact, a term foundational to Williams's entire body of work. While contact has been understood as an interpenetration of subject and object, arising from an engagement with the ordinary and the daily, *In the American Grain* makes clear that Williams's perception of contact involves alternative notions of authority and is grounded – philosophically, metaphorically, linguistically, and ontologically – in an idea of the feminine. The task of Chapter 2 is to untangle just what this idea of the feminine entails. Continuing from Chapter 1 an analysis of the privileged place of the maternal within Williams's concept of creativity, this second chapter examines the configurations of the maternal and the feminine in *In the American Grain,* particularly as they coalesce within the figure of the Native American. In this text, Williams develops a poetics of the maternal that is characterized by inclusion, contact, and disruption (of the masculine status quo), and is manifested largely through the American Indian. The link between the feminine and the Native American developed throughout the essays constructs the category of "female," as Schmidt suggests, as a metaphor for "all that has been excluded by a dominant culture." In effect, the feminine is provisionally politicized as an inclusive and interventionary category; while building an approach to history and culture within this feminine matrix, Williams moves between the poles of essentialism and constructivism to provide a forceful critique of patriarchy that ultimately depends upon the material basis of constructions of gender identity and interaction in America.

In debating Williams's essentialist tendencies, critics have by and large been interested in identifying particular images and treatments of women that are then advanced to illustrate a fixed and universal idea of the feminine. However, as this study argues, Williams's texts continually problematize their own essentialist gestures; moreover, the work as a whole develops complex interactions between fixed ideas of the feminine and socially constructed ideas of gender. In rethinking the issue of essentialism as inescapably a part of Williams's writings and poetic theories, it becomes important to ask *how* essentialism is deployed within specific contexts. Recent reassessments of the essentialist debate among feminist theorists and critics offer helpful points to consider. While an earlier feminist refutation of essentialism has been valuable in challenging naive and reductive notions of an original sexed self, a certain polarization of positions has often resulted in an unquestioning dismissal of essentialism. However, theorists like Diana Fuss and Janet Wolff have argued, with different emphasis, that essentialism need not be automatically condemned but instead investigated for its "possibilities and potential usages" (Fuss, *Essentially Speaking,* xi). Claiming that "essentialism and constructivism are deeply and inextricably co-implicated with each other," Fuss persuasively encourages us to "investigate what purpose or function essentialism might play in a particular set of discourses," and to become attentive to essentialism's "certain tactical or interventionary value, especially in our political struggles and debates" (xii). The assumption that essentialism is "bad" is itself an essentializing gesture that renders unproductive judgments rather than grappling with the contextual particulars of the so-called essentialist act. Fuss shifts the focus from evaluation to analysis in asserting that "in and of itself, essentialism is neither good nor bad, progressive nor reactionary, beneficial nor dangerous. The question we should be asking is not 'is this text essentialist (and therefore "bad")?' but rather, 'if this text is essentialist, *what motivates its deployment?*' " (xi).

Thus, while all four poets in this study can, on occasion and to different degrees, be described as using essentialist tactics, my interest is in how this essentialism is evoked, what motivates it, and what distinguishes one kind of essentialism from another. Often deconstructing and constructing female essences simultaneously, these poets anticipate a strategy Fuss identifies in the work of Luce Irigaray – the act of essentializing the female as a displacement of phallocentric essences: "to give 'woman' an essence is to undo Western phallomorphism and to offer women entry into subjecthood," a subjecthood prohibited within the mainstream of Western thought arising from Aristotle's association of woman with matter or with lack of soul and essence (71). Levertov's need, for example, to evoke a linguistic essentialism in speaking of women as a collective group becomes a political interventional strategy supported by an evolving ontological category of "woman" in her poetry – that is, the category of woman based upon an experiencing of reality particular to a woman's consciousness. Simultaneously, however, Levertov investigates the construction of gender in relationship to discourses of power, exploring how the category of woman (particularly in its relationship to the category of "poet") is produced. Rather than getting bogged down in apologies for or laborious castigations of each poet's participation in essentialist notions of "woman," this study calls attention to the interaction between essentialism and constructivism in their works.

Looked at in their particular historical moments, then, these poets might be read as essentializing "against the grain," as provisionally (at least) laying claim to a feminine power that exposes and challenges masculinist assumptions marking poetry and language. What this means, of course, for a male poet must be questioned carefully, and a major objective of this study is to investigate Williams's need to create a decidedly feminine ground for his poetry – for the poetry of a self-asserted male voice and consciousness. This becomes an unresolved conflict for Williams, while at the same time rendering a poetry remarkable in its own investigations of gendered authority. It is here that I locate Williams's usefulness to later women poets, as well as his strong link to women modernists who wrote contemporaneously.

The inclusion of Mina Loy in the story of moderism changes many conceptions of that movement, particularly its relationship (whether reactionary or congenial) with feminism's attack upon institutionalized forms of gender. Loy's works clearly exemplify Rita Felski's definition of "feminist literature" as "texts that reveal a critical awareness of women's subordinate position and of gender as a problematic category" (14). In addition, her radical innovations with language – which, like Stein's, preceded the high modernist experiments of Joyce, Pound, and Eliot – coalesce with an explicit feminist politics and produce what Wolff terms "the radical potential of the deconstructive strategies of modernist culture" (63). Loy's strategies of language rupture, montage, and self-reflexiveness work to defamiliarize and question gender ideologies prevalent in her time, and retrieving her work serves to repoliticize modernism's potential.

Bringing Loy's work into a reconsideration of Williams's early radical period illuminates his concern with "gender as a problematic category" and recasts his aesthetic evolution in political terms that link language, gender, and power. A poet who has never fit easily into the academic canon of modernism, Williams, by the 1940s, wanted desperately to be recognized as an important modernist who continued to define himself in opposition to the classical model he perceived in Pound and Eliot. It is arguable that Williams suffered exclusion from New Critical appraisals of moderism for many of the same reasons women like Loy have disappeared. Williams, like Loy or Stein or Moore, inhabited a relationship to "*male avant-garde hegemony,* simultaneously within it and subversive of it," as DeKoven describes the female modernist tradition ("Male Signature" 79). Obviously, Williams's relationship to a masculinist modernism is distinct from that of a female counterstrain; of significant concern, however, is the overlap between the modernisms Williams and his women contemporaries practice as a subversion of masculinist ideologies.

Relocating Williams helps us understand the *potential* his poetic strategies hold for women poets, and also demonstrates his tendency to overwrite the women who most aided him in realizing the gender dimensions of artistic production and expression. Williams certainly places Moore and Stein in his pantheon of poets, and his essays on these writers (from the late twenties and thirties) clarify his debt to their language innovations, particularly as he sees through their example the inextricable tie between language and cultural forms of power. Yet writers like Loy or Dickinson or H.D. are rarely mentioned, or are pushed patronizingly forward for a brief moment before suffering poetic eclipse by a Pound or Poe. Nonetheless, a careful analysis of Williams's work demonstrates his absorption of various linguistic strategies, linked in his work to cultural revisions, that characterize the radical stylistics of these women. In *Spring and All,* written at the culmination of his most experimental period, we see Williams turning to the strategies used by women to subvert masculinist modes of modernism; the ramifications of these choices, of these models, is not merely textual or stylistic but resonates into questions of poetic authority, language, and gender.

These questions lead us to consider the constructions of tradition and poetic imagination that evolve in Williams's work, often in clear relationship to models of the maternal. Throughout his career, Williams claims a maternal lineage for his creativity and, by the time he is writing the first books of *Paterson,* has articulated a model of artistic production based upon female-gendered notions of creativity and tradition. One might argue that he is appropriating the feminine in the service of defining himself as a male poet – and to a degree, such appropriation occurs. More is at issue here, however, for in the course of his career and in ways often similar to women poets of this century, Williams both resists and reconstructs a traditional masculine model of poetic lineage and creative empowerment. Although he most clearly describes this reconstruction, and its cultural implications, in his 1946 "Letter to an Australian Editor" (see Chapter 2), his yearning toward the maternal as a configuration of poetic creativity is evidenced in his earliest works. Chapters 1 and 2 explore the development of the maternal in the works of the 1910s and early 1920s, questioning what it means for the male poet to construe the maternal as a model for his poetics. These questions are inherently intertwined with issues of gender and authority as Williams pursues his attraction to and valorization of the maternal at the same time that he wrestles with a male-encoded poetic tradition and a male-identified concept of the poet. Moving from his incipient statement of a modern poetics in "The Wanderer" through his critique of patrilinear and patrilocal forms of power in *In the American Grain,* these chapters discuss Williams's construction of the maternal in conjunction with his uneasy oscillations toward and away from cultural constructions of gender. Within the broadly essentializing strokes painting the maternal as a mode of contact, touch, or contiguity, Williams works toward an understanding (although unsystematic) of gender identity resembling what Judith Butler describes as "a personal/cultural history of received meanings subject to a set of imitative practices, which refer laterally to other imitations" (138). Recognizing, while often in a sustaining manner, the regulatory nature of gender formations, these texts are striking in their recurrent attentiveness to the structures of power that produce the category of woman. Uncannily at times, a poem or prose passage will comment upon its own representations of women, approaching the representational politics that Butler describes as a task of feminism: a "representational politics... [that offers] a critical genealogy of its own legitimating practices" (8). In looking at Williams's various representations of women – a methodological strategy too often labeled as naive or outdated – I do not merely assume an interest in the images of women per se. More insistently, concern is with Williams's own investigation of the very sources of authority ennabling him to construct these images. Surprisingly often, in exposing the gender-based conventions and practices (of language, of power) legitimating his role as poet, he effectively delegitimizes or undercuts the authority of his poetic voice.

This exploration leads in two directions. First, what historically specific circumstances encourage Williams continually to question his authority to speak and to recognize in discursive systems gender-related issues of power? To begin to deal with this complex question, numerous texts that characterize this self-questioning practice are discussed in relationship to first-wave feminism, Pound's masculinist modernism, and Mina Loy's alternative feminist poetics. The discussion then extends into a reading of *In the American Grain,* contending that Williams projects what begins as a self-directed questioning onto the more public arena of historical narrative. This self-reflexive text continually foregrounds the process of constructing narratives of history, problematizing a traditional association between history and objective truth while underscoring a masculinely biased relationship between the authority of history and conscriptions of gender.

Second, if in putting forth the "sign" of woman while simultaneously undermining his own authority in such production, what potential does Williams's work offer to women who read him and who write? In dealing with this specific question and its broader implications for reading women within a male-dominated tradition of poetry and criticism, I have drawn upon two immensely helpful theoretical frameworks. The first is adapted from Rita Felski's discussion of the "duality of structure" as a dynamic "dialectical interrelation between subject and structure" in which "human beings do not simply reproduce existing structures in the process of action and communication, but in turn modify those structures even as they are shaped by them" (*Beyond Feminist Aesthetics* 58, 56).[5] While the constraints of a white, male tradition and its conventions have significantly been recognized by writers belonging to excluded groups, the action arising from that recognition can potentially transform those structures into enabling forces. Within a process of revision and critique on the part of the woman poet, masculine cultural structures such as literary history and tradition can be seen as serving both as constraint and empowerment, leading to developmental change rather than a static state of oppression. This dialectical process provides a basis for considering the position of the poetic daughter within a tradition of fathers, particularly in the discussion of Denise Levertov's poetry, her poetic and personal relationship with Williams, and her rewriting of the older poet within her work. Pursuing Levertov's investment of the maternal with poetic power and her concomitant need to negotiate a male-dominated world of poetry, Chapter 3 traces the investigation of authority her work undertakes and the authorization of a writing self as a strategy of resistance. A central part of this analysis concerns the reading of Williams that emerges for Levertov in this process of constructing a social and poetic self.

Radiating outward from this question, of course, are other questions aimed at the idea of "the self," a "writing self," subjectivity. The analysis of both Levertov and Fraser concerns this fundamental issue within feminism and is informed by the concept of subject-positions shifting within ideological structures. Particularly in terms of social and familial structures, this study is interested in the position of the poetic daughter – in Levertov's case, within the context of Williams's self-delegitimizing authority as poetic father, and in Fraser's case, within the context of a retrieval, by the daughter, of an alternative female tradition. Here a second theoretical framework is usefully derived from Diana Fuss's work on the female reader and from Janet Wolff's related arguments for a feminist engagement with the dominant culture that destablilizes and deconstructs its categories of subjectivity through "guerilla tactics" of intervention and subversion (*Feminine Sentences* 87).

Building upon Lacan's notion of the dispersed subject and Foucault's concept of "subject-positions" in devising a feminist theory of "the subject who reads and is read," Fuss is primarily concerned with the relationship between gender and text, while seeking a way to speak of the female reader without advancing the binarisms of essentialism and anti-essentialism or diluting the political imperative for the female subject within the feminist project (*Essentially Speaking* 30).[6] Fuss joins such critics as Teresa De Lauretis in theorizing subjectivity as a site continually undergoing the process of construction (Fuss 33).[7] While claiming that "we always read from *somewhere*," Fuss raises important questions concerning the shifting, evolving ground of the subject-position and its relationship to discursive texts: "What are the various positions a reading subject may occupy? How are these positions constructed? Are there possible distributions of subject-positions located in the text itself? Can a reader refuse to take up a subject-position the text constructs for him/ her? Does the text construct the reading subject or does the reading subject construct the text?" (32). From these questions, which clearly mark points of intersection with Felski's materialist structuration theory, Fuss derives the notion of "double reading": "We bring (old) subject-positions to the text at the same time the actual process of reading constructs (new) subject-positions for us" and, in occupying several positions at once, are often caught between opposing or conflicting positions (33). It is important to note that Fuss emphasizes a fluidity between multiple subject-positions rather than stressing a taxonomy of difference, warning us against a cataloguing of each position that rigidifies and totalizes what she sees as a continual, dynamic interaction.

If we agree, given this site of shifting, multiple subjectivity, that the reading process is a "negotiation amongst discursive subject positions which the reader, as a social subject, may or may not choose to fill" (Fuss 34), then we can begin to consider the impact upon women writers of the male tradition within which they must contend and of their individual choices – or movements amongst subject-positions – in relationship to the subjectivities a particular male-authored text constructs or that male-identified conventions encourage. For the woman writer, the position as literary daughter (traditionally minimalized and subject to male approval), the position of poet (historically male-defined), the position of woman (socially constructed and subject to change), and a myriad of other positions assigned by race, class, ethnicity, and so on coexist and continually mediate one another. If readers, "like texts, are constructed," and if "reading positions are constructed, assigned, or mapped" by historical and cultural variables, then it behooves us to consider the process through which this construction and the action of double reading is written – either implicitly or self-reflexively – into the woman-authored text (Fuss 34).

Denise Levertov, who begins writing well before the women's movement of the 1960s and 1970s, is distinctive early on in her attention to woman-centered experience and her clear articulation of a female poetic voice. Although by the late sixties a virtual revolution in women's poetry affirms women's concerns, experiences, and voices as legitimate subject matter in American poetry, Levertov's first volumes in America (published in the late 1950s) anticipate this affront to a male-dominated tradition. However, Levertov herself acknowledges that her early success in publication and reception had much to do with being "chosen" by a variety of men – poets, editors, publishers – as the exception to the rule that poets are men. Levertov's poetry, following her immigration to America in the 1950s, develops directly out of Williams's influence and her association with the Black Mountain poets, in particular Robert Creeley, Robert Duncan, and Charles Olson. The relationship of gender to Levertov's early affiliation with male poets raises the issue of her own self-perception as a woman poet and her need to occupy seemingly contradictory roles or positions. Chapter 3 looks at the relationship between Levertov's process of reading and writing from conflicted subject positions, Williams's position as poetic father to her, and the focus upon authority and power that expansively pervades the development of her work.

Reading Williams's works from the perspective of a literary daughter, Levertov's continual return to his poetry informs her negotiations with various forms of literary, religious, and social authority. This process involves a stress on female identity and an implicit enactment of "double reading" in the concurrent reception of representations of female subjectivity and an active construction of a female writing subject. Along with representations of women and the maternal, Levertov finds in Williams's poetics of contact a poetry imbued with social concern and resistant to conventional patriarchal constructs of power. Examining poetry and prose spanning her career, Chapter 3 traces connections between her interpretation of Williams as a central presence in her work, her position as cultural daughter, her evocation of a maternal lineage, and her revisionary concern with authority. Numerous questions inform the discussion of these connections: How is the position of poet constructed by a male-dominated tradition and particularly by those male poets important to Levertov? How does Levertov reshape or reconstruct masculinist conventions of the poet and of poetry from her position as "woman"? How does this position of woman itself shift and change through the historical specificity of Levertov's career? What dialectic develops between the woman poet and structures like family, religion, government, marriage? What structures appear most constraining or enabling? How is Levertov positioned as (or constructed as) a "daughter" by structures of poetic inheritance? Who are the "sons," and how does she see this gendered position constructed differently? How does she choose, at different times, to occupy the position of daughter, especially in relationship to Williams? How does she reconstruct Williams to enable her own negotiations with various forms of literary, religious, and social authority? How does she construct a maternal lineage in resistance to a male-dominated tradition, and how is Williams repositioned, in this complex revision of a received literary framework? How do these various revisions and developments suggest what Felski has called "the potential for self-reflexivity and critique on the part of social actors"?

These questions remain constantly in the background as Chapter 4 moves on to discuss the poetry of Kathleen Fraser in relationship to Williams's innovative *Spring and All*. However, the questions become reformulated through the mediation of three historically specific considerations. First, Fraser begins writing at a different historical moment than Levertov, fully a generation later, during the most militant years of the feminist movement. Second, her work passes through (in the late seventies and eighties) the impact of poststructural theory, particularly the ideas of Roland Barthes and French women theorists such as Luce Irigaray, Julia Kristeva, and Hélène Cixous. Third, Fraser takes an active part in the retrieval of female modernist writers that academic literary feminism has helped stimulate in the last fifteen years. Thus, Fraser's work is informed by a sense of language and subjectivity in relationship to cultural constructions of authority (of which gender and literary tradition are central in her work) that is compatible with strains of poststructural theory, grounded in a feminist politics, and enabled by the innovations of earlier women modernists.

In its concern with structures of language and representations of gender, Fraser's work from the 1980s until the present takes part in the cultural politics of the postmodern as described by Janet Wolff. Rather than "playful practices which fragment and disrupt narrative and tradition, and which refuse any grounding or closure in favour of a true play of signifiers," Wolff advocates a politically invested art that performs cultural work through its engagement with the dominant culture: "The most useful definition of the postmodern . . . is that work which self-consciously deconstructs tradition, by a variety of formal and other techniques. . . . Such an interrogation is informed by theoretical and critical consciousness" (*Feminine Sentences* 93). Fraser's grounding is feminist, and her work demonstrates a feminist postmodernism aimed at exploring the roles of language and representation in the construction of female subjectivity; her texts seek, in Wolff's description of postmodern art, "to reposition the spectator in relation to . . . images and ideologies of contemporary culture" (95). Producing an interventional poetics, Fraser links feminist politics and language innovation to investigate dominant forms and discourses within a patriarchal culture, particularly those systems underlying categories of gender.

My choice of Fraser in this study has to do with her self-articulated project of dismantling the masculinist ideology of modernism in order to both renew and continue a radical and deeply politicized strain of modernism. This project takes active form in her critical essays, her literary works, and her founding editorship of *HOW(ever)*, a journal that provided a forum for women writers and critics working in experimental directions. Finding resistance on the part of (primarily male) publishers and editors to her experimental work, Fraser began the journal as a way of redressing obstacles of production and reception confronting women experimentalists. Although the journal recently ended, its five volumes offer a rich site for examining the efforts current women writers are making in devising a feminist and postmodern cultural politics. Their efforts coincide with the critical insistence (by such critics as Wolff and

Andreas Huyssen) that we must distinguish between modernism as institution and modernism as practice. Fraser's practice of a deconstructive modernism, enabled through the recovery of female writers, reconnects language innovation and disruption with gender politics. Her modernist strategies draw heavily from women writers whose inclusion in the history of modernism repoliticizes that narrative and the products of its participants. Therefore, Fraser's texts offer a way of understanding and examining postmodernism as, in important ways, a continuation of modernism, but one which causes us to reconsider received ideas of that movement. Within this reconsideration of modernism, initiated within the context of a feminist postmodern practice, Williams's alignment with the gender politics and language disruptions of female modernists can be brought into focus. While locating the closest point of alignment in the texts of the early twenties, particularly *Spring and All,* this study argues that his continued and often conflicted concern with authority is embedded within much later texts that bear the ideological and formal marks of this countertradition.

Focusing primarily on Fraser's poetry and prose from the 1980s, Chapter 4 discusses her use of formal strategies to explore the areas of subjectivity and the female body – an application of strategies she often derives and sees modeled in the texts of earlier female modernists. Identifying the humanist self-contained subject as essentially male, Fraser's texts develop and linguistically explore a notion of the shifting subject or the subject in continual process of construction. These texts trace a female subjectivity moving amidst the regulatory practices of gender formation, institutionalized forms of gender, and systems of gendered power. In searching out alternate ideas of subjectivity that emphasize a self-reflexive and liberating (for Fraser) negotiation with socially inscribed subject-positions, these texts enact assertions of female identity continually played against its dismantlement. This refusal of a stable female identity is not a nihilistic extinguishment of subjectivity but resembles Jane Gallop's resistance to merely replacing an "old" identity with a "new":

> I do not believe in some "new identity" which would be adequate and authentic. But I do not seek some sort of liberation from identity. That would lead only to another form of paralysis – the oceanic passivity of undifferentiation. Identity must be continually assumed and immediately called into question. (*The Daughter's Seduction* xii)

A recognition of identity as contingent rather than essential or inherent underlies Fraser's forays into female subjectivity. At the same time the clear emphasis placed upon female identity often derives from treatments of the female body.

Even in Fraser's first lyrical works, the female body is a gendered body, psychically and socially produced. It is a body experienced by women, while at the same time Fraser's recognition of social mediation vitiates any claim to a "direct" experiencing of the natural, precultural body.[8] Affirming the female body as a material factor in a female identity while also foregrounding its social formation, Fraser's work takes part in a "body politics" that speaks "*about* the body, stressing its materiality and its social and discursive construction, at the same time disrupting and subverting existing regimes of representation" (Wolff, *Feminine Sentences,* 138). Fraser's retrieval of formal devices from a tradition of women modernists becomes part of this body politics, a restructuring of language involved in cultural transformations of gender.

From this point, Chapter 4 focuses upon Williams's *Spring and All.* Drawing upon the practices of women modernists, this expression of resistance to the modernism of Pound and Eliot foregrounds the interlocking powers of language and ideology. Developing the poetic tenets of measure and contact, *Spring and All* turns to the formal innovations of women poets – particularly Loy, Stein, Moore, and Dickinson – to reconsider poetic form's relationship to structures of authority.

Thus, the last chapter circles back to the first in reading Williams through the women contemporary to him. As with the formation of literary history, however, the accomplishments of these women are clarified through the examples of their descendants, which in turn alters our reading of a received version of literary history that has excluded these women. The Conclusion of this study considers Williams's own acknowledgment, in *Paterson,* of the treatment of women in literary tradition – be they authors, poetic subjects, muse figures, or allegorical essences. This acknowledgment is deeply troubled, infused with questions of poetic authority explored in his earlier work while also desperately attracted to that authority and its masculinist premises. This conflict and the tensions it generates riddle the late epic, choreographing its experimental dance in uncertain steps through the echoing question of who "shall have the mastery?" (*Paterson* I.ii: 30). The same question pervades Williams's first modernist endeavors, reformulated time and again as a central issue of gender, authority, and the poetic enterprise.

# 1

## "The Full of My Freed Voice"

### Williams and Loy,
### Feminism and the Feminine

As the final poem in William Carlos Williams's 1917 *Al Que Quiere!*, "The Wanderer" articulates Williams's aesthetic and philosophical tenets, commenting on the collection it concludes and looking forward to poetry that will follow. Confronting the poet's relationship to the rapidly transforming modern world, the speaker asks, "How shall I be a mirror to this modernity?" (*CP1* 108). Generating the poem and engrossing the poet, the question derives not from his own mind but from "Her mind" (108), the mind of the poem's "marvelous old queen" (111), the "horrible old woman" (110) who initiates the young poet into a "new wandering" (117), a "new marriage" (111) with the earth, and who empowers his voice as poet.

This repulsive and tattered character resonates with an explosive power to reveal, through her speech and action, a new world to the poet. The poem begins with this question of modernity, "Which she had put on to try me," and sets up the expectation that the question will be answered (108). Indeed, in the second section, "Clarity," the poet affirms that "certainly somewhere here about us / I know she is revealing these things" that make up "the beauty of all the world" (109). However, in "recreating the whole world" for the poet, the old woman changes not the world but the poet's method of seeing and hearing (109). Dipping him into the "filthy Passaic," she consecrates the poet's communion with the earth and with her voice; her powers of speech and sight will be bestowed upon the "child" poet *if* he strives to remember their source (115, 113). By the poem's end, his task is no longer to "mirror this modernity" but to engage in an active re-visioning of it, just as the initial question that motivates the poem ("How shall I be a mirror...") is reconsidered and revised. Rejecting an art of mimetic representation, the poem shifts its interest to interactions between language and experience, suggesting an early focus within Williams's poetics upon the construction of experience or "reality" through language alongside a concern with the impact of material circumstances upon forms of discourse. The poem points toward a modernist poetics that is both deconstructive and revisionary. Significantly, the figure of the female embodies this deconstructive capacity; "The Wanderer" sets forth a poetic task encouraging a different way of seeing that is figured in the old woman's fierce power to strip away, reveal, and recreate the world. For the early Williams, poetic authority derives from the "old queen," and we must ask what implications this claim to lineage has for considering Williams's relationship to questions of authority and gender.

As an expression of an evolving poetics, the poem is generated by a struggle between gendered notions of poetic authority – between the "din and bellow of the male wind" and the "female chorus / Linking all," a struggle that shapes and characterizes Williams's modernist aesthetic (*CP1* 114). Far from residing in an ethereal or transcendent realm, the modernism practice by Williams is engaged in the material world, insistently investigating links between constructions of poetic authority, language, and culture; this investigation progresses to a large extent through the category of gender. Particularly in the poetry marking his transition toward and embrace of a radical, linguistically innovative poetry that culminates with *Spring and All* in 1923, Williams's poetry not only takes on figures of the female as frequent subjects, but casts that very act of appropriation into the center ring of his modernist endeavor, where it is problematized (even when celebrated) by a self-reflexive attention to the gendered dimensions of power evoked in the act of making poetry.

Significantly, the poetry of this period (1914–23) coincides with the cultural and political impact of the century's first wave of feminism in America. Williams's developing conception of the poet, of creativity, and of the poetic voice occur and should be read within the cultural backdrop of a prewar feminism that actively unsettled traditional ideas of sexual difference and masculine power. Situating Williams's work within this historical context, this chapter considers the interaction between feminism and modernism, joining such critics as Carolyn Burke, Rachel Blau DuPlessis, and Marianne DeKoven in reconsidering the modernist movement as ideologically charged with issues of gender and power.[9]

Early avant-garde journals, both in England and America, disclose many of the ideological tensions suffusing the development of modernism. This chapter begins by focusing upon Williams's relationship with the *Egoist*, the British journal editorially directed by Pound to provide a forum for modernist art and thought in the teens and early twenties. Williams's presence within the journal – the text of his poetry within the context of the *Egoist*'s development – manifests an unease with Pound's masculinization of modernist poetics. Reading Williams's contributions within the context of the journal's frequent expressions of misogyny, this chapter first focuses upon his use of women as central figures in these early poems. His treatment of female subjects and feminized imagery suggests ideological differences with the egoist project of an individual aggrandizement configured in masculine terms; specifically, the chapter questions what these poems suggest to us about Williams's developing notions of artistic power through the distinctions he makes between masculine and feminine that relate to a struggle with his own position as a male poet. These poems are joined by a series of letters published in the *Egoist,* a correspondence on gender between Dora Marsden, who founded the journal as the *New Freewoman,* and Williams. In his letters, Williams works to theorize "the feminine," an articulation significantly combining essentialized notions of the feminine with a nascent attention to the cultural construction of gender. This early investigation of "the feminine," then, embodies the often contradictory movement within Williams's work between a naturalized essentialism and a materially based constructivism, but also suggests that his essentialist gestures are often underscored by a keen sense of gender's cultural frameworks.

Just such an argument is advanced through examining Williams's publications in *Others* and *The Masses,* two American journals of the teens, and by considering the 1921 volume *Sour Grapes* in relationship to the historical moment of feminism. Williams is linked to this moment through the poetry of Mina Loy, a central figure in New York avantgarde circles in the late 1910s. Her project of defining a feminism for herself grounds her poetry of this period, drawing upon ideas circulating within the multifaceted feminist movement. To look at Loy and Williams together forcefully reveals their shared concerns over sexual desire, gendered authority, and the social construction of the gendered self. Inflected by feminism's challenge to conventional hierarchies of power, Williams's poetry during his years of closest poetic and personal association with Loy throws the assumption of male authority into question. The second part of this chapter analyzes the poems of the late teens and early twenties in their tendency to problematize masculinity. Additionally, it suggests Williams's ideological intersection with women modernists whose notion of "making it new" included the category of gender and counterpointed a retrenchment into masculine privilege enacted by the modernism of Pound and Eliot. Williams, more so than his fellow male expatriates, stands with one foot within a female line of modernism and one foot within a male tradition, a position whose tensions give rise to a modernist poetry registering a self-conscious awareness of gender and power.

*The* New Freewoman, *the* Egoist, *and the Feminine as Resistance*

During the years 1914–19, Williams published nineteen poems, three letter-essays, and an improvisation in the British journal the *Egoist*. His presence in the journal is no surprise, as his friend Ezra Pound had gained control of the literary content in August 1913, prior to the adoption of the name *Egoist*. Begun in Britain in June 1913 as an ostensibly feminist periodical by Dora Marsden and entitled the *New Freewoman*, the journal changed its name in January 1914, reflecting Pound's influence and suggesting fundamental developments in its intellectual and political orientation.[10] In December 1913, at the same time that Pound aggressively battled with Harriet Monroe over altering the policy of *Poetry* magazine, he successfully convinced the editorial board of the *New Freewoman* to rename the magazine. Unhappy with the implications of the journal's title and with the feminist focus, he drafted a letter to editor Dora Marsden requesting that a new name be chosen, "which will mark the character of your paper as an organ of individualists of both sexes, and the individualist principle in every department of life" (Pound in Levenson, *A Genealogy of Modernism*, 70). The new name, the *Egoist*, aligned the journal with the radically individualist philosophy of Max Stirner, the nineteenth-century German author of *The Ego and His Own* (1845), whose writings and thought experienced a revival in the early twentieth century. Stirner advocated the supremacy of the individual ego and attacked social institutions that limited its development. As the journal's intellectual direction progressively embraced the philosophy of egoism, the poetic direction was carefully channeled (by Pound and Richard Aldington) into the imagist and then vorticist camps. Though proclaiming herself a feminist, Marsden already espoused Stirnerian egoism in the *New Freewoman,* and she acceded to the request. Marsden's "feminism," however, was of her own fashioning, shaped primarily by egoist thought and often in conflict with a mainstream feminism fighting for women's rights. As Bruce Clark argues, and as the following discussion will demonstrate, an examination of Marsden's writings in the *New Freewoman* (presumably her feminist phase) "shows that (1) an explicit 'eogistic' current ran consistently from the first to the last issue, and (2) it was never devoted to advancing women's suffrage and was not, strictly speaking, a 'feminist' periodical, but rather an anarchist one" (93). Newly titled as the *Egoist,* the publication defined itself during the next two years through a progressively more exclusive focus upon egoism.[11]

The *Egoist*'s importance to the modernist movement during the years before, during, and just after World War I has been well documented. Published from 1914 until the early twenties, its volumes contain central essays on and examples of imagism, vorticism, and high modernism, as those categories are conventionally understood. As such, the journal charts the continual redefinition of a modernist aesthetic carried out by such men as Pound and Aldington, and later, by Joyce and Eliot. Williams's resistance to this British and expatriate group in London has been treated variously, though most commonly as a claim to an American poetic ground that countered the expatriates' refutation of native sources for a viable modern art. This resistance, this counterpoetics, works to a significant degree against the impulse of a Poundian modernism to reclaim the masculine as the realm of poetry and, of necessity, to denigrate the feminine – both as a naturalized notion and as a social construct. The gender politics developing in the course of Pound's prewar modernism find partial (though tenacious) roots in the Stirnerian egoism that provides the philosophical basis for Pound's aesthetic formulations in the midteens. Within the pages of the *Egoist,* Williams's conceptualization and representation of the feminine signals a resistance to the modernist aesthetic of this period and, by extension, places him in opposition to a masculinized glorification of power and mastery espoused by the editorial board and many of the artists involved with the *Egoist.*

Ideologies of gender underlie the journal's role as a forum for the modernist project defined by Pound and Eliot. However, recent discussions of Pound's involvement with the journal have obscured the actual antifeminist slant revealed in Dora Marsden's pre-Poundian polemics. In charting the shifts in editorial policy from the *New Freewoman's* "feminist" orientation to the *Egoist's* Poundian aesthetic, Shari Benstock claims that Pound and Aldington's tactics were designed to move "against the localism and feminism of the original journal," using it to publicize imagism and "squeezing the 'local feminist' perspective of the journal into smaller and smaller space" (*Women of the Left Bank* 364). Benstock correctly asserts that Pound "was determined to turn the *Egoist* into an avant-garde paper with no special interest in feminism" – causing Rebecca West, for instance, to sever connections with the magazine – and that "in the first five years of its publication, male writers including Ezra Pound and Ford Maddox Ford [then Hueffer] dominated the *Egoist's* pages, and while its literary content increased, the feminist writing gradually diminished" (364). Though Benstock's general formulation of Pound's aggressive and controlling hand reveals his indifference toward "trivial" women's issues and provides a striking example of the gendered conflicts recently exposed through critical reexaminations of the modernist period, it is also pertinent to note Marsden's own participation in this polemical silencing of feminism and the related masculinization of a developing modernist aesthetic. Because an actual dialogue emerges in the pages of the *Egoist* between Marsden and Williams, and because this correspondence centers upon language and gender, a closer look at Marsden helps us understand Williams's relationship to two movements often in ideological conflict, modernism and feminism. Placed within a context informed by the egoism of Max Stirner and Allan Upward, an egoism of individualist will and power voiced by Marsden, Pound, Aldington, and Wyndham Lewis, Williams's essays and poems reveal an important distance in his own world-view and aesthetics from certain central tenets of Pound's modernist movement.[12]

Marsden's essays provide not only a clear example of egoism's incompatibility with feminist thought of the time but also manifest the journal's conscious movement away from any association with feminism. This resistance to feminism finds expression even in the early issues of the *New Freewoman*, despite its ostensibly feminist origin. Marsden certainly addresses women's issues and speaks in terms familiar to her feminist contemporaries (on both sides of the Atlantic) of woman's need to attain economic independence and assert individual worth. However, her arguments are grounded in Stirnerian notions of will and power, and she consistently criticizes feminist efforts as weak and ineffective precisely because the movement lacks an egoist ideology.[13] Marsden's vision of a "better society" prefigured fascist sympathies later experienced by numerous modernists, a political distinction characterizing Marsden's discussions of gendered and nongendered issues alike. In the August 1913 *New Freewoman*, Marsden states in "The Heart of the Question" that "the question we are concerned with is the meaning of the disturbance regarding the position of women," particularly the growing resistance among "intellectuals" to such terms as "feminism" and such ideas as economic self-sufficiency for women (61). She goes on to link economic independence – a major feminist concern of the time – to individual power in an argument celebrating the elite power of material ownership. Echoing Friedrich Engels's contention that the ownership of women underlies capitalist structures of hierarchy, Marsden reaches conclusions that differ markedly from Engels, who advocates the dissolution of hierarchy. In Marsden's thinking, the social, economic, and political structures of hierarchy should not be disturbed, for they support her definition of power as "ownership, which in turn means the power of using one's possessions in the service of one's own satisfactions.... Ownership is synonymous with worth.... The more extensively he owns, the more augmented is his worth, his power" ("Heart of the Question" 61). Because women "on the whole own little or no property" (63), they inevitably "sell what their power of sexual attraction will fetch, either in marriage or prostitution," and thus are rendered powerless (62).

Although her argument for economic independence and her recognition of the effects of women's economic dependence upon men coincides with economic arguments made by feminists at the time, her emphasis upon the exercise of power through ownership becomes central to a politics that condescends to the weak and unprivileged, while glorifying privileged holders of power. Defining egoism in the editorial column of this same issue, Marsden expresses her belief in the self-creative capacity of the individual's will and power, she sees such self-creation necessarily manifesting itself through isolation from a society that strives to weaken the individual through its demands for convention and uniformity. As a member of a larger community "one is good for others only by being good for oneself: that is, by being a power in oneself. . . . The only end which it is worth while for the individual to give his attention to, is the increase of his own power, of which he is the only one who may be expected to know what is required for its increase" ("Views and Comments," *Egoist* 1.1, 65). Social movements, given such thinking, prove to be not only ineffective but unnecessary. In response to the Labour Movement, for example, Marsden condescendingly proclaims: "The poor will cease to be poor when they refuse to be: the downtrodden will disappear when they decide to stand up: the hungry will have bread when *they* take it" ("Views and Comments," *Egoist* 1.1, 4). Her contempt for the masses justifies itself in a blur of Social Darwinist and Stirnerian thought that emphasizes the legitimate power of the fittest, who by virtue of their power owe nothing to lesser members of society.[14]

Although Pound appointed Harriet Shaw Weaver editor in 1914 after the June issue, relegating Marsden to the role of contributing editor, the issues of the journal published under Marsden's control are no more feminist than those under Weaver's (or Pound's) control. Though she claimed to be a suffragist, Marsden's politics were infused with egoism. She encouraged women to emulate men of power and mocked those who refused, as her writings reinscribed culturally oppressive relationships within an unaltered hierarchical structure. Even examples of outright misogynist thought appear in the earliest issues of the *Egoist,* still edited by Marsden.[15] In her final editorial prior to assuming the status of contributing editor, Marsden addresses the issue of suffrage and of the *New Freewoman*'s origins within the movement, effectively severing the journal's link to the British movement. Responding to an American woman's letter asking "where the 'Freewoman' (now the EGOIST) stands in relation to the suffrage movement," Marsden answered: "Replying on impulse, we would say 'Nowhere,' since the suffrage is wholly a matter of indifference" ("Views and Comments," *Egoist* 1.12, 224). Criticizing the suffragists for failing to realize that freedom actually means power, Marsden unequivocally aligns herself with an egoism that preempts demands for social equality with a searing criticism of the "weakness" such demands in themselves indicate.[16] As the topic of war entered the pages of the *Egoist,* the treatment of women descended further into ridicule.[17] With the war as backdrop, Marsden consistently reiterated her claim that freedom equals power, and in the essay "Women's 'Rights'," printed in the October 1914 issue, she insists that women should mold themselves as men to gain real equality through power. She reasons that women's physical weakness evidences their inability to attain power and pathetically results in their subsequent status as war booty.[18] To break out of the "normal womanly protected sphere," modern women must acquire the "elements of self-defensive and aggressive force" characteristic of men, particularly in circumstances of war. In Marsden's view, gendered difference arises from the culturally imposed set of characteristics that "passive womanliness" has fostered and which must be overcome through woman's emulation of the standard of power, the masculine norm.

While expressing the decidedly antifeminist stance of the journal, Marsden's example significantly reveals the extent to which such misogynist attitudes were encouraged by the Stirnerian revival. Pound's aesthetic embrace of this egoist philosophy excluded at its deepest level of thought the possibility of valuing models or experiences of feminine difference.[19] This concept of creativity is linked to Pound's developing sense of the artist in conflict with the common masses.[20] As Marsden's egoism progressively denigrated feminism and women in general, the magazine's egoism moved in elitist and isolationist directions, positing the artist as an individual existing on a plane above the comprehension of the common man. In one of his most extreme statements of egoism, Pound proclaims in a 1914 essay on Wyndham Lewis that the " 'man in the street' cannot be expected to understand the 'Timon' at first sight. Damn the man in the street, once and for all, damn the man in the street who is only in the street because he hasn't intelligence enough to be let in to anywhere else, and who does not in the least respect himself for being in the street" ("Wyndham Lewis" 233). In "The New Sculpture," an essay published in the *Egoist* on February 16, 1914, Pound assaults the social order, places the artist in violent conflict with that order, and denigrates the race of humans inhabiting it, while he elevates the egoist artist-creator: "Modern civilisation has bred a race with brains like those of rabbits and we who are the heirs of the witch-doctor and the voodoo, we artists who have been so long the despised are about to take over control." The artist "knows he is born to rule but he has no intention of trying to rule by general franchise," since democracy has proved to be "folly"; hence, as artists leave behind such foolish notions, they "shall mount again into our hierarchy" as "the aristocracy of the arts is ready again for its service" (68).[21]

Williams did avow a certain affinity to the egoist position, claiming in a July 1914 letter to Viola Baxter, "An egoist is simply a person who owns himself to bestow himself perfectly" (in Weaver, *William Carlos Williams*, 24). Williams's own regard for the priority of individual experience links him partially to the egoists, but his coexistent yearning to "connect," to make contact, colors that individualistic bent with anything but Stirnerian hues. In 1914, just as the journal most loudly insists upon its extreme egoist position, Williams's voice within the journal undercuts the antidemocratic, elitist elevation of the individual (artist) and posits a type of individual and artistic power that has little in common with the dominating and controlling power advocated by Pound, Marsden, and other egoists. The divergent notions of poetic authority that so strikingly distinguish the voices of the two friends and contemporaries, Pound and Williams, implicitly surface within the textual field of the *Egoist*. What Denise Levertov calls the poet's "long stem of connection" characterizes his poetry and also his life,[22] and the poems Williams printed in the magazine demonstrate the investment of this "connection" with a feminine presence that dramatically contrasts with the journal's emerging egoism (*CIB* 60). Although at this point, Williams's poetic treatment of women cannot be deemed "feminist," these early female figures point toward a more explicit concern with authority and constructions of gender characterizing poems that will follow in the next few years. Thus, in looking at the images of women in these poems, I am most interested in an incipient tension between Williams's ideas of the feminine, his appropriation and representation of female subjects, and his position as a male poet – a position continually in process as Williams begins to problematize its authority.

Something of this tension is suggested in the selective process by which Williams revised a 1914 poem published in the *Egoist*. Appearing again in *Collected Poems 1934*, "The Revelation" has undergone cuts and changes that have not only tightened it but have diminished the role of the poet as a mediator of experience, particularly of gendered experience. The original version and the version printed in *Collected Poems 1934* are printed below:[23]

> *The Revelation* (1914)
> I awoke happy, the house
> Was strange, voices
> Were across a gap
> Through which a girl
> Came and paused,
> Reaching out to me
> With never a word.
>
> Then I remembered
> What I had dreamed:
>
> A beautiful girl
> Whom I know well
> Leaned on the door of my car
> And stroked my hand

While her soul
Streamed up to me
From her quiet eyes.

I shall pass her on the street,
We will say trivial things
To each other,
But I shall never cease
To search her eyes
For that quiet look
Henceforth.

*The Revelation* (1934)

I awoke happy, the house
Was strange, voices
Were across a gap
Through which a girl
Came and paused,
Reaching out to me—

Then I remembered
What I had dreamed—
A girl
One whom I knew well
Leaned on the door of my car
And stroked my hand—

I shall pass her on the street
We shall say trivial things
To each other
But I shall never cease
To search her eyes
For that quiet look—

In revising, Williams strives to focus upon or objectify the experience itself without commentary, a tactic in keeping with the overall direction of his poetry. Significantly, though, his cuts and alterations reject the earlier poem's more conventional poetic treatments of the girl. No longer does her soul stream "up to me / From her quiet eyes," nor is she even "beautiful," suggesting a dissatisfaction with poetic conventions in writing about women. The Dickinsonian dashes, which refuse closure to each stanza and to the poem itself, open the revised poem to both hesitancy and multiple possibility; the poet's shaping vision is both deconventionalized (in relationship to the original poem) and destabilized as an imposing force. The poem's revisions in form and content suggest a recognition of the male poet's authoritative relationship to images of women and conventions of poetic treatment.

Just as significantly, however, the lines retained from the first to second versions reveal a distinctive rhetoric articulating experience through language and imagery that Williams will continue to associate with the feminine: the girl comes "across a gap," for instance, a nothingness or absence that becomes a central motif for Williams in ways that prefigure more recent feminist critical discussions of the feminine as residing in gaps, erasures, and silences. At the same time, however, the poem and its revision enact a scene familiar within the Western tradition of poetry, for the woman is inspiration to the male poet, enabling his creative effort. Interestingly, the 1914 "Revelation" is published in the same issue as the first version of "The Wanderer," a poem that also dramatizes creative empowerment of the male poet by the female figure; however, the old woman inverts the conventional muse in her active role, while the poet is suggestively feminized. Rather than statically defining Williams's notion of "the feminine" in relationship to his poetry, these poems reveal the central and yet unstable focus upon a feminine source for vision and language. At the same time, they mark the initial steps in a process through which Williams's work continually reconsiders itself in relationship to ideas of the feminine.

Published several months before "The Revelation," another poem, "Woman Walking," also uses the central motif of a female's appearance out of nothingness to inspire the poet. The corporeal, self-assured presence of a woman selling fresh eggs moves into the cinematic vision of the poet, who first describes a wide-angle view of the village, then narrows his vision to a particularized spot and zooms in on the figure of the woman:

> —what a blessing it is
> to see you in the street again,
> powerful woman,
> coming with swinging haunches,
> breasts straight forward,
> supple shoulders, full arms
> and strong, soft hands (I've felt them)
> carrying the heavy basket.
>
> (66)

Enacting a pattern of imagery that identifies woman as a source of regenerating power, the poem ends with an image of bleak nothingness out of which this "powerful woman" has emerged and which threatens to reclaim the scene once she moves out of sight: "you walking out toward me / from that dead hillside! / I might well see you oftener" (67). Images of women in Williams's poetry often are linked to the production of art; the question of producer and product becomes complexly involved with the relationship between gender and language.

Williams commented years later, in the 1950s, on the origin of "Rev-

fjelation" and the source of "that quiet look" from the woman that
motivates the poem: "I saw an old woman on the street the other day
and something emanated from her to me. I am still looking in every face
for that rare combination. 'That's for me.' It's always a woman. It may
be a man, since there's no sex. The essence of art – Demuth, Sheeler"
("Notes," *CP1,* 478). Williams deliberately confuses the very proclamations he makes: Is the "essence of art" "always a woman"? How is
it so, if it "may be a man, since there's no sex"? This manuever to
confuse gender dualities (for the binaries of man/woman are removed)
employs a series of moves privileging an idea of the feminine in relation
to artistic generation, while retaining the role of the artist for actual men.
A similar confusion informs another poem of 1914, published in the
December *Egoist.* Of "Transitional" Williams would later say, "My definition of what the poet's attitude to the world should be. Not philosophical, not practical, but poetic – a view of life" ("Notes," *CP1,* 478).
The poem, written in the "transitional" period between *The Tempers* and
*Al Que Quiere!,* situates itself in a dialogue between two voices, which
although male, undergo a blurring of gender identities:

> First he said:
> It is the woman in us
> That makes us write—
> Let us acknowledge it—
> Men would be silent.
> We are not men
> Therefore we can speak
> and be conscious
> (of the two sides)
> Unbent by the sensual
> As befits accuracy.
>
> I then said:
> Dare you make this
> Your propaganda?
> And he answered:
> Am I not I—Here?
>                  (40)

What does Williams mean when he claims that "the woman in us / makes
us write"? One might argue that he follows in a traditional line of male
poets invoking a female muse, or that the poem enacts a classic appropriation of "the feminine." Others might argue that this woman, like
others in his poetry, represents an aspect of himself, the anima of his
psyche.[24]

However, the poem also offers a complex reworking of subjectivity
through the constituents of language and gender. Evoking the logos in

the first line ("he said"), the poem proceeds to contradict the linear, univocal promise of this opening allusion. The final assertion of self syntactically equates, and even merges, presence ("Am I . . . Here") and absence ("not I") in an answer that is itself a question. The logocentric concept of self suggested in the Biblical echoes of the first line has, by the final line, been rendered fluid and shifting by the poem's formal strategies in concert with its language of ambivalence. Dashes and question marks litter the poem and in the final line disrupt the definitive logic presupposed by the colon ending the penultimate line. Categories of meaning and syntax are dislodged just as gender categories lose their demarcation and as the poem generates itself through contradiction. The "he" proclaims, "We are not men" for "It is the woman in us / That makes us write"; the final line, with its repetition of "I," further confuses the gendered distinctions earlier played upon.[25] The male speaker's claim to "the woman in us" (us, presumably, being male writers collectively) accompanies a linguistic wrenching of binarisms – of the "two sides" – and suggests a collapsing of gender polarity, an affront to stable gender identities based upon the sexed body. This claim to "woman," in this regard, suggests both a decentering of masculine authority and an identification with a marginal position "conscious / (of the two sides)," processes that encourage consciousness and speech. Traditional associations of women and the sensual are reversed ("Unbent by the sensual"), as are time-honored assumptions of women as silent and silenced. These reversals and disruptions are daring, the second speaker notes ("Dare you make this / Your propaganda?"), and even the seemingly clear category of propaganda or polemic as unsuitable for poetry is confused by the deferring gesture of the final line, which while labeled an "answer" is neither logical nor in the form of an answer: "Am I not I—Here?" This simultaneity of selves – the I-am and the not-I – like the interplay of gendered selves earlier, works against or resists the boundaries of a humanist self-contained subjectivity; additionally, the operation of language resists the logical and the rational, producing meaning through ambivalence, contradiction, disjunction, reversal. Stable meaning through linguistic structures is abandoned, in direct correlation to a refutation of stable identity.

Where does this reading leave us? On the one hand, the poem enacts a revision of subjectivity by calling into question the categories of gender; on the other hand, why is it still troubling to read the voice of a "he" claiming the feminine for male writers? Can the poem, or can we as readers, escape the binarisms the poem ultimately depends upon? This question reverberates through readings of Williams's work, for it poses a central dilemna – it *is* the "he" who speaks and who is enabled to speak by "the woman in us." The authority to speak remains grounded in the male subject, while at the same time that authority is rendered uneasy by the poems. What is placed before us is the reenactment of cultural scripts of gender that are, in the linguistic manipulation of their assumptions, revealed as unstable inscriptions of selfhood. Gender itself, in seeming to provide a natural and transparent category of subjectivity, is held up as "propaganda"; thus termed, gender is questioned as a culturally and linguistically produced category of meaning. As "propaganda," it is shown to be quintessentially unstable ("Am I not I—Here?") and changeable within variants of time and circumstance. "Here," and its attendant question mark, emphasizes Williams's obsession with the present moment as a site for contact, and more complexly, poses a notion of self continually contextualized.

As this reading of "Transitional" argues, then, the gender politics of Williams's work are tied to revisionary concerns with subjectivity, language, and authority. Against this backdrop, I would like to return to "The Wanderer" and focus upon Williams's location of creative power within a maternal line of imaginative inheritance. This claim to lineage, like the claim to "the woman in us," compels Williams's sense of himself as a poet while generating serious questions within his writing concerning forms of authority.

These questions arise throughout *Al Que Quiere!*, and in the final version of "The Wanderer," the interplay between male-poet novitiate and the maternal figure enacts a feminization of the poet recalling the blurring of gender identity in "Transitional." Language and imagery suggest that in learning from the powerful old woman, the poet, in effect, claims "the woman in us" through the maternal line, contradicting poetic conventions of a paternal inheritance. The paternal, in fact, is rendered suspect. Significantly, the one poem (among the many written to or about his ancestors) in *Al Que Quiere!* that is addressed to his actual father begins with qualified praise for "You who had the sense / to choose me such a mother," the highest praise he offers. The father's creative capacity is an almost accidental result of doing nothing, of possessing "the indifference / to create me" ("Invitation," *CP1*, 99). The maternal presence, on the other hand, teaches and speaks and acts. In "The Wanderer," the old woman first addresses the poet as "my son," and remarks upon her strength: " 'See how strong my little finger is! / Can I not swim well? / I can fly too!' " (*CP1* 108). (The "little finger" calls to mind Williams's description of his mother's imaginative power to break "life between her fingers" in the prologue to *Kora in Hell*.) The speaker repeatedly calls attention to "Her mind," "her eyes" (108), "her might," "her voice," and her will – at the same time presenting the physical details of her "diminished state" as an old, tattered "wanderer of the by-ways / Walking imperious in beggary!" (109). Her might allows them both to fly, and succeeds in "recreating all the world" (109) by teaching the poet to see and touch and connect, and to " 'Be mostly silent' " (116), an admonishment perhaps to present the thing itself without commentary but through engagement with it; however, it is also a phrase reverberating with gendered associations. We are reminded of the male voice of "Transitional," who admits "men would be silent," which implies an association between silencing the masculine and allowing the feminine full play and power. The old woman is both silent and voiced, as "Silent, her voice entered at my eyes," suggesting an interaction of vision and speech. Her voice, mighty *and* silent, speaks in "a low thunder," contrasting with the poet's, a "seed in the wind," sperm without womb (113, 114). In the ensuing lines, however, conventions of procreation are reversed; the seed does not impregnate but is impregnated through the "queen's" bestowal of vision and the "voice of leaves and varicolored bark," and it will grow to convey "the full of my freed voice," she tells her initiate (113). As patrilineage is displaced by matrilineage, the seed becomes the womb or the site that nurtures the "full freed voice."

In fully beholding the old woman, the poet begins the process of seeing himself differently. Part of this different vision arises from a movement in and out of gender identities, an unresolved identification with masculine and feminine prompted by "contact" with the maternal figure and her earthiness. Dabbling her "mad hands" in the filthy Passaic (*CP1* 115), the old woman shocks the poet's vision into greater clarity:

> And then for the first time
> I really saw her, really scented the sweat
> Of her presence and—fell back sickened!
> Ominous, old, painted—
>
> (110)

He is commanded to behold himself old and sees himself in two ways: "winding with slow might— / A vine among oaks," a connection between things of the earth; however, his "might" is also envisioned as "the din and bellow of the male wind" that moves through forests, "Tipping sound, the female chorus— / Linking all lions, all twitterings / To make them nothing" (114). This vision seems to contradict the old woman's example (a voice both silent and mighty), and her advice to be "mostly silent"; the overpowering male wind topples, upsets, strikes (connotations of "tipping") the "female chorus" to make "nothing." The word "tipping" also suggestively incorporates a phallic image of a projection (a tip), inserted into "sound," marked female.[26] This "din and bellow" links things only by oppressing them, by overpowering them; is this the vision of the poet the speaker endorses or must accept? Or a vision of what he does not want to become? Or is this a potential alternative, a choice of the masculine that the speaker both resists (as oppressive) and is drawn to (as powerful)?

Whether this vision of a future, masculine self comes to be, the dual nature of the novitiate's choice is conveyed by the old woman's warning, which suggests that her gift of speech to him can be either positive or negative: " 'Good is my over lip and evil / my under lip to you henceforth' " (*CP1* 114). Imagistically, this "might" has been set up oppositionally as either the "vine," which is connective, or the male wind, which combines violence and eroticism in a destructive flattening of the "female chorus." By the poem's final section, the speaker accepts the maternal inheritance in a ritual baptism in the Passaic, and in this experience the "young man" is figured in decidedly (although stereotypically) feminine terms. The grandmother leads him to the river, where she speaks to the river of their union, before crying, "Enter youth into this bulk! / Enter river into this young man!" As the poet enters the river, he himself is entered, and his receptivity evoked as feminine:

> Then the river began to enter my heart
> Eddying back cool and limpid
> Clear to the beginning of days!
> But with the rebound it leaped again forward—
> Muddy then black and shrunken
> Till I felt the utter depth of its filthiness,
> The vile breath of its degradation,
> And sank down knowing this was me now.
>
> (116)

The river, with phallic energy, thrusts itself into the poet in a simulation of rape that leaves the poet experiencing both disgust and self-revelation; he collapses from the degradation while "knowing this was me now." In identifying the novitiate with the female victim of rape, Williams prefigures his use of the rape motif in *Kora in Hell* a few years later, in which submission to such experience metaphorically produces both self-revelation and access to creativity. While suggesting an awareness of power as gendered and even an identification with the powerless, this claim to rape both elides the political realities of abuse and idealizes a feminine submissiveness as a mode of contact. As dangerously, it plays into romances of rape fantasy, those myths claiming that all women really want to be raped, an experience that can transform them into "real" women. The poem's allusions to these ideas of rape reveal the tenacity of sexual stereotypes in Williams's thinking; however, it is this fascination with gender's relationship to power that will motivate his most interesting examinations of masculinity.

At this early point in developing his poetics, Williams conceives of the feminine as embodying a powerful relationship between language and sensory experience; the maternal line is posited as a source of contact with the earth for the male; the process of contact feminizes the poet. This valorization of a feminine essence is complicated by the idealization of female submissiveness to rape as epitomizing "contact" simultaneous with the celebration of an active, creative female power. Unorthodox conceptions of woman as the agent and producer of knowledge (the old woman, for example) seemingly conflict with the stereotype of woman as the passive receptacle of male desire. Although Williams's choice of rape as a central analogy to the creative process is wildly problematic, within the context of the poem it suggests an attentiveness to issues of gendered power that characterize the work he will produce in the following few years. His identification with the powerless, the degraded, the violated remains a central impulse often embattled with the awareness that his own position, as male, grants him power. This conflict leads, in the work, to a self-reflexive and even deconstructive textualization of sexual essence, as though the texts themselves begin to question and take apart the very essences they assert. Thus, even the conceptualization of rape as an idealized mode of contact that generates *Kora in Hell* gets turned on its head by subsequent work that problematizes elisions of gendered power performed by his own theories.

One of his earliest articulations of language theory can be found in the *Egoist*. The 1917 letter-essays, "The Great Sex Spiral," reveal Williams's attempt to express a theory of the feminine and its relationship to poetry. While this theory generally depends upon essentialized and often conventional ideas of the feminine, it paradoxically puts forth enigmatic suggestions of the material power dynamics involved in the process of constructing a fixed, idealized feminine. He wrote the letters in response to Dora Marsden's essays on creativity and language, or what she called "lingual psychology." These "chapters" of her study ran regularly from July 1916 until the journal's demise in 1919 and dealt with questions of language, perception, and creativity, while attacking the "abstract" tradition of speculative philosophy. The egoist bent of her philosophical revisioning appealed to Pound and intrigued Williams, but for arguably different reasons. Williams's interest in the first chapter reveals much more about his own notions of the individual's relationship to language and the material world than they illuminate Marsden's actual text. Williams (mis)reads Marsden, filtering her ideas through his own thoughts on perception, language, gender, and sex.

"The Great Sex Spiral" responds to Marsden's first essay on lingual psychology, in which she criticizes traditional philosophy for its speculative methods of inquiry into an "unknown" reality. What obviously engages Williams is her insistence upon man's tendency, through the abstractions of language, to distance himself from himself, and her concomitant emphasis upon the validity of the human senses in approaching "Reality." She sets herself in contrast with the conventional "belief. . . . that the answers to philosophy's ultimate questions lie forever beyond the apprehension of the human senses" ("Lingual Psychology" 98). As Marsden states in other essays, the equation of "perception" with "being" elevates the "I" or the ego into a position of mastery, and her war against grammar, syntax, and abstractions aggressively asserts the means to invert what she saw as language's mastery over man.[27] Language must be recognized as man's servant and the result of his own construction, rather than metaphysically equated with the "Great Unknown": though men have created language, "this latter-day creation: this waiting-maid of men, has become invested with Authority as Lord Master and Begetter with men's own acquiescence. . . . To blast the Word, to reduce it to its function of instrument is the enfranchisement of the human kind: the imminent new assertion of its next reach in power" ("I Am" 2). As his response suggests, Williams is drawn to Marsden's insistence upon the human senses as the route to knowledge, rather than her assertions of mastery over language. He isolates her thoughts on sensory forms of knowledge and reads them as expressing a "feminine psychology"; although Marsden never uses this term, Williams attributes this omission to her unawareness of the true import of her statements.

As a close look at his response makes clear, Williams's concept of the individual and of individual perception relies not upon mastery but upon relatedness or connectedness, thus distinguishing his from the articulated ideas of the expatriate modernists at a very early stage in the movement's development. The relationship between concrete, sensory experience and the "blasting" of language provides the egoist position with a drive to mastery through assertion of the ego as the only valid reality, whereas for Williams this relationship constitutes the feminine and its connective capacity, which is freed or made possible through the blasting of logic, polite syntax, and convention. In Williams's writings on the imagination, on poetics, and on poets themselves, it is evident that he wants, like many of his female contemporaries, to break open tyrannical (i.e., mastering) forms and structures to allow more inclusive, democratic, and multiple spaces. This process coheres with gendered paradigms within his thinking, and that collusion begins to be articulated in "The Great Sex Spiral."[28]

Applauding Marsden for expressing for "the first time" a "philosophy from the female standpoint: militant female psychology," Williams heralds this "vigorous and fruitful female psychology" as supplanting outworn structures of thought, or male psychology ("The Great Sex Spiral," *Egoist* 4.3, 46). In this first of two letters responding to Marsden's initial chapter on lingual psychology, however, Williams accuses her of committing the same fallacy found in the system she tries to overturn, of attempting to replace one narrow, insufficient vision with another. Criticizing Marsden's approach, while praising the implications of her argument, Williams sprinkles his comments with gendered terms. He declares that, in her zeal to attack "male psychology," Marsden misses the point of her own argument, which is the promise of an "establishment of a truly *pregnant female* psychology" (46). In committing the error of narrowness characteristic of the epistemology she attacks, Marsden has "sounded a most *penetrant* almost a romantic, *sex-note*"; however, Williams has detected the "by-product of her investigation," which is the "real profit of her *labour,* i.e. the establishment of female psychology" (46; my emphasis throughout). The poet constructs his argument through body-oriented language that is punningly gendered; the labor of fecundity becomes analogous to a new way of thinking, while phallic penetration suggests a narrow, restrictive direction for thought. We are reminded here of the two choices posed in "The Wanderer" between the "vine" and the "wind."

As is typical with Williams's prose, his terms lack specificity in this first letter, while they gesture toward a more elaborate context. Marsden, responding in an Editor's Note to the letter, wishes Williams would make "clearer what the distinction is which he draws between male and female psychology. Is it anything beyond the fact that the one is written by a man, the other by a woman?" Thus, in a second letter published in August 1917 (*Egoist* 4.7), Williams goes to much greater lengths to explain his ideas. Within this discussion of male and female psychologies, at times drawing incipient distinctions between what we now understand as gender (socially constructed) and sex (biological body), he comments upon tradition, upon woman's perception of reality, and upon gendered relationships to language and experience.

Williams begins by asserting his belief that the age is experiencing changes that "have as their basis a domination of female psychology over an outworn male psychology," a process that is preceded by and "parallel to that which came over objective science in Bacon's time" (110). Although he employs the binary terms male and female, he views them here (though not consistently throughout the essay) as gendered rather than biological labels:

> I do not mean necessarily a psychology limited to men on the one hand, or to women on the other. I mean two essential parts of the one thing, psychology, either of which may become predominant at any given period in any given field, and govern all activities in that field for the time being. But though influencing both sexes, it will be typified none the less by an identity with *male or female sense-experience* as the case may be. (110; my emphasis)

The value Williams places upon the difference between the sexes is rooted in a difference in sensory perception that he further develops into notions of intellectual difference. Unlike Marsden, he does not assume that female experience is or should be like male experience, and his valuing of sexual difference becomes evident in his later commentaries on women writers, such as Gertrude Stein, Mina Loy, Marianne Moore, and Anaïs Nin. Here, Williams clearly suggests that the construction of reality occurs within gendered paradigms that are based upon "sense-experience" or the body. The essay goes on to essentialize the female's close connection to the earth, through her capacity to give birth, and to argue from this essentialist base a different form of knowledge to which women are privileged but with which men can identify themselves. This desire to identify with a feminine essence echoes, of course, "The Wanderer" and other poems of this time, and Williams sees such potential for identification threatened by Marsden's attempt to subsume the feminine within a gender-blind notion of the universal, "to blend the two sexual concepts in her search for reality." Such blending, "an attempt to obliterate the difference between the sexes," would lead only to "death." Williams advocates instead a union that does not extinguish difference or multiplicity, for it "is the union of these elements, each separately contributed, that gives life to the whole."

While invoking an essentialized feminine, Williams's essay also stresses the material erasure and exclusion of women from Western systems of thought and culture. The omission of "female psychology," Williams explains, historically characterizes the accepted fields of knowledge and tradition itself. Traditional structures of thought, as contained within the discipline of philosophy, reflect "an age dominated by male thought" and should be termed more aptly "male psychology." These systems of thought have erroneously considered a single viewpoint (male) as expressive of all humankind; Marsden, argues Williams, falls into the same trap by defining traditional "philosophy" as "psychology," "using a single term *psychology* to express two things completely dissimilar: *male psychology and female psychology*" (110). The very apperception of reality "depending on sense-experience – differs for the two sexes," and it is in this "apperception of reality that the divergence between male and female psychology lies." The desire to disrupt "male psychology" or constructions of reality with a "female psychology" develops as an interesting maneuver, for the absent, erased feminine is here granted subjectivity through the act of essentializing as presence that which has historically been essentialized as nothing, or absence. This strategy requires that Aristotelian polarities between matter (as female) and soul (as male) be undone, and by the essay's conclusion, Williams has reversed the value of matter and soul, while also suggesting their archaic dualism. The body, in effect, is stressed as material to disrupt the traditional hierarchy in Western thought that places the soul/male above matter/female.

While subtle, the process of stressing the body's materiality – even to the point of essentializing it – to actually subvert representational narratives of gender seems to occur in the course of the essay. How, first, does the essay stress the body, and how does it employ essentialized ideas of the feminine? Second, how does the essentialization call attention to the dominance of male-defined reality and to the the constructed quality of that "apperception of reality"? Although at times Williams argues that male and female psychology are not necessarily bound to one's biological sex, at other times his argument clearly places the experience of reality within the physical body. Difference, for example, "is transient, it exists only while sex lasts to enkindle life; it may even appear at first superficial, but it is all the difference there is, and between its two extremes lies every conceivable activity of thought" (111). Activities of thought, as directly related to the sexual, sensual body, distinguish one "psychology" from another. Both are figured in active, physical terms: "to maintain life two things are necessary . . . a male and a female element: an engendering force and a definite point of action" (110). Metaphorically equating the womb and gestation with "a definite point of action," Williams reconceptualizes the conventionalized idea of woman as a passive receptacle.

However, such revision still relies upon an idea of a natural, precultural body. Particularly important to Williams is the potential for each female body to transform into the maternal body, creating an essential closeness between women and the material world. Furthermore, in keeping with his notion that the capacity for gestation naturally ties woman to the earth, Williams suggests two ways in which the male may attach himself to the "objective world." The most obvious and "positive connexion with the earth is in the fleeting sex function. When not in pursuit of the female man has absolutely no necessity to exist." The outline of Williams's oft-remarked, expansive libidinal economy obviously finds justification in such a view, but Williams rather pessimistically admits the futility of such pursuit: "But this chase [of the female] can never lead to satisfaction in the catch, never to objective satisfaction, since as soon as the catch is made the objective is removed and nothing remains but to make another catch of the same kind" (111). Although here essentialized, the "male pursuit" later is explored within the contexts of culture and history. As in this essay, Williams chooses to reject the pursuit as a mode and metaphor for creativity. Instead, Williams inserts another possible alternative, which he offers quickly and almost dismissively, but which nonetheless holds importance in suggesting the empowerment gained through the male's recognition of his maternal lineage. While also underscoring lineage itself as a cultural construct, Williams claims that male psychology is "characterized by an inability to concede reality to fact" and proceeds to explain his reasoning:

> This has arisen no doubt from the universal lack of attachment between the male and an objective world – to the earth under his feet – since the male, aside from his extremely simple sex function, is wholly unnecessary to objective life: the only life which his sense perceives. He can never be even certain that his child is his own. From this may arise some of the *feeling a man has for his mother, for in her at least is a connexion with the earth,* if only a passive one, though even here he cannot be certain that his mother is his own . . . (110; my emphasis)

This emotional attraction to the maternal grows out of a desire for "connexion with the earth," while expressing explicit recognition of the narratives of origin that connect the child to the parent, and thus to the earth. The father "can never be even certain that his child is his own." Foundational to Western culture, patrimony is revealed as a constructed fiction by the disruptive "factual" knowledge of the mother, the only member of the family romance who can assuredly claim a blood connection to the child she bares. Even the child "cannot be certain that his mother is his own" and must depend upon narratives of origin passed down. Thus, even in the act of essentializing the maternal, the text reminds us of reality's discursive construction, coinciding with the construction of a poetics identified with the feminine.

The male physical pursuit he discusses here "leads only to further pursuit, that is not toward the earth, but away from it – not to concreteness, but to further hunting, to star-gazing, to idleness" (111). In contrast, Williams's definition of female psychology sounds like a description of his own poetic efforts. Female psychology

> is characterized by a trend not away from, but toward the earth, toward concreteness, since by her experience the reality of fact is firmly established for her. Her pursuit of the male results not in further chase, at least not in the immediate necessity for further chase, but to definite physical results that connect her indisputably and firmly with the earth at her feet by an unalterable chain, every link of which is concrete. Woman is physically essential to the maintenance of a physical life by a complicated and long-drawn-out process. (110)

Williams's inscription of the feminine as a combination of the sexual and the maternal provides him with the basis of his poetics and helps shape a theory of the imagination and its operations in linking the feminine with "the reality of fact."[29] While partaking of socially produced definitions linking woman to nature, the essay proceeds to simultaneously construct and deconstruct essence by placing its deployment within the context of an Aristotelian tradition of philosophy. Refuting the "central contradiction at the heart of Aristotle's metaphysics . . . [that] woman has an essence and it is matter; or put slightly differently, it is the essence of woman to have no essence" (Fuss, *Essentially Speaking*, 72), Williams culminates his argument by relating the feminine's attachment to the concrete with articulation and language. This relationship, as presented by Williams, insists upon a subjectivity denied women by a tradition of Western philosophy. Williams's text essentializes the feminine while, in connecting it with language and material contact, also reveals the Aristotelian "contradiction" of essence-less woman; it is precisely in focusing upon discursive constructions that an insistence upon female subjectivity and its erasure takes place. Calling attention to the constructed nature of "truth," Williams's letter refers to narratives that deny female subjectivity. Turning to the psychologist Otto Weinberger, Williams attributes a common error to this thinker and Marsden, locating it in a perspective derived "from [and distorted by] the male side":

> In *Sex and Character,* Weininger claiming for man a soul, denying it for woman, means just this: man philosophically or psychologically denies the earth, woman proclaims it. To improve man's position and to save him from the inevitable charge of futility – since his use on earth is so slight – Weininger borrows the worn-out term "soul," with which he proceeds to endow man, meanwhile disparaging woman's practical symbolization. But his most palpable error . . . is that in his eagerness to make out a case for man, he *deliberately perverts and transposes facts*. Man is the vague generalizer, woman the concrete thinker, and not the reverse as he imagined. Man is the indulger in "henids," and woman the enemy of "henids." (111)[30]

Weinberger (and, in the reference to "soul," a whole tradition of philosophy endowing only men with subjectivity) is accused of male supremacy. Identifying the bias of its male perspective – a casting of facts to "improve man's position" – Williams locates "truth" within the material making of a narrative. In his corrective reading of Weininger, Williams sees himself recovering facts that Weininger "perverts and transposes" in misconstruing woman's relationship to speech and experience. His goal here, revealed more fully in *In the American Grain,* is to remake the narrative, to reconsider the facts in a way that questions the framework supporting "man's position"; in other words, this essay begins a process of investigating naturalized truths as cultural constructions open to change and debate. Signaling a recognition that "empirical facts are always ideological productions" (Fuss, *Essentially Speaking*, 118), this essay suggests what his American "history" will later explore in its attention to "facts" as the products of "definite practices, theoretical or ideological, conducted under definite real conditions" (Hindess and Hirst in Fuss 118).

These practices and conditions, for Williams, are clearly involved with gender and the production of gendered roles and assumptions; "facts" are not the naively pure basis of empiricism – the notion that experience is knowledge – but are investigated within the context of the ideological work they perform, the structures within which they produce knowledge. Experience, hailed as the bedrock of Williams's poetics, can be understood as functioning for him as an access to the working of our culture, or ideologies; experience, in these incipient modernist works, is not raw material but comes to us, to the poet, already invested with and mediated by material and ideological circumstances. As with Weinberger, the "fact" of man's soul (and woman's lack) serves an ideological purpose that, in its historical endurance, has come to be seen as empirically natural. Revising this interpretation of gender, the essay uses essentialism to call attention to the operation of essentialism itself, and thus to question not only the authority of Weinberger's narrative but that of Williams as well.[31]

Thus, the essay's notion of the feminine seems constructed in resistance to naturalized denigrations of women. This resistance lies at the heart of Williams's envisioned project of cultural regeneration, and, as a self-consciously male poet, he will investigate the possibilities and implications of approaching the feminine within his art. In "The Great Sex Spiral," although Williams insists that one sex cannot "concede the reality of the experience that underlies the psychology of the other," nor can it "enter the other's consciousness" without relinquishing "its sense of reality," he seems to be caught between defining the sense experience of each sex on the one hand and the sensibility that arises (in a culture, or a field of knowledge) when one "sense of reality" dominates an age. In these short letter-essays, Williams implicitly envisions an overall sensibility growing from and originating in the physical experience of woman; although the male cannot experience the female consciousness, perhaps such a sensibility can be acquired from another direction – through cultural forms (such as art) and through a striving toward the concrete, the objective fact, the literal. An act of the engaged imagination and an investment of vision and creative power can carry the poet within a feminine and maternal locus. This essentialist notion of the feminine, however, joins with an awareness of cultural constructions of gender in Williams's poetry, suggesting the impact of the prewar feminist movement upon his avant-garde rebellion against authority. We will discuss this awareness as it develops out of his involvement with *Others* and his exposure to the feminist poetics of Mina Loy.

*The Feminist Movement, Mina Loy, and* Others

During New York City's "Little Renaissance" in the years just prior to America's entrance into World War I, the artistic avant-garde intermingled freely with various political and social movements, all striving to challenge convention and provoke change. Regardless of whether particular artists actively embraced political or social "isms" active at the time, the ideas spawned by socialism and feminism permeated New York's artistic circles and left recognizable traces in their works. Williams, for example, writes of the Paterson strike as early as "The Wanderer," and socialism's resistance to class hierarchy more subtly complements Williams's own egalitarian embrace of diverse groups, classes, and individuals.[32] Although Williams never fully endorsed a specific political movement, he absorbed much from the political talk and activity surrounding him during this formative period of experimentation in his own work. As Williams wrestled with questions concerning a possible poetry of modernity (a "new wandering"), socioeconomic and sexual struggles continually traversed his local environs pursuing variants of that very question: how to form a modern world, how to change or forsake an unusable inheritance and proclaim a better alternative.

While modernist artists launched a lively assault upon "the old," traditional ideas of gender were typically retained by the male writers, manifesting what DeKoven terms "an ambivalence toward the radical remaking of culture" and even a terror over the possible loss of masculinity (*Rich and Strange* 20).[33] Feminist activitists, on the other hand, focused their battle with convention upon the very issue of restructuring society through obliterating and rebuilding gender relations. Feminism intersects with the works of modernists upon the revolutionary grounds most touted; for some modernists, this intersection is threatening, and the responses range from indifferent condescension to brutal hostility. Yet for others, and particularly for women writers, feminism posed questions that naturally intertwined with the modernist revolt against outworn ideas and forms. While Williams is certainly not entirely free from the biases of his time, his work demonstrates a compatible response to feminism's criticism of conventional gender roles, especially in its recognition of the workings of power within such structures.

Centered in Greenwich Village, the feminist movement exploded upon the American scene in the decade preceding the war. Engaging the interest of a large and varied audience, feminism quickly became a popular topic of discussion and was extensively addressed within the media. At the end of 1913, *Harper's Weekly* noted that "within a year the Feminist Movement has become of interest to everyone" and comprises "the stir of life, the palpable awakening of conscience." A few months later, in

the spring of 1914, the lead editorial of the general feature magazine
*Century* reflected the growing importance of feminism to a modern
world: "The time has come to define Feminism; it is no longer possible
to ignore it. The germ is in the blood of our women. The principle is
in the heart of our race. The word is daily in the pages of our newspapers.
The doctrine and the corollaries are on every tongue" (in Cott, *The
Grounding of Modern Feminism,* 14, 13). Even America's premier star of
the silent screen, Theda Bara, claimed that in developing her film persona
as a powerful vamp, "I am in effect a feministe" (in Cott 45).

This widespread intrigue with feminism reflected the movement's multiple areas of concern and activity. Although the late twentieth century
tends to equate the first wave of feminism with the political fight for
suffrage, the feminist movement captivated public interest by challenging
the most deeply ingrained conventions defining women at the time. The
movement contained various factions, "all loudly voiced and mutually
recognized as part of the same phenomenon of female avant-garde self-
assertion," demonstrating the plurality of issues involved (Cott 49).
Though efforts for universal suffrage cut across all factions of the movement, different feminist groups concentrated on issues of professional,
psychic, and sexual freedom, birth control, labor conditions, and domestic roles. The radical feminist journal *Woman Rebel,* edited by Margaret Sanger, expressed the cultural transformation envisioned by
feminists eager to enact reforms that would, in the words of one of its
writers, "necessarily shake all established things, creating conscious disturbance and distress, where now habit blinds us." Such radical feminists
considered suffrage a limited political goal, deeming the vote by itself
an insufficient tool in reformulating patriarchy's socioeconomic constructs; like the *Woman Rebel* contributor, they sought to "remodel social
life, to create another industrial revolution, to purge sex relations of
barter and property, to set up a new type of home and family relation."[34]
The feminist movement encouraged a critique of the ideologies supporting patriarchal structures of family, religion, government, and capitalism; moreover, insisting upon historical reasons for these structures,
feminists countered naturalized beliefs and definitions restricting wom-
en's activities and expression.

As a forceful presence within the public discourse, feminism brought
issues of gender and authority to the attention of social and artistic re-
volutionaries alike. Writing amidst the disruptive feminist voices emerging from Greenwich Village, which he frequented with other artists and
intellectuals, Williams ventured into the arena of cultural critique through
a poetry inflected by feminist concerns of the day. Most notably, Williams's writing during these years of artistic revolution signifies a conflicted relationship with authority revealing itself repeatedly in terms of

gender. Particularly, his early avant-garde experiments with subject and form often claim gender ideologies as sites for challenging authority. To varying degrees, certainly, participating in patriarchal constructs attacked within the feminist movement, Williams evidences gender-blind assumptions about the cultural revolution he and other artists propounded; nonetheless, his work continually explores cultural connections between power and gender. Provoking a doubled vision of poetic and social authority, these poems explore and undercut the authority of creation and mastery supporting the traditional paradigm of the male poet. As part of a historical moment invigorated by feminist opposition, Williams's poems of the teens develop into a poetry of modernity also resisting masculine authority. Williams's literary relationship with the *Egoist* suggests his unease with Pound's masculinized ideas of society and poetry; in American feminism, he found alternative ideas and began to recognize more clearly the workings of cultural constructs of gender.

In the fight for unionization and fairer labor laws, working–class women in the early years of the century protested intensively for equal wages, better working conditions, child labor laws, and protective legislation for women. Between 1909 and 1914, women's involvement in a "strike wave" across the country "announced to the world women's wage-earning presence" (Cott 23). This strand of feminism joined naturally with socialist efforts for the worker and emphasized, as a point of political intersection, the capitalist perpetuation of sexual inequality through the patriarchal institutions of marriage and family. Though "most moderate socialists were hesitant to support changes in morality," more radical socialist voices found expression in the New York journal *The Masses* (Wertheim, *The New York Little Renaissance,* 80). Active participants in the feminist movement, editors Floyd Dell and Max Eastman gave speeches, wrote articles, and attended mass meetings in support of feminist causes. They considered feminism and socialism "copartners in the struggle for economic and sexual changes," and they "printed articles attacking the double standard, discriminatory divorce laws, and job discrimination" (Wertheim 82). Prompted by the increasing number of women leaving the domestic sphere to enter the work world, *The Masses* printed a "Woman's Citizenship Number" in 1915, choosing as its cover illustration a drawing of a woman riding the subway to work. Dell and Eastman avidly supported Margaret Sanger's campaign for birth control, but their rationale reveals the submergence of gender concerns within the broader socialist vision of a workers' revolt. Birth control, for the socialist, was important primarily for the revolution, not the woman. Arguing that poverty was a direct effect of overpopulation, the editors reasoned that birth-control restrictions limited working-class independence and the "worker's propensity for revolt" (Wertheim 83).

While reiterating Sanger's conviction that the working–class woman suffered the most extreme oppression from birth-control legislation, socialism's concern with "the worker" elided the issues important to Sanger's movement – a woman's right to control her own body and determine her sexual freedom. Many feminists, including Sanger, gradually dissociated themselves from the socialist movement, partially because of its appropriation of feminism for the ultimate benefit of men.[35]

Williams responded to *The Masses* critically, interpreting the political poetry it published as evincing only a superficially polemical concern with the oppressed. He complained in 1917 that the socialist magazine "cares little for poetry unless it has some beer stenches upon it – but it must not be beer stench. It must be beer stench – but not beer stench, it must be an odor of hops and malt and alcohol blended to please whom it is meant to please. Oh hell!" ("America, Whitman, and the Art of Poetry" 35). In his study of Williams's early politics, David Frail comments upon Williams's conviction that "the editors wanted poetry either written by members of the working class or which spoke for them, but wanted it to be poetry of the genteel sort as well" (*Early Politics and Poetics* 104). Frail convincingly speculates that the two poems submitted by Williams to the magazine in 1917 exhibit the poet's unease with the polemics he found in the magazine. He reasons that the poems "Sick African" and "Chinese Nightingale" represent a political gesture intended to "comment on political poetry" by presenting the working-class characters themselves (a sick black man and his wife, and a Chinese laundryman), without comment (Frail 105). This interpretation limits Williams to a naive empiricism in ignoring the poems' significations of ideological networks and circumstances that comment upon the politics of race and gender. These networks extend to the journal itself, which for a time provided "a major voice for radical feminism" (Wertheim 80). Especially once the magazine's connection to feminism is acknowledged, Williams's political gesture unfolds even more complexly into a critique of forms of male privilege ironically shared by both the magazine's socialism and the institutions it opposed. In "The Sick African," the maternal figure is not only "for Williams . . . the stronger of the couple," as Frail notes (105), but more significantly, Grace's maternity contests traditional patriarchal texts of gender:

> Wm. Yates, colored,
> lies in bed reading
> The Bible—
> And recovering from a dose of epididymitis
> Contracted while Grace
> Was pregnant with
> The twelve day old

Baby:
There sits Grace, laughing,
Too weak to stand.
(*CP1* 59)

The poem divides neatly into contrasting halves, each an arrangement
of details and images around a central figure. Grace, the mother, is
associated not only with pregnancy and the baby but also with laughter.
Either from the labor of birth or laughter, she is "too weak to stand."
Through its allusion to common misapprehensions of pregnancy as sickness or debilitation, this final line ironically emphasizes the strength of
maternal labor, a strength the doctor-poet would often witness. Grace's
"sickness" has produced the twelve-day-old baby, an image of regeneration related to Grace and her laughter; in sum, her "weakness" is a
strength, her "sickness" a revitalizing and natural process except when
viewed through a male-centered understanding of pregnancy and birth.
On the other hand, Wm. Yates suffers "a dose of epididymitis," a disease
afflicting the testicles. While Grace's maternal image suggests creation,
Yates's paternal state converts logocentrism's central image of creative
power as male potency into a vulnerable, ineffective, and diseased state.
Clustered around this symbolic phallus are allusions to its social, artistic,
and religious manifestations. Yates bears the English name passed from
the master culture to his own in an assimilating imposition of Anglo-
European identity upon the African; furthermore, the name recalls William Butler Yeats, the "father" poet of the British/European modernist
strain Williams resists. Afflicted with epididymitis, Yates turns to the
Bible, the book of the fathers and a central text of male potency. As an
African, however, Yates's metaphoric illness derives from his white fathers since he suffers a sickness that, like his name and religion, is of
their culture: The poem's careful selection of detail suggests that patriarchy's privileging of male potency as the primary generative power is
itself a disease traversing levels of class, sex, and race. Grace's laughter,
coming from the margins of these patriarchal images, asserts a ludic
revaluation of the system granting power exclusively to men. Her child
and her response suggest a creative source welling up from that marginal
(and maternal) space of race and gender.

Such a reading of "The Sick African" proposes an ideological connection to a pluralistic chorus of feminist voices speaking out at the time
against male-authored norms defining and controlling the female body.
Throughout the 1910s, feminists attacked the marriage institution and
the legal regulation of a woman's body, pressing in speeches, articles,
and protests for birth-control reform and sexual freedom. Anarchist
Emma Goldman "criticized marriage as an institution exploiting women
as property and urged free love based on mutual equality" (Wertheim

80). Goldman believed that female emancipation would be possible only when feminists themselves understood that "independence from external tyrannies" in labor, professional, political, or domestic spheres was insufficient as long as women remained subservient to the "internal tyrannies . . . [of] ethical and social conventions" within a patriarchal, capitalist society (Goldman in Burke, "New Poetry," 42). Both Goldman and Margaret Sanger fought against the Comstock Law of 1873, which "made it a crime to import or disseminate any drug, medicine, or article designed to prevent conception or to induce abortion. Such items and information were lumped together and classified as lewd, lascivious, and pornographic books and illustrations" (Baskin, "Margaret Sanger," viii). An insistent and vocal resistance to this law helped publicly heighten the issue of a woman's right to control her body. Sanger waged an active, prolonged, and widely publicized movement that demanded (as the journal she founded in 1914 proclaimed) that a woman's "right to decide" the fate of her body comprised the first step toward total liberation: "If a woman is to free herself effectively, she must make herself absolute mistress of her own body," a self-control invalidated and suppressed by "a ridiculous idea of love and of the act of reproduction, an idea handed down from the infamous Christian religion" (Méric, *Woman Rebel* 1.2, 10).

Founded to provide a forum for radical feminists who felt that the suffrage movement too narrowly directed its energies toward altering "external tyrannies," the *Woman Rebel* gained notoriety with its 1914 indictment by the American Postal Authorities. Accused of publishing "a pamphlet of obscene, lewd, and lascivious character, containing articles of such vile, obscene, filthy, and indecent nature that a description of them would defile the records of the United States District Court," Sanger went to trial in a case that generated international publicity (in Burke, "New Poetry," 42). The articles in question discussed birth control and abortion, which violated the Comstock Law, and the trial underwent repeated postponement as supporters from Greenwich Village and abroad protested Sanger's indictment through a stream of editorials, speeches, and protest meetings.[36] Sanger attributed the February 1916 dismissal of charges against her to "the power of public opinion and active protest" (Baskin, "Margaret Sanger," xiv). In these two years, birth control had became "the central issue of the period" (Burke, "New Poetry," 42), and continued activism helped open the silence surrounding the subject of women's bodies. By 1916, birth control and sexuality had become the "topic of discussion and interest among strap hangers in subways and housewives at home . . . [and by] many who some months earlier would have only broached the subject in hushed and secretive tones" (Baskin xvi).

Amidst this upheaval caused by threats to the basic tenets of patriarchal authority over women's bodies and activities, the avant-garde journal *Others* appeared. The magazine invigorated Williams's poetry, providing an aesthetic forum for what he considered the newest, most exciting poetry being written in the years 1915–19. During the lifespan of *Others,* Williams claimed: "Whatever I wrote at this time, the poems were written with *Others* in mind; I made no attempt to publication anywhere else; the poems were definitely for *Others*" (*IWTWP* 19). Not only did he reserve his work for publication in *Others,* but he edited one issue and participated in the general production of its other issues, making "weekly trips, winter and summer, to help read manuscripts, correct proofs" (Williams, *IWTWP,* 19). While the pages of the *Egoist* document the ideological shifts and developments of the London modernist movement as it progressed through imagism and vorticism to the classicism of Eliot and Pound's "high modernism," the pages of *Others* reveal that in many senses, the art world of New York remained more than an ocean away. The exclusivity of Pound's editorial policy disturbed Williams, and he accused his old friend of acting "positively disgusted with the work of everyone" but his "little group of proselytes" ("America, Whitman" 36). The self-conscious marginality experienced by many American artists is rather aptly signified by the title Alfred Kreymborg chose for the little magazine in 1915; *Others* presented itself as a radical alternative to magazines controlling the poetry world, most particularly Harriet Monroe's *Poetry,* and claimed to open its pages to the new, unknown, and more revolutionary verse that Monroe's editorial hand had excluded. When *Others* appeared, Williams found that "the yeast of new work in the realm of the poem was tremendously stirring," prompting him to go "madly in my flivver to help with the magazine which saved my life as a writer" (*Autobiography* 136, 135). He wrote in the *Egoist* of the artistic energy this new magazine supplied, recalling that "a strange quickening of artistic life" accompanied its initial publication, an issue that opened significantly with Mina Loy's "Love Songs I–IV." The publication of her work subsequently provoked a stir of public outrage, gaining the magazine immediate attention.

This outrage is important to examine, for the initial response to *Others* was, in large part, a response to Loy's handling of female sexuality, and Williams's contact with Loy suggests a strong affinity with her feminist poetics. Loy's first published poems appeared in New York's little magazines, all familiar to Williams, and her name was well known among the *Rogue* circle, the Stieglitz *291* circle, the Arensberg circle, and of course the Kreymborg *Others* circle. The poems that appeared prior to her arrival in America criticize traditional morals and conventions, clearly speaking from a woman's perspective of economic oppression through institutionalized virginity and marriage, of psychic oppression through male supremacist attitudes, of physical oppression through sexual and reproductive experiences.[37] "Three Moments in Paris" and "Virgins Plus Curtains Minus Dots" (*Rogue* 1915) conflate woman's economic subjugation with society's moral standards; "Parturition" (*Trend* 1914) explicitly presents the female experience of giving birth, an unacceptable subject at the time, suggesting the creative capacity arising from such specifically woman's pain, as opposed to (Loy's depiction of) the shallow and calculated lust of male sexuality; "Love Songs I–IV" (*Others* 1915) express female sexuality in radically explicit and nonromantic terms.[38]

Grouping these poems as "poems of the female self," Virginia Kouidis comments upon their revolutionary subject matter:[39]

> They construct the metaphysics that shapes all her poetry and ground the spiritual autobiography in uniquely female experience. . . . They introduce the technical and structural experiment that is one of Loy's major contributions to American modernism. And they are a distinctive statement in the feminist debate, filling in their metaphysics with a tough-eyed analysis of woman's sexual-psychological and, to a lesser extent, socioeconomic oppression. *Few, if any, of the other female poets of the era speak so honestly about the quotidian life of woman.* (47; my emphasis)

In Loy's poetry the rhythms of her life as a woman are inseparable from the artistic process. Writing from a specifically female perspective, she regarded that perspective as central to her life's philosophy and her aesthetic efforts: "My conceptions of life evolved while . . . stirring baby food on spirit lamps – and my best drawings behind a stove to the accompaniment of a line of children's clothes hanging round it to dry" (*The Last Lunar Baedeker* lxvi).[40] For Loy, the exploration of her sexuality constituted a crucial part of this perspective, and Carolyn Burke comments that several "groups of poems from the early 1910s constitute a kind of aesthetic and personal self-analysis, in which images of gender and sexuality are dredged up from the subconscious" ("New Poetry" 49). In a 1915 letter to Carl Van Vechten, Loy specifies a path to self-knowledge that necessarily begins with sexuality: "I know nothing about anything but life – and that is generally reducible to sex! But soon I shall have written through all I think about it – and then I shall develop some other vision of things." She then criticizes a modernist "revolt" that avoids such honesty, suggesting that the unveiling of sexual attitudes is central to any deeply effective cultural revolution: "Also I think the Anglo-Saxon covered up-ness goes hand in hand with a reduction of the spontaneous creative quality . . . all this modern movement – is keeping entirely on the surface – and gets no further psychologically" (in Kouidis, *Mina Loy,* 28). A feminist poetics, on the other hand, would open up this tightly sealed surface and encourage a creative freedom in life and art. As she commented to Mabel Dodge in 1914, "Do tell me what you are making of Feminism. . . . Have you any idea in what direction the sex must be shoved – psychological I mean – bread and butter bores me rather" (in Kouidis 28). Loy's way of pushing "the sex" into liberation depended upon proclaiming female sexuality and experience as a basis for poetic form and subject matter, a belief that gained her notoriety as a woman poet even in popular media. Choosing her as the exemplar of the new "Modern Woman," the *New York Evening Sun* interviewed Loy in a February 1917 article that asked, " 'Who is . . . this 'modern woman' that people are always talking about?' "[41] As Carolyn Burke significantly establishes, the interview "makes explicit the connection between the politics of the new woman and the principles of the new poetry," as the reporter proceeds to reflect that " 'some people think that women are the cause of modernism, whatever that is,' " and comments on the " 'new female perspective' " of Loy's " 'original kind of free verse' " (in "New Poetry" 37).

The editorial decision to open *Others* with "Love Songs I–IV," written by a woman whose poetry was well known in New York avant-garde circles as radically feminist in voice, subject matter, and perspective, suggests that the magazine's innovative principles – the principles marking its otherness – could be manifested directly through the poetry most effectively marginalized by tradition: the poetry of the female erotic. Helping to lift the silence concerning female eroticism, as perceived from the female perspective, *Others* instantly made an American place for itself within a literary dialogue dominated by such luminaries as Ezra Pound and Harriet Monroe. During its four-year run, the magazine continued to publish Loy's poetry, dedicating one whole issue to the completed love songs, "Love Songs to Joannes, I–XXXIV," in 1917. Such women as Lola Ridge, Helen Hoyt, Djuna Barnes, Marianne Moore, Mina Loy, and Mary Carolyn Davies were published alongside Williams, Stevens, Pound, and Kreymborg, signifying the magazine's relative openness to women's voices.

A special "Woman's Number" (*Others* 3.3), printed in September 1916, opened with guest editor Helen Hoyt's call to women to write as women. Justifying the issue's exclusive focus, she argues in the introductory "Retort" that woman's poetry communicates a gendered difference too long suppressed within a literary tradition composed predominately of male voices and perspectives erroneously regarded as "universal":

> "Why a 'Woman's Number' " asked someone. "Art is surely sexless. There isn't man's poetry and woman's poetry. A poem must satisfy the same canons whether it happens to have been written by a man or by a woman." These contentions are true, but . . . is there not as great

difference, in physical make-up, in psychology, custom and history [as
between cultures], between the people called Men and the people called
Women? Yes, alas.

At present most of what we know, or think we know, of women
has been found out by men. We have yet to hear what woman will tell
of herself, and where can she tell more intimately than in poetry? If
only she is able to be sincere enough; and rather brave! (n.p.)

The clamor "to hear what woman will tell of herself" reached unprecedented proportions in prewar America, and Hoyt's call to greater consciousness of woman's identity reflects the larger cultural presence of the
vigorous feminist movement while also coinciding with Williams's analysis of male systems of knowledge in "The Great Sex Spiral." The *Others*
group participated in the feminist ideological challenge to conventional
definitions and expectations of women by opening its pages to women's
voices – voices not merely attached to women's names but calling pointed
attention to ideas of sexual difference. In both its artistic and philosophic
inception and its public reception, *Others* reveals itself as a measure of
the intersections of artistic and feminist ideas in New York circles.[42]
Moreover, as a fulcrum for Williams's aesthetic life during these years,
*Others* suggests the influence of feminist thought upon the development
of Williams's poetry and poetics.

Published in the midst of "the stir of new life, the palpable awakening
of conscience" that *Harper's Weekly* called the feminist movement, the
first issue of *Others* stimulated a similar stir (Cott, *Grounding of Modern
Feminism,* 14). Williams, remembering this issue as a landmark, observed,
"Never shall I forget our fascination with Mina's 'Pig Cupid, his rosy
snout rooting erotic garbage' " (*Autobiography* 147). His comment refers
to the "Love Songs" and Loy's treatment of male and female sexuality,
spoken from a perspective distinctly claimed as female, that demystifies
notions of romantic love, brazenly calling attention to the "suspect
places" of the sexual organs. Greeted with wild extremes of enthusiasm
and disgust, the first issue caused what Kreymborg called a "small-sized
riot" over matters of form and subject matter, particularly in response
to Loy's poetry. He recalled: "Detractors shuddered at Mina Loy's subject
matter and derided her elimination of punctuation marks and the au-
dacious spacing of her lines" (*Troubadour* 235). The *Others* editor significantly points to Loy's formal originality in using techniques later
attributed to male poets (including Williams) but developed by Loy earlier
during her association with the Italian futurists and European art movements. The subject matter, derived from her ability to go "about expressing herself freely," unsettled the sensibility of a country that had
recently labeled articles on birth control obscene (Kreymborg, *Troubadour,* 236). As Kreymborg reasons,

In an unsophisticated land, such sophistry, clinical frankness, sardonic conclusions, wedded to a madly elliptical style scornful of the regulation grammar, syntax and punctuation horrified our gentry and drove our critics into furious despair. The nudity of emotion and thought roused the worst disturbance, and the utter nonchalance in revealing the secrets of sex was denounced as nothing less than lewd. . . . I remember how some of the reviews puzzled, rather than injured her. . . . Had a man written these poems, the town might have viewed them with comparative comfort. But a woman wrote them, a woman who dressed like a lady and painted charming lamp-shades. (*Our Singing Strength* 488–9)

Loy's insistence upon telling "what woman will tell of herself" generated charges of obscenity that rested upon three interrelated factors: the unorthodox language, syntax, and form; the female sexuality; and most damning, the authorship of the poems by a woman. Such overstepping of propriety, in the eyes of many contemporaries, clearly linked Loy's poetry with the scandalous writings of the New York feminists who were receiving constant publicity. Like Sanger and Goldman, who wrote political pamphlets out of and about women's experience and who defied male regulation of this experience, Mina Loy based her poetry in the physical, psychological, and emotional materiality of her life as a woman.[43] *Others* endorsed her work, publishing her radically feminist pieces throughout its four-year run, despite or perhaps because her poems were regarded as "lewd and lascivious writing, in the same class as the pamplets of Margaret Sanger or the lectures of Emma Goldman" (Kreymborg, *Singing Strength,* 488–9).

Loy's poetic efforts were directed toward a psychic and social liberation for women, continually exposing and critiquing the construction of gender through agencies of religion, economics, family, and art. Although she saw her poems as political expressions, she did not feel comfortably contained within any particular niche of feminist activism. She wrote to Carl Van Vechten in 1915 about her feminism: "What I feel now are feminine politics – but in a cosmic way that may not fit in anywhere" (in Burke, *New Poetry,* 41). Before arriving in New York, she had been kept abreast of its feminist movement through Mabel Dodge, and in November 1914 she sent her American friend a copy of her "Feminist Manifesto," declaring in the opening line: "The Feminist Movement as instituted at present is INADEQUATE" (*Last Lunar Baedeker* 269).[44] Emphasizing the need for women to reject male-defined ideas of womanhood in gaining liberation, she declared: "Leave off looking to men to find out what you are *not.* Seek within yourselves to find out what you *are.* As conditions are at present constituted you have the choice between Parasitism, Prostitution, or Negation" (269). Although she asserted that sexual power relations divided men and women against one another, she felt that this polarity could be collapsed potentially through sex, for the "only point at which the interests of the sexes merge is the sexual embrace" (269). Loy advocated the "Absolute Demolition" of such socially constructed fictions as "mother," "mistress," "virtue," or "virginity," and called for voluntary motherhood that was independent of marital state. The body and mind, the sexual and psychological, Loy insisted, must be reconsidered by women for political or economic solutions to be truly effective: "In defiance of superstition I assert that *there is nothing impure in sex* except the mental attitude toward it. The eventual acceptance of this fact will constitute an incalculably wider social regeneration than it is possible for our generation to acquire" (271).

Loy's feminism, she felt, could be expressed more fully in an American atmosphere than in a British and European one. Though English herself, Loy was not attracted to the London art scene, and her major outlets before 1920 were neither English nor European, despite her movement within European circles of modern artists. Moreover, Loy's interest in American cultural and artistic activities are specifically characterized by an attraction to feminist ideas and to the possibility of feminine expression within the American literary scene. In addition, Loy found in Williams's precursor, Walt Whitman, an expression of "the essential sexual dimension of selfhood" that encouraged her own expressions of female sexuality (Kouidis, *Mina Loy,* 27). Loy herself drew such a connection in a 1915 letter from her Florence home to Carl Van Vechten, in which she defends the sexual honesty of her poems and places them within an American context: "I believe we'll get more 'wholesome sex' in American art – than English after all... but that is to be expected – we haven't had a Whitman" (in Kouidis 27). While Williams is struggling to build an American ground for a distinctly modern poetry, Loy locates that ground in her sex and proclaims it through her feminist poetics.

In Loy, we have access to a body of modernist poetry directly engaged in the feminist movement's agenda to restructure society. The revolt against tradition informing the modernist project, for this modern woman, depended upon a feminist commitment to radical change of sexual conventions. Gender politics lie at the heart of Loy's assault upon what Williams would call "hangovers from past generations," a phrase he uses in the 1920 manifesto to the journal *Contact* in which a poem by Loy refutes her "forebears' excrements" ("O Hell"). Drawn to Loy and her poetry, Williams foregrounded her works in the two avant-garde journals he helped edit, *Others* in 1917 and *Contact* in 1920. Founded and edited by Williams and Robert McAlmon, urging American artists to free themselves of European models, *Contact*'s first issue includes two pieces by Loy, "Summer Night in a Florentine Slum" and "O Hell."

Significantly, Williams also wrote the introduction for the 1958 printing of Loy's *Lunar Baedeker*, praising this poet who had been silent since the thirties. Although in the teens and early twenties, "it was common to couple the names of Mina Loy and William Carlos Williams"[45] (Yvor Winters in 1926 proclaimed Williams the poet "closest in spirit" to Loy[46]), not much has been made of this coupling except to note each poet's radical experiments with form and obvious fascination with sexuality. These important points of intersection are worthy of further reflection; Carolyn Burke observes that of all the male modernists, Williams, "like Loy . . . learned to make sexual difference a poetic subject, and . . . undoubtedly agreed with her that women's experience differed radically from men's" ("New Poetry" 52). Moreover, in their focus upon sexual difference, both poets open into broader considerations of the relationship between gender, authority, and art.

Although Williams disapproved of the polemical poetry in *The Masses,* he admired Loy's poems, in which Loy, as self-defined feminist, transformed the personal into the political.[47] Her frank treatment of sexuality gained Williams's attention, helping him to open his own poetry to the sexual; moreover, Williams's receptiveness to Loy's work during a formative period in his own development suggests ways in which his own notions of gendered relationships are mediated by her feminist example. The woman-centered poetry he inaugurates with "The Wanderer" in 1914 begins to incorporate a set of sexualized and gendered tensions that question traditional assumptions of both cultural and poetic authority. As Williams delves into the sexual, he, like Loy, recognizes the interplay between erotic sexuality and gendered authority. Both poets found themselves resisting aesthetic movements that emphasized the artist's capacity and function to control and master; Loy reacts very explicitly against the Italian futurists, while Williams more covertly resists the Stirnerian egoism informing Pound's (and the London modernists') notion of the artist. The resistance embedded in Williams's work of the period emerges more vividly when the poems are read in relationship to Loy's poetic treatment of male authority and power.

During the *Others* years, Kreymborg observed, Williams "frankly and fearlessly undressed himself down to the ground" in his explorations of sexual feelings and erotic desire (*Troubadour* 242). Like Loy, Williams deliberately rebuked a sentimental tradition of love poetry through emphasizing a physical eroticism that, in his case, extends into the natural world. Loy's treatment of love in poems like "Human Cylinders" and especially "Love Songs to Joannes" forcefully demystifies romantic love while retaining a central focus upon the relationship between the sexes. Her example demonstrated to Williams an alternative to his earlier romanticized love poetry; moreover, Loy's poetic confrontation with the physical through a visceral, sensual language exhibited a vocabulary of eroticism that Williams would take up. It is a vocabulary reveling in the body's functions, dwelling upon its skin and tissue and fluids as ways of figuring love. Deliberately resisting the idealization of the body, Loy's treatment ranges from disgust to delight with the flesh while accepting the entire spectrum of reactions; in her attempt to render desire fully incarnate she must confront the cultural attitudes toward the body that alternately reify and denigrate it. In "The Dead," such language connects the maternal and the sexual within the female body: "Our tissue is of that which escapes you / Birth-breaths and orgasms" (*LLB* 7). The maternal body, entering the transcendent realm of "cosmic reproductivity" in "Parturition," earns its final identification with "infinite Maternity" only after the intensely physical experience of labor, which is depicted through an unprecedented attention to the woman's body during birth:

> Against my thigh
> Touch of infinitesimal motion
> Scarcely perceptible
> Undulation
> Warmth   moisture
> > (*LLB* 69)

Most infamously, "Love Songs to Joannes" explicitly situates love in the physical body, beginning with a collision between fairy-tale versions of romantic love ("erotic garbage") and eroticized images of nature:

> Spawn of Fantasies
> Sitting the appraisable
> Pig Cupid
> His rosy snout
> Rooting erotic garbage
> "Once upon a time"
> Pulls a weed
> White star-topped
> Among wild oats
> Sown in mucous-membrane
> > (*LLB* 91)

This first section lingers on the "suspect places" of sexuality, the "Constellations in an ocean / Whose rivers run no fresher / Than a trickle of saliva" (91). Suggestive of sexual tumescence, these images give way in the second section to distinct images of male sexuality: "The skin-sack . . . Something the shape of a man" (*LLB* 91–2). Loy speaks of the male's libidinal experience from a woman's perspective, describing it as "a clockwork mechanism/Running down against time/To which I am not paced"

(*LLB* 92). Here, her focus upon sexual difference locates itself in the body.

Loy's mixture of the surreal and the natural in "Love Songs" heightens the physical eroticism permeating her treatment of sexual love. Williams's own "Love Song," written in 1915 and significantly revised in 1916 after he would have read Loy's sequence, similarly confronts the reader with images of physical love akin to the "trickle of saliva" or "skin-sack" or "wild oats sown in mucous membrane" in her verse. In the 1915 version, highly sentimental stanzas surround the core section that survives into the final version. Williams chooses to cut these exclamations of love's grandeur, strengthening the central image of desire and release as "the stain of love." The final version concentrates upon this stain:

> I lie here thinking of you:—
>
> the stain of love
> is upon the world!
> Yellow, yellow, yellow
> it eats into the leaves,
> smears with saffron
> the horned branches that lean
> heavily
> against a smooth purple sky!
> There is no light
> only a honey-thick stain
> that drips from leaf to leaf
> and limb to limb
> spoiling the colors
> of the whole world—
> you far off there under
> the wine-red selvage of the west.
> (107–8)

A poem suggesting masturbation, "Love Song" evokes the male's sensual experience through words such as "honey-thick stain," "drips," "smears," "horned branches." Like Loy's "Love Songs," the speaker in Williams's poem acknowledges the erotic substance of his act while also revealing its isolation: the woman remains "far off there under / the wine-red selvage of the west," and the stain of love is "spoiling the colors / of the whole world." This sense of alienation within erotic experience develops, in Loy's poetry, out of imposed attitudes toward sexual difference that prohibit connection: though "We might have coupled / In the bedridden monopoly of a moment," she writes, the act is one of "broken flesh . . . At the profane communion table" – there is no communion between the lovers (*LLB* 92). Culturally imposed gender boundaries prevent "communion" between the sexes.

For both Loy and Williams, the emphasis upon erotic desire signifies a self-exploration devoted to the final goal of communion with others. What is discovered in this process of working through desire is neither consistently pleasant nor praiseworthy but suggests the degree to which these two poets attempt to investigate a culturally and psychologically repressed subject, to get beyond the "Anglo-Saxon covered up-ness" derided by Loy. More importantly, their concern with sexuality in turn leads them to consider fundamental issues of authority inextricable from the sexual dimension; they continually find communion or contact blocked by forms of authority shaping gender. For Loy, acknowledging sexual desire and sexual difference compels her feminist critiques of masculine authority; Williams, as a male poet, evokes the phallic as a way of demystifying romantic love conventions, but he then goes on, significantly, to see and critique the conventions of phallic power sustaining cultural constructs of authority.

Williams evokes a phallic eroticism in any number of ways, although one of his most prevalent tendencies involves an eroticization of nature. As in "Love Song," the imagery of "Spring Strains" (1916) creates a decidedly sexual overtone. The "blue-grey buds / crowded erect with desire," imbued with the physicality of male eroticism, imagistically build into the multiply climactic depiction of birds and their "swift convergings to a point that burst / instantly" (97). The tension of the imagery – the "buds crowded erect" on "hard, rigid jointed trees" – and its energetic, upward release eroticizes the natural landscape (97). A similar sense of pressure underlies the approach of spring in "April": "too many opening hearts of lilac leaves, / too many, too many swollen / limp poplar tassels on the / bare branches!" (144).

In the 1919 "Romance Moderne," an eroticism of place and nature combines with a highly libidinal monologue to deromanticize physical love. Printed in *Others* two years after the journal devoted an entire issue to Loy's complete "Songs to Joannes I–XXXIV," the poem recalls Loy's treatments of love. The narrative element recedes into the background as a surrealistic and eroticized landscape comes to suggest the sexual energy of the poem. Traveling in the back seat of a car, the male speaker flirts with a female companion while fantasizing about her. Rapidly juxtaposed images of the changing landscape create a kaleidoscopic impression; as inner and outer worlds intertwine, the landscape takes on a sexual atmosphere and the speaker's excitement heightens:

> Swim around in it, through it—
> all directions and find
> vitreous seawater stuff—
> God how I love you!—or, as I say,
> a plunge in the ditch. The end. I sit

examining my red handful. Balancing
—this—in and out—agh.

(149)

Brutally illustrating the "male pursuit" Williams criticizes in "The Great
Sex Spiral," this sequence results in a "deliberately crude demystification
of the phallic principle" through juxtaposing "romantic declarations of
love with violently anti-sentimental references to its physical apparatus"
(Burke, "New Poetry," 52). Recalling Loy's image of the "clock to which
I am not paced," the male's sexual energy takes over the poem, infusing
its language and tone with an aggressive forcefulness. Following a jagged
movement of abrupt changes in tone and image, the poem generates
itself through a rapidly paced rise toward climax, a frenetic heightening
informed by fantasies of speed and violence. At one point, the speaker
imagines smashing the driver: "Lean forward. Punch the steersman /
behind the ear. Twirl the wheel! / Over the edge! Screams! Crash!" (148).
Sexual energy and masculine power drive toward images of violence,
and finally, to the fantasy of the woman's death. The final lines reveal
this fantasy as the ultimate objectification of the woman: "I wish that
you were lying there dead / and I sitting here beside you" (150). A
frightening enactment of male erotic fantasies of dominance, the poem
replicates the patriarchal dynamic between sexuality and power; as such,
it demonstrates a "romance moderne" privileging a male potency erected
upon the elimination of the feminine. As an object of desire, the woman
is culturally abused through fantasies of possession and mastery by the
male.

Where does Williams stand in relationship to this "male pursuit," as
he terms this construct of masculine potency? In this poem, he connects
the phallic principle to violence toward women, and it is troubling to
say the least to read the poem as an ecstatic endorsement of the masculine.
However, the poem is too riddled with crude exaggeration to be a celebration of a masculine eroticism that thrives on force and aggression;
moreover, it is too full of a self-conscious disgust to suggest the poet's
endorsement, although it clearly admits to his complicity in this phallocentric construct of sexuality. It is also too aware of discourse as a
construct: The poem foregrounds the artificial nature of verbal arrangements through emphasizing the artist's structural manipulation of words
and images, as in the lines "rain, rock, light, trees—divided: / rain-light
counter rocks-trees or / trees counter rain-light-rocks or—" (150). Just
as the artist constructs the poem, such formal play suggests, the man
constructs the fantasy. The power derived from the arrangement of
words underlies both the power and the fiction of social orders; to view
the masculine presumption of authority and mastery as a fantasy leads
the way toward its possible dismantling.

Loy's feminism reacts specifically against masculine authority as a construction based upon cultural fictions of phallic power. Such a perception was surely intensified by her involvement with the overtly misogynist Italian futurists in the early 1910s. Their aggressively male supremacist attitudes encouraged the deliberate exploitation of women, which they justified on a basis of woman's inferior and animallike intuitional existence as opposed to man's forceful intellectuality.[48] After rejecting their sexist postulates and severing ties with the futurists – ties that included affairs with the leading figures, Marinetti and Papini – Loy satirized their sexist ideas in a number of 1915 poems and a play, *The Pamperers*. Vehemently and articulately opposed to futurist misogyny, Loy also found their worship of machines an alien and even dangerous expression of the will to power. However, she did credit the futurist movement with helping her develop certain characteristics of her own experimental aesthetic, an aesthetic thereby formed in simultaneous attraction to and revolt against futurism. Marinetti's "aggressive assertion of selfhood" and his "structural experiment" affected Loy tremendously (Kouidis, *Mina Loy*, 8), encouraging her to write poems of selfhood that radically spoke from a female-centered experience while leading her to question the cultural forces shaping the gendered subject. In her attentiveness to such forces, Loy was aware that her feminist appropriation of futurist tenets contradicted the movement's glorification of male creativity; furthermore, she accused this avant-garde of dismissing female creative power in the very act of appropriating it for their benefit. In a futurist satire, she writes of "a manifesto / notifying women's wombs / of man's immediate agamogenesis," clearly mocking the movement's aggrandizement of a masculine creative power ("Lions' Jaws," *LLB* 58).

Loy's satires of male–female relationships and gendered roles both ridicule and subvert the male supremacy of the futurists, exposing the ideological construction of a supposedly fixed and natural gender hierarchy. In "The Effectual Marriage," she mocks the idea of the poet's creative power as a form of male potency through the characters of Miovanni and Gina (Giovanni Papini and Loy herself). Satirizing the gendered division of work, Loy places Miovanni in the library, and Gina in her kitchen "where he so kindly kept her" (*LLB* 33). Each exists with a proper sense of purpose: "To man his work / to woman her love" (33). Subversively, Gina will sometimes "write a poem on the milk bill," yet she will not visibly or verbally interrupt the "scrubbed smell of the white wood table" or the perfectly ordered universe of her male-defined world. As a footnote to the poem, Loy writes: "This narrative halted when I learned that the house which inspired it was the home of a mad woman," signaling the madness of repression and self-effacement threatening any woman (and here, the female poet in particular) in a male-defined society (35).

In the special issue of *Others* that featured Maxwell Bodenheim, Kreymborg, and Williams, entitled "Three Others," Williams includes various portraits of women who resist their distinctly disenfranchised status. "K.McD." (later changed to K.McB.) suggests a feminine power that operates subversively to resist masculine oppression. As Loy's poems uncover male-defined boundaries and the female's covert transgressions of such lines, Williams often locates in female figures the dismantling of mastery that his own aesthetic attempts to enact. In "K.McD.," written to the nursemaid who tended his young sons during World War I, he encourages her to transform what others scorn or look down upon into a strength that can subversively empower her:

> You exquisite chunk of mud
> Kathleen—just like
> any other chunk of mud!
> —especially in April!
> Curl up round their shoes
> when they try to step on you,
> spoil the polish!
> . . . . . .
> Do they expect the ground to be always solid?
> Give them the slip then;
> let them sit in you;
> soil their pants . . .
>
> (106)

The "ground" projects derogatory associations back upon those who hold them, disordering the relationship between low and high elements. Contact becomes a form of resistance in the image of the "exquisite chunk of mud," a way of upsetting dualistic hierarchies and empowering the oppressed.

Cultural validation of male authority, the "indisputable male voice" that "roars" through the female speaker's brain and body in Loy's "Three Moments in Paris," echoes within numerous other poems she writes during this period. The "male voice" defines and controls, as in "Giovanni Franchi" (*Rogue* 1916), in which "Three women . . . skipped parallel / To the Progress / Of Giovanni Franchi." The "three women" are one, a division of the female self perpetuated by male privilege and female self-effacement:

> The threewomen was composed of three instincts
> Each sniffing divergently directed draughts

> The first instinct     first again     (may
> Renascent gods save us from the enigmatic
> penetralia of Firstness)
> Was to be faithful to a man     first
> The second     to be loyal to herself first
> She would have to find which self first
>                         (*LLB* 51–2)

This attempt to "find which self first," to locate a female self free of masculine definitions, is repeatedly expressed as a breaking through the boundaries of male-defined spaces. "Parturition" most emphatically acclaims feminine space and energy as a "leap with nature / Into the essence / Of unpredicted maternity" (69). Though the speaker's male lover leaves her during her labor for a dalliance with another woman, the experience of giving birth affirms her femaleness in ways that he cannot. "The irresponsibility of the male / Leaves woman her superior Inferiority," an inferiority inverted through this experience into a transcendent union with a feminine principle:

> Mother I am
> Identical
> With infinite Maternity
> Indivisible
> Acutely
> I am absorbed
> Into
> The was-is-ever-shall-be
> Of cosmic reproductivity
>                         (*LLB* 70)

This image of the maternal, derived from the woman's definition of her own experience, stands in contrast to the cynical final image of mothers, the "woman-of-the-people," who come to help the next day. They are the angels of the house, each "Wearing a halo / A ludicrous little halo / Of which she is sublimely unaware" (71). Emphasizing Christianity's ideology of gender, the poem satirically acknowledges the roles attributed to male and female; the master (male) creator has constructed these women, and Loy concludes that "I once heard in church / God made them" (71). Attacking patriarchal authority in the church, Loy writes in "The Black Virginity": "It is an old religion that put us in our place" (76). Within a theology based upon a male creator, women are

> Preposterously no less than the world flesh and devil
> Having no more idea what those are
> What I am

to mastery, Williams enacts a critique of a poetics, and ultimately of a cultural ethos, that chooses mastery over contact. The act of representation, of methophor-making, is recognized within the poem as an act of violence within gendered frameworks of power.

### The Feminine as Resistance to Authority

The feminist challenge to masculine forms of authority surfaces in Williams's struggle to defy tradition and claim an American ground for poetry. His efforts to historically reconstruct an enabling American tradition rely upon a critique of authority that most clearly coincides with feminist ideology in *In the American Grain*, written in the early twenties. A revisionary history of the New World, this work examines manifestations of power within patriarchal systems while envisioning an alternative creative power configured as feminine and maternal. At the same time, his history questions the cultural meanings of masculine, feminine, and maternal, further deconstructing patriarchal definitions of gender. Between the years of "The Wanderer" and *In the American Grain,* Williams's poetry returns again and again to issues of authority. Primary among these issues is the assumption of artistic authority as a masculine prerogative, of creativity as derived from male potency.

*Sour Grapes,* published in 1921, contains numerous poems revealing Williams's preoccupation at the time with the relationship between gender and authority. Sorting through personal and cultural attitudes toward women, reflecting upon masculine sexuality and privilege within a male-dominated culture, these poems display a range of contradictory attitudes. "Romance Moderne" is joined in this volume by other poems openly derived from male sexual fantasies of women. "Arrival" imagines an illicit liaison with a woman in a "strange bedroom," where her "tawdry veined body emerges / twisted upon itself / like a winter wind . . . !" (164, 165). In "The Cold Night," the speaker tentatively escapes the frigid barrenness of winter by envisioning "the round and perfect thighs / of the Police Sergeant's wife" that he will see again in spring (154). This thought sustains him in the cold, metaphorically offering a regenerative hope after winter's death:

> White thighs of the sky! a
> new answer out of the depths of
> my male belly: In April . . .
> In April I shall see again—In April!
> the round and perfect thighs
> (154; Williams's ellipses)

Here, male desire is configured through the male gaze, blatantly disembodying and objectifying the woman into a pair of thighs that satisfy the need arising from the "male belly." Even in asserting the gaze, though, the poem complicates this move toward objectification by simultaneously evoking the maternal body. Twice the thighs are mentioned, each time in conjunction with the woman's maternity. Initially, the speaker imagines "the bare thighs / of the Police Sergeant's wife— among her five children"; in the final lines, he sees the thighs again, "perfect still after many babies" (154). In a twist on the catalogue tradition, Williams introduces the image of the mother into a romance convention that typically excludes the maternal body when admiring a woman's attributes. The maternal mediates the male gaze, commenting upon the gaze itself while subtly suggesting the poetic tradition's delimitation of female sexuality in defining women in terms of their functions of wife and mother.

Paternal authority, on the other hand, partakes of this gaze and regards women as objects of exchange and subjugation. "Youth and Beauty" offers an allegory of the father's possession of his daughter:

> I bought a dishmop—
> having no daughter—
> for they had twisted
> fine ribbons of shining copper
> about white twine
> and made a tousled head
> of it, fastened it
> upon a turned ash stick
> slender at the neck
> straight, tall—
> when tied upright
> on the brass wallbracket
> to be a light for me
> and naked
> as a girl should seem
> to her father.
>
>                    (167)

The "daughter," a domestic tool, is made and displayed for the father's benefit. She provides a "light" for him, although to do so she must be "tied upright" and kept in place. The sexual possessiveness underlying this paternal authority is disturbingly exposed in the final three lines. The emphatic image of the daughter, "naked / as a girl should seem / to her father," ends the poem with the deliberate shock of satire, following Loy's example in such poems as "Virgins Plus Curtains Minus Dots," "The Black Virginity," or "Three Italian Pictures." In these satires, virgins are locked in patriarchal homes where they wait to be purchased, and any disobedience elicits a horrible fate. Angered at her daughter's love for a man, the Italian father of the latter poem magically transforms her into a wild animal, and Loy suggests a sexual, incestual undercurrent to the father's act:

> It is unnatural in a Father
> Bewitching a daughter
> Whose hair   down   covers her thighs
> (*LLB* 48)

Williams's version of paternal authority inserts itself in this genre, critiquing through satire the patriarch's possession and abuse of his daughters.

This possession extends into all levels of cultural inscription of the feminine. "Portrait of a Lady," written in 1920 though not included in *Sour Grapes,* consciously parodies the catalogue convention and calls into question poetic inscriptions of the feminine. In an image linking it to "A Cold Night," the poem begins: "Your thighs are appletrees / whose blossoms touch the sky" (129). Proceeding, as is customary within the catalogue structure, to comment (gaze) upon the lady's knees and ankles, the poem interrupts itself in a fashion uncustomary of its genre. With each image of a body part, questions break the sequence, until the syntax disintegrates into uncertainty:

> it is
> one of those white summer days,
> the tall grass of your ankles
> flickers upon the shore—
> Which shore?—
> the sand clings to my lips—
> Which shore?
> Agh, petals maybe. How
> should I know?
> Which shore? Which shore?
> I said petals from an appletree.
> (129)

Through suffering a disruption of the catalogue convention, the poem has undergone a process of revision on numerous levels. It comments upon the genre (and, by extension, a whole tradition of love poetry) and its reliance upon the male gaze as an objectifying, controlling authority of vision, for the gaze no longer commands the poem once the questions unsettle the eye's directive control. Based on a painting by Watteau, the poem reconsiders the representation of women by male artists. Repeatedly interrogating both the selection and creation of images, it rejects the extended metaphor of the catalogue: "Which sky?"; "What / sort of man was Fragonard?"; "Which shore?" The poem also revises its verbal construction; the opening metaphor evolves into the direct statement ending the poem, suggesting that the woman's body escapes metaphorical dismemberment. Line by line, the poem derails the direction it initially established until it implicitly questions its own authority as a cultural inscription.

This strategy of revision provides Williams with a formal approach to the problem of poetic authority. To include revision as a part of the poem acknowledges the poet's mediating presence while challenging his mastery over the poetic subject; in the endless proliferation of revision, the subject continually escapes inscriptive closure. "Portrait of the Author," a closing poem in *Sour Grapes,* complements "Portrait of a Lady" in bringing to the surface through formal means the issue of the poet's authority to inscribe:

> The birches are mad with green points
> the wood's edge is burning with their green,
> burning, seething—No, no, no.
> The birches are opening their leaves one
> by one. Their delicate leaves unfold cold
> and separate, one by one. Slender tassels
> hang swaying from the delicate tips—
> Oh I cannot say it. There is no word.
>
> (172)

The poet relinquishes control, though not without ambivalence. This is a poem filled with both despair and hope; the hope hinges upon a springtime of human contact and communion, a possibility that asks how language may become an inclusive force rather than a barrier.

This questioning demands, on multiple levels, a revision of myriad forms of authority. Williams's response to authority – whether it be religious, literary, or social – progressively takes form within feminine configurations as he writes his experimental works, particularly *In the American Grain* and *Spring and All.* Emerging out of a decade traversed by feminist concerns, these works consider a "feminine" that is both essentialist and materialist – both evoking a feminine essence and witnessing the feminine as a cultural construct. Before moving on to a more explicit discussion of *In the American Grain* as a critique of patriarchal authority, I will conclude with a discussion of two poems in *Sour Grapes* that suggest the evolving, multifaceted, and fluid notion of the feminine informing Williams's early work.

While the maternal remains central to Williams's understanding of the poetic imagination, his developing modernism signals an awareness of the pernicious danger of idealization. In "Complaint" the doctor-poet employs his medical experience to oppose the idealized status of motherhood. The reality of maternal experience not only contradicts the idealized version but also demonstrates the actual oppression such idealization of women's procreation masks. This oppression is conveyed through the juxtaposition of physical detail and mock celebration in the following lines, describing the woman the doctor has traveled to care for:

> Here is a great woman
> on her side in the bed.
> She is sick,
> perhaps vomiting,
> perhaps laboring
> to give birth to
> a tenth child. Joy! Joy!
>                 (153–4)

As a doctor practicing medicine during the years the Comstock Law restricted the dissemination of information on birth control, Williams would repeatedly confront the harsh reality such legal prohibitions caused for women, particularly working-class women. "Complaint" points to the burden of bearing children without cease while also exposing the myth of maternal "joy" that renders the burden invisible. A certain helplessness pervades the final lines the doctor speaks: "I pick the hair from her eyes / and watch her misery / with compassion" (154). As witness to the ramifications of the social, legal, and religious circumstances prescribing women's procreation, the poem reiterates a view central to feminism's contemporaneous birth-control movement.

In this vignette, Williams's voice figuratively joins with Margaret Sanger and Emma Goldman in decrying sanctioned oppression of women's bodies. He engages this cultural viewpoint most often in treatments of working-class women, but its insight often underlies his own attempts to represent female difference. As the preceding discussion of his *Others* period begins to suggest, Williams's poetic renderings of female figures and his grappling attempts to understand the feminine are accompanied by a self-conscious apprehension of his gendered position of cultural and poetic authority over the female subject. This self-consciousness belies an unease with patriarchal constructs and further coincides with his efforts to define or locate a maternal and feminine sensibility within which to situate his poetics. Yet this sensibility continually shifts its ground within his poetry, just as the feminine as a concept eludes his never-ending efforts to understand, define, and absorb its enabling promise. Despite the many representations of women and proclamations of a feminine essence present within Williams's oeuvre, he intuits a quality his verbal constructs cannot circumscribe. "Queen-Anne's-Lace" suggestively evokes a feminine desire ultimately unrepresentable through language and, hence, ultimately resistant to poetic control:

Her body is not so white as
anemone petals nor so smooth—nor
so remote a thing. It is a field
of the wild carrot taking
the field by force; the grass
does not raise above it.
Here is no question of whiteness,
white as can be, with a purple mole
at the center of each flower.
Each flower is a hand's span
of her whiteness. Wherever
his hand has lain there is
a tiny purple blemish. Each part
is a blossom under his touch
to which the fibres of her being
stem one by one, each to its end,
until the whole field is a
white desire, empty, a single stem,
a cluster, flower by flower,
a pious wish to whiteness gone over—
or nothing.

(162)

The poem begins with the female body and moves to the final one-word utterance of "nothing." In between the lines proceed by negation ("not," "nor," "no") to a final series of imagistic reversals and inversions: the "tiny purple blemish" becomes a "blossom," the field is full of white flowers yet "empty," the "single stem" is a "cluster." Singleness is plurality, fullness is emptiness, depletion is replenishment: These dualities merge within a field of "white desire," the desire of "her body," which is both "the wild carrot taking / the field by force" and "empty," "nothing." It is a desire marked and blemished by "his hand," but it "blossoms under his touch"; here, the difference in nuance between his hand (an image connoting force) and his touch (an image of contact) suggests alternative ways to approach this desire. Touch leads to blossom and to the paradoxical empty–fullness of the field. This is the paradox of the imaginative process for Williams and the "nothing" of a feminine creative capacity; this is feminine desire as a force overtaking the field while remaining empty to discourse – a void in language but what language continually yearns for.

When Mina Loy's *Lunar Baedeker and Time-Tables* was issued in 1958, after years of artistic silence on Loy's part, Williams was eager to write one of the introductions. In his remarks, Williams calls attention to Loy's forgotten status and attributes it to her insistence (like Stein and Moore) on the word: "When she puts a word down on paper it is clean; that forces her fellows to shy away from it because they are not clean and will be contaminated by her cleanliness," and the "undisciplined word, seeking a new discipline, was prominent in everything she set her hand to" (unnumbered). These comments could apply to any number of modernist writers, but Williams strikingly focuses upon her female viewpoint: "This is a record of a beautiful woman who has fearlessly taken her part in a disturbing period of the life about her," Williams writes, somewhat sentimentally. But the verses he chooses to quote completely undercut any sentimental notion of the beautiful, brave poetess and demonstrate the unorthodox feminist voice, challenging conventions of sexuality, love, and gender, a voice that had startled and affected Williams years earlier. He praises, for example, the following excerpts:

> A silver lucifer
> serves
> cocaine in cornucopias

and

> until you turn on us your smoothfools' faces
> like buttocks bared in aboriginal mockeries
> We are the sacerdotal clowns
> who feed upon the wind and stars
> and pulverous pastures of poverty.

He also quotes her "best known" passage, the opening to "Love Songs," with its infamous references to "Pig Cupid" and "erotic garbage." The passage he deems "one of her most brilliant" expresses her oft-voiced criticism of masculinized concepts of power in no uncertain terms, and his choice iterates Williams's own resistance to patriarchal dualisms of flesh and spirit:

> The elderly colloquists
> the Spirit and the Flesh
> are out of tongue
> The Spirit
> is impaled upon the phallus

The poems he finds "some of the most moving" are excerpted sections from Loy's 1925 autobiographical long poem, "Anglo-Mongrels and the Rose," which follows the awakening consciousness and psychological development of the heroine, Ova, from the time of birth. Williams is particularly attentive to the portrayal of "the determining factor of . . . alliances upon the mind" (of the young female) that seek to mold her (such as religion and parental authority).[49] He singles out "Ova Begins to Take Notice" as one he most admires. Significantly, this poem presents the experience of the young female coming to language, and does so in terms strikingly similar to those Williams employs in discussing (both separately and together) the imagination, creativity, language, and the feminine. In the poem, Ova is immersed in total sensory experience when "the word" first makes cognitive sense:

> And instantly
> this fragmentary
> simultaneity
> of ideas
>
> embodies
>     the word
>
> A
> lucent
>     iris
> shifts
>     its
> irradiate
>     interstice

The poem resists the logocentric understanding of the word, celebrating a "fragmentary / simultaneity / of ideas" rather than a monolithic, unified logos. In his own articulations of the imaginative process, Williams often describes an intersection of simultaneous and multiple loci, and the resulting interstices, that he relates to feminine sense-experience. More complexly, he sees in this process a revolutionary approach to language that challenges not only language propriety but conventions of cultural constraint and oppression.

Confronted in the 1910s with a developing modernist aesthetic, as proclaimed from London by Ezra Pound, that conceived of poetic authority and creative power in explicit terms of masculine mastery, Williams resists this conception of his own artistry by valorizing what he himself defines as a feminine attribute – to make contact, to touch, and thus, in Loy's words, "to extract / a radium of the word" (*LLB* 26). In an early poem on Gertrude Stein, Loy imbues Madam Curie and Stein with the powers of contact and disruption – a deconstructive capacity to dismantle defined assumptions and to liberate the word from logocentric control. The poem, "Gertrude Stein," celebrates this relationship between the writer and the word:

> Curie
> of the laboratory
> of vocabulary
> she crushed
> the tonnage

of consciousness
congealed to phrases
to extract
a radium of the word
(*LLB* 26)

Loy's comparison of Stein and Curie provides Williams with a conception
of the poet's relationship to the world and its language that will later
become a central motif in his long poem, *Paterson*.[50] Curie's experience
is the experience of the poet, who, through the process of contact allows
a luminosity, an imaginative leap, a poetic newness. Conflating her pregnancy, the labor of her experiment, and her discovery, Williams recasts
Loy's Madame Curie:

—with ponderous belly, full
of thought! stirring the cauldrons
.  in the old shed used
by the medical students for dissections.
Winter. Snow through the cracks

Pauvre étudiant   .
en l'an trentième de mon âge
Item .   with coarsened hands
by the hour, the day, the week
to get, after months of labor   .

a stain at the bottom of the retort
without weight, a failure, a
nothing. And then, returning in the
night, to find it   .

LUMINOUS!
(177–8)

As an image of the poet, the figure of Curie is more aptly a figure of
the poetic process, a process Williams progressively understands in feminine and maternal terms akin to the feminist poetics of Loy and the
cultural feminism informing the prewar years. The authority of tradition,
of the fathers, must be broken if the "American verse of today" can be
a "new verse," Williams writes in 1917: "It must be new verse, in a new
conscious form. But even more than that it must be free in that it is free
to include all temperaments, all phases of our environment, physical as
well as spiritual, mental and moral. It must be truly democratic, truly
free for all" ("America, Whitman" 29). This insistence upon inclusiveness
continues to evolve in feminine configurations in *In the American Grain*
and still later in *Paterson*, questioning the conventional understanding of
the creator as male and the poetic precursor as father, and resisting the
modernist insistence upon such a lineage. As he writes in 1947, "to do

as Pound did, strike back toward the triumphant forms of the past, father to father," makes "No mother necessary," and ultimately results in a sterile poetics ("Letter" 208). In looking back to modernism's poetic mothers, we can begin to reconstruct a fuller sense of Williams's negotiations with the feminine as a part of his embattled stance within tradition.

# 2

# *In the American Grain*

## *Proclaiming a Feminine Ground*

By 1923, Williams had written much of his American history, *In the American Grain*. Though the essays go only as far as Lincoln's assassination (Williams originally planned a second volume to complete the history), the entire text implicitly addresses its own particular moment in a rapidly changing America. Within the five years preceding 1923, the country had fought in a devastating war and had granted women, after decades of suffrage, the vote; only twenty-seven years before its entry into World War I, the federal government had waged its final battle with the Native Americans at Wounded Knee, and, as the book went to press in 1925, Indians had just received citizenship in the country they had inhabited for centuries.

These events stand as moments inextricably involved in and evolving from the history of America Williams chooses to tell. As a historical narrative that both searches for and critiques the cultural inheritance of a modern American ethos, *In the American Grain* refuses a historical objectivity by foregrounding the bias of race, nationality, and gender in the process of producing history. History, in this text, is not claimed as a form of scientific truth but is revealed as a constructed narrative, ideologically invested. In the text's insistence upon its own historical moment of making (especially in the "Jacataqua" chapter) and in its self-reflexive attention to structures of narrative, *In the American Grain* enacts a continual tension between myth, history, and narrative manipulation that results in various revisions and refractions of a monolithic "American identity." Williams focuses on the early Spanish, British, and French explorers, the Puritan leaders, the Founding Fathers, the first pioneers; he places his own interpretations alongside primary texts by such men as Cotton Mather and Christopher Columbus in a collage of fact, narrative play, and myth that blurs clear demarcation between history and fiction[51] and calls attention to the making of history as a reaction to and production of cultural myths.

Commenting upon the power of myth within a collective cultural identity to both enable and limit its peoples, Richard Slotkin writes that myth "describes a process, credible to its audience, by which *knowledge is transformed into power;* it provides a scenario or prescription for action, defining and limiting the possibilities for human response to the universe" (*Regeneration Through Violence* 7; my emphasis). Williams's historical text recognizes the process of mythmaking and its intimate ties to systems of power while simultaneously emphasizing the links between fiction making and the development of central historical narratives that define an American mythos and identity. The text's foregrounded awareness of itself as a narrative construct distinguishes between the conventional notion of history as a form of objective truth and a recognition of history as a set of culturally mediated texts. The self-reflectiveness of Williams's text includes the overt manipulation of fictive devices – such as voice, form, and selection and arrangement of detail – and is signaled in numerous ways: through the use of multiple (and often contradictory) voices that undermine a unitary voice of authority; through the juxtaposition of primary and secondary materials; through the contextualization of voices within specific ideological and/or historical confluences; through the presentation of Williams's own voice as a fictional construct. Williams's textual strategies demonstrate that he was "strongly aware of the irremediable gap between the past and its narrative representations. And in writing *In the American Grain,* he eschews the standard practices by which historians create the illusion of a well-ordered past" (Conrad, "Deceptive Ground," 24).[52] As authority is consistently shown to be mediated by nonobjective forces – as authority is revealed as subjective, relative, and temporal – Williams's own authorial voice calls itself into question, pointing toward this version of history as a necessary fiction, as a renaming without claims to final authority.

In the only book-length study on this text, Bryce Conrad perceptively asserts that the "underlying premise" of *In the American Grain* "is that a history of America must be, in part, a history of language in America, a study of the tropes and verbal configurations which have historically defined the place" ("Deceptive Ground" 22). Exploring the making of history and place, these essays look to the "tropes and . . . configurations" of gender that have permeated, shaped, and sustained America's identity. In recognizing the "fictive grounds of history" (Kronick, *American Poetics of History,* 227), Williams returns repeatedly to the fictive grounds of gender, and in his most explicit critiques of modern America (found most vehemently in "Jacataqua"), he links its spiritual and moral unhealthiness with meanings Western society has constructed for each gender. Within the text's insistence upon history's kinship with fiction and myth, gender narratives are shown as primary shaping forces of history;

examining, furthermore, the process of gender construction as a fundamental activity underlying American culture, *In the American Grain* suggests breaking open history's sexual/textual narratives to gain a new vision of past and present. As Joseph Kronick points out, "Williams suggests that in recognizing the fictive grounds of history, the reader frees *himself* to reinterpret the past and uncover whatever is usable for *man*. Writing history, then, is reinterpreting the texts and interpretations that have solidified into accepted truths" (227; my emphasis). Williams emphatically looks to texts of gender as a way of reclaiming a New World history, freeing the reader to "reinterpret the past and uncover what is usable" for woman *and* man. His text questions the gendered meanings of "male" and "female" preserved and affirmed in the canonized myths of America.

Williams's reinterpretation of American history identifies the country's grounding in patriarchal ideologies, focusing upon various manifestations of masculine authority and its gendered transmission. Obsessively employing tropes and rhetoric of masculine sexuality to describe the Old World's military, political, and religious conquest of the New, the essays self-reflexively deploy an essentialized masculinity and a monolithic patriarchy to reveal the ideological underpinnings of America's "discovery," conquest, and settlement. Tropes of masculinity emphasizing potency as penetration and dominance structure many of the essays, creating overlapping links between familial structure, inheritance by patrilineage, imperialism, and Christianity. Movement from the local instance to the larger structure of power characterizes the movement of the essays, as does a continual exploration of systems of male dominance historically enacted within private and public realms and enfolded within patriarchal myths of male dominance and European supremacy.

Within this movement, a notion of the feminine and the maternal emerges as a form of resistance, inclusiveness, newness, and contact. Opposed to the hierarchical dominance of the European explorers and settlers, this feminine sensibility crosses gender and race, but is most often figured in association with the American Indian. The cluster of meanings that develop around Native American figures, on the one hand, romanticize and idealize this group; simultaneously, through the Indian, Williams's history links the status of subordinated groups to patriarchal myths of mastery that, to maintain their power, necessitate the ideological "mashing" of "Indian, child, and matron into one *safe* mold" that will not disrupt the status quo (*IAG* 112). Williams's aversion to sameness and conformity is rooted in an understanding of systemic ideologies that require and coerce such unity; his history encourages an openness to multiplicity that arises from a maternally imagined contact with the world, represented most prominently by Williams in the Native American's systems of belief and social codes. His task is not to write the history of native cultures; rather, his text reveals the way received representations (including his own) of subordinated groups are constructed to support the dominant ideology. He locates points of disruption and subversion within a "feminine" sensibility operating alternatively to the masculine potency inscribed upon the New World.[53]

The feminine ground he seeks to uncover and reclaim involves an examination and refutation of a paternal model of inheritance and the envisioning of a maternal model. This potentially enabling reconsideration of cultural inheritance recalls "The Wanderer" and its claim to a maternal poetic inheritance for the individual poet, who comes to understand the maternal as a source of creativity; similarly, it echoes the insistence upon the maternal as a source of contact in the Marsden correspondence. Significantly, this claim also anticipates a later revisionary articulation of literary tradition and models of lineage. Written in response to Ezra Pound's paternal model of tradition (as Williams describes it), "Letter to an Australian Editor" in 1946 proposes a maternal alternative, provocatively setting forth the ideological assumptions, grounded in political and socioeconomic contexts, underlying traditional and male-centered concepts of literary inheritance. This theoretical position did not evolve late in Williams's career but is present in incipient form from the very beginning and, as the 1946 essay makes clear, develops in part in resistance to Pound's conceptualization of a masculine modernist poetics. Because the essay is little discussed and because it expresses ideas earlier explored in *In the American Grain,* a close consideration of the maternal model of tradition in "Letter to an Australian Editor" will serve as backdrop to a fuller exploration of gender texts in Williams's history.

### A Maternal Model for Tradition

"The Wanderer" grounds Williams's work within a matriarchal locus of vision and creative power, signifying his early construction of the maternal as an enabling site and source of the imagination. Like the poem's "old queen," the maternal is valued in the 1917 Dora Marsden correspondence for providing the male "a connexion with the earth" ("Great Sex Spiral" 110). These concepts are echoed when Williams credits his biological mother, Elena Williams, a painter, with influencing his creative nature through her example. In his preface to *Kora in Hell,* written in 1919, Williams constructs aesthetic arguments to present himself as a poet of importance in the modern world, and he begins his defense by presenting his mother as the quintessential exemplar of imaginative power.[54] He writes of Elena Williams:

> Thus, seeing the thing itself without forethought or afterthought but with great intensity of perception, my mother loses her bearings or

associates with some disreputable person or translates a dark mood. She
is a creature of great imagination. I might say this is her sole remaining
quality. She is a despoiled, molted castaway but by this power she still
breaks life between her fingers. (*Imaginations* 8)

In Williams's understanding of the imaginative process, this "great intensity of perception" provides a matrix of feminine contact that makes
possible creative acts of transformation. This construction of the maternal, in the poet's life and in his work, ties Williams to both language
and experience – a connective force dramatized in "The Wanderer,"
theorized in "The Great Sex Spiral," and paradigmatically offered in the
Preface to *Kora in Hell*. The relationship between his notions of the
feminine and the maternal, and those of language, form, and experience,
reveals itself in the poet's continual reiterations of contact as the foundation for poetry, for contact remains for Williams associated with feminine energies.

The mother's imaginative power derives from her ability to experience
directly, to make contact with "the thing itself," unburdened by a web
of associations. This celebration of the maternal, however, raises questions concerning the relationship between the masculine subjectivity of
the poet and the function of the feminine and the maternal. Does the
maternal, in these formulations, reside outside of culture or previous to
it? Does the correlation between the maternal and the literal (a language
of direct experience) merely reiterate conventional and derogatory associations between woman and nature, both of which are conventionally
positioned below man and culture, just as the literal is undervalued in
relationship to the figurative? Moreover, how does a poet who appears
keenly aware of the discursive shaping of reality so naively evoke a pure,
prediscursive reality in "the thing itself"? The maternal figure who makes
contact with this prediscursive reality enables the male poet to also make
contact and to derive a language from this experience: Is the maternal
body the site for the male's contact with the world, with experience, and
is this an appropriation of the maternal for the benefit of the male subject?
In other words, is the maternal valued and celebrated primarily in its
function of enhancing and making possible masculine subjectivity?

At certain points in Williams's work, I would agree that such an appropriation occurs and signals his partial entrenchment within traditional
structures of gender. However, although strong arguments could be and
have been based upon an affirmative answer to the previous questions,
my sense is that this stance remains too inattentive to the function of the
maternal to disturb privileged sites of power (as Williams's work develops
in the late teens and early twenties). The maternal provides for Williams
an alternative source or basis for constructing a world-view in which
creativity and imagination are understood through their opposition or

affront to a masculinist (for Williams) and patriarchal world view; at the same time, Williams's conflicted attachment to this masculinist identity shapes his thinking about the maternal, while his thinking about the maternal becomes a mode of questioning that very (masculine) subjectivity and its constructed nature. In discussions of the maternal in Williams's work, it seems necessary to ask how this masculine subject is to be understood.

The relationship between masculine identity, the male body, and the maternal body provides the central focus for a provocative reading by John Palattella of Williams's concept of the maternal. Relying upon the Dora Marsden correspondence, *Kora in Hell,* and "Three Professional Studies," all written within the wartime period, Palattella argues that in these works Williams is asserting a masculine authority and credibility after suffering a sense of masculine loss linked to the Great War. In this Kristevan reading, "the maternal body is the place where the wounded male body acquires a literal language and makes good its lack" (" 'In the Midst of Living Hell' " 31); the maternal body functions to enable the male poet to recover his masculine subjectivity. This valorization of the maternal is joined by a "depiction of loss and negativity as essentially feminine," creating a duality through representations of the maternal that reveals "how he uses the maternal to make good his lack; he either sees the promise of recuperation in the literal language which the maternal bears, or he denies lack and loss by making it a condition biologically specific to femininity" (33). While Palattella raises excellent points, the methodological reliance upon Kristevan notions of the maternal and the abject[55] excludes a consideration of the relationship of subjectivity to larger structures of power within Williams's writing. Even in the Marsden correspondence, which Palattella reads as a theory of language acquisition based upon essentialized categories of gender, the act of essentialism is made questionable through suggestions, on Williams's part, of cultural systems of power. By *In the American Grain,* the concern with cultural constructs (including those authored or sustained by Williams himself) comes into much fuller play with fixed universals of gender, so that essentialism itself is revealed as a construct. This applies particularly to a notion of masculine subjectivity, which Palattella seems to read as a stable and unchallenged category in Williams's thinking and writing. I argue instead that it is precisely through constructions of the maternal and the feminine that Williams's texts problematize, question, and take apart masculine subjectivies that ground masculinist systems of power.

This process underlies his epic poem *Paterson,* written in the 1940s and 1950s. The poem, as I argue in the Conclusion, evolves as a troubled site for charged interactions between gendered notions of cultural authority and its transmission. In 1946, during a period of concentrated work on the epic, Williams wrote an essay that defines literary tradition in gendered terms, proposing a maternal model in opposition to the paternal model he associates with Pound. Attempting with *Paterson* to place himself at the center of modernism, Williams concurrently in this essay defines his poetry within a maternal and feminine model, just as decades earlier he had affirmed his imaginative power through the example of his mother. The essay "Letter to an Australian Editor" describes a conflict between what Peter Schmidt calls "two very different cultural traditions" (the Old World and the New World), linked to the paternal and the maternal – a conflict, Schmidt suggests, dramatized in *Paterson* ("Introduction" 4).[56]

"Letter to an Australian Editor" responded to a request by Flexmore Hudson, an editor in Australia, for Williams's definition of the poet's role in the world. In the essay, Williams distinguishes his own emphasis upon contact from Pound's intellectualized and classical formulation of poetic creativity; in so doing, he explicitly argues against the interpretation of tradition he sees advanced by the modernism of Pound, Eliot, and Joyce. The essay's focus on models of literary tradition develops into considerations of patrilineal and matrilineal descent that are significantly linked to different notions of the relationship of poetry to socioeconomic and political contexts. The foundation for poetry, Williams insists, must be based in the material conditions of a historical moment, a relationship between literature and culture that the paternal model of Pound systematically suppresses. Williams accuses the modernist movement of erroneously, even disastrously, working within a classical, masculinist model of poetic influence and inspiration that abstracts experience and leads to poetic sterility. Within the classical model of a patrilineal tradition, "women are generally considered only accessory to the arts," and the modernists have continued this convention of exclusion through privileging the father–son dynamic: "Man, as it has been drummed into our ears since Joyce discovered Hamlet, is out to seek his own father – his spiritual father, that is" (205). This patrilineal model, argues Williams, develops from the conviction that "minds beget minds," a belief motivating Pound's expatriation:

> He left the States under the assumption that it was mind that fertilizes mind, that the mere environment is just putty and that – assuming one's self great the thing to do in this world, is or was then, to go to Europe, which he did.
>     The mind, you see, is a sort of bird bred of air *without female,* or in fact nest of any sort. It leaps ages and places and if it is not perpetuated by fission it at least emerged whole in this case from the shoulder of,

well, Guido. It is an attractive belief that has ruled the classic world immemorially and led to the best of Ezra Pound's earlier poems. (205; my emphasis)

These poems, derived from a masculine tradition, are more precisely "translations," great on their own terms but ultimately sterile as poetry. In their reliance upon "the riches of the ages," such poems are composed "in the forms of the past," and even in their deviations from fixed classical forms, "it is nevertheless precisely the established and accepted work of the masters . . . by which they are asserting their greatest originality" (206). If the creative process depends upon the intellectualized transfer of mind to mind, "without female" or the "environment," only "translations" of the father texts issue forth, only works "bred androgynetically from the classics which father [the poet's] every thought" (206). Williams sees himself and his own relationship to tradition as "diametrically opposed to the mind to mind fertilization of the classical concept," which he further qualifies as essentially elitist, exclusionary, and autocratic. On this point, his own work most dramatically opposes Pound's:

> The forms of the past, no matter how cultivated, will inevitably carry over from the past much of the social, political, and economic complexion of the past. And I insist that those who cling basically to those forms wish in their hearts for political, social and economic autocracy. They think in terms of the direct descent of great minds, they do not think in terms of genius arising from the great movements of the people – or the degeneracy of the people, as known in the past.
>
> I look for a direct expression of the turmoils of today in the arts. Not *about* today in classical forms but in forms generated, invented, today direct from the turmoil itself. . . . (207)

Here, Williams associates the classical model of patrilineal poetic inheritance with an exclusionary sensibility conveyed through (what he considers) the closed nature of the forms employed; moreover, to his mind, an autocratic consciousness supports a modernist aesthetics that "cling[s]" to the "forms of the past" while suppressing the "social, political and economic complexion of the past." Such writers "wish in their hearts for political, social and economic autocracy" and "think in terms of the direct descent of great minds," or of androcentric genius, passed from father to son. Significantly, throughout the essay, Williams insists upon the relationship between art and its historically specific social, political, and economic contexts; culture arises from and reacts against the "turmoils of today." The poet's "difficult task" is "to wrest from society, the politics and the economic phantasm before me new worlds of art. New forms" (207).

The perceived need for new forms is a deeply politicized yearning here, for Williams asserts that the cultural production of knowledge within the paternal, "classical" tradition sustains the power of the fathers – economically and socially – while "new forms" of production disrupt that power. Pointing to the radical nature of this thinking, Peter Schmidt describes the analogy between literary tradition and socioeconomic power that the essay develops:

> Thirty years before the word "patriarchy" was widely used, the author of a long poem emphasizing pater/son transmission here deploys the word "androgynetic" to describe how one male genius' mind is dynamized by a male predecessor's mind in the "classical" tradition. Williams implies further that patriarchal power reproduces itself by first establishing some cultural forms as universal and eternal and then by allowing "originality" in selected individual talents who may consciously make minor innovations in these forms. In such a process, the authority of a literary tradition is validated generation to generation, "mind to mind," in a way analogous to how political and economic power is passed down. ("Introduction," 5)

Therefore, the creation of new forms, "new worlds of art," demands according to Williams a dismantling of the "tyrannies" that reign within a "classical" patriarchal consciousness: "We must be destructive first to free ourselves from forms accreting to themselves tyrannies we despise. Where does the past lodge in the older forms? Tear it out. I am not speaking of anything but forms" (207). Because both invention and form "arise from the society about him," the artist's cultural work does not separate form from the material world but recognizes and makes use of their interdependence. The *process* by which form will "arise from the society" is contact, a feminized process in Williams's thinking (208). Significantly, Williams describes the origin of form as a mode of contact impossible within the classical conception of poetic inheritance, of (male) minds begetting (male) minds. Form arises from contact, and a poet "will continue to produce only if his attachments to society continue adequate. If a man in his fatuous dreams cuts himself off from *that supplying female,* he dries up his sources – as Pound did in the end heading straight for literary sterility" (208; my emphasis). Such poets as Pound have "divorced themselves from the primary source of their fertility," a severance manifested in their regard for poetic tradition and inheritance as necessarily patrilineal. As Schmidt suggests, Williams's "designation of what is 'female' is both revolutionary and repressive" ("Introduction" 6). We see Williams operating still within the concept of the artist as male, who draws from a "female" world to create; at the same time, gender classifications operate in the essay to illuminate political, social, and economic systems of power and to locate the production of art precisely within these systems characterized as masculine. Arguing against a purely essentialist reading of "the supplying female," Schmidt comments that the poet's "emphasis on the cultural and historical contexts in which all art must be understood suggests that the 'female' is his metaphor (or personification, giving voice) to all that has been excluded by a dominant culture. Therefore, his definition of the 'supplying female,' of what is excluded and silenced, may be seen as a cultural construction subject to contestation and revision – which is precisely what Williams' essay does" (6).

In this sense, the "female" becomes a deconstructive process of contact arising from a fluid engagement between poet and world. Without contact there are "no mothers" and no new forms: "The scholarly thing (adopted frequently out of disgust for the raw oders and other aspects of the manure heaps) is to do as Pound did, strike back toward the triumphant forms of the past, father to father. No mother necessary" (Williams, "Letter," 208). Attributing autocratic sensibility and structure to the concept of a father–son lineage, Williams reacts against linear models of tradition and the creative process. He sees Pound's historical method as operating within such hierarchical dynamics: "He has taken the classic attitude. He has written, here and there appreciatively, of a few of the men, 'measuring' them, pontificating about their qualities. And in this he thinks he has been a great leader in the matter" (206). Because Pound's approach depends upon such linearity, according to Williams's argument, his genius limits itself: "The great must rule, not only in literature but in politics. . . . When he has summed up another mind – the process stops" (206). Williams's historical method rejects this hierarchy of father-minds and focuses upon an alternate and more multiple source, a suggestion of the "necessary" maternal:

> . . . there may be another literary source continuing the greatness of the past which does not develop androgynetically from the past itself mind to mind but from the present, from the hurley-burley of political encounters which determine or may determine it, direct. This is definitely not the academic approach to literature. It is diametrically opposed to the mind to mind fertilization of the classical concept. Whereas the academic approach may speak *about* us always in the forms of the past or their present day analogues, the direct approach *is* the spectacle of our lives today, raised if possible to the quality of great expression by the invention of poetry. (207)

In the "Letter to an Australian Editor," the critique of patrilineal formulations of creativity and tradition articulates the inextricable connections between poetry, culture, and history that Williams perceived and first examined fully in *In the American Grain*. The figure of Pound exemplifies these connections in the 1946 essay, for Pound as poet is inseparable from Pound as political individual, since the same model of order and energy encompasses all he does or says. Written soon after Pound's incarceration in St. Elizabeth's Hospital and during Williams's experiments with history and poetic form in *Paterson* (Book I was published in the same year as "Letter"), the essay's own historical moment bears consideration. The philosophical differences between Pound and Williams that surface in the early *Egoist* period have become clearly articulated oppositions, and Pound's political fate an inevitable – or at least, for Williams, an understandable – circumstance within his masculinized structure of values. Careful to distinguish himself from the values that have simultaneously generated Pound's poetry and his politics, Williams writes:

> I am not pretending to decide the controversial issue between Ezra Pound and the United States Government. I am merely saying that Pound has acted in a perfectly logical and understandable manner when you know his mind and that this illustrates perfectly his attitude also toward literature and goes along with all he has written. (208)

In its opposition to Pound's patrilineal model, Williams's implicitly matrilineal model reclaims the "supplying female" as an affirmation of the quality of direct contact informing the poetic process. Rather than a mind-to-mind fertilization, this matrilineal model draws from and extends to multiple sites at once. For the poet,

> not only his fertility but those forms themselves – arise from the society about him of which he is (if he is to be fed) a part – the fecundating men and women about him who have given him birth. Let me insist, the poet's very life but also his forms originate in the political, social and economic maelstrom on which he rides. (208)

While Pound seeks to reclaim the greatness of the past, as embodied in the (male) figures he selectively admires within his constructions of lineage, Williams looks to the present to gain an understanding of what we are, to the past to understand how we have become. The use of history, then, resides in constructions of ideas, myths, and facts that, in turn, construct the ideas, myths, and facts of the present. Williams does not want to glorify a past but to dig within it for clues to understanding how and why his American society has come to hold certain values, to express itself through certain mythologies, and alternately to generate and destroy itself through certain fictions. By looking through the "hurley-burley" of the present, the past can be seen to interact simultaneously with the present rather precede it within a linear chronology. This process involves the revisionary "newness" of opening forms to what has been excluded and silenced, to pursue a cultural "crosspollenization" (a term Williams coins in *In the American Grain*) rather than transmitting cultural authority in a narrow linear fashion. This process becomes both theme and method for *In the American Grain,* which examines the "classical" model of patriarchal authority in America's history.

### History's Myth of Discovery: Mastery's "outward thrust"

*In the American Grain* asks us to recognize the frame of classical patriarchy through which we are taught to view the country's history. The essays reveal this frame partially through obsessive images of male sexual potency and patrilineage that characterize the quests of the early explorers and settlers as phallocentric attempts to possess and master the New World. Only recently have the text's dynamics of gender been studied closely, most extensively by Bryce Conrad in the sole book-length study of *In the American Grain.* Recognizing the essays' focus upon male virility, Conrad argues that Williams repeatedly celebrates the moment of insemination: "ritualized inseminations of the land are Williams' metaphor for the germination of a distinctively American culture" (*Refiguring America* 105). Conrad sees these moments as providing the "founding mythos of *In the American Grain* – the birth of a poet out of fertilizing contact with the female body." Central to this myth, the New World is characterized "as a woman who can castrate the determining power of an old world patriarchy" (107). Yet Conrad sets up a reading that depends upon and participates in a system of sex and gender that places the phallus at its center, a system that *In the American Grain* continually – though imperfectly – challenges. We can go a step further and approach the text by examining its own questioning of the "ritual insemination" so central to Conrad's interpretation (along with earlier critics) and to Western culture itself. From within a patriarchal context of the maternal, the feminine becomes associated with a negative maternal horror, and the primacy of the phallus as regenerative is threatened by the possessive force of female sexuality; *In the American Grain,* however, begins to disturb the primacy of the inseminating moment by associating masculine potency with degeneracy and sterility, and by positing a feminine "possession" and "regeneration" that locates an energizing, creative power – not an engorging, castrating horror – in the female body.[57] As we read the text, we must ask whether Williams is "forcing an inscription upon the female, writing upon the body of the mother" (Conrad, *Refiguring America,* 146), or whether his text reveals the textual process through which history enacts such an inscription, a process infused by the American dream of discovery and private possession. In asking such questions, we can approach the repeated "ritualized insemination" of the New World not as a central, celebratory moment in the text, but as a dangerous mythos in need of revision.[58]

Within a patriarchal value system, the text suggests, discovery is necessarily conquest and conquest is necessarily violent. In choosing the

Icelandic saga of Eric the Red as a beginning, Williams opens history to the deep level of violence and oppression that marks the first entry of Western patriarchy in the Americas. This initial essay sets up a pattern of patriarchal lineage and power that prefigures the European and English colonization of the New World.[59]

Red Eric, accused of murder and "marked" as other and evil, rejects the authority of the powerful Christians reigning in Norway but must also reject their world and find refuge in Greenland. Upon his exile, Eric claims:

> Rather the ice than their way: to take what is mine by single strength, theirs by the crookedness of their law. But they have marked me – even to myself. Because I am not like them, I am evil. . . . Because their way is the just way and my way – the way of the kings and my father – crosses them: weaklings holding together to appear strong. But I am alone, though in Greenland. (*IAG* 1)

This first historical essay calls attention to the fictionalization inherent in historical narrative, which has both marked and marginalized Eric. Eric recognizes that the weak can be strong if "they in effect have the power" of "holding together," and he claims that his exclusion from power is a result of his otherness, "because I am not like them" (1). Part of his difference is constructed through the bias of history, or, more precisely, of authoritative documents that become history: Christ's "bishops that lie and falsify the records, make me out to be what I am not – for their own ends – because we killed a man" (1). As Williams continually reminds us, no narrative of history can claim untainted objectivity, and we remain conscious that Eric's own retelling is likewise biased. Decentered by history, Eric tries to center himself as father and leader – though this is a center that will not hold – as he speaks from the perspective of the patriarch who bases his authority on the power of domination. Endorsing systems of male authority ideologically tied to the powers that have "marked" him, Eric consciously places himself in a line of fathers (as opposed to Williams's final figure, Lincoln, who ends the book by associating himself with his mother), and rationalizes the violence and murder he has committed by linking these acts to a masculine concept of self. Thus, in this case, the process of victimization (Eric's exile from Norway, and his mark of otherness from history) leads the dispossessed male victim to reinscribe the ideology that has oppressed him. Within the text of Eric's manhood, the possessor of enough strength to destroy any threat to that strength maintains power: "If my slaves cause a landslide on Valthioff's farm and Valthioff's kinsman slays them, shall I not kill him? Is it proper for me to stand and to be made small before my slaves? I am not a man to shake and sweat like a thief when the time comes" (2). Eric's comments, while proclaiming a masculine power, also expose the potential victimization of anyone – male or female – within a power-based culture; like other figures Williams chooses to retrieve from history, Eric exemplifies patriarchy collapsing upon itself.

Thus, while patriarchal power demands masculine potency, in classical Oedipal fashion that potency plays itself out in forms of self-destruction. Eric's sons figuratively kill the father whose potency issued them forth in, ironically, "the way of the kings and [their] fathers" that first led to Eric's exile. Lief converts to Christianity and enters the Norwegian court of Olaf, who had once exiled Eric as murderer. Red Eric responds: "So they chopped me up. The Pope wins Olaf. Lief at court – Olaf commissions him to carry the thing back to Greenland. It grows like fire" (3). Christian conversion destroys Eric's identity as father, husband, and man: "Thorhild bars me, godless, from her bed. Both sons she wins to it. Lief and Thorstein both Christians" (4). Moreover, the discovery of America coincides with the metaphoric overthrow of the father:

> Then Lief, Eric's son, sails to Norway.... But on his return, Lief the Lucky, he is driven westward upon a new country, news of which he brings to Brattahlid. At the same stroke he brings me back pride and joy-in-his-deed, my deed, Eric moving up, and poison; an edict from Olaf – from my son's mouth – solid as an axe to cut me, half healed, into pieces again. (3)

The act of discovery becomes figuratively equated with the act of patricide, the most primal form of conquest in patriarchy. Though Eric is an outsider to Christianity, he shares a similar concept of order and power with such Christian fathers of the New World as Columbus, Cortez, or Ponce de León, all portrayed in Williams's text. An authority of dominance and violence, this is "the curse" that Eric and his offspring cannot escape, for it portends the self-destruction of patriarchy.

In the figure of Freydis, Eric's daughter, we see the cross-gendering of this lineage, for the daughter also inherits the curse of patriarchy through initiating power struggles based upon conquest. Freydis travels to Vinland with her brothers, Karlsefni and Snorri, and other settlers to found the New World. Though they begin on peaceful trading terms with the Indians, or Skrellings, the Viking leaders soon turn to displays of aggression and a battle erupts.[60] As the Indians gain the upper hand, Freydis emerges from her cabin and cries to the fleeing Vikings: "Why do you flee from these wretches, when ye should slaughter them like cattle?" Here, Freydis reenacts an imposition of otherness as her father did in his relationship to Christian power, though now the Indian is marked as other to the point of dehumanization. Freydis, large with child, grabs a sword, bares her breasts, and slaps her "breast with her bare sword. At this the Skrellings were terrified and ran down to their boats" (5). Although Bryce Conrad sees in the "truculent Freydis" a "defender of the New World's matriarchal essence," Freydis, despite her anatomy, ideologically reinscribes her father's ways and asserts a violence derived from her paternal inheritance (139). She seizes the power of patriarchy abdicated by the Viking male lineage; the weapon against the breast suggests her renunciation or displacement of maternal nurture for the power of the phallic sword passed from her brothers. She strengthens this power through deceiving her husband into believing her brothers have wronged and beaten her. He rouses his men and leads them in slaughtering her brothers' household, much as Eric defined his own manhood in the context of potent revenge. Finding the women in her brothers' home untouched by the massacre, Freydis grabs an axe and falls "upon the five women . . . [leaving] them dead" (6). In her rout of the natives and her murder of the women, Freydis enters into complicity with a destruction of the feminine that will mark American history as Williams interprets it. Just as the death of women, at the hands of a woman who emulates her father, concludes the opening essay – looking forward to the remainder of the text – the birth of a woman who transforms the father image of Lincoln into a maternal, "unearthly reality" born out of violent deaths ends the final essay and looks beyond the narrative ending of either history or Williams's text.

Extending the focus upon the gendered dynamics of cultural authority set up in "Red Eric," the remaining essays on the early explorers define American history as a narrative of patriarchal violence, or violence repeatedly enacted against the feminine, thus reinterpreting the prevailing Eurocentric notion of discovery: "History begins for us with murder and enslavement, not with discovery" (39). The slaughterers, however, as he sees it, inherit the souls of their victims, though that inheritance is suppressed and erased within the collective American consciousness: "No, we are not Indians but we are men of their world . . . the spirit, the ghost of the land moves in the blood, moves the blood. . . . These are the inhabitants of our souls that lie . . . agh!" (39). Recovery of these aboriginal American inhabitants, a recognition of feminine contact, motivates Williams's revisionary project as he asks: "Do these things die? Men do not know what lives, are themselves dead. In the heart there are living Indians once slaughtered and defrauded – Indians that live also in subtler ways" (42). As Americans, Williams implies, we live with the internalized struggle between Indian and European, contact and conquest, life affirmation and slaughter. Of this heritage, he writes:

> If men inherit souls this is the color of mine. We are, too, the others. Think of them! The main islands were thickly populated with a peaceful

folk when Christ-over found them. But the orgy of blood which followed, no man has written. We are the slaughterers. It is the tortured soul of our world. (41)

What and how we "inherit" becomes a central focus of the essays dealing with the early European explorers – Columbus, Ponce de León, de Soto, Cortez, and Raleigh. Representing the Old World ethos as it invades the New World, the values and consequent actions of these men draw upon and perpetuate a masculinized heritage of conquest, possession, and mastery that Williams continually associates with phallic imagery and a patrilineal ideology. Significantly, prefiguring his later criticism of Pound's classical model of literary tradition as paternal and therefore sterile, Williams presents male generative power as degenerative rather than regenerative, as destructive and deforming rather than creative and enabling.

The essays on the early explorers comment upon the Old World's efforts to destroy the otherness of the New World, an otherness figured as feminine and represented most emphatically by the Indian.[61] In Williams's representation, Columbus descends from the mythic status of America's heroic discoverer to a power-hungry man who falls victim to the greed of the religious and political powers his own actions have sustained. However, on his first of four landings, he momentarily responds to the *unlikeness* of this new land. He comments upon the "many trees very unlike those of our country" and the "fish so unlike ours that it is wonderful" (26). The Indians who visit, bearing gifts, are admired in their difference, and Columbus finds he cannot categorize them in terms of European orders, commenting after lengthy descriptions that they are "neither black nor white" (25). As he walks among the trees, he experiences a contact with the New World in all of its difference. The contact, however, is brief and interrupted by Old World visions of the New.[62] Equating discovery with possession, Columbus comes to view this New World through the vision of "the illusive bright future of a great empire founded, coupled with a fabulous conquest of heathendom by the only true church" (9). He carts captives and New World exotica back to Spain, where "his triumph was acclaimed," further fueling his own desire for power (9). In regard to the lands and civilizations he "discovers," he proclaims "that henceforth I should be called Don, and should be Chief Admiral of the Ocean Sea, perpetual Viceroy and Governor of all the islands and continents that I should discover and gain in the Ocean Sea, and that my eldest son should succeed, and so from generation to generation forever," following the traditional form of Biblical patriarchy underlying European forms of political power.

The discovery of the Indies brings "wealth and renown for Spain and great increase to God and to his Church" (11). These political and religious institutions of patriarchy replicate, on a larger scale, the desire for authority and power Columbus experiences, and this desire inscribes itself upon the land's cultures and histories through conquest. This process perversely generates itself through self-destructive energies, as exemplified by Columbus's fate. Usurpers overthrow his Santo Domingo rule and the Spanish king imprisons him; Columbus's personal dreams of multigenerational power over the new lands are foiled by the betrayal, deceit, and violence arising from the competing quests for power. Conquered by the institutional powers his actions have helped sustain, Columbus participates in his own demise by denying the initial contact he felt with the New World and seeking instead to master it. As Kutzinski claims, this mastery involves the imposition of Old World myths upon the New, and rather than discovering the New World, Columbus "conquered it by depriving it of its historical autonomy and its otherness" (33).

However, in the brief historical moment of Columbus's first landing, his embrace of the New World's "unlike" elements provides a glimpse of the contact Williams seeks to reestablish within a New World mythos. Here, discovery of the new does not involve conquest but openness, sensuality, and the possibility of inclusion. This approach thrives in the New World's native peoples but is disastrously suppressed by the hierarchic imperialism informing the early exploration and colonization of the New World. Though European notions of value are alien to the Indians who first greet Columbus (they are pleased by gifts of glass beads of "little value," and Columbus later notices an Indian carrying "some dried leaves which must be a thing highly valued" in his culture [25, 26]), the imposition of concepts of private property and material possession accompanies and aids the genocide of the Indians.[63] Williams links the introduction of this concept of property into the New World to the hierarchical ordering of the sexes, races, and classes. His insistence upon the relationship between Christian Europe's lust for property and wealth and the oppression of groups excluded from power reaches its greatest intensity in the essays on Cortez and Ponce de León.

Justifying New World conquest as a process of civilization and positing European society as the norm, Cortez razes an ancient site of Indian culture, as Williams reports in "The Destruction of Tenochtitlan." As his soldiers destroy the Indian city, they invoke European orders of civilization, claiming to act "under the names of King or Christ or whatever it may be" (27). These labels given to distinctly patriarchal orders of civilization are actually only "the awkward names men give their emptiness"; rather than signifying divine or absolute forms of authority or order, these labels mask "instincts, ancient beyond thought" (27), a description recalling Williams's discussion of the male pursuit in his 1917 essays, "The Great Sex Spiral." This pursuit, in distancing man from the concrete, from an earthly reality, cyclically grows from and replenishes these ancient "instincts" for power and domination. Conquest, the actualized result of the "pursuit," generates further conquest and destroys the "dark life" or otherness of the New World, never to be rekindled "save in spirit . . . a spirit lost in that soil" (27). Contact with the material world most sharply distinguishes the Aztecs from the Spaniards and particularly characterizes the different prehistoric "instincts" and the different notions of "civilization" held by the two groups. The conquering Europeans view the material world as something to be possessed, and possession grants both power and civilized status; even their religion supports this world-view, Williams implies, in its desire to accumulate swelling numbers of converts. The Aztecs, whose religion dwells intensely within the physical – as human sacrifices attest – are pulled by "the earthward thrust of their logic; blood and earth; the realization of their primal and continuous identity with the ground" (33). Though the explorers are horrified by the "savagery" of human sacrifice, Cortez's destruction of Tenochtitlan, performed with malicious intent, displays a more horrific sacrifice of humanity based not on a "continuous identity with the ground" but upon an adversarial relationship with it, a desire to possess and deplete it. Interchangeably called "the Conqueror" and "the Christian," the figure of Cortez links the monolithic ideology informing patriarchal religious and socioeconomic systems.

In further demonstrating these ideological roots of American culture – and more local to the text, of Indian genocide – Williams chooses Ponce de León to exemplify the "orgy of blood" that "no man has written" (41). Writing of this historical figure, Williams isolates the religious discourse used by European settlers to justify the murder of Indians: "Indians have no souls; that was it. That was what they said. . . . On all sides 'heavenly man' bent on murder, self-privilege" (4). Similarly, in "The Great Sex Spiral," Williams had objected to the classical insistence that women lack souls, a strategy ensuring male privilege by regarding the male as standard norm and subject, while viewing all others as deficient. As Williams details Ponce de León's slaughter and enslavement of the Indians, as "heavenly man" claims to bring "culture" to the New World, the feminine and Indian presences merge in images of both victimization and resistance. The Indians' vulnerability to Spanish subjugation is conveyed through numerous images of women murdered, raped, and mutilated. Captured while doing laundry in the river, for example, the women suffer violently misogynistic acts as their breasts are slashed off; in effect, this particularly antifeminine violence emblematizes the Spaniard's enslavement of the Indian race as "the whole free population was brought into slavery or killed off" (42). A purveyor of patriarchal ideology, Ponce de Léon either violently extinguishes otherness or confines it within boundaries he constructs for his own well-being.

Significantly, resistance to these regulating boundaries emerges in the figure of an old Indian woman whose subversive manipulation of the Spaniard's hunger for power upsets his tyrannical designs. Recalling both the "despoiled, molted castaway" Williams saw in his own mother (whom these words describe and who also was Caribbean), and the "marvelous old queen" of "The Wanderer," this old woman is seemingly broken by life: "an old woman, loose tongued – loose sword – the book, her soul already half out of her with sorrow: abandoned by a Carib . . . her children enslaved" (42–3). Her power, however, to move out of this nothingness and generate transformation constitutes a particularly feminine power within Williams's oeuvre, which she displays in telling de León the legend of the fountain filled with "clearest water of virtue to make old men young" (42). With this story, she becomes a feminine figure of the "real, the thing destroyed turning back with a smile" (42); she is the poet's mother, who "by this power [of great imagination] . . . still breaks life between her fingers"; she is the African Grace, "laughing / Too weak to stand" (CP1 59); she is Madame Curie, facing "a failure, a / nothing. And then, returning in the / night to find it  .  / LUMI-NOUS" (Paterson 177–8). Of her story, Williams muses, "Think of that! Picture to yourself the significance of that – as revenge, as irony, as the trail of departing loveliness" (IAG 42). Indeed, believing the old woman's story as she knew he would, Ponce de León undertakes a long, exhausting, and futile search for the fountain of eternal youth, a quest that leaves "the murderer, the enslaver, the terror striker, the destroyer of beauty" both physically and spiritually depleted. Like Columbus, he is driven by images of great power, while the pursuit of grandeur writes itself upon the land as destruction within a lineal procession of conquerors. Williams's text insists on this repetition, as de León lands his boat at Guan-ahini, "Columbus' first landfall." In contrast, however, de León does not find the "unlike" trees, peoples, and creatures Columbus first beheld but the result of that first moment's betrayal: The island, "then populous, inviting [is] now desolate, defeated, murdered – unpeopled" (43). His desire for power exceeds his predecessor's in seeking control over the natural processes of life, aging, and death – an extreme attempt to master nature. As with Columbus, however, this desire serves his own destruction. Weakened by his failed quest for the fountain, de León stirs to life again only when he hears of Cortez's triumph, and he sails to Florida hoping to discover (or, rather, conquer) another Tenochtitlan. The Ya-masse Indians respond to his intended conquest by depleting the source of his power; they end his life, and his death parallels the impotent search for the fountain. Shooting an arrow into his thigh, the Indians "let out his fountain" in an act that Williams metaphorically relates to both his failed quest and a failed potency; the sexual image of the fountain is "let out," made fully and finally impotent. The old woman's story and the arrow that lodges in his thigh are both aimed at his masculinized potency and power, and both weapons derive from another kind of power: "the real, the thing destroyed turning back with a smile."

This feminized power speaks in the voice of the New World, the voice of She who continually comments upon and interrupts the narrative of de Soto's four-year march into the Florida wilderness. Personified as feminine, the New World is the "recreative new," the site of a regenerative power that inverts European notions of material possession and religious conversion. Though threatened by de Soto's "lust," She speaks in a sensual voice that challenges his overtures. Inviting him to enter into a state of contact with her (a conversion on his part), She bears a resemblance to the seductive femme fatale of male-authored literary conventions, but the resemblance remains superficial and actually works to subvert such conventions.[64] This subversion operates both through the essay's form and its gendered imagery as the language of She breaks through the formal narrative de Soto constructs.

Williams structurally interrupts the "historical" account of de Soto's exploration with the sporadic, fluid voice of the wilderness itself, reflecting the disruptive force of both natural and native elements to the Spanish project in the New World. She has a voice unheard in History: It is a voice combining the erotic with maternal powers of creation and disruption, sharing a strong kinship with the primary female deities of Indian cosmologies to whom we can turn as embodying alternative mythic modes of feminine power. Unlike the Westernized perception of maternity as a "limit on the power inherent in femininity," many Indian cosmologies hold maternal power central to all varieties of creation, and in myths that cross multiple tribal theologies, the Old Woman figure provides the dominant myth of the prime mover. Variously manifested as the Old Spider Woman, White Calf Buffalo Woman, and Thought Woman, these deities "testify that primary power – the power to make and to relate – belongs to the preponderately feminine powers of the universe" (Allen, *The Sacred Hoop,* 17). Enabling all forms of transformation, woman's power encompasses both creation and destruction in native American myth. Ixchel, the goddess of the Moon and of weaving in the Yucatan, possesses the "power of fruitfulness" yet is also connected with the "power to end life . . . her power to weave includes the power to unravel, so the weaver, like the moon, signifies the power of patterning and its converse, the power of disruption" (Allen 27).

The voice of She is similarly a voice that unravels and disrupts. She warns de Soto that his attempt to possess her is futile, and that she will possess him through the conversionary experience of contact. If he resists, the experience can only occur through death, an undoing of the material titles and possessions he holds in life, a letting go that must precede any "possession" of She, as She defines the term. She croons to him, "you are vigilant, sagacious, firm besides. But I am beautiful. . . . You shall receive of me, nothing – save one long caress as of a great river passing forever upon your sweet corse . . . You are mine, Black Jasmine, mine" (45). Reverberating with sexual overtones, the possession she claims occurs through contact, not invasion or seizure, denoting important gender-specific distinctions between these two modes of possession. Though She fears defeat from the "lust" of de Soto's drive and envisions him straddling her in a position of sexual dominance, her own call to connection and contact vitiates complete mastery. She warns him, "Ride upon the belly of the waters, building your boats to carry all across. Calculate for the current; the boats move with a force not their own, up and down, sliding upon the female who communicates to them, across all else, herself" (53). The "female who communicates . . . herself" merges sexual, feminized possession with maternal contact, creating a female presence undivided in its maternity and sexuality, investing the maternal and the feminine with a power denied by patriarchy's dualism of the two and its insistence upon male potency as power. Her child is the Indian, whose intimate connection with the land is figured as a habit of listening to the maternal language of She.

To enter into the maternal, to hear her "wild language," is to undergo a conversion that reverses the European efforts to Christianize the Indians (46). Such has been the fate of Juan Ortiz, a captured Spaniard, who lives with the Indians and reappears with a small group staging an unsuccessful ambush of de Soto's men. He has been "nursed tenderly" for twelve years while She has been "teaching him the wild language," a language of contact (46). Recaptured by de Soto, Juan Ortiz acts as translator of the wilderness language and the Indian tongue, and the troops survive by responding in degrees to this language. Their subsequent adaptation of Indian dress and hunting methods suggests the conversion She has foreseen: "And if, to survive, you yourself in the end turned native, this victory is sweetest of all" (50). Yet the motives compelling the army's transformation never fully diverge from the ethos of conquest, for de Soto's men appropriate Indian ways and dress to overpower, not to emulate, the Indians, seeking to possess rather than to connect. Unconverted, de Soto and his men are left without language when Juan Ortiz dies, and they fear "to enter the country, lest [they] might get lost" (54).

Just as the voice of She disrupts the linear narrative of de Soto, the "wild language" of the land and Indian now thwarts and resists the Spanish advance:

> [Ortiz's] death was so great a hindrance to our going, whether on discovery or out of the country, that to learn of the Indians what would have been rendered in four words, it now became necessary to have the whole day; and oftener than otherwise the very opposite was understood to what was asked. (54)

Language itself becomes a site of resistance, a heritage Williams will trace through such writers as Edgar Allan Poe and Gertrude Stein.

Only in death does de Soto finally join with this maternal power through the conversion of contact, for his death represents the abandonment of material possession and hierarchical authority. Williams details the heritage de Soto leaves behind – consisting of "two male and three female slaves, three horses, and seven hundred swine" (58) – and elucidates his titles of power in a catalogue reminiscent of that of Columbus: "the magnanimous, the virtuous, the intrepid captain, Don Hernand de Soto, Governor of Cuba and Adelantado of Florida" (57). In death, his attempted mastery surrenders to the New World's otherness, and imagistically his potency is subsumed within the utter difference of She. De Soto's body is dropped into the river, and its description both recalls and dispels the masculine "lust" of his drive through the wilderness. The potency sustaining his movements in life changes in death into a drifting kind of contact: "Down, down, this solitary sperm, down into the liquid, the formless, the insatiable belly of sleep; down among the fishes there was one called a bagre . . . " (58). The paragraph goes on to describe the distinctly New World fish – the peel-fish, the shad, the pereo, the unnamed varieties Columbus first observed as "unlike" the European. Significantly, the focus is not upon the engendering power of the sperm; rather, de Soto's body, a "solitary sperm," drifts amidst a difference imagistically feminized as a womblike "liquid, . . . belly." An inclusive space of connection and contact, it is "unlike" the Old World while analogous to the New.

However, one cannot read descriptives such as "liquid" and "belly" without confronting stereotypical ideas of gender, as most critical readings of the de Soto section demonstrate. This language and these images echo traditional representations of the maternal womb as a passive receptacle, while de Soto's submergence suggests the anxiety of the maternal abyss, in which the maternal is psychologically experienced as a place of engorgement, a swallowing up of the masculine. Nonetheless, while calling upon such representations of the feminine derived from a masculine system of meaning, the text simultaneously redirects the focus from the engendering power of the sperm's movement to the connective power of the "belly," displacing masculine potency with the inclusive fluidity of interaction. In figuring de Soto's corpse as a solitary sperm, the metaphor provides a significant shift in the text's sexual imagery – or, more precisely, in the conventional expectations associated with the procreative experience and process. If we read this image from a male (hence, a standard) perspective, we focus on the "failure" of the solitary sperm to join the egg and engender life.[65] From this perspective, the success or failure of male generative power depends upon the moment of insemination. However, Williams's imagery suggests a contradictory reading. The image of sperm is not an image of an originating force, nor does its movement suggest pursuit; rather, the imagery of the entire passage suggests an interactive process through foregrounding the feminine space of She. Rather than describing the sex act purely in terms of male experience, the text emphasizes feminine contact, not male penetration and virility, as a generative power.

Concurrently, the cultural meanings associated with these gendered images come into play, enacting what Marianne DeKoven has recently termed the "*sous-rature* – the unsynthesized dialectic or unresolved contradiction that characterizes modernist form" (*Rich and Strange* 25). Considering modernist writing within the context of first-wave feminism and the anxieties it produced in both men and women, DeKoven theorizes a modernist strategy of "contradictoriness" in which the "representation and its own negation coexist in the text in an oscillating simultaneity, an unresolved contradiction" (23). De Koven's analysis of this representational process can be applied in sorting through the contradictory nature of the de Soto text. She sees the representation of gender, under the pressure of feminist and socialist activity, undergoing a simultaneous reiteration and deconstruction through modernist forms of juxtaposition and disjunction, creating "a system that coexists within one figure with its own undoing" (21). For Williams, this "system" is humanist masculine subjectivity, figured by the corpse of de Soto and the belly of She, coexisting with its own undoing in the imagistic disorientation of the masculinely privileged perspective. The de Soto passage both evokes gender dualisms and encourages an alternative perspective to the conventional privileging of the phallus, enacting what DeKoven refers to as Kristeva's " 'impossible dialectic,' simultaneously acknowledging dualism and repudiating both its hierarchical imbalance and its rigid self–other exclusivity." This process offers "a *passage* out of our masculine economy of representation, given the fact that we are now inevitably located within it and can only see a passage out within its terms" (30). Rejecting the traditional dualism of "both/and" (of sperm/womb in this instance), the Williams text alters the relationship between sperm and womb from hierarchical to a "simultaneity enabled by an open 'passage' between them," as DeKoven describes this alternative to masculine representation (37).

The workings of masculine representation are explored in the essay on Raleigh, which follows the de Soto episode in a clear pairing with it. The masculine subjectivity emphatically asserted in this section provides the "undersong" of de Soto's pursuit. The feminine space of the womb emphasized in this final image of de Soto, a sexual metaphor of contact as potentially regenerative, stands in startling contrast to the obsessively masculine sexual language used to describe Sir Walter Raleigh and his exploits. While de Soto's masculine subjectivity, imaged as sperm, undergoes a conversion from the standard representation of phallic potency to a passage through and contact with difference, Raleigh's experiencing of the New World throws into stark relief the contours of patriarchal masculinity. Like the Spanish explorer, Raleigh embarks on a "pursuit of beauty" likened to a lustful passion, practically a rape. As a founder of colonies, "plunging his lust into the body of the new world" after having "penetrated to the Queen," Raleigh's relationship to the New World and his relationship to Queen Elizabeth become conflated within imagery of male sexuality and seemingly echo the eroticized dynamics of possession enacted between de Soto and She (59, 60). However, the figurative language of sexuality continually redefines notions of power within the complexly compact space of the essay. While opening with archetypal images of male virility as the primary essence of achievement and discovery, the essay ends with dual images of the paternal line destroying itself: Raleigh sends his son to death, and the king condemns Raleigh to death.

Seeking "an England new again," Raleigh's pursuit of beauty is a pursuit of a mythic, Arcadian realm, an England renewed and reborn. With this vision, "he penetrated to the Queen" as the "whetter, the life giver to the Queen" (60). His "outward thrust, to seek" turns out to be a "voyage on the body of his Queen: England, Elizabeth – Virginia!" (60). Images of Elizabeth oscillate between stressing her body and her patriarchal authority. Hers is "the body of the Queen stirred by that plough" of colonization, but "withdrawn" (in a phallic association) from Raleigh as she and England desert him. The body of the Queen, the Virgin of English mythos replicated in the Virgin land of the New World, is violated by the lustful plunge of imperialist design – of which Raleigh is an agent and the Queen herself a controlling power. Under the queen's authority, Raleigh is the male vehicle through which her patriarchal power is transmitted to the New World. Unlike the wounded body of She, whose virginity exists only in the European myths of invaders seeking to deflower her, the Queen's "body" reacts to desires of possession and control, for she herself wants mastery. Speaking, for example, of Raleigh's relationship with one of her ladies, she rages: "What have you dared to do? How have you dared, without my order, to possess yourself of what is mine?" (61). She forces Raleigh to marry her "possession," a patriarchal treatment of the female as currency or exchange. Though a woman herself, Elizabeth's strategies of power historically involved careful negotiations with gender and authority as she attempted to both masculinize her image (through her insistence upon likening herself to her father and to the role of king) while retaining the virtuously elevated status of virgin.[66] As virgin, she approached more closely the male gender than would a married woman within the traditional distinctions of her culture, occupying a place more masculine than feminine in relationship to power. Williams's text stresses her political authority while simultaneously emphasizing her sexual body, suggesting her manipulation of sexual status as a political tool. Furthermore, in replicating the rule of the fathers, the figure of Elizabeth contrasts with the feminine energies of the New World. She remains England, not the Virginia bearing her inscription, and the text syntactically effects this contrast through a repetition of the pronoun "she" that recalls the New World She:

> ... she, Elizabeth, she England, she the Queen – deserted him; Raleigh for Leicester, Essex now for Raleigh; she Spenser whom he friended, she "The Faery Queen," she Guiana, she Virginia, she aetheist, she "my dear friend Marlowe," she rents, rewards, honors, influence, reputation, she "the fundamental laws of human knowledge," she prison, she tobacco, the introduction of potatoes to the Irish soil ... (61)

Unlike the maternal and sexual She, Elizabeth stands as a complex figure embodying both male-defined feminine virtue and patriarchal power; her body, in effect, rapes itself with Raleigh, and in this way, Raleigh – in all his lust and virility – is "the tool of a woman," a woman in the mold of patriarch (60). In effect, patriarchy is the rapist, a degenerative force within the New World. The paternal line of succession – the "legal fiction" of paternity that ensures male dominance – fails as that very male potency turns in on itself in acts of self-destruction. The essay ends by querying, "Why did he send his son into that tropic jungle and not go himself, upon so dangerous an errand? And when the boy had died why not die too? Why England again and force the new king to keep his promise and behead him?" (62).

Raleigh's paternal line of succession literally ends with the death of his son, just as the Tudor line ends with Elizabeth's demise, yet a cultural line continues through the Pilgrims, the "seed of Tudor England's lusty blossoming," as the ideology of invasion is transferred into themes of colonization (63).[67] The seed, "hard and little," moves "not toward ger-mination but the confinements of a tomb" (63, 66); subsequently, the lineage of the fathers is sterile, and the inherited dualism of "spirit against the flesh" produces "a race incapable of flower" in "the most lawless country in the civilized world, a panorama of murders, perversions, a terrific ungoverned strength" (66, 68). Williams does not merely react against (his perception of) Puritan repressiveness and its relationship to modern perversities; more complexly, he links the metaphor of male potency to structures of knowledge as they are constituted by language. The "jargon of God" central to Puritan identity (the logocentrism "by which they kept themselves surrounded as with a palisade") and "the seed" (the phallocentrism of male power) interact within a Puritan ide-ology revealed in the text as ordering systems of thought that, through language, construct gender identity; moreover, the construction of gen-der identities is shown to be at the heart of the American identity, itself an idealized construction Williams attempts to take apart and to discredit largely through attacking the sanctuaries of meaning associated with gender.

### The Feminine Ground of Contact: "a moral source not reckoned with"

In the first third of *In the American Grain*, the history of Old World explorers develops as a history of a masculine subjectivity founded upon the goals of conquest and domination, thereby fueling imperialist and Christian projects alike in the New World. The feminine, in these essays, is represented as both victim and resistant force; against the text's construction of masculinity as mastery over the feminine, the feminine is constructed as the power of contact. The central essays, significantly, begin to relate historically specific constructions of the feminine within male-authored cultural texts, ranging from prescriptions for Puritan women to denigrations of Indian women to idealizations of modern women. In the inclusion, for example, of Cotton Mather's sermons and the records of witch trials, the text alerts us to specific historical deter-minants affecting the formation of the concept of the feminine in Amer-ican thought and the regard for women in American society. These historical constructions of the feminine are linked, through the essays' symbiotic development of meaning, with the failure of Americans to generate an enabling energy except through violence and destruction.

What seems important to stress is the interaction between Williams's own construction of the feminine as contact and the context he weaves out of historical documents and anecdotes that define and regulate actual historical women. In effect, the collocation of such documents glaringly exposes their constructed and biased nature, denaturalizing their claims to inscriptive authority over women. It also has the effect of making us constantly aware that Williams's notion of the feminine is offered as yet another construct rather than claiming to define an absolute essence; the essentialization of the feminine as a mode of touch or contact occurs within the context of previous and powerful texts purporting to define "woman," and their very exposure as ideologically invested narratives reflects back upon the rubric of gender that *In the American Grain* develops. As American history is revealed within the frame of its ideological enclosures, the text links the feminine and the Indian as disruptive concepts capable of illuminating and breaking through those enclosures.

The French explorer Champlain exemplifies this ideologically enclosed perspective through the grids, maps, and charts that produce "a country almost invented . . . out of his single brain" (70). In "The Founding of Quebec," which accompanies the Puritan essays, Williams employs two speakers, one of whom finds the violent origin of Quebec "too amusing" and "marvelous – all through" (73). The second speaker replies: "To hell with all that: collecting pictures for France – or art! What for the New World?" (73). The double narrative voice undercuts the authority presumed by a single "objective" version of history; in this way, Williams's formal strategy reacts against the categorical mapping of the colonized lands. Champlain's mapping of New France, "with his maps, for France, for science, for civilization," attempts to "convert" the New World to Old World concepts of civilization, an attempt built upon an illusory notion of civilization:

> It is why France never succeeded here. It is the Latin, or Gaelic or Celtic sense of historic continuity . . . planting a drop of your precious blood in outlandish veins, in the wilderness and fancying that that addition makes them French – that by this the wilderness is converted! Civilized, a new link in the chain. (74)

Anticipating Williams's later criticism of Pound's classical and patrilineal notion of tradition, the text equates a seminal act ("planting a drop of precious blood") with the desire to map and categorize in an effort to eliminate difference. Imposing a conversion upon the land, Champlain's actions are analogous to the Puritan "mapping" of God's will upon the New World, a mapping that creates distance and separation while asserting a form of mastery that suppresses contact. Still, Williams presents such gestures toward mastery as finally unable to contain the force of contact, a "force to leap up and wrench you from your hold and force you to be part of [the land]. . . . That is generous. Open. A break through" (74). The force of contact is a force of disruption, a breaking that Williams values in both poetic and political contexts.

In rewriting the story of American conquest and colonization, Williams inverts conventional praise of civilizing forces as heroic or divinely manifest, stressing instead that this inheritance disastrously represses the Indian's "continuous identity with the ground" (33). The true heroic figures of Williams's history somehow turn "native" by exhibiting the capacity for contact and acting upon this capacity through "crosspollenization" – Williams's term describing a cross-cultural opening to difference (121). Such figures are not the founders and fathers, but individuals like Père Sebastian Rasles, Daniel Boone, and Aaron Burr, who act as sites of cultural interaction in Williams's essentially feminine imaging of heroism:

> It is *this* to be *moral:* to be *positive,* to be peculiar, to be sure, generous, brave – TO MARRY, to *touch* – to *give* because one HAS, not because one has nothing. And to give to him who HAS, who will join, who will make, who will fertilize, who will be like you yourself: to create, to hybridize, to crosspollenize – not to sterilize, to draw back, to fear, to dry up, to rot. (121)

Touch or contact is clearly associated with the feminine and, early on in Williams's thinking, with the female and especially the maternal body. The body becomes a foundation for new systems of interaction – interpersonal, economic, societal, linguistic, and so on. The female body supplies a metonym for an epistemology to displace masculinist traditions of thought. Rather than a literalist reading of the female body as a biological entity for contact, I would suggest considering the ways in which this set of associations (female body / maternal / contact) operates within the text's system of tropes to expose the centrality of phallomorphism to Western thinking and to begin to displace it.

Williams's essentializing gesture, in this respect, intersects with the later efforts of Luce Irigaray. Irigaray's dependence upon the biological body, and particularly her representation of the feminine through the image of two labial lips,[68] has met with much criticism for seemingly regressing to a reductive anatomical essentialism of sex. However, a number of recent critical works have begun rethinking Irigaray's configurations in a more complex and useful manner.[69] In a central essay, Irigaray describes a feminine touch that touches upon but never wholly absorbs:

> As for woman, she touches herself in and of herself without any need for mediation, and before there is any way to distinguish activity from passivity. Woman "touches herself" all the time, and moreover no one can forbid her to do so, for her genitals are formed of two lips in continuous contact. Thus, within herself, she is already two – but not divisible into one(s) – that caress each other. (*This Sex* 24)

Rejecting a purely literalist reading of this figure of two lips, Diana Fuss writes that "Irigaray's production of an apparently essentializing notion of female sexuality functions strategically as a reversal and a displacement" of Western phallomorphism (particularly as revealed in Lacan). Reading "the relation between language and the body as metonymic" (62), Fuss sees that the "figure of the two lips as a model for a new kind of exchange 'puts in question all prevailing economies' (Irigaray, *This Sex*, 31)" (64). Irigaray's deployment of essentialism is steeped in erudite knowledge of and reference to a tradition of Western philosophy, and her challenge to that tradition is highly systematic (in an unorthodox fashion); obviously, no such claim can be made for Williams. However, the strategy Irigaray uses casts light upon Williams's own less sytematic or consistent critique of a patriarchal tradition. Like Irigaray, Williams proceeds associatively through connections between gender and language; unlike the French philosopher, however, Williams's own sense of his relationship to a masculine authority in language perplexes the movement of his thought. Just when he might seem to be breaking into radical reconsiderations of gender, his need to reassert a masculine subjectivity along traditional lines might intensify. This double gesture often typifies his most anxious and lambastic utterances, and marks the generative movement of his epic, *Paterson*.

In these essays on American history, however, Williams rebels against a form of discovery associated with the masculine. He insists that discovery is contact, not conquest or penetration; therefore, to create and to make is to "join" and to "crosspollenize," and the "new" is the newness of cross-cultural regeneration, not the "newness" or discovery of an ethnocentrically defined origin. From this perspective, history offers an opportunity to discover and to regenerate the present through uncovering the intersecting forces and influences informing both past and present. In so doing, Williams rejects a Puritan morality that praises sterility labeled as purity, a morality that forces the Puritan to "reproduce its own likeness, and no more" (68); instead, the different purity of contact affirms the inextricability of the maternal and the sexual as a way to touch, essentially moral in its regenerative openness.

The patriarchal fear of contact, or what Irigaray terms the "prevailing" economy, provides Williams with the major theme of his history. In such essays as "Maypole at Merry-Mount," "Mather's Wonders," "Père Sebastian Rasles," and "Jacataqua," he traces the manifestation of this fear in cultural texts that regulate women's activities, sexuality, and identity. Recounting the May Day revelries of Thomas Morton, Williams focuses upon the Puritan reaction to Morton's open relationship with local Indians and particularly their horror of his intimacy with the women. Alongside this reaction, Williams juxtaposes various treatments of the native women's sexuality by male historians, such as Stratchey, Parkman, Wood, Jossellyn, and LeJeune. The imposition of Western conventions of womanhood upon Native American women stands as a paradigm within the text for the patriarchal interpretation and suppression of the feminine.

For Williams, Thomas Morton represents a figure of conversion from the Old World to the New. Author of the seventeenth-century *The New English Canaan,* which presented an Arcadian image of the New World, Morton aroused Puritan ire by holding pagan revelries and developing close, intimate ties with the Indians. To the Puritans, Morton exemplified the danger of the Christian's exposure to the wilderness, seen as an innately evil realm tempting the faithful away from civilization into the powers of Satan.[70] Morton's frontier plantation, his contacts with the Indians, and his deliberately pagan activities confirmed for the Puritans their conception of the wilderness. Reconsidering Morton's experience from outside the Puritan mentality, Williams seeks to "relieve him from that imposition of his time and seriously to show up that lightness, his essential character, which discloses the Puritans themselves as maimed" (76). To disclose Morton's New World character, Williams pieces together various historical commentaries from the colonial period that undo one another's authoritative status. He finds this deauthorizing process already underway between Morton's own text and its preface by C. F. Adams, who advocates the Puritan disgust with Morton and thus undercuts the outcast's autobiographical narrative. Adams agrees that the Puritans were "dead right" in violently objecting to Morton's relationships with the Indians – both his trading relationships with the men and his more intimate commerce with the women. Focusing on Puritan responses to native American women, the text reconsiders historical opinions on the sexuality and morality of Indian women. As Williams quotes one historian after another,[71] their gendered and ethnocentric bias is revealed not only in and of itself, but as a powerful and concealed discourse of gender and race.

The Indian woman is repeatedly defined in terms of such Anglo-European womanly virtues as chastity, fidelity, and modesty. Josselyn and Wood both praise responses they interpret as the modesty of Indian women, and Parkman records that "chastity in women was recognized as a virtue by many tribes" (77). Yet Williams reveals the imposition of cultural biases in such history as he reports that Morton, who lived in close contact with the Indians, finds the concept of chastity does not exist in the Indian mind; furthermore, Morton claims, "adultery does not seem to have been looked upon as a very grave offense among the Indians of the vicinity of which they live" (77). Stratchey records that young girls go naked until pubescence, at which time they put on a "kind of semecinctum lethern apron before their bellies and are very shamefaced to be seen bare" (78), therefore exhibiting the sexual guilt and shame considered proper to women. But Williams contradicts Stratchey in quoting yet another opinion that ambivalently concludes since the women are " 'wantons before marriage and household drudges after, [therefore] it is extremely questionable whether they had any conception of it' (i.e. female chastity)" (78). Through such misogynist Westernized images, many early American writers constructed familiar stereotypes of Indian women, operating under the assumption of universal morals regulating woman's sexuality and the family unit.[72] Likewise, unable to conceive of alternative cultural values or structures, the Puritans draw solely upon their own morality as absolute in their condemnation and praise of Indian women.

Moreover, as Richard Slotkin documents, the Puritans equated Indian eroticism with a demonic power that sought to "seduce and racially debase white Christianity," an eroticism (for the Puritans) most evidenced and empowered by the Indians' relationship to nature; subsequently, the Puritans judged this relationship as fundamentally related to the Invisible Kingdom of witchcraft in Salem (*Regeneration Through Violence* 117). Hence, Morton's relationship with Indian women inspired Puritan fear as much as disgust and, eventually, triggered a violent reaction. When Morton sets up a Maypole "upon the festival day of Philip and Jacob," he plans, in his own words, "Revels and merriment after the old English custome" to commemorate the new name of his plantation, Ma-re Mount. As Williams notes, "Bradford's account [of the revelries] was very different" from Morton's, for the Puritan leader views the revels celebrating the fertility rite of May Day as pagan and lascivious, objecting strongly to the interaction of the Englishmen with Indian women. Comparing the revels to a revival of "the feasts of the Roman Goddess Flora, or the beastly practices of the madd Bacchinalians," Bradford condemns Morton and his men for setting up the Maypole, "drinking and dancing about it many days together, inviting the Indian women, for their consorts, dancing and frisking together, (like so many fairies, or furies rather) and worse practices" (79). Morton, in contrast, believed the Indians were descended from the heroic Greeks, and he foresaw a renewal of Christianity in its merger with native cultures (Slotkin 61–2).[73] As Williams's text reports, during the revels Morton's men seemingly transform into Indians to sleep with Indian women, donning Indian garb and engaging in dances that combine English, Greek, and Indian paganism.

For the Puritans, the lack of Christian morality among the Indian women evidenced the presence of Satan, and they feared the power of such women to seduce Christian men to the Devil's ways. This logic, the intertextual play of these essays suggests, extends to the Puritan woman also, through whom Satan most easily can enter and infect a Christian society. Williams writes that the Puritans, "forced by Morton's peccadillo . . . countered with fantastic violence," both in their immediate destruction of Morton's plantation and in the incendiary antifeminine ferment of the witch trials:

> As Morton laid his hands, roughly perhaps but lovingly, upon the flesh of his Indian consorts, so the Puritans laid theirs with malice, with envy, insanely, not only upon him. . . . Trustless of humane experience, not knowing what to think, they went mad, lost all direction. Mather defends the witchcraft persecutions. (80)

Making this explicit link between the Maypole incident and the Salem witch trials, the text moves from (mis)readings of Indian female chastity to (mis)readings of English female deviance, self-reflexively commenting upon the inscription of the female by male "authors" of history, culture, and religion.

Cotton Mather's success in stimulating the hysterical fear of witchcraft in 1692–3 partially depended, in complex and multivalent ways, upon the Puritan's conceptual regulation of womanhood. Mercy Short, the young woman responsible for the onslaught of accusations of witchcraft against the villagers (largely elderly women) of Salem, had undergone captivity by the Indians prior to her hallucinations.[74] For Mather, Mercy Short became an archetypal symbol of New England's condition – the pure, white female in danger of possession by Indian demons. To preserve and protect this virginity, the New Englanders were encouraged by Mather to eliminate the demons rather than passively submit to them. Mather's Puritan mythology established the violent extinction of the Indians as the only possible route to salvation within the New World's wilderness: "the only acceptable communion between Christian and Indian, civilization and wilderness, was the communion of murder, hunger, and bloodlust" (Slotkin, *Regeneration Through Violence,* 117). By envisioning the civilized New England colonies as conventionally female – helpless, pure, chaste – the Puritans justified violence as the manly Christian response. The witch persecutions manifested yet another form of masculine protection of the virginal female in condoning, as a societal exorcism of Indian demons, the execution of those convicted of witchcraft. Encouraged by Mather's manipulation of her story, Mercy Short's vengeful accusations against fellow villagers enacted one form of "violent retribution" against evil in the name of redemption, mirrored on a larger scale by the response to the Indian as evil and, therefore, requiring extermination (Slotkin 117).

The selection of Mather's work effectively demonstrates historical links between misogyny, fear of women, and the genocide of the American Indian within the rubric of a Christian ideology defined by men to maintain the supremacy of white, Anglo-European males. By including Mather's own unmediated text, Williams emphasizes the process through which male-authored cultural texts define and regulate the feminine and, further, how this historically specific regulation ideologically justifies for the Puritans both the witch trials and the aggressive hatred of Indians. In placing Mather's defenses of the trials next to excerpts from historians' responses to Indian female sexuality, Williams calls attention to the Puritan regulation of the feminine and the relationship of its regulation to the concept of the Indian as evil. Hence, the accusations of witchcraft leveled against Bridget Bishop and Susanna Martin invite comparison with the historical accounts of Indian women. In both cases, men act as authoritative witnesses to female virtue, and women seen as deviant from the "pious and prudent wife" (praised by Mather) are condemned. Both Martin and Bishop are accused of acting quarrelsome and prideful, that is, of exhibiting unwomanly traits for a Puritan woman. Moreover, reports that Martin repeatedly attacked men in bed associate a female eroticism with both power and evil, and suggest a related horror of the customarily open sexuality of Indian women as threatening to corrupt Christian goodness.

Williams's text frames the reports of the two women's trials, significantly, by Mather's arguments against acculturation of the English into the wilderness and Indian civilization, a theme common to his revival sermons attacking Puritan complacency. The revulsion to a marriage with the wilderness that links the witch persecutions and a hatred of the Indians lies at the heart of Mather's admonitions against acculturation to the New World. Mather's own verbal artistry remains intact within *In the American Grain* as a text that re-presents the center of authority, the speaker of the Fathers, whose fear of contact pushes both Indian and woman to the margins, where they remain silenced and distorted. Unlike Morton, who considered the mingling of the races and the embrace of the wilderness a source of renewal, Mather sees only debasement. In his first argument against acculturation, Mather asserts the Puritan belief that the "first Planters of these Colonies were a chosen Generation of Men" and urges a return to the idealized (because untainted by the New World) ways of the English fathers. He blames the degeneration of the younger generation upon its closer contact with the New World, "once the Devil's territories," representing a concomitant distance from God that constitutes the "cause of our Afflictions": "the Devil is now making one Attempt more upon us" in the form of witchery (83, 84). His second argument, offered after detailing the accusations of witchcraft leveled against Bishop and Martin, goes on to relate the "Witchcraft now upon us" to a few "Matchless Curiosities" that he shall report "with Good Authority" (100). The First Curiositie describes the Devil's "Impious and Impudent imitation of Divine Things" through his chosen people, the Indians. Mather interprets an Indian migration from Mexico to New England as the Satanic reversal of the Israelite's journey through the wilderness and considers Indian religious rituals to be evil imitations of the Mass and sacraments. The Salem witches are privy to these "Bloody Imitations," for they join the Indians in the worship of the Devil. In reality, numerous individuals accused of witchcraft, particularly the men, were known to maintain relations with the Indians, and accusations of connubial relations were especially damning, recalling the treatment Thomas Morton received at the hands of Puritans who viewed the open sexuality and erotically charged religiosity of the Indians as a threat to Christian purity.

The Indian's sexuality appeared most un-Christian in its female manifestation, and the threat of female eroticism seducing the male Pilgrim was much more real in the minds of the Puritans than any fear of the white female being seduced by the Indian male, since the conventional image of the chaste Christian woman did not allow for the possibility of such sexual attraction on her part. White female relations with the Indian male could be imagined only in terms of rape, rather than marriage or voluntary communion, revealing once again the imposition of Anglo-European gender systems upon the Indians; though the Western lore of the conqueror presumes the rape of women as part of the possession of plundered goods, such a mythos did not exist within the codes of the eastern Indian warrior.[75] Although Cotton Mather, among others, would instill fear of the Indian as rapist in the hearts of the Puritan communities, rape was not a part of the Indian's institution of maleness.

The text of Mather's unmediated words is immediately disputed by Williams's own narrative voice in the essay that follows Mather's defense, explicitly critiquing its ideological substructure and implicitly refuting the notion of language transparency. All words, the essay suggests, are mediated by cultural forces, and no narrative voice, including his own, is pure or transparent. As one of two speakers in "Père Sebastian Rasles," Williams carefully places himself in Paris, "this center of old-world culture," where he engages in dialogue with the Frenchman Valéry Larbaud on the uses of history (105). The conversational form questions the role of historian through explicitly showing each speaker's personal circumstances and his intent to mediate his views of American history. As he has earlier deauthorized the historian's voice through suggesting ethnocentric and gendered bias, in "Père Sebastian Rasles" he presents his own voice as historicized rather than existing outside of history, and he looks to the process of making historical narratives to understand how "our conception of the New World has been fabricated" (125). As the two men converse, Larbaud expresses his affinity with European attitudes imported to the New World. Williams assaults two such attitudes explicitly: the glorification of violent regeneration – as Larbaud praises the Spaniards for giving "magnificently" to the New World, and Mathers for adhering to a clarity of order – and the concept of historical origin as coincident with the heroics of conquest and violence. America's history, for Larbaud, "begins with giants – cruel, but enormous, who eat flesh" (113). Most perniciously to Williams's mind, Larbaud views history as theory separate from life and considers its books remote tales of the past. Williams protests: "I cannot separate myself... from this ghostly miasm. It grips me. I cannot talk of books, just of Mather as if he were some pearl" (115). His refusal to view history as a hermetically sealed artifact is to "seek the support of history . . . [to] wish to understand it aright, to make it SHOW itself" (116).

History resides not in books but in the concrete, everyday shaping force of its mythologies and ideologies upon America's morals, actions, expressions, and modes of interaction. To seek the support of history is to seek and proclaim a "ground on which to stand," a ground Williams feels America fails to recognize or claim, choosing instead a selective amnesia in viewing its past. Speaking of his own historical writings, Williams explains his reclamation project to Larbaud:

> It is an extraordinary phenomenon that Americans have lost the sense, being made up as we are, that what we are has its origin in what the *nation* in the past has been; that there is a source IN AMERICA for everything we think or do; that morals affect the food and food the bone, and that, in fine, we have no conception at all of what is meant by moral, since we recognize no ground our own – and that this rudeness rests all upon the unstudied character of our beginnings. . . . That unless everything that is, proclaim a ground on which it stand, it has no worth; and that what has been morally, aesthetically worth while in America has rested upon peculiar and discoverable ground. (109)

Williams looks to the French Jesuit Sebastian Rasles to reclaim this New World ground as a "moral source not reckoned with" by the inherited Puritan imagination, a source that is "peculiarly sensitive and daring in its close embrace of native things . . . opening, reviving – not shutting out" (121). Rasles is "another root" for "a new spirit in the New World" because he "recognized the New World" for itself (120). Newness is not origin, but discovery of a ground that enables change and transformation – the new partakes of the old without destroying it or shutting it out. If newness derives from contact, not conquest, in a moral and cultural sense there can be no New France or New Spain or New England; there can only be the newness of cross-cultural regenerativeness or the stale repetition of the old. In a figure such as Père Sebastian Rasles, the moral source of heroism locates itself in contact, a contact enacted most obviously in his relationship to the Huron Indians. Through Rasles, Williams "proclaims a ground" that recognizes the prior claim of the Indian: "In Rasles one feels THE INDIAN emerging from within the pod of his isolation from eastern understanding, he is released AN INDIAN. He exists, he is – it is an AFFIRMATION, it is alive" (121). An alternative to the Puritan's violent battle against the wilderness, Rasles's interaction with the native peoples and land provides an ethical model and moral base within American history; it is the "quality of this impact upon the native phase that *is* the moral source I speak of, one of the sources that has shaped America and must be recognized" (122).

Through figures such as Rasles, Williams redefines concepts of purity and morality while simultaneously uncovering the Puritan understanding of these words. While Larbaud praises the "clarity and distinction" of Mather's world-view, Williams interprets this "rigid clarity" as an "*inhuman* clarity" in its "steel-like thrust from the heart of each isolate man straight into the tabernacle of Jehovah. . . . Its virtue is to make each man stand alone" (111). This rhetoric again repeats the gesture of male sexual conquest informing the earlier essays, and here its ideology is shown as a repressive force. Fearful of the corruption of their civilized and Christian purity, the Puritans "could not afford to allow their senses to wander," and the rigidity of their social definitions assumes the purpose of preserving this claim of purity. Inextricably tied to a denigration of earthly existence, this repression of sensory experience resides at the heart of Puritan definitions (via Mather) of social deviance. Such definitions institutionalize the oppression of those seen to exist in closeness to the earth or who are led by senses that "wander." In Williams's historical configuration, both the Indian and women suffer from the denigration of earthly contact:

> The Puritan, finding one thing like another in the world destined for blossom only in 'Eternity,' all soul, all emptiness, then here, was precluded from SEEING the Indian. They never realized the Indian in the least save as an unformed PURITAN. The *immorality* of such a concept, the inhumanity, the brutalizing effect upon their own minds, on their SPIRITS – they never suspected. (113)

The Indian, as unformed Puritan, is defined by that sect in the mold of the savage, "men lost in the devil's woods, miserable in their abandonment and more especially damned" (110). Likewise, women are defined within a mold that seeks to contain their otherness and to separate them from their bodies:

> Is there another place than America (which inherits this [Puritan] tradition) where a husband, after twenty years, knows of his wife's body not more than neck and ankles, and four children to attest to his fidelity; where books are written and read counselling women that upon marriage, should they allow themselves for one moment to *enjoy* their state, they lower themselves to the level of the whore? (112)

Williams perceives this molding force ideologically embedded within "books," and goes on to focus upon the genre of the captivity narrative. According to Puritan "formula," any wandering from convention justifiably invites punishment, as with Hannah Swanton, who was *"punished by captivity and* TEMPTATION among the Catholics in Quebec" (111). Mather, in fact, historically exerted tremendous influence upon the emerging, developing mythology of America, and his "use of the captivity myth to suppress natural tendencies... ultimately produced the brief tragedy of the witchcraft hysteria and the enduring tragedy of a permanently distorted image of the American wilderness and the dark American races" (Slotkin, *Regeneration Through Violence,* 114–15). The same authorizing impulse regulating female sexuality is "this abortion of the mind, this purity" that, in Williams's history, compels the Puritans to commit "horrid atrocities in the name of their creed" against Indians, women, supposed witches, and other deviants (113).

Williams rereads the captivity narrative of Hannah Swanton, enabled by Rasles's "presentation of the Indian point of view [through his letters], toward the raids on the English settlements" (121). Viewed from the perspective of the Abnaki tribe's values and lifestyle, the "hardships that Hannah Swanton endured following her captivity, were little more than those of any Indian woman on the march.... She must walk or die" (122). Yet within this "life of the savage," generosity and interdependency coexist with hardship as all struggle for mutual survival:

> On this trip they had little to eat for days at a time. Once she had a part of a turtle they had killed. Once an Indian gave her a piece of moose liver. Once, on an island in the river with her Indian mistress, she had hailed a passing canoe filled with squaws, who, seeing her condition, gave her a roast eel to feed upon. (122)

The Puritan interpretation of Swanton's experience as punishment for deviance is challenged by the inclusion of an Indian perspective, albeit one derived from a non-Indian source. By shutting out the native perspective, the text suggests, history fixes a unitary form of cultural understanding and subsequently justifies the oppression of those it has silenced. Evoking what Slotkin calls the "enduring tragedy of a permanently distorted image of... the dark American races" (115), Williams laments: "but we are used only to the English attitude bred of the Indian raid. This is FIXED in us without realization of the EFFECT that such a story, such a tradition, entirely the product of the state of mind that it records, has had upon us and our feeling toward the country" (124).

Against this "fixed" tradition of the Indian, Williams poses a "countering legend" in Jacataqua, the native American woman and sachem. She also provides a countering legend to the patriarchal myths of the feminine brought to the New World by European explorers and settlers. With the essay "Jacataqua," the text confronts for the first time a modern America as Williams launches into a severe critique of the country's greed for wealth and power, its love of violence, and its fear of contact. One can see the starved and deadened state of the country itself, he asserts, most clearly in its women, for they have been most starved by their cultural heritage. Within patriarchy's textualization of the feminine, Williams suggests, women are deadened to themselves as women, and by extension, an entire culture is deadened to the feminine in itself.

"Jacataqua" deals extensively with the dynamics of gender perpetuated through the historical division between the maternal and the sexual underlying American myths of womanhood. Prior essays also begin to interpret this dualism as a fundamental tool of masculine power. In his conversation with Larbaud, Williams points out the duplicity behind Puritan regulations of sexuality, a duplicity that historically threatened women's lives. Their "plight . . . is heavily shadowed" by the simultaneous condemnation of "unofficial sexual indulgence" and the accepted practice of "official sexual excess" (119). Williams informs Larbaud that "other means being denied them, the Puritans ran madly to OFFICIAL sexual excess – during the long winters. . . . It was a common thing for men to have had as many as seven wives. Few had less than three. The women died under the stress of bearing children, they died like flies under the strains and accidents of childbirth" (119). With his doctor's eye, Williams reads woman's experience into the New England records of marriages and deaths that hold these statistics, and from this perspective he condemns the Puritan rationale for reproduction.[76] Reduced to "shooting children against the wilderness like cannonballs" (179), the Puritan women find their sexuality defined by male need; their maternal capacity to create is valued by men primarily as a tool in conquering the wilderness. Their bodies become sites of weapons production, while their sexuality is objectified in serving masculine sexual indulgence – both of which deaden the women, literally and spiritually. While he criticizes these masculine attitudes and their consequences, Williams admires the women's refusal to accept the powerless status of victim. He reports that the Puritan women of Groton choose to assert their sexuality, however mildly in modern terms, by wearing ribbons in their "hitherto plain bonnets" and resisting the commands of the male elders to remove the bit of color (119). This resistance, admired by Williams, culminates in a symbolic attack on the patriarchal stronghold of virginity; one young woman wears a wedding dress "of scarlet satin with a purple velvet shoulder cloak over it," exhibiting the "unknown pride" of sexuality condemned by the Puritan fathers (119).

Williams's reading of history argues against this division within the feminine of the sexual and the maternal, and he draws implicit contrasts between Western and Indian notions of the maternal as it is related to sexuality. He praises the fertility dance of the Chippewas, outlawed by the Puritans because it celebrated an eroticized fecundity that, to their minds, illicitly and publicly condoned the sexual dimension of the generative process. Puritan fear motivates

> the suppression of the superb corn dance of the Chippewas, since it symbolizes the generative processes – as if morals have but one character, and, that, – SEX: while morals are deformed in the name of PURITY; till, in the confusion, almost nothing remains of the great American New World but a memory of the Indian. (157)

Modern America, Williams complains, is a culture of "Men weaving women, women spouting men," a culture that associates procreation with its women and creation with its men. Culturally, the very words "production" and "reproduction" are underwritten by the "familiar dualism of mind and body, a key component of Western patriarchal ideology. Creation is the act of the mind that brings something new into existence. Procreation is the act of the body that reproduces the species" and, in functional terms of production, shoots babies against the wilderness (Friedman 75). Most explicitly in Williams's history, the voice of She undoes the premise traditionally separating the maternal from the sexual through embodying a native American understanding of the maternal, and it is this voice that resonates associatively through Jacataqua's presence.

Before looking specifically at the treatment of Jacataqua, it is helpful to elaborate upon the context of the essay itself, which asserts that America's heritage of conquest and violence suppresses this image of (feminine) resistance, making "us the flaming terror of the world, a Titan, stupid," where, "through terror, there is no direct touch," only an increasing "gap between touch and thing" (177). Silenced and defined by this masculine ethos, the feminine loses or hides its resistant power, Williams suggests, as women internalize the image of the feminine that Western culture provides and thereby participate in its continuance. In a culture that insists that "the ideal woman should end at the eyebrows and have the rest filled in with hair," the "whip-like intelligences" of American women too often atrophy through suppression and misuse of the intellect

(181). While women's assertion of intelligence has been historically discouraged by Western patriarchy, their value as physical, sexual beings for male benefit simultaneously encourages male desire and female self-loathing. Internalizing patriarchal notions of sexuality, women learn most unequivocally to hate their bodies, their sexual selves. Virginity, the "central lie," effectively convinces the female that she is "a low thing (they tell her), she is made to feel that she is vicious, evil" if she acknowledges her sexuality (183). Admired for their bodies, yet forbidden to experience them as erotically feminine, women are transformed into objects "fit only to be seen in shows," a dehumanization Williams admits to perpetuating with his own male response: "I have often watched, as who has not," he confesses. The American female, in submitting to this gaze, in believing and embodying her culture's definitions of woman, learns most to hate herself when responding to her own sense of womanliness and transgressing the sanctified boundaries. Thus, in America it "means *everything*" to a girl to lose her virginity: "It means that she gets such a violent jolt from her past teaching and such a sense of the hatred of the world . . . against her that she is ready to commit suicide" (184).

Arguing against this destructive process of female acculturation, Williams urges that "a woman must see with her whole body to be benevolent," or must learn "touch" (182, 179). On a cultural level, he locates a spiritual and aesthetic barrenness in the split of body and mind, in a silencing of a feminine erotics, in the refusal of contact:

> NEVER to allow touch. What are we but poor doomed carcasses, any one of us. . . . It is the women above all – there never have been women, save pioneer Katies. . . . Poets? Where? They are the test. But a true woman in flower, never. Emily Dickinson, starving of passion in her father's garden, is the very nearest we have ever been – starving. (178–9)

Assuming a stance admittedly troubling in its claim of authority to assess "true" womanhood, Williams enacts a simultaneous valorization of women and reiteration of repressive gender associations. The women are "closer to earth – the only earth. They are our cattle, cattle of the spirit – not yet come in" (181). As discussed in an earlier section of this chapter, this association of woman with the literal and the earthly is problematic in relationship to the masculine authority of the speaker; on the other hand, this association works to suggest the needed inclusion of marginalized and silent voices in an American culture. Poetic power, in Williams's aesthetic, derives from contact with the earth and with the ordinary, a modern inversion of conventional poetic and cultural values. In the feminine, Williams locates a poetics of contact limited and silenced by an American culture that analogously suppresses its women. The "discouraging" American aesthetic is "the annunciation of the spiritual barrenness of the American woman," a barrenness that represents yet another form of sterility within the country's patriarchal inheritance that partially arises from women's internalization of (rather than resistance to) patriarchal definitions of the feminine. The retrieval of the feminine offers a possibility for a new aesthetic based in the "cattle of the spirit," the chthonic ordinariness that for Williams provides the ground for a new poetics. It is also the ground for a new cultural politics of feminine contact, and even as he worked on *Paterson,* he was to write in 1948:

> With woman there's something under the surface we've been blind to, something profound, basic. We need, perhaps more than anything else today, to discover woman; we need badly to discover woman in her intimate (unmasculine) nature – maybe when we do we'll have no more wars, incidentally, but no more wars. ("Woman as Operator," n.p.)

As a source for poetry, Williams looks to the power of the feminine freed from patriarchal definitions. Emily Dickinson, he claims, in choosing to remain "in her father's garden" rather than adopt the accepted role of womanhood, enacts a choice that allows her to be a poet. Choosing to "live against [the] stream" (180) of America's socioeconomic constraints (the "garden's" rules), Dickinson's life can be read as a subversive act of resistance that results in a poet who is "the very nearest we have ever been" to "a true woman in flower," true womanhood being impossible within the strictures of American society (178–9). Notwithstanding, Williams sees her realm of choice as providing insufficient sustenance for both poet and woman, for the self-confinement making the poetry possible leaves her "starving of passion," forced to operate within the split of woman and poet. Williams associates himself with this split, claiming "I salute them, because only for American women, have I any deep fellow feeling" (185). American women are "great experimenters with the emotions" (185), who too often resist their father's gardens by leaving the country itself. Alluding somewhat longingly to the poetic daughters of Dickinson who have leapt the garden walls (expatriates such as Hilda Doolittle, Gertrude Stein, or Margaret Anderson), Williams muses, "I wish they could live at home" (185).

To live at home, to draw from a particularly American ground a source for poetry, early on becomes Williams's insistent requisite for the American poet, his defense for his own fears of provincialism, and his primary criticism of the expatriate poets. However, in its focus upon gender constructs within American history and culture, a focus that shifts in kaleidoscopic fashion from seemingly random to sharply delineated designs, *In the American Grain* reveals an American landscape that has not been "home" to women, to the feminine, or to the poetic. The construction of an enabling tradition, for himself as an American poet, involves an opening for the feminine at the very same time – to proclaim a new ground for an American poetics means to "discover woman," or to retrieve a ground of contact almost obliterated within the New World's history and mythology.

Appearing at the end of this essay named for her, yet focused more obsessively on modern America, the figure of Jacataqua offers a mythic articulation of the feminine within a New World context. In Williams's words, Jacataqua provides a "counter legend" to the American myth of the murderous savage. By placement, she also constitutes a "counter legend" to the mythic American woman whose value is assessed by her willingness to perpetuate, rather than rupture, the patrilineal passage of authority. Jacataqua's mixed Indian and French heritage identifies her with an inclusive New World, a crosspollenized newness, and her status as sachem, or chief, clearly signifies a culture far different in its gender constructions than the patriarchy imported from Europe. Williams further identifies Jacataqua with the poet, but particularly a poet of the feminine, for she gives "shape to the formless age as by a curious die," providing a measure that "gave to womanhood in her time, the form which bitterness of pioneer character had denied it" (186). The measure she provides grows from the combined elements of her powerful status, her sexuality (the "wild pulses of her heart"), and her egalitarian self-possession before the white male, Aaron Burr. Her womanhood asserts itself not in obedience to man but in the complementarity of the challenge: "Primitive and direct, it was she who opened the conversation and opened it with a challenge: 'These,' with a wave of her brown hand toward Howard and the group of officers, 'these want meat. You hunt with me? I win' " (187). She stands outside of the Western dualisms of mind and body, of virgin and whore, that Williams views as preventing women from awakening to themselves as women, or what Emma Goldman called the "internal tyrannies [of] . . . ethical and social conventions" enacted within a patriarchal society (in Burke, "New Poetry," 42). Singularly embodying the continual overlay of Indian and feminine that runs through the text, Jacataqua is a figure of challenge and resistance to the patriarchal order, a resistance enabled by a clear assertion of her sexuality.[77]

### Language and the Local: "a woman drawing to herself . . . myriad points of sound"

Jacataqua, more than any other single figure in the text, actualizes the enabling predecessor Williams seeks in American history, yet she is both an imaginary creature and one treated only briefly. Why does he resort to a fictive character as the central figure of womanhood in his history of America? In the historical record, he condescendingly asserts, "there have never been women" of significance, "never a character to raise into story" (185). It is with these statements that Williams seems most obtuse about his own complicity in a patriarchal treatment of women that his text condemns while simultaneously enacting. Indeed, it would seem that "Williams demands of the female a role that can only be fulfilled by the products of his own imagination, rather than actual women of historical record. . . . Though Williams declares the primacy of the female, his reigning women are all got out of Williams himself, a repetition of the founding myth of patriarchy – Eve got out of Adam's rib" (Conrad, *Refiguring America,* 133). This accusation points out a serious shortcoming in Williams's historical project, and I do not mean to refute its insight; however, I would like to stress that the text's relationship to this "founding myth" is complex and conflicted, and I have attempted to demonstrate a measure of Williams's attempt to criticize an ideology of mastery and domination through attention to the constructions of gender. Although his text does not treat any one woman fully, in its concern with the construct of masculinity as a potent force in our culture, it begins the process of dismantling that construct as it has defined the feminine. While rejecting many a male author's inscription of womanhood and recognizing the impact of cultural definitions of gender, Williams avoids depicting *at length* an actual woman in history who might exemplify the limitations of such definitions, although he mentions such women as Emily Dickinson and Gertrude Stein in this regard.

Whether this blind spot bespeaks an anxiety on Williams's part or a misogynist participation in the tradition of writing history that has neglected women's cultural contributions is difficult to gauge. Intentionality aside, the inclusion of women that does occur and how it occurs operates in a significantly disruptive manner. Textually, women appear fleetingly and often anonymously, but they are *everywhere* in the text, woven like resistant bits of steel wool into the fabric of patriarchy textualized by so many male figures and voices. Focusing primarily on male figures within the contours of a patriarchal culture, *In the American Grain* leaves women's experiences fragmented and submerged within the text, yet these very fragments threaten the unitary narrative of masculine history through exposing its ideological basis of gender hierarchy. Although his choice of words is regrettable, and his opinion flat wrong, Williams's assertion that women have not been significant in history also stands as an indictment of a society that has circumscribed their activities and written them out of history. Williams's historical method aims toward opening history and tradition beyond the limits of history's authorial voice, suggesting a process of revision that can rectify, to an extent, this erasure. In other words, the text employs conceptual tools to use in approaching history – even Williams's history – to retrieve a fuller picture of the past than the authoritative versions provide. Speaking of Aaron Burr, he emphasizes this process: "I say that what Burr stood for – and that this is typical of us – is lost sight of in the calumny that surrounds his name, through which the truth is not so easily to be discovered. Let us dig and we shall see what is turned up – and name it if we can" (196). In this way, tradition can (and must) "leave a vantage open" for demands counter to it (197).

As he digs into the bed of facts and fictions clustered around Aaron Burr, in "The Virtue of History," Williams measures his findings in terms of Burr's relationship to women. Though considered immoral by his contemporaries, he was "perhaps the only one of the time who saw women, in the flesh, as serious" (204). Living with all "the senses waking," which is "what a democracy must liberate" (195), Burr is depicted as worthy of Jacataqua's attention, for he is alert to the feminine "spirit":

> [Other men] were frivolous with women. The rest denied them, con-
> doned the female flesh, found them to be helpmates at the best and at
> the worst, horses, cattle, provincial accessories, useful workers to make
> coffee and doughnuts – and to be left to go crazy on the farms for five
> generations after – that's New England, or they'd hide the bull behind
> the barn, so that the women would not think it knew the cows were
> – Bah, feudal dolls gone wrong, that's Virginia.
>
> Women? necessary but not noble, not the highest, not deliciously a
> free thing, apart, *feminine,* a heaven. . . . Burr found the spirit living
> there, free and equal, independent, springing with life. (205)

The text associates the feminine with a state of sensory alertness that recalls earlier descriptions of both the maternal figure and the Indian, especially in the latter's capacity to derive a freedom from contact with the New World land. Significantly, the "spirit living there," in both the Indian and the feminine, enters and informs Burr's speech. His is a distinctly New World speech, an inclusive oratory intermingling multiple cultures that is characterized by "its immediacy, its sensual quality, a pure observation, its lack of irritation, its lack of pretense, its playful exaggeration, its repose, its sense of design, its openness, its gayety, its unconstraint. It frees, it creates relief" (206). In this understanding of speech that "frees" through its "*feminine* . . . spirit," Williams theorizes language and its structures as ideologically invested discourses shaping reality. Williams shared this recognition with Gertrude Stein, under-standing her experimental techniques as forms of cultural revolution that involve the deepest levels of social meaning. "For everything we know and do is tied up with words," he writes of Stein in 1935, "with the phrases words make, with the grammar which stultifies, the prose or poetical rhythms which bind us to our pet indolences and medievalisms" (*SE* 163). With his history, Williams, like the Stein his words describe, "is striking . . . at the basis of thought, at the mechanism with which we make our adjustments to things and to each other. This is the significance of the term culture and an indication of literature's relation thereto" (*SE* 165).

This idea of culture is tied to a notion of the "local," which returns us again to the "supplying female" of social and historical contexts. For Americans, the idea of culture has always been problematic, and for Williams the culture inherited from England and Europe lacks the "locality upon which originality is rested" (224). Such "plagiarists" as Longfellow and Bryant wrote from a "desire to have 'culture' for America by 'finding' it, full blown – somewhere," and their work has "NOTHING of the New World in it," replicating the Old World's ideology of colonization (224). In Edgar Allan Poe's approach to language, Williams detects the "local" and the "original," both of which he defines within a concept of culture tied to its etymological roots – to cultivate, "to work with a thing until it be rare" rather than to "build an unrelated copy upon it" (224). Old and imported forms, which "cover" New World qualities, represent a literary coercion analogous to the tyranny of Ponce de León or the regulatory sexism of the Puritans; therefore, it is "NOT culture to *oppress* a novel environment with the stale, if symmetrical, castoffs of another battle" (225). Instead, culture "is still the effect of cultivation," and Williams goes on to assert: "This is culture; in mastering them, to burst through the peculiarities of an environment" (224–5). His use of the word "master" might seem contradictory, as though espousing the very qualities of dominance and control that the text has critiqued and formally undercut; however, given his understanding of the "local" as "the sense of being attached with integrity to actual experience" (*SE* 118), an understanding informing the essay on Poe and all of *In the American Grain*, his use of the word suggests a mastery that is knowledge through contact – a coming to know the "peculiarities" of the environment, not the oppression of them. He suggests this knowledge when he speaks of the desire for "aesthetic satisfaction . . . [which] in America, can only be filled by knowledge, a poetic knowledge, of that ground" (213).

For Williams, Poe stands as the first writer who proclaims this New World ground and who recognizes a form of artistic mastery that involves contact, not coercion. Through Poe, Williams explicitly brings gender tensions into play in relationship to the male artist, the female ground of the local, and the feminine process of contact. The nineteenth-century writer is "the first to realize that the hard, sardonic, truculent mass of the New World . . . was, in fact, not a thing to paint over, to smear, to destroy – for it WOULD not be destroyed, it was too powerful, – it smiled!" (225). This image of resistance echoes the earlier image of the old woman, "her soul already half out of her with sorrow," who tricks Ponce de León into his futile quest for eternal youth (42). She is an image amalgamating Jacataqua, Emily Dickinson, the Salem witches, the Puritan women who deviantly weave ribbons into their bonnets – all are the voice of She, living "against the grain." In Williams's recreation of him as an enabling precursor, Poe enters this feminine voice as a "new de Soto," and "one is forced on the conception of the New World as a woman" who speaks the language Williams strives to hear (220). Although such comments partake of a familiar gender dualism, they also gesture toward a wavering of binary categories as Williams develops a deconstructive notion of language. The local, in a sense, is the deconstructive capacity of language that encourages a break (that all-important word for Williams) with habits of thought. Although Poe seems a strange choice to exemplify this idea of the local, it is highly significant that Williams reads him and, in effect, recreates him, through the language experiments of Gertrude Stein and in feminine terms of contact and disruption.[78]

As with the voice of She, the site of language provides a ground for the local and the original:

> Poe's work strikes by its scrupulous originality, *not* 'originality' in the bastard sense, but in its legitimate sense of solidity which goes back to the ground. . . . It is the New World, or to leave that for a better term, it is a *new locality* that is in Poe assertive; it is America, the first great burst through to expression of a re-awakened genius of *place*. (216)

However, what Poe "wanted was connected with no particular place; therefore it *must* be where he *was*" (220). His locality suggests to Williams a Steinian "articulation with existence" (*SE* 119) that reveals itself in the methods and forms of articulation:

> With Poe, words were not hung by usage with associations, the pleasing wraiths of former masteries, this is the sentimental trap-door to beginnings. With Poe words were figures. . . . Sometimes he used words so playfully his sentences seem to fly away from sense, the destructive! with the conserving abandon, foreshadowed, of a Gertrude Stein. The particles of language must be clear as sand. (221)

Williams's sense of "differing conceptions of language" in some ways resembles the "feminine text" described by Cixous and various feminist critics as subverting and challenging traditional texts and the patriarchal assumptions underlying them. Cixous writes: "A feminine text cannot fail to be more than subversive. It is volcanic; as it is written it brings about an upheaval of the old property crusts, carrier of masculine investments; there's no other way" ("The Laugh of the Medusa" 316); "Such is the strength of women that, sweeping away syntax, breaking that famous thread (just a tiny little thread, they say) which acts for men as a surrogate umbilical cord, assuring them – otherwise they couldn't come – that the old lady is always right behind them, watching them make phallus, women will go right up to the impossible" (315). Although I would like to resist a purely biological reading of the concept of the feminine text, Cixous's formulation suggests a socially contextualized notion of the feminine as an ideologically disruptive discourse, exposing conventional discursive forms as the "carrier[s] of masculine investments" (316). This subversive, "feminine" language works toward opening spaces for alternative ("original") understandings of culture, history, and literature.

This is a language that understands itself as language, a deconstructive capacity he learns from Stein and, I would argue, from other women modernists (see Chapter 4 for a discussion of women modernists and *Spring and All*). In a 1930 essay on Stein, through whom he reads Poe, Williams clarifies the revolutionary range of her experiments:

> Stein's theme is writing. But in such a way as to be writing envisioned as the first concern of the moment, dragging behind it a dead weight of logical burdens, among them a dead criticism which broken through might be a gap by which endless other enterprises of the understanding should issue – for refreshment.
>
> It is a revolution of some proportions that is contemplated, the exact nature of which may be no more than sketched here but whose basis is humanity in a relationship with literature hitherto little contemplated.
>
> And at the same time it is a general attack on the scholastic viewpoint, that medieval remnant with whose effects from generation to generation literature has been infested to its lasting detriment. It is a break-away from that paralyzing vulgarity of logic... (*SE* 115–16)

The relationship between a culture and its literature, "hitherto little contemplated," involves a complexly interwoven set of deeply ideological constructs that are sustained and validated by "grammatical, syntactical and prosodic grounds" (216); both Stein and Poe "clear the ground" and turn Williams's attention to the gaps in the tightly woven fabric of the dominant ideology. Opposed to the conventional boundaries of logic and representation (Poe criticizes Hawthorne's "lifelike copying of the New England melancholy"; 228), Poe's method moves against the grain of cultural and social conventions that effectively oppress the "peculiarities of an environment," or "the real, the thing itself." Poe, in his sentences that "fly away from sense," is "of [this]... very ground," the ground that "WOULD not be destroyed, it was too powerful, – it smiled" (225). To "let the real business of composition *show*" (230), Poe opts for a method that foregrounds and disrupts conventional modes of language, emphasizing process over mimetic product and illuminating the materiality of language. Language, understood as a system that speaks us through its discursive modes, offers a place for disruption of oppressive traditions and claims to absolute truths. In language, Williams locates a resistance to fixed absolutes: "Language is the key to the mind's escape from bondage to the past. There are no 'truths' that can be fixed in language. It is by the breakup of the language that the truth can be seen to exist and that it becomes operative again" (*EOK* 19). For Williams, this formal revolution draws from and empowers the New World ground, the resistant and disruptive feminine that "smiled."

In theorizing this different language, this different system of exchange, Williams creates a concept of the feminine that is both essentialized and cognizant of social structures. The conflated figure of the feminine and the maternal often operates to invert social conventions of value and, in the process, to demonstrate their basis in gender divisions. The New World ground that "smiled" recalls once again Cixous's depiction of the feminine text as a "laughing Medusa," a resistant alternative to the "opposition, hierarchizing exchange, the struggle for mastery which can end only in at least one death . . . [which] all . . . comes from a period in time governed by phallocentric values" (320). Such a figure is evoked within the final essay, "Abraham Lincoln," as an American "father" metaphorizes into a feminine and maternal presence. Placing himself within a maternal line of inheritance, Lincoln is quoted as claiming, "All I am or ever hope to be I owe to my angel mother" (234). Though suggesting the Victorian angel-in-the-house, Lincoln's initial statement is subverted by further associations of the maternal with perception and language. His inheritance is linked to speech as Lincoln repeats "day after day" an act of maternal contact. Borrowing a neighbor's baby, he paces with the child "sleeping inside his cape upon his shoulder to give him stability while thinking and composing his coming speeches" (234).

The feminine is further associated with artistic creation, as a process of simultaneous receptivity and command that operates within multiple intersections of loci. In describing the orchestra and its conductor, the gender terms syntactically blur:

> Mengelberg, a great broad hipped one, conducts an orchestra in the same vein. It is a woman. He babies them. He leans over and floods them with his insistences. It is a woman drawing to herself with insatiable passion the myriad points of sound. . . . It is the balm of command. (234)

As the woman draws "to herself" multiplicitous sounds, the typically passive connotation of woman-as-receptacle is transformed into an image of receptivity as an active form of engagement, of contact. Interestingly, it is often in the work of his women contemporaries that Williams detects this language of contact, learning from their example. In a 1931 essay on Marianne Moore, Williams describes the poet's imaginative process in similar terms of multiplicity:

> A course in mathematics would not be wasted on a poet, or a reader of poetry, if he remember no more from it than the geometric principle of the intersection of loci: from all angles lines converging and crossing establish points. He might carry it further and say in his imagination that apprehension perforates at places, through to understanding – as white is at the intersection of blue and green and yellow and red. It is this white light that is the background of all good work. . . . it is a quality present in much or even all that Miss Moore does. (*SE* 122)

The Lincoln essay presents this image of woman as the "intersection of loci," juxtaposed with yet another female image, an image resembling Lincoln in that it associates a cultural father, Socrates, with the feminine. Somewhat enigmatically, Williams writes, "Brancusi should make his statue – of wood – after the manner of his Socrates, with the big hole in the enormous mass of the head, save that this would be a woman –" (234). Although this image dangerously suggests the stereotype of woman without mind or intellect, it turns around on itself through the reference to Socrates. How can Socrates, the philosopher, be represented by an "enormous mass of the head" that contains a "big hole"? And what does this image have to do with Williams's understanding of the feminine? The image can be read as emphasizing a capacity for a non-abstract understanding that Williams sees as Socrates' feminine quality. In a more complex and subtextual sense, the image of nothingness does not carry negative connotations for Williams throughout his works. Nothingness is not a *lack* but a space within which the imagination moves and labors; out of nothingness, the creative process brings forth what is "LUMINOUS"; the imagination "breaks life between her fingers" in a process of regeneration and transformation. And, as *In the American Grain* demonstrates in its historical method and as experimental works like *Spring and All* emphasize formally, negative spaces – traditionally ignored or backgrounded – provide an alternative way of perceiving, an alternative way of measuring. The engagement with negative space, for Williams, serves as a way of moving from sensory perception to poetic expression. Writing to John C. Thirwell in 1955, he explains:

> The first thing you learn when you begin to learn anything about this earth is that you are eternally barred save for the report of your senses from knowing anything about it. Measures serves us as the key: *we can measure between objects;* therefore we know that they exist. Poetry began

> with measure, it began with the dance, whose divisions we have all but forgotten but are still known as measures. Measures they were and we still speak of their minuter elements as feet. (*SL* 331; my emphasis)[79]

"The in-between," the space of the feminine text for Cixous, is the space for a feminized imaginative process for Williams, and the image of empty space becomes the way we come to know the world, the way we connect ourselves with the positive or foregrounded spaces.[80]

Williams's treatment of Lincoln's assassination enacts this process. The murder itself, usually the focal point when the story of Lincoln's death is told, is never described, and what emerges instead – from between the spaces of the more minute details of the experience – is a highly feminized space. When Lincoln is shot, a private finds a "woman to caress him," and in Williams's rendering of this maternal image, the woman syntactically merges with Lincoln himself. The American Father eerily transforms into a female presence recalling, once again, the old Indian woman: The presence is "a woman to carress him, a woman in an old shawl – with a great bearded face and a towering black hat above it, to give unearthly reality" (234). What is killed – in Lincoln, in the Indians, in the land – is what is reborn, as the "destroyed thing" turns back "with a smile" to regenerate itself "with a woman, born somehow, aching over it, holding all fearfully together" (235). Regeneration is figured within matrilineage; a woman is born of the woman/Lincoln figure, and this birth signifies the end of "THAT period," the period of patriarchal history the text has described. This birth concludes the text in a closure that ends this narrative and at the same time resists closure by opening to visions of a feminized future; indeed, in "The Great Sex Spiral," Williams speculates that the world is moving into a feminine age. Embodying a transformational maternal power, this final image of woman recalls the central figure of "The Wanderer," whose ties to the earth generate her power and through whom, in various manifestations, Williams proclaims a new ground for a New World poetry.

# 3

## Denise Levertov

### *The Daughter's Voice*

> Well, I think Denise has a sense of metrical arrangement of lines which is not the conventional thing, but it has a unity. . . . I feel closer to her than to any of the modern poets. She is more alert – very much more alert to my feeling about words – As Flossie says, she is America's woman poet of the future.
>
> – William Carlos Williams[81]

To read the profuse writings of Denise Levertov is certainly to read within a Williams tradition; Levertov's critics and the poet herself have amply documented the influential presence Williams maintains in Levertov's lyrical affirmation of the ordinary, her adoption of an American idiom, and her understanding of form. Williams's enthusiasm for Levertov's work, as the opening quote suggests, grows in part from a recognition of a poetic heir who, in carrying on his own project, mirrors and affirms for the older poet his struggle to develop a distinctly American poetry. However, in an interesting moment of validation, Williams turns to Flossie for the authority to comment upon "America's woman poet," distinguishing both his wife and his literary daughter from a mainstream, male American poetry. This moment is loaded with an unresolved ambiguity, for on the one hand it can be seen as a subtle slighting of "women's poetry." On the other hand, in turning to Flossie's opinion, Williams suggests that this poetic daughter speaks vividly within a female continuum and that the closeness he feels to her arises in part from his efforts to locate himself and his poetry within a similar continuum.

What does this "continuum" mean? For both Williams and Levertov, the feminine and the maternal become important figures for alternative authority, which is at times cast in idealized terms – through mythologizing, essentializing, generalizing – but is also insistently developed through the material contexts of cultural activity. The feminine, as a quality of connection and contact, provides a reference point for advancing ethical and political concerns, a reference point for beginning to remap the realm of authority within a world dominated by men. Although in instances this category is used naively and reductively by each poet, we need to move beyond a quick dismissal of these efforts and consider the ongoing interaction of the feminine – as a figure, a cluster of associations, a mode of action – and social critique.

Literary history chooses most often to align Levertov with Williams on the basis of stylistic similarities and a shared (and often misunderstood) commitment to immediacy, which even recently is read by some critics as a poetry concerned with surface and not with ideas.[82] In arguing against this notion by considering a range of Levertov's poetry as it develops in relationship to Williams's work, this chapter traces the concern for each poet with ideological constructions and their relationship to language; moreover, the ensuing discussion of these two poets seeks to discern ways in which this concern reflects back upon the construction of their positions within literary history – as poetic father and daughter. However, rather than consider Levertov primarily within the example of Williams, this chapter considers Williams within the example of Levertov, exploring most particularly her readings and rereadings of this predecessor within the context of the social critique grounding her poetic project. Examining the process through which the cultural daughter reads the father, considering the conflicts involved and the selective attention enacted, I hope to suggest the need in constructing versions of literary history to consider the interaction between the poet-subject and the structures she inherits. What does she steal, revise, continue, or reject? What complications, for father and daughter, arise from a shared resistance to cultural definitions of authority that extend into filial structures of descent, involving a turn to the maternal that qualifies the work of both poets?

Through much of their poetry, Williams and Levertov seek an alternative mode of authority that sustains connectedness. Charles Olson, Levertov's Black Mountain contemporary, both praised and criticized the authority of Williams's epic, *Paterson,* on just this basis. In the "Mayan Letters" (1951), Olson compares Pound's "ego–system" to Williams's "emotional system": "Ez's epic solves problem by his ego: his single emotion breaks down to his equals or inferiors . . . Bill HAS an emotional system which is capable of extensions and comprehensions the ego-system . . . is not" (*Selected Writings* 81–2). Olson's comments point to an essential link between Levertov and Williams in distinguishing a form of authority that "cuts through this orderly universe with feelings that connect us" to other people and to the earth itself (Jones, "On Authority," 121). At the same time, Levertov's deflection of Williams's "emotional system" through a woman's voice suggests both the impact of gender upon her own particular reading of Williams's poetic authority and her developmental transformation of its "extensions and comprehensions" into an active politics of connection.

As a "daughter of her culture," Levertov experiences dominant modes of literary, religious, and sociopolitical authority within the position she inherits. While interrogating the modes that would silence her, she seeks ways to empower the daughter's position: to revise filial ties to cultural fathers and to proclaim a maternal line. Within this framework, I will consider Levertov's interpretation of Williams by suggesting links between her readings of his works and her evocations of the maternal. Joining Williams in his affirmation of contact and connection, Levertov extends his poetic concerns explicitly into the public realm. I will examine Levertov's political poetry as it develops toward an authority of compassion and community; merging public and private experience, this authority derives from a contact between self and other. Finally, I will turn to Levertov's negotiations with the paternal traditions of literature and religion, again paying attention to the daughter's continual retrieval of the maternal and her rewriting of the paternal as efforts to redefine authority.

### A Maternal Mode of Authority: "The voice / a wave rising"

Levertov's entry into the American poetic tradition involved both the act of choosing, on her part, and the circumstance of being chosen by a group of male poets who aided her acceptance as a publishing writer in the United States. A British expatriate to America in the late 1940s and 1950s, Levertov turned away from the neoromantic style of her first book, *The Double Image* (1946), which developed out of a specifically British tradition. She chose instead to align her poetic voice and sensibility with the most insistently American of the modernists, Williams, and with the projectivist poets following in his lead, particularly Robert Creeley, Robert Duncan, and Charles Olson. Her early association with these Black Mountain poets and with such men as Kenneth Rexroth, Lawrence Ferlinghetti, and Jonathan Williams – who all promoted her work prior to and just after her arrival in America – benefitted Levertov both practically and aesthetically. She has claimed that her personal relationships with Creeley and Duncan, and particularly her deep and conflicted friendship with the latter, have been crucial to the development of her poetry; additionally, she considered them the two most important American poets in the early sixties, and she looked to Charles Olson's formulations of projective verse as a basis for her own statements on organic form. Williams, of course, would always remain a central presence in her poetry, and the two corresponded and visited regularly in the last years of his life. Grieving the loss of the modernist voices important to her – Pound's silence, Williams's strokes, H.D.'s seeming reticence – "September 1961" responds to a letter from Williams following a severe stroke in June of that year, in which he wrote, "I can't describe to you what has been happening to me" (in Mariani, *William Carlos Williams: A New World Naked*, 764). In the poem, which quotes his letter, she writes that "the old great ones / leave us alone on the road," yet "we have the words in our pockets," for they have "given / the language into our hands" (*Poems 1960–1967* 81–2). Yet her claim to a place in this tradition alongside Olson, Creeley, Duncan, Ginsberg, and others was largely an association with men, determined by men, and, as she later would realize, sustained by certain male prerogatives. Levertov, as the female exception to the rule, gradually came to realize the masculine assumptions supporting the authority of the poets she learned from, and her poetry begins more explicitly to claim a different shape of authority.

Levertov speaks of this recognition in a 1973 introduction to a group of poems by women, which she selected for the literary journal *Trellis*. Her introductory comments reflect upon the conventional authority of male poets, an authority justifying the typical dismissal of female poets. Referring to her own experience, she writes:

> What I used not to realize was that I had, without my noticing or understanding what it meant, been chosen, tacitly, by some group of male poets, or by individuals, as the exception that proved the rule – the rule that poetry was a masculine prerogative and that women were, by and large, either Muses or servants. ("Poems by Women" 98)

"The rule" of "masculine prerogative" describes a cultural framework Levertov inherits from both British and American literary traditions, and within this framework her position is conflicted. As woman, she is the "exception" and gains credibility as a poet, while her poetry is praised most often within the auspicious category of "woman's poetry," as Williams's comment to Flossie demonstrates. The relationship of the woman poet to a male-dominated tradition has been fruitfully explored by feminist criticism, and such critics as Suzanne Juhasz and Alicia Ostriker early on suggested the "double bind" and self-division experienced by the woman poet. Split between the conflicting cultural expectations for women and for poets, these critics have observed, women writers often feel opposing binds to each set of expectations.[83] Sandra Gilbert and Susan Gubar, in their three-volume study of twentieth-century women writers *No Man's Land*, have advanced the theory of the "anxiety of authorship," based upon Freudian categories of female development and stipulating that women writers experience conflict over their allegiance to a male or female tradition.

Rather than assuming, however, that Levertov's relationship with a male tradition and powerful male contemporaries involves a conflict with a female "authentic self," implicit in the paradigms of Freudian stages of female selfhood or the double bind, I find it helpful to rely upon notions of subjectivity suggested by such critics as Diana Fuss, Teresa De Lauretis, or Mary Gentile. These "recent feminist reconceptualizations of the subject as a site of multiple and heterogeneous differences" posit the " 'I' as a complicated [rather than unitary or binary] field of multiple subjectivities and competing identities" (Fuss, *Essentially Speaking*, 33). This notion of subject-positions recognizes the vast intersections of gender, race, class, religion, and so on that interact within the category of "woman"; additionally, and most pertinent to this discussion of Levertov, the subject as a "site of differences," continually in the state of construction, allows for choice on the part of the social subject in moving among subject-positions. By choice, I do not refer to a humanist concept of an autonomous subject somehow outside of these positions, but suggest a reflective and critical capability arising from the negotiation of several subject-positions at once. This claim to choice deviates from poststructuralist formulations of the "fragmented, or intermittent, identity of a subject constructed in division by language alone, an 'I' continuously prefigured and preempted in an unchangeable symbolic order" (De Lauretis, *Feminist Studies*, 9). Instead of the nihilation of self, these feminist reconceptualizations of a posthumanist subject focus upon the continual shifting or construction of subjectivity through the interaction of multiple subject-positions that are historically and culturally specific. Hence, Levertov, in occupying simultaneously the subject-positions of poet, wife, mother, immigrant, and Jew (to mention a few possibilities), enacts particular choices in negotiating this "site of differences." To think of Levertov as a reader of various cultural texts, including the American poetry by men she encounters, is to think of "the reading process as a negotiation amongst discursive subject-positions which the reader, as a social subject, may or may not choose to fill" (Fuss 34). A "double reading" process results, in which Levertov brings "(old) subject-positions to the text at the same time [that] the actual process of reading constructs (new) subject-positions" for her (Fuss 33).

The first section of this chapter will focus upon the construction of various subject-positions located within Levertov's work and arising in relationship to cultural frameworks of masculine authority, necessarily beginning with the construction of a female self and voice in the poetry of the late 1950s and early 1960s. The convergence of historical circumstances – Levertov's arrival in a postwar America retreating into the cult of the private and the domestic, her entry into motherhood, her social activism, her exposure to Williams's poetry – will provide a context for considering the communal female self the poetry proposes and the woman/poet conflict it relates. This construction of a female self becomes a reference point for advancing an ethical revision of authority within a communal and collective sensibility that refutes the authority of individualism. Levertov develops the maternal as a mode of such authority, emphasizing a nonpossessive form of discovery and a fluid, interactive form of contact between self and other. Finally, in considering Levertov as a reading subject, I link her self-proclaimed debt to Williams with her enabling construction of a female voice and of a maternal mode of authority. Claiming to reread and reexplore Williams's work, Levertov engages in this process as a context for advancing a revisionary critique of authority.

Perceived by others and herself as a poetic heir to Williams, Levertov is positioned clearly as a daughter figure. Although such a position may bring prestige, the cultural daughter also inherits a tradition in which her particular position has been muted, objectified, and made invisible. Within a male-dominated literary tradition and a masculine model of the poet, the daughter faces structures of value, language, and convention that affect her poetic production and reception in ways related to gender. However, she need not merely receive and reproduce structures that privilege masculine dominance and encourage feminine subservience but can engage in a "complex appropriation, revision, and development of existing cultural frameworks," as Rita Felski describes feminist practices of writing (*Beyond Feminist Aesthetics* 59). Rejecting both the "inadequate voluntarism" of the poststructural self (in which "individuals remain unconscious of and unable to reflect upon the discursive structures through which they are positioned as subjects"; 52–3), Felski adopts a structuration theory based upon the "dialectical interrelation between subject and structure" (58):[84]

> The conceptualization of the duality of structure, applied to the specific interests of a feminist analysis of language and culture, thus allows for a more differentiated understanding of *structure as not only constraining but enabling,* a precondition for the possibility of meaningful choices . . . As Gidden argues, "structure thus is not to be conceptualised as a barrier to action, but as essentially involved in its production." (60; my emphasis)

Felski's comments help us to define Levertov's poetic relationship to Williams in its dynamic of daughter and father, without condemning her to an unaware reliance upon a masculine model or the father's law. Williams's example, as read by Levertov, enables her to an important degree in making "meaningful choices" as both poet and person. Significant to this point is Williams's own critique of the masculine structure of literary tradition and of culture in general, combined with his ambivalence concerning his position within such a system.

During the years of her American tutelage, Levertov first began reading Williams upon Robert Creeley's recommendation. Describing her first encounter with his poetry, she elucidates her attraction to Williams's ideas and work:

> Between the publication of *The Double Image* and my next book, *Here and Now* (1957), eleven years elapsed. I had married in 1947 and come to the U.S. in 1948. My son was born in 1949. The early '50s were for me transitional and not very productive of poems; but I was reading a great deal and taking in at each breath the air of American life. William Carlos Williams became the most powerful influence on my poetry, and at that time, seeking as I was to engage my capacities as a poet with the crude substance of dailiness, as I had notably *not* done in the 1940s, I took as influence from Williams nothing of the profound mythic element we find (especially, but not only) in *Paterson*, but rather the sharp eye for the material world and the keen ear for the vernacular which characterize his earlier and shorter poems. (*PIW* 68)

In a broad sense, Williams's "dictum that the universal is found only in the local" encouraged Levertov to speak out of her "local" experience as a woman, stressing much earlier than subsequent feminist poets the image and voice of the woman poet as an active maker (*PIW* 41). While a poet such as Adrienne Rich confesses to a fear, which continued until the early 1960s, of doing "without the authorities" and speaking as a woman, a glance at Levertov's poetry of the fifties reveals numerous poems celebrating a feminine and often maternal creative power (Rich, *On Lies*, 45). These poems were written while Levertov experienced "the most powerful influence" on her poetry in the works of William Carlos Williams (*PIW* 68) and also, significantly, in the "transitional period" that included the birth of her son. In relationship to this concurrence of influences, Levertov isolates Williams's *earlier* poetry – work obsessively linking a notion of the feminine to the poetic operation and exploring the construction of masculine authority – as central to her formative apprenticeship to American poetry. Preferring the earlier poems, she admits that the later masterwork, *Paterson*, failed to engage her own developing sensibility as a poet. It is clear, from this and numerous other comments, that she admires the epic poem, claiming that Williams's "profound longing for, and striving toward, a language and a form with which life might be quickened, renewed, grasped, gave [him] the majestic image of *Paterson*" (*PIW* 83). Yet the "majestic" epic does not enable her own early efforts in the extensive way that Williams's poems of the daily underlie her "transitional" stage from British neoromantic to American poet, or from a gender-neutral speaker to a self-consciously female voice.

Writing (and read) among male poets working from the modernist sources of Williams and Pound, Levertov was influenced tremendously through her early association with the Black Mountain poets; at the same time, her poems from this period repeatedly insist upon the woman as maker.[85] Though she shares with Olson, Creeley, and Duncan concepts of poetic form developed out of modernism, her gendered response to her predecessors and contemporaries includes a need to claim her womanliness as a necessary condition of her artistic voice and vision. Although the 1960s would see a tremendous blossoming of women's poetry in America, as Levertov is writing in the 1950s models for a woman-centered poetry are few. Moreover, models of womanhood in postwar America increasingly stressed the ideal of submission and self-sacrifice within the private sphere (although in reality larger numbers of women than ever were working), partially to help reestablish the male position of authority in American families and culture after the relative absence of men (especially from the workplace) World War II had necessitated.

To enter America and motherhood in this decade meant entering an ideological period, supported by government, media, labor, the psychological profession, and other powerful regulators of gender roles, encouraging self-denial and repression for American women and instilling fears of deviance from a proclaimed female norm. During these years, however, Levertov began combining her roles as mother and wife with social activism, participating in antinuclear demonstrations in New York in the 1950s. Coming from a family "that had a strong social conscience," Levertov's political engagement in the 1950s involved both an inherited social sensibility and a degree of detachment as an immigrant and a new mother:

> The Ban the Bomb demonstrations in New York started in the Fifties and I had begun to participate in them. I did not participate in the Civil Rights movement. I come from a family that had a strong social conscience, but I was still pretty new in America, and my son was little, and I had not yet reached an understanding of the relationship of public and personal lives in a radical way, not until later in the Sixties. I certainly admired what people were doing with voter registration and all that, but I felt detached from it. I was not assimilated into America enough to feel impelled to do that kind of thing myself. (Levertov in Smith, "An Interview with Denise Levertov," 596)

The Vietnamese War catapulted Levertov out of detachment and into the center of activism. By 1963 and 1964, Levertov and her American husband, Mitchell Goodman, had become actively involved in the antiwar movement, and in 1967 became organizing members of RESIST, a group supporting draft resisters.[86] The development of Levertov's social and political engagement in America, from a follower in the 1950s to an organizer in the 1960s, offers an important framework for considering the representations of women in the poetry of the earlier decade. The construction of a female identity and voice that challenges the cultural norms of the 1950s and the poetic conventions of literary tradition becomes in this poetry a way of working toward understanding the relationship of public and private, a foundation for political involvement and for the overtly political verse of the 1960s. In asserting a female self, these earlier poems need to be considered as part of a process of cultural transformation located initially within the site of female subjectivity and expanding or connecting outward. Through these poems, we can begin to investigate in Levertov's work "the status and value of subjectivity as a source of cognition and a reference point for political and cultural activity," as Felski describes theorizing the "function of subjectivity in relation to oppositional practices" (*Beyond Feminist Aesthetics* 51, 52). These poems chart the first necessary stage of a feminist politics in claiming a subjectivity and go on to recognize that such a claim is not alone sufficient for accomplishing cultural change but is integrally involved in the process. Invoking a female self who makes and creates, transvaluing the personal and the domestic, these poems incipiently involve a feminist art practice that Janet Wolff speaks of as repositioning the reader "in relation to the hitherto unquestioned images and ideologies of contemporary culture" and suggest the "clear, if complex, relationship between woman as cultural producer and woman as 'sign' " (*Feminine Sentences* 95, 113).

Numerous early poems link vision and acts of making to the domestic, maternal, and marginal roles culturally encouraged for women. Surrounded by masculine models, Levertov expresses an awareness of the need for a self-making as woman poet that mediates and shapes the influences she absorbs and the structures she operates within. "A Woman," written in the early 1950s, describes a woman's eyes that "are looking, looking for a door / to open in a wall where / there's no door, none unless she make it" (*CEP* 13). Her 1957 volume, *Here and Now*, adopts a clearly female-identified voice, drawing upon traditional forms of women's making. In "Something to Wear," for instance, the poet imagines a waiting attitude of discovery to be "like a woman knitting," hoping her creation will "make something from the / skein unwinding, unwinding" (*CEP* 36). Anticipating Adrienne Rich's celebration of a "new kind of poetry forming" in the piecing together of scraps from a woman's life (Rich, *Dream of a Common Language* 76), the poem "Mrs. Cobweb" tells of a mad woman who makes "a collage of torn leaves," "a glass moon-reflector," and creates from the materials of her own life:

"whatever she could touch, she made" (*CEP* 43). The "old / bandanna'd brutal dignified / woman" who opens the volume in "The Gypsy's Window" descends from Williams's "The Wanderer" and similarly embodies the connective force between the ordinary and the poetic: Through such figures, the "courage / of natural rhetoric tosses to dusty / Hudson St. the chance of poetry" (*CEP* 29).

Although these figures from the early poetry convey a feminine vision and creativity, "The Goddess," published in 1960, mythologizes the woman poet's confrontation with her own feminine power. Figured as a goddess, this power remains external to the woman speaker who passes her time in "Lie Castle" (*CEP* 110). Having only paid "lipservice" to the idea of the goddess, the woman experiences a violent awakening when the goddess finally "came upon me where I lay in Lie Castle":

> Flung me across the room, and
> room after room (hitting the walls, re-
> bounding—to the last
> sticky wall—wrenching away from it
> pulled hair out!)
> till I lay
> outside the outer walls!
>
> There in cold air
> lying still where her hand had thrown me,
> I tasted the mud that splattered my lips:
> the seeds of a forest were in it,
> asleep and growing! I tasted
> her power!
>                                   (*CEP* 110–11)

To speak without tasting this power is to speak in someone else's voice, and the final lines of the poem carry much resonance for the woman poet within a male tradition: Without the goddess, "nothing / speaks in its own tongue, but returns / lie for lie!" Alicia Ostriker, in discussing the poem, points out that to "identify an active, aggressive woman with Truth is to defy a very long tradition that identifies strong females with deception and virtuous females, including muses, with gentle inactivity" (*Stealing the Language* 220). Levertov's gesture of defiance toward one tradition draws strength through another tradition of feminist thought, represented by the person and works of Jane Harrison, the early twentieth-century classicist, and continued through various muse-goddess poems that span her works. Sandra Gilbert calls attention to a piece in the same volume, "Girlhood of Jane Harrison," which "suggests one of the forces that shaped her thought on this matter, for in her [Harrison's] monumental *Prolegomena to the Study of*

*Greek Religion* (1903) the British feminist-classicist had sought to document the dominance of the Great Mother in ancient Greek culture" ("Revolutionary Love" 344–5).[87] Gilbert enumerates other muse-goddess poems that develop Harrison's theories of "the goddess who empowers not only the flowering grounds on which the earthwoman lives but also the strange songs of the waterwoman,"[88] including "The Well," "Song for Ishtar," and "To the Muse" as examples from her first few books. These poems also reflect Williams's defiance of the muse tradition in his representation of a female creative power as an active intertwining of speech, body, and mind in "The Wanderer," a poem Levertov greatly values. For Williams, such defiance involves a critique of masculine conventions and authority concurrent with a complicity in the tradition of masculine inscription and appropriation of the feminine. As "daughter," it means something quite different for Levertov to claim an idealized mythos of feminine power as a process of self-construction in opposition to the masculine authority Williams both represents and holds up to question. It is particularly interesting to see these assertions of female identity within the poetry most clearly written under the tutelage of Williams and his example.

"Song for Ishtar," which opens the Williams-influenced *O Taste and See* (1964) with a clear assertion of feminine power, inverts poetic conventions of language and inspiration in restating conceptions of the woman writer:

> The moon is a sow
> and grunts in my throat
> Her great shining shines through me
> so the mud of my hollow gleams
> and breaks in silver bubbles
>
> She is a sow
> and I a pig and a poet
> When she opens her white
> lips to devour me I bite back
> and laughter rocks the moon
>
> In the black of desire
> we rock and grunt, grunt and
> shine
>                    (*Poems 1960–1967* 75)

Evoking "images for what is divine and mundane, spiritual and animal, delicate and violent in female sexuality and female art," the poem proclaims a woman-authored poetry that encompasses all of these oppositions (Ostriker, *Stealing the Language,* 220). Levertov rejects conventional notions of the "poetess" precisely by applying a Williams-like celebration of an earthy eroticism to the woman poet and her muse, who demonstrates a clear connection to his chthonic muse; at the same time that this connection suggests a way in which Williams's example enables his daughter, it also shows Levertov's ability to make that inheritance her own by transforming Williams's muse into a muse specifically for women. This transformation also reflects back upon Williams's empowerment by his unconventional muse. "Song for Ishtar" imagines a same-sex empowerment that involves not loss but valuable gain for the woman as poet; "The Wanderer" imagines an empowerment that calls for a diminishment of masculine identity. The old woman serves not to increase the poet's male potency; instead, the initiate poet must accept the inheritance of the maternal godhead, his poetic voice replicating hers. This muse demands creative energies of reciprocity and connection – the reciprocal "grunt and shine" of Levertov's female poet and goddess. As a man, Williams cannot *be* his muse; however, under the influence of a muse of connection, his surrender of a masculine claim to creativity allows him to transfigure his responsiveness to the world around him. Moreover, while Williams's adaptation of a female muse as an active figure creates a degree of tension and anxiety over his position as male poet, Levertov's claim to a female power registers the consequences of such transgressive behavior on the part of a woman. A conflicting sense of roles, a conflicting array of subject-positions, bespeak the anxiety familiar to readers of women-authored poetries; the poet-self, based upon a masculine norm, suffers a dualistic antagonism with the culturally prescribed woman-self.

As early as 1957, the folklorish piece "The Earthwoman and the Waterwoman" contrasts the domestic, strong earthwoman with the waterwoman, who "sings gay songs in a sad voice" and "goes dancing . . . in dragonfly dresses and blue shoes" (*CEP* 31, 32). A later manifestation of the waterwoman appears in "In Mind" as a "turbulent moon-ridden girl" and as an old woman, "both / dressed in opals and rags," both knowing "strange songs." These women who sing are "not kind," unlike the poem's other female figure: the woman "of innocence" who "is kind and very clean" but who has "no imagination" (*Poems 1960–1967,* 143). A later poem, "The Woman," contextualizes the problem within gender relations, for the "bridegroom" desires "the one in homespun" and wearies of "the one in crazy feathers," a weariness the woman shares under the stress of the dualism:

> Alas,
> they are not two but one,
>
> pierce the flesh of one, the other
> halfway across the world, will shriek,

her blood will run. Can you endure
life with two brides, bridegroom?
(*FOD* 53)

This dualism includes the patriarchal opposition of the erotic and the
maternal. The waterwoman's alienation from the earthwoman denotes
a split from the maternal, and hence, in the poet's mind, from an earthbound contact. The earthwoman "has oaktree arms" and "tends her cakes
of good grain" that keep her children vigorous; the waterwoman's
"moonshine children," in contrast, "are spindle thin" (*CEP* 31). What
we can read into this poem's image of division is not only the female
poet's "double bind," but the suppression of models of the maternal
within a poetic tradition and, moreover, the repression of the female
body within Western history and society.

Cultural norms dividing the erotic from the maternal perpetuate such
suppression; in response, Levertov's poems of erotic desire work to oppose this division and consequently to help redefine the woman-authored
lyric.[89] Speaking as woman, mother, and poet in such pieces as "Our
Bodies," "Song Praising the Hair of Man's Body," and "Remembering,"
as well as in tributes to other women, Levertov joins the erotic and the
maternal. The 1949 poem, "Who He Was," enfolds the erotic within the
maternal as the pregnant speaker experiences both identification with and
alienation from the child within her body. To her husband she marvels
at the life to come from their passion, "only because / the strange flower
of your thighs / bloomed in my body. From our joy / begins a stranger's
ride" (*CEP* 11). The flesh that knows the erotic and the maternal, Levertov's poems tell us, is the impetus for her song:

When I am a woman—O, when I am
a woman,
my wells of salt brim and brim
poems force the lock of my throat.
("Cancion," *FOD* 49)

In constructing a female self, emphasis on the body problematizes a
tradition that has circumscribed for women their flesh. In "Fantasie-
stück," from the 1978 volume *Life in the Forest,* the daughter's body is
figured as a source of creative power that illuminates the repressive (for
women) authority of tradition and offers an alternative to it. The daughter's voice speaks from an intriguing perspective as Caliban's half-sister
– intriguing partially because her father is Prospero, the archetypal figure
of poetry and power in *The Tempest* who, within literary legend, is
Shakespeare's projection of himself. Levertov creates a mythic "bastard
daughter," born of the union of Prospero and the witch Sycorax, the
absent (because dead) mother of the play. As Ariel was imprisoned within

a tree, the sister is imprisoned within her body, a cell from which Prospero's power can never liberate her. The poem, addressed to Ariel, begins with a question:

> 'My delicate Ariel'—
> can you imagine,
> Caliban had a sister?
> Not ugly, brutish, wracked with malice,
> but nevertheless
> earthbound half-sibling to him,
> and, as you once were,
> prisoned within a tree—
> but that tree being
> no cloven pine but the sturdy wood
> her body seemed to her
>
> (*LIF* 79)

This female Caliban, earthbound daughter of an entire poetic tradition embodied in Prospero, must turn to her own body for a song that the legitimate daughter Miranda could not sing:

> Spirit whose feet touch earth
> only as spirit moves them,
> imagine
>     this rootbound woman,
> Prospero's bastard daughter,
> his untold secret, hidden from Miranda's
> gentle wonder.
>     Her intelligent eyes
> watch you, her mind
> can match your own, she loves
> your grace of intellect.
> But she knows
> what weight of body is, knows her flesh
> (her cells, her magic cell)
> mutters its own dark songs.
>
> (*LIF* 79)

Appropriating an entire privileged, male tradition in undermining its assumptions of paternal lineage and male creativity, the poem enacts a politics of the body similar to that encouraged by Janet Wolff:

> There is every reason [despite negative cultural definitions of woman's bodies] . . . to propose the body as a privileged site of political intervention, precisely because it is the site of repression and possession. The body has been systematically repressed and marginalized in western culture, with specific practices, ideologies, and discourses controlling

and defining the female body. What is repressed, though, may threaten
to erupt and challenge the established order. (*Feminine Sentences* 122)

For both of Prospero's daughters, Miranda and the nameless offspring
of Sycorax, the body is systematically repressed and regulated: Miranda,
who through her father's (and, by extension, all patriarchal systems of
authority) control over her body becomes an object of exchange to be
kept pure and valuable; Caliban's half-sibling, who inherits the banish-
ment of her mother and carries it within her own body. This sister's
earthbound status suggests the restrictive association traditionally and
derogatorily made between woman and nature, but the poem proceeds
to invert this devalued link. This "rootbound woman" encompasses both
the "weight of body" and "intelligent eyes"; these binarisms are not
exclusive and their coalescence is manifested in the "dark songs" her
"flesh . . . mutters," for her songs arise from body and intellect, from a
"magic cell."

Significantly, the song metonymically recalls the absent mother. Caliban's sister, who like her brother suffers a form of exile inherited from
their mother, implicitly looks to this earthbound side of her lineage to
empower her song. In its comment upon a male tradition, the poem is
reminiscent of Williams's "Letter to an Australian Editor." Like Williams, Levertov here notes that "no mothers" seem necessary within a
patriarchal tradition; in fact, they are erased. Whereas Williams alludes
to the "supplying female" as a source for disrupting and revising this
tradition, Levertov mythically proposes the female body as the "privileged site of political intervention" (Wolff 122) that calls attention to the
systems of inscription, metonymically represented by Prospero and en-
compassing literary tradition, familial structure, and historical imperialism (to name a few), that repress and define the feminine and the female
body.

Reading this poem as an allegory of lineage, it is tempting to think of
Williams as a Caliban figure, resisting a tradition in which the mother
is invisible and registering a continual search for her enabling presence
in his poetry. In fact, Levertov associates Williams with Caliban and
Ariel through a cluster of poems. In "Freeing the Dust," she writes of
the poet's task: "Let Ariel learn / a blessing for Caliban / and Caliban
drink from the lotus" (*FOD* 113); in the later "Williams: An Essay," she
uses identical imagery to praise the poet: "He loved / the lotus cup" and
"the wily mud" (*CIB* 60). These images again recur in "The Dragon-
Fly Mother," furthering the connotation of a maternal link between
Williams and Levertov within their reliance upon an earthbound creativity. Both Levertov and Williams find themselves writing under the

rule of Prospero, muttering dark songs of the flesh that are enabled by a muse of feminine power, an absent but reclaimable mother.

For Levertov, this reclaiming involves transgression, as in "The Dragon-Fly Mother." This poem reworks the earlier "Earthwoman and Waterwoman" by making the nourishing mother the inspiring muse: She brings food to her daughter while also enabling her to write. But to listen, the daughter must break with duty and heed the maternal messages: "we told one another dreams, / I stayed home breaking my promise" to speak at a rally (*CIB* 14). The external promise is replaced with

> . . . a tryst with myself,
> a long promise that can be fulfilled
> only poem by poem,
> broken over and over.
>                        (15)

The daughter of the dragon-fly mother is kin to Caliban's sister and Ariel at once: "I too, / a creature, grow among reeds, / in mud, in air." The mother is "a messenger" who moves the daughter through "winds / of passage," and the final stanza connects the broken promise to a necessary act of passage:

> There is a summer
> in the sleep
> of broken promises, fertile dreams,
> acts of passage, hovering
> journeys over the fathomless waters.
>                        (15)

The spirit Ariel and the earthbound Caliban join here, as do the earthwoman and waterwoman, within the maternal creatrix. Moreover, Levertov's rendering of the dragon-fly mother's speech relates the maternal to a notion of language as listening:

> When she tells
> her stories she listens; when she listens
> she tells you the story you utter.
>                        (14)

Within a maternal configuration, Levertov imagines a language she has always desired in her poetry. In "Craving," a poem published seven years earlier, Levertov describes this language as reactive and organic:

> A language
> of leaves underfoot.
> Leaves on the tree, trembling

in speech. Poplars
tremble and speak
if you draw near them.
          (*FOD* 45)

Although elicited by one's movement toward it, at the same time this
language demands a listening to its "trembling" speech. The act of listening becomes a process of speech, and speech a process of listening:
"when she listens / she tells you the story you utter." This reciprocity
between speech and listening contributes to an ethics of connection that
underlies Levertov's sense of poetry's relationship to the world.

   Like other contemporary women poets, Levertov has imagined maternal myths that empower the daughters to speak the poems that unlock
their throats. The maternal figure of "The Soothsayers" submits that
"my daughters" will know the "weight" of their "fruit" only when the
maternal line is claimed as a source of vision and speech (*CIB* 4). Addressing her daughters, she is the old woman, "the weaver / of fictions,
tapestries," the maker of texts. Like a tree, she "blossoms year after year,
/ random, euphoric," both rooted and nurturing (4). Speaking, it seems,
to a tradition of women writers discovering their maternal lineage as a
source of knowledge and legitimacy, she predicts:

     My daughters
     have yet to bear
     their fruit,
     they have not imagined
     the weight of it.
               (*CIB* 4)

Like Williams, Levertov looks to the maternal as a constellation linking
contact, vision, and language, thereby providing a ground for imaginative power.

   Although this construction is often mythologized, both poets often
evoke their biological mothers as sources for poetic creativity. Levertov's
Welsh mother, Beatrice Spooner-Jones Levertov, receives continual tribute in her daughter's poetry. In a 1977 memoir, she writes of her mother,
"it was she who . . . 'taught me to look, / to name the flowers when I
was still close to the ground, my face level with theirs' " (*LUC* 243).
Claiming, "I could never have been a poet without that vision she im-
parted," Levertov's short memoir reveals the basic premise she gained
under her mother's tutelage; learning to "look" and to "name," she
perceives a reciprocity between vision and language that she later describes as "an attention, at once to the organic relationships of experienced
phenomena and to the latent harmony and counterpoint of language itself
as it is identified with those phenomena" (*PIW* 54). This attention,

when accompanied by a relinquishment of possessive or defining forms of control, leads the eye to discover the world. In "The Garden Wall," an open but nondirected vision reveals a world unseen by a more controlled or commanding gaze. The garden wall behind the flowers goes largely "unnoticed—"

> but I discovered
> the colors in the wall that woke
> when spray from the hose
> played on its pocks and warts—
>           (*Poems 1960–1967* 132)

This discovery "can't be looked for, only / as the eye wanders, / found" (132). This lesson is learned from her mother in "Earliest Spring" (*LIF* 44–5). Remembering her first awareness of spring's flowering landscape, Levertov invests this moment of transition from baby to child with the clarifying vision her mother teaches. Moving through the garden, the mother cries out at the sight of flowers and "stoops to show me precise / bright green check-marks" on their leaves, and "she brings my gaze" to details of color and texture (*LIF* 44, 45). This process of moving with the mother "step by step, / slow, down the path" metaphorically recapitulates the poet's insistence upon form as a revelation of content, in which the path of the poetic line registers revelation and, as with the garden walk, "[e]ach pause / brings us to bells or flames" (45).

A similar sense of discovery informs "The Instant," a poem from Levertov's 1958 volume, *Overland to the Islands*. Mother and daughter leave the house early to collect mushrooms, and the poem moves carefully through the physical details of the morning:

> Mushrooms firm, cold;
>     tussocks of dark grass, gleam of webs,
> turf soft and cropped. Quiet and early. And no valley,
> no hills: clouds about our knees, tendrils
> of cloud in our hair. Wet scrags
> of wool caught in barbed wire, gorse
> looming, without scent.
>                          (*CEP* 66)

This scene is framed by two instances of the mother's speech, and the poem generates itself through the maternal voice. The opening two lines initiate the journey, a domestic and ordinary task: " 'We'll go out before breakfast, and get / some mushrooms,' says my mother" (65). The scene then unfolds in earthy, sensuous textures, establishing a connective richness between mother, daughter, and earth that leads to the mother's second utterance, a response to her sudden vision of Mt. Snowdon:

        then ah! suddenly
the lifting of it, the mist rolls
quickly away, and far, far—

        'Look!' she grips me, 'It is
                Eryi!
                        It's Snowdon, fifty
        miles away!'—the voice
a wave rising to Eryi,
falling.

                            (66)

The scene's obvious allusion to Wordsworth's Mt. Snowdon excursion in *The Prelude* alerts us to the formative nature of this moment in the poet's life but also redefines that moment within feminine and maternal terms. The mother's spontaneous utterance of the Welsh name, Eryi, displaces Wordworth's English Snowdon; at the same time, the Romantic sublime's essential concern with mastery within the creative act (what Keats called the Egotistical Sublime) here transforms into the open and attentive immanence[90] that Levertov's poetry strives to reenact. The sublime spectacle of "Snowdon, home / of eagles, resting place of / Merlin, core of Wales" undergoes a feminine transformation in the final lines, as "Light / graces the mountainhead": "mountainhead" carries the soundtrace of "maidenhead" in a vision suffused with light and grace, in contrast with Wordsworth's dark sublime. Wordsworth's apprehension of the sublime is wrought with agonized claims to the "majestic intellect" and to the creative act as a coercive, combative effort, and he feels he must look upon Mt. Snowdon with the commanding gaze of the artist. Levertov and her mother experience a visionary moment like that articulated in "The Garden Wall," one which provokes speech and a "conversation" with the world. The mother's speech is a "voice / a wave rising to Eryi." The "instant" of vision and speech, occurring between mother and daughter, replaces the myth of the Romantic sublime. Situating poetic vision and speech within a feminine sphere, the poem reflectively alters traditional aesthetic assumptions that exclude or objectify female experience. This expression of a maternal lineage coincides, significantly, with Levertov's move away from a British tradition. Additionally, "The Instant" is important to consider as a poem written by a woman joining an American tradition stemming from Williams and Pound.

    In this light, however, it is essential to consider Levertov's reading of this tradition, and particularly her self-proclaimed rereading of Williams in the late 1960s and early 1970s. The "revelation of Williams" Levertov experienced in the 1940s led the younger poet to trust the "spirit of the here-and-now" that continues to provide the basis for her poetry (*PIW*

159, 80). However, as she will insist, Williams has been all too often misread in this vein, and Levertov's comments upon his work demonstrate a more complex attempt to read the here-and-now as an ethical and moral possibility. She looks to Williams and his love of "the long stem of connection" (*CIB* 60) to validate the integration of the poetic and the ethical within an inherently political realm defined as the "reciprocity between poem and action" (*PIW* 116). Her translation of Williams's famous coda, "No ideas but in things," relates the connective power of the here-and-now to an ethical world-view:

> "No ideas but in things," said William Carlos Williams. This does not mean "no ideas." It means that "language [and here I quote Wordsworth] is not the dress but the incarnation of thoughts." "No ideas but in things," means, essentially, "Only connect." And it is therefore not only a craft-statement, not only an aesthetic statement (though it is these things also, and importantly), but a moral statement. *Only connect. No ideas but in things.* The words reverberate through the poet's life, through *my* life, and I hope through your lives, joining with other knowledge in the mind, that place that is not a gray room full of little boxes. . . . (*PIW* 116; Levertov's brackets)

A commitment to the ethics of connection prompted Levertov's antiwar activism, and as her poetry developed in overtly political directions, she turned back to Williams to examine his drive "to connect" in its broader social implications. A 1972 essay, written during the height of Levertov's political activism, explores Williams's political sensibility as a "theme of defiance" revealed through a struggle of "love and compassion," a resistance to oppressive authority, and (as Levertov's choice of examples demonstrates, though she makes no overt connection) manifested through feminine evocations in his work.

Discussing Williams's political poetry, the essay "Williams and the Duende" rhetorically relates the elder poet's revisioning of authority to the maternal presence in his works. Transfiguring the authority of willed dominance into the authority of compassion, Williams's political, historical, and social sensibility "rails against stupidity and gracelessness and man's inhumanity to man" (*PIW* 257).[91] Many of his poems "in differing degrees of overtness, are of political import; so pervasive was the historical sense in him that there is virtually nothing he wrote that does not – especially within the context of his work as a whole – have social implications" (259). To further her point, Levertov selects "In Chains," a poem Williams first published in 1939 and included in the 1944 volume *The Wedge*. It considers possible responses to oppression, while warning of the ease with which the victim can become the victimizer:

> When blackguards and murderers
> under cover of their offices

accuse the world of those villainies
which they themselves invent to
torture it—we have no choice
but to bend to their designs,
buck them or be trampled while
our thoughts gnaw, snap and bite
within us helplessly—unless
we learn from that to avoid
being as they are, how love
will rise out of its ashes if
we water it, tie up the slender
stem and keep the image of its
lively flower chiseled upon our minds.
                    (*CP2* 65)

Admiring the poem, Levertov nevertheless worries that it fails to adequately "develop a definition of what 'bucking them' – resistance – might
be" (260). The poem, she feels, does not clearly envision the form resistance might take, leaving the reader with an "incomplete" directive.
However, she claims a "theme of defiance" or resistance runs throughout
his work, and she turns to an example, "A History of Love," to help in
clarifying Williams's notion of resistance:

> And would you gather turds
> for your grandmother's garden?
> Out with you then, dustpan and broom;
> she has seen the horse passing!
>
> Out you go, bold again
> as you promise always to be.
> Stick your tongue out at the neighbors
> that her flowers might grow.
>                     (*PIW* 260)[92]

Necessitated by tending the grandmother's garden, resistance takes form
within the ordinary and the banal, Williams's regenerative source for the
imagination. Calling upon this poem's matrilineal image of growth,
Levertov can then reread the "incomplete" notion of resistance that troubles her in "In Chains," seeing within the context of other poems "that
resistance *without* keeping the image of love's 'lively flower chiseled on
our minds' is self-defeating, because a struggle uninformed by love and
compassion makes of the rebel a mirror image of the executioner" (260).

   To reveal and lay claim to a politically and socially conscious Williams,
Levertov insists upon a corrective reexploration that looks to his earliest
works. Defending his work against the then customary accusations that
it was "lacking in intellectual force," an opinion encouraged by "an-
thologists who try to reduce him to a sort of witless imagist miniaturist,"

Levertov complains that "a recent tendency [in reading his works]...
has been a *reverse* chronology that does not even lead all the way back
to the beginnings but leaves readers ignorant of all the earlier work except
for the small selection Randall Jarrell edited" (261, 263–4). Particularly,
she marvels, readers are too often ignorant of "The Wanderer," "the
early poem in which so many clues to the understanding of *Paterson* are
embedded (which is in fact one of those early works in which the whole
subsequent development of an artist is shadowed forth prophetically)"
(263). Arguing that a fuller reading of Williams reveals "the high degree
of his relevance to contemporary concerns," Levertov defies the canonized version of his accomplishment: "How different Williams, *re-
explored,* is from the stereotype in which he has been cursorily presented
to many minds" (264; my emphasis). Levertov's argument comes to rest,
significantly, upon the image of the old woman in "The Wanderer": "—
the face of a Muse who is both wild gull and godhead, 'marvelous old
woman' and 'horrible old woman,' mighty, crafty, feared and beloved"
(266).

The old woman's power of speech and poetic vision, her role as creatrix, implicitly underlies Levertov's admiration of Williams's 1948 poem,
"The Sound of Waves" (*CPV2*, 114–15), in which the poet repeats the
question motivating his "new wandering" in the earlier poem: "... the
poet-voyager asks himself... How to proceed...? Williams moves by
a process of elimination toward an image in which the mist, rain, sea-
spume of language is blown against jutting rock, and takes its hard shape"
(265). This image connotes Pound's imagism and his directive to "be
concrete," so often applied simplistically to Williams's insistence on contact. In the lines of the poem that Levertov quotes, the poet moves

> Past that, past that image:
> . . . . . . . . .
> above the waves and
>
> the sound of waves, a
> voice      speaking!
>                    (*PIW* 265)

The final line registers a voice of silence and speech, of absence and
presence, which Levertov reads as an almost mystical otherness. To her
mind, the poem

> suggests a twentieth-century poetics: not an "applied metrics," but a
> poetics inseparable from the rest of human experience and – not because
> of its content but by its very nature, its form, its sensuous forms that
> are its very essence – expresses and defines the nature of humanness;

and in so doing arrives at the edge of the world, where all is unknown,
undefined, the abyss of the gods. From there at last, beyond the human,
a voice    speaks.   (*PIW* 265)

The placement of Williams's poem within the essay juxtaposes this
"voice    speaking," with the maternal figure from "The Wanderer"
that concludes Levertov's discussion of Williams's political and social
concern. She sees Williams writing under the aegis of this "godhead,"
and her essay rhetorically relates this maternal presence to matters of
language and authority.

As this sense of a maternal relationship continues to evolve in Levertov's own work, the idea of community or connectedness remains
central. This authority of community develops in opposition to a notion
of the self and of social power based within an ideology of individualism.
In an essay that explores Levertov's sense of community, Harry Marten
criticizes what he sees (in other poets) as the primacy of individualism
in the American poetic tradition. He equates the myth of individualism
with isolation from others and an impersonal distance from community
that has led, he feels, either to a poetry of excessive privacy or to objective
denials of self through strategies of irony and form. Thinking in gendered
terms, we can also see this tradition of individualism developing from a
privileged construct of masculine subjectivity that values autonomy and
separation from others. Although his analysis does not engage the category of gender, Marten calls for a poetry that "must find its authority
in the ways both feeling and thought, form and statement conjoin. It
must be an art of community" ("Exploring the Human Community"
53). He finds this art in the work of Levertov and her poet-activist friend,
Muriel Rukeyser, two women whose concepts of community involve a
fundamental collapse of the traditional separation between private and
public discourse.[93] Marten offers a valuable discussion of the "authority
of community" sustaining the poetry of both writers and deeply motivating the political dimension of their lives and work. He quotes Rukeyser's definition of action, developing her insistence that "art is action
... [because] it prepares us for thought": Deriving her idea from Karen
Horney, Rukeyser suggests that action is defined "in terms of relationship, so that the individual is seen not only as an individual, but as a
person moving toward other persons, or a person moving away from
other persons, or a person moving against other persons" (in Marten
53).[94]

Although Marten's reading of these poets remains silent on the issue
of gender (nowhere does he ponder the fact of a woman's signature as
related to this authority of community), his analysis nonetheless provides
material for developing valuable connections between ideas of community, gender, and authority. Rukeyser, writing in 1949 and drawing

from her readings of Horney, whose early feminist rereading of Freud challenged his a historical neutrality and rejected the concept of the male as norm, makes comments within the context of a psychological theory foregrounding a female development of self. As such, Rukeyser's definition of action derives from a woman-centered epistemology, while also articulating (and very likely influencing) the grounds for Levertov's continual concern with social action.

The authority of community that Marten perceives in Levertov's work involves a concern with process, which she clarifies as "the *process* of thinking/feeling, feeling/thinking rather than focusing more exclusively on its *results.*" Examining Levertov's use of the linebreak as a way to "make manifest . . . the interplay or counterpoint of process and completion,"[95] Marten observes that she "works logical syntax against the pauses of perception that determine line ends . . . [transforming] detached observation into active participation in the selecting and seeing process" (58). Process, then, becomes a mode connecting self and non-self, a communal action.

Interestingly, although Marten does not acknowledge a maternal link to the authority of community as it appears in Levertov's work, his choice of poems to discuss moves in the direction of such acknowledgment. He selects "A Daughter (I)" and "A Daughter (II)" from *Life in the Forest* (1978), describing them as the "intense and poignant, deeply personal evocations of her mother's death" and using them to demonstrate the "message and technique of discovery . . . the process by which self and non-self meet in mutual opposition and definition, each becoming other" (60). Tending her mother as she nears death, the daughter becomes mother and "mother is child, helpless" (*LIF* 27). The fluid interaction between daughter and mother makes Levertov's authority of community possible (though Marten does not assert this generalization); subsequently, the central loss of the maternal connection, the maternal body, prompts numerous "daughter" poems in this volume and future ones. The two "A Daughter" poems join "Death in Mexico," "The 90th Year," "A Visit," "Death Psalm: O Lord of Mysteries," and "A Soul-Cake" in a series of meditations on her mother's life and death, to which the daughter has acted as witness. The poems resound with a longing for maternal touch, arms "once / strong enough to hold her and rock her" and a voice that "used to chant / a ritual song that did magic" (27). The meditations culminate with "Earliest Spring," a record of the poet's first memory of spring in the garden, learning from her mother an attentive vision. Indeed, in "The 90th Year," Levertov claims (with a line she quotes in her later memoir), "It was she / who taught me to look" and marvels at "how much gazing / her life has paid tribute to the world's body" (24). Vision, as taught and practiced by the mother, is a gaze of tribute; in poems about her mother and about vision, Levertov directly relates this gaze to an empathy with and embrace of otherness.

In this sense, vision offers a moral and political alternative to the gaze of objectification she struggles against in her society and in herself. "The Long Way Round," spoken from the perspective of a white American, addresses the fear of otherness that Levertov recognizes she has shared with other members of her race. The goal of assimilation – the myth of America's melting pot – grows from this fear:

> 'The solution,' they said to my friend,
> 'lies in eventual total'—they said (or 'final'?),
>    'assimilation. Miscegeny. No more trouble—'
> > > *Disappear*, they said
> > > > (*LIF* 53)

Although conceding complicity with this view, Levertov underscores the awakening she experienced through her antiwar activism, during which she perceived the war effort as part of an ideology of assimilation justifying oppression. Only after combatting this ideology's manifestation in Vietnam does she begin to understand its local reality. She realizes that she

> had to lean in yearning towards
> the far-away daughters and sons of
> Vietnamese struggle
> before I could learn,
>     begin to learn,
> by Imagination's slow ferment,
> what it is to awaken
> each day Black in white America
> > (53)

Though imagination allows an empathic connection, she also comes to realize that she can never know "in the flesh" what it is like to wake each day to one's body as

> something that others
> hated,
>     hunted,
>        haunted by its otherness,
> something they wanted to see disappear.
> > (54)

The final stanza envisions the world as a giant pool that contains all races, but grants whites the "right of way" over the other swimmers. Only touch disrupts this design's well-enforced rules and boundaries; sometimes, "scared and put off our stroke / but righting ourselves with a gasp," she writes, "sometimes we touch / an Other" and discover the "breathing and gasping body," the humanness revealed through touch (55).

### A Discourse of Compassion: "Revolution in the poem"

As Levertov's poetry of the sixties engages in political issues, the maternal authority of compassion coalesces with a poetics of connection derived from Williams's example and ascends through layers of literary, religious, and social authority. In her political poetry, Levertov begins to engage Williams's example on a more insistently ethical level through exploring alternative forms of authority underlying his concern with contact. Emphasizing continually that the personal is political and expanding her use of the lyric to include public utterance, Levertov looks toward moments within literary tradition to validate her attempt to fuse the lyrical and the polemical. In so doing, she questions the nature of the public voice, altering it by acting upon her claim that the personal is political; Levertov's realignment of the lyric voice within the public sphere demonstrates an intersection of literary revision and feminist ideology by refusing to view the political as a set of "external pressures" and recognizing instead the workings of power on the most daily and intimate levels of interaction. For a woman to assume a public voice that is responsible to her experience as a woman exerts pressure upon conventions of public utterance and necessarily changes the nature of a private/public dichotomy of speech. The hostility directed toward Levertov's body of activist verse rarely considers the difficulty with which a woman assumes a public voice, when she has no models other than men, and the way in which she must restructure those models to accommodate her voice rather than fitting her voice to them. Although a long tradition of women's political poetry in America extends at least back to the colonial poet Mercy Warren, this tradition has been suppressed; moreover, female models available from earlier and contemporary poets have generally been devalued. We can approach Levertov's overtly political works as attempts to authorize a public voice of empathy and connection that draws upon the daily as a legitimate source of human activity and conceives of the imagination as a potential site of contact. As such, Levertov's work joins the feminist effort to interrogate models of authority that naturalize hierarchy and dominance while also following in the tradition of Williams's revisionary texts, such as *In the American Grain*.

Levertov sees her political poetry as fusing engagement with lyricism, summarizing her viewpoint in a 1985 interview:

> There is no reason why a poetry of political and social engagement
> can't be as good as any other poetry. It very often isn't, and that applies

to some of my own, too. But the hope of writing poems which were both politically engaged and have the qualities of lyricism I found very challenging and very exciting. I would like to write poems of such a character that people wouldn't be able to say, this is a political poem, and this is a lyric poem. (Smith, "An Interview," 597–8)

In articulating this possibility, Levertov echoes a stance that had sustained her for over a decade.[96] Striving for an "osmosis of the personal and the public, of assertion and song," in the 1960s and 1970s her work explored the possibility of a lyric poetry in which the "didactic would be lyrical, the lyrical would be didactic" (*LUC* 128). Significantly, Levertov's comments on the possibility of an American poetry of political and social engagement often involve questions of poetic tradition, demonstrating the high degree of self-consciousness with which she viewed a relationship between her own poetry and the tradition out of which she chose to write. Looking to sources like the poetry of Pablo Neruda, she would claim that it is "harder for American poets, or any English-speaking poets, to write engaged poetry than it is for Hispanic poets, for the simple reason that there isn't an accepted tradition" (Smith, "An Interview," 599).

In the 1975 essay "On the Edge of Darkness: What Is Political Poetry?" (*LUC*), Levertov tries to discern an "acceptable tradition" of Anglo-American lyric poetry of social engagement. This requires that she first isolate reasons for the standard division of the two impulses within the literary categories of the lyric and the epic. She takes issue with the Romantic notion of the lyric as a private form that excludes the public, while criticizing the modernist elevation of the epic as the proper didactic form. Disagreeing with Pound's definition of the epic as "a poem containing history," she argues that "the presence of history – or of politics, as we call our immediate social environment when it is critically examined" – neither makes a poem an epic nor remains outside of other poetic modes (*LUC* 115–16). Tracing the elevation of the lyric mode in the nineteenth century, "because it was the most *personal* mode," Levertov condemns the egotism of the Romantic period that intensified the isolation of poet (and poetry) from social concern by "seeing the artist as endowed with a special sort of temperament... which made him at all times supersensitive" (116). The lyric can retain its characteristic intimacy, Levertov argues, but still be charged with historical consciousness, and she urges a twentieth-century lyric form that "does not isolate the personal from the social" (121). In such a poetry, the lyric's sensuous and emotive power, rooted in "song, magic, and the high craft... makes itself felt as exhilarating beauty even when the content voices rage or utters a grim warning" (126). In another essay, she claims that Williams's "few classifiably political poems... are lyrical and polemic" and that "all of his work is imbued with a social concern" (*LUC* 130). She turns to his words to express the lyric form that she envisions for a modern poetry responsible to the urgent need for cultural and social change. She quotes Williams's assertions:

> Everything else is secondary, but for the artist *that,* which has made the greatest art one and permanent, that continual reassertion of structure, is first . . . The altered structure of the inevitable revolution must be *in* the poem, in it. Made of it. It must shine in the structural body of it . . . Then, indeed, propaganda can be thoroughly welcomed . . . for by that it has been transmuted into the materials of art. It has no life unless to live or die judged by an artist's standards. But if, by imposing . . . a depleted, restrictive and unrealized form, the propagandist thinks he can make what he has to say by merely filling in that wooden structure with some ideas he wants to put over – he turns up not only as no artist but a weak fool.[97] (*LUC* 127; Levertov's ellipses)

Revolution found its roots for Williams in language. His insistence upon a poetry derived from a distinctively American idiom was in large part a desire to break open the privileged forms of power embedded within linguistic conventions. In his late essay, "The American Idiom," he wrote that "the English tongue was a tough customer with roots bedded in a tradition of far-reaching power. Every nursery rhyme gave it a firmer grip on the tradition and there were always those interested in keeping their firm hold upon it" (*IWCW* 101). Speaking in a similar vein, Levertov focuses on the relationship between poetic and political challenges to power: "I believe our survival demands revolution, both cultural and political. If we are to survive the disasters that threaten, and survive our own struggle to *make it new* – a struggle I believe we have no choice but to commit ourselves to – we need tremendous transfusions of imaginative energy" (*PIW* 99). The imaginative energy Levertov calls upon is an imagination of connection – what Driscoll calls the "empathic sensibility" that marks all of her writing and that undergoes a "blossoming and maturation" in her political writings ("A Sense of Unremitting Emergency" 292). I would like to examine the maternal model of empathy and connection evident in Levertov's earliest work as it validates the imagination of revolution sustaining her polemical works, and then to consider the intersection of this model with Williams's investment of poetic authority within a maternal construct.

When Levertov speaks, using Pound's phrase, of "making it new," she specifically calls upon Williams's understanding of newness as a process of rediscovery and adaptation that reveals "the neglected worlds that lie around us" through "the focus of that energetic, compassionate, questioning spirit that infused even the most fragmentary of Williams's poems" (*PIW* 90). In a 1970 defense of Williams's poetics, she describes his concept of invention and discovery, ideas this study discusses in regard to *In the American Grain:*

> [In his] recognition of the rhythmic structure of the American language . . . what he was after was origins, springs of vitality: the rediscovery, wherever it might turn up (in language or incident), of that power of the imagination which first conceived and grasped *newness* in a new world, though the realization was ever and again nipped in the bud, blighted, covered over with old habits and strangling fears. Read him – the short early and later poems, and *Paterson,* and the longer poems of the great final flowering, from *The Desert Music* on; and the prose: *In the American Grain* and essays like "The American Background," as well as the specifically "literary" essays such as those on Pound, Sandburg, or Stein, and the unclassifiable pieces such as "The Simplicity of Disorder." It is all there, said many ways, but clear and profound. Williams emphasizes the necessity of the poet to deal with specifics, to locate himself in history – but never at the expense of the imagination. (*PIW* 91)

Levertov then goes on to quote Williams from "The American Background," speaking of the first settlers who arrive in America, "at a place whose pressing reality demanded . . . great powers of adaptability, a complete reconstruction of their most cultural make-up, to accord with the new conditions" (Williams in *PIW* 91). The imagination, interacting with the specifics of history, ideally generates a cultural reconstruction that responds to "new conditions" rather than excluding or suppressing them – so that "newness" demands responsiveness and adaptability, an imaginative energy of reciprocity that stands in contrast to the mastery fueling the "discovery" of the New World. Levertov defines this concept of newness as central to Williams's modernist project: "It is the failure, over and over, to make that adaptation – the timid clinging to forms created out of other circumstances – that he deplores, grieves over; the rare leap of imagination into the newly necessary, the necessary new, that he rejoices in" (*PIW* 91–2). Levertov's reading of Williams's modernism locates his formal experiments firmly within a context of cultural remaking, allowing her to regard him as a poet of political and social vision, a clear predecessor for her own political poetry. It would be helpful now to consider Levertov's poetry against the pervasive backdrop of Williams's explorations of and negotiations with forms of cultural authority – a project that her own ongoing interpretations of his writing demands. Levertov follows Williams in a tradition of cultural revision that questions the very basis of our national mythos and its relationship to language; her questioning, like his, reveals the impact of feminist thought at heightened moments within feminism's history. Each poet's critique of American society delves into the roots of myth and history nurturing an identity continually regenerated through violence, to paraphrase Williams's words. Through their revisionary content, these critiques seek to dismantle a body of ideas sustaining authority as separation and oppression and, in turn, to rediscover "new" worlds of contact and inclusion.

"Another Journey," published in *With Eyes at the Back of Our Heads* (1960), signals a revisionary awareness that links Levertov backward to Williams (especially his historical writings) and forward to such cultural feminists as Adrienne Rich (for example in "When We Dead Awaken"). The poem expresses a resistance to "a world composed, closed to us" and calls for an awakening to the "brutal dream of history" through reconstructing the idea of history – a history that is inclusive and immediate in each individual, private life:

> Not history, but our own histories,
> a brutal dream drenched with our lives,
> intemperate, open, illusory,
>
> to which we wake, sweating to make
> substance of it, grip it, turn
> its face to us, unwilling . . .
>
> (*CEP* 95)

Levertov shares this approach to history with Charles Olson, and both poets draw upon Williams's example.[98] In an important poem that for many critics signals the inception of her political voice, Levertov incorporates Olson's definition of "social action, for the poet." She begins "Three Meditations," included in the 1961 *Jacob's Ladder*, with an epigraph taken from Olson's *Maximus Poems*:

> the only object is
> a man, carved
> out of himself, so wrought he
> fills his given space, makes
> traceries sufficient to
> others' needs
>    (here is
> social action, for the poet,
> anyway, his
> politics, his
> news)
>       (*Poems 1960–1967* 31)

Olson's insistence upon self-making appeals to Levertov, and the integral relationship between filling one's own space and connecting with others remains central to her concept of "social action." Two interesting observations arise from this point of conjunction between these two descendants of Williams: On the one hand, this model of the poet speaks of "a man," "his politics," "his needs" – a conventional masculinization of the poet that Levertov herself employs in prose and poetry through the 1960s and 1970s, but one that Olson rather unrelentingly incorporates within his poetics as a phallic potency. However, at the same time that Levertov's poetry undertakes the tasks of social action, she is writing explicit critiques of the denigration of women. Investigating the cultural position of women, she simultaneously establishes a public voice for herself from this position.[99] Her activist poetry interweaves with poems calling attention to forms of cultural misogyny; the politics supporting one merges within the politics of the other. Secondly, and not unrelated to this voice of feminine experience, Levertov focuses more emphatically upon one aspect of Olson's equation than the other; for Levertov, the "traceries . . . to others' needs" assume a primary importance or focus throughout her development, while for Olson, containment (filling one's given space) becomes the primary act.[100] Each poet values the inseparable nature of these two processes, but each enters the arena of "social action" through a different door.[101]

"Three Meditations" provides a suitable point to begin considering how Levertov's understanding of the poet's "social action" progressively focuses upon the "traceries . . . to other's needs." Olson's presence is clear in the poem, not merely in the epigraph, but in the particular phrases that underscore the poetic and philosophic juncture between the two poets: "Stand fast in thy place"; "Live / in thy fingertips"; "sharpen / thy wits to know power and be / humble" (*Poems 1960–1967* 31).[102] These phrases reiterate Olson's insistence upon containment. The second meditation acts as a midpoint in the process between filling one's space and responding to others. The meditation moves to a point of subjectivity (the "I") that then exfoliates into multiple "traceries" of I and other:

> Who was it yelled, cracking
> the glass of delight?
> Who sent the child
> sobbing to bed, and woke it
> later to comfort it?
> I, I, I, I.
> I multitude, I tyrant,
> I angel, I you, you
> world . . .
>
> (32)

About this section, Kerry Driscoll observes that Levertov bridges "the gap between self and other" by projecting "her identity progressively outward until she encompasses the entire world," a Whitmanian gesture "with one crucial difference: whereas Whitman identifies primarily with the downtrodden and oppressed . . . Levertov is able to place herself in the antithetical positions of oppressor and oppressed" ("A Sense of Unremitting Emergency" 300). More like Williams than Whitman, Levertov's identification with both oppressed and oppressor registers the same danger she reads in his poem "In Chains" – that it is not enough to overthrow the oppressor if the oppressed takes on that position once gaining power; instead, new models of authority must be constructed that do not replicate the hierarchical dualisms the tyrant's power holds in place. In Levertov's political poetry, as in many of Williams's works, there is a struggle to remain clearsighted on this issue, and a tension is produced between the critique of authority and the recognition (or lack thereof) of one's own complicity with forms of authority seemingly condemned.

This struggle plays itself out in Levertov's works, underlying the political poetry of the mid-1960s and early 1970s, in which she calls for cultural change and ends by projecting those demands back upon herself, realizing the self-revision that must take place. In this way, Levertov finally collapses the distinction between lyric and didactic, personal and political – by subjecting herself to the political and didactic criteria that she had directed outward, by making the poet a part of the material conditions of the political system that needs to be changed. She is enabled in this move by an increasingly careful and absorbing attention directed along the "traceries . . . to others' needs" and a recognition that in "filling one's space" one can still never fully ostracize the "devil" that ends "Three Meditations." In the final lines, she returns to Olson's image of containment as the path for the poet:

> to be
> what he is
> being his virtue
>
> filling his whole space
> so no devil
> may enter.
>                (32)

By the time Levertov puts together the revisionary volume *Relearning the Alphabet,* in 1969, and the antiwar volume *To Stay Alive,* in 1971, she repeatedly confronts the "devil" in the external world – in its mutable forms of militarism, racism, sexism – and slowly begins to recognize that in "filling one's whole space" one cannot help but incur the inner devil. The poet never occupies a place of separation from the world nor embodies a self innocent of its systems of power, and Levertov's confrontation with her own complicity in the corruption she fights signals an important point in her work's engagement with the world. Between "Three Meditations" and her poetry of the 1970s, Levertov tries to un-ravel what is meant by one's "whole space": what constitutes this space and this self? How does one exist within it, change it, understand it? Rachel Blau DuPlessis, discussing Levertov's poetry of critique, com-ments that "within lyric poetry, [she] enact[s] a personal awakening to political and social life, and . . . situate[s her] consciousness and its for-mation at a specific historical moment" ("Critique of Consciousness" 199). In relationship to these questions, socially realized "traceries" be-come keys for Levertov, for the traceries must be traveled in coming to know the "space" – an interfacing of self and other that becomes her imagination's task.

In "Origins of a Poem" (1968), Levertov discusses the poem as a place of communion and the act of writing the poem as intrinsically "an action *toward others*" (*PIW* 49). Levertov extends Olson's definition of social action in this essay into a vision of an authority of compassion and connection. She refers back to Olson's words, placing emphasis upon the social action of connection:

> Olson is saying, as Heidegger is saying, that it is *by* being what he is capable of being, *by* living his life so that his identity is "carved," is "wrought," *by* filling his given space, that a man, and in particular a poet as a representative of an activity peculiarly human, *does* make "traceries sufficient to others' needs" (which is, in the most profound sense, a "social" or "political" action). (*PIW* 51–2)

Here, the moment of connection *is* the political, and the self-carving a necessary component of this moment, whereas, for Olson, the nuance is slightly different as the connective moment seems the by-product of self-containment.[103] Levertov clarifies her own emphasis by further de-fining this moment as the imagination's purpose. The "clue to what must make the poet's humanity *humane*" is:

> *Reverence thyself.* . . [which is] the recognition of oneself as *life that wants to live* among other *forms of life that want to live*. This recognition is indissoluble, reciprocal, and dual. There can be no self-respect of others, no love and reverence for others without love and reverence for oneself; and no recognition of others is possible without the imagination. The imagination of what it is to *be* those other forms of life that want to live is the only way to recognition; and it is that imaginative recognition that brings compassion to birth. Man's capacity for evil, then, is less a positive capacity, for all its horrendous activity, than a failure to develop man's most human function, the imagination, to its fullness, and con-sequently a failure to develop compassion. (*PIW* 52–3)

One exercises this compassion, or reverence for life, through "Atten-tion," a "Reverence for the 'other forms of life that want to live' "

(54). Such attention makes possible an active connection to others and is the "ground for poetic activity." Though Levertov speaks customarily in more transcendent terms than Williams, this sense of the imagination as compassion echoes his preoccupation with contact and squarely situates it, as he does in *In the American Grain*, in the historical and the social.

Levertov began writing overtly political poetry as a "natural process of becoming more politically involved" in the peace movement of the 1960s and of writing out of her "daily experience" (Levertov in Smith, "An Interview," 596). Connecting the personal and the political, Levertov's political poetry, like Williams's historical writing, confronts the processes by which history is recorded, stored, and transmitted, questioning what is left out or written over, and at what point the private becomes separable from the public. This challenge to the authority of historical narratives and selectivity coincides with the efforts of post-modern feminisms, which recognize that "to represent the past in language and in narrative is to construct the past" and that this construction is related to "inextricable links between the personal and the political" (Hutcheon, *The Politics of Postmodernism*, 166). The notebook form Levertov employs in *The Sorrow Dance, Relearning the Alphabet,* and *To Stay Alive* denaturalizes history through conflating the personal and the political; this strategy insists upon personal memory as a form of resistance to a public history indifferent to the private experiences Levertov chooses to record and remember. These make up the daily and individual modes of political being or historical consciousness that lead her to consider personal and national responsibilities at once. In the overtly activist poems, and particularly in the notebook sections, the idea of self is inseparable from material and historical circumstances, and the self's recording of these circumstances admits or allows personal distortions in forsaking the idea of an objective history. Levertov's use of the notebook form as a conflation of the private and public joins with "a very feminist awareness of the value of experience and the importance of its representation in the form of 'life-writing' – however difficult or falsifying that process might turn out to be. It may be the case that we can 'no longer tell exactly what we have experienced,' " but we recognize that an attempt must be made (Hutcheon 167). Levertov's approach to history exemplifies an intersection between feminist and postmodernist challenges to cultural authority that Linda Hutcheon describes as part of what

> feminisms have brought to postmodernism, sometimes to reinforce already existing concerns, sometimes to unmask cultural forms in need

of "de-toxification." I am thinking not only of an increased awareness of gender differences, but of issues like the complexity of the representation of experience; the paradox of the inevitable distortions of recording history and yet the pressing drive to record nevertheless; and the unavoidable politics of the representation of both the past and the present. (167)

Levertov's desire to eliminate the boundaries between the lyrical and the didactic leads her to envision a poetry compelled by an inclusive historical consciousness. Her poetry inverts the language of authority traditionally associated with public speech; instead, she imagines a discourse of compassion and connection that can be relearned in language.

Levertov works toward articulating this discourse in her 1971 introduction to *To Stay Alive,* a volume that reprints poems found earlier in *Relearning the Alphabet* and *The Sorrow Dance,* along with new compositions. The book is a deliberate attempt to arrange her socially engaged poetry from the previous decade into an aesthetic whole and to emphasize the artist's work as an ongoing and interrelated process. In contrast to a Romantic or high modernist regard for the poem as self-contained artifact, Levertov asks that the artist's experience in history and society be considered inseparable from the work produced within a specific historical moment. Countering a narrow academic approach to poetry, Levertov defends the artist's work as one of ongoing composition and recomposition:

> I have heard professors of literature snicker with embarrassment because a poet quoted himself: they thought it immodest, narcissistic. Their attitude, a common one, reveals a failure to understand that though the artist as craftsman is engaged in making discrete and autonomous works . . . yet at the same time, more unconsciously, as these attempts accumulate over the years, the artist as explorer in language of the experiences of his or her life is, willy-nilly, weaving a fabric, building a whole in which each discrete work is a part that functions in some way in relation to all the others. (*Poems 1968–1972* 105)

Here, Levertov sets up terms crucial to reading her poetry as an ongoing process, an interaction of poet, language, and culture, rather than as isolated units of aesthetic completeness. She sees her poems within a field that includes the subjective experience of history – a history, moreover, perceived and revealed through life's daily and personal details. Although the activist poems place a value upon the daily, Levertov hopes that, when read with attention to their interrelated wholeness, the poems stand apart from "mere 'confessional' autobiography" (105). Taken together as a continuing process, the poems provide "a document of some historical value, a record of one person's inner/outer experience in America during the '60's and the '70's, an experience which is shared by so many and transcends the peculiar details of each life, though it can be expressed in and through such details" (107). Mudane details of the ordinary reveal systemic connections with and between realms of power; the poetry of this period deals obsessively with the abuse of power manifested by the country's participation in the Vietnam War, but her reactions "cannot be separated from opposition to the whole system of insane greed, of racism and imperialism, of which war is only the inevitable expression" (106). As the daughter addressing a patriarchal system she has taken part in, she experiences a growing need for self-critique and an awareness that the forms of address must themselves be rethought. Essential to the cultural and poetic daughter's processes of critique is the reoccurring figure of the maternal that provides the daughter with an empowering and revisionary poetics based upon a discourse of compassion. Such a discourse stipulates an "I" that is multiply constituted, in which there is no clear split between the "I" and the "not-I."

I have chosen three poems to discuss as points along the path leading toward such a discourse: "Relearning the Alphabet" (1967), "The Malice of Innocence" (1972), and "The Cry" (1984). These three poems exhibit Levertov's progressive investigation, replete with significant changes and unfoldings, of the relationships between language and power. The title piece of her 1967 volume, "Relearning the Alphabet," urges a rediscovery of language that recognizes and resists corrosive distortions of it, particularly by individuals in positions of institutional power. In the same volume, "An Interim" laments the loss of language as a common ground or "touchstone." Set against the ubiquitous backdrop of war, the poem compares the language games of young children to the official language of war. Just as the five-year-old brother can offer his younger sister gum, and then say "yes means no,/so you can't have any," the United States military twists language to its own desired effect by depleting it of meaning or integrity. Murder and bombing of civilians, in the mouth of the officer, becomes a paradox in which "yes" means "no" and "to save" means "to destroy": " 'It became necessary/to destroy the town to save it,'/a United States major said today" (*Poems 1968–1972* 20). As the brutal experience of war is redefined through language, the issue of political, personal, and poetical control of language looms as an ominous cloud over the poet's own claim to words. What is this claim and how is its shape revealed by the historical moment? The poem continues:

> O language, mother of thought,
> are you rejecting us as we reject you?

Language, coral island
accrued from human comprehensions,
human dreams,

you are eroded as war erodes us.

(21)

"Relearning the Alphabet" responds to this erosion by considering the
ideological attachment to order within conventions of language. A series
of twenty-six units arranged by the letters of the alphabet, the poem
returns to the elemental signifying basis of this "coral island," the letters
themselves. As a poem about its own materials, it attempts formally to
free language from an ordering ego, a liberation enacted paradoxically,
however, within the same orders of language that have enabled oppression. The order (here, the alphabet) of human interactions, the poem
suggests, must be rediscovered beneath the layers of power that sever
the connective potential of words. Contact and connection make up the
letter B, as "to be" becomes an embrace of otherness: "To be. To love
an other only for being" (*Poems 1968–1972* 91). However, wrapped up
in language, enclosed by dominant structures of discourse, the "I" seems
unable to experience this love – as both reverence for self and reverence
for others – and the poem follows a movement of descent as the speaker
stumbles to find the "I-who-am-I again" (92):

> Lost in the alphabet
> I was looking for
> the word I can't now say
> (love)
>
> (93)

To relearn love, the speaker slowly realizes she must relearn the alphabet,
and by extension other forms of order, apart from the "rules of the will":

> . . . it
> slowly becomes known to me:
> articles of faith are indeed
> rules of the will—graceless,
>        faithless
>
> (97)

She seeks, through "utterance" to "step by hesitant step" move "to
continuance," which is "not what the will/thinks to construct for its
testimonies" (99). She desires an altered vision and way of being not
"under the will's rule" and imagines a vision of rootedness and engagement in the poem's key section:

*U*

Relearn the alphabet,
relearn the world, the world
understood anew only in doing, understood only as
looked-up-into out of earth,
the heart an eye looking,
the heart a root
planted in earth.
Transmutation is not
under the will's rule.

(99)

She circles back to a relationship between vision and discovery epitomized in "The Instant," written almost twenty years earlier. Discovery, rather than manifesting the will's authority through dominance and possession, results from the oneness of heart and eye, grounded in a "continuance" with the earth. This relationship between imagination and reality echoes Williams's understanding of contact as an interactive engagement leading to discovery:

*V*

Vision sets out
journeying somewhere,
walking the dreamwaters:
arrives
not on the far shore but upriver,
a place not evoked, discovered.

(99)

And, a few sections later, this type of vision is explicitly set against the will:

*Y*

Vision will not be used.
Yearning will not be used.
Wisdom will not be used.
Only the vain will
strives to use and be used,
comes not the fire's core
but cinder.

(100)

As a poem of descent, "Relearning the Alphabet" shares a common spirit with the descent passage beginning Book 2 of *Paterson,* which accepts both defeat and despair as opportunities for moving from the self-absorbed ego to the "renewal" of "new / places":

No defeat is made up entirely of defeat—since
the world it opens is always a place
                formerly
                                        unsuspected. A
        world lost
                            (*Paterson* 77)

To look "for that nul . . . that's past / all being" suggests to Williams an
openness to "unsuspected" places (77), to a newness of discovery not
engendered through the willed transformation of the "nul" into the new,
nor through the willed transmutation of absence into presence that Levertov's final section also refuses:

        absence has not become
        the transformed presence the will
        looked for,
        but other: the present
        that which was poised already in the ah! of praise.
                            (100)

The penultimate line recognizes the presence of the other, formerly
understood as absence and approached through the will with a desire to
transform it, for to view difference as absence is to sustain sameness.
    The antiwar poetry of the sixties and early seventies revolves around
a critique of the will to power that, in "Relearning the Alphabet," takes
place simultaneously as a relinquishment of mastery and a discovery of
otherness. Her poems attack American culture and its war machine as a
display of power seeking to extinguish otherness (the poor, the nonwhite,
the Vietcong). In "Enquiry," one of her harshest war poems, she directs
her critique – a barrage of accusations – at the individual soldier:

        You who go out on schedule
        to kill, do you know
        there are eyes that watch you,
        eyes whose lids you burned off,
        that see you eat your steak
        and buy your girlflesh
        and sell your PX goods
        and sleep?
            (*Poems 1968–1972* 126)

The anger expressed in this poem exemplifies a self-righteously polemical
tone, often conveyed by the antiwar poems, that has routinely received
criticism. The tone of accusation belies a more complex problem than
propagandizing when considered within Levertov's own philosophical
and poetic terms, for the stance it assumes suggests she is outside the
will to power that she condemns. In attempting to so totally speak for

the "other" – the Vietcong woman victimized by war – the poem remains blind to the poet's struggle with that will, a struggle nonetheless registered within the larger body of her poetry.

However, as Levertov has urged, no poem is self-contained, and in "The Malice of Innocence," published in the 1972 *Footprints,* she implicitly reflects upon her liturgy of protest. The poem describes her nursing days in the 1940s, recapturing the "night routine" of checking the ward, "noting all we were trained to note" while making rounds (*Poems 1968–1972* 247). The order of the nightly routine (recalling the "schedule" the soldier is trained to follow in "Enquiry"), she realizes, was an order that attracted her in and of itself:

> —the well-rehearsed
> pavanne of power. Yes, wasn't it power,
> and not compassion,
>                    gave our young hearts
> their hard fervor?
>
> . . . . . . . . . . . . .
> But I loved the power
> of our ordered nights . . .
>
> (247)

Part of the speaker's power derives from the "writing" of details, the inscription of agony that shapes our perception and experience of it. The poem moves through detail after detail of these ordered nights; in the poem's final stanzas, a relationship surfaces between this love of power, enacted on the intimate and local level, and the love of power played out through international conflict:

> . . . I got lost in the death rooms a while,
> remembering being (crudely, cruelly,
>
> just as a soldier or one of the guards
> from Dachau might be) in love with order
>
> an angel like the *chercheuses de poux,* floating
> noiseless from bed to bed,
>
> smoothing pillows, tipping
> water to parched lips, writing
>
> details of agony into the Night Report.
>
> (247)

The final line, with its chilling allusion to the nightly news broadcasts that brought Vietnam's death count into America's living rooms, likens the nurse to the soldier. Recognizing how she is like the soldiers she once condemned, Levertov establishes a new "tracery" to others. The condemnation continues but is redirected away from the individual toward the "well rehearsed / pavanne of power" – the dance of power individuals are trained to follow and encouraged to love. The "ordered nights" of nurse and soldier replicate the dance and exclude compassion; in reaction, Levertov posits compassion as a way to break through these orders and reconnect human to human.

This poem begins an intensive reconsideration of orders of authority, in which Levertov admits her own participation while she considers ways to revise, not just relearn, these orders. In "A Poem at Christmas, 1972, During the Terror-Bombing of North Vietnam," Levertov spews forth angry visions of assassinating Nixon and his "friends and henchmen" (*FOD* 37). The visions "imagining murder" in explicitly gory terms involve the weapons and strategies employed in Vietnam – napalm, rounds of bombs dropped on civilian victims: "*O, to kill / the killers!*" the poem exclaims within the dementia of its vision. But the poem reverses itself upon a recognition of an even greater evil than the war or its advocates:

> It is
> to this extremity
> the infection of their evil
> thrusts us . . .
> (*FOD* 38)

Evil is intensified when those fighting its purveyors replicate their actions. The poem recalls a political choice offered and rejected by Williams in "In Chains," the poem cited by Levertov in her essay (also written in 1972) on Williams as a political poet. First published in 1939 as World War II began, "In Chains" is included in the 1944 volume *The Wedge*. Containing a number of poems written in direct response to the war, this book opens with an introduction that claims the "arts have a complex relation to society" (*CP2* 53). Voicing an argument Levertov will continue, Williams asserts that poetry emerges within a material, historical context: "The war is the first and only thing in the world today. The arts are not, nor is this writing a diversion from that for relief, a turning away. It is the war or part of it, merely a different sector of the field" (*CP2* 53).

Williams's insistence upon the interrelationship of art and sociohistorical phenomena is not at all new for him by this time, yet faced with the immensity of this second war, he evidently finds it necessary to strengthen his argument for poetry's engagement with reality by using combat diction. Art is not sealed off from the war, as an aestheticist argument would have it, but is a part of the war's artillery; hence, Williams's famous statement comparing the poem to a "small (or large) machine," put forth in this introduction, desentimentalizes poetry while also empowering it with a capacity to maintain a resistant space within a world scarred by war machines. The poem-as-machine, rather than endorsing a machine worship complicit with the world's destruction, offers the choice to "learn from that [oppression] to avoid / being as they [the oppressors] are" ("In Chains," *CP2* 65). The "machine" becomes another form of connection, an "intimate form" in which all parts are related; this gives "language its highest dignity, its illumination in the environment to which it is native" (55). Against the backdrop of global war, poetry becomes a "continuous" war for humanity, and its machinery the forms engendered by contact. It is no accident that the introduction – a call, in effect, to this war of resistance – is followed by "A Sort of Song," the poem asserting Williams's famous statement of contact: "No ideas / but in things!" (55). The short poem concludes with an image of breaking open: "Saxifrage is my flower that splits / the rocks" (55). The frail plant, the poem, the machine – these are Williams's images of a resistance, or an opening, that pushes its way through oppression and blooms into the "lively flower" of love that ends "In Chains" and later affirms for Levertov her own poems of resistance. "In Chains" warns, however, that the love that "will rise out of its ashes" must be tended to; it will rise if "we water it, tie up the slender / stem and keep the image of its / lively flower chiseled upon our minds" (65). Otherwise, we bend to the torturers' designs or become "as they are," recognitions registered progressively more clearly through Levertov's activist poetry, in such poems as "Malice of Innocence" and "A Poem at Christmas."

Levertov returns often to Williams's image of the "stem" of love, most emphatically connecting her own poetics with his in "Williams: An Essay," the central poem (structurally and in spirit) of *Candles in Babylon* (1982). The final stanzas gather images that quote from her own poetry and his, conflating the daughter and father within a poetics joining the lotus flower of Ariel and the mud of Caliban:

> He loved
> the lotus cup, fragrant
> upon the swaying water, loved
>
> the wily mud
> pressing swart riches into its roots,
>
> and the long stem of connection.
>                (60)

Not only is this a significant statement of their shared aesthetic ground, but also an allusion to its ethical and political force. Connection, compassion, contact – realizing "one's traceries to others' needs" – offer a power to counter the world's self-destruction. Levertov describes this power in "Freedom," a poem that comes out of her Vietnam experience and appears in the postwar volume *The Freeing of the Dust* (1975). She compares the "acts of choice / made in solitude" to the "other acts," unseen, that

> not even vanity,
> or anxious hope to please, knows of—
> bone doings, leaps of nerve, heart-
> cries of communion: if there is bliss,
> it has
> been already
> and will be; out-
> reaching, utterly.
> Blind
> to itself, flooded
> with otherness.
>
> (112)

The radical and even utopian vision of a society based upon this notion of self has much in common with Irigaray's association of the feminine with "nearness," an association effective in exposing the ideologically masculine foundation of individualism and its tropes:

> Woman always remains several, but she is kept from dispersion because the other is already within her and is autoerotically familiar to her. Which is not to say that she appropriates the other for herself, that she reduces it to her own property. Ownership and property are doubtless quite foreign to the feminine. At least sexually. But not *nearness*. Nearness so pronounced that it makes all discrimination of identity, and thus all forms of property, impossible. Woman derives pleasure from what is *so near that she cannot have it, nor have herself*. She herself enters into a ceaseless exchange of herself with the other without any possibility of identifying either. This puts into question all prevailing economies. ... (*This Sex* 31)

Here the self exists within fluid communion, a state of contiguity and touch with "otherness," a rejection of humanism and its ideological orders of separation and hierarchy. The essentialized feminine acts as an interventionary strategy rather than as a representation of the authentic self, a notion this alternate economy, or system of exchange, puts into question.[104]

Also in the manner of Irigaray, Levertov employs the female body to metonymically refer to and investigate material systems of power. "The Cry" offers an example; included in *Oblique Prayers* (1984), the poem deals with the insufficiency of language to sustain this being "flooded / with otherness," and reflects back upon her own use of polemical speech. Written in Williams's triadic foot,[105] the poem begins with a recognition of the failure of language to fully articulate the dread experienced "in this time" or to radically alter it:

> No pulsations
> > of passionate rhetoric
> > > suffice
> in this time
> > in this time
> > > this time
> we stammer in
> > stammering dread
> > > or
> parched, utter
> > silence
> > > from
> mouths gaping to
> > 'Aayy!'—
>
> > > > (44)

The world faces its "last choice" as it threatens to "erase / is / and *was* / along with / *will be*" (45). The "sibling lives" of animal and vegetable

> we've lorded it over,
> > the powers we've
> > > taken in thrall

on the earth are threatened with complete erasure (45). To "turn away from / that dis- / solution" becomes the cry of the poem, brokenly articulated in a powerfully maternal image that bridges the earthly and the cosmic. To resist, to turn away from the "dis- / solution" (an echo of the "final solution") is to hope for

> only, O
> > maybe
> some wholly,
> > holy
> > > holy
> unmerited call:
> > bellbird
> > > in branch of
> snowrose
> > blossoming
> > > newborn cry
> demanding
> > with cherubim
> > > and seraphim
> eternity:
> > being:
> > > milk:
>
> > > (45–6)

The movement of immanence, from bellbird and snowrose to cherubim and eternity, inverts itself in the last three words as "eternity: / being: / milk:" unfold in a Trinity of maternal touch, a being "flooded with otherness." The colon that ends the poem admits the possibility of continuance, an inclusive opening rather than a definitive closure within this triadic matrix. As a strategy of ideological intervention, in "The Cry" the maternal intersects with the political and the religious in a manner characteristic of Levertov's evolving poetics of community.

### The Houses of Tradition: "rise up / with changed vision"

As Levertov's political activism intensified during the Vietnam War, highlighted by her work with draft resisters, with her participation in the establishment of People's Park in Berkeley, and by a 1972 protest trip to Saigon, her poetry registers an important shift in awareness of sexual politics and cultural systems of authority that shape her personal life as a poet. Although, as we have seen, Levertov's poetic voice speaks clearly as a woman through the span of her works, it is not until the mid-sixties that a tension arises between that voice and a larger set of poetic assumptions defined by gender bias. From this tension arises a revisioning of the poet as specifically female, positioned both oppositionally and marginally in relationship to "the rule that poetry was a masculine prerogative" (Levertov, "Poems by Women," 98). Particularly through this emphasis upon the *marginalized position* of female perspectives and experiences, Levertov's poetry reconsiders the overlapping cultural frameworks of the poet figure, literary tradition, and the Judeo-Christian tradition. The masculine individualism underlying these frameworks is displaced by the authority of community developing in her works of the 1960s. As the poetry evolves from political activism to spiritual examination, the communal self is explored in terms of the maternal body, culminating with Mary – who opens herself "utterly" to otherness – and extending across gender lines in the figure of Christ, whose self exists "in kinship" with the not-I. To map out this development, this section begins with readings of poems expressing an oppositional female position, followed by a close reading of the long poem "Pig Dreams" as a mythic treatment of literary tradition, focused upon gendered values defining inclusion. The issue of inclusion is then considered in relationship to narratives central to the Christian tradition through a group of recent poems; these poems insist upon and enact interpretive shifts precipitated by a shift in perspective from the male center to the female margins of these narratives.

Levertov's sense of marginality – of being the woman poet in a group of men – was early on noted by Williams. Their correspondence in the mid-fifties includes letters from Williams concerned with her experience as a woman in a male-dominated realm. Interestingly, in one group of letters that seem an attempt to establish a common ground between them, he articulates Levertov's "difference" and relates it to a maternal heritage he feels they both share in Sappho; at the same time he recognizes his position in relationship to this poetic mother as different from Levertov's within the context of cultural constructs of gender. His comments on Sappho as a woman poet call attention to gender conventions as obstacles for the poet who is not male, a material point of connection he draws between the ancient poet and Levertov. On August 30, 1954, he wrote, "Sappho must have been a powerful wench to stand what would have torn a woman apart otherwise. The tensions she must have withstood without yielding have made her poems forever memorable" ("Letters to Denise Levertov" 163). To live fully aware as a woman, Levertov's poetry records, is to exist in a state of radical resistance to cultural norms and constructs of power. The poetic mother Sappho demonstrates how the woman's hand on the pen inevitably ensues a wrenching of her relationship to culture.

Again on June 13, 1956, Williams reflects on Sappho:

> It may be that women are different from men in that, they may have to strip themselves barer than men do, the history of Sappho seems to indicate it – nothing held back, absolutely nothing, complete incontinence, but the cost is exhorbitant. Women can rarely do it, they are physically ruined. Not that they should not be but the cost is more than they can endure. And nothing less than completely laying themselves bare is any good. They frequently do as Sappho did, is reported to have done, turn to love of individuals of their sex – though Sappho turned to a sailor at the end – presumably a young sailor. What could she do, men apparently proved impossible to her. They only wanted the one thing soon exhausted. But she was satisfied only with the greatest subtleties which existed only in herself. Only the putting down of the deeply felt poem in its infinite and resourceful variety could relieve her. No man could give her what she required. ("Letters to Denise Levertov" 165)

Here, Sappho's artistry arises from a feminized continuum between her inner and outer experiences, a self-touching that the masculine world prohibits. Although Williams's words may effect a paternalistic tone, they also articulate a space within tradition defined by a female difference linking body and desire to language.

This difference finds expression frequently in Levertov's poetry, as we have seen in discussing the body politics motivating representations of the female body in her work. In redefining the figure of the poet as both marginalized and female, Levertov often employs female-associated allegorical terms and images that link poems written at different points in her career. Whereas, for example, the poem "The Earth Worm," included in the 1967 *The Sorrow Dance,* complements the figure of the poet drawn from Charles Olson's metaphor of "digging"[106] and from Williams's chthonic sensibility, Levertov's next book includes "The Snail," which retracts the previous poem and proclaims an arena of gendered difference. "The Earth Worm" echoes Olson's tenets:

> The worm artist
> out of soil, by passage
> of himself
> constructing
> .  .  .  .  .
> He throws off
> artifacts as he
> contracts and expands the
> muscle of his being,
> ringed in himself,
> tilling. He
> is homage to
> earth, aerates
> the ground of his living.
> (*Poems 1960–1967* 176)

Reminiscent of Williams, this image of the artist emphasizes place and rootedness; the poet is self-contained, "ringed in himself / tilling," re-calling Olson's construct of the poet. However, in "The Snail," the poet sees the earthworm figure as explicitly masculine. The worm's "lowly freedom," for which the snail once yearned, allows him to go "under earth" where his "slow arrow pierces / the thick of dark" (77). The snail thinks "to crawl / out" of its shell, but comes to understand that "in my shell / my life was" (77). With its feminine associations of enclosed, domestic, private space, the shell is both "burden" and "grace"; the moment of grace occurs when the snail claims a particular vision from within the shell. Once the shell is claimed as the locus of "my life"

> I remembered
>
> my eyes adept to witness
> air and harsh light
>
> and look all ways.
>                 (77)

Through a trail of allusions, the poet claims herself as woman and her shell as difference; significantly, she locates her power of vision within that difference. This poem continues in the line of "The Instant" and "The Garden Wall," only now the concept of poetic vision is carried into a reconsideration of poetic models: The worm's "slow arrow pierces / the thick of dark," implying a masculine model the snail tries to emulate. This occurs at the cost of forgetting her own vision and its source in her "shell," a feminine model finally "remembered" as a mode of witnessing rather than endured as a brittle prison.

This poem joins other revisionary works in *Relearning the Alphabet* concerned with gender values and associations shaping literary conventions. "Adam's Complaint" again alludes to the earthworm poet, suggesting that Eve's desire somehow is not contained within this model, much to Adam's bewilderment: "Some people," he complains, "no matter what you give them, / still want the moon"; "And water: dig them the deepest well, / still it's not deep enough / to drink the moon from" (54). "Wings of a God" looks to yet another ancient myth, that of Leda and the swan, and reconsiders Yeats's modernist rendering of Leda's rape. Told from Leda's perspective, the poem illuminates the traditionally ignored moment after the blow falls and imagines a Leda who rises up in strength and "changed vision," her own power a "singing" in her ears. Whereas Yeats portrays a helpless, staggering girl, "mastered by the brute blood of the air," and focuses upon the rape (*Poems* 218), Levertov imagines Leda's poetic empowerment as distinct from the violence. Her "changed vision" derives not from the rape but from her phoenixlike rise after the "blow":

> The wings unheard
> > felt as a rush of air,
> > of air withdrawn, the breath
> taken—
> > the blow falls,
> > feather and bone
> > > stone-heavy.
> I am felled,
> > rise up
> > with changed vision,
> a singing in my ears.
> > (Poems 1968–1972 39)

The "changed vision" suggests the power of re-visioning from the perspective of the woman whose story is usually written for her by longstanding cultural narratives. The woman as writer changes this pattern in claiming and telling her own stories, rather than repeating history as "his story."

By the time Levertov puts together the 1982 *Candles in Babylon,* her poetry insists upon the revisionary potential of the female writer. "She

and the Muse" clearly disputes the hero/heroine dichotomy of traditional
romance by presenting the heroine as "scribe" and valuing the moment
when the lovers part *because* it allows the writer to return to her desk.
The poem initially follows conventional narrative; the man rides away
on his horse, replete with the marks of the male hero. He wears a plumed
hat and carries a saddlebag full of "talismans, / mirrors, parchment histories," all of the "indecipherable clues to destiny" that accompany his
ride "off in the dust cloud of his own / story" (67). Refusing convention
at this point, however, the story does not end with his story of masculine
adventure. Instead, it traces the heroine's return to her domestic world,
the "flagstoned kitchen" where she "clears honey and milk and bread /
off the table" and sweeps the hearth. Here she is empowered, and

> . . . Returned to solitude,
> eagerly she re-enters the third room,
>
> the room hung with tapestries, scenes that change
> whenever she looks away. Here is her lectern,
> here her writing desk. She picks a quill,
> dips it, begins to write. But not of him.
>
> (67)

What happens when the woman, culturally inscribed by endless narratives, begins to inscribe herself? What happens when Leda takes on a
voice? What do the cultural daughters have to say that the sons cannot?

These questions run through the long sequence that makes up the
second section of *Candles in Babylon*. Comprising a maternal and sororal
mythopoesis, a call to feminine creative powers, "Pig Dreams" allegor-
ically speaks of the woman writer in a male tradition, which is a house
not her own but one she has been "chosen" to enter. The sequence tells
the story of Sylvia, a pig chosen to leave the sty for the human house
and become a pet. It is spoken in Sylvia's voice, with the exception of
the final poem in which the goddess Isis prophesies for Sylvia a house
of her own. The figures of poet, pig, and goddess expand upon the earlier
poem, "Song for Ishtar": "The moon is a sow / and grunts in my throat";
"She is a sow / and I a pig and a poet" (*Poems 1960–1967* 75). In "Pig
Dreams," the pig-poet retraces her destiny in what becomes an act, Isis
tells her, of "redreaming the lore of your destiny" (*CIB* 40). As the
concluding line, Isis's prophecy refers back to the sequence's beginning,
the poem "Her Destiny," in which Sylvia remembers her origin in maternal presence. The initial stanza establishes this earliest sense of the
maternal as both touch and vision:

> The beginning: piglet among piglets,
> the soft mud caking
> our mother's teats.

Sweetsqueal, grunt:
her stiff white lashes, the sleepy
glint of her precious
tiny eyes.

(25)

The humans, however, choose Sylvia as a house pet, removing her from
the sty and her mother:

But I am Sylvia. Chosen.
I was established
*pet.* To be
the pig of dreams, the pig
any of us could be,
    taken out of the sty,
    away from the ravaged soil of pig-yards,
    freed from boredom and ugliness.
I was chosen to live without dread of slaughter.

(25)

Once chosen, she is brought to the human house, where for three days
she hungers for her mother: "Nowhere a teat to suck from, / no piglet
siblings to jostle and nudge" (25). The He-human, "naked and white as
my / lost mother," bends to her bowl of food and shows her how to
eat, "Gave me / the joy of survival" (25, 26). As a young piglet, she
learns to love human cuddling and to play with the other domestic
animals; the house accommodates her and she finds "brothers" in the
other creatures there. In "Dogbrothers," she tells of being "Pigalone . . .
Sylvia Orphan Onlypig" until "I found / my Dogbrothers," with whom
she plays and sleeps, "almost believing / I, Sylvia, / am dog not pig"
(26–7). Her difference almost forgotten when among her brothers, Sylvia
experiences fraternal companionship in much the same way that Levertov
wrote within the male group of Black Mountain poets. In a letter written
to Levertov on October 5, 1955, Williams had observed an unease in her
while amidst a group of solely male poets:

You seemed absent and lost at times yesterday among all the masculine
concerns about which we were talking. We just touched the edge of
something that seemed to interest you but no one seemed inclined to
follow it up. For a woman, as in the case of Creeley's wife, it must be
puzzling in a male world to find a way to keep the mind alive. ("Letters
to Denise Levertov" 165)

The letter provides an apt image of the woman poet's marginal position, existing among "brothers" but still the exception to the rule who
lingers on the fringe of the inner circle of "masculine concerns." The

next poem in the sequence, "The Catpig," recalls even more specifically
her relationship with Robert Duncan.

> John the Cat
> is most my brother,
> almost pig
>
> even though he
> leaps among branches,
> climbs to high shelves . . .
>                   (27)

It is certainly likely that Duncan's homosexuality allowed him a greater
degree of empathy with Levertov's marginal position as a woman and
enhanced their sense of connection. Writing openly as a gay man in the
forties, Duncan "wrote self-consciously as an outsider to the literary
establishment, a gay writer in a homophobic society," generating poetry
through this "commitment to marginality" and its attention to gender
identity (Davidson, "Marginality in the Margins," 278).[107] For both, the
gendered position of marginality becomes an important point from which
to read and write; Duncan's reading of the modernists (especially H.D.
and Williams) from this position seems to have offered Levertov an
important opening into American poetry. Their connection predated
their actual meeting, for Levertov read his *Heavenly City, Earthly City*
in 1948 while living in Florence and awaiting a move to America. This
reading, she would later claim, provided her first sense of connection to
an American poet and the literature of her adopted country. In an essay
written in 1975, reflecting upon their close friendship and its fracturing
under the strain of political disagreements,[108] Levertov remembers her
initial attraction to his poetry: "So here, I must have intuited, was an
*American* poet whose musical line, and whose diction, were accessible to
me. It must have made my emigration, which I knew was not far distant,
seem more possible, more real" (*LUC* 198). In "The Catpig," Sylvia
fondly recalls

> Black and white Catpig,
> I outgrew you,
> but once we matched.
>                   (27)

Following his death in 1988, Levertov wrote "To R.D., March 4th 1988,"
a poem that echoes Sylvia's lines. Revealing a dream in which Duncan
appears to Levertov in a church where the two are reconciled, the poem
begins: "You were my mentor. Without knowing it,/I outgrew the need
for a mentor" (4). After the dream, "I was once more/your chosen sister,
and you/my chosen brother" (4). Of Duncan's presence in her life, despite

their conflicts, Levertov claims that "none of my many poet friends has
given me more" (*LUC* 232). Like the cat for Sylvia, he seems "most
my brother" among the poets sharing Levertov's poetic house.

As Sylvia grows older and larger, the poems focus more extensively
on her femaleness, which comes to define her sense of herself as pig, as
different. "The Bride" tells of Sylvia's breeding with a "beautiful, imperious boar," during a "week of passion and feasting," a "sensuous
dark" that carries her to the "depths/of desire" (29). The humans send
her to be bred; although her initial fear is replaced by erotic desire, shame
overcomes her once she is separated from the boar. Her "maiden cham-
ber," her pig-house, is now too small for her "swill-swollen body," and
she lies on the ground outside it, passing her days "silent and humble"
like a penitent woman. Erotic pleasure, in this narrative, allows only
shame and repentance. Maternal experience, however, marks Sylvia's
reclaiming of a pig-world – a recognition that the human ([hu]man) world
that chose her as pet (p[o]et) is not hers, nor can she be human, though
to dwell in the human house ensures survival. With motherhood, Sylvia
embarks upon a subversive relationship with the house that shelters her.
In "Her Task," her piglets cling to her:

> These shall I housetrain, I swear it,
> these shall dwell like their mother
> among dextrous humans, to teach them
> pig-wisdom. O Isis, bless
> thy pig's piglets.
>
> (30–1)

The matriarch, under the aegis of the goddess, begins to collect and
build a world for her piglets from bits and pieces of the human environment. The objects she retrieves and hides would seem trivial to the
humans beside the "fine things" of their world, but they signify a culture
and heritage passed from Sylvia, the mother, to her offspring:

> In my neat A-frame
> they think there is nothing,
> only the clean straw of my bed.
> But under the floor I gather
> beautiful tins, nutshells, ribbons,
> shining buttons, the thousand baubles
> a pig desires.
>
> They are well hidden.
> Piglets shall find one day
> an inheritance of shapes,
> textures, mysterious substances—
> Rubber! Velvet! Aluminum! Paper!

Yes, I am founding
    stick by stick,
    wrapper by wrapper,
    trinkets, toys—
Civilization!

          (31)

Levertov's aesthetics of the domestic and the ordinary here appears as
the mother's heritage – shapes hidden and mysterious, to be discovered
and reclaimed, and to be recognized as a shape of civilization omitted
and suppressed within the dominant patriarchy.

In "Her Nightmare," Sylvia reveals a dream of transgressing civilization's "Law" by doing what "is forbidden to pigs" – swimming (32).
In the dream, her flailing feet cut her throat and the river fills with blood
as she sinks "screaming and then / voiceless" into "the sticky / crimson
blood" (32). Blood imagery permeates the dream, and in fact, the "dream
is blood"; this is the blood of menstruation and birth, signifying female
transgression in the primal myth of Eve as the first breaker of the Father's
Law. Sylvia remembers a time before she was conscious of the Law:
"When I was young, / not knowing the prohibition, / I did swim" (32),
and the swimming is sweet and easy. But, as she grows "heavier, thick
in the throat, / properly pigshaped," she "learned the Law" (32). With
this consciousness, the nightmare begins, filling up her "bowl of sleep
/ with terror, / with blood" (33). She realizes in "Her Lament" that she
has outgrown her humans and their house, has become "Sylvia the Sow":
"How could a cherished piglet / have grown so tall?" (34). And in "Her
Judgement," she warns her offspring of the human race:

I love my own Humans and their friends,
but let it be said,
that my litters may heed it well,
*their race is dangerous.*

          (37)

Sylvia most condemns the human disdain for otherness, their drive to
possess and make objects of exchange out of everything nonhuman. She
warns, "they breed us not that our life/may be whole, pig-life/thriving
alongside" all of the "lives of earth-creatures" (38). In contrast is Kaya,
her "Jersey cowfriend" in "Her Sister" – although they are different
creatures, as sisters Kaya and Sylvia "worship/the same goddess" (40).
The proclamation of sisterhood includes an admission and love of difference – the sororal crosses boundaries and connects the creatures. Coming near the end of the sequence and written in Williams's triadic foot,
the poem anticipates "Williams: An Essay," which appears later in the
volume. Sylvia traces "the mud in pigpatterns," leaving her signs upon

the earth in a dance of contact with her sister, and the sororal opens here to the suggested presence of Williams, connecting mud and flower, Caliban and Ariel.

The final poems of the sequence evoke, as did Williams's earliest works, a creative female power. Levertov draws upon a female source, however, in a more deliberate effort to shape a tradition speaking specifically to women. The goddess Isis prophesies a future that the poet joins in constructing from and for women poets. In "Isis Speaks," the concluding poem, the goddess foretells that

> the time shall come
> when you shall dwell,
>      revered,
> in a house of your own
> even finer than that you have.

There, the goddess tells Sylvia, "you shall live long, and at peace, / redreaming the lore of your destiny" (40). Isis speaks in response to Sylvia's prayer, which asks the goddess to "forget not thy pig" (40): the final invocation to a feminine power echoes the initial presence of the maternal and encloses the entire sequence within a poetic space explicitly feminized. Sylvia speaks upon various levels of authority (as pet, as mother, as wise pig), but they are all levels reached through a feminized sensibility of contact and power of creation.

Affirmation of this power shapes Levertov's reading of the Christian tradition in the poetry that follows *Candles in Babylon,* undercutting cultural associations between creation and male potency as they derive from the story of the Logos, generated by a father God. In *Oblique Prayers* (1984), *Breathing the Water* (1987), and *A Door in the Hive* (1989), Levertov takes as her subject the Christian religion, revealing her intensified commitment to spiritual matters. Her worship within a religion privileging the Father and the Son involves both a rereading of its sanctioned moments and an illumination of the mother and daughter in relationship to those moments; in many of her spiritual poems, Levertov focuses upon women's experiences of divinity as apprehensions of the Godhead mediated through a female. Reclaiming a feminine agency for Christianity and challenging its paternal base of authority, Levertov seeks to emulate Julian of Norwich, the fourteenth-century mystic who is a major figure in recent poems, in conveying a vision of Christ as the embodiment of an "Imagination" of "kinship" (*BW* 69). In this way, Christ manifests the maternal empathy of vision, discovery, and touch so central to Levertov. Poems such as "The Servant-Girl at Emmaus," "On a Theme from Julian's Chapter XX," "The Showings: Lady Julian of Norwich, 1342–1416" (*BW*), and "Annunciation" (*DH*) reveal instances of religious vision attained through the agency of a woman. Julian of Norwich stands as a paradigm of feminine vision in these poems. A witness to the microcosm's revelation of the macrocosm, she is a "vivid woman" (*BW* 77) grounded in the physical world yet one who

> ... witnessed
> with your own eyes, with outward sight
> in your small room, with inward sight
> in your untrammeled spirit—
> knowledge we long to share:
> *Love was his meaning.*
>
> (*BW* 82)

To articulate a vision of love, Levertov chooses Julian as her guide: "I turn to you, / you clung to joy though tears and sweat / rolled down your face like the blood" (82). Through Julian's words, Levertov understands Christ as embodying an imaginative force capable of opening to otherness. This marks the divinity in Him: "*The oneing,* she saw, *the oneing / with the Godhead* opened Him utterly / to the pain of all minds, all bodies" (68). This openness manifests the "utmost Imagination" and its sorrow "in kinship" with the world (69).

Based upon a painting of the same name by Velázquez, "A Servant-Girl at Emmaus" dramatizes a moment of witnessing and locates it within a marginal space – the black woman servant in the kitchen. Not only is the intersection of the divine and human revealed in the ordinary, but that "ordinary" is explicitly associated with feminine space (the kitchen) and with a cultural position triply marginalized by gender, class, and (when read through the Eurocentric version of Christ as a blond-haired, blue-eyed Caucasian) by race. Before she sees the face, the servant-girl recognizes the voice of Christ, having previously heard him preach and remembering the voice of he "who had looked at her, once, across the crowd, / as no one ever had looked":

> Those who had brought this stranger home to their table
> don't recognize yet with whom they sit.
> But she in the kitchen, absently touching
>     the winejug she's to take in,
> a young Black servant intently listening,
>
> swings round and sees
> the light around him
> and is sure.
>
> (*BW* 66)

The movement of immanence from feminine space to divine vision involves touch and aural attentiveness, an active engagement with the physical. In a poem like "The Cry," this immanence is traced in reciprocal fashion, from divine to maternal in the triadic movement of "eternity: / Being: / milk:" (*OP* 46). Rather than the transcendent mode, the immanent returns to the earthly, engaging the divine and the material worlds in a continual dialogue that Levertov configures within the feminized energies and spaces of contact.

In Christological terms, the preeminent feminine space is the womb of the Virgin Mary, the chosen receptacle for the Word made flesh. Levertov's poem "Annunciation" opens with an epigraph from the Agathions Hymn celebrating this space: "Hail, space for the uncontained God" (86). The transference of this Christian idealization of the womb, as passive receptacle, into secular currency demonstrates a central understanding of the feminine inherited from Christian thought; however, "Annunciation" reconsiders this space as grounded in a female body, possessed not by God but by Mary herself, whose choice to accept God fundamentally involves her as an active agent in the Incarnation. The poem focuses upon "the minute no one speaks of, / when she could still refuse," when God must wait upon her consent (88). Through revealing a moment often omitted in official narratives of Christ, the poem reconsiders the patriarchal idea of conception as a male action, of creation as a male prerogative. From the countless representations of that familiar narrative, "We know the scene: the room, variously furnished, / almost always a lectern, a book; always / the tall lily" (88). As we think we know the scene – this feminine, domestic space where Mary waits – the poem suggests that we think we know also the space of the womb and its purpose in the Annunciation. Yet, when the angel arrives, the poem imagines a moment that the narratives rarely consider:

> But we are told of meek obedience. No one mentions
> courage.
> > The engendering Spirit
> did not enter without consent.
> > > God waited.
>
> She was free
> to accept or to refuse, choice
> integral to humanness.
>
> > > > > (86)

The poem's logic is multilayered here. Not only does it uncover a hidden moment and reinscribe what has been erased, but it does so by appealing to the core of Judeo-Christian thought – the concept of free will as the quintessential measure of humankind in its relationship to God. The poem illuminates the degree to which free will, though deemed a universal human quality, is ideologically and historically represented as a masculine prerogative. Interpretations of the Biblical narrative, disregarding the element that makes Mary most human, misinterpret the moment of conception and the experience of gestation, which Levertov interprets as a time and space of power brought on by the courage of Mary's choice:

> to bear in her womb
> Infinite weight and lightness; to carry
> in hidden, finite inwardness,
> nine months of Eternity; to contain
> in slender vase of being,
> the sum of power—
> in narrow flesh,
> the sum of light.
>     Then bring to birth,
> push out into air, a Man-child
> needing, like any other,
> milk and love—
> but who was God.
>
>                          (87)

The fundamental basis of Christianity depends upon the corporeality of Christ, and yet, this poem insists, that human inheritance derives from Mary, whose own full humanity is denied by separating her motherhood from the maternal body and from the exercise of free will. The poem connects the corporeal maternal body to Mary's free will; the Annunciation becomes a moment affirming the human elements of free will and flesh, rather than a moment so insistently excluding female sexuality through the traditional need to retain a virginal state for Mary. The final section of the poem links the utterly human moment of Mary's free will to a recognition of her being as a physical woman. While the Spirit waits, a "breath unbreathed" and "suspended," Mary makes her choice:

> She did not cry, 'I cannot, I am not worth,'
> nor, 'I have not the strength.'
> She did not submit with gritted teeth,
>
>                          raging, coerced.
> Bravest of humans,
>
>                          consent illumined her.
> The room filled with its light,
> the lily glowed in it,
>
>                          and the iridescent wings.
> Consent,
>     courage unparalleled,
> opened her utterly.
>
>                          (88)

Consent, as an act of courage, ceases to be a passive state. The final line simultaneously grounds the Annunciation in the reality of Mary's female body – the sexual body opening in the moment of love and conception and the maternal body opening to birth – as inseparable from the spiritual body that is opened "utterly." As we see in this powerful image of Mary, Levertov's continual return to the maternal as a grounding for critique, for reevaluation, for vision, and for discovery, her poetry imagines a communal notion of self, empowered and continually altered through connection with others.

# 4

## Kathleen Fraser
### A Tradition of Marginality

> Breaking rules, breaking boundaries, crossing over, going where you've been told not to go has increasingly figured in the writing of the contemporary woman poet as a natural consequence of the restraints placed upon her as a child being socialized to the female role her class and culture prefer. The poem becomes her place to break rank: her words, her line lengths and placements, her "stuff."
>
> – Kathleen Fraser[109]

The chosen daughter of an acknowledged American tradition of modern poetry, Denise Levertov writes directly out of a male-dominated line. Nonetheless, she imagines the unexperienced fullness to come when the daughters write from their mothers. A generation after Levertov's entry into an American tradition, Kathleen Fraser and other experimental women writers actively began seeking out their literary mothers, a project giving rise to many questions concerning a tradition of poetic fathers.

This tradition, as experienced by contemporary writers, extends to and sustains the poetic world of the present. Associated in her early career with Frank O'Hara's New York School, Fraser quickly became sensitized to the exclusion of women (such as Barbara Guest) from serious treatments, anthologies, and groupings of that movement, whether by critics or by the poets themselves. More recently, Kathleen Fraser's work is often placed within the expansive category of Language poetry where a similar pattern of gender disparity haunts the critical treatment of a diverse and expansive group of poets whose works, Stephen Fredman tells us, put "into question . . . our assumptions about poetry, language, and discourse" (*Poet's Prose* 150).[110] In its responses to poststructuralist theories, Language poetry has engaged in a relationship with theoretical discourse that self-consciously foregrounds the political nature of language and of theory itself. Yet, as such critics as Marianne DeKoven remind us, much of the discussion of this new avant-garde, and the most prominent recognition of its practitioners, involves primarily the major male figures, while many of the most interesting women engaging in language innovations remain "safely buried" from general regard:

> The fact that one hardly ever sees [women] writers . . . mentioned in print except by one another is particularly surprising given the widespread interest among feminist critics in "French theory," which emphasizes precisely the kinds of formal dislocations these writers employ. One hears of the "language poets," a current, predominantly male American avant-garde: they occupy a margin which has become a recognized position, a firmly established niche, in the American literary scene. . . .
> . . . As long as the experimental writer whose "signature" is female aligns herself with the language poets, for example, as many of them sometimes do, she has a place on the literary map. The price she pays, a price familiar to all of us, is twofold: the question of gender will be erased, declared a non-issue, and at the same time it is less likely than if her signature were male that she will become one of the stars, even in that tiny firmament. ("Gertrude's Granddaughters" 13)[111]

DeKoven, here as elsewhere in her comments on the relationship between feminist and postmodern aesthetics, calls attention to the danger of invisibility threatening women categorized within – or subsumed by – an avant-garde tradition whose writings are addressed primarily as postmodern and only secondarily (if at all) as woman-centered both in form and content; moreover, she finds a precedent for such gender bias in the conventional disregard for an earlier tradition of female modernists.[112]

Recognizing this bias, many women poets involved in a current avant-garde descending from modernism have brought questions of language and tradition into play within a feminist-informed poetry. In the late 1970s and the 1980s, Kathleen Fraser and other experimental women writers, such as Beverly Dahlen, Frances Jaffer, Susan Howe, and Rachel Blau DuPlessis, actively began seeking out literary mothers who had explored language innovations earlier in this century. Reconstructing a forgotten line of avant-garde women writers, these poets and critics have authorized their own language innovations by placing themselves within a modernist counterstrain emerging from the works of Emily Dickinson, Gertrude Stein, Mina Loy, Djuna Barnes, H.D., Virginia Woolf, Marianne Moore, Laura Riding, Lorine Neidecker, and others. In 1983, to further this effort, Fraser founded the journal HOW(ever) as a forum for both new projects and for explorations of the tradition enabling them.[113] Largely, this reclamation project grew out of a desire to find a poetic tradition investigating relationships between gender and language. In helping to rewrite the history of modernism to include the women artists "experimenting in aesthetic form . . . [and] formulating the specifically female experience of modernity" (Wolff, *Feminine Sentences* 61), these contemporary women writers represent a significant cultural moment within a postmodern sensibility that registers an awareness of the processes through which structures (of self, tradition, language, etc.) are ideologically mediated. For these women, ideologies of gender are inseparable from their (dis)placement within literary history and culture at large.

In the past decade, amid vigorous debates over the meanings of the cultural phenomenon of postmodernism, Kathleen Fraser has become an important voice in locating the postmodern through the impact of feminism and the practices of women writers. Since 1988, two significant essay collections dealing with postmodern poetics have included essays by Fraser, in which she articulates valuable approaches to reading the experimental works of women in this century.[114] These essays, along with shorter pieces addressing notions of literary history, pose intriguing questions concerning the formal elements women experimentalists explore, their relationship to cultural inscriptions of the feminine and the material realities of women, and the possibility of a feminine writing or *écriture féminine*. Her own collections of poetry and prose poems engage the theoretical, historical, and literary questions her essays pose, joining in an ongoing conversation with other women writers of the past and present. Examining the formal strategies at play in Kathleen Fraser's work, I would like to suggest the nature of this conversation, particularly in its concern with the interaction between linguistic innovation, feminist politics, and literary tradition, and in its implications for reading the modernism practiced by Williams.

Throughout her work, Fraser foregrounds the confrontation of women-authored texts with male-authored inscriptions of the feminine. Through embracing the displacement she experiences as a woman, her works seek to transform the relationship between her experience of marginalization and cultural forms of authority. This effort involves an investigation of subjectivity in direct relationship to the boundaries, codes, and texts of the gendered self encouraged by a (Western) male-dominated society. Retextualizing "woman," these works perform the oppositional cultural politics Janet Wolff describes as "destabilization," borrowing the term from Sandra Harding to describe strategies of "exposing the ideological limits of male thought" through "engaging with, and destabilizing, the images, ideologies, and systems of representation of patriarchal culture" (81–2). Particularly in referring to Fraser's work as postmodern, I am guided by this idea of a writing that is deeply informed by and invested in a cultural politics attentive to language's relationship to gendered authority. Wolff's definition of a politically motivated and deployed postmodernism aptly applies to the convergence of feminism and language innovation in Fraser's work: Her writing demonstrates an "engagement with the dominant culture itself. . . [and] engages directly with current images, forms, and ideas, subverting their intent and (re)appropriating their meanings, rather than abandoning them for alternative forms, which would leave them untouched and still dominant" (*Feminine Sentences* 88); moreover, "such an interrogation is informed by theoretical and critical consciousness" (93).

As such, Fraser's postmodernism is both a direct inheritance from modernism and a revision of it. It is precisely in her recovery of women modernists and their formal strategies that we can locate an important intersection of modernism and feminism, one which redefines modernism to have "critical and radical potential for woman writers and artists" (Wolff 53). Reacting against the exclusion of women writers and their experiences from received definitions of modernism, Fraser has sought to claim an alternative lineage through those marginalized writers. Central to this project is a challenge to a masculinist ideology of modernism that reveals a politics of gender and power as foundational to modernism.[115] Because of her conscious efforts as poet, essayist, and editor to recover a tradition of women modernists and her incorporation of their strategies within her culturally politicized works, Kathleen Fraser is an experimental woman writer whose efforts offer us a way of examining this tradition's language innovations in light of gender politics – of recognizing formal and linguistic experimentalism within the context of political and cultural work.

Traversing relationships between language, form and authority, Fraser's work looks back to her poetic mothers for alternatives to and challenges of modernism's self-conscious assertion of poetic authority. Fraser's hindsight is enabled by the historical specifics of feminism's second wave and of the introduction of European poststructuralist theory in America. Both have increased her awareness of the political nature of language; this awareness informs her reading of modernist women and particularly her interest in their formal strategies. Fraser's work, then, combines the retrieval of a female modernist tradition with a feminist politics that interactively draws upon deconstructive notions of discourse. Her readings of this recovered tradition aid us, in turn, in reconsidering the political possibilities of modernism's formal techniques and aesthetic concerns. Reading Williams in light of Fraser's recasting of modernism we can detect his own formal and ideological interaction with a modernism practiced by women. To my eye, the work Williams asserts most emphatically as "modernist" is that most marked by the impact of his female contemporaries, a debt he variously celebrates and overwrites.

Concentrating first on Fraser's experimental work of the eighties, this chapter argues a connection between her feminist politics and her formal innovations, contextualized within a destabilization of modernism's canonical and ideological masculinity. The interaction of form and ideology underscores Fraser's retrieval of women modernists; through her project, we can approach the modernist tradition and its artists, rereading both aesthetic concerns and formal devices in relationship to the politics of gender authority revealed within the historical moment of the movement's emergence. While Chapter 1 situated the concerns of Williams's early work within the historical context of first-wave feminism, this chapter looks to *form* as politically and historically invested, primarily in reading the 1923 *Spring and All* through the strategies of women modernists. Working from Fraser's discoveries within this alternative tradition, which highlight its often subversive gender politics, this analysis locates within *Spring and All* the interaction of modernist strains in Williams's writing characterized primarily in terms of gender and authority.

In the works of her literary mothers, Fraser finds formal strategies that resist patriarchal structures and suggest models for expressing a range of feminine experience. She overtly develops these strategies in her own work, and her efforts clarify the often subversive characteristics of her precursors' linguistic innovations. In effect, when we read this daughter, we read back through an entire tradition, marginalized by literary history. We also read the dismantling of a patriarchal tradition that has "written" woman and whose assumptions of male creativity have disqualified women writers and their editorial input from serious consideration. Williams repeatedly validates his linguistic innovations through the works of women modernists: How are these innovations revealed to us anew when considered in relationship to the tradition Fraser and other poets have brought into the present? How do these linguistic strategies mediate his representations of women? How do the maternal lines he claims in his poetry include an active tradition of women writers? What literary mothers have sustained him, and how is their "difference" brought into his works? Is this a form of patriarchal appropriation, or does it suggest an interchange that alters the assumptions upon which we read both poetry and its tradition? Although answering these questions in all of their complexity requires a more careful study of Williams and the modernist tradition of women writers than can be provided here, I would like to approach these issues from the angle of Kathleen Fraser's work and its relationship to Williams's book of the imagination, *Spring and All*.

*Language Innovation and a Feminist Poetics: "to re-write the flood"*
Fraser's writing of the eighties has built upon feminist concerns evident from her earliest works, concerns that increasingly develop in relationship to matters of language, subjectivity, and literary tradition.

With her first book of poetry, *Change of Address* (1967), Fraser joined other feminist poets in the mid-1960s whose works challenged poetic convention by openly speaking about women's experiences. Invigorated by the second wave of feminism, Fraser's earliest poems question gender roles encouraged for women while also investigating her own female identity in relationship to prescribed standards of beauty, romance, sexuality, motherhood, and so on. At this early point, Fraser was not familiar with many of the women modernists whose work would later become so important to her; however, along with her contemporaries, she realized that a vast tradition of Anglo-American poetry had dismissed the female perspective. Fraser and other women began questioning the power of this male-dominated lineage: "What were young women poets to do, understanding clearly by then the rules of the game and how we must submit our language to the scrutiny of those in power?" A desire to "locate a poetics on our own terms" developed alongside a keen awareness that women "had always been the marginalized sex, looking towards the center, and from our point of view there was reporting yet to be done" (Fraser, "Tradition," 24).

As women's poetry flowered in the early seventies, a new center defined itself within this marginal space. The political need for "reporting" women's stories led to a central "call for the immediately accessible language of personal experience as a binding voice of women's strength" (Fraser, "Tradition," 24). Fraser, however, found herself exploring the assumptions behind the idea of an "accessible language"; her subsequent experiments with language structures distanced her from feminist circles emphasizing content over form as the primary locus for a feminist poetics. Her efforts deviated from the poetry produced and encouraged within these circles, a woman's poetry "committed . . . to a belief in the transparency of language and its ability to represent adequately, through relatively conventional literary forms, the specificity of women's experience" (DeKoven, "Male Signature," 75–6). However, Fraser's feminist project focused instead upon patriarchal structures of language, exploring the linguistic play she had begun to discover in Stein and Woolf as a gender-marked resistance to these structures. She recognized in these predecessors "a structural order of fragmentation and resistance to the patriarchal models that confirmed my perspective" and claimed, "I wanted this difference in my own work" ("Tradition" 25).

This "difference" not only hindered the reception of Fraser's poetry in the most dominant feminist circles, but the hostility directed toward her avant-garde practice caused Fraser to feel doubly marginalized – as a woman and as an experimental writer. Writing from this double margin, Fraser sought out other women concerned with connections between language, perception, and cultural constructs of gender. Reading Barbara

Guest, she became intrigued with her "tenacious insistence on the primacy of reinventing language structures in order to catch one's at-oddness
with the presumed superiority of the central mainstream vision" ("Tradition" 24). In San Francisco, she met Frances Jaffer, Beverly Dahlen,
and other women poets whose "focus" brought her to a

> different kind of attentiveness: it wasn't the witty polish or posturing
> of 'great lines,' but a listening attitude, an attending to unconscious
> connections, a backing-off of the performing ego to allow the mysteries
> of language to come forward and resonate more fully. ("Tradition" 25)

In the seventies, Fraser turned to journal writing as a way to explore
this "different attentiveness" through her relationship, as a woman, to
linguistic, literary, and cultural constructs. The fragmented, spontaneous, and private journal sequences of these years offered formal options
for conveying personal experience outside the traditional lyric and opened
her work to the possibilities of a female "difference located in usage"
("Tradition" 25). She embraced the journal as "a form of writing that
didn't bully me into the traditional beginning, middle and end – the linear
model of organizing a poem that had so largely comprised my university-
educated ideas about writing poetry" ("How Did Emma Slide?" 13).
The form of notational writing used in keeping a journal provided a
"place of entry, [a] place of breaking away from public received forms
of intimacy, *while yet linked* to poetic practice."[116] Employing a language
engaged with process, Fraser's journal writings led her to imagine and
explore alternative subjectivities she considered more suited to her experience as a woman: the "shifting subject," the "I" undergoing continual
change in relationship to "romance, politics, nature, culture, etc." as
"each ensuing change in consciousness pummeled or undermined the
assumptions I'd been living and writing with most of my adult life"
(Fraser, "Line," 167, 166). A series of short journal entries first appears
in *What I Want* (1974), exploring the poetic possibilities of journal writing
through compression of language combined with a notational associa-
tiveness. Fraser's play with such possibilities culminates in the long poem,
"The Story of Emma Slide," which is written as fictional journal entries
but is highly conscious of the crafting of line and the use of page space.
Fraser discusses this poem in a 1979 essay, "How Did Emma Slide? Or
the Gestate: A New Poem Form for Women." Using the poem to illustrate the possibilities of poetic form drawn from an inextricability of
female body and female subjectivity, Fraser connects the formal qualities
of journal writing – its circularity, lack of closure, inclusion of interruption, and self-generating form – with the distinctly feminine experience
of reproduction and child-rearing. Referring to the "unfolding process
of gestation" and "all the uneven physical and emotional curves," Fraser

coined the noun "gestate" to articulate a tentative model for feminine discourse grounded in the maternal body: "a poetic form of unnumbered discrete phases, unfolding and proliferating as rapidly or as slowly as one's perceptions do. . . . recognizing the value of precise detail and the use of formal devices while welcoming those unexpected and mysterious and necessary leaps in human consciousness" ("How Did Emma Slide?" 14). Emerging in these early statements of poetics, issues involving the shifting relationship between body, self, and language mark the direction Fraser's experiments with poetic form take in the more radical works of the eighties.

*New Shoes* (1978) marks Fraser's transition from a style influenced by the New York school's embrace of the ordinary and the accidental to one more specifically exploring the intertwined nature of language and gender. Speculating at the time on the potential for a feminist approach to form and discourse, she writes:

> The limits of language present us, continuously, with the limits of what we might know about ourselves. The woman poet should be able to face her text as a speculative journey, a process of writing in which she does not know what the limits will be ahead of time. Poetry is the place where she can resist making a commodity and can push against or extend the formal directives of a literature shaped by a poetics largely developed out of the experiences and pleasure principles of men writing. (*Feminist Poetics* 7)

Fraser's 1978 volume explores this "place" or "text," authored by a woman uncovering her own language needs within a phallogocentric culture. Concerned with codes and laws, erasure and revision, the poems imagine a female self-empowerment through the dismantling and re-constructing of this "text" of woman. It is particularly the internalization (by women) of Western patriarchy's myths, ideas, and images of the feminine that these works explore. The poems of *New Shoes* urge a "rewriting" of the feminine, imaging the female body as a locus for knowledge and change. At the same time, the crafting of the poems demonstrates a growing attentiveness to the visual and spatial aspects of form – to the movement of words on the page and the perceptual links or breaks attained through such movement. The textual forms interact with the retextualizing of the feminine.

"Locations" offers up this feminist project:

> To give up
> finally   to stop holding
> the infant idea   how deep
> you've been told to hurt,
> to dissemble the structure

of wounds which choose
to resemble one another

. . . . . . . .

A home inside yourself
Your body held unto itself.
                (80)

Only in dissembling "the structure of wounds" marking the female body
can women reclaim their bodies from cultural idealization and degradation. In "Flood" (35–7), Fraser responds to the imaging of women in
male-authored texts. The poem reads like the book's manifesto, urging
an awakening "out of the old / female sleep." Lines arranged down the
page, moving back and forth through white space in irregular distancings
from the left margin, the poem is like the "body / seen / in motion"
that the speaker looks toward at the poem's conclusion. This body, which
she wants "to re-write," would break, in its motion, the static and even
violent inscriptions of the feminine reified in art and cultural artifacts.
The poem's attention to spacing and visual space suggests this break as
the speaker thinks of Gauguin's woodcut, in which he cut the words
"Soyez Mystérieuses" (Be Mysterious)

> above the backside of
>     a female body
> lying perfectly
>         voluptuous
>             in mud
> or sleeping (was it?)
>     as if pillowed
> and dreamy with her legs
>     explicitly
>         not there
>   but held in darkness
> under the wild waves curling
>   where his tool entered
>         wood
>     showing us
>       his choice for her
> in the prolonged watery beat
>     always sleeping
>         face sideways
> with flesh of body
>     soft   white   wanting
>   to nod out
>     of what the next cut
>     might reveal.

The phallic tool carves while it erases the feminine, her legs "explicitly
/ not there" but held in darkness, the body mysterious, awaiting the

tool's defining entrance to show "his choice for her," his mark, his cut. "You get the joke," the poem continues, "Babyhood becomes us," a model of womanhood coexisting with "Lady mamma, queen somebody." These alternatives, written out of the male gaze, are forms of female somnambulism, a sleeping through life as artifact. The poem describes a movement out of slumber, a freeing of the body:

> Aslant,
>         you appear
>                     in relief
>     but feel yourself
>         moving out of the old
>                 female sleep.
> You hear the intellect
>                 of cells
>                         turning over,
>         recognize
>             in another's gaze
>     a different subject, not merely
>         "you" and "me" not even
>     representational or
>                 seductive
>                     but hungry for breakfast
>         under waking Pacific sky
>             and eager to swim out.
>             I want
>                     to turn this body
>         over,
>     show you her face
>                 awake and askew,
>     imperfectly ready
>         to re-write
>                 the flood
>     nothing in the way,
>             all of the body
>                     seen
>         in motion.

Fraser's dance, like Isadora Duncan's modernist free-footed dance, choreographs itself in reaction to a specifically male-defined pattern of steps, the male-authored texts of the feminine.

To "rewrite" the female body becomes Fraser's project of the eighties, centered on the awakening of a "body" or "flood" of women's language. This awakening, for Fraser, has involved an ongoing excavation of "safely buried" avant-garde women from past and present, an "urgent shifting and digging," writes Fraser, meant "to reconstruct that preexisting tradition of modernist women who need us to acknowledge them as much as we need them to fall back on . . . so that *we* may set out a light for whatever next unknown voices are laboring in the dark" ("Tradition" 26). Explorations of writings by early women modernists have directed Fraser into further inquiries concerning the interlocking gender experiences of language, culture, and tradition:

> Why was there no acknowledged tradition of modernist women's poetry . . . as there clearly was for men (and women) working out of the Pound/Williams tradition or the Stevens/Auden lineage? Why had most of the great women modernists been dropped cold from reading lists and university curricula? Why were most feminist and traditional critics failing to develop any interest in contemporary women poets working to bring structure and syntactic innovation into current poetic practice?
>
> Then there were the puzzling questions of language and gender. Did female experience require a totally different language, as Luce Irigaray seemed to be suggesting? How was that difference located in usage, a usage that had perhaps occurred and been ignored, dismissed as insignificant, or dropped out of the canon and quickly absorbed – even appropriated – by powerful figures such as Pound and Graves? How is gender expressed and imprinted socially? (25)

*Language Dis-ease: "What structure gagged me?"*

As readers, we are confronted with these compelling questions in Fraser's language experiments of the eighties, which gather together her earlier concerns and begin to work more explicitly through the influence of a modernist tradition of women writers. *Each Next* (1980) extends a concern with language and gender into formal prose experiments that break open narrative structures while investigating imposed orders of culturally gendered authority. *Something (even human voices) in the foreground, a lake* (1984) carries these experiments further into the disruption of syntax and the dissociation of detail in sequences deliberately evoking the possibility of a feminine discourse. *Notes Preceding Trust* (1987) claims a feminine discourse and explores its new measure in poems and prose directly linked to a tradition of women modernists.

*Each Next,* a collection of prose-poem narratives and poems, confronts what one piece calls woman's "dis-ease" with traditions of language, literature, and authority. This confrontation takes place on a formal level as much as a level of content, for Fraser's "narratives" break from sequential, conventional forms and rely instead on discrete units of thought, perception, and experience that self-reflectively comment upon the medium of communication they employ. With a doubleness of vision, the narratives read themselves as opposing conventions of language while simultaneously residing within them. Recording snatches of inner dialogue, these narratives develop out of Fraser's experiments with the journal structure, but as Suzanne Juhasz points out, now the private writing is intended to be read by an other: *Each Next* "uses the forms of private writing, and its capacity for understanding and rendering the hidden moment, for the purposes of telling the other person, too, so that the space of the relationship might be more fully experienced by both people" ("The Journal as Source" 19). Use of prose techniques (character, plot, setting) "both amplifies and condenses the journal structure" into recognizably narrative form, resulting in a continual tension between the narrative conventions (as assumptions that shape and define a reality) and experience that seems excluded by those conventions ("The Journal as Source" 19). *Each Next* attempts to negotiate this tension, to find formal ways of communicating a specifically female reality – a reality at base informed by her relationship to language and its shaping of power along lines of gender. Asking a central question running through these narratives, the female speaker of "Talking to Myself Talking to You" ponders her silence before men: "What structure gagged me?" (28).

For a woman to "assert [her] language in the powerful field" of a reality structured by male experience entails an effort of resistance leading to the dismantling of the structures that "gag" her (34). In approaching these experimental narratives, we must ask how resistance marks them and how these arrangements of words upset habits of thought and behavior that, intentionally or not, render women deficient, inferior, or invisible. The opening narrative, "this. notes. new year." reads, as its title suggests, as a series of notes, associatively generated and moving forward without a predetermined order or significance. This is the mind listening to itself but with a doubleness that includes a listening to *how* one is speaking. This first piece sets out notes for the rest of the volume, like marginal notations that Fraser will take up and expand upon in other pieces. These are also notes that sketch language itself as a communal space that the poems try to construct: "Someone's rhythm sneaking in again. Sharing a language. The osmosis of rubbing up. Communing" (13). Fraser addresses these notes to an "other," whose echoes and responses she invites: "Dear other, I address you in sentences. I need your nods and I hear your echoes." A language formed between speech and response, it could compel "a forward movement still, as each word is a precedent for what new order," or, as Williams detected in Stein's work and sought to emulate, a movement by process, not "purposed design," in which the composition of words determined "not the logic, not the 'story,' not the theme even, but the movement itself" (*Each Next,* "Stein," 17). In contrast with a purposed design, or what Fraser later calls "pre-fabricating significance" (*Notes* 48), movement by process includes accident. Long valued by Fraser as both an aesthetic and a life principle, accident here becomes a matter of language interpretation or translation – or, more precisely, a revisionary openness to mistranslation. The second prose unit, a parenthetical "shift into another's past" that is a memory of her previous "self," recalls a transition from design to process. The woman is " 'in a fury' " because her lover's "letter told the usual stories in all the old ways. She swallowed them whole. Then came the nausea. She wanted a 'flow' she thought, but in the translation it was corrected, displacing the *o* and substituting *a*. She could give herself to an accident. She was looking out the window" (*Each Next* 11).

Process, accident, and betweenness alter the sense of language order, allowing one to look out a different window, to enjoy a different per-spective. Picking up on the evocation of "sentences" in the opening line, the speaker later muses:

> One man said of another that he was committed to the sentence. I sentence you. I could hear the terseness of his sentences and how se-ductive it seemed to move the words always towards a drop in the voice. What did it mean to be flat? Was there a principle of denial? Of manipulation? (12)

The sentence and its tonal utterance bespeak an authority, implicitly sustained by male "commitment" in its order. She thinks then of the French workers she would hear on the streets from her Paris apartment, who spoke sentences as questions, "voices raised at the ends of sentences, as though all were in question. I question that. I like that. It made you want to look out the window" (12). Shift in tone, then, makes the sentence like the question not only in rhythm but in eliciting a gesture of response, in provoking another "look out the window." This mimicry of the authoritative sentence finds a poetic precedence in Marianne Moore's parodic alterations of syntax, rhythm, and poetic structure; Fraser elsewhere identifies Moore's "refusal of pre-existing forms and the continuous search for her own modalities and formal shapes" with alternatives available for a feminist poetics interested in "the structural re-invention of the poem's terms, as well as the range of female expe-riences informed by those structures" (*How(Ever)* 4.3 [Jan. 1988], 17).[117] Or, as Rachel Blau DuPlessis observes, Moore "takes away what you are used to (meter, rhyme, conventional stanzas), but gives back some-thing almost the same (syllabics, slant 'rhyme,' unique but exact stanza shapes based on syllable count)." Drawing on Luce Irigaray's terms, DuPlessis claims Moore's mimicry

> "works at 'destroying' the discursive mechanism." . . . [and] mimics all the rituals of poetic order and excellence in order to substitute her own. (*How(Ever)* 4.3 [Jan. 1988], 15)

Fraser, in the narrative, also thinks of the French theorists she had begun reading and teaching at the time of writing *Each Next*.[118] Her own insistence upon contact and contiguity has found affirmation in Hélène Cixous's notion of the maternal touch and Luce Irigaray's feminine poetics of two lips touching, while their writing serves as model for a feminist dismantling of patriarchal ideologies embedded within language. In this narrative, she describes their writing: "I wanted, suddenly, to speak French because of certain French women thinking about layers, thinking *in* layers, but as yet not translated. They had moved ahead but not in a line" (12). She goes on to comment upon the authority these women possess – an authority implicitly inaccessible to the American feminist writer because of a marginalization of her tradition and cultural position. But for the French, "growing up inside of, yet opposing, a tradition peculiarly French and masculine appeared to give them a certain authority because the tradition itself assumed a dialectical plane and invited the next position, while echoing 'I baptize thee in the name of the father and the son' " (12). Though there is a certain ambivalence here toward the paternal line of the French tradition, there is also a recognition of its invitation to dismantlers, a doubleness inflecting the works of the poststructuralist fathers, Lacan and Derrida, from whom the female theorists descend. In the example of these daughters carefully taking apart their fathers' homes, often with the tools placed paternally in their hands, Fraser gains a useful strategy and a sense of her own doubleness, within and opposed to a literary tradition dominated by men. And she remembers her own early embrace of this tradition's poetic tenets, unconscious at the time of their gender bias disguised as claims to authority. Recalling a line of Stanley Kunitz's, a favorite of hers at twenty-one, she reflects: "That was a peculiar passion I do not often encounter in the poetry of the late '70s, but do not want to deny. That urgency we call romantic, but which might actually be, in part, the willingness to be told lies. That rush. How I've wanted it. His romance" (13). This is one of the "half-truths" she questions, at the same time questioning "why I sink into silence around them." Questions open her to speech, to her own sentences, as "now that I've made the decision to attempt a separation from their hold on me, I am released into sentences" (12).

The issue of the woman poet's particular "dis-ease" with a male tradition that defines both poetry and the poet from the vantage of male writers appears frequently, as in "Piling up about to pour over." Composed of nuanced details and fragmentary reflections, this narrative suggests an unease that almost completely pushes plot into the background, so that the "plot" *is* the unease, signaled early on by a reference to the mythos of the serious poet: "Black notebooks. Poets carried them full of pages. These, tonight. She thought about her notebook covered with needlepoint, the flowers stitched to their colors. At the garage sale, someone had left it and she had found it. No heavy bindings. No black think"(42). Confronted with traditional signs of a poetic sensibility, she asks herself, "Have I refused a certain sign of seriousness?" The power of signs also occupies the woman in "The decision," as she looks through her "collection of black silk beauty marks" and explains, "I was looking for a mark. A sign to place abruptly there, on the white field of the paper. To hold your attention for an instant only" (17). Playing on the dual meaning of the word "occupied," Fraser comments, "She had been occupied. As in 'occupied zone' " (17). This zone is diagnosed as a sickness in "Side Drawer," but a sickness that refers to itself within a literary tradition. In the poem's final lines, the woman's malaise is diagnosed: "You've got dark night of the soul, he said, shaking his plastic thermometer," alluding most immediately to Eliot's aesthetic of the negative way and its root in the mystic tradition of St. John of the Cross. The woman responds with a counterallusion, to Pound's *Cantos* and their place within the Homeric epic tradition: "I've got wine-dark sea, she replied." Within the "zone" of male modernism, encompassed by the ubiquitous zone of literary history, the woman poet resides with disease.

In searching for a language "both watchful and fluent, allowing the variants of yourself to have voice" (55), Fraser discovers language constructions that mitigate the authority of forms or precedents she terms "bullying." An apt example occurs in the final poem, a series of fictionalized and poetically compressed journal fragments entitled "Notes re: Echo." The entry for September 6 reads: "Elements of disorder. A sweet disorder in the dress. The idea of order in Key West. Disorder and Early Sorrow. Order me a beer" (50). Continuing her earlier experiments with journal writing, here Fraser employs notational forms to undermine the authority of canonical writers through the repetitive and associational movement of her language. Robert Herrick's "sweet disorder" recalls an entire tradition, spanning from the Renaissance to the modern era. Wallace Stevens and Thomas Mann, each notable for his concern with the artistic temperament and the creative capacity of the poet, exist here amidst colloquial assertion ("order me a beer") and the individualized fragmentariness of the woman's thoughts. Fraser recognizes these figures of poetic authority but does not regulate her discourse to theirs; rather, they become part of her discursive process.

The series of notes from Echo to Narcissus admit this dual gesture toward tradition as she asks, "Why, then, do I trust your language enough to enter it?" (55). The trust grows from a recognition of language as "both watchful and fluent," a language in which meaning is formed between speech and answer, open to a multivalency of self and other. Looking for herself in language, Echo writes to Narcissus: "Is language, in fact, the pool? Looking into your words as if they represented a surface of water (Narcissus gazes with longing, trying to find himself), do I then find me, a word I know? Yes. No. Some deflection, in-flexing of where we might overlap" (51). But, rather than an overlapping or in-flexing pool, language between Echo and Narcissus continually defines him, and she finds herself only through his self-definition. The note ends: "Echo is She, who watches Narcissus look for himself and returns him to himself, slightly altered, by her very attentiveness. Where am I?" (51). The September 10 entry "echoes" back to the book's opening notes and their comments on the French tradition. Using the image of a fist, Fraser suggests the doubleness of woman's relationship to language and its forms:

> Walking up to a new edge, I discovered in myself an old mute. But I stayed, allowing my curiosity to teethe on the silence. . . . It was, of course, a question of language. Of a code shared by the interior of four fingers and a thumb who knew each other's openings and closings. Knew how to make a fist, the form of which I recognized and hated, while feeling an odd affection and curiosity for each of the parts. (54)

The fist, both familiar and hated, cannot merely be severed, but its code need not be limited to "His words. How they tone up, then polarize or identify certain pleasures. Activate some as yet unexercised part" ("September 11" 56). Without denying the beauty of this language, the "beautiful surface" of Narcissus's pool, Echo warns that its beauty "is always involved with seduction" (56). Invoking an image of water and depth, a plumbing of the deep waters below the surface of the pool, Echo asks, "And what of the darker, colder water? One cannot deny its pull" (56). In these waters, the self shifts and is multiple and variant: "How, then, to hold on to the *who* you think you are. The image in water shifts, according to the light's impact, and currents we cannot wholly predict" (56).

Echo's apprehension of a deeper pool comments back upon a key piece in the volume, "Green and blue piece for Francie, swimming, in which Grace enters." Written for the artist Francie Shaw and the poet Grace Paley, the narrative conflates a pool, language, and the maternal body in an interweaving of imagery that fluidly shifts within the lights and currents of a "wet pool" the poet swims through. As the speaker swims, thoughts of Paley speaking as a woman poet, of Shaw painting with wet pools and floods of pigment, of embryos developing, of her own mother's eighth-grade body, of the pregnant body, all swim together within this pool of language. The pool is the maternal body, which is the "colorless language" that "surrounds us all," and the creative act is linked to the engagement with an experience of otherness embodied in the gestate, the pregnant body:

> Bump into Francie's body swimming while thinking only yesterday of
> her, swimming with baby inside her in other pool, different neigh-
> borhood. But here they both are, swimming past me in water. I see
> *her,* here, but think in past tense, located in images of Langton St., or
> morning light in her loft skimming paintings, or *Life* magazine's "De-
> velopment of Embryo," seeing who *would* be my child, now David,
> had fins and eye sockets. (20)

Fraser relates the woman artist's creativity to the experience of gestation
as an experience of contiguity with otherness, the wet pool/womb containing a difference nonpossessible but connected. This is the "fourth
language," the maternal pool of interconnection:

> Three languages making Grace's heart go bump, behind her warrior
> strength-and-courage. Dukes up. I kick and breathe while she reads.
> Wanting to be water for her. Fear pulling down on limbs. This fourth
> language. This colorless language surrounds us. Who is the shadow?
> These faces, to be there in her. And she, at that same table, a small
> thing in her mother's lap, fifty years before the embryo which swims
> each day with Francie. Doing laps. All is astir.

> Francie stirred the paint, dripping green leaves all over it. Black edge
> seeking what that form might identify. The next aspect, she is bringing
> to it. Wet pool of it. Red and black. Background. On her back, swim-
> ming through cheesecloth and yellow sun where infant presence is also
> a field. Speeding along the graph, sinuous, all ways. (22)

Defining a poetic "field" tied to a maternal consciousness, produced not
so much by the exclusively physical experience of maternity but by the
socialization of women in regard to their bodies, Fraser's impressionistic
rendering of the pool suggests what she elsewhere terms a "female collective consciousness, a spiritual and erotic set of valuings essentially
ignored by the dominant culture" ("Line" 155). The pool conflates maternal and "infant presence," as past and present converge in circular
contiguity. The artist evolves within these waters and, like the wet pools
of paint, merges with the "colorless language" of the womb, connecting
with other women creating from this fluid space.

    Fraser's next volume, *Something (even human voices) in the foreground,
a lake* (1984), continues to examine matters of gender and language. In
many ways, this collection and *Each Next* strive, through a compressed
and self-reflexive narrative form derived from notational writing, to find
ways of trusting oneself with language. DeKoven suggests that "the
effect of her [Fraser's] writing is to open out the world-as-language,
making us feel our own subliminal connections between disjointed emotions and the sequences of perceived objects and partially articulated
thoughts they attach themselves to" ("Gertrude's Granddaughters" 14).
Marking a greater dislocation of language and rupture of syntax, these

prose paragraphs also swell ripely with sensuous details of landscape, bodyscape, and domestic environs, employing a painterly love of color and shape as the writing "offers a nonreferential combination of precision and generality. We get very particular expressions of emotion . . . combined with . . . rigorous refusal, in the abstract diction, of specifying context or narrative coherence" (DeKoven, "Gertrude's Granddaughters," 13). The first section, made up of seventeen prose paragraphs in which an unspecified group of people gathers near a lake, deliberately obscures identity, distinct location, and narrative sequence. Palpable but inarticulable states of feeling emerge, riding upon a textured surface of precise detail interwoven with a connotative discursiveness, so that the texture creates its own context and generates its own pattern and design.

Moving between emotion, thought, and observation, the prose values the weight and feel of each word as the materiality of language is brought into a flattened foreground beside meaning. "Becoming famous and powerful" exemplifies the overall style:

> To each other, she is as if the sun were oddly powerful, borne in her palinquin mind, her grammar moving in the lag (into) a narrower cut, slammed on a map of fixed color, crimson perhaps, like a tear in the surface of isolation, her brain the extenuated appreciation, the cold space it leaves as it blows by. Oh happy speed, marshes here, mahogany blue boats for one foot (startled by that flatter water's intimacy), clenched in the same style he remembers. Beautiful hair to take care of. The selfish ruined shine of her. (4)

The string of clauses making up the first long sentence refute the linear sentence, reading more like overlays of thought and observation (recalling the French women Fraser thought of as writing in layers). Antecedents are unclear: Is the sun "borne in her palinquin mind"?; is "her grammar" or "art" "slammed on a map"?; what is "like a tear"?; what is "the cold space"? The interchangeability of meaning encouraged by this sentence structure allows multiple and simultaneous perspectives, nuances of feeling in a spectrum of possible meanings that refuse to locate any one point of stable, isolated meaning.

Although a disruption and indeterminacy of syntax certainly characterize experimental works by male writers, Fraser ties her language strategies to a female identity and particularly to a female experience with language. Visualizing, in the structure of the sentence or the narrative, "that marginal and unspoken region [contemporary women poets] claim as difference," Fraser conveys the "resistance" that she calls the "ongoing condition-of-being for most women poets" ("Line" 155, 166). She explains this condition as "the inability to say how it is or *not wanting* to say, because what *wants* to be said and who wants saying can't be expressed with appropriate tonal or spatial complexity in confident, firm [masculine] assertions" ("Line" 166). This feeling of inarticulateness – or at least of deficient speech – is expressed in "In white, she who bathed," the final prose paragraph of the first long section: "Everywhere, rooms are leading to other rooms. The brain, she thinks, is her corridor and her strict casement when she is a window. It is believed that she understands partially, but cannot speak, except haltingly, and about nothing in particular" (17). For the woman, enclosed by patriarchal structures of language, "what wants to be said is both *other* and of 'the other world.' It wants words and worlds to be registered in their multiple perspectives, not simply his or yours" ("Line" 166). In these prose paragraphs, possibilities for multiplicity of perspective arise from the Dickinsonian movement between the particular and the general, producing a continual decentering of attention and logic. Fraser's own term for Dickinson's inscription of otherness within her poetry, "the knowledge of rupture," applies to her own legitimation of "the disturbed otherness of a mind not in sync" with a "masculine thought and poetry" that seems "unruptured, smoothly in control" ("Line" 154).

Exploring the female self's otherness in language becomes the focus of the final section, "Energy Unavailable for Useful Work in a System Undergoing Change," an excerpt from *Leda. & Swan.*, termed a work-in-progress. This meditation on artistic process unfolds from an initial, small detail of domestic order as the female subject ("She") notices the loose corner of a drawing pinned to the wall and "has instructed herself to go get another pin" for the "fourth corner [that] has been unanchored for days" (24). "Pin it down," she directs herself, but "as soon as she leaves this room, there is the back porch with its large old windows to look out towards the valley, the bridge, Mt. Diablo's pale oriental cone on a clear day" (24). Her mind and attention wander, compelled by external details into various musings and memories, "a demonstration of how I lose sight of the fourth corner" (25). Whenever she regains sight of it, however, she feels inadequate and yet resistant to this internalized judgment as she questions her own desire to "touch" rather than anchor down. This tension evolves into a consideration of her poetics:

> Back at her place, she notices a tear in the lining of the lamp. She wonders if it has always been there. She notices a large piece of cracked paint peeling back from the perfect Desert White of the ceiling. The light fixtures are naked, dusty Sylvania bulbs bulging asymmetrically for years from their sockets. Exposed. One could spend a life fixing, arranging, mending, covering, improving, touching-up. She'd rather touch. Yet there did remain this yearning for completion, symmetry, a formal ascendency to the next level. Her attempts were full of falterings and lurchings. They were insufficient, awkward, premature, repetitive.

> They were loose threads, a button missing. A pin falls. The drawing is unanchored.
>
> Trying to become perfect, a way of pulling against this displacement. (32)

Only when she embraces the experience of "displacement" does she transform her relationship to poetic (and linguistic) forms of authority: "Not to ask for a prize. A little Hershey's kiss, with a message for you tucked inside the foil wrap. She is breaking the code. She is a system undergoing change" (32). This effort to construct what DeKoven calls "a (writing) self" ("Gertrude's Granddaughters" 14) involves a new structure of trust in one's discovered (not received) relationship with language and all that language encloses: "After months of starting and stopping, not liking what I write, not finishing, I have, meanwhile, been building the difficult structure of trust" (29). A process of self-empowerment specifically relating gender and writing, this "system undergoing change" rewrites tenets of the old system:

> A phoenix in her with a different sort of song. A reclassification of duck into swan. Sunday into Monday. Dross into slippers that fit. Her desire was on a grand scale and she empowered it as vision. Slowly, belief. Then a seizure of voice. Asking for, saying *this*. This is what I want. (33)

As DeKoven comments, the "mundane duck *becomes,* rather than being raped by, the swan: Fraser's feminist rewriting of the patriarchal myth of empowerment" ("Gertrude's Granddaughters" 14). This rewriting follows H.D.'s lead in taking the form of palimpsest, "writing 'on top' of other writing," as Fraser explains her predecessor's linguistic innovation; Fraser writes over the patriarchal tradition (with Yeats as the specific allusion) while also writing over her own previous writings ("Line" 155). With the phrase "what I want," she recalls a fragment of her earlier work[119] and with it her whole history within a feminist aesthetics, retrieving "bits and pieces of language, single words, alphabet fragments whose traces and marks suggest the challenge of coded hermetic messages, both from recovered past writings and from one's own unconscious" ("Line" 155). In effect, she is reinscribing a myth of empowerment over her own fragments, which rise to the call of "a seizure of voice." At the same time, her formal strategy links her back to a poetic mother, empowering her through this maternal line.

Seizing or claiming a voice affects the medium of language; for Fraser, the feminist assertion of voice cannot merely mean entering a slot available within a necessarily masculinist ideological continuum that underlies habitual linguistic forms. Language itself is changed through a defamiliarizing process that calls attention to notions of linguistic (and cultural) norms, while suggesting alternative ways to interpret experience and to articulate the process of thought involved in acts of interpretation or translation. Fraser's style ruptures phallocentrically sanctioned meaning and authority by revealing "the mechanism by which meaning is constructed through language," while helping us "recognize the irrational, disjointed substratum beneath our processed, homogenized, male-coherent assimilation of life's raw data to acceptable interpretive models" (DeKoven, "Gertrude's Granddaughters," 13).

### Language, Gender, and Tradition: "inside / (jittery / burned language)"

Furthering concerns developing from her earliest work, Fraser's more experimental work of the 1980s reveals an influential recognition and embrace of a marginal tradition of women modernists that begins to provide *other* interpretive models for her to pursue. In *Notes Preceding Trust* (1987), a book of poems and prose, Fraser reassembles language and poetic form within her experience of gender, mapping a shifting terrain of feminine cognition. Her letter to Andrea, part of "five letters from one window, San Gimignano, May 1981," describes the poetics informing this volume and the two preceding it:

> My writing is changing. One might sometimes think I was returning to the style of work I did twenty years ago, except that my line is surer and my eye more exacting. Still, I am just as uncertain and resistant, at the beginning of each work attempted, as I ever was. In fact, my bursts of confidence are fewer, my self-doubt greater. I'm trying to find a way to include these states of uncertainty . . . the shifting reality we've often talked about – fragments of perception that rise to the surface, almost inadvertently, and come blurting out when one has lived in intense desire and frustration. We need to be able to map how it is for us, as it changes . . . but are often half-choked by awkwardness in the face of the mot juste. But why deny this partialness as part of our writing? Why not find formal ways to visually articulate its complexity – the ongoing secret life – without necessarily making it a candidate for the simple-minded "confessional?" Writing *is*, in part, a record of our struggle to be human, as well as our delight in reimagining/reconstructing the formal designs and boundaries of what we've been given. If *we* don't make our claim, the world is simply that which others have described for us. (47)

To "make our claim," *Notes Preceding Trust* redescribes not just the world ("which others have described for us") but the language and formal designs employed in making that claim. Though she has urged this direction continually, it is with this latest work that Fraser poetically enacts a feminine claim to language, a full and powerful seizure of voice.

The volume begins with a densely lineated poem, its title familiar yet made strange by the transposition of letters that alters a key word in Fraser's poetics, as "boundary" becomes "boundayr"; this visual disjunctiveness is counteracted by the aural quality now admitted into the production of the word's meaning, for we realize that "boundary" is a form of "bound air," or "boundayr." Our habits of perception are further defamiliarized by the intangibility of a subject (or subjects), moving among an array of colors used to create verbal canvases in which the words themselves float unattached to referential objects, yet evoke strong emotional and psychological moments and nuances. As the opening section demonstrates, the suppression of the noun's specificity combines with forcefully connotative verb forms and an adjectival framework of color. Parts of speech interact within a linguistic negative space, flowing around and between the sentences' shifting, undefined subjects:

> The seizing of the blue social level, the red duality inert the yellow
> body forming intimate contact, essential string, the beige of hemp and
> wall, green responding, green sado/shadow bottle, the plum enables
> us, the black beyond our hours will satisfy this encounter,
>                                                   substantial
> white of chair the presence in the world of non-primary blue. Red en-
> ables us to be distinct *and* substantial, at some point we must inhabit
> ourselves, the evidence is mauve and lively with grey borders, to know,
> to feel, even *be* the inheriting white, the celery, that light with which
> we regulate, become pink and peach, we blush and are fruit, we bruise
> but did blossom formally, we are halfway there, we are capable of
> giving the ultra aquamarine, we are absence of carnelian. Now
>                                                   you are
> in the violet world and she is turquoise and you want to tangle in each
> other's altro. Inside the border, the heightened concern between her
> and a color she feels is appropriate in this hour. (9)

Distinct and yet related, the colors make up a map of a self, both singular ("you") and collective ("we"), that follows movements of overlap, separation, conflict, and contiguity. It is a map, however, without north or south, without stable borders, without legends of "measure or invention" (10). It suggests the dimensions of "the year of breaking thread around the boundayr, the primacy of embroidered meanings, petal of each pool and mouth, poppies opening in spite of every border or the yellow diminishing" (9). Movement occurs through and within borders, as the "inheriting white" with which "we must inhabit ourselves" is both the "light with which we regulate" and also the light with which we "become pink and peach, we blush and are fruit." Without this light, if "the white besieged by red" shuts out other colors, the white is an absence, a nonhabitation of space, associated with borders and categories that organize and separate: "White appears and reappears and disappears, boundaries of field, some owning or lowing, the subtracted smallness, the dots in focus, magenta snow screen, all that falls away from you, black letters through the page, your mother's name you did not keep" (10). Whereas the red that "enables us to be distinct *and* substantial," circumscribed with "lively" grey borders, suggests a form of becoming in the first two segments, by the poem's final segments this quality of distinction disallows contact or contiguity. The purple, previously an "enabling" color, now suggests the hardness and impenetrable objectivity of a created artifact: "and the purple figs, the marble figs also, the inedible green marble with its purple objectivity, she who was almost there without measure or intervention" (10). As the piece has progressed, the colors themselves take on different psychic weights, imbuing the prose with washes of changing overtones. We are left with questions of plot, setting, character: Who is "she," "you," "we"? What is happening and where? Is the landscape inner or outer? Where is the important "almost there" of the final line? Perhaps what we need to ask, however, has more to do with language: How does boundary become boundayr? How are borders of language and self moved, altered, or enlivened, and how are they enforced, exclusive, objective? When is one "inside the border" of another color, an other color, and when can one both regulate and become "pink and peach"? How can this fluid self be measured through language, through formal structures of any kind? What "measure or intervention" prevents or excludes or suppresses this shifting self? Again, we circle around to the title's implicit question – when is a boundary a boundayr?

A boundary, for one thing, defines a space as a focus of attention, distinct from surrounding space that, through the boundary's demarcation, becomes the margin. Fraser claims the margin as feminine and, in "Written in the margins" (20), she considers woman's marginal position within the borders of a language privileged and sustained by phallogocentric traditions of thought. The piece begins with a reference to Karl Marx that suggests language as the male seduction and erasure of the feminine: "The governess is in white. Helen lags with a letter from Karl M. When Jenny arrives at the scene of the seduction, a voice is overheard saying: '*I am not interested*' " (20). Karl M. "assigns a working-class gesture to one hand on each of their bodies," emblematic of the philosophical and historical subsumation of women within Marxist class concerns, obscuring gender with the overriding mark of class. As "their bodies" are written upon, their language is silenced. Karl M. can enter language with ease, as he "asks questions wherever he goes and studies every day, moving from cookbooks to soccer, choosing science texts always in the preferred language of the country currently inhabited." On the other hand, language for women resides in silences, linking the feminine body (as culturally erased and inscribed) to a feminine language: "Jenny's words are gaps. Olive. Oil. Spreads. Further. Makes. An. Enlarged. Spot. In. Several. Places. And 'you pay for your choices.' (This, in her mother tongue.) She wants to write in English, with some slighted resistance to her situation." The words themselves, restrained by insistent periods, evoke a visceral sense of the feminine body, a feminine jouissance of fluidity and multiplicity, that is halted and broken into noncontiguous words, so that the gaps between words are important to consider. To write in English, yet resist its logocentrism, forces the poet to resist the periods, to open the gaps, to somehow transform language by creating forms for the feminine. The piece concludes with a suggestion of a transformation, as "Jenny returns to her conjugations," singing them "like scales," and grammar becomes *her* song, her structure of music. She sings "as if in a fever, but with perfect lucidity."

This process of resisting seduction and seizing language with one's own voice underlies the entire collection. The first section, *boundayr* (which includes the two prose pieces already discussed), moves through various tasks of rethinking the structures of seduction, or from another angle, the structures of "measure or intervention." The poem "Notes preceding trust" speaks of the "interim" space that Fraser is learning to trust:

> We are after difficulty
> Our love is effulgent and the world
> at each edge surrounds
>
> creeping at the peripherals
> We are a zone we can have
> and take each morning
>
> first in the different light
> what inhabits
> the full air
>
> of who spoke in the interim
> There are shifts we learn
> to trust behind their split seconds
> (13)

The contact between self and other occurs in the space between them, the "interim" that continually "shifts." As this "zone" shifts, so do the participants involved in its space, and they must learn to trust to a fluidity of self. A process of labor that moves each lover into the "zone" or "full air" of a shifting interim space between them, this trust can too easily give way to an inattentive "habit of viewing," in which shapes are merely repeated: "Some one else's / distance / determining a thickness / not between us" (14, 13).

The shapes and boundaries of representation compel the rather enigmatic "Bresson Project: Forget you are making a film," a two page layout of prose, poetry, and line drawings. The drawings – two incomplete rectangles, a line containing a bump, a bull's eye, a piece of barbed wire – all suggest forms of measurement, containment, and definition. In cultural representations of women, a formulaic positioning of the feminine conceals a violence toward women, a misogyny hidden beneath the adoration of feminine beauty. Consider the juxtaposition of the "he" and "she":

> he is particularly aggravated
> agger. vated    inner.vated
> he is violent        ultra-
> violet   She is
> the wow of his silver screen
> cinnamon queen with
> freckles, she's so fine,
> so fi-yi-yine
>
>                    (18)

Beneath the "fictional hairlocks," a "new bump on her scalp forms," suggesting again a violence that marks her feminine appearance, making it "a little gold tomb, with an / old singing in it" (18). Representations are accepted as "real" in their formulaic accessibility, "as a popular love song we remember from our childhood is real when it wets the heart with satisfying equations" (19). The final line of the poem isolates a single statement in quotes, placed next to a three-sided rectangle, its unclosed side opening toward the white margin of the page. The line reads, punningly, " 'I'm drawing a blank just tell me a position' " (19).

The next piece, "Written in the margins," finds a position by claiming the white space left open by the incomplete rectangle, and in the final prose piece of the section, the speaker returns to the matter of trust that this claim requires. In "Everything you ever wanted," the speaker confesses, after having depended for so long on the "positions" provided by cultural instructions, that "I do not trust these glaring invitations to break into green. . . . First comes the comma, then the period. Walking on water, then stepping into a long breath trying to catch up. I am having trouble finding where to take the first step" (22). There are no maps, except what emerges in the process of movement forward. She dreams of being blind, of seeing "only light and the dark shapes of things" as an "undeciphered part of me" separates from the "body I left behind on the bed . . . densely heavy and a stranger" (22). When she awakes into a reintegrated body that can "*think* of moving my legs and *feel* their movement at the same instant," she runs in place until a person she "desires" places a key in her wine glass: "I choose to lift the glass and drink every drop. This silence grows jittery and shifts its weight. I have come to the end of the list of necessary distractions. Each task has a check mark next to it, a little gesture on the map's white silence" (22). The map evolves, "reimagining / reconstructing the formal designs and boundaries of what we've been given" (47).

*Electric railway, 1922, two women,* the second section, is a series of poems and one short prose poem that begins this reimagining. The opening poem, which provides the section title, presents two nameless women riding the train in Italy. We initially see them as distanced observers, looking at the passing world through the framework of prescribed femininity:

> Hair of old railway posters, yellow
> helmet, some sort of
> gold bracelet
> above the elbow one notices
> as her left hand appears to make a social gesture.
>
> .   .   .   .   .   .   .   .   .   .   .   .   .
>
> your companion wears the black watchstrap and leans forward and
> is pulling at her pearls
> with a sentiment you imagine.
>
> (25)

The train's mahogany window, from which the women watch the passing scenery, keeps them safely enclosed within a perspective they have chosen:

> At every moment
> a body is being violated,
> although the mahogany window frame was designed for safety
> when you chose this method of seeing
>
> (25)

The train's power and motion, like the power fueling vehicles of patriarchy, subsumes the woman addressed as "you," giving her "surcease from personal density and a diminishing will" in the crowd of voices surrounding her. The voices, or styles of speech, "remain as disembodied prowlers" on the train, belonging to others but ominously threatening to her. Then, in the final stanzas, a voice in the crowd sounds familiar; its style of "hesitation" implicitly female, it alerts her to her own disease on this powerful train:

Someone's hesitation is American and feels so comfortable
you alert yourself: You are in a woman's body,
you are expected to act a certain age although
you retain an interior childhood of dread
and being caught at every border.

This randomness changes color when you speed
south, in your mind your body
slowly removing its cotton garments.

(26)

The expectations and borders circumscribing the "woman's body" are like her clothes, which she mentally removes, piece by piece, undoing external roles and confronting the "interior childhood of dread." As the body is revealed, borders are transgressed and reimagined, and a feminine discourse begins to be constructed and retrieved.

Recovering a sense of this discourse in a tradition of women writers, the poem "Botticelli: from Bryher's imagined notes" searches for a way to write the feminine into a language that provides an ill-fitting garment for the woman poet. The poem, in the voice of Bryher, a writer and H.D.'s lover, begins with the problem: "To write it (you or I) / this plan / something like a dress you didn't choose" (27). Bryher finds in the stress patterns of other languages an awakening of silenced syllables that is suggestively feminized:

Svelto does not mean svelte
The language crosses over and is wet

In Venice we said Venezia

In any small town the beat flew
to a middle syllable

(27)

This "wet" language too often becomes frozen and static when brought into public: "Bodies standing / in pools of sound with their tongues / buried so, crushed ice around canisters" (27). In the poem's next lines, we can read an allusion to the modernist "pool of sound," within which H.D.'s tongue is buried. Recalling the modernist trope of the city, Bryher queries, "If / a city is an invention / why are we not there" (28). Instead, H.D. constructs the imagist poem along the rhythms of an alternate (an other) space and time:

We divide time into little containable parcels
which can fit on one page

You write in the heat
but I continue to draw

a fresh calendar for each month
I begin with clear white space

and follow with sharpened divisions
For one evening I can sleep
unarmed before the desired
eventfulness.

(28)

The "little containable parcels," the imagist poems surrounded by so
much white space, allow an intimacy, a disarmed openness "before the
desired / eventfulness," or, as the lineation insists, before the desire. The
acts of demarcation and arrangement (Bryher's calendars, H.D.'s poems)
suggest a poetic authority unlike the sound of power and authority in
works by Eliot or Pound, "the sea-surge modulating into the didactic
in Pound, the liturgical, magisterial tones of Eliot" (Ostriker, "No Rule
of Procedure," 20–1). Ostriker continues: "Hold H.D. up to the eye and
ear and we have something quite different, something which includes a
great deal more space, more silence around the words as if pausing were
as important as speaking . . . rather like a still small voice: not 'authoritative' but intimate" (21). So long denigrated as slight or trivial, H.D.'s
imagist poems are linked in these imagined notes by her lover to a
language of wetness, a poetics of awakened stresses and syllables, a form
that includes the white space of silence and, thus, the conventionally
silenced feminine. The imagist poems are like the

more than hundred
flowers in "Primavera"
or rather that Botticelli wanted
each singleness his pleasure.

(28)

We are reminded of the botanical detail rendered in H.D.'s imagist
poems, an attention to nature that links her to a tradition of women
poets, although critically relegating her to the status of minor poet until
recently. The varnish of literary history, obscuring H.D.'s poetic achievement, is lifted and cleared by the restorative care of her literary daughters,
whose labors reveal to them the multiple "flowers" of a feminine discourse.

Suggesting her own struggle for a feminine discourse, Fraser has written in another poem:

(My words are intentional and discover themselves pictorially
as they emerge and continue
to struggle from their white
bits of netting.)

("Agosto, Puccini, Gabriella" 30)

This interaction between intentionality, discovery, and contextuality (the
"white bits of netting") makes up the artist's struggle with language,

self-consciously foregrounded by the modernists' experiments with the word. This section ends with "re:searches," a series of fragments dedicated to Emily Dickinson. Fraser's "searches" reveal Dickinson as modernism's revolutionary precursor, although her "latent content/[and] extant context" have been traditionally misinterpreted. Considering her achievement within a male tradition, many readers have insisted on an image of Dickinson as a lonely spinster, suffering the loss of love and penning demure gemlike poems. In contrast to this image, Fraser's first fragment suggests a poet and poetry more recently revealed:

> inside
> (jittery
> burned language)
> the black container
> (36)

A modern lyric tradition, a poetry of the internal, descends from this jittery, burned language, these poems that are black containers. Their power stems as much from desire, from sensuous pleasure, as from the poet's internal world. The second fragment reads as a litany of feminine desire for the feminine:

> white bowl, strawberries
> perfumy from sun
> two spoons      two women
> deferred pleasure
> (36)

   These first two fragments suggest an intimacy between women, alongside the linguistic decentering performed by Dickinson's poems. From this connection of burned language and the deferred pleasure of two women – threatening and unacceptable forms of power – the fragments pile up without coherent order, a linearity forsaken for layers, a palimpsest that provides only bits and pieces and does not pretend an authority of completion or coherence. Dickinson's own poetry provides a model: "pious   impious / reason could not take / precedence" (36). A contradictory poetry within the boundaries of reason, containing oppositions within one line, it must be read outside of reason's directives. Her poetry, "Pronounced with / partially closed / lips" (39), subversively bears the imprint of her gender and her awareness of women's invisibility and voicelessness. The act of writing, an act of translating perception, articulates a self otherwise muted:

> the fact of her
> will last only

> as long as she continues
> releasing the shutter, she thinks
>
> (37)

The subversive quality of Dickinson's poetry, largely unrecognized long after her publication, meant a certain erasure of her radical innovations, and particularly of their base within a gendered apprehension of language. Fraser calls attention to this erasure, then transfigures it through linguistic manipulation:

> pink pearl eraser
> erasing her face her
> eee face ment
> her face meant
>
> (39)

The entire series of fragments enacts this transfiguration, moving out of effacement into what "her face meant." The strawberries, associated with the two women, are recalled in fragments that suggest Dickinson's departure from a logocentric notion of language transparency:

> just picked—
> this red tumbling mound
> in the bowl
> this fact and its arrangement
> this idea and who
> determines
>
> this strawberry is
> what separates her tongue
> from just repetition
>
> (36–7)

Demonstrating what "her face meant," Fraser ends her "re:searches" by placing this Dickinson at the head of a modernist lineage, upsetting a lineage conventionally codified as a search for literary fathers. In these final fragments, Pound, Joyce, and Williams (respectively, by stanza) are embedded in the word play:

> this above
> all to be who,
> be nature's two,
> and though heart
> be pound-
> ing at door,
> cloud   cuckoo

radial activ-
ity, who cow now,
who moo

not random, these
crystalline structures, these
non-reversible orders, this
camera forming tendencies, this
edge of greater length, this
lyric forever error, this
something embarrassingly clear, this
language we come up against
                    (40)

In "researching" Dickinson, the woman poet finds the male modernists
crowding in, their prescriptions for a modern form and measure offering
authoritative models: "this above / all to be who." Who is the model
for the modern women poet? Pound is "pound- / ing at door" with his
constructed lineage (synecdotally suggested by "cuckoo," from the medieval song he rewrote as "Ancient Music") and his vorticist form ("radial
activ- / ity"); Joyce's version of the young (male) artist's evolution joins
Pound's example as the opening lines of his *Bildungsroman* are recalled
("who cow now, / who moo"); Williams's objectivism appears with its
"camera forming tendencies." An entire tradition of women's lyric poetry and its dismissal as a minor form ("this / lyric forever error") enters
into this litany. For the woman poet, language and its poetic measures
derive from the fathers; however, Fraser's "re:search" funnels all of these
models into the poem's final line, asking how the modernist revolution
of the word is mediated by Dickinson's prior confrontation with "this
/ language we come up against." To move behind the fathers is to find
the mother who prefigured their own radical experiments.

Such "re:search" becomes part of Fraser's effort to remap her own
poetic identity and relationship to language. When Fraser writes, "We
need to be able to map how it is for us, as it changes," she calls for a
fundamental change in the idea of mapping and measuring. Her "Five
letters from one window, San Gimignano, May 1981" revolve around
types of measurement that one uses to locate oneself, to detect change,
to understand relationships between different objects and spaces, and to
perceive multiple phenomena simultaneously. The five letters, to five
individuals, are written in one afternoon and arranged in the order they
were written, beginning at four o'clock and ending at seven thirty-nine.
Thus, we receive five views out of one window, producing both a cubist
simultaneity of perception and an impressionist attention to momentary

flux. From the letter form – spontaneous, unplanned, yet attentive to imagery and lyric reflection – develops a series of meditations on measurement that is affected by the measure of multiplicity and simultaneity the form itself employs.

Fraser's studio window provides a standardized space for measuring and mapping what she sees, and the first letter, to Michael, establishes its framing perspective: "A car, sky-blue, is rolling as easily as a marble across the two middle panes of my studio window. It follows the road to Certaldo. Call the left and right sides of my window points A and B. Point A is a tree still leafing out in the grassy green brightness of April . . . " (43). Measurement through comparison alerts one to difference and proportion: "Point B is a house at the edge of the road to Certaldo, at the top of the hill in front of me. The house is longer than tall; its roof of brick-red tiles breaks into three sections" (43). The letter goes on to consider, before ending, an important image of multiple differences contained within (rather than assimilated or subsumed by) and defining a shape. "A patch of trees quite particular in their varying height and cut of leaf yet dominated, finally, by the shape made from their overlapping differences" suggests a dynamic of relationship between the individual identity and defining context (43). This image speaks of a possible shape measured not by the individual, not by the homogeneous group, but by the "overlapping differences" that create a new shape.

To Andrea, at 6:18 P.M., Fraser writes that the view from her window "is divided almost equally between green hills and a Della Robbia blue sky" (46). The view transforms itself by the moment, as mist replaces "big puffs of white cloud," and she wonders: "What happened in those brief moments, when I looked down, absorbed?" The desire to include "what the writer's eye lights on when she looks up from the page" in the movement from word to word recalls Gertrude Stein's "use of landscape, or the detail of the immediate physical environment . . . as a focus for the effort to transform into language, or to use language to create, a complicated emotional / intellectual 'moment of being' " (DeKoven, "Gertrude's Granddaughters," 13). Landscape and detail suggest modes of measure suitable to Fraser's process–oriented poetics, and she observes that "having a horizon to measure by alerts one to change" (46). Measure, then, does not reify or impose an absolute order but enhances one's perception of change, movement, and proportion; likewise, the horizon changes with one's location, remaining a measure tied to individual placement and, significantly, to choice. Fraser chooses, for example, the studio window as viewpoint, as she chooses to reject " 'the planned deviousness of a story.' " Like Martha Gellhorn, the author she quotes in her final letter, she is "tired, finally, of pre-fabricating significance in human events" through imposed measures and structures (48).

Both the strategy of simultaneity and the issue of measure occupy the final poem in *Notes Preceding Trust*. Interweaving multiple voices and stories, "Four voices telling stories about dark and light" looks at standards of measurement that prefabricate significance based upon measurements derived from male experience. The poem explores a "new measure" derived from Fraser's "re:search" into language, tradition, and gender, suggesting a multiform narrative as four voices create a continually shifting texture that combines glimpses of narrative, bits of lyric reflection, and imagistic refrains. "Four voices telling stories about dark and light" does not clearly distinguish between four individual voices, though two distinct stories emerge and each discrete stanza can be taken as a different voice. At times a voice is singular, at other times a collective "we" appears; the stanza units vary in length and some present a story with plot and character, while others offer fragments of perception, single images charged with emotional weight, or seemingly random comments. One voice tells of riding a train through Tacoma that hits a young boy; another voice – the voice that weaves itself through the poem most vividly – retrieves a memory from elementary school. Fraser's formal strategy is to place all of these fragments within a structure that does not determine their relationship but encourages their interaction. The poem's structure requires a reading and thinking in layers; Rachel Blau DuPlessis described this strategy when Fraser first began exploring a layered conception of thought:

> . . . how to get dualism without an order of priority. That is recognizability without valorizing one side of anything. Where there are no sides . . .
>
> Homans says it another way – how to get a linear poem in a deconstructed space. (linear because language is read forward, period) You have to read the poem in a linear fashion and yet oppen [sic] the space so that hierarchy & dualisms do not set the value tone of the piece. This is the challenge to any new poetry and – it is the challenge that Silliman has taken up. For one. ALSO KATHLEEN! But also – Oppen (see "Freud slip," above) How to get dualism without an order of priority, without gender asymmetry. Homans says it is almost inconceivable. Is it? is it? ("A Note" 113)

Fraser's poem attempts to be "a linear poem in a deconstructed space," taking apart the collective consciousness of gender asymmetry. The assumptions of a collective consciousness – exemplified by the "we" on the train – provide a source of measure that comes to seem both natural and universal. In contrast, another voice, an alternate measure, unravels the gender particularities informing the universalized notion of the artist, challenging the male bias that claims gender neutrality.

The poem begins with a visualization of perception's relative accuracy, and immediately our attention is called to the effect of context and the changing nature of perception. "Black dresses make people smaller / but lights seen behind an edge make an apparent notch in it," the lines read, warning us away from absolute forms of measure (51). A longer stanza follows, introducing the first story and the figure of the "master" artist, the young boy Bobby, whose artistry is represented as control of a "new shape":

> fireflies that summer after supper
> then September came and the new boy at his desk drawing war
>     planes. Everyone
>                                                        wanted
>
> a drawing made by Bobby
> and some boys paid him a nickel and
> copied his cockpits and wings,
> trying to master the clear poise
> of a new shape.
>                                                         (51)

The poem's voices are all concerned with shapes: the shape of guilt when the train hits a boy, the shape of a discursive space between two people, the shape of a doorway that interrupts a "formal surface," the shape of gender experience (54).

Bobby's talent dazzles his schoolmates, who observe him "every day at his desk, / drawing and drawing." His activity becomes a source of measure as "all luxury lost its meaning, in that order" (52). Other voices deflect off of this narrative, suggesting unease with this measure and the mastery of these new shapes:

> The blank page
> was merely an interval or
> an intrusion. We could not rescue it
>
> nor could we huddle, as if the page were
> big enough. (52)
>     . . . .
> These experiments may be modified to infinity.
> That airplane appears to be traveling from the right,
> making an arc over every head
>
> but we are not its children
>
> .
>
> and we do not make little drawings of airplanes.
>                                                         (53)

The drawings are linked to gender experience; in addition, certain analogies develop between the airplane and the train, both vehicles of movement that contain multiple individuals, although as shapes of power they claim the individuals as a homogeneous "we":

> "We are in Tacoma,"
> and when it hit the boy
> they said, "We hit him,"
> as if all of us had done it.
>                     (53)

This collective voice provides its own structure of language: "Something travels circuitously and we give over / even our list of words" (53). Words are surrendered to an order that excludes listening: "It is clear from his description who prefers to make his or her own order and who waits for a listener" (54).

Halfway through the poem, one voice provides an image of a different measure, interrupting the formal order and dismantling its structure: "First, they pulled the balcony away, ripping out the floor and safety guards to reveal simple light. Then we saw the white original wall with a makeshift door, also of white, nailed into what had been a doorway or an interruption of the formal surface" (54). Imaging the feminist reclamation of women's voices that interrupt assumptions of aesthetic and cultural order, one voice goes on to dismantle her own seduction by the "master" drawings and clear poise of Bobby's airplanes.

> We covered the floor with paper airplanes and PT boats.
> We were inside his obsession when the lamp cast its shadow.
> Our fingers repeated his shapes
> until we could amaze someone with a little war
>                                         (56)

The mentality of war and the shape it provides the imagination quickly appears as a gendered experience of culture similar to the mythos empowering the "discovery" explored in Williams's *In the American Grain* or the "plagiarizing imagination" he condemns in *Spring and All*. From this basis for artistic measure, the final voice(s) claim difference:

> "When I was a boy . . . "
>
> You were in training. You were in the sky
> looking for a place to land.
>
> Bobby was pretending to be "you"
> or someone saluting the flag in your khaki shirt.
>
> I was on the rug with crayons
> inventing substitutions. Inside primary shapes
> it was red or it was yellow.
> We were warned

about stars on flags in windows
when someone's father went away.

. . . . . . . . . . . .

When I was young, I wasn't like you and I'm not now.
(56–7)

The ideological grounds of measure undergo scrutiny as "substitutions" are devised and reclaimed. Measure renews itself in the shifting self's relationship to language, a relationship permeated by the cultural and historical process of gender difference.

In Fraser's feminist poetics, measure is tied to the betweenness and responsiveness of a feminine discourse she explores and envisions throughout her work. Striving through language to shift our habits of thought, Fraser's writing offers a way of speaking about a feminine aesthetic that bridges formal strategies and lived experience within a matrix of a woman's tradition. To read Fraser and to read this tradition encourages us to alter collectively assumed notions of poetry and modernist aesthetics by considering the gendered apprehension of language as it relates to the material world. On this basis, we can approach the works of William Carlos Williams, sensitive to his (often conflicted) participation in a marginal tradition and to the effects of his own notions of gender on his poetic theories and practice.

Spring and All: *New Forms and a Hidden Tradition*

Like Fraser's *Notes Preceding Trust*, the experimental work *Spring and All* (1923) carries the imprint of the women modernists whose writing influenced each poet, although in the older poet's case the imprint is often occluded. Through retrieving the strategies of the women writing in this hidden tradition, we can refocus our reading of Williams's modernist manifesto to detect his incorporation of the subversive modernisms practiced by writers like Marianne Moore, Gertrude Stein, H.D., Mina Loy, and Emily Dickinson. Reaching this point of recognition, we can then go on to consider the impact of formal elements, derived from a female counterstrain of modernism, first upon the cultural work the text undertakes and, secondly, upon that work's relationship to the aesthetic tenets of contact and measure, long considered central to Williams's poetics.

Williams's insistence upon the materiality of language continually recalls Gertrude Stein, who sought much earlier than he "an escape from crude symbolism, the annihilation of strained associations, complicated ritualistic forms designed to separate the word from 'reality,' " as Williams describes his efforts in *Spring and All (CP1)*.[120] Praising her unlinking of words "from their former relationships in the sentence," Williams's 1930 essay on Stein notes in her new arrangements of words what Fraser later describes as a form of "overlapping differences": Each word "has a quality of its own," and yet together they "are like a crowd at Coney Island, let us say, seen from an airplane" (*SE* 116). The penultimate poem in *Spring and All* coincides in metaphor and spirit with his statement on Stein's writing, as "the crowd at the ball game / is moved uniformly" but "is laughing / in detail" (233, 234). Like the trees that Fraser observes in "Five letters," this image of the crowd suggests a unifying shape or arrangement containing yet not eradicating multiple differences – or, rather, that the shape of "beauty" admits "the power of their faces" (234), a power of "overlapping differences" (*Notes* 43). For Williams, this shape images the imagination, the "fraternal embrace" of oneness that refuses a "horrid unity" for this crowd, who "in detail . . . are beautiful" (233) – a Steinian composition, a paratactic collage. This image of the crowd reflects the linguistic principle of parataxis that informs Williams's (and Stein's) experiments and that resists the predetermined logic naturalized by our language assumptions. Stephen Fredman writes that

> the hypotactic sentence can be diagrammed hierarchically; it has a logical order. The plot of the paratactic sentence works by a continual sidewise displacement; its wholeness is dependent upon the fraternal [or, we might add, sororal] bonds of a theoretically endless proliferation of familial resemblances rather than the dynastic bonds of filiation. Thus the conscious sentence writer can subvert, deny, or replace the authority of the hypotactic sentence through the alogical plot and the aural structure of the paratactic sentence. (*Poet's Prose* 31)

Williams, like Fraser, investigates concepts of order that cross over from language into cultural thought, and his choice of parataxis as a literary strategy reveals Stein as an ideologically subversive presence in his works.

If Stein's ideas ground Williams's approach to language, Marianne Moore stands explicitly as his poetic model, the modern poet proclaimed most significant to his work in *Spring and All*. Tributes to Moore are plentiful, significantly cast in opposition to the modernism of Eliot and Pound; she "escapes" the "empty symbolism" of her contemporaries, her revisionary imagination "contending with the sky through layers of demoded words and shapes" (188). She "cleaves herself away" from the compositional strategies of the traditionalists and "is of all American writers most constantly a poet" (188, 230). Writing "from the source from which poetry starts" (230), Moore's example suggests to Williams an attentiveness to language interaction, a listening process within the "overlapping differences" of linguistic forms: "Of course it must be understood that writing deals with words and words only and that all discussions of it deal with single words and their association in groups.

. . . Marianne's words remain separate, each unwilling to group with the others except as they move in one direction" (231). Unable to quite grasp Moore's verbal choreographies – what he elsewhere calls a "rapidity of movement" that forms "an anthology of transit" (*SE* 123) – he concludes: "Her work puzzles me. It is not easy to quote convincingly" (231). Rather than quote her, he pays her (and her brand of poetic authority) homage in the poem that follows his comments, "Somebody dies every four minutes" (231–2). Collocating advertisements, statistics, slang, and train directions within a paste-up collage drawn directly from Moore's example, he legitimates his own "antipoetry" through her authority, inscribing her impact upon his poetic vision into this book of the imagination (177). Replicating Moore's famous disdain for "poetry," the poem's second stanza rejects the "illusion" or barrier of "art" that Williams takes to task. "To hell with you and your poetry," the poem states as it asserts its own unconventional sources and movement, leaping from fragment to fragment:

> AXIOMS
> Don't get killed
> Careful Crossing Campaign
> Cross Crossing Cautiously
> THE HORSES          black
>                &
> PRANCED            white
> outings in New York City
> Ho for the open country
>                    (232)

The poem's final line, "Interborough Rapid Transit Co.," provides a gloss on the poem's technique and a bow to its source, as Moore's poetics of rapid transit compels Williams's linguistic and formal movement in this and other poems.

   The metaphoric comparison between Moore and a "Rapid Transit Co." provides Williams with a central expression of her poetics. In an essay he wrote while composing *In the American Grain* and *Spring and All*, Williams identifies and praises this "rapid" movement in the work of Moore, linking her to Emily Dickinson and a poetics of multiplicity and betweenness:

> Unlike the painters the poet has not resorted to distortions or the abstract in form. Miss Moore accomplishes a like result by *rapidity of movement*. A poem such as "Marriage" is an anthology of transit. It is a pleasure that can be held firm only by moving rapidly from one thing to the next. It gives the impression of a passage through. There is a distaste

for lingering, as in Emily Dickinson. As in Emily Dickinson there is too a fastidious precision of thought where *unrhymes* fill the purpose better than rhymes... it is at most a swiftness that passes without repugnance from *thing to thing*. (123–4)[121]

In Moore and Dickinson there is "a distaste for lingering," or as Fraser describes the movement of a Dickinson line:

> We often see the starting and stopping movement of doubt within her line, as well as between lines, as we watch each unit lurching forward – both separated by a dash *and* rushing forward through the seeming haste of that dash – to the next perception or extension – the argument of parts – one Emily hesitant to say – another Emily eagerly rushing in – if stammering – with a further ironic shift of view. ("Line" 153–4)

Fraser's comments help flesh out Williams's point in alluding to a "fastidious precision of thought" expressed by *un*rhymes – near rhymes that create an unsettling, destabilizing, and halting quality in Dickinson's poetry, while combined with a simultaneous "swiftness." Williams learns from Dickinson's poetic line, incorporating a similar play between movement and hesitation that is consciously foregrounded in *Spring and All*.

This movement allows a multiplicity of perception and an attention to negative space, the space of "unrhymes." In the essay, aligning himself with this poetic lineage stemming from Dickinson, Williams characterizes its quality of multiplicity in numerous ways:

> Good modern work, far from being the fragmentary, neurotic thing its disunderstanders think it, is... a multiplication of impulses that by their several flights, crossing at all eccentric angles, might enlighten. As a phase, in its slightest beginning, it is more a disc pierced here and there by light; it is really distressingly broken up. But so does any attack seem at the moment of engagement, multiple units crazy except when viewed as a whole. (*SE* 123)

In Moore's work, there is "a multiplication, a quickening, a burrowing through, a blasting aside, a dynamization, a flight over" as it enacts "the geometric principle of the intersection of loci: from all angles lines converging and crossing establish points" (*SE* 121, 122). This movement of multiplicity directs the eye to the "in between" space of intersection, for it "grows impossible for the eye to rest long upon the object of the drawing. The unessential is put rapidly aside as the eye searches *between* for illumination" (*SE* 123; my emphasis). In this verbal and poetic negative space – literally compared by Williams to the negative space of a drawing – engagement or contact is possible.

Moore's collage method, which Williams admires and discusses at length, evokes this negative space in the process of "wiping soiled words or cutting them clean, removing the aureoles that have been pasted about them or taking them bodily from greasy contexts." "With Miss Moore," he goes on to say, "a word is a word most when it is separated out by science, treated with acid to remove the smudges, washed, dried and placed right side up on a clean surface. Now one may say that this is a word. Now it may be used, and how?" (*SE* 128). Moore's method of collage depends upon the placement of such acid-cleaned words in arrangements that maintain each word's defined edge, each word's materiality. The word "may be used . . . in such a way that it will remain scrupulously itself, clean perfect, *unnicked beside other words in parade.* There must be edges" (128). The thing, the word, is itself, but also makes "edge-to-edge contact with the things which surround it," and in the "inevitable connective" of poetry (rather than editorial, grammatical connectives), the word/thing takes on a presence that is relative and depends upon contiguity and context. Like Stein's definition of a nonhierarchical modern composition as a paratactic process equalizing all parts, an insistence upon the lack of center and the importance of all parts that she saw in Cézanne's works, Moore's collage does not subsume its parts in serving the overall composition: "The effect is for the effect to remain 'true': nothing loses its identity because of the composition, but the parts in their assembly remain quite as 'natural' as before they were gathered" (*SE* 129). Williams considered Moore's collage approach akin to his own efforts to connect the thing and the idea, and in fact, to use the idea as a material thing within the poem: "If a thought presents itself the force moves through it easily and completely: so the thought also has revealed the 'thing' – that is all. The thought is used exactly as the apple, it is the same insoluble block. In Miss Moore's work the purely stated idea has an edge exactly like a fruit or a tree or a serpent" (*SE* 129). She is able to do this, Williams suggests, in refusing "ex machina props of all sorts . . . rhyme, assonance, the feudal master beat" and following instead "her own rhythm," as did her predecessor Dickinson.

Though not mentioned by name, the examples of Dickinson and Mina Loy further inform such poems as "Crustaceous / wedge" (211–12) or "The rose is obsolete" (195–6). The weighty quality of the words in "Crustaceous wedge" read as though chosen from a poem by Loy: The extreme physicality and density of words are emphasized by short, often one-word lines that isolate like granite blocks the verbal materials of the poem. Words like "crustaceous," "pulverize," "swarming," "triphammers," "stancions," "ventricales," draw upon Loy's lexicon of nonmelodic sounds and syllables and the dense rhythms they create. A concrete specificity calls attention to the physicality of detail, yet combines with a cerebral or conceptual vocabulary in a movement that seems constantly off balance, much like Loy's early poems and satires. The penultimate stanza suggests her rhythms, charting this perceptual-linguistic movement as a dense compression of consciousness:

The aggregate
is untamed
encapsulating
irritants
but
of agonized
spires
knits
peace
            (212)

The same unyielding quality of material and form, noted by Yvor Winters in his 1926 *Dial* article as characterizing the verse of Loy and Dickinson, appears frequently in this volume. Loy's specific influence imbues "The rose is obsolete," which follows the female poet's lead in deromanticizing the language and symbols of romance: "The rose carried the weight of love / but love is at an end – of roses" (195). Williams constructs lines that replicate what Fraser calls Dickinson's "rupture of knowledge," and the final lines of the first stanza exemplify his debt to her line's acknowledgment of hesitancy and indeterminacy through the devices of paradox and the dash:

—the edge
cuts without cutting
meets—nothing—renews
itself in metal or porcelain
whither? It ends—

Carrying the impulse of the dash even further, he forsakes the authority of completion by leaving lines syntactically incomplete:[122]

What

The place between the petal's
edge and the

From the petal's edge a line starts
that being of steel
            (195)

This interruptive pattern, replicating a movement of fragmentary perception, cannot verbally reach the "place between" the petal's edge and an unnamed space, a space left blank in the poetic line. This is an interesting moment of silence in the poem, for its evocation of negative space suggests an attempt to reach or communicate the space where "at the edge of the / petal that love waits" (195). However, to regenerate itself in language, the poem turns to a masculinization of the rose; unable to verbalize the betweenness, the poem focuses on the line drawn as boundary:

> infinitely fine, infinitely
> rigid penetrates
> the Milky Way
> without contact—lifting
> from it—neither hanging
> nor pushing—
>                      (196)

This image links to the earlier "copper roses / steel roses" that the "sense" makes, and the poem's formal strategy questions how one reads the "edge" of these various roses: Does one read the edge as a "between space," unexpressed and inexpressible, that is left in the poetic line as unfinished or opening out; or does one read the edge as the stanza that follows, suggesting an edge that is "infinitely rigid . . . without contact"? The final stanza collapses these two choices, suggestively reintroducing the capacity for touch in the image of the "fragility of the flower / unbruised," while endowing it with the kinetic spatial quality the previous stanza evokes. The flower's fragility "penetrates space," and the words "fragility" and "penetrates" pull together verbal oppositions in much the same way that Dickinson's verse undermines dualistic habits of thought through the irresolvable pairing of paradoxical or oppositional words. This move replicates in the poetry a prose strategy Stephen Fredman examines in Williams's *Improvisations,* in which the "paradoxical figure" enacts a conflation of "two pairs of mutually exclusive images, two sets of the basic oppositions that structure our Western cultural assumptions" (*Poet's Prose* 25). When the romantic ideologies associated with the rose are dismantled, the realm of love is no longer structured by gender oppositions that the "illusion of art" sustains. Rhetorically, paradox allows a mode of contact, an investigation of the oppositions of discourse that enter experience.

As *Spring and All* demonstrates, Williams's poetic ground establishes itself within a tradition of women writers whose resistance to a sanctioned tradition is inseparable from negotiations with poetic authority. Like Fraser, Williams often felt that tradition played the bully, and in this volume, he pits his concept of the imagination as a connective force against the powerful "plagiarizing imagination" of tradition that erects barriers through its art of "beautiful illusions" (178). Early on he writes that "nearly all writing, up to the present, if not all art, has been especially designed to keep up the barrier between sense and the vaporous fringe which distracts the attention from its agonized approaches to the moment. It has always been a search for the 'beautiful illusion.' " Even the modernist quest for the "new," in its claim to destroy old forms, repeats the evolutionary process of art, "repeating move for move every move that it made in the past" until a "perfect plagiarism results. Everything is and is new. Only the imagination is undeceived" (182, 181). The first prose sections of *Spring and All* concern this plagiarizing imagination and "THE TRADITIONALISTS OF PLAGIARISM" who oppose the true imagination. The apocalyptic violence that Williams sardonically heralds, often read as his nihilistic endorsement of a destruction that will allow newness to flourish, defines the power of the plagiarizing imagination, and Williams's caustic sarcasm condemns rather than condones its rationale.[123]

The out-of-sequence "Chapter 19" describes the world's annihilation, America's "monster project of the moment: Tomorrow we the people of the United States are going to Europe armed to kill every man, woman and child in the area west of the Carpathian Mountains (also east) sparing none" (178). Coming as it does so early in the book, before we can get a sense of Williams's tone or project, this proclamation can seem a shocking and extreme Dadaist call for complete destruction, its literal intent negligible beside its metaphoric basis in an authority of aggression and dominance. But to even accept the metaphoric element as a direct expression of Williams's poetics of the new completely ignores the unease with authority his poems constantly display and, most obviously, the critique of this very attitude in *In the American Grain*. With this swaggeringly apocalyptic vision, Williams offers yet another version of the peculiarly American imagination, "regenerated by violence," as he states in his history, an imagination distorted by a tradition combining repression and dominance into a dangerous misapprehension of "the new." *In the American Grain*'s critique of this imagination reiterates Williams's description of this "monster project," America's modern extension of its founding imagination, its authorizing mythos. This is the imagination "intoxicated by prohibitions" that "rises to drunken heights to destroy the world. Let it rage, let it kill. . . . Then at last will the world be made anew" (179).

The order and peace that result from this "final and self inflicted holocaust" reenvision the narrow unity of sameness espoused by the Puritan fathers. The "love" fueling the holocaust succeeds in eliminating cultural and racial difference:

> that together the human race, yellow, black, brown, red and white, agglutinated into one enormous soul may be gratified with the sight and retire to the heaven of heavens content to rest on its laurels. There, soul of souls, watching its own horrid unity, it boils and digests itself

within the tissues of the great Being of Eternity that we shall then have become.

(180)

In contrast with the newness of cultural "crosspollenization" proposed in *In the American Grain,* this vision of a "horrid unity" requires the suppression of difference. This imagination, again "drunk with prohibitions, has destroyed and recreated everything afresh in the likeness of that which it was. Now indeed men look about in amazement at each other with a full realization of the meaning of 'art' " (181). Like the Old World's settlement of the Americas, the "new" is merely a repetition of what came before, and "art" resides within the province of "THE TRADITIONALISTS OF PLAGIARISM." Their effort to "try to get hold of the mob" and maintain the status quo is a power struggle involving cultural weapons: "Those who led yesterday wish to hold their sway a while longer. It is not difficult to understand their mood. They have great weapons to hand: 'science,' 'philosophy' and most dangerous of all 'art' " (185).

Philosophy, in Williams's mind, had traditionally been a product of male experience; in his 1917 essays to Dora Marsden, "The Great Sex Spiral," he explicitly made the connection between a masculine perception and what he now calls "the plagiarizing imagination." Williams even mentions Marsden's writings as an example of a totalizing system's insufficiency to deal with important questions: "Emptiness stares us once more in the face. Whither? To what end? Each asks the other. . . . Why are we here? Dora Marsden's philosophic algebra" (184). The imagination that resists the constraints of philosophy, of plagiarism, of tradition's claim to power, appears as a female figure derived from the modern dancer Isadora Duncan, whose bare feet and free form scandalized New York society and inspired the artistic avant-garde: "The imagination, freed from the handcuffs of 'art,' takes the lead! Her feet are bare and not too delicate. In fact those who come behind her have much to think of" (185). *Spring and All,* "addressed – To the imagination," and to the female dancer whose steps embody the imagination's movements and its risqué revelations, is working out of a creative matrix we have seen developing from "The Wanderer" through *In the American Grain.* Like Fraser's dance of the daughters, this barefooted imagination dances against masculinely coded forms of power and authority, while invoking a femininely coded creative power historically realized in the person of Isadora Duncan.[124] At the same time, an ambivalent assertion of masculine identity accompanies this tribute to the barefoot dancer, whose body falls within the gaze of "those who come behind her." The pun, whether intended or not, on the word "come" couples a lecherous, self-satisfied male gaze with a climactic arousal to textually insist upon the appropriation of the feminine for the satisfaction of masculine desire and subjectivity. This instance of doubleness prefigures the tensions underlying *Paterson,* a poem marked by what Merle Altman defines as "a male lyric gaze that appropriates, interpolates, masters what it takes in" (15) but also continually questions its claim to masculine authority.

The imagination of spring is, at base, a poetics of contact. This work of prose and poetry combines forms that run into and through one another rather than remain separate, and the formal element of contiguity reflects Williams's notion of the imagination as a space of contact. The piece's opening asserts that there is "a constant barrier between the reader and his consciousness of immediate contact with the world" (177). Art and writing, he goes on, have been "designed to keep up the barrier," and he issues an invitation to dissolve the barrier: "In the imagination, we are from henceforth (so long as you read) locked in a fraternal embrace, the classic caress of author and reader. We are one. Whenever I say 'I' I mean also 'you' " (178). The prose and poetry of *Spring and All* suggests the imaginative space as more of a *maternal* embrace, more like the "fourth language" of the womb / pool in Fraser's "Green and blue piece," with its emphasis upon a contiguity of a discrete self and other. For Williams, who associated both the imagination and language with the maternal, linguistic play offered a route into this space of contact. As he spoke of his mother "breaking" life upon her fingers, or of Moore's verse as "a break through all preconceptions of poetic form and mood and pace, a flaw, a crack in the bowl" (*SE* 121), or of Elsie as speaking with a "broken" brain, or of Stein as "unlinking" words, Williams connected this rupture and poetic creativity with ideas of the feminine.

Williams's experimental defamiliarization of language and poetic form, like Fraser's, develops from a desire to encourage contact, not alienation, through stimulating a process of revaluing or re-visioning the world. DeKoven observes that Fraser's style allows "her language to defamiliarize the world, to 'break the reader's emotional as well as visual habits of expectation.' . . . This is the great power of experimental writing, to make us see the world through a lens that would subvert, at their linguistic-perceptual root, habits of consciousness comfortable with the predominant cultural givens" ("Gertrude's Granddaughters" 13). At the end of *Spring and All,* Williams reiterates his desire to liberate words from familiar habits of mind, not by dissociating words "from natural objects and specified meanings," but by defamiliarizing and, thus, freeing them "from the usual quality of that meaning by transposition into another medium, the imagination" (235). Williams traces this movement, this transposition, as a re-visionary process that leads to contact:

> So long as the sky is recognized as an association
>
> is recognized in its function of accessory to vague words whose meaning it is impossible to rediscover
>
> its value can be nothing but mathematical certain limits of gravity and density of air
>
> The farmer and the fisherman who read their own lives there have a practical corrective for—
>
> they rediscover or replace demoded meanings to the religious terms
>
> Among them without expansion of imagination, there is the residual contact between life and the imagination which is essential to freedom                                    (187)

This process of linguistic dissociation, Williams was careful to maintain, enhanced connective possibilities: "the attempt is being made to separate things of the imagination from life, and obviously, by using forms common to experience so as not to frighten the onlooker away but to invite him" (194). Here, Williams interrupts his sentence with two poems that seek to revise "demoded meanings" – "The rose is obsolete" and "The sunlight in a / yellow plaque." His sentence resumes in mid-structure: "things with which he is familiar, simple things – at the same time to detach them from ordinary experience to the imagination" (197).

Far from denigrating ordinary experience or personality, this poetics seeks to "revalue experience" and to demonstrate "the importance of personality, by showing the individual . . . that his life is valuable" (203, 194). Williams later confesses that "my whole life has been spent (so far) in seeking to place a value upon experience and the objects of experience that would satisfy my sense of inclusiveness without redundancy" (202). In "the creation of new forms, new names for experience," Williams links the poem's formal structure with personal experience, seeking ways to embrace poetically those experiences excluded by conventions of the "plagiarizing imagination," and he considers his most linguistically experimental work, *Kora in Hell*, an attempt to "revalue experience" through "their [the Improvisations'] placement in a world of new values" (203). Dislocation of syntax, linear development, or the word itself affirm rather than annihilate a material reality, while also encouraging habits of consciousness to shift away from a rigid center of cultural givens: "As birds' wings beat the solid air without which none could fly so words freed by the imagination affirm reality by their flight" (235). In this flight of language, the word is "able to communicate release from the fixities which destroy it" only when "it is accurately tuned to the fact which giving it reality, by its own reality establishes its own freedom from the necessity of a word, thus freeing it and dynamizing it at the same time" (235).

The flight of a defamiliarized language, lacking the strong currents of linearity and conventional coherence, takes wing through a surrender of mastery to the accidental and improvisational. An early poem, "Aux Imagistes," prefigures Williams's comparison here of birds' wings and words freed by the imagination. To a springlike presence that has "exalted" him, he writes, "You shall not take wing / Except wing by wing, brokenly" (*CP1* 40–1). Again, we return to the word "broken," and perhaps can discern the antiauthoritarian impulse behind this concept in Williams's works. Looking at Moore's verse while he was writing *Spring and All*, Williams compared her poetry to a broken bowl that completely upsets the reader's values, using this image to explain what "one means when he says destruction and creation are simultaneous" (*SE* 121). In *Spring and All,* an apocalyptic vision represents and dramatizes a misapprehension of "destruction" as the forceful, oppressive poetics urged by factions of the avant-garde, bent on fueling their creative efforts with the idealization of mastery. Williams places himself within a different milieu, one characterized by an unlinking, a breaking, a rupturing that distinguishes itself, through its directives of revision and contact, from the "monster project" of violent dominance.

It is through these directives and the poetics they engender for Williams that we can look within the poems to the figures and images associated with the feminine. The volume's first poem, "By the road to the contagious hospital" (183), announces the approach of a "sluggish / dazed spring," noting the minute, initial signs of a natural rebirth. The personified birth imagery signals a dual apprehension of the maternal body we later discover as helping to define Kathleen Fraser's feminine discourse. The birth process is both separation and contact, alienation and contiguity. As new sprouts and green leaves push through the "broad, muddy fields" and interrupt the gray winter sky,

> They enter the new world naked,
> cold, uncertain of all
> save that they enter. All about them
> the cold, familiar wind—

This maternal process of labor bears these "objects [that] are defined" in their otherness by "clarity, outline of leaf." All the while, the feminized quality of contact underlies the process, as "rooted, they / grip down and begin to awaken." Contact or touch, associated most insistently with the maternal, opens into an indeterminacy, a multiplicity, and a betweenness that enables the imaginative process.

However celebratory, we are constantly reminded that the essentializing gesture of such maternal imagery occurs within a text that is male-authored. This very circumstance and its relationship to representation are problematized by one of the most anthologized poems in the volume, "The pure products of America," or "To Elsie." A poem that takes as its subject the very dynamics of representation it enacts, it turns essentialized conventions of the feminine inside out by situating them within material frameworks of power involving sex, race, and class. A poem also about the imagination, it ties a cultural diminishment of imaginative potential to the workings of masculine systems of control and desire marking the female body. The poem's first nine stanzas describe the "pure products" of America, the "peasant" class of workers and "mountain folk" who live "desolate" lives because their imaginations have been severed from "peasant traditions to give them / character." Escape from deprived conditions occurs through gender-specific means; the men can take to "railroading / out of sheer lust of adventure," their mobility assured by their sex, their "lust" assuring their mobility. The women may only escape through the stasis of sexual surrender, and the "young slatterns," in "succumbing / without emotion" to the conventions of male desire, face their submission through "numb terror / . . . which they cannot express." The women are defined (as sluts) and silenced through the operations of male desire, or more precisely, when the mechanisms of male desire are enabled through the severance of the "imagination," through the rigidification of habits of thought rooted in male supremacy.

Elsie embodies both the result of this system and the potential to disrupt or break it. Recalling the feminized cross-culturization of Jacataqua as well as the old Carib woman who resists Ponce de León, Elsie is a product of a "marriage / perhaps / with a dash of Indian blood." Yet she is also "hemmed round," closed in by the conditions the poem has described in terms of gender and class. Her movement to better circumstances, financially speaking, retains much of the old, for as a young woman she remains "hemmed round" by the male-identified institutions that continue to define her: the agent who rescues her, the state who rears her, the suburban doctor who employs her – the "us" about whom Elsie's "broken / brain" expresses the "truth." Against these sanctuaries of public authority, this "us," the poem suddenly insists upon Elsie's body, the "voluptuous water," the hips and breasts; moreover, in a significant doubling back upon itself, the poem goes on to alert us to the process of reading the female body within the contexts of masculine power that the poem both describes and joins. The poem begins to deconstruct itself, its own representation and objectification of the female body linked to the hierarchies of state, class, and gender that "read" and "re-present" women in our culture:

> . . . some Elsie—
> voluptuous water
> expressing with broken
>
> brain the truth about us—
> her great
> ungainly hips and flopping breasts
>
> addressed to cheap
> jewelry
> and rich young men with fine eyes
>                         (218)

The hips and breasts, "addressed" like a written text to the male gaze or the "fine eyes" of men, also undergo the objectifying gaze of the poet who here defines the female body according to cultural standards of beauty, male systems of desire. But even as we are told that her hips are "ungainly" and her breasts "flopping," the poem confronts us with the mechanism underlying definitions of the feminine, metonymically signified by the "fine eyes" of rich men. The devil-may-care men, the agent, the state, the doctor, the poet all join in creating this bodily text of "woman." The repressed, oppressed body, however, is a site for exposing this process, the "truth about us" that is revealed in how we "read" our culturally sanctioned texts of convention and meaning; the textualization of the female body, performed by the fine eyes of men and the representational gestures of the poem, is underscored by hierarchies of gender, class, and race that shape a reading of the female body and, furthermore, is self-conciously linked to a lack of imagination – a lack that "seems to destroy us." The objectification and suppression of the female body is contextualized within a denigration of earth and nature, a binarism necessary to perpetuate such hierarchy. Elsie's body is submitted to the male gaze

> as if the earth under our feet
> were
> an excrement of some sky
>
> and we degraded prisoners
> destined
> to hunger until we eat filth
>
> while the imagination strains
> after deer
> going by fields of goldenrod in

the stifling heat of September
Somehow
it seems to destroy us
(218–19)

The "imagination" here is not liberating for it is not transformational; it is the imagination without peasant character, the imagination of the "plagiarists" earlier criticized in *Spring and All*. This imagination labors and strains after desired but absent forms of beauty rather than generating itself through contact with the material world; it reads itself through convention and habit of thought, the "stifling heat of September," longing for a pastoral or illusory vision of the world – deer in fields of golden rod. This seems a pretty poetic image precisely because we are taught that such subjects and images are "poetic." Here, the poetic privileging of tradition (suggested by the pastoral vision) is part of what denigrates Elsie and what seems "to destroy us."

Thus, in contrast with the young women who "cannot express" the sexual terror engendered by male authority, Elsie expresses "with broken / brain the truth about us." More precisely, the speaker's recognition of linked systems of power that inscribe, represent, and "hem round" the female body unfolds in the act of his own participation, through his inscription and representation of Elsie. The poem problematizes the act of representation and its place and power within a (masculinely authored) poetic tradition yearning after deer in goldenrod; or within a middle-class suburb where the exotic and voluptuous racially mixed woman represents an objectified sexuality of otherness to the "rich young men with fine eyes." The poem identifies itself as a "hemming round" of the female Elsie while seeking the "broken" expression she embodies and that conventions exclude. The final lines of the poem recall this expression, a brokenness that reveals "isolate flecks":

It is only in isolate flecks that
something
is given off

No one to witness
and adjust, no one to drive the car
(219)

This final stanza revises, in a sense, the earlier poem "The Young Housewife," which associates the car's power with a poetic mastery that destroys (through erecting metaphoric boundaries) the poem's subject (see Chapter 1). The car image in "To Elsie" recalls the railroading men of the first stanzas and stands as an emblem of male power and mobility, enabled in part by female submission and terrified silence. Here, though, there is no adjustment, no control of the car's movement; significantly, it is not that there is "no one to witness," but that there is no one to witness *and adjust* when the "driver" opens to the imagination's broken, isolate flecks. The labor of this process, a painful relinquishment of authority on various levels of language, culture, and epistemological habit, is a movement in and out of the "filth" that one discourse perceives and the deer that the plagiarizing imagination desires: "Somehow / it seems to destroy us." The poem itself moves in and out – Williams witnessing and adjusting, while realizing the "broken" truth and the "isolate flecks" such adjustment (or the habit of thought encouraging this adjustment) diminishes. Elsie is both diminished (by one reading of Williams's description of her) and stands free from diminishment through the deconstructive act the poem suggests, leaving us to strain after the isolate flecks, the traces, the feminine betweenness that the dominant text ("the rich young men with fine eyes"; Williams himself) overwrites. The poem is painful in its desolation over the loss of authority to "drive the car," yet by these final lines it has held this desire up for self-implicating inspection.

The poet's "adjustment" of language, Williams's own formal innovations suggest, is tied to sanctioned forms of authority that he consistently associates with gender. As poet, his is like "the artist figure of / the farmer—composing / —antagonist"; although resisting codes and laws of art, he also derives a certain legitimation from them (186). He tries not to "set values on the word being used, according to presupposed measures," but he benefits from those measures all the same (206). His insistence upon process is, in part, an altering of the concept of measure. In the poem that precedes and "explained partially" this last comment, Williams considers the interaction between types of measure. He again associates driving the car with a form of authority, a measure of imposed order:

> In passing with my mind
> on nothing in the world
>
> but the right of way
> I enjoy on the road by
>
> virtue of the law—
> (205)

Here, the driver's movement and place are enabled by "the law," but the law does not define the movement because the driver proceeds without a "presupposed measure":

> Why bother where I went?
> For I went spinning on the
>
> four wheels of my car
> along the wet road until

> I saw a girl with one leg
> over the rail of a balcony
>            (206)

Driving a car without a predetermined goal in mind; writing, like Stein, without the freight of "purposed design"; opening, like Fraser, to the moment's perception rather than anchoring the fourth corner of a drawing. For Williams, the process leads him to the image of the girl in the final lines, who, like Elsie, suggests a feminization of process as a mode of witnessing without adjusting, of driving the car without running over the thing seen.

Fraser's struggle with notions of measure and definition is pertinent to Williams's lifelong desire to find a modern measure that is not "presupposed." His intuitive and often inchoate conceptualizations of measure are due to a resistance to imposed form that indicates a larger effort, like Fraser's, to completely revise what measure means and does. And again like Fraser, Williams's search for measure cannot be separated from a continual effort to wrench himself and his readers away from habits of thought and cultural values that empower the act of measure as an act of controlling mastery, a demarcation of the will to power. Pound's "classic attitude" exemplifies the type of measure Williams opposes, for Pound has "written about a few good men, 'measuring them,' pontificating about their qualities" ("Letter to an Australian Editor" 206). When Williams writes that "poetry does not tamper with the world but moves it" (206), he echoes the final lines of "To Elsie" and anticipates the volume's final vision of "art" as a site of cultural "fixities" that the imagination can liberate: "To free the world of fact from the impositions of 'art' and to liberate the man to act in whatever direction his disposition leads" (235). He does not want to make "nature an accessory to the particular theory" a writer holds, an appropriation that only "blinds him to the world," but to engage with the world as an observer/participant akin to Fraser's "self-in-progress." A new measure, then, helps one detect a changing, shifting world – like Fraser's window or the horizon glimpsed through it in "Five letters," through which form is engaged, not imposed. Williams writes that the

> inevitable flux of the seeing eye toward measuring itself by the world it inhabits can only result in himself crushing humiliation unless the individual raise to some approximate co-extension with the universe. This is possible by aid of the imagination. Only through the agency of this force can a man feel himself moved largely with sympathetic pulses at work – (192)

Williams advocates a measure that is more precisely a *way* of measuring that posits "co-extension" and "sympathetic pulses" instead of a destructive (or self-destructive) "crushing" measure. In essence, Williams calls for a way to inhabit the world based upon patterns of contiguity rather than control. This opens "patterns" into sites of flux and multiplicity, a measure exemplified by Marianne Moore's poetry. Unlike Moore's example, the "aristocratic compositions of the earlier times, the Homeric inventions," while still vital as classics, do not provide forms for modernity, for they were written when "life had not yet sieved through its own multiformity" (189). Measure, therefore, must embrace and reinstate this "multiformity," and it is in the women poets and the female experience that Williams apprehends the possibility – the linguistic and lived examples – of this measure.

Kathleen Fraser's exploration of a feminine discourse, tied to cultural and historical structures, suggests an alternative shape to Williams's poetics of contact. Emphasizing the contiguous touch, the betweenness of negative space, and the mutually shaping influence of self and other as they touch, Williams's notion of "contact" goes beyond the collage model of edges meeting, of objects juxtaposed. When we reconsider Williams from within Fraser's poetic tenets, we begin to see how his concern with contact is shaped by a sense of the feminine as touch, as an embrace of "crosspollenization"; that his feminization of process provides a mode of discovery and a model for organic form; that feminine touch encourages an inclusive multiplicity and suggests a source for measure in contiguity.

A female image concludes *Spring and All,* an image of the enabling feminine presence written into Williams's work of the 1910s and 1920s. The poem collects together many of the images we have discussed: Elsie, Grace, the old Carib woman, Jacataqua, Lincoln's transfiguration, the old woman in "The Wanderer," and from life, Elena Williams.

> Black eyed susan
> rich orange
> round the purple cone
>
> the white daisy
> is not
> enough
>
> Crowds are white
> as farmers
> who live poorly
>
> but you
> are rich
> in savagery

Arab
Indian
dark woman
    (236)

This poem enacts a double gesture that, by now, seems familiar, and specifically recalls "To Elsie." The reference to the "dark woman" exoticizes the woman of color, singling out her "rich . . . savagery" in a replication of Western culture's objectification of non–Anglo-European cultures and particularly their women as embodying an animal sexuality, a savage eroticism. This is regrettable, but should also be considered within his developing sense of an American identity that embraces cultural otherness and of his own identity as shaped by mixed cultural heritages. The poem, in its reference to the "dark woman," pays tribute to his various mothers, literally drawing upon his own mother's multicultural heritage. As Kerry Driscoll so aptly demonstrates, Elena Williams's Puerto Rican ethnicity provided her son's imagination with an inclusive and multiple idea of New World culture that, in turn, shaped his visions of an American tradition (*William Carlos Williams and the Maternal Muse*). As DuPlessis comments, Williams's " 'possession of America' was of multi-cultural America(s), and his possession of language 'out of the mouths of Polish' – and other – 'mothers' was deeply inflected by and mediated through his own Caribbean mother and the matrilineage which helped form him as an artist" ("Review" 51). We have been hindered in reading this matrilineage by a lack of ways to speak of it, for we are accustomed to thinking of Williams in relationship to other men or to a male-defined tradition; in a larger sense, we simply have not spoken enough of maternal lines (in our culture as well as our literary traditions) to fully perceive their presence or to understand the poetics they engender. Kathleen Fraser's poetics, descending from a displaced feminine tradition, offers a part of what we lack and enables us, as readers, to reconsider both mothers and fathers and to find ways to speak of their difference, a difference of and within language.

# Conclusion

## Paterson *and the Question of Authority*

How strange you are, you idiot!
So you think because the rose
is red that you shall have the mastery?

—William Carlos Williams[125]

Writing from an analogous position to the one taken in this study, Rachel Blau DuPlessis confronts *Paterson* in the essay "Pater-Daughter." She asks:

> What is missing what   what is missing what omitted. what is missing?
> a way of mediating between Mme. Curie's creative stubbornness and
> the voiceless / over-voiced other woman – Cress. A way of mediating
> between sex and text, between gender and writing as a struggle within
> the production, so a struggle within the reading of this work. (40)

How the daughter reads this text is intimately bound up with the positions of father, daughter, and son in the poem. These positions, in turn, are inextricably linked to matters of authority and tradition that we have investigated within Williams's early works and in his relationship to women poets. How does Williams's "magnum opus," as he called it, translate the issues of authority embedded within gender scripts from his earlier experimental works to his late epic (*SL* 163)? In the move from a defamiliarizing language of contact to a symbolic mythic structure asserting a familiar epic authority, "what is missing" and what remains?

Despite the criticism of a "father to son" modernism leveled by Williams against Joyce and Pound in the 1946 "Letter to an Australian Editor," he had incorporated just such a scheme in the first book of *Paterson,* published contemporaneously. Williams followed with envy the epic poem Pound began publishing in 1917 and would continue writing for the rest of his life. Throughout the thirties, Williams agonized over his failure to sustain a modern epic; in this decade, he had "been

237

patronized by Blackmur, Winters, Jarrell, Tate, and . . . dismissed by most of the other critics because he had not fit the acceptable university molds" (Mariani, *William Carlos Williams: A New World Naked*, 499). The appearance of *Paterson* I elevated his status among these powerful critics, especially Randall Jarrell, who generously praised Williams's achievement. Traditionally considered the mature poet's form, the epic represented to Williams (among other things) a way to equal his expatriate friend, Pound, and a way to achieve the regard seemingly reserved for Pound and Eliot as the most important practitioners of a high modernist aesthetics. In concluding this study of poetic lineage, I would like to consider briefly *Paterson* as a poem in which lines of lineage cross and scripts of gender conflict: a poem written in the authoritative form of the epic, yet uncertain as to the basis for that authority.

In his biography of the poet, Mariani tells us that Williams, capable of incorporating myriad voices into his work, sought in *Paterson* I to find "the voice of authority to hold the others together" (499). Michael Bernstein argues, however, that the "proper direction for a modern epic, in Williams's eyes, is a total revitalization of the poem's assertive authority; emotionally and structurally the text must present itself as a 'testing,' as an exploration which is always willing to recognize false directions and adjust its expectations accordingly" (*The Tale of the Tribe* 222–3). Adopting a symbolic framework from Joyce's *Ulysses* – the city, the wandering man – Williams goes even further in affiliating his epic with Joyce's mythic structures: "Behind the motif of Paterson the sleeping giant, [is] the primal father-son whose bride is the very landscape of the poem" (207). In this way, he "appropriated and simplified the imaginative constructs of the very tradition *Paterson* was intended to subvert" (207). Bernstein goes on, however, to argue that *Paterson*'s symbolic structure undermines itself, mixing the accidental and the designed in a narrative of plural voices that accepts its own incoherence and continually revises itself. The epic form is revitalized, "providing an alternative to the inflexible hierarchies of Pound's *Cantos*" (220). The strategies Williams employs in this "deliberate overthrow of the work's mythic structure" contest the idea of a poem's totality, of a voice's "final authoritative privilege" (221).

We can further contextualize Bernstein's argument by extending it backward through the chronology of Williams's works. The pluralistic voice and the questioning of mythic structures are not at all new for Williams, for he employed these approaches in *In the American Grain* for the express purpose of critiquing patriarchal modes of authority. He questions these modes even earlier in the poetry of the 1910s, in works that undermine his authority as the male creator. As I have argued throughout, Williams's persistent investigation of gendered constructs of authority demonstrates a cultural link to contemporaneous feminist challenges of patriarchal givens, and his participation in a tradition of women modernists exposed him to linguistic innovations that resist and dismantle such givens. When he applies the formal strategies that arose from these challenges and critiques to the epic form, a certain schizophrenia ensues; to recall DuPlessis's struggle in reading, something is missing. Though Williams's "flexible, tentative responses, his openness to new experiences, actually challenges the very authority of his symbolic coherence" until "that coherence is . . . effectively deconstructed within *Paterson* itself," how is this deconstructive movement gender-informed (Bernstein 220)? Why is it necessary for the poet, through his mythic framework, to so strongly assert a patriarchal authority in the first place? Is that authority actually deconstructed, or does it continually reassert itself against the danger of deconstructive elements that Williams had unleashed with revolutionary zeal twenty-five years earlier in proclaiming a maternal ground for poetic authority?

Reading the poem as the Jungian dramatization of "paternal and maternal archetypes . . . played out explicitly in terms of Williams's complicated relationships with his mother and father," Albert Gelpi asserts that *Paterson* takes form as Williams's Oedipal conflict with the "father-critic" (*Coherent Splendor* 324). Quite unlike Bernstein, Gelpi considers the epic a deliberate effort to control and master the feminine "expressive medium" and its "inchoate materials" (332, 322). A corrective of his earlier submission to maternal flux and dissolution (in the experimental works), *Paterson* "proclaimed [its masculine] drive toward form . . . [in its lines:] 'Paterson, / keep your pecker up' " (324). Does the maternal reside merely in the "medium," the feminine that is silenced, overvoiced, mastered by the epic's phallic drive? Does *Paterson* replicate the cultural script of mastery Williams had so vigorously protested in *In the American Grain*?

Bernstein and Gelpi offer two divergent readings of authority in this poem. Offering a third view, DuPlessis isolates the poem's "great moments" as those times when the epic's authority – its mastery – is abandoned: "when Williams allows his poem to pass beyond composition into a world of meanings which offer contradictory and unreleased swarmings into the world" ("Pater-Daughter" 40). These moments, "in short, follow *Spring and All* (1923), *Kora in Hell* (1918), *The Great American Novel* (1923), *A Novelette* (1932)" (40). DuPlessis focuses on the semiotics of these texts, regretting *Paterson*'s incorporation of the symbolic order as a discourse of mastery.

*Paterson* is also about a different kind of authority – the authority of lineage. A poem generated within and against an acknowledged lineage of epic predecessors, *Paterson* at once claims a place within this line while pushing against its limits. In writing an epic poem, Williams strives to enter a tradition defined by the critics then in power, led by Eliot's example, who viewed the mythological and historical structures employed by Pound, Eliot, and Joyce as quintessential modern qualities of the form. Drawing upon the entire epic tradition, the authors of the *Cantos* and *Ulysses* sought to revitalize the epic structure through a modern context and modern form. In taking on the epic, then, Williams engages the genre's long and privileged history, along with its modern manifestations, as the most serious vehicle for the poet's voice. He also engages the singularly masculine authority the epic assumes; written by men, adopting a public voice, the classical epics make up a tradition reserved for the mature male poet. However, where Pound or Joyce look to Homer, Williams often looks to Sappho as one of his models, particularly in the "defiance of authority" revealed through her lyric fragments (III.ii: 119), her "broken tongue" (V.ii: 217). As a counterpoint to Pound's classical lineage (which Williams quotes in a letter from his friend just after evoking Sappho's poems in Book III), Sappho stands apart from the epic tradition in multiple ways – as a woman, as a lesbian, as a lyricist. All of *Paterson* is informed by this countermove: The poem strains toward a legitimate and masculinely associated tradition while continually questioning its authority by evoking a marginal, feminine line.

This doubleness is most evident, thematically, when the epic celebrates the figures of Curie and Sappho as originating sources. We will return to these moments shortly and suggest their formal import within the epic structure; first, however, it is necessary to look at the paternal role Williams designates for himself through the inclusion of letters from younger poets. While the creation of an epic initiates him into a line of fathers, this son in turn takes on a fatherly role for those poets who follow him. By gesturing toward a future tradition, these letters are infolded within the epic's inherent call to the tradition stretching behind it. At the same time, the letters from Marcia Nardi (Cress in the poem) and Allen Ginsberg expose the poetic tradition, which privileges the epic form, as mired in "patriarchal muck," to use DuPlessis's phrase ("Pater-Daughter" 40).

Ginsberg's first letter to Williams is carefully placed in *Paterson IV*, following the opening sequence of the father speaking to his son. A letter of self-introduction, it replicates the theme of filial relationship in clearly establishing the younger poet's feeling of kinship with the "unknown old poet," asserting that they are "brotherly children of the muses" who should recognize one another "across the generations" (IV.ii: 173). Ginsberg briefly divulges his "history" and his "literary liking" before launching into a description of his style: "youthful attempts to perfect, renew, transfigure, and make contemporarily real an old style of lyric machinery" (IV.ii: 174). Ginsberg's letter, though exuding confidence in his poetic ability, reads as the son's attempt to claim his place within the tradition of his fathers. He regrets failing to establish contact with Williams through an earlier opportunity: "I had nothing to talk about except images of cloudy light, and was not able to speak to you in your own or my own concrete terms" (IV.ii: 174). This failing haunts him as he now seeks the older man's approval, although it is by virtue of his feeling of inheritance that he can approach Williams in a confident fashion. As a native of Paterson, Ginsberg delights in his connection to the evolving epic, seeing himself as heir to Williams's modernist treatment of the city: "This place is as I say my natural habitat by memory, and I am not following in your traces to be poetic: though I know you will be pleased to realize that at least one actual citizen of your community has inherited your experience . . . " (IV.ii: 174). Enclosing poems for Williams's perusal, this heir locates them within an acknowledged tradition of verse: " . . . a kind of dense lyric I instinctively try to imitate – after Crane, Robinson, Tate, and old Englishmen" (IV.ii: 175). The letter, in effect, shows Ginsberg generating a poetic identity through placing himself as son and heir within a tradition of poets. In addition, the son's words become part of the father's issue, the epic.

Ginsberg's second letter, written in May 1956, appears in *Paterson* V. By then a part of the beat movement, he writes to thank Williams for his introduction to *Howl:* "Your foreword is personal and compassionate and you got the point of what has happened," he writes to his "big sad poppa" (V.i: 212). Mariani tells us that, by 1956, "Ginsberg wanted his 'father' to know, there were other sons of Williams' out there in San Francisco having a grand old time with him," such as Robert Creeley and Gary Snyder (705). During the years of the epic's production, its author experienced the growing adulation of poetic heirs and came to see himself more and more as a father figure within the American tradition. This is the Williams Denise Levertov would meet and correspond with, and she willingly embraced her position as daughter.

However, before Levertov, Marcia Nardi had resided for a brief moment under Williams's tutelage and sponsorship. Nardi met Williams in 1942, and he wrote an introduction to a collection of her poems published that year in *New Directions*. In an essay on Anaïs Nin's *The Winter of Artifice,* printed in the same volume, Williams emphasizes the need for women "as women, to exploit the female in the arts" (429). He goes on to discuss the "many special difficulties" women are forced to "overcome" in the arts (429) because of a male tradition's "failure to recognize that there is an authentic female approach. . . . [that] has been submerged" by the belief that "the greatest masterpieces are the work of males as well as of the male viewpoint" (432). Urging women to write from their "secret source of power . . . a secret having to do profoundly with her sex" (435), he singles out Marcia Nardi's work:

> In a woman, something that links up her womanhood with abilities as a writer will allow her to draw abundantly upon that for her material. . . . A young poet, Marcia Nardi, succeeds in it more seriously and unaffectedly than any woman writer I can recall at the moment. (433)

Had he thought harder, he might have remembered Mina Loy (who for years had chosen silence over publication), whose work Nardi's resembles in its frankness and density. Readers of Williams's essay on Nin could flip back a few pages in the magazine and find out for themselves what he saw as distinguishing Nardi's poems. "A Group of Poems," introduced by Williams, begins with the editor's note: "Marcia Nardi was discovered by William Carlos Williams . . . " (413). In praise of his protégé, he claims that she is "so much better at her best than some of the best known professional poets about us that I am willing to say that by moments no one surpasses her" (414). Significantly, after continually emphasizing the fact of her womanhood, he locates her writing in the body: "She uses language for a purpose, the purpose is to make poems which in themselves tell what her whole body is screaming to make clear" (413).

In these comments, Nardi comes to represent the modern female poet writing out of a gendered experience of language and culture that Williams, in *In the American Grain,* had seen prefigured in Emily Dickinson. Moreover, he claims to have discovered this poet. Nardi's letters, included in *Paterson* I and II, respond specifically to Williams's endorsement of women writing from their "secret source of power" and to his discovery and sponsorship of her poetry. On both counts, she finds him a sham:

> My attitude toward woman's wretched position in society and my ideas about all the changes necessary there, were interesting to you, weren't they, in so far as they made for *literature?* That my particular emotional orientation, in wrenching myself free from patterned standardized feminine feelings, enabled me to do some passably good work with *poetry* – all that was fine, wasn't it – something for you to sit up and take notice of! . . . all that fine talk of yours about woman's need to "sail free in her own element" as a *poet* [in the Nin essay], becomes nothing but empty rhetoric in the light of your behavior towards me. No woman will ever be able to do that, completely, until she is able *first* to "sail free in her own element" in living itself – which means in her relationships with men even before she can do so in her relationships with other women. The members of any underprivileged class distrust and hate the "outsider" who is *one of them,* and women therefore . . . will never be content with their lot until the light seeps down to them, not

from their own, but from the eyes of changed male attitudes toward
them . . . (II.iii: 86–7)

Nardi's angry words, particularly in this long letter ending the second
book, describe the situation of the woman writer that feminist critics
and writers have examined in recent years. She speaks of the devastating
split between her poet self and her female self, a division she feels the
male tradition (including Williams) imposes. In addition, she enumerates
the economic difficulties facing a woman trying to establish a room of
one's own, a place to write.

Embedded within this male-authored epic is a treatise on the woman's
position in relationship to the tradition authorizing the genre itself. Moreover, in accusing Williams of appropriating her words to turn them into
"literature," the letter calls into question his lifelong focus upon the
feminine and his support of women artists: "And you saw in one of my
first letters to you (the one you wanted to make use of, then, in the
Introduction to your Paterson) an indication that my thoughts were to
be taken seriously, because that too could be turned by you into literature
. . . " (II.iii: 86). Nardi calls attention here to the appropriation and objectification of "woman" within male-authored representations of
women. Significantly, this letter concludes a book framed by mirrored
gestures toward the feminine. Opening the book with an image of the
male poet's inscription upon the female body, Williams replicates the
epic's proclaimed symbolic structure:

> The scene's the Park
> upon the rock,
> female to the city
>
> —upon whose body Paterson instructs his thoughts
> (concretely)
>
> (II.i: 43)

Nardi's letters accuse Williams of just such an inscription, penned by a
powerful "literary man's ego" upon the body of the woman poet in his
gestures of authorization toward her poetry: "That literary man's ego
wanted to help me in such a way, I think, that my own achievements
might serve as a flower in his buttonhole, if that kind of help had been
enough to make me bloom" (II.iii: 91). In her relationship to the father
poet, the daughter is inscribed and possessed; the son, on the other hand,
is released into a "whitmanic mania" (V.ii: 212). Even in presenting these
letters, the epic asks how it can possibly enable the woman writer.

Like Phyllis, who in Paterson IV cannot stop writing to her drunken
father despite her repeated pledges to be "through" with him, Nardi's
letters evidence a bitter thralldom to Williams's authority. At the same
time, they emphasize the male privilege of that authority and point to

the traditional inscription and silencing of the feminine within constructs of male authority – the poet, the epic, the father all included. Taken together, the appearance of the letters from Nardi and Ginsberg qualifies Williams's authority as epic author and poetic father: On the one hand, Williams lays claims to a phallic potency for the poet, while on the other hand the poem reveals (as had *In the American Grain*) the brutal and oppressive manifestations of this potency within socially sanctioned frameworks of gender. We must question whether noting destructive differences *in itself* is a positive gesture; in tangling with this question, we also are led to ask whether we can ever feel comfortable with Williams as a benign figure after he has placed this painfully unresolved material before us. The poem's depictions of male privilege further a sense of this conflicted complicity in the oppressions his earlier works challenge. Instances of fathers' cruelty riddle the epic, and for each assertion of phallic potency as a creative force, the epic spits up another reprehensible version of its power to kill, maim, or silence. The female body becomes a "lost body," bathed in masculine "opinions" and words (III.i: 105): Even the maternally imaged landscape concluding *Paterson* I is elided through language as the "Earth" becomes the "father of all speech" (I.iii: 39). The female, if not erased, is marked by violence: Their bodies sites for male pleasure, women are impregnated and abandoned, or raped, or murdered, or they commit suicide. *Paterson* III, in particular, reads as a litany of such violence, born of the male desire to possess the female:

> till I must believe that all
> desired women have had each
>     in the end
>     a busted nose
> and live afterward marked up
>             (III.ii: 127)

Analogously, the "beauty" of the page of verse suffers this violence, "beaten by whips" held in the poet's hand – a distinctly masculine image of writing as the violation of the blank page (III.ii: 126). But this violation spreads, like a cancer, into all forms of gendered authority in the poem: The farmer breaks his wife's jaw because she is too sick to work, then composes a song to make her happy (III.iii: 141). Is this how Williams sees the poet, composing a song whose origins reside in overpowering the feminine? Or is this what the epic form traditionally enacts? In writing the epic, must Williams replicate the crime of the young father in *Paterson* IV who kills his infant daughter by "snapping the wooden tray of a high chair in the baby's face" because "her crying annoyed him" (IV.iii: 196)? Or is this violence the result of the ode preceding this grim story, praising the "peak / from which the seed was hurled" (IV.iii: 193)? Does the

phallic power privileging the son seek to "Smash the wide world / a
fetid womb, a sump!" (IV.ii: 171)? Or does the son turn to the mother's
"ponderous belly, full / of thought" (IV.ii: 177)?

Moving between such unresolved questions, the epic dances "to a
measure / contrapuntally" through its claims to lineage (V.iii: 239). The
poem's final three books, in which the poet's assertions of "I, Paterson,
the King-self" increase, paradoxically center upon two female models of
creative power, Curie and Sappho. As Ginsberg had written his lineage
into the first letter sent to Williams, now the father-poet writes his lineage
into the epic. The pregnant Curie discovers radium, bringing a luminosity out of "nothing," a process of "breaking down" analogous to the
imaginative process, the search for the radiant gist (IV.ii: 178). Sappho
offers the formal means, the "broken tongue," to convey this process in
language. The epic takes on the self-contradictory project of reclaiming
a poetic mother.

Amidst the raging fire of *Paterson* III, an image of a bottle reglazed by
the flame's heat comes to emblematize Williams's epic project:

> An old bottle, mauled by the fire
> gets anew glaze, the glass warped
> to a new distinction, reclaiming the
> undefined.
>                    (III.ii: 118)

Transforming the image of fire from destruction to renewal, the "Poet
Beats Fire at Its Own Game!" (III.ii: 118). The flame's destructive
"game," on the other hand, is played out historically in the deliberate
suppression of Sappho's "defiance of authority": this flame "—burnt
Sappho's poems, burned by intention (or are they still hid / in the Vatican
crypts?)" (III.ii: 119). In "reclaiming the undefined," Williams imagines
his epic as a form that reclaims these hidden Sapphic fragments, this
"anthology suppressed" (119). The formal qualities that Bernstein notes
– the multiple voices, the insertion of the accidental, the conflation of
public and private materials – trace themselves back to Sappho with the
assertion of the epic's task to reclaim her "broken tongue" (V.iii: 217).

Williams brings Sappho into the epic most reverently with his translation of her lyric. Opening the second section of the fifth book, the lyric
reveals Williams's own idea of a woman's poetry – a feminine discourse
linked to the body. Williams chooses to translate Sappho's passion in
emphatically physical (and conventionally unladylike) terms: "Sweat
pours out: a trembling hunts / me down" (V.iii: 217). This woman poet
speaks from her passion with a "broken tongue," an image amalgamating
Williams's view of Stein, Moore, Dickinson, his mother, the old "queen"
of "The Wanderer." Sappho's lyric is soon followed by Williams's own

lyric in praise of the "woman in our town" who "walks rapidly, flat bellied / in worn slacks upon the street" (V.ii: 219). She disappears from his view – "she was gone!" – and he writes:

> if ever I see you again
> as I have sought you
> daily without success
>
> I'll speak to you, alas
> too late! ask,
> What are you doing on the
>
> streets of Paterson? a
> thousand questions:
> Are you married? Have you any
>
> children? And, most important,
> your NAME! which
> of course she may not
>
> give me—though
> I cannot conceive it
> in such a lonely and
>
> intelligent woman
>
> have you read anything that I have written?
> It is all for you
>
> (V.ii: 220)

This well-known segment of *Paterson* epitomizes the unresolved tensions within the poem. Addressing the "lonely and / intelligent woman" as its privileged reader, the lyric asks that we mediate between sex and text, as DuPlessis described the process of reading the long poem in the opening quote to this Conclusion. The "woman" is the "supplying female" sought for his poetry, the material that the poet draws from but also the context within which he writes and is received. The poet's masculine self-definition depends upon this search, while the elusiveness of the woman suggests an acknowledgment that "woman" cannot be appropriated. Indeed, it is "woman" as reader who validates the epic, but an epic in which "woman" is repeatedly positioned in the service of male authority, while also positioned (like Sappho) in resistance to it. The anxiety of the father-poet, the epic author(ity), translates itself through this dual positioning. "Woman" becomes, in these schizophrenic movements, the excluded and oppressed, metaphorically building an(other) epic or anti-epic within an epic celebrating the male city, the one-horned unicorn, the King, the son, the "pecker." In a sense, two gender-inflected modernisms coexist, in uneasy tension, throughout the long poem that brought Williams recognition as an important father of "modernism" within the New Critical camp. We can now see that the poem itself demonstrates the fallacy of categorizing modernism solely through the literary accomplishments of men or of disregarding the masculine impulse of received modernist texts; indeed, the monolithic structure of modernism cannot contain the varieties of modernist practice nor the unresolved wildness of *Paterson*.

Writing to Mary Barnard in 1958, Williams positions himself between gendered lines of American poetry. In a gesture both paternalistic and sensitive to the impact of gender upon literary history, he presents himself as a poetic vehicle for transmitting Sappho to modern women, who, "not vocal enough in their own support," needed poets like Sappho as models (in Mariani 739). Through Williams, we can understand the many dangers to accure from the male writer's assumption that he can communicate the "feminine" to women; however, at the same time, these dangers do not cancel out the strength that can be gained from reading his works within a context of women writers and recognizing the interweaving influences at play across generations, across genders. *Paterson*, in its contradictory complexity, weaves a text figuring such influence, full of gaps and knots and broken threads. We can unravel the ties back to the poetic and imaginative mothers who enable Williams's work within a tradition of women and who continue to speak through contemporary poets of both sexes.

# Notes

## Introduction

**1** Identifying a tradition of modernism practiced by women that is ideologically antipatriarchal (often subversively so), critics like Janet Wolff, Rachel Blau DuPlessis, Marianne DeKoven, Shari Benstock, Carolyn Burke, Sandra Gilbert, and Susan Gubar share in a project that is reshaping our understanding of texts and writers by insisting upon a retrieval of this counterstrain. Wolff directly and succinctly summarizes the need for such retrieval: "Three things are clear. First, the definition of the modern, and the nature of modernism, derived from the experience of men and hence excluded women. Second, women, of course, had their own experience of the modern world, and were engaged in articulating this in literature and painting. And third, there is no doubt that women writers and artists were as much involved in the revolution in literary and visual languages as men. That is why it is both possible and essential to rewrite the history of modernism, showing women's role in it. . . . we need to look again at the classics of modernism, to discover what we can now see as their very particular perspective on 'the modern' " (Wolff, *Feminine Sentences,* 58–59).
**2** See, for example, Audrey Rodgers (*Virgin and Whore: The Image of Women in the Poetry of William Carlos Williams*); Bryce Conrad (*Refiguring America*); Albert Gelpi (*A Coherent Splendor*); Theodora Graham (various essays; dissertation); Kerry Driscoll (*William Carlos Williams and the Maternal Muse*); and Rachel Blau DuPlessis ("Pater-Daughter").
**3** My argument here does not involve an equation of avant-garde writing with the feminine, a strategy familiar to varieties of poststructural critics. Like Rita Felski and Marianne DeKoven, I am uncomfortable with the categorization of experimental writing as *écriture féminine*. Acknowledging that avant-garde experiments often sustain misogynist attitudes, DeKoven poses a crucial point: "Feminist analysis of experimental stylistics, rather than pretending either that the avant-garde tradition does not exist or that it is the same thing as écriture féminine, should acknowledge the antipatriarchal potential of form in historical, male-signed avant-garde writing, but at the same time acknowledge the self-canceling countermove of the writing toward male supremacism and misogyny"

248

("Male Signature" 79). Rita Felski elaborates a further problem in aligning all experimental writing with the feminine. Critiquing psychoanalytic theories of gender and text that "frequently seek to ground a theory of resistance in characteristics traditionally associated with the feminine (hysteria and pleasure, for example)," Felski finds a problem in that "subversion is located everywhere and nowhere; the valorization of the 'feminine' as a site of resistance fails to acknowledge that woman's assignment to a distinctive 'feminine' sphere has ... been a major cause of their marginalization and disempowerment" (11). Thus, although my analysis certainly involves the links drawn by the poets themselves between language innovation or disruption and either a feminine or antipatriarchal potential, my consideration of these links remains grounded in certain historically specific conditions of textual production and reception, such as the frameworks of feminist thought and modernist aesthetics circulating in the post–World War I years. Janet Wolff partially expresses my objective when she claims that "it is worthwhile to pursue the question of the congruence of modernism and feminism, and ... that modernism (carefully defined) had and continues to have critical and radical potential for women writers and artists" (*Feminine Sentences* 53).

4  See Carolyn Burke's essays, "The New Poetry and the New Woman: Mina Loy," and "Getting Spliced: Modernism and Sexual Difference"; Marianne DeKoven's *Rich and Strange: Gender, History, Modernism;* Janet Wolff's *Feminine Sentences: Essays on Women and Culture;* Shari Benstock's *Textualizing the Feminine* and *Women of the Left Bank;* and Sandra Gilbert and Susan Gubar's projected three-volume study, *No Man's Land.*

5  Felski's feminist reading of Giddens's structuration theory argues for "a more differentiated understanding of structure as not only constraining but enabling, a precondition for the possibility for meaningful choices" (60).

6  Fuss's argument continues the point of her book, *Essentially Speaking,* that essentialism and anti-essentialism (or constructionism) actually coimplicate one another. Concerning the anti-essentialist use of the concept of "subject-position," she claims that "the essentialism in 'anti-essentialism' inheres in the notion of 'where I stand,' of what has come to be called, appropriately enough, 'subject-positions' " (29).

7  Fuss begins with Foucault's poststructuralist definition of the subject as " 'not the speaking consciousness, not the author of the formulation, but a position that may be filled in certain conditions by various individuals" (Foucault, *The Archaeology of Knowledge,* in Fuss 32). Advancing Foucault's concept as "compatible with recent feminist reconceptualizations of the subject as the site of multiple and heterogeneous differences ... [or] a notion of the 'I' as a complicated field of multiple subjectivities and competing identities" (33), Fuss considers this feminist work important in moving "beyond the self/other, 'I'/'not-I' binarism central to Lacan's understanding of subject constitution" (33). She quotes De Lauretis's *Feminist Studies/Critical Studies* on this notion of identity: "For it is not the fragmented, or intermittent, identity of a subject constructed in division by language alone, an 'I' continuously prefigured and preempted in an unchangeable symbolic order. It is neither, in short, the identity of the individualist, bourgeois subject, which is male and white; nor the 'flickering' of the posthu-

manist Lacanian subject, which is too nearly white and at best (fe)male. What is emerging in feminist writings is, instead, . . . a subject that is not divided in, but rather at odds with language" (Fuss 9).

8   Janet Wolff's assessment of women's necessary claim to bodily experience helps describe Fraser's work, which begins "from the lived experience of women in their currently constituted bodily identities – identities which are *real* at the same time as being socially inscribed and discursively produced" (*Feminine Sentences* 138).

### 1. "The Full of My Freed Voice": Williams and Loy, Feminism and the Feminine

9   For discussions of first-wave feminism and modernism, see DuPlessis's *The Pink Guitar;* DeKoven's *Rich and Strange: Gender, History, Modernism;* Carolyn Burke's "The New Poetry and the New Woman: Mina Loy."

10   See Bruce Clark's "Dora Marsden and Ezra Pound: *The New Freewoman* and 'The Serious Artist' " for a recent analysis of the journal's history. Clark provides valuable archival information and seeks to retrieve Marsden as an important figure in the development of modernism. However, in his reading of Marsden's politics, he seems uninterested in noting the masculinist assumptions of her egoist position.

11   Michael Levenson's *A Genealogy of Modernism* traces the intellectual development of the modernist movement in London as a "recognizable lineage in a specific geographic centre during a confined period" (x). Though he does not discuss Williams or the women modernists, his exclusive focus on the male London modernists galvanized by Pound (Hulme, Lewis, Ford, Eliot) clarifies aspects of "Poundian Modernism" that Williams resisted on a number of grounds. Levenson examines the polemical and repeatedly revised nature of a modernist aesthetic undergoing self-conscious articulation even as it constantly transformed itself under the influence of such thinkers as Bergson, Stirner, and Upward. Looking at the concepts of image, symbol, tradition, expression, and objectivity, and the successive doctrines of impressionism, imagism, vorticism, and classicism, Levenson charts the movement from subjectivity to egoism to objectivity. I am indebted to his careful and thorough scholarship, and particularly to the detailed attention paid to the time period of 1914–17, during which aggressive, elite, and exclusive individualism marked the pronouncements of the London modernists.

12   Levenson's chapter "Egoists and Imagists" (*A Genealogy of Modernism* 63–79) establishes the connection between Pound and Allen Upward, particularly in regard to Pound's changing attitudes about the artist's relationship to society. Michael Weaver's discussion of Williams's letter-essay dialogue with Marsden provides important documentary information on Williams's own concept of egoism (*William Carlos Williams* 23–29).

13   Weaver provides a cogent discussion of Marsden's advocacy of "egoism as an alternative to feminism" (*William Carlos Williams* 23–24). Levenson charts the philosophical links between Marsden and Pound, noting that the journal might claim the feminist movement as its founding impetus, "but the editorial policy

was feminist only in a greatly strained sense. . . . The *New Freewoman*'s principal and overriding concern was to trumpet Stirnerian egoism, and the rhetoric was deafening" (66). David Frail's chapter on the *Egoist* builds on the scholarship of these men, but focuses more explicitly on the conflict between Williams's "ethic of service" and egoism (*The Early Politics and Poetics of William Carlos Williams* 97–108).

**14**  Attacking the abstract concept of "liberty" in the first issue of the *Egoist* (Jan. 1914), Marsden expresses the glorification of individual will exemplifying the connection critics have made between the intellectual strain of egoism within modernist aesthetics and later reactionary, even fascist, leanings: "We are one another's daily food. . . . Where the limiting line falls is decided in the event, turning on the will, whim and power of those who are devoured and devourers at one and the same time. Life is feasting and conflict: that is its zest. The cry for peace is the weariness of those who are too faint-hearted to live" ("Liberty, Law, and Democracy" 2).

**15**  See Richard Aldington's essay on Violet Hunt, which relentlessly relegates the woman novelist in general to second-class status, or the short piece "Venus and Mars" by M.C., which reiterates stereotypical and conventional notions of gendered responses to love, clearly attempting to debunk notions of the "new woman."

**16**  In this essay, Marsden writes of the suffragist claims: "Such claimants are, in fact, asking for protection, i.e., that others should forgo the exercise of their power in order to give them an *appearance* of power. Claims are the reproaches of the powerless: whines for protection. All the suffragists' claims are of this order, and it was to disentangle the journal from association with these and with the long list of whines, Free Speech, Free Love, Free Assembly and what-not, the 'Freewoman' became EGOIST, which title is a sign hung out above the seat of authority: the centre of power; the self. One has the 'freedom' if one has the 'power,' and the measure of one's power is one's own concern" (224).

**17**  See the short poem "The Song of the Sock" by Josephine Wright, which satirizes the domestic sphere's war effort as comprised of ineffectual gestures that ironically dispelled claims of women's equality by demonstrating the female sex's seeming inability to defend the country as do the men: "For when by war their country's hit / English ladies always knit" (*Egoist* 1.18, Sept. 15, 1914, 338).

**18**  Mardsen writes in "Women's 'Rights'": "The question is whether women *have* the power, the genuine self-supplying power, and not the bogus counterfeit of conferred power. . . . [Moreover] every form of self-responsible power demands – not last, but first – capable physical self-defence. One might venture to say it would be impossible to find in these islands any 'advanced' woman who has not felt herself made into something of a fool by the unequivocal evidence as to the position of women presented by the war. . . . They find that they may busy themselves with efforts to assist their less 'protected' sisters toward maintenance; they may form an admiring audience: they may have the honour of being allowed to share in their country's defence by dint of knitting socks. . . . In the war-area itself, they form part, along with the rest of the property, of the spoils of the conquered" (363).

**19**  See Carolyn Burke's "Getting Spliced: Modernism and Sexual Difference," in which she maps out Pound's exclusion of the feminine and his emphasis upon a masculine concept of creativity. As she convincingly argues, Pounds's ideas "about relations between the sexes can only be described as increasingly phallic in emphasis" (103). Linking writing and sexuality, he could only see "intelligent women poets [like Moore or Loy] . . . as honorary men," and his conceptualization of creativity insisted upon masculine potency (106). Burke quotes, for example, a 1919 statement on creativity, in which he likens the creative process to "an act like fecundation, like the male cast of the human seed"; "Even oneself has felt it, driving any new idea into the great passive vulva of London" (104).

20   For an analysis of modernism's feminization of mass culture, see Andreas Huyssen's "Mass Culture as Woman: Modernism's Other."

21   This essay precedes the vorticist journal *Blast* by a few months (its first issue was published in July 1914), and these developments in Pound's aesthetic illustrate that he has come, Levenson comments, "to a position as anti-democratic and as anti-humanitarian as that of Stirner, Nietzsche or Upward. The social justification for art, as found in 'The Serious Artist' [a 1913 essay by Pound], has disappeared. Social amenities and social responsibilities . . . are obstacles. The pressing need is for an aesthetic individualism that recognizes its antagonistic relation to the social whole" (*Genealogy of Modernism* 76).

22   David Frail, studying the early poetics and politics of Williams, cites the mediating effect of Williams's "ethic of service" upon egoism as the poet interpreted the philosophy through his grounding in the care of others (as a doctor) and through Unitarian thought (by which he was raised) (*Early Politics and Poetics* 99).

23   These poems are taken from *The Collected Poems of Williams Carlos Williams*, Volume 1, 1909–1939. The 1914 version is found in the Notes (477–8); the 1934 version is printed in the collection (39). Unless otherwise indicated, parenthetical citations of Williams's poetry will refer to this volume.

24   See Gelpi's chapter on Williams in *A Coherent Splendor* for a discussion of the feminine/masculine interplay along these lines. Gelpi contends that Williams "wanted the interplay of the masculine with the feminine which would give form to his intuitive openness to experience." In Williams's understanding of the creative process, writes Gelpi, the "masculine represented the inclination toward clarity, definition, unity; the feminine, the inclination toward instinct, indeterminacy, multiplicity" (323). Gelpi's wide-ranging analysis covers the span of Williams's career, reading the poetry as "the psychological and aesthetic drama of resolving empathy and form, energy and direction" that is "thrown back on the paternal and maternal archetypes and . . . played out explicitly in terms of Williams' complicated relationships with his father and mother" (324).

25   Rachel Blau DuPlessis, in her essay "No Moore of the Same," comments upon this poem as disrupting gender authority in much the same way that Moore's syntactical manipulations question such (male) authority.

26   To my ear, the voice of Shakespeare's Iago is recalled, as this manipulator of language and illusion maliciously warns Barbantio that "an old black ram / Is tupping your white ewe" (*Othello* I.i. 88–9).

27   See, for example: "The Science of Signs" (Aug. 1916); "The 'I' and the 'Ego' " (Sept. 1916); "The Verbal Form 'Be' " (Nov. 1916).

**28**   See John Palattella's article " 'In the Midst of Living Hell,' " which discusses the Marsden correspondence, for a somewhat different reading of the gender dynamics, particularly in their relationship to World War I. Palattella brings the ideas of Julia Kristeva to bear upon a group of WWI texts by Williams that include these letters.

**29**   Williams intuits a relationship between women and the literal that contemporary feminist psychology explores: "Margaret Homans in *Bearing the Word* suggests that women may value the liberal languages that the son represses at the time of his renunciation of his mother. Unlike men, whose entry into the symbolic or figurative order is, according to Freudian-Lacanian theory, a crisis, women's 'entry' into the symbolic order is only a gradual shift of emphasis. Men thus privilege the figurative and assign the literal a place as devalued as the place assigned women themselves" (Leonardi, "Recipes for Reading," 344).

**30**   Weaver tells us that "*henids*" is a "term coined to suggest undifferentiated thought and feeling received in inarticulate form" (*William Carlos Williams* 25).

**31**   As Diana Fuss describes Luce Irigaray's project within the context of Western philosophy, a "strategic deployment of essentialism . . . [can clarify] for us the contradiction," for "to give 'woman' an essence is to undo Western phallomorphism" (*Essentially Speaking* 72, 71).

**32**   See David Frail, *The Early Politics and Poetics of William Carlos Williams*, for an analysis of Williams's relationship to socialist thought.

**33**   DeKoven provides a groundbreaking study of modernism as a historically specific cultural movement with far-reaching implications for the present: "The modernists themselves were highly self-conscious concerning the cultural and social implications of their 'new' aesthetic practices, and the polemics they initiated have been extended by many of this century's most influential Western aesthetic theorists, from a widely diverse range of historical-cultural-ideological positions" (7).

**34**   Teresa Billington Greig, "Feminism," 3.

**35**   See Wertheim's chapter on the feminist movement in New York City for a discussion of male feminists; see Cott for a fuller understanding of the interaction of male and female feminists and socialists of the time.

**36**   Goldman, speaking out on birth control, was arrested and briefly jailed during this period between Sanger's 1914 indictment and the February 1916 suspension of charges.

**37**   See Kouidis, *Mina Loy*, and Burke's essays for fuller readings of these poems.

**38**   At the same time, Loy writes her "Feminist Manifesto," sending it to Mabel Dodge following their discussions of the American feminist movement, and submits "Aphorisms on Futurism" to Alfred Stieglitz (which is printed in *Camera Work* 1914); together, these two polemical prose pieces define her ideas of feminism and individualism.

**39**   Kouidis's study of Loy provides the only full-length examination of the entire body of Loy's work. Her reading of the poetry has been invaluable to my analysis of a Williams–Loy connection.

**40**   Unless otherwise noted, future citations of Loy's work will refer to this volume.

**41**   "Selecting Loy from a list of candidates that included Baroness Else von

Freytag Loringhaven, Ida Rauh, Margaret Sanger, Louise Bryant, Margaret Anderson, Jane Heap, and Loy herself, the newspaper clearly regarded Greenwich Village and its mixtures of artists, feminists, and radicals, as the logical place to find the 'new woman' " (Conover, "Introduction," xliii).

**42** See Carolyn Burke ("New Poetry") for additional discussion of this intersection.

**43** Loy developed an active interest in the New York feminists while still living in Florence, and requested information from Mabel Dodge, in Greenwich Village, on the movement's activities. She and Dodge discussed feminism in the years between Dodge's arrival in New York (1912) and Loy's American debut (1916). Carolyn Burke's essay, "New Poetry," documents their relationship, and argues the mutually influential feminist and aesthetic principles of the time.

**44** The "Feminist Manifesto" is included in this collection.

**45** Roger L. Conover, "Introduction" to *The Last Lunar Baedeker*, xxii. For a historically informative discussion of Loy and Williams and their reception by contemporaries, see pp. xxii–xxxii.

**46** The *Dial* 80 (1926), 498–9. Conover's introduction (see note 45) includes a discussion of Winters's comments.

**47** As editors of *Contact*, Williams and McAlmon chose two pieces by Loy to include in their opening issue (1920). In 1958, Williams expressed his longstanding admiration for Loy's work in an introduction to her *Lunar Baedeker and Time-Tables*.

**48** See Kouidis, *Mina Loy*, for a full account of Loy's interaction with the futurists.

**49** In "The Subject as Text: Mongrel-girl in No Man's Land in *Anglo-Mongrels and the Rose*," a paper presented at the February 1992 Twentieth Century Literature Conference in Louisville, Kentucky, I examine Loy's poem in its concern with the construction of female subjectivity.

**50** In the textual notes to this poem contained in *The Last Lunar Baedeker*, the editor informs us that "Joseph Riddell and Mike Weaver attribute the Madame Curie section of William Carlos Williams's *Paterson* to M.L.'s earlier use of the same metaphor in this poem, which originally appeared as the opening epigraph of a letter on Gertrude Stein addressed to Ford Madox Ford" (324).

## 2. *In the American Grain:* Proclaming a Feminine Ground

**51** See Bryce Conrad's recent book-length study, *Refiguring America*, for a valuable reconstruction of Williams's historical sources and methods.

**52** Conrad's assessment of Williams's historical method has been helpful: "Williams's attempt to base a knowledge of history not on words that have been written *about* the past, but on language written *in* the past is prescient of recent developments in historiographic theory. Work by Arthur Danto, Louis Mink, and Hayden White has shown how ordinary modes of history-writing invent stories about the past according to narrative conventions rather than historio-scientific laws. ... Even in its most objective descriptions of the past, White claims, written history linguistically constitutes its subjects and events, ordering them into narrative schemes of organization" (23).

**53**  In *Refiguring America*, Bryce Conrad offers an alternative reading of the text's sexual dynamics; see especially Chapter 4, "The Poetics and Politics of Sex" (105–55). Although Conrad and I agree that the text focuses upon the destruction of the feminine, we disagree as to what constitutes the feminine and how it appears through *In the American Grain*. Conrad reads Williams's history as valorizing the male pursuit and the engendering power of insemination; he accuses Williams of inscribing the feminine, yet does not acknowledge Williams's awareness of his complicity in this cultural process and his critique of it. Conrad's analysis is groundbreaking and thoroughly thought provoking, although at times the terms of his discussion do not clearly distinguish ideologies of gender from biological sex (for example, in his treatment of Freydis as the "feminine" because she is female), and he is reluctant to attribute to Williams much awareness of masculinity as a cultural construct.

**54**  Kerry Driscoll's study of Williams's relationship to his mother, *William Carlos Williams and the Maternal Muse*, examines his "textualization" of Elena Williams as he associated her with "the ethnic diversity of the New World" (139). Focusing primarily on his work *Yes, Mrs. Williams*, Driscoll studies Williams's numerous portrayals of his mother and argues that his conception of her is crucial to the development of his poetics. She concentrates on the link between Elena Williams's language (a "hybrid dialect – that curious melange of colloquial expressions, foreign words, and nonstandard syntax") and Williams's literary experimentation with language (138). Driscoll argues that the conversation form of *YMW* allows a "harmonious interplay of objective and subjective realities in the creation of art" through which Williams can identify with the feminine other (62).

**55**  The abject, as Palattella draws from Julia Kristeva's *Powers of Horror*, refers to "ambiguous objects that threaten the social order. Society ceremoniously labels certain objects filthy – menstrual blood, disease, excrement – and jettisons them because, as objects lost from the body but still familiar, they cross boundaries and upset the symbolic and rational stability on which the social order is based" (Palattella 25). Because the abject "triggers remembrances of pre-objectal relationships, or the unrepresentable sensations a subject experienced prior to the entry into language," it is related to the maternal or the "lost pleasure of the mother's body." To evoke the abject pushes against the limits of rational language through "the possibility of naming the pre-nominal, in this case the mother's body," and generating "a literal language of figurative plenitude that exists beyond the stultifying rational limits of language" (26). The "restoration of the male body depends on contacting through maternity a literal language of abjection," but at the same time, Williams locates "the negative aspects of abjection in maternity" (30).

**56**  Schmidt's Introduction attends the first reprinting of Williams's essay since its original publication in the United States in *Briarcliff Quarterly* 3.2 (Oct. 1946), edited by Norman McLeod. The essay was printed in Australia in 1947.

**57**  I find Luce Irigaray's articulation of a "different" feminine economy of desire helpful here: Women's "desire is often interpreted, and feared, as a sort of insatiable hunger, a voracity that will swallow you whole. Whereas it really involves a different economy more than anything else, one that upsets the linearity of a project" as advanced within a phallic economy (*This Sex* 29–30).

**58**   I do not mean to suggest that Williams or his text are free from the cultural ideas I see critiqued in *In the American Grain;* as numerous studies and even a cursory reading of his work demonstrate, he is certainly a writer exhibiting the gender ideologies of his culture. However, what interests me is the continual, although conflicted, attempt to dismantle the very ideologies his works often explicitly or implicitly endorse. His own imperfect apprehension of the implications of his critique create a tension in his work informing an ongoing obsession with gender relations.

**59**   Williams thus insists upon a history that precedes European discovery, and a New World literary heritage that disrupts the classic canon of American literature by including "nonliterary" and non-European sources, as Vera Kutzinski perceptively argues in *Against the American Grain.* However, even as he steps outside of canonized history, Williams brings into New World history a deeper level of violence and oppression that marks the entry of patriarchy into the Americas prior to the arrival of Columbus. While decentering the Italian as discoverer of America, Red Eric also prefigures him as both a bearer of a phallocentric world-view and, ultimately, a victim of its power structures.

**60**   Williams significantly alters the emphasis in the Norse saga on the violence of the natives and instead attributes the Vikings with hostility and unwarranted aggression. Richard Slotkin writes: "In Norse sagas, which recount an attempt to colonize Vinland a good half a millennium before Columbus, the dark spell of the land atomizes and ruins the colony. Although the settlers find the land fruitful, the natives are brutish *skrelings,* hostile and bloody-minded; and in that far place, assailed by the fears natural to isolated men in a hostile world, the Norsemen turn on one another in murder and fratricide, breaking the order of the colony in fragments, leaving only a dark saga of jealousy and slaughter" (*Regeneration Through Violence* 34–35). Williams's interpretation of the "dark saga" indicts the invaders, not the natives, for the disintegration of the settlement.

**61**   Vera Kutzinski argues that Williams is insisting upon cultural exchange and the inclusion of difference. She sees the text as challenging Eurocentric versions of America and attempting to reinvent a New World tradition and literature. Examining the ideological substance of European colonization, she writes: "As Europe conceived of itself as 'history's paradigm,' the possibility of a plurality of worlds was an outright heresy. It is thus not very surprising . . . that certain conceptual and/or ideological mechanisms were developed to circumvent and defer the ultimate acknowledgement of such a potential pluralism: Europe imagined America not as a different world but as a *new* world, or better perhaps, as a new part of the same whole" (*Against the American Grain* 16). As a result, "the New World, stripped of its difference and its radical otherness, could become the immaculate embodiment of European thought . . . the divine revelation of a lost Paradise" (31).

**62**   Richard Slotkin discusses various myths of the New World and offers two "antagonistic pre-Columbian conceptions of the West: the primitive belief in the

West as the land of the sea, the sunset, death, darkness, passion and dreams; and the counterbelief in the West as the Blessed Isles, the land of life's renewal, of rebirth, of reason and a higher reality" (*Regeneration Through Violence* 27). Slotkin defines the major theme of these mythic versions of the New World as "European renewal through discovery and conquest of the New World" (30). The Puritan version of this myth expresses a desire for "a tabula rasa on which they could inscribe their dream: the outline of an idealized Puritan England, a Bible commonwealth, a city on a hill exemplifying the Word of God to all the world. Thus Bradford's first thoughts on the New World emphasized the virtual emptiness of the land and dismissed the few Indians present as having little claim to humanity and less to the land" (38).

63  Slotkin comments upon the native American conceptions of economic value and the significance of value exchanges: "The Indian feared that all economic exchanges were potentially productive of evil – either simple ill will or the magical malice of witchcraft. . . . The giving of wampum was 'medicine,' protecting the giver of wampum and the recipient against 'spiritual infection,' purging the transaction from latent evil force. The European concept of 'intrinsic value' currency (with its concomitant ideas of the methods for economic success) was antithetical to the Indian concept of currency as a mask for 'spiritual and supernatural interplay' " (*Regeneration Through Violence* 43).

64  "She" has often been read in just such terms. James Breslin (*William Carlos Williams: An American Artist*), for example, describes the voice of She as "fiercely seductive" (114) and claims "De Soto and this mighty earth-goddess are lovers, but she offers him little more than violence and frustration" (115).

65  For example, Breslin describes this metaphor in terms of male generative power: "At the end, De Soto has gained – nothing; but it is a nothing . . . that is synonymous with everything. A series of reversals, cutting away conscious egotism, have opened him, immersed him in the new environment. . . . The language in which this action [his body entering the river] is described suggests the act of love, defining the moment as more a beginning than an ending. . . . Now completely identified with the spirit of the place, De Soto becomes a generative power – a seed" (*William Carlos Williams: An American Artist* 115–16).

66  Leah S. Marcus examines ways in which Elizabeth "emphasized the male component of her identity, her participation in the kinship of her father" ("Erasing the Stigma of Daughterhood" 408). Particularly interesting in relationship to the body imagery associated with the Queen in Williams's essay is Marcus's discussion of Elizabeth's own manipulation of such imagery. According to the medieval concept of the King's Two Bodies, the monarch was at once mortal and immortal: "It was left to Elizabeth to explore the doctrine's rhetorical potential: she frequently appealed to her composite nature as queen. Her 'body natural' was the body of a frail woman; her 'body politic' was the body of a King, carrying the strength and masculine spirit of the best of her male forebears" (409).

67  The Puritans, explains Slotkin, embody the archetypal ideology of American colonization: "In many ways our Puritan ancestors seem to have shown in exaggerated form, almost in caricature, the patterns of thought and behaviour, the religious and literary tendencies, and the sociopolitical and psychological preoc-

cupations of all the Europeans who colonized the islands and forests of the primitive New World. The Puritans were perhaps the archetypal colonizers; they were certainly the most extreme antipathetic to the culture and institutions native to the aboriginal population of America" (*Regeneration Through Violence* 42). Slotkin's assessment provides an apt gloss on Williams's treatment of the Puritans.

**68** See Irigaray's essays, "When Our Lips Speak Together" and "This Sex Which Is Not One," in the volume sharing the latter's title.

**69** See Diana Fuss, *Essentially Speaking;* Margaret Whitford, *Luce Irigaray;* and Elizabeth Grosz, *Sexual Subversions.*

**70** Slotkin discusses Morton's relationship to the Puritans and the Indians (*Regeneration Through Violence* 58–65).

**71** Bryce Conrad, in *Refiguring America,* clarifies the source of these historical excerpts; they are all contained in Adams's Introduction. Williams's lifting of Adams's quotes suggests further the deconstructive play of his selections and arrangements, for while Adams turns to history for "proof" of his own ethnocentric bias, Williams allows the quotes to demonstrate that very bias.

**72** See Carol Devens, "Separate Confrontations," for an enlightening discussion of historical stereotypes of Indian women.

**73** For a comprehensive discussion of Mather and the genre development of the captivity narrative, see Slotkin, Chapters 3–5 (pp. 57–145).

**74** As Slotkin skillfully demonstrates, the occasion of her captivity, followed by her "demonic possession" upon her return to Salem, provided Mather with the concrete framework of the captivity narrative for linking the assaults of "Indians and frontier paganism . . . [and] the assaults of the Quakers [who interacted peacefully with the Indians] . . and the final assault of the witches" (*Regeneration Through Violence* 129).

**75** The eastern Indians "because of their tribal mores . . . almost never committed rape" (Slotkin, *Regeneration Through Violence,* 125). Projection onto the Indian of Western concepts of maleness, based on mastery and domination, elided differences between Indian and white, for ironically, "as the court records show, [the Indians of the area] differed from their white counterparts" in the actual incidence of rape, which remained predominately a white male crime (Slotkin 125).

**76** Similar insight informs poems dealing with women's reproductive experience, such as "The Complaint," which demythologizes motherhood by insisting upon its material conditions, or "The Sick African," which criticizes cultural texts of paternity. (See discussion of these poems in Chapter 1.)

**77** This resistance finds historical parallels. The resistance of Indian women to European systems of gender, religion, and economics has been studied by Carol Devens, whose work on the native women of New France documents their responses to Christian conversion ("Separate Confrontations"). She identifies their resistance to conversion and locates its source in a consciousness on the part of the women themselves of their debased status within Christian patriarchal constructs. Opposed not only to the control of their activities and sexuality, many native women vigorously and even violently opposed conversion, in marked contrast to the numbers of Indian men who accepted Christianity. The French system of trade, favoring the male activities of hunting for furs, subsequently denigrated the previously valued and high-status camp activities of the women. Thus, as the economic system sanctioned production and private property, the Christian world-view insisted upon male authority within the nuclear family. As economic and religious forces disrupted the native culture and ideology, the men tended to acquiesce to new systems that would benefit them, while the women proved a major stumbling block to conversion efforts. Devens generalizes that the effects of this resistance to Western forms of patriarchy have fostered the perpetuation of native culture and ideology largely through woman's identity. Without claiming that Williams possessed in any way the historical perspective on the native American woman that recent scholarship is opening, I do find his intuitive treatment of Jacataqua remarkably coincident with such investigations of the gynocentric elements in native American cultures.

**78**  Particularly given Poe's chivalric sexism and blatant racism, I would like to emphasize Williams's selective attention to matters of tradition, language, and syntax in his reading of Poe. Though his inattention to Poe's misogyny reveals the degree to which Williams is embedded in the cultural structures his text criticizes, his particular attraction to this predecessor enacts itself through re-creating Poe in Steinian terms.

**79**  Kronick comments on this letter from a deconstructive perspective: "Measure is the spatio-temporal play between which writing begins – poetry originates in/as *différance*" (*American Poetics of History* 207).

**80**  Alice Fulton talks about Emily Dickinson's use of negative space as particularly feminine: "Dickinson defines subtle states by saying what they are *not,* possibly because no word exists for the emotional realm she's creating. She describes what she can't do as a means of evoking her obscured achievement... or her entrapment. . . . Such negative locutions might well be influenced by gender. Women are defined in terms of what they are not (not man, not central; the Other, the peripheral, the distaff) and constructed according to what they lack rather than what they have. The female self is seen as the negative space that allows the positive pattern to emerge. Dickinson created a language embedded with this gendered attrition, a world in which What-Is-Not is something in itself" ("Her Moment of Brocade" 9).

### 3. Denise Levertov: The Daughter's Voice

**81**  Williams's comments are made in an interview with Walter Stafford (*IWCW* 40).

**82**  See Marjorie Perloff, "Toward a Wittgensteinian Poetics." She contrasts recent experimental poetry and its concern with language with the " 'O Taste and See!' [a Levertov title] formula of an earlier generation" that ostensibly did not realize that "the Keatsian life of sensations is always already mediated by language" (207).

**83**  Since Suzanne Juhasz's landmark feminist study in 1976 of a modern American tradition of poetry by women, *Naked and Fiery Forms,* this split or "double bind" has been recognized as a characteristic distinguishing modern American women's poetry as early as Emily Dickinson's verse. Levertov's poetry has been variously discussed in this regard, placing her within a lineage of female poets whose writing reveals this double bind. Juhasz first described this condition in her study: "The woman who wants to be a poet... needs to exhibit certain aspects of herself that her society will label masculine. She is in double-bind situation, because she is set up to lose, whatever she might do. The conflict between her two 'selves' is an excruciating and irreconcilable civil war, when both sides are in fact the same person. If she is 'woman,' she must fail as 'poet'; 'poet,' she must fail as 'woman.' Yet she is not two people. She is a woman poet whose art is a response to, results from, her life.... If and when a woman chooses to be poet, the double bind exists within the writing itself. Her models have all been men; her criteria and standards of excellence have been created by men describing the work of men. Because the masculine has always been the norm in our society, familiarity with the nature of masculine expression and its formalization in art is long-standing and to a great extent determines our very definitions and evaluations of art" (2–3).

**84**   Felski adapts the structuration theory articulated by Anthony Giddens to her feminist analysis. See pp. 55–62.

**85**   For discussions of Levertov in the context of the Black Mountain or projective poets, see Roberta Berke's "The Will to Change: The Black Mountain Poets," *Bounds Out of Bounds,* Rudolph Nelson's "Edge of the Transcendent," and Diana Surman's "Inside and Outside in the Poetry of Denise Levertov."

**86**   Levertov's husband was arrested for his activities. See interviews with Levertov by Lorrie Smith and E. G. Burrows for fuller comments by the poet on her antiwar activities, including involvement with RESIST.

**87**   Levertov also quotes Harrison in the essay "Great Possessions" (*PIW* 96).

**88**   Gilbert refers here to the early Levertov poem "Earthwoman and Waterwoman," which I will discuss in the coming pages.

**89**   Levertov is certainly not the first woman poet to express erotic desire in conjunction with the maternal, but earlier poets most often became marginalized, such as Mina Loy.

**90**   I am indebted here to Charles Altieri's study of postmodern poets, *Enlarging the Temple: New Directions in American Poetry During the 1960s.* I am drawing from the connections he makes between Romantic and postmodern poets; in particular, I am incorporating his influential discussion of immanence. Within an "essentially *immanentist* vision of the role of poetry," he claims, "poetic creation is conceived more as the discovery and the disclosure of numinous relationships within nature than as the creation of containing and structuring forms. Hence its basic commitment is to recovering familiar realities in such a way that they appear dynamically present and invigorate the mind with a sense of powers and objective values available to it. Where the symbolist poet seeks to transform nature into satisfying human structures, the immanentist poet stresses the ways an imagination attentive to common and casual experience can transform the mind and provide satisfying resting places in an otherwise endless dialectical pursuit by the mind of its own essences and of Transcendental realities" (17).

**91**   All further citations from "Williams and the Duende" are taken from *PIW*.

**92**   "A History of Love" was originally published in *The Clouds,* 1948. The poem appears in Williams's *CP2*, p. 134.

**93**   Levertov and Rukeyser participated together in numerous antiwar activities, including a 1972 trip to Saigon to protest the war. Each woman's activism dramatically enters her poetry.

**94** These quotes are from Rukeyser's *Life of Poetry*, 15 and 8–9.

**95** In Marten (57); quotes are from Levertov's *Light Up the Cave*, p. 62.

**96** For more extended and well-argued defenses of Levertov's political poetry, see Paul Lacey's "The Poetry of Political Anguish"; Kerry Driscoll's "A Sense of Unremitting Emergency: Politics in the Early Work of Denise Levertov"; Nancy Sisko's "To Stay Alive: Levertov's Search for a Revolutionary Poetry"; and Rachel Blau DuPlessis's "The Critique of Consciousness and Myth in Levertov, Rich, and Rukeyser." Also, for a discussion of Levertov within the context of other poets writing on the Vietnam War, see James F. Mersmann's book, *Out of the Vietnam Vortex: A Study of Poets and Poetry Against the War*.

**97** Levertov quotes from Williams's 1939 essay "Against the Weather," included in *The Selected Essays of William Carlos Williams* (1969).

**98** Discussing Olson and a postmodernist view of history, Charles Altieri writes: "History so often means conservatism and seems to insist that we must remain with the hierarchies of Western analytical thinking. . . . Moreover, claims to the importance of historical thinking tend to beg the question of whose history – a question pertinent to both the subjects and objects of historical inquiry. . . . History, however, need not be primarily analytic and interpretive. The postmoderns . . . look to history as a way of extending the energies of the present. Once we learn how to look the past can become a dimension of the present" ("From Symbolist Thought to Immanence" 631).

**99** Such poems would include, among others, "Sunday Afternoon" from *Overland to the Islands;* "Partial Resemblance," from *Jacob's Ladder;* "Hypocrite Women," from *O Taste and See!;* and "The Mutes," from *The Sorrow Dance* (all in *Poems 1960–1967*). I have chosen not to discuss them specifically because of constraints of space, but also because this group of poems has been perceptively treated by various feminist readings of Levertov's work. See, for example, Sandra Gilbert's "Revolutionary Love" and Rachel Blau DuPlessis's "The Critique of Consciousness and Myth in Levertov, Rich, and Rukeyser." Gilbert surveys Levertov's woman-centered poetry, and DuPlessis examines the "critiques of culture and ideology" that these poems provide in analyzing "women's assumptions and patterns of action, revealing the cultural norms that uphold the traditional consciousness of women" (199).

**100** I am relying here upon Stephen Fredman's discussion of containment in his book, *The Grounding of American Poetry*.

**101** Here we can detect Levertov's affinity with Rukeyser's definition of social action and postulate a difference in emphasis (from Olson) as related to a cultural construction of gender and an understanding of self within gender-mediated terms.

**102** See Olson's 1951 essay, "Human Universe," in *Selected Writings,* a central moment in his formulation of projective verse, in which he describes the skin as the place of contact between internal and external worlds and urges a living in the flesh that demands total engagement and allows total presence.

**103** For Levertov, politics is inseparable from "traceries" to others. In a 1985 interview, Levertov distinguishes Olson's "cultural statements" from a socially engaged poetry, and in her comments suggests that she follows more in the line of Williams in this regard: "In this century you get Williams making lots of social and sometimes very political statements and allusions. And Stevens writing about war, and Pound making valuable points, usually, but also mixed up with his odd politics. It's very hard to separate. Olson makes *cultural* statements which obviously have a social aspect and political implications, but I don't think he's really a poet who deals with politics head on" (Smith, "An Interview," 600).

**104**   The essay quoted, "This Sex Which Is Not One," provides a good example of Irigaray's contextualization of the essential and the biological within the material. Following the quote just cited, she goes on to urge "the analysis of the various systems of oppression brought to bear upon" women and offers a materialist reading of woman as commodity and use-value for man (31–2). She also notes the insufficiency of universal categories like class in resolving the "historical problem" of women's suppression (32). Here as elsewhere, the essentialized feminine is offered as a strategic and interventionary conceptual tool for challenging a phallocentric tradition of thought, not as a fixed or authentic essence naively based upon anatomy. See Whitford (Luce Irigaray) and Fuss (*Essentially Speaking*) for excellent discussions of Irigaray's essentialism.

**105**   In discussing this poem in an interview with Lorrie Smith, Levertov describes her use of the triadic foot to achieve an "adagio effect," or to slow the reading pace through a lineated structure "in which each segment has the same duration in time" (601–2). She comments that Williams's use of the triadic line does not always operate in a way that relates content to form, that "there are some late Williams triadic line poems whose subjects don't seem to call for that adagio pace," and perhaps "the slight confusion of mind after his strokes might have affected him" (601). Although Williams maintained that the triadic foot made the spaces between words a part of the line's measure, Stephen Cushman also relates this formal device to the influence of the visual arts and observes that "typographic spacing gives a sense of rest within a visual field" (*William Carlos Williams and the Meanings of Measure* 68–9). The distinction between the aural and the visual may provide the distinction between Levertov's sense of her use of the triadic foot and that of Williams.

**106**   Digging, for Olson, provides a primary metaphor for grounding oneself. In "A Bibliography on America for Ed Dorn," he writes: "Best thing to do is *to dig one thing or place or man* until you yourself know more abt [*sic*] that than is possible to any other man. It doesn't matter whether it's Barbed Wire or Pemmican or Paterson or Iowa. But *exhaust* it. Saturate it. Beat it. / And then U KNOW everything else very fast: one saturation job (it might take 14 years). And you're in, forever" (*Additional Prose* 11).

**107**   This recent article has an excellent discussion of the homoerotic basis of Duncan's poetry and the relationship between Duncan's formal developments and gender identity.

**108**   Reading Levertov's antiwar poetry, Duncan felt she refused to admit or accept her own responsibility in the corruption she condemned. Accusing her of resorting to sensational effects through graphically violent, sexualized details, his increasingly strident objections to her political poetry led to an estrangement between the poets. See Mersmann's chapter on Duncan in *Out of the Vietnam*

*Vortex;* also see Levertov's essay on her relationship with this "mentor" in *Light Up the Cave.*

### 4. Kathleen Fraser: A Tradition of Marginality

**109**  "Line," p. 170.

**110**  Recently, Charles Bernstein brought together a valuable collection of essays (which does include contributions by women: Susan Howe, Rosmarie Waldrop, Nicole Brossard, Erica Hunt, and Hannah Weiner) addressing the multiple concerns of Language poets: *The Politics of Poetic Form: Poetry and Public Policy.*

**111**  See Rae Armantrout for an alternate view.

**112**  DeKoven addresses at length the issue of the relationship between feminist and postmodern aesthetics in her essay "Male Signature: Female Aesthetic," in *Breaking the Sequence: Women's Experimental Fiction,* a collection that provides a wonderful range of essays involving women's experimental writing.

**113**  Although in 1983, *HOW(ever)* was the only journal committed to the publication of works by women experimentalists, it has given rise to a second generation of women-edited literary magazines, such as *6ix, Black Bread, big allis,* and *f(lip.).*

**114**  See Fraser's essay "Line" in *The Line in Postmodern Poetry* and "One Hundred" in *Breaking the Sequence: Women's Experimental Fiction.*

**115**  For an analysis of this masculinist ideology, see: Andreas Huyssen, "Mass Culture as Woman: Modernism's Other," and Janet Wolff, *Feminine Sentences: Essays on Women and Culture.*

**116**  Fraser, unpublished personal correspondence with the author, December 1992.

**117**  Williams recognizes in Moore's careful and crafted patterning of words a resistance to the patterned rhythms and content of "ritual" – a synecdotal term suggesting the modernist regard for myth and ritual embodied in the works of Pound, Eliot, and Joyce: "And to organize into a pattern is also, true enough, to 'approach the conditions of a ritual.' But here I would again go slow. I see only escape from ritual in Miss Moore's work: a rush through wind if not toward some patent 'end' at least away from pursuit, a pursuit perhaps by ritual. If from such flight a ritual results it is more the care of those who follow than of the one who leads. 'Ritual,' too often to suit my ear, connotes a stereotyped mode of procedure from which pleasure has passed, whereas the poetry to which my attention clings, if it ever knew these conditions, is distinguished only as it leaves them behind" (*SE* 127).

**118**  Fraser incorporated ideas of the French feminists in a writing workshop she taught in 1982. The class, entitled "Feminist Poetics," published much of its work, including the syllabus and essays by guest speakers, class members, and Fraser, in a volume under the same name. Carolyn Burke and Rachel Blau DuPlessis were among the women to address the ideas of these French theorists.

**119**  Fraser's volume of selected poems is entitled *What I Want* and includes a poem of the same name dealing with pregnancy.

**120**  All future citations for *Spring and All* are taken from this volume.

**121**   Published in the May 1925 issue of the *Dial,* this essay was written in 1923. See Paul Mariani, *William Carlos Williams: A New World Naked,* p. 216.

**122**   Stephen Fredman's distinction between *completeness* and *wholeness* in relationship to Williams's syntactical experimentation is pertinent here. He writes: "*Wholeness* and *completeness* represent the two modes of order and closure available in a sentence . . . throughout the rest of this study, *wholeness* will represent organic, implicit, or generative forms of the sentence (often employing parataxis), and *completeness* will represent normative, explicit, or preconceived forms of the sentence (often exhibiting hypotaxis)" (*Poet's Prose* 30).

**123**   In the 1946 "Letter to an Australian Editor," Williams links Pound to a tradition of plagiarism, which is also a tradition of fathers, "without female" (205).

**124**   Carolyn Burke traces the impact Duncan's dance made upon the writing and reception of avant-garde works. In "The New Poetry and the New Woman: Mina Loy," Burke explains that Loy chose Isadora Duncan, "an acquaintance from the expatriate colony in Florence," as her model for "the predicament of the modern woman as avant-garde artist": "Possibly she recalled her fellow radicals' high esteem for the dancer's art: when Duncan appeared in New York in 1915, she seemed to represent 'women's emancipation, sexual liberation, artistic freedom and political protest' all in one. . . . Her unfettered movements, which seemed to the modernists to express creativity in its pure state, soon suggested a metaphor for the 'free feet' of free verse. The image of bare feet, emancipated from the stiff shoes and outworn choreographies of classical ballet, recurred whenever reporters began to write of the revolution in poetry" (45–6).

## Conclusion: *Paterson* and the Question of Authority

**125**   *Paterson* I.ii: 30.

# Bibliography

Aiken, William. "Denise Levertov, Robert Duncan, and Allen Ginsberg: Modes of the Self in Projective Verse." *Modern Poetry Studies* 10 (1981): 200–40.

Aldington, Richard. "Violet Hunt." *Egoist* 1.1 (Jan. 1914): 17–18.

Allen, Donald, and Warren Tallman, eds. *Poetics of the New American Poetry*. New York: Grove Press, 1973.

Allen, Paula Gunn. *The Sacred Hoop: Recovering the Feminine in American Indian Traditions*. Boston: Beacon Press, 1986.

Altieri, Charles. *Enlarging the Temple. New Directions in American Poetry During the 1960s*. Lewisburg, PA: Bucknell UP, 1979.

"From Symbolist Thought to Immanence: The Ground of Postmodern American Poetry." *boundary 2* 1.3 (1973): 605–37.

*Self and Sensibility in Contemporary American Poetry*. Cambridge: Cambridge UP, 1984.

Altman, Meryl. "The Clean and the Unclean: William Carlos Williams, Europe, Sex, and Ambivalence." *William Carlos Williams Review* 18.1 (Spring 1992): 10–20.

Armantrout, Rae. "Why Don't Women Do Language-Oriented Writing?" In *In the American Tree*. Ed. Ron Silliman. Orono, ME: National Poetry Foundation, 1986. 544–6.

Balestrieri, Elizabeth. "Audrey T. Rodgers' *Virgin and Whore: The Image of Women in the Poetry of William Carlos Williams*." *William Carlos Williams Review* 15.1 (1989): 64–8.

Bartlett, Jeffrey. " 'Many Loves': William Carlos Williams and the Difficult Erotics of Poetry." In *The Green Tradition: Essays and Poems for Sherman Paul*. Ed. H. Daniel Peck. Baton Rouge: Louisiana State UP, 1989. 135–54.

Bartlett, Lee. "From Walport to San Francisco: Art and Politics Make Peace." *The Literary Review* 32 (1988): 9–15.

Baskin, Alex. "Margaret Sanger, *The Woman Rebel* and the Rise of the Birth Control Movement." In *Woman Rebel*. Ed. Alex Baskin. New York: Archives of Social History, 1976. i–xxii.

Beck, Joyce Lorraine. "Denise Levertov's Poetics and *Oblique Prayers*." *Religion and Literature* 18 (1986): 45–61.

Beis, Patricia. "Cold Fire: Some Contemporary American Women Poets." Diss. Saint Louis University, 1972.

Benstock, Shari. "Beyond the Reaches of Feminist Criticism." In *Feminist Issues in Literary Scholarship*. Ed. Shari Benstock. Bloomington: Indiana UP, 1987. 7–29.

 *Textualizing the Feminine: On the Limits of Genre*. Norman: University of Oklahoma Press, 1991.

 *Women of the Left Bank, Paris 1900–1940*. Austin: University of Texas Press, 1986.

Berke, Roberta. *Bounds Out of Bounds: A Compass for Recent American and British Poetry*. New York: Oxford UP, 1981.

Bernstein, Charles. *Content's Dream: Essays, 1975–1984*. Los Angeles: Sun & Moon Press, 1986.

 ed. *The Politics of Poetic Form: Poetry and Public Policy*. New York: Roof Books, 1990.

Bernstein, Michael. *The Tale of the Tribe: Ezra Pound and the Modern Verse Epic*. Princeton: Princeton UP, 1980.

Berry, Eleanor. "The Williams–Oppen Connection." *Sagetrieb* 3.2 (Fall 1984): 99–116.

Berry, Wendell. "A Secular Pilgrimage." *The Hudson Review* 23 (1970): 401–24.

Blaydes, Sophie B. "Metaphors of Life and Death in the Poetry of Denise Levertov and Sylvia Plath." *Dalhousie Review* 57 (1977): 494–506.

Block, Sandra Jean. "The Archetypal Feminine in the Poetry of Denise Levertov." Diss. Kansas State University, 1978.

Boose, Lynda E. "The Father's House and the Daughter in It: The Structure of Western Culture's Daughter–Father Relationship." In *Daughters and Fathers*. Eds. Lynda Boose and Betty Flowers. Baltimore: Johns Hopkins Press, 1989. 19–74.

Bowles, Gloria Lee. "Suppression and Expression in Poetry by American Women: Louise Bogan, Denise Levertov, and Adrienne Rich." Diss. University of California, Berkeley, 1976.

Breslin, James E. B. *From Modern to Contemporary: American Poetry, 1945–1965*. Chicago: University of Chicago Press, 1984.

 *William Carlos Williams, an American Artist*. New York: Oxford UP, 1970.

Breslin, Paul. *The Psycho-Political Muse: American Poetry since the Fifties*. Chicago: University of Chicago Press, 1987.

Brinnin, John Malcolm. *William Carlos Williams*. Minneapolis: Minnesota Pamphlet Series, 1963.

Burbick, Joan. "Grimaces of a New Age: The Postwar Poetry and Painting of William Carlos Williams and Jackson Pollock." *boundary* 10.3: 109–23.

Burke, Carolyn. "Becoming Mina Loy." *Women's Studies* 7.1, 7.2 (1980): 136–58.

 "Getting Spliced: Modernism and Sexual Difference." *American Quarterly* 39.1 (1987): 98–121.

 "The New Poetry and the New Woman: Mina Loy." In *Coming To Light: American Women Poets in the Twentieth Century*. Ann Arbor: University of Michigan Press, 1985. 37–57.

"Without Commas: Gertrude Stein and Mina Loy." *Poetics Journal* 4 (1984): 43–52.

Burrows, E. G. "An Interview with Denise Levertov." *Michigan Quarterly Review* 7 (1968): 239–42.

Butler, Judith. *Gender Trouble: Feminism and the Subversion of Identity*. New York: Routledge, 1990.

Carruth, Hayden. "Levertov." *The Hudson Review* 27 (1974): 475–80.

"What 'Organic' Means." *Sagetrieb* 4.1 (Spring 1985): 145–6.

Christensen, Paul. "William Carlos Williams in the Forties: Prelude to Postmodernism." In *Ezra Pound and William Carlos Williams: The University of Pennsylvania Conference Papers*. Ed. Daniel Hoffman. Philadelphia: University of Pennsylvania Press, 1983. 143–63.

Christenson, Inger. *The Shadow of the Dome: Organicism and Romantic Poetry*. Bergen, Norway: University of Bergen, 1985.

Cixous, Hélène. "The Laugh of the Medusa." In *Critical Theory Since 1965*. Eds. Hazard Adams and Leroy Searle. Tallahassee: Florida State UP, 1986.

Clark, Bruce. "Dora Marsden and Ezra Pound: *The New Freewoman* and 'The Serious Artist'." *Contemporary Literature* 33.1: 91–112.

Coles, Robert. "Instances of Modernist Anti-Intellectualism." In *Modernism Reconsidered*. Eds. Robert Kidy and John Hildebile. Cambridge: Harvard UP, 1983. 215–228.

Conover, Roger L. "Introduction." *The Last Lunar Baedeker*. Highlands, NC: The Jargon Society, 1982. xv–lxi.

Conrad, Bryce. "The Deceptive Ground of History: The Sources of William Carlos Williams' *In the American Grain*." *Williams Carlos Williams Review* 15.1 (1989): 22–40.

"Engendering History: The Sexual Structure of William Carlos Williams' *In the American Grain*." *Twentieth Century Literature* 35.3 (1989): 254–78.

*Refiguring America: A Study of William Carlos Williams and In the American Grain*. Urbana: University of Illinois Press, 1990.

Costello, Bonnie. "Flooded With Otherness." *Parnassus* 8 (1979): 198–212.

" 'Polished Garlands' of Agreeing Difference: William Carlos Williams and Marianne Moore, an Exchange." In *The Motive for Metaphor: Essays on Modern Poetry*. Eds. Francis Blessington and Guy Rotella. Boston: Northeastern UP, 1983. 64–81.

Cott, Nancy. *The Grounding of Modern Feminism*. New Haven: Yale UP, 1987.

Cushman, Stephen. *William Carlos Williams and the Meanings of Measure*. New Haven: Yale UP, 1985.

Davidson, Michael. "Marginality in the Margins: Robert Duncan's Textual Politics." *Contemporary Literature* 33.2: 275–301.

DeKoven, Marianne. "Gertrude's Granddaughters." *The Women's Review of Books* 4.2 (1986): 13–14.

"Male Signature: Female Aesthetic." In *Breaking the Sequence: Women's Experimental Fiction*. Eds. Ellen G. Friedman and Miriam Fuchs. Princeton: Princeton UP, 1989. 29–37.

*Rich and Strange: Gender, History, Modernism*. Princeton: Princeton UP, 1991.

De Lauretis, Teresa. *Alice Doesn't: Feminism, Semiotics, Cinema.* Bloomington: Indiana UP, 1984.

ed. *Feminist Studies/Critical Studies.* Bloomington: Indiana UP, 1986.

*The Technologies of Gender: Essays on Theory, Film, and Fiction.* Bloomington: Indiana UP, 1987.

DeShazer, Mary K. *Inspiring Women: Reimagining the Muse.* Cincinnati: Xavier UP, 1986.

Devens, Carol. "Separate Confrontations: Gender as a Factor in Indian Adaptation to European Colonization in New France." *American Quarterly* 38.3 (1986): 461–80.

Diamond, Irene, and Lee Quinby, eds. *Feminism and Foucault: Reflections on Resistance.* Boston: Northeastern UP, 1988.

Dickie, Margaret. *On the Modernist Long Poem.* Iowa City: University of Iowa Press, 1986.

Dijkstra, Bram. *The Hieroglyphics of a New Speech: Cubism, Stieglitz and the Early Poetry of William Carlos Williams.* Princeton: Princeton UP, 1969.

Dow, Philip. *19 New American Poets of the Golden Gate.* New York: Harcourt Brace Jovanovich, 1984.

Doyle, Charles. *William Carlos Williams and the American Poem.* New York: St. Martin's Press, 1982.

ed. *William Carlos Williams: The Critical Heritage.* Boston: Routledge & Kegan Paul, 1980.

Driscoll, Kerry. "A Sense of Unremitting Emergency: Politics in the Early Work of Denise Levertov." *Centennial Review* 30 (1986): 292–303.

*William Carlos Williams and the Maternal Muse.* Ann Arbor: UMI Research Press, 1987.

Duffey, Bernard. *A Poetry of Presence: The Poetry of William Carlos Williams.* Madison: University of Wisconsin Press, 1986.

DuPlessis, Rachel Blau. "The Critique of Consciousness and Myth in Levertov, Rich, and Rukeyser." *Feminist Studies* 3 (1975): 199–221.

"No Moore of the Same." *HOW(ever)* 4.3 (Jan 1988): 14–15.

"No Moore of the Same: The Feminist Poetics of Marianne Moore." *William Carlos Williams Review* 14.1 (Spring 1988): 6–23.

"A Note: (Reflections on Louise Bogan)." *Feminist Poetics: A Consideration of the Female Construction of Language.* San Francisco: San Francisco State University, 1982. 108–13.

"Pater-Daughter." *Soup* 4 (1985): 40–54. (Reprinted in *The Pink Guitar.*)

*The Pink Guitar.* New York: Routledge, 1990.

"Review: Kerry Driscoll, *William Carlos Williams and the Maternal Muse.*" *William Carlos Williams Review* 15.2 (Fall 1989): 51–5.

Elder, John. *Imagining the Earth: Poetry and the Vision of Nature.* Chicago: University of Illinois Press, 1985.

Feinberg, Harvey. "The American Kora: Myth in the Art of William Carlos Williams." *Sagetrieb* 5.2 (Fall 1986): 73–92.

Felski, Rita. *Beyond Feminist Aesthetics: Feminist Literature and Social Change.* Cambridge: Harvard UP, 1989.

Foucault, Michel. *The Archaeology of Knowledge and the Discourse on Language.* Trans. A. M. Sheridan Smith. New York: Pantheon Books, 1972.

Frail, David. *The Early Politics and Poetics of William Carlos Williams*. Ann Arbor: UMI Research Press, 1987.

Frank, Robert, and Henry Sayre, eds. *The Line in Postmodern Poetry*. Chicago: University of Illinois Press, 1988.

Fraser, Kathleen. *Each Next: Narratives*. Berkeley: Figures Press, 1980.

——— ed. *Feminist Poetics: A Consideration of the Female Construction of Language*. San Francisco: San Francisco State University, 1982.

——— "How Did Emma Slide? Or the Gestate: A New Poem Form for Women." *Trellis* 3 (1979): 12–14.

——— *In Defiance of the Rains*. San Francisco: Kayak Books, 1969.

——— "Interview from a Treehouse." In *19 New American Poets of the Golden Gate*. Ed. Philip Dow. New York: Harcourt Brace Jovanovich, 1984. 69–74.

——— "Introduction: Taking It On." In *Feminist Poetics: A Consideration of the Female Construction of Language*. Ed. Kathleen Fraser. San Francisco: San Francisco State University, 1982. 7.

——— "Line. On the Line. Lining Up. Lined With. Between the Lines. Bottom Line." In *The Line in Postmodern Poetry*. Eds. Robert Frank and Henry Sayre. Chicago: University of Illinois Press, 1988. 152–74.

——— *New Shoes*. New York: Harper & Row, 1978.

——— *Notes Preceding Trust*. San Francisco: Lapis Press, 1987.

——— "One Hundred and Three Chapters of Little Times: Collapsed and Transfigured Moments in the Fiction of Barbara Guest." In *Breaking the Sequence: Women's Experimental Fiction*. Eds. Ellen Friedman and Miriam Fuchs. Princeton: Princeton UP, 1989.

——— *Selected Poems*. Orono, ME: National Poetry Foundation. (forthcoming)

——— *Some (even human voices) in the foreground, a lake*. Berkeley: Kelsey Press, 1984.

——— "A Tradition of Marginality." *Frontiers* 10.3 (1989): 22–7.

——— *What I Want*. New York: Harper & Row, 1974.

Fredman, Stephen. *The Grounding of American Poetry: Charles Olson and the Emersonian Tradition*. New York: Cambridge UP, 1993.

——— *Poet's Prose: The Crisis in American Verse*. New York: Cambridge UP, 1983.

Friedman, Ellen, and Miriam Fuchs, eds. *Breaking the Sequence: Women's Experimental Fiction*. Princeton: Princeton UP, 1989.

Friedman, Susan Stanford. "Creativity and the Childbirth Metaphor: Gender Difference in Literary Discourse." In *Speaking of Gender*. Ed. Elaine Showalter. New York: Routledge, 1989.

Froula, Christine. "The Daughter's Seduction: Sexual Violence and Literary History." In *Daughters and Fathers*. Eds. Lynda Boose and Betty Flowers. Baltimore: Johns Hopkins Press, 1989. 111–35.

Fulton, Alice. "Her Moment of Brocade: The Reconstruction of Emily Dickinson." *Parnassus* 15.1 (Spring 1989): 9–44.

Fuss, Diana. *Essentially Speaking: Feminism, Nature, and Difference*. New York: Routledge, 1989.

Gallop, Jane. *The Daughter's Seduction: Feminism and Psychoanalysis*. Ithaca: Cornell UP, 1982.

Gelpi, Albert. *A Coherent Splendor*. Cambridge: Cambridge UP, 1987.

——— *The Tenth Muse: The Psyche of the American Poet*. Cambridge: Harvard UP, 1975.

Gilbert, Sandra M. "Purloined Letters: William Carlos Williams and 'Cress'."
    *William Carlos Williams Review* 11.2 (Fall 1985): 5–15.
  "Revolutionary Love: Denise Levertov and the Poetics of Politics." *Parnassus*
    12–13 (1985): 335–51.
Gilbert, Sandra M., and Susan Gubar. *No Man's Land: The Place of the Woman
    Writer in the Twentieth Century. V.I: The War of the Words.* New Haven: Yale
    UP, 1988.
Gitzin, Julian. "From Reverence to Attention: The Poetry of Denise Levertov."
    *Midwest Quarterly* 16 (1975): 328–41.
Goldman, Emma. *Anarchism and Other Essays.* New York: Mother Earth Pub-
    lishing Association, 1910.
Goodridge, Celeste. "Private Exchanges and Public Reviews: Marianne Moore's
    Criticism of William Carlos Williams." *Twentieth Century Literature* 30
    (1984): 160–74.
Graham, Theodora R. " 'Her Heigh Compleynte': The Cress Letters of William
    Carlos Williams's *Paterson.*" In *Ezra Pound and William Carlos Williams: The
    University of Pennsylvania Conference Papers.* Ed. Daniel Hoffman. Philadel-
    phia: University of Pennsylvania Press, 1983.
  "Myra's Emergence in William Carlos Williams' *A Dream of Love.*" *Sagetrieb*
    3.2 (Fall 1984): 71–9.
  "Williams, Flossie, and the Others: The Aesthetics of Sexuality." *Contemporary
    Literature* 28.2 (1987): 163–86.
  "Woman as Character and Symbol in the Work of William Carlos Williams."
    Diss. Penn. State, 1974.
Greig, Teresa Billington. "Feminism." *Woman Rebel* 1.1 (1914): 3.
Grosz, Elizabeth. *Sexual Subversions: Three French Feminists.* Sydney, Australia:
    Allen & Unwin, 1989.
Guimond, James. *The Art of William Carlos Williams: A Discovery and Possession
    of America.* Urbana: University of Illinois Press, 1968.
Hallisey, Joan. "Denise Levertov – . . . 'Forever a Stranger and Pilgrim.' " *Cen-
    tennial Review* 30 (1986): 281–91.
  "Denise Levertov's 'Illustrious Ancestors': The Hassidic Influence." *MELUS*
    9.4 (Winter 1982): 5–11.
Hamalian, Linda. "The Genesis of the San Francisco Renaissance: Literary and
    Political Currents, 1945–1955." *The Literary Review* 32.1 (1988): 5–8.
Harris, Victoria. "The Incorporative Consciousness: Levertov's Journey from
    Discretion to Unity." *Exploration: Journal of the MLA Special Session on the
    Literature of Exploration and Travel* 4 (1976): 33–48.
Hindess, Barry, and Paul Hirst. *Pre-capitalist Modes of Production.* London: Rout-
    ledge, 1975.
Hoffman, Daniel. *Ezra Pound and William Carlos Williams: The University of
    Pennsylvania Conference Papers.* Philadelphia: University of Pennsylvania
    Press, 1983.
Holden, Jonathan. *Style and Authenticity in Postmodern Poetry.* Columbia: Uni-
    versity of Missouri Press, 1986.
Howe, Susan. *My Emily Dickinson.* Berkeley: North Atlantic Books, 1985.
Hoyt, Helen. "Retort." *Others* 3.3 (1916): n.p.

Hunt, Jean. "Denise Levertov's New Grief-Language: *The Sorrow Dance*." *University Review* 35 (1969): 171–7.

Hutcheon, Linda. *The Politics of Postmodernism*. New York: Routledge, 1989.

Huyssen, Andreas. "Mass Culture as Woman: Modernism's Other." *After the Great Divide: Modernism, Mass Culture, and Postmodernism*. London: Macmillan, 1988.

Irigaray, Luce. *This Sex Which Is Not One*. Trans. Catherine Porter. Ithaca: Cornell UP, 1977.

Jackson, Richard. "A Common Time: The Poetry of Denise Levertov." *Sagetrieb* 5.2 (Fall 1986): 5–46.

Johnson, Honor. "New Feminism and Painterly Techniques: Kathleen Fraser." *Ironwood* 12.2 (Fall 1984): 139–45.

Jones, Kathleen. "On Authority: Or, Why Women Are Not Entitled to Speak." In *Feminism and Foucault: Reflections on Resistance*. Ed. Irene Diamond and Lee Quinby. Boston: Northeastern UP, 1988. 119–34.

Juhasz, Suzanne. "The Journal as Source and Model for Feminist Art: The Example of Kathleen Fraser." *Frontiers* 8 (1984): 16–20.

*Metaphor and the Poetry of Williams, Pound, and Stevens*. Lewisburg: Bucknell UP, 1974.

*Naked and Fiery Forms: Modern American Poetry by Women*. New York: Harper & Row, 1976.

Koch, Vivienne. *William Carlos Williams*. Norfolk, CT: New Directions, 1950.

Kouidis, Virginia. *Mina Loy: American Modernist Poet*. Baton Rouge: Louisiana State UP, 1980.

Kreymborg, Alfred. *Our Singing Strength: An Outline of American Poetry, 1620–1930*. New York: Coward-McCann, 1929.

*Troubadour: An Autobiography*. New York: Boni & Liveright, 1925.

Kristeva, Julia. *Powers of Horror: An Essay on Abjection*. New York: Columbia UP, 1982.

Kronick, Joseph. *American Poetics of History: From Emerson to the Moderns*. Baton Rouge: Louisiana State UP, 1984.

Kutzinski, Vera M. *Against the American Grain: Myth and History in William Carlos Williams, Jay Wright, and Nicolas Guillen*. Baltimore: Johns Hopkins Press, 1987.

Kyle, Carol A. "Every Step an Arrival: 'Six Variations' and the Musical Structure of Denise Levertov's Poetry." *Centennial Review* 18 (1973): 281–96.

Lacan, Jacques. *Écrits*. Trans. Alan Sheridan. New York: Norton, 1977.

Lacey, Paul A. *The Inner War: Forms and Themes in Recent American Poetry*. Philadelphia: Fortress Press, 1972.

"The Poetry of Political Anguish." *Sagetrieb* 4.1 (Spring 1985): 61–71.

Leonardi, Susan J. "Recipes for Reading: Summer Pasta, Lobster à la Rieseholme, and Key Lime Pie." *PMLA* 104.3 (1989): 340–7.

Levenson, Michael H. *A Genealogy of Modernism: A Study of English Literary Doctrine 1908–1922*. Cambridge: Cambridge UP, 1984.

Levertov, Denise. *Breathing the Water*. New York: New Directions Press, 1987. (*BW*)

*Candles in Babylon*. New York: New Directions Press, 1982. (*CIB*)

*Collected Earlier Poems, 1940–1960*. New York: New Directions Press, 1979. (*CEP*)

*A Door in the Hive*. New York: New Directions Press, 1989. (*DH*)

*The Freeing of the Dust*. New York: New Directions Press, 1975. (*FOD*)

"The Ideas in Things." In *William Carlos Williams: Man and Poet*. Ed. Carroll F. Terrell. Orono, ME: National Poetry Foundation, 1983. 141–52.

*Life in the Forest*. New York: New Directions Press, 1978. (*LIF*)

*Light Up the Cave*. New York: New Directions Press, 1981. (*LUC*)

*Oblique Prayers*. New York: New Directions Press, 1984. (*OP*)

*Poems 1960–1967*. New York: New Directions Press, 1983.

*Poems 1968–1972*. New York: New Directions Press, 1987.

"Poems by Women." In *Denise Levertov: In Her Own Province*. Ed. Linda Wagner. New York: New Directions Press, 1979.

*A Poet in the World*. New York: New Directions Press, 1973. (*PIW*)

Lipking, Lawrence. *Abandoned Women and Poetic Tradition*. Chicago: University of Chicago Press, 1988.

Loy, Mina. *The Last Lunar Baedeker*. Ed. Roger L. Conover. Highlands, NC: The Jargon Society, 1982. (*LLB*)

*Lunar Baedeker and Time-Tables*. Highlands, NC: Jonathan Williams, 1958.

M.C. "Venus and Mars." *Egoist* 1.2 (June 1914): 218–19.

Marcus, Leah S. "Erasing the Stigma of Daughterhood: Mary I, Elizabeth, and Henry VII." In *Daughters and Fathers*. Eds. Lynda E. Boose and Betty S. Flowers. Baltimore: Johns Hopkins Press, 1989. 400–17.

Mariani, Paul. *A Usable Past: Essays on Modern and Contemporary Poetry*. Amherst: University of Massachusetts Press, 1984.

*William Carlos Williams: A New World Naked*. New York: McGraw-Hill, 1981.

*William Carlos Williams: The Poet and His Critics*. Chicago: American Library Association, 1975.

"Williams: La Gioconda's Smile." *William Carlos Williams Review* 11.2 (Fall 1985): 55–60.

Marling, William. *William Carlos Williams and the Painters, 1909–1923*. Athens, Ohio: Ohio UP, 1982.

Marquis, Harriett Hill. "Cries of Communion: The Poetry of Denise Levertov." Diss. Drew Univ., 1984.

Marsden, Dora. "The Heart of the Question." *New Freewoman* 1.1 (1913): 61–4.

" 'I Am.' " *Egoist* 2.1 (1916): 1–4.

"The 'I' and the 'Ego'." *Egoist* 3.9 (1916): 129–31.

"Liberty, Law, and Democracy." *Egoist* 1.1 (1914): 1–3.

"Lingual Psychology." *Egoist* 3.7 (1916): 97–102.

"The Science of Signs." *Egoist* 3.8 (1916): 113–17.

"The Verbal Form 'Be'." *Egoist* 3.11 (1916): 161–4.

"Views and Comments." *Egoist* 1.1 (1914): 3–5.

"Views and Comments." *Egoist* 1.12 (1914): 224.

"Views and Comments." *Egoist* 1.19 (1914): 223–6.

"Women's 'Rights'." *Egoist* 1.19 (1914): 361–3.

Marten, Harry. "Exploring the Human Community: The Poetry of Denise Levertov and Muriel Rukeyser." *Sagetrieb* 3.3 (Winter 1984): 51–61.

Martin, Biddy. "Feminism, Criticism, and Foucault." In *Feminism and Foucault:
Reflections on Resistance*. Eds. Irene Diamond and Lee Quinby. Boston:
Northeastern UP, 1988. 3–20.

Marzan, Julio. "Mrs. Williams's William Carlos." In *Reinventing the Americas:
Comparative Studies of Literature of the United States and Spanish America*. Ed.
Gari Laguardiz. New York: Cambridge UP, 1986. 106–21.

Mazzaro, Jerome. *William Carlos Williams: The Later Poems*. Ithaca: Cornell UP,
1973.

Méric, Victor. "The First Right." *Woman Rebel* 1.2 (1914): 10.

Mersmann, James F. *Out of the Vietnam Vortex: A Study of Poets and Poetry Against
the War*. Wichita: Kansas UP, 1974.

Messerli, Douglas, ed. *"Language" Poetries: An Anthology*. New York: New
Directions Press, 1987.

"A World Detached: The Early Criticism of William Carlos Williams." *Sagetrieb* 3.2 (Fall 1984): 89–98.

Middlebrook, Diane Wood, and Marilyn Yalom, eds. *Coming to Light: American
Women Poets in the Twentieth Century*. Ann Arbor: University of Michigan
Press, 1985.

Miki, Roy. *The Prepoetics of William Carlos Williams: Kora in Hell*. Ann Arbor:
UMI Research Press, 1983.

Miller, J. Hillis. *Poets of Reality*. Cambridge: Harvard UP, 1966.

ed. *William Carlos Williams: A Collection of Critical Essays*. Englewood Cliffs,
NJ: Prentice-Hall, 1966.

Mills, Ralph. "Denise Levertov: Poetry of the Immediate." In *Denise Levertov:
In Her Own Province*. Ed. Linda Wagner. New York: New Directions Press,
1979.

Mottram, Eric. "The Limits of Self-Regard." *Parnassus* 1 (1972): 152–62.

Nardi, Marcia. "Group of Poems." *New Directions* 7 (1942): 413–28.

Nash, Charles. "Women and the Female Principle in the Works of William Carlos
Williams." *Publications of the Missouri Philological Association* 3 (1978): 91–
100.

Nay, Judith. "William Carlos Williams and the Singular Woman." *William Carlos
Williams Review* 11.2 (Fall 1985): 45–54.

Nelson, Rudolph L. "Edge of the Transcendent: The Poetry of Levertov and
Duncan." *Southwest Review* 54 (1969): 188–202.

Notley, Alice. "Dr. Williams' Heiresses." *Tuumba* 28 (1980).

Oliphant, Dave, and Thomas Zigal, eds. *William Carlos Williams and Others:
Essays on Williams and His Association with Pound, Doolittle, Duchamp, Moore,
Romano, Stevens, and Zukofsky*. Austin: Harry Ransom Humanities Research
Center, University of Texas, 1985.

Olson, Charles. *Additional Prose: A Bibliography on America, Proprioception and
Other Notes and Essays*. Ed. George Butterick. Bolinas, CA: Four Seasons
Foundation, 1974.

*Selected Writings*. Ed. Robert Creeley. New York: New Directions Press, 1966.

Ostriker, Alicia. "In Mind: The Divided Self and Woman's Poetry." *Midwest Quarterly* 24 (1983): 351–6.

"No Rule of Procedure." *HOW(ever)* 5.4 (Oct. 1989): 20–1.

*Stealing the Language: The Emergence of Women's Poetry in America.* Boston: Beacon Press, 1986.

"What Do Women (Poets) Want?: H.D. and Marianne Moore as Poetic Ancestresses." *Contemporary Literature* 27 (1986): 475–92.

Ostrom, Alan B. *The Poetic World of William Carlos Williams.* Carbondale: Southern Illinois UP, 1966.

*Others.* New York: Kraus Reprint Corporation, 1967.

Palattella, John. " 'In the Midst of Living Hell': The Great War, Masculinity, and Maternity in Williams' *Kora in Hell* and 'Three Professional Studies'." *William Carlos Williams Review* 17.2 (Fall 1991): 13–38.

Pearce, Roy Harvey. *Continuity of American Poetry.* Middletown, CT: Wesleyan UP, 1987.

"The Metaphysics of Indian-Hating: Leatherstocking Unmasked." *Historicism Once More.* Princeton: Princeton UP, 1969. 109–136.

*The Savages of America: A Study of the Indian and the Idea of Civilization.* Baltimore: Johns Hopkins Press, 1965.

Perloff, Marjorie. *The Dance of the Intellect: Studies in the Poetry of the Pound Tradition.* Cambridge: Cambridge UP, 1987.

*Frank O'Hara: Poet Among Painters.* New York: George Braziller, 1977.

*The Poetics of Indeterminacy: Rimbaud to Cage.* Princeton: Princeton UP, 1981.

"Toward a Wittgensteinian Poetics." *Contemporary Literature* 33.2: 191–213.

Pound, Ezra. "The New Sculpture." *Egoist* 1.4 (1914): 67–8.

"Wyndham Lewis." *Egoist* 1.12 (1914): 233–4.

Radloff, Bernhard. "Name and Site: A Heideggerian Approach to the Local in the Poetry of William Carlos Williams." *Texas Studies in Literature and Language* 25.2 (Summer 1986): 140–63.

Reid, Ian. " 'Everyman's Land': Ian Reid Interviews Denise Levertov." *Southern Review: Literary and Interdisciplinary Essays, South Australia* 5 (1972): 231–6.

Rich, Adrienne. *Dream of a Common Language: Poems 1974–1977.* New York: Norton, 1978.

*On Lies, Secrets, and Silence: Selected Prose 1966–1978.* New York: Norton, 1979.

Riddel, Joseph. *The Inverted Bell: Modernism and the Counterpoetics of William Carlos Williams.* Baton Rouge: Louisiana State Press, 1974.

Robbins, Bruce. "Modernism and Professionalism: The Case of William Carlos Williams." In *On Poetry and Poetics.* Ed. Richard Waswo. Zurich: Swiss Association of University Teachers of English, 1985. 191–205.

Rodgers, Audrey T. "The Female Presence: Women in the Poetry of William Carlos Williams, 1910–1950." *American Poetry* 3 (1986): 2–17.

*Virgin and Whore: The Image of Women in the Poetry of William Carlos Williams.* Jefferson, NC: McFarland, 1987.

Rosenfield, Alvin H. " 'The Being of Language and the Language of Being': Heidegger and Modern Poetics." *boundary* 2.4 (1976): 535–53.

Ross-Bryant, Lynn. "Imagination and the Re-Valorization of the Feminine."

*Journal of American Academy of Religious Thematic Studies* 48.2 (1981): 105–17.

Rukeyser, Muriel. *Life of Poetry*. New York: A. A. Wyn, 1949.

Sayre, Henry M. *The Visual Text of William Carlos Williams*. Urbana: University of Illinois Press, 1983.

Schmidt, Peter. "Introduction to William Carlos Williams' 'Letter to an Australian Editor' (1946): Williams' Manifesto for Multiculturalism." *William Carlos Williams Review* 17.2 (Fall 1991): 4–7.

*William Carlos Williams, the Arts, and Literary Tradition*. Baton Rouge: Louisiana State UP, 1988.

Schriker, Gale C. "The Case of Cress: Implications of Allusion in *Paterson*." *William Carlos Williams Review* 11.2 (Fall 1985): 16–29.

Segal, Charles M., and David C. Stinebeck. *Puritans, Indians, and Manifest Destiny*. New York: Putman, 1977.

Silliman, Ron. "Language, Realism, Poetry." *In the American Tree*. Orono, ME: National Poetry Foundation, 1986.

Simpson, Louis. *Three on the Tower*. New York: Norton, 1975.

Sisko, Nancy. "To Stay Alive: Levertov's Search for a Revolutionary Poetry." *Sagetrieb* 5.2 (Fall 1986): 47–60.

Slatin, John. "American Beauty: William Carlos Williams and Marianne Moore." *Library Chronicle of the University of Texas* 29 (1984): 49–73.

" 'Something Inescapably Typical': Questions About Gender in the Late Work of Williams and Moore." *William Carlos Williams Review* 14.1 (Spring 1988): 86–103.

Slotkin, Richard. *Regeneration Through Violence: The Mythology of the American Frontier, 1600–1860*. Middletown, CT: Wesleyan UP, 1973.

Smith, Lorrie. "An Interview with Denise Levertov." *Michigan Quarterly Review* 24 (1985): 596–604.

Stirner, Max. *The Ego and His Own*. Trans. Steven T. Byington. New York: R. Tucker, 1907.

Surman, Diana. "Inside and Outside in the Poetry of Denise Levertov." *Critical Quarterly* 22 (1980): 57–69.

Sutton, Walter. "Denise Levertov and Emerson." *Notes on Modern American Literature* 1 (1976): item 1.

Tapscott, Stephan. *American Beauty: William Carlos Williams and the Modernist Whitman*. New York: Columbia UP, 1984.

"Williams, Sappho, and the Woman-as-Other." *William Carlos Williams Review* 11.2 (Fall 1985): 30–44.

Terrell, Carroll, ed. *William Carlos Williams: Man and Poet*. Orono, ME: National Poetry Foundation, 1983.

Townley, Rod. *The Early Poetry of William Carlos Williams*. Ithaca: Cornell UP, 1975.

Wagner, Linda W. *American Modern: Essays in Fiction and Poetry*. Port Washington, NY: Kennikat Press, 1980.

*Denise Levertov*. New York: Twayne Publishers, 1967.

ed. *Denise Levertov: In Her Own Province*. New York: New Directions Press, 1979.

"Levertov and Rich: The Later Poems." *South Carolina Review* 11.2 (1979): 18–27.

Wakoski, Diane. "The Birth of the San Francisco Renaissance: Something Now Called the Whitman Tradition." *The Literary Review* 32 (1988): 36–41.

"William Carlos Williams: The Poet's Poet." *Sagetrieb* 3.2 (Fall 1984): 43–7.

Walker, David. *The Transparent Lyric: Reading and Meaning in the Poetry of Stevens and Williams*. Princeton: Princeton UP, 1984.

Weatherhead, Andrew Kingsley. *The Edge of the Image: Marianne Moore, William Carlos Williams, and Some Other Poets*. Seattle: University of Washington Press, 1967.

Weaver, Michael. *William Carlos Williams: The American Background*. Cambridge: Cambridge UP, 1971.

Wertheim, Arthur Frank. *The New York Little Renaissance: Iconoclasm, Modernism, and Nationalism in American Culture, 1908–1917*. New York: NYU Press, 1976.

Whitford, Margaret. *Luce Irigaray: Philosophy in the Feminine*. New York: Routledge, 1991.

Whittemore, Reed. *William Carlos Williams, Poet from Jersey*. Boston: Houghton Mifflin, 1975.

Williams, William Carlos. "America, Whitman, and the Art of Poetry." *The Poetry Journal* 8.1 (Nov. 1917): 27–36.

*The Autobiography of William Carlos Williams*. New York: New Directions Press, 1967.

*The Collected Poems of William Carlos Williams*, Vol. 1, 1909–1939. Eds. A. Walton Litz and Christopher MacGowan. New York: New Directions Press, 1986. (*CP1*)

*The Collected Poems of William Carlos Williams*, Vol. 2, 1939–1962. Eds. A Walton Litz and Christopher MacGowan. New York: New Directions Press, 1988. (*CP2*)

*The Embodiment of Knowledge*. New York: New Directions Press, 1974. (*EOK*)

"The Great Sex Spiral: A Criticism of Miss Marsden's 'Lingual Psychology'." *Egoist* 4.3, 4.7 (1917).

*I Wanted to Write a Poem: The Autobiography of the Works of a Poet*. New York: New Directions Press, 1977. (*IWTWP*)

*Imaginations*. Ed. Webster Scott. New York: New Directions Press, 1970.

*In the American Grain*. New York: New Directions Press, 1956. (*IAG*)

*Interviews with William Carlos Williams: "Speaking Straight Ahead."* Ed. Linda Wagner. New York: New Directions Press, 1976. (*IWCW*)

*Kora in Hell: Improvisations*. Boston: Four Seas Co., 1920.

"Letter to an Australian Editor." *Briarcliff Quarterly* 3.2 (1946): 205–8.

"Letters to Denise Levertov." *Stony Brook* 1/2 (1968): 163–4.

" 'Men . . . Have No Tenderness': Anaïs Nin's *Winter of Artifice*." *New Directions* 7 (1942): 429–36.

"Mina Loy." *Lunar Baedeker and Time-Tables*. Mina Loy. Highlands, NC: Jonathan Williams, 1958. unnumbered.

*Paterson*. New York: New Directions Press, 1971.

*Pictures from Brueghel and Other Poems 1950–1963*. New York: New Directions Press, 1967.

*A Recognizable Image: William Carlos Williams on Art and Artists*. Ed. Bram Dijkstra. New York: New Directions Press, 1978.

*The Selected Essays of William Carlos Williams*. New York: New Directions Press, 1969. (*SE*)

*Selected Letters*. New York: McDowell & Obolensky, 1957. (*SL*)

*Something to Say: William Carlos Williams on Younger Poets*. Ed. James Breslin. New York: New Directions Press, 1985.

*Yes, Mrs. Williams: A Personal Record of My Mother*. New York, McDowell & Obolensky, 1959. (*YMW*)

"Woman as Operator." *Women: A Collaboration of Artists and Writers*. New York: Samuel M. Kootz Editions, 1948.

Winters, Yvor. "Mina Loy." *Dial* 80 (1926): 498–9.

Wolff, Janet. *Feminine Sentences: Essays on Women and Culture*. Cambridge, UK: Polity Press, 1990.

Wright, Josephine. "The Song of the Sock." *Egoist* 1.18 (1914): 358.

Yeats, W. B. *The Poems of W. B. Yeats*. Ed. Richard J. Finneran. New York: Macmillan, 1983.

Younkin, Ronald. "Denise Levertov and the Hasidic Tradition." *Descant: The Texas Christian University Literary Journal* 19 (1974): 40–8.

# Index

Adams, Charles Francis ("A. C. Adams" in *In the American Grain*), 104, 258n71
Aldington, Richard, 22, 23, 24, 251n15
Altieri, Charles, 260n90, 261n98
Anderson, Margaret, 115, 254n41
Arensberg, Walter, 49
Aristotle, 9, 38
Armantrout, Rae, 263n110
Auden, W. H., 193

Bara, Theda, 44
Barnard, Mary 247
Barnes, Djuna, 51, 184
Barthes, Roland, 16
Baxter, Viola, 26
Benstock, Shari, 23, 248n1, 249n4
Bergson, Henri, 250n11
Berke, Roberta, 260n85
Bernstein, Charles, 263n110
Bernstein, Michael, 238–9, 245
*big allis*, 263n113
Bishop, Bridget, 107
*Black Bread*, 263n113
Black Mountain Poets, 14, 174–6, 260n85.
    *See also* Olson, Charles; Duncan,
    Robert; Creeley, Robert
Blackmur, Richard P., 238
*Blast*, 252n21
Bodenheim, Maxwell, 61
Boone, Daniel, 102
Bradford, William, 105, 257n62
Brancusi, Constantin, 123
Breslin, James, 257n64, 257n65
Brossard, Nicole, 263n110
Bryant, Louise, 254n41
Bryant, William Cullen, 119

Bryher (Winifred Ellerman), 209–10
Burke, Carolyn, 20, 48, 50, 51, 55,
    248n1, 249n4, 250n9, 251–2n19,
    253n37, 254n42, 254n43, 263n118,
    264n124
Burr, Aaron, 102, 116, 118
Burrows, E. G., 260n86
Butler, Judith, 11–12

*Camera Work*, 6, 253n38
captivity narrative 111–12, 258n73, 258n74
*Century* (magazine), 44
Cezanne, Paul, 222
Champlain, Samuel de, 101
Christ, 169, 178–82
Cixous, Hélène, 16, 120–21, 122, 124, 196
Clark, Bruce, 22, 250n10
Columbus, Christopher, 75, 88, 90–1, 93,
    96, 256n59, 256n60
Comstock Law of 1873, 48, 69
Conover, Roger L., 254n41, 254n45,
    254n46
Conrad, Bryce, 76, 86, 89, 248n2,
    254n51, 254–5n52, 255n53, 258n71
*Contact*, 54, 254n47
Cortez, Hernando, 88, 90, 91–2, 93
Cott, Nancy, 43–4, 45, 46, 253n35
Crane, Hart, 241
Creeley, Robert, 3, 14, 127, 128, 131,
    132, 241
Curie, Marie, 72–3, 93, 245, 254n50
Cushman, Stephen, 262n104

Dahlen, Beverly, 184, 189
Danto, Arthur, 254n52
Darwinism, social, 25

279

Continued from the front of the book